WEB DESIGN

BASICS

ROCKPORT

GLOUCESTER MASSACHUSETTS

WEB DESIGN

BASICS

ROCKPORT PUBLISHERS

Ideas and Inspiration for Working with Type, Color, and Navigation on the Web

First published in the United States of America by
Rockport Publishers, Inc.
33 Commercial Street
Gloucester, Massachusetts 01930-5089
Telephone: (978) 282-9590
Fax: (978) 283-2742
www.rockpub.com

Library of Congress Cataloging-in-Publication data available

ISBN 1-56496-890-1

10 9 8 7 6 5 4 3 2 1

Grateful acknowledgment is given to Jeff Carlson, Toby Malina, Glenn Fleishman, and Richard Karl Danielson for their contributions to this book.

Design: Leeann Leftwich Zajas
Cover Design: Deep Creative Ltd.

Printed in China

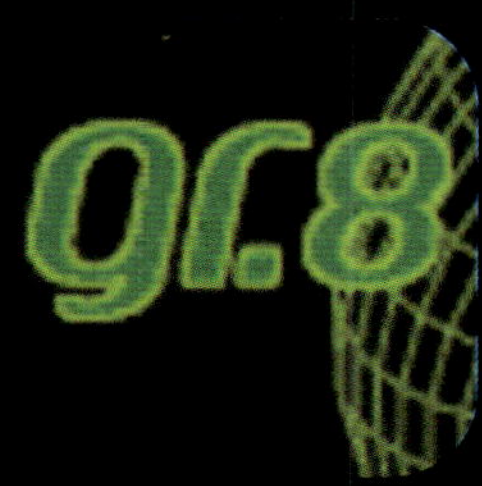
gr.8

contents

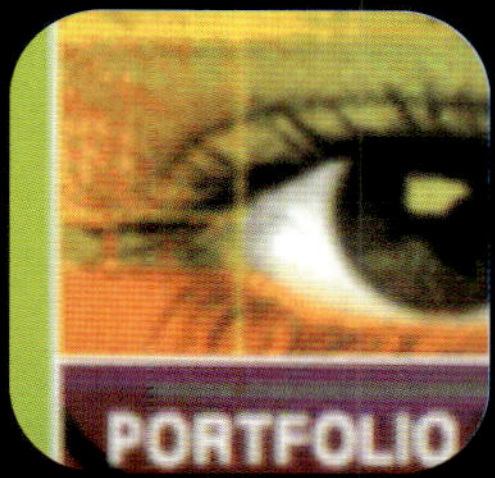
PORTFOLIO

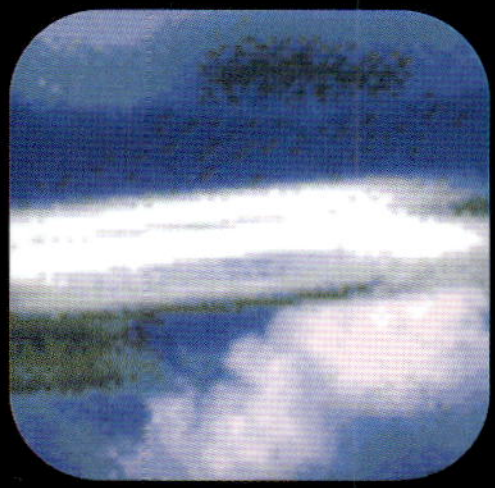

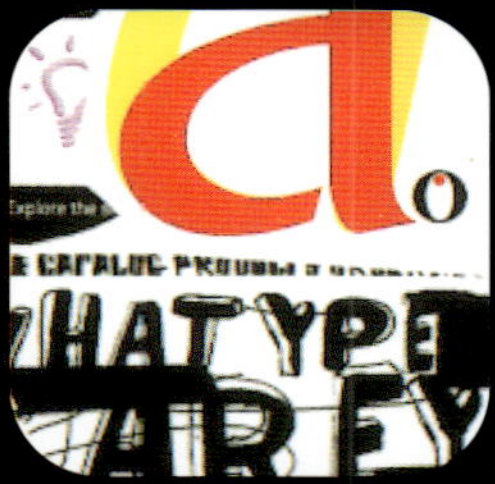

introduction

While the Web is a constantly changing medium, no matter how the technology evolves, there are a few elements that remain essential ingredients for good Web site design—typography, color, and navigation. This book showcases hundreds of Web sites that show the best examples of these basic elements in use. Each site is critiqued in terms of its strength, highlighting the elements and design techniques that show an innovative and creative use of these basic Web design elements.

For most traditionally trained designers, the Web is a limiting medium. The designs featured in the book are selected to show the work of designers who have struggled against these limitations and achieved ingenious solutions to the challenges of the Web's design restrictions.

Pushing the envelope of traditional design has always been a theme of the digital and Web design world, but it's often done at the cost of effective design results. Understanding the fundamentals of the basic design elements provides design innovators with the tools to push their work beyond the norm—and to succeed.

color

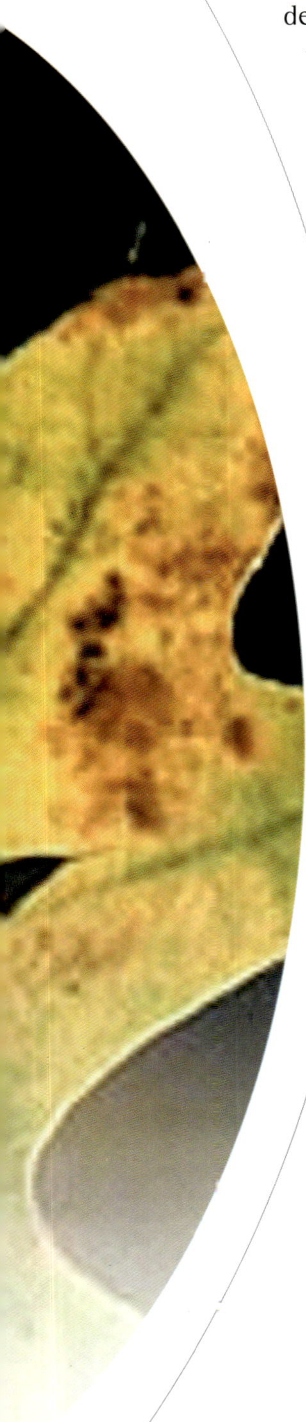

A palette of 216 colors might have daunted any artist except for the pointillist Georges Seurat, but it is the defining scheme for most of today's World Wide Web sites. Some designers rebel against this limitation, but the practical world intrudes.

If you want some sense that your work will appear similarly on many different machines, you must choose a small set of colors, typically from the so-called Web-safe palette. Choosing more than 216 colors, or going nuts and using 24-bit color (millions of colors), means that the majority of viewers will see dithered, pixelated, corrupted renditions of your original intent.

For certain audiences, you can rely on deep color and ignore these limitations. A software company selling three-dimensional animation software deals mostly with folks who have more than the average eight bits of color (256 colors). Similarly, a site that presents art might attract surfers, but can't make a *Starry Night* out of ten blues.

The challenge for all designers is to make each color count, whether you're drawing from a deep pool or a paint-by-numbers scheme. The sites appearing in this book have made design choices that allow them to work within the constraints they've put upon themselves, rather than working outside the frame and allowing Web browser software to interpret colors in whichever way it sees fit.

Some sites choose to push the saturation envelope, taking advantage of the fact that bright colors can fight each other on screen with often surprising results. They borrow from video games, silk-screened posters, television cartoons, and laser light shows. Other pages find great interest in using tiny differences: one shade and its nearest discernible neighbor forming all the contrast on a page.

It's clear that the best sites educate their visitors by giving them a message spelled out in hue and tonality: without even reading the words, we know where we've landed. And unlike a finely-dappled Seurat painting, we don't have to take several steps back in order to get the full picture.

"The challenge for all designers is to make each color count, whether you're drawing from a deep pool or a paint-by-numbers scheme."

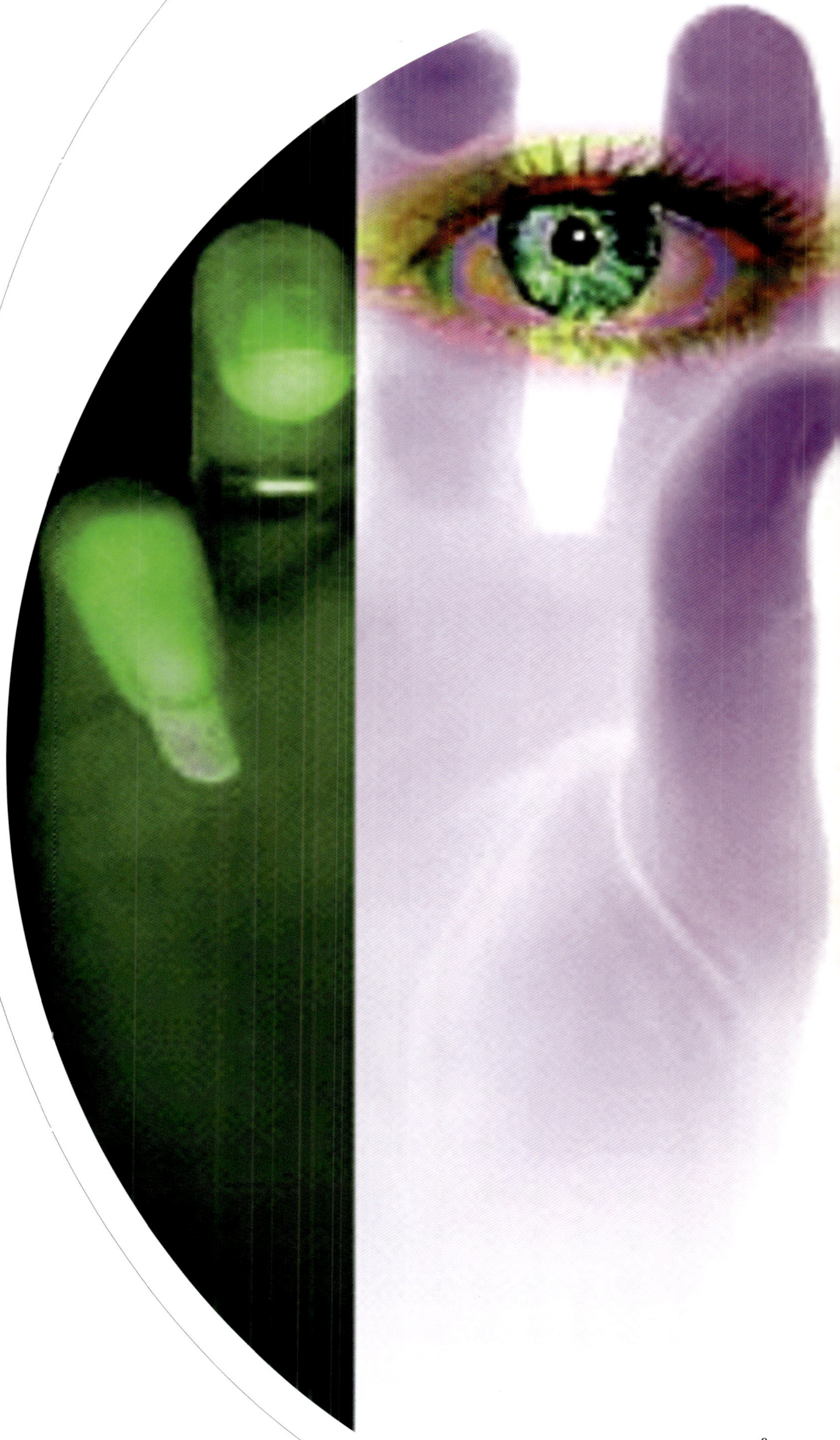

title
Bodyflow
URL
http://www.qmm.com.au/hon/
designer/illustrator/
programmer
Hon Hiew

The Bodyflow site is an excellent example of how color can be used effectively without dumping it over every inch of screen space. Each section carries its own color designation. Although not necessary for navigation (locations are prominently displayed in text form and in each window title bar), the color consistency adds a smooth professionalism to the site. Plus, the pages load extremely fast.

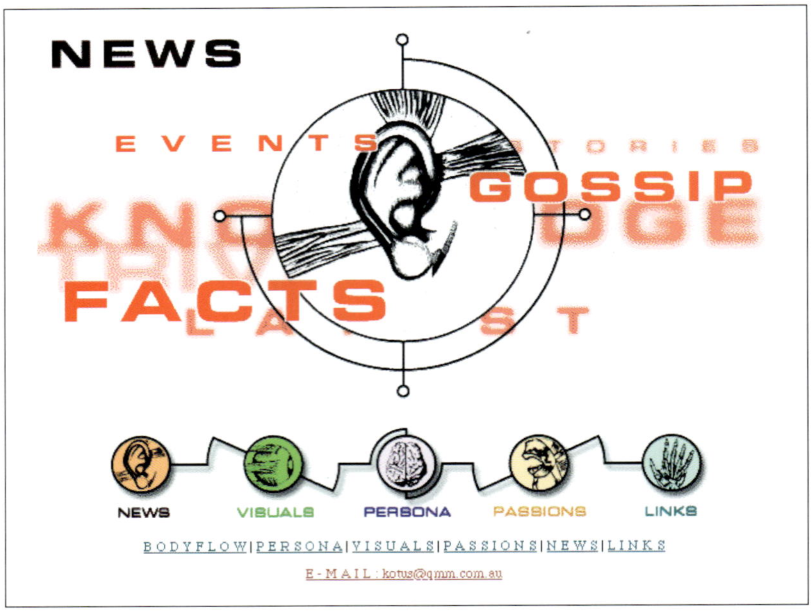

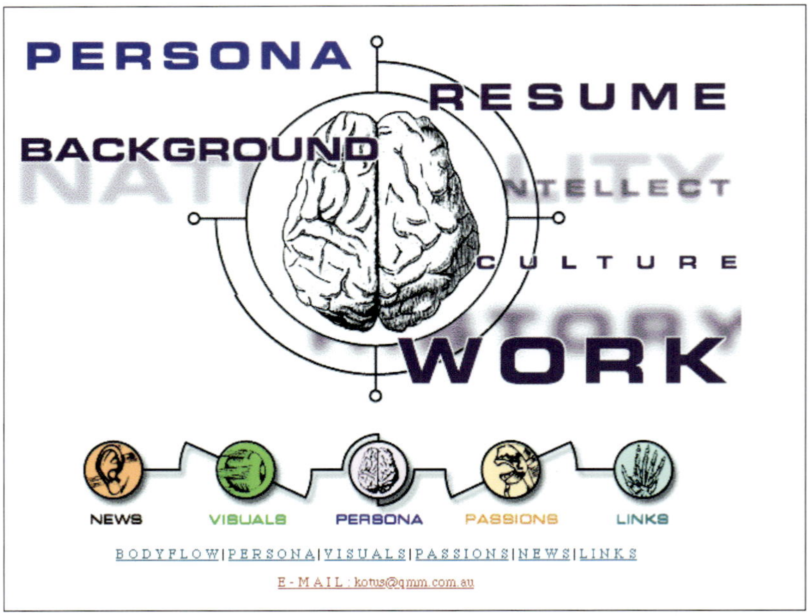

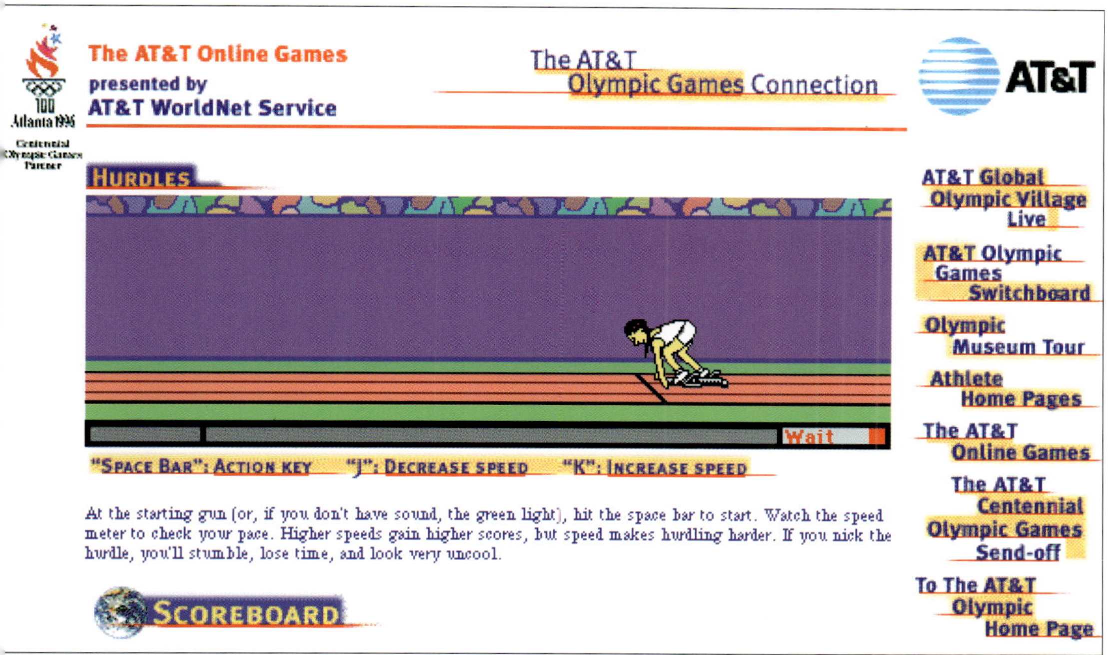

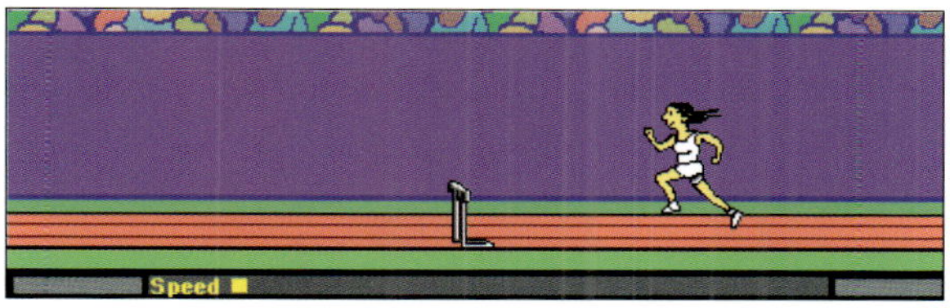

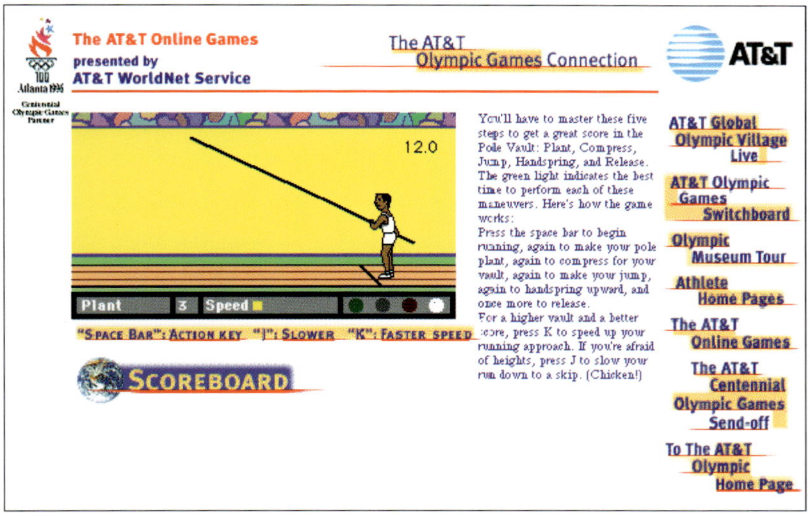

title
AT&T 1996 olympic games
URL
http://www.olympic.att.com/
design firm
Modem Media
creative director
Joe McCambley
associate creative director
David J. Link
art directors
Tracy Long, Stefanie Trinkl
producers
Joseph Salvati, Glen White, Bob Carelli

Can you use a lot of color and still get good performance? Definitely. Although the site looks like a bandwidth-waster, the frugal color palette used here keeps download times to a minimum. Particularly eye-catching are the Shockwave-based online games, with bright, pixelated graphics that respond to your commands.

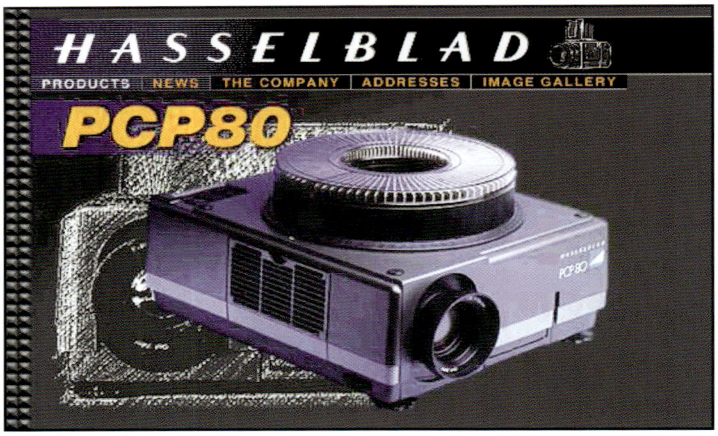

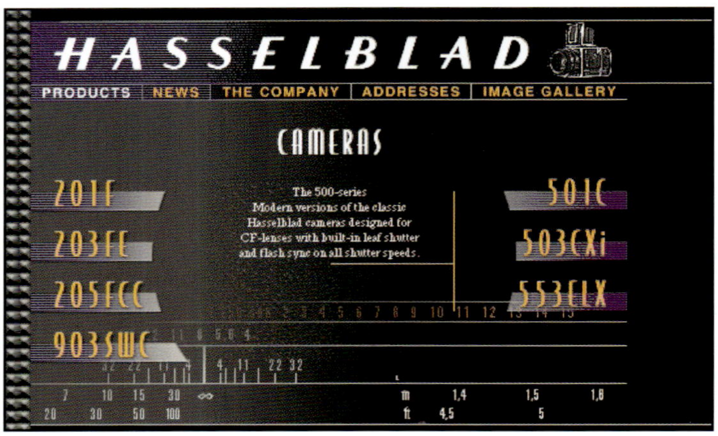

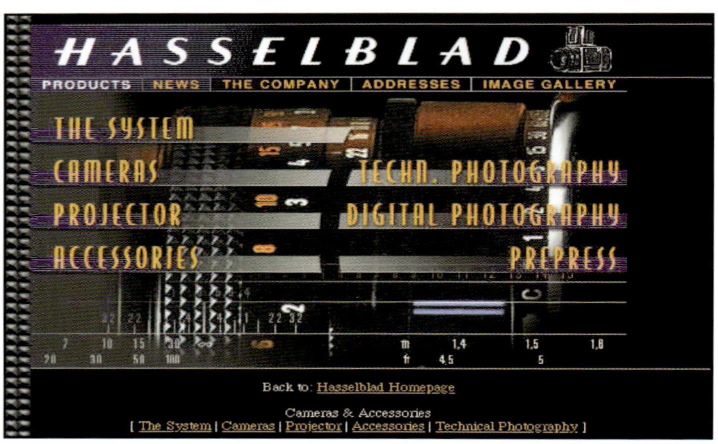

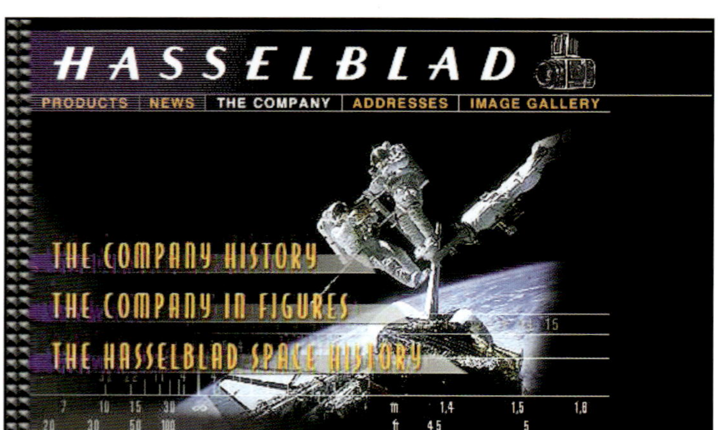

Title
Hasselblad
URL
http://www.hasselblad.se/
Design Firm
Adera Digital Media AB
Designers
Jaanus Heeringson, Ola Carlberg
Illustrators
Jaanus Heeringson,
Laszlo Nagy
Photographers
Jens Karlsson,
Victor Hasselblad AB
Programmers
Jaanus Heeringson,
Ola Carlberg, Thomas Friberg

As one would expect from a leading manufacturer of photographic equipment, the images on Hasselblad's Web site are superb. However, one aspect that makes them work so well is the tightly controlled color palette that drives the site. Blue and orange are prominently featured in the navigation as well as many of the product shots.

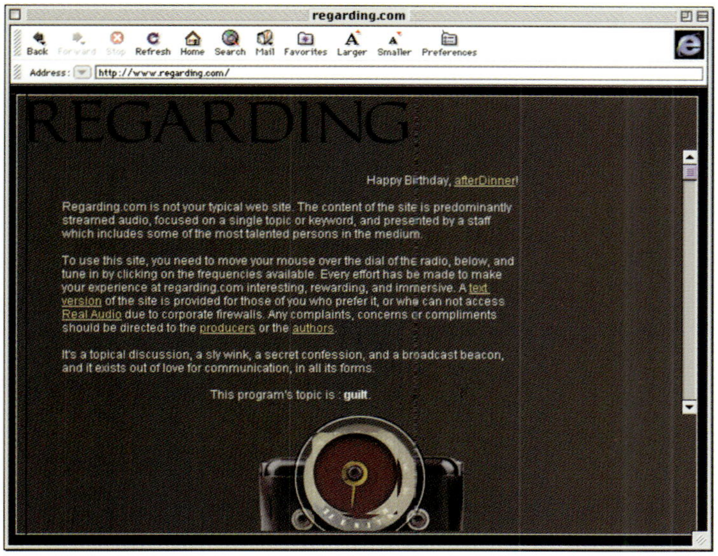

Title
Regarding.com
URL
http://www.regarding.com/
Design firm
Hushville Interactive
Designers
Alexis Massie,
Gregory Alkaitis-Carafelli
Authoring platform
Mac

Serious themes require serious colors. Regarding covers issues through audio explorations, and the metaphor is a dark, comfortable room, where one might tune in the dark Bakelite radio. The link color picks up from the brass color of the dial; the background green provides enough contrast for the link color to stand out, as well as the reversed type.

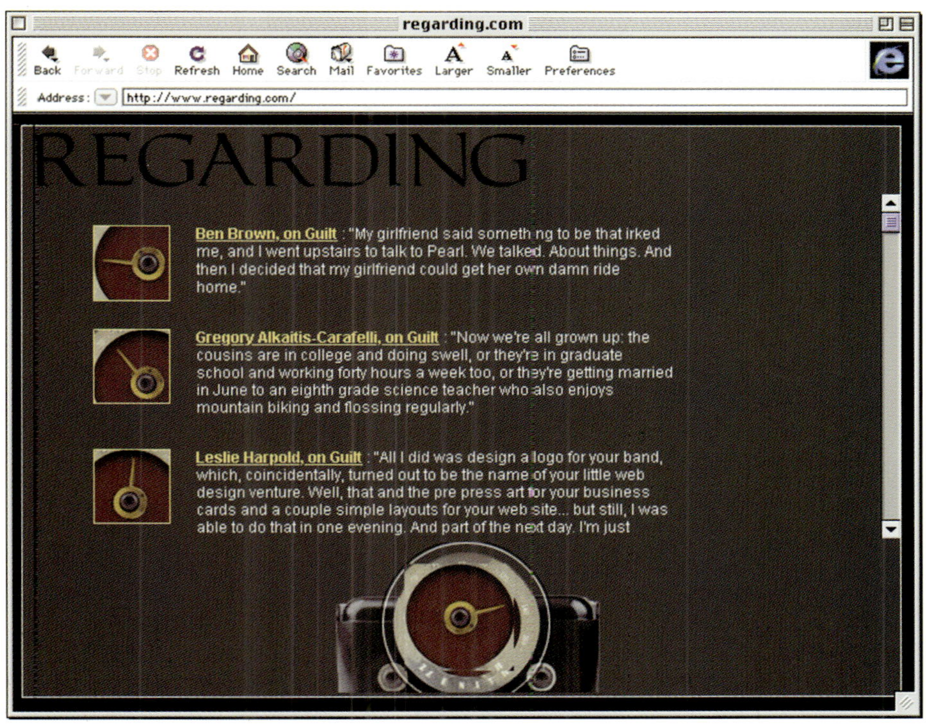

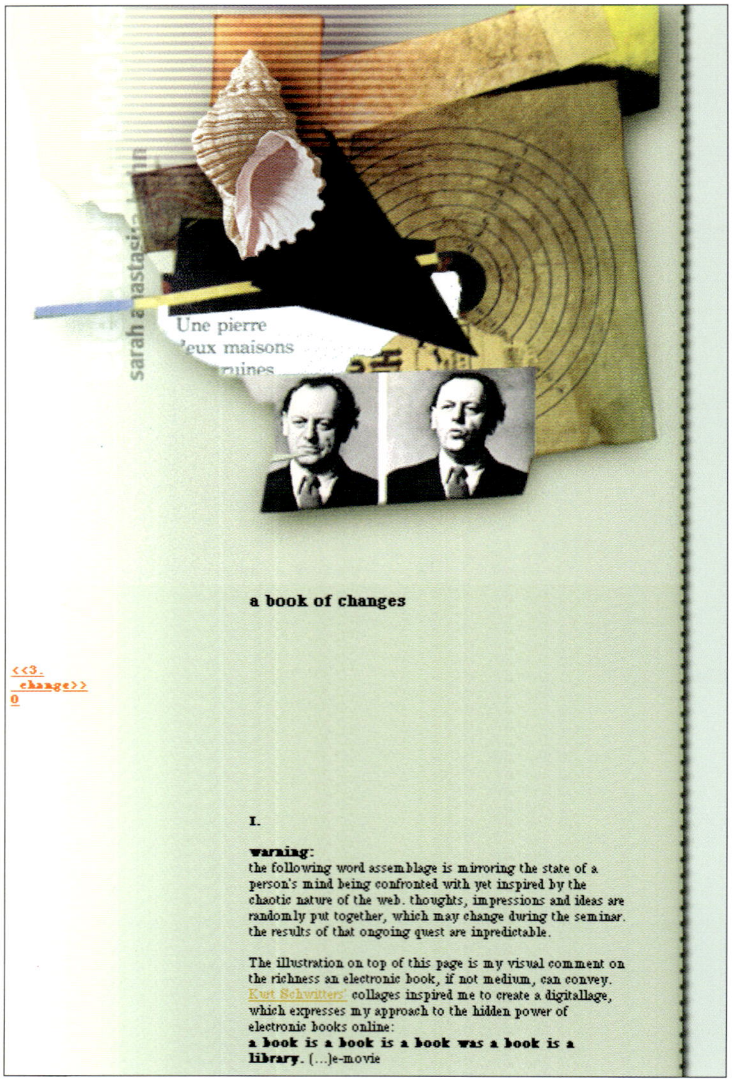

Title
BRODY Electronic Books
URL
http://www.newmedia.co.at/brody/e_books/
Design Firm
BRODY newmedia
Designers
Florian Brody, Sarah Anastasia Hahn

Color comes from light, yet it is rare to see light expressed on the Web. One of the notable aspects of this site's color is the way the designers have introduced a virtual light source at the left edge of the screen. Although most apparent on the opening page, subsequent pages employ a soft transition between white and light olive that soothes the eye and draws its gaze.

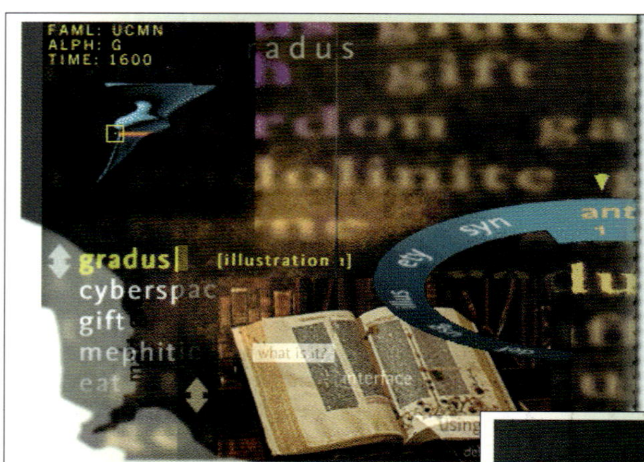

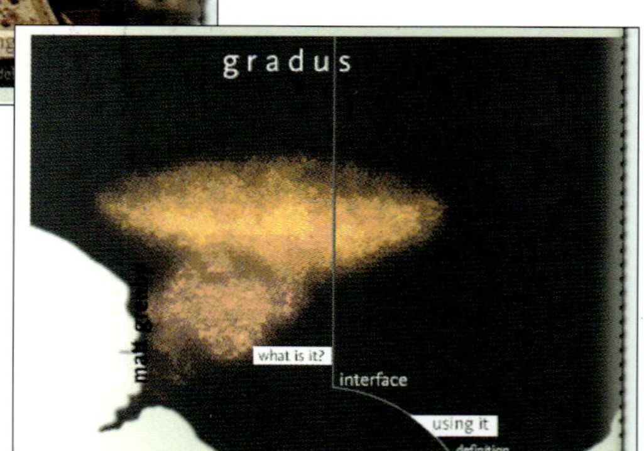

Title
Lekrummet online
URL
http://www.ot.se/lekrummet/
Design firm
Lekrummet Design
Designer
Jorgen Joralv
Photographers
Mikael Wehner, Jens Petersen
Programmers
Jorgen Joralv, Alex Picha

Demonstrating that basic is often better, the color scheme of Lekrummet Online is easy on the eyes and quick to load. Rather than fighting for screen space with every color in the palette, this page's two dominant colors are striking on a simple, white background.

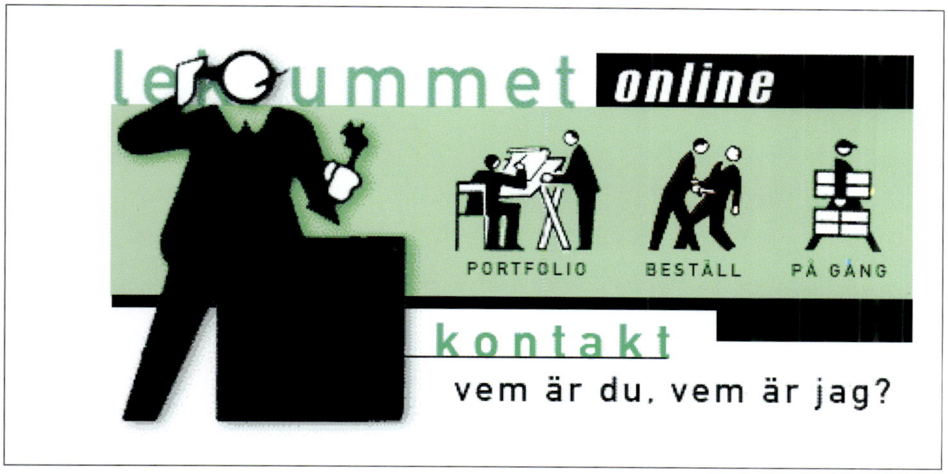

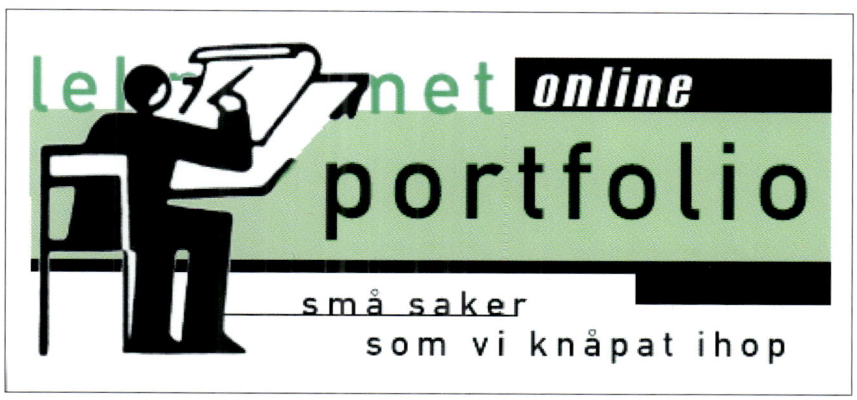

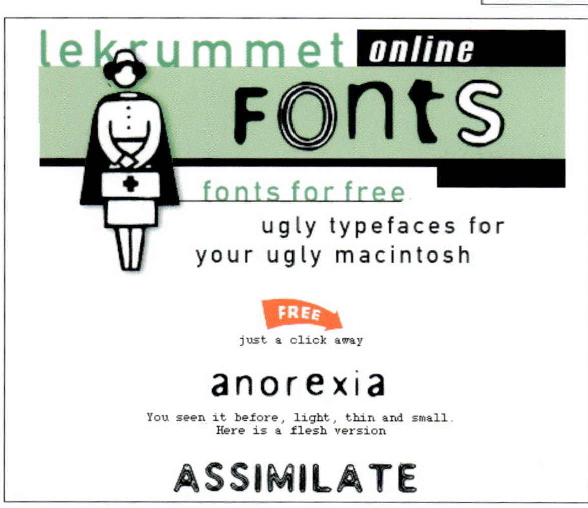

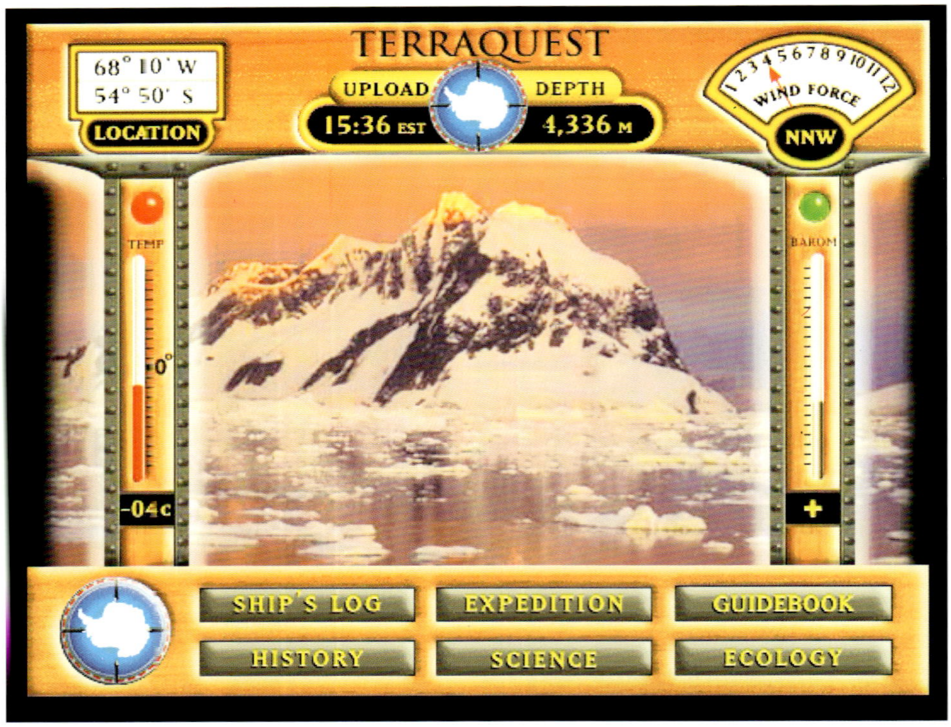

title
Mountain Travel • sobek's virtual Antarctica
URL
http://www.terraquest.com/va/index.html
designer
Brad Johnson
principal photographer
Jonathan chester

The View from the Bridge page of the Virtual Antarctica site is most interesting not because of its faux-wood grain, but because of its approach to displaying the simulation. No attempt has been made to create a photorealistic bridge: edges are smoothly rounded, the windows are not distorted or subjected to perspective. The color here is deliberately soothing and welcoming.

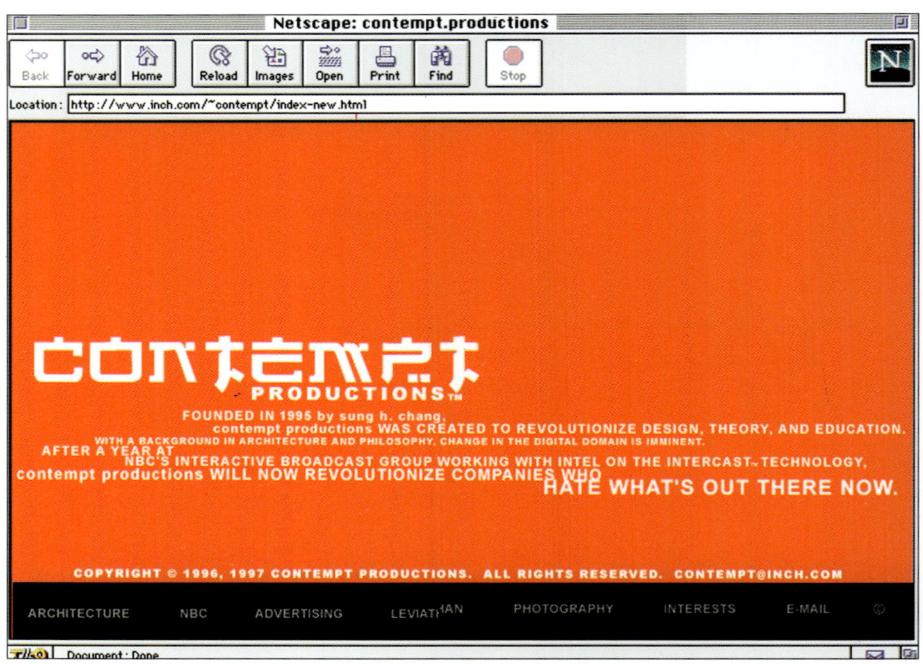

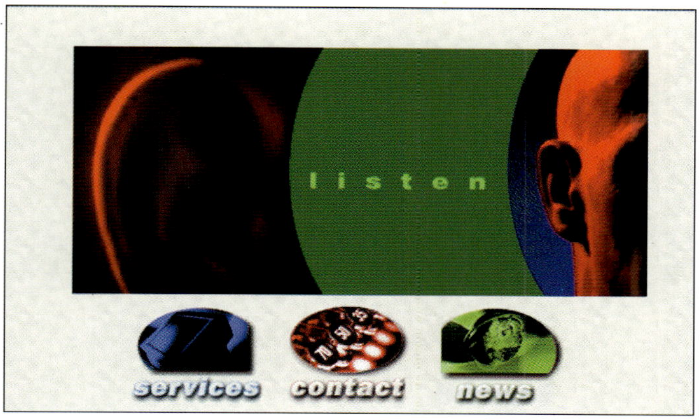

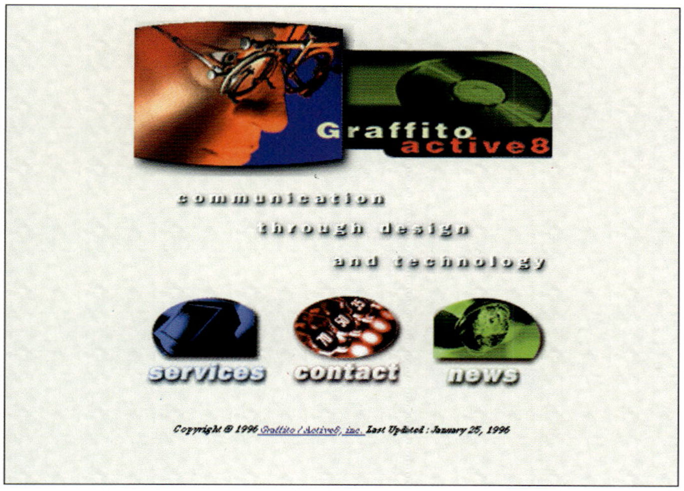

Title
Graffito/Active8
URL
http://www.gr8.com/
Design firm
Graffito/Active8
Designers
Tim Thompson,
Jon Majerik
Illustrator
Josh Field
Photographers
Ed Whitman, Taran Z,
Michael Northrup
Programmer
Jon Majerik

You don't often see these color combinations on the Web. Deep-orange, dark-maroon, violet, and organic-green pairings make the site's atmosphere unnerving, but not quite jarring. Eye-catching, yes, but hard to tell at first just what has grabbed your attention.

Title
Contempt Productions
URL
http://www.comtempt.net/
Design firm
Contempt Productions
Designer
Sung H. Chang

Everything about the Contempt Web site suggests a desire for power and control. Its colors strike at extremes: stark, white text on a deep-red background, supported by a foundation of black. Visitors must delve a few layers into the site before the red gives way to violets and other hues.

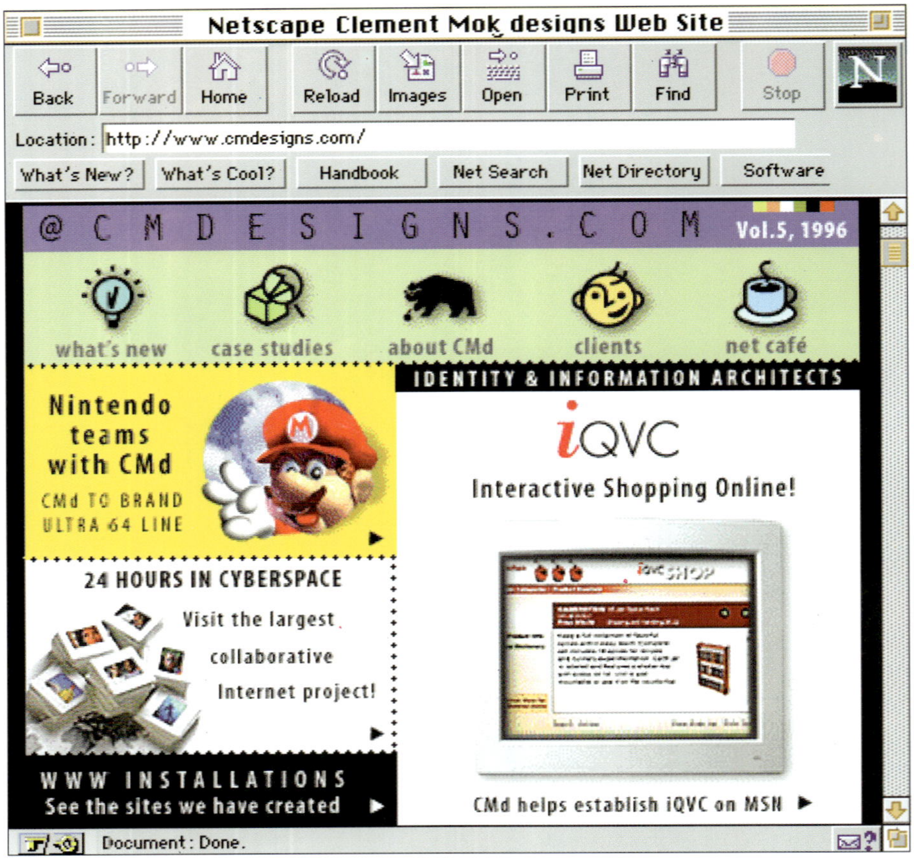

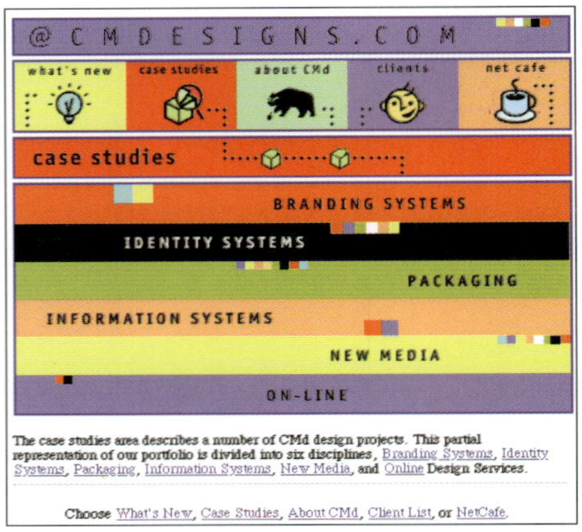

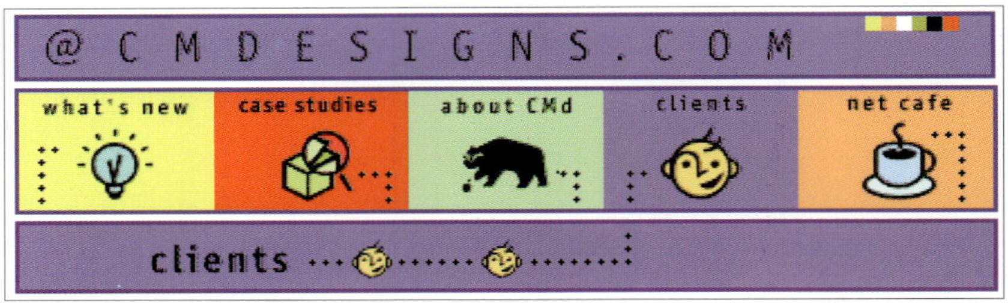

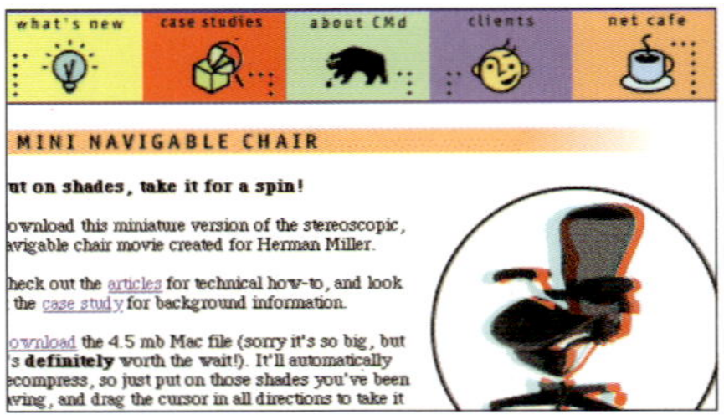

Title
studio Archetype (formerly clement mok designs)
URL
http://www.cmdesigns.com/
Design firm
studio Archetype
producer
sheryl Hampton
creative Director
clement Mok
Associate creative Director
claire Barry
illustrator
Andrew cawrse
programmers
Mark Anquoe, Michael clasen, stephan Bugaj

Bright colors not only make these pages pop, they also function as unobtrusive navigational aids and content separators. The tiered subsystem of sections is a straightforward guide to where in the site the visitor is located, while the small color swatches in the upper-right corner make it easy to jump to other sections and do not waste screen real-estate.

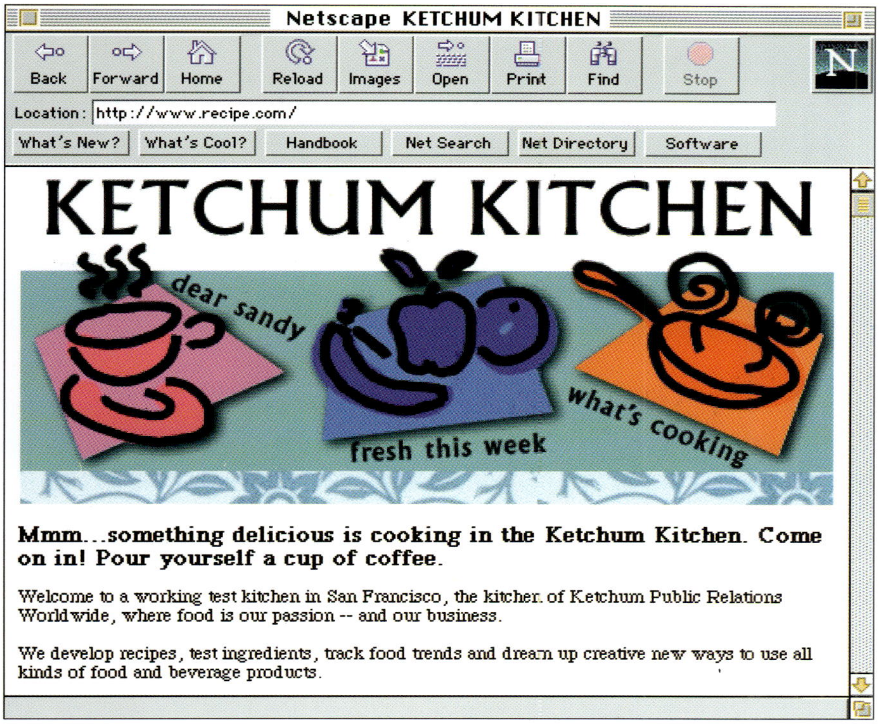

Title
Ketchum Kitchen
URL
http://www.recipe.com/
Design Firm
Red Dot Interactive
Creative Director
Judith Banning

This site, which has held up well since the early stages of Web design, relies on color and patterns to draw the visitor, rather than the frames, tables, and other trappings of modern Web design. The straightforward HTML loads quickly, as do the controlled color palettes, which impart the warmth of a premium kitchen.

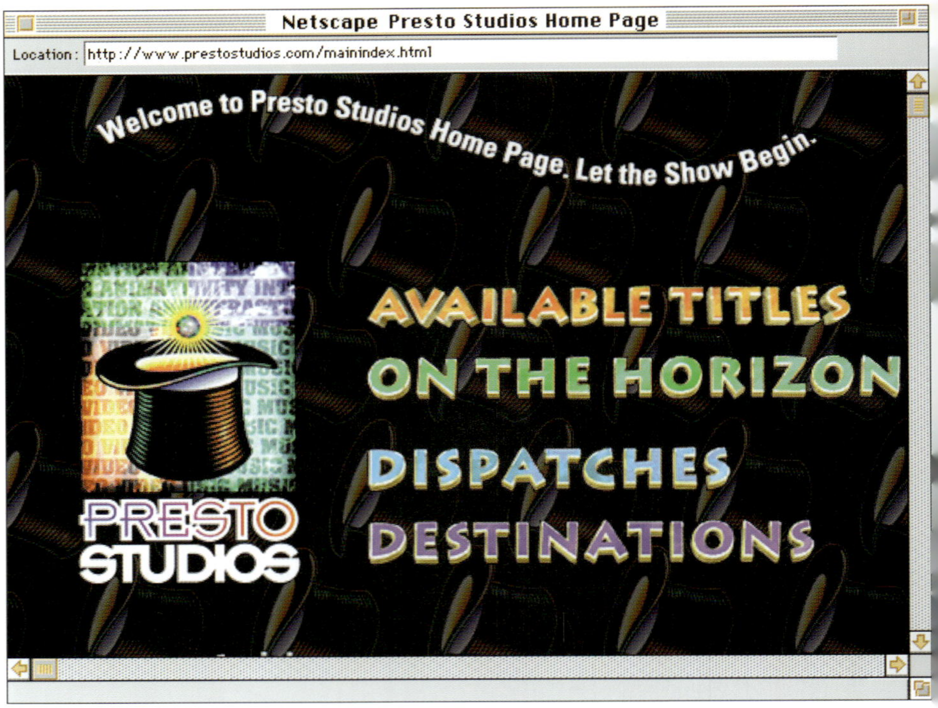

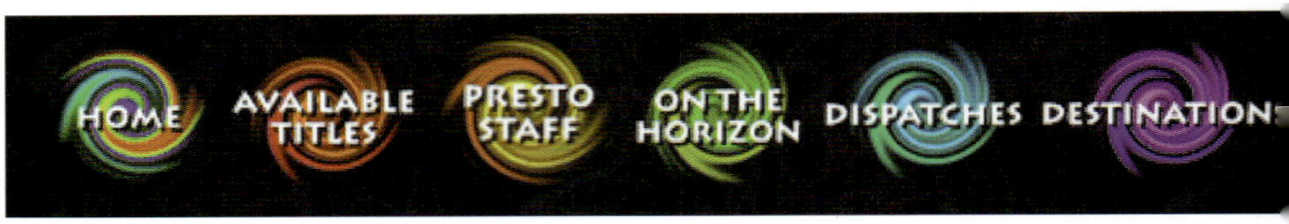

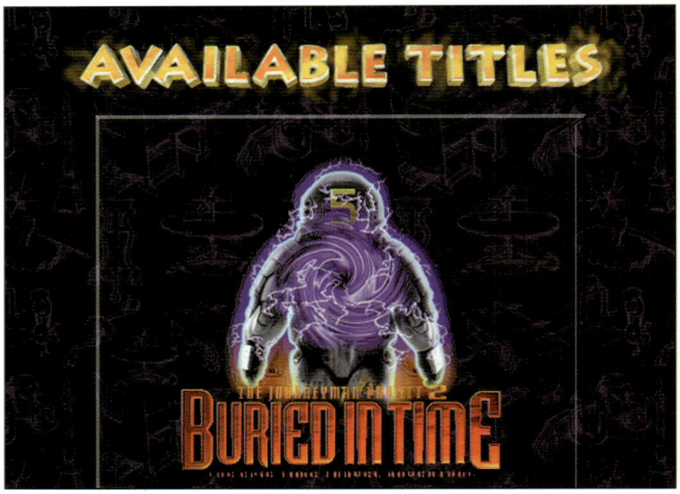

Title
presto studios
URL
http://www.prestostudios.com/
Design firm
presto studios
Designers
frank vitale,
eric fernandes
Programmers
eric fernandes,
prakash kirdalani

Although the multicolored blends decorating the logo and titles are eye-catching, it's the background pattern that makes this site attractive. Repeating a single object is usually a fatal blow to any page, but here, the soft hues of the repeated logo are accentuated by the page's graphics.

Title
DigitalFacades
URL
http://www.dfacades.com/
Design Firm
DigitalFacades
Designer
Oliver Chan
Programmer
Jane Lin

It's always refreshing to find sites that use a single color effectively, as in this example. It allows your eye to be drawn immediately to the navigation, while still savoring the texture of multiple images. Hints of more color appear as you get further into the site, culminating in the site's gallery: The single color gives way to the full-colored examples, which now have more emphasis.

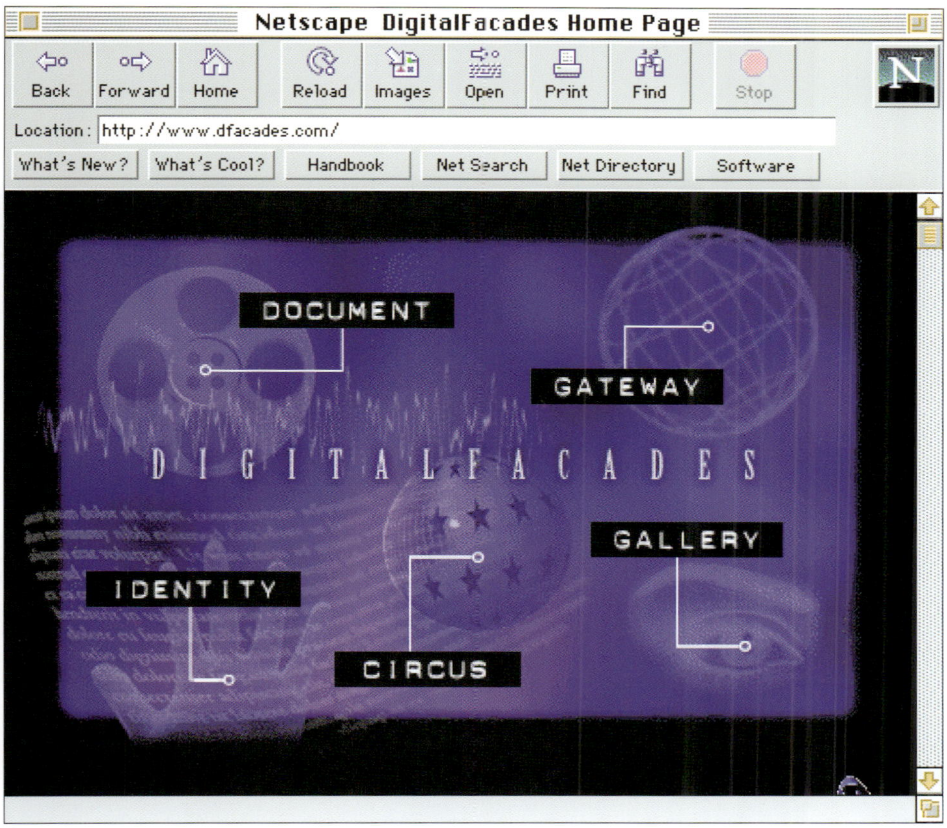

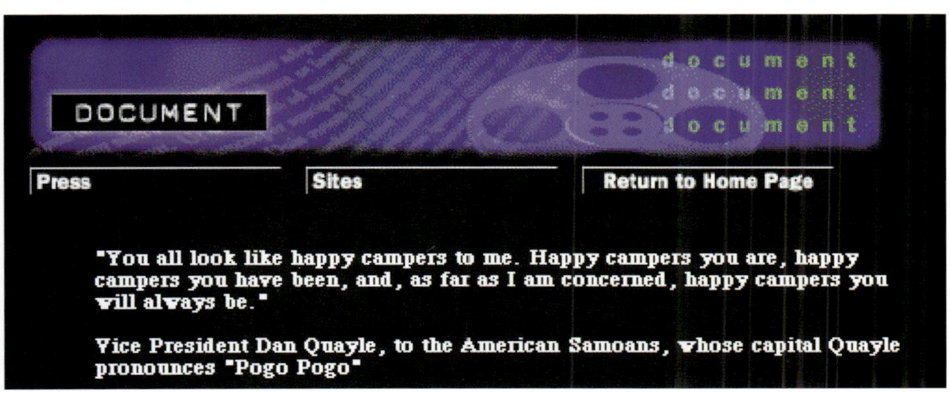

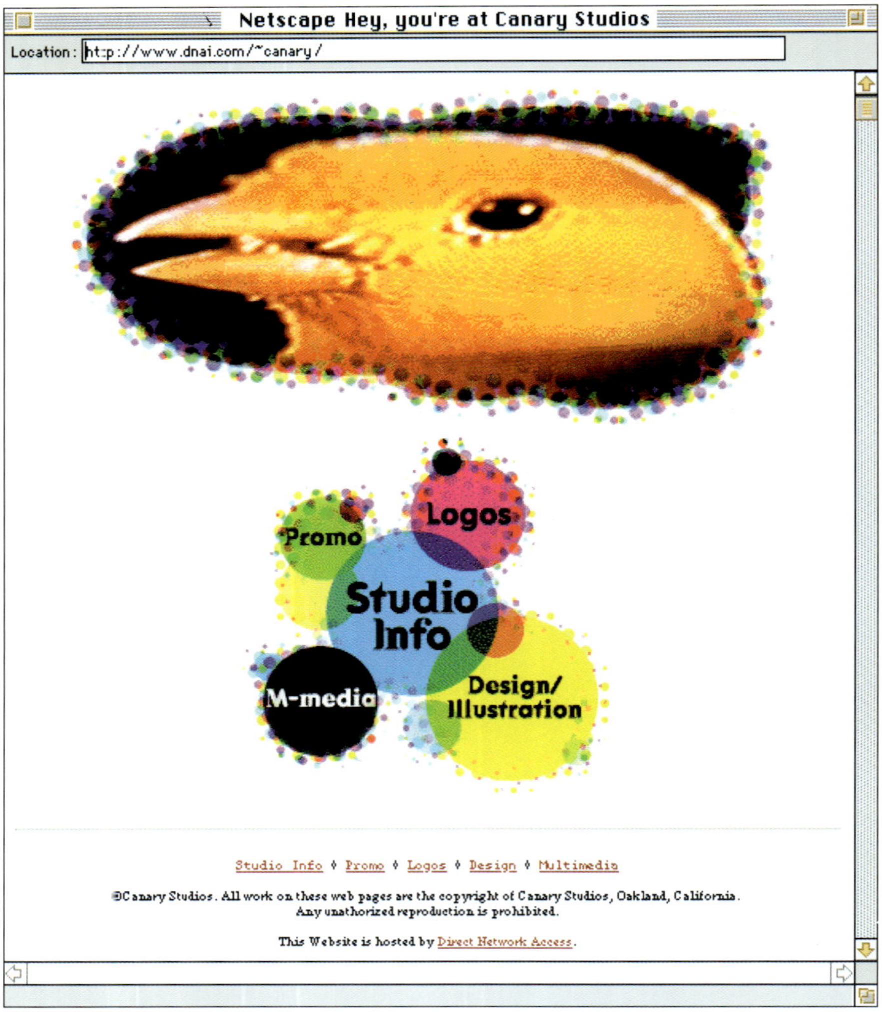

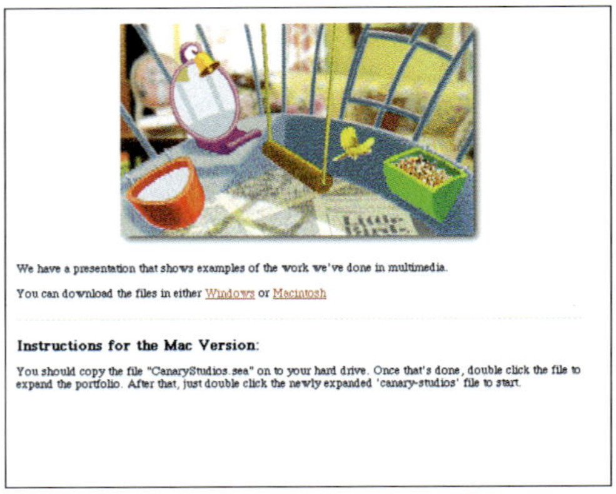

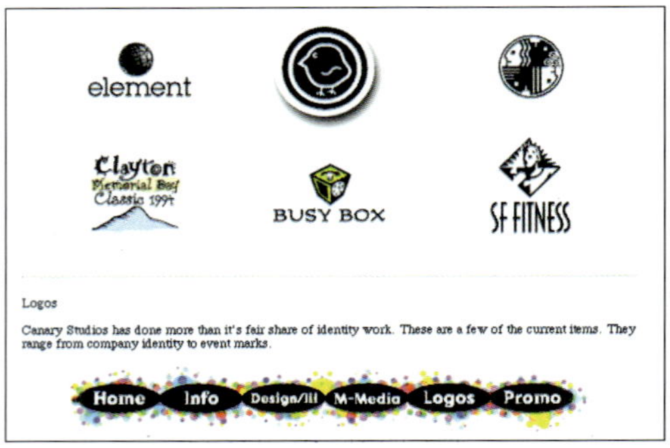

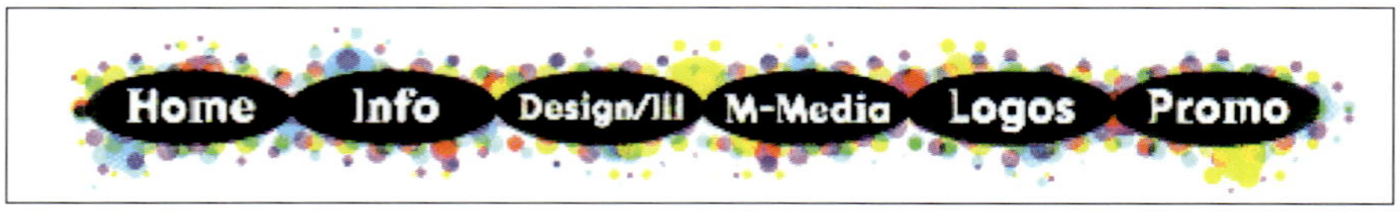

Title
canary studios
URL
http://www.
canary-studios.com/~canary/
Design Firm
canary studios
Designers
Ken Roberts, Carrie English
Illustrator
carrie english
Photographer
Robert Sondgroth
Programmer
Ken Roberts

Who says a canary must be colored canary? The oversaturated image at top suggests that what you'll find here is beyond the normal range of design. The splotchy navigation elements, a seemingly randomized collage of color halftones, reinforce this notion. Once inside, however, the cleanliness of the designers' work adds a professional polish to their image.

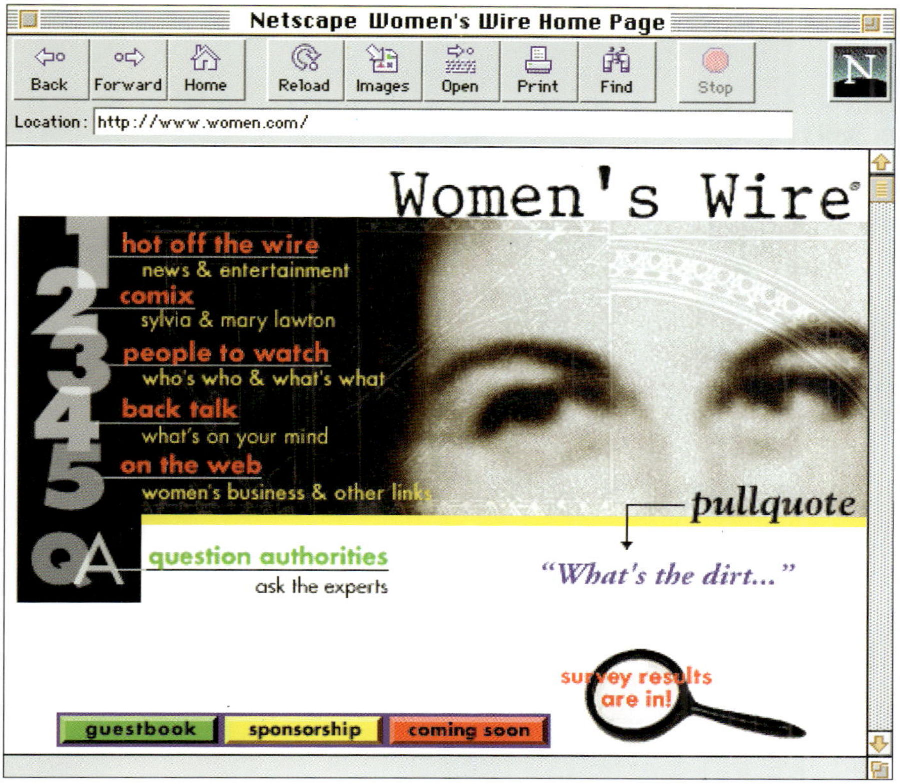

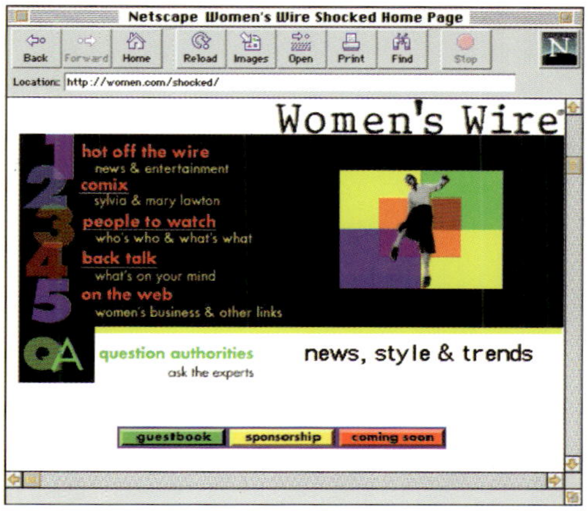

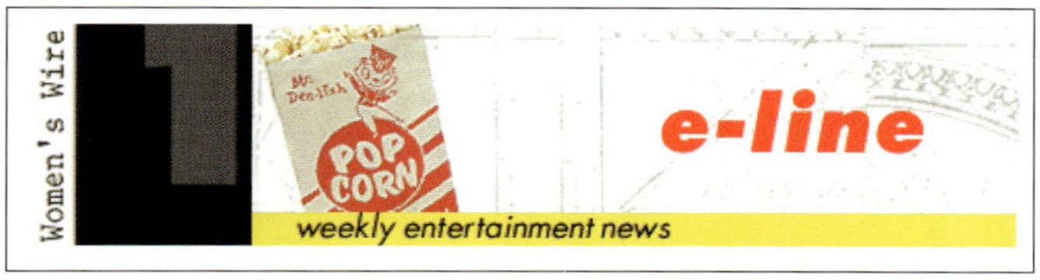

Title
women's wire
URL
http://www.women.com/
Design firm
Lisa Marie Nielsen Design
Designer
Lisa Marie Nielsen

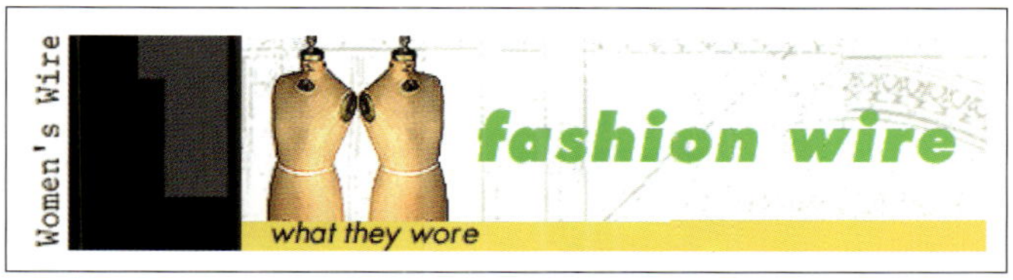

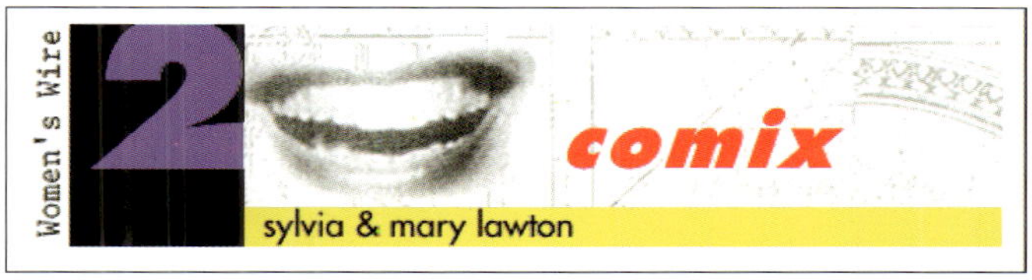

Bright colors are often unfairly reserved for ultra-cheerful sites that occasionally repel viewers due to an overdose of sugarcoating. Not so here. The bright colors on these pages, combined with the grayscale photographs and bitmapped texture, create an upbeat look that respects the intelligence of the site's target audience.

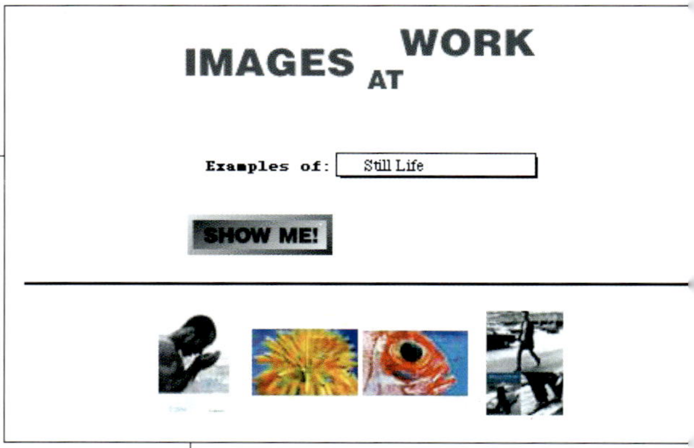
IMAGES AT WORK
Examples of: Still Life
SHOW ME!

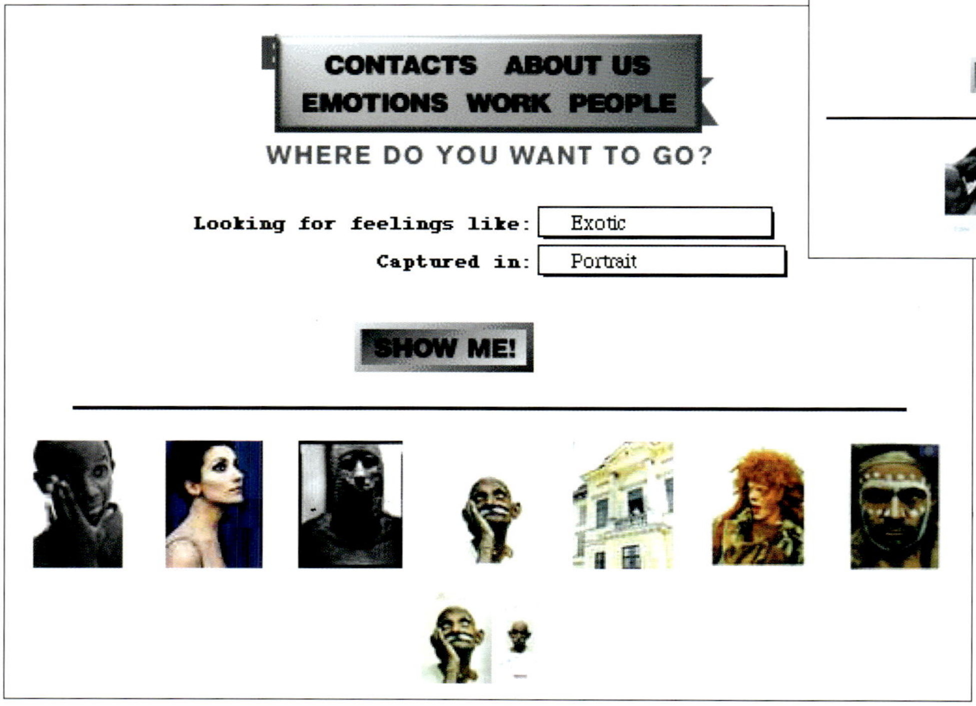
CONTACTS ABOUT US
EMOTIONS WORK PEOPLE
WHERE DO YOU WANT TO GO?
Looking for feelings like: Exotic
Captured in: Portrait
SHOW ME!

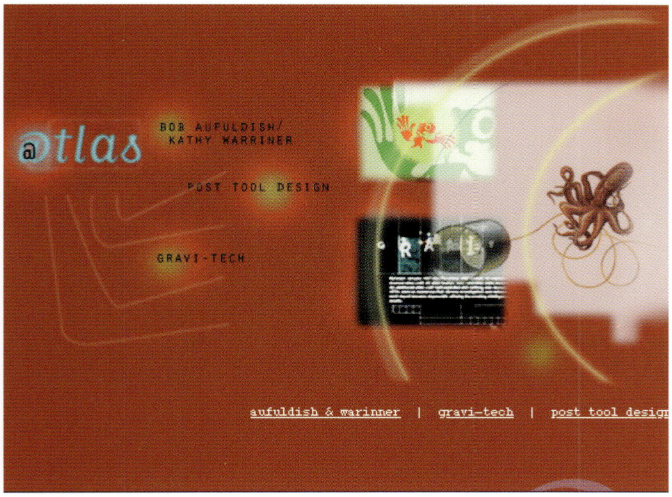

Title
@tlas
URL
http://www.atlas.organic.com/atlas/win97_f3.html
Design Firm
@tlas Web Design
Senior Designer
Amy Franceschini
Co-designer
David Karam
Programmer
Michael Macrone

Using a different colored background isn't necessarily notable on the Web. What makes @tlas different in this respect is the way the background and foreground elements blend well together. The blurs provide a soft context upon which rests the harder-edged highlights of each page.

Title
Camera Link AB
URL
http://www.cameralink.se/
Design Firm
Robot
Designers
Raket/Robot
Programmer
Jesper Weissglas

With a potential palette of millions of colors, why choose to create a largely grayscale Web site? As aficionados of classic black-and-white movies are aware, the starkness of grayscale can bring more drama to a medium dominated by color. When colored images are introduced, they make a bigger impact.

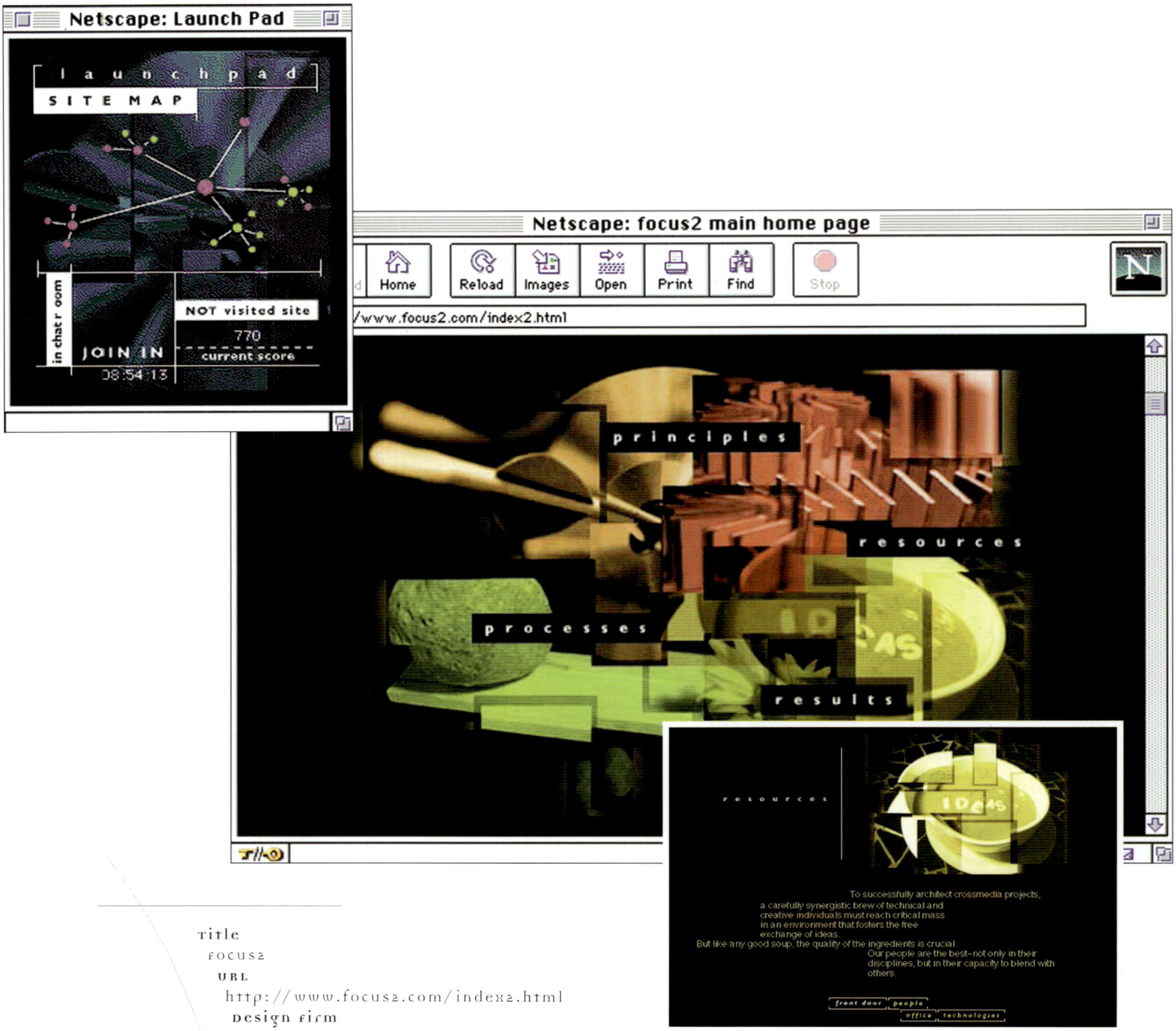

Title
focus2
URL
http://www.focus2.com/index2.html
Design firm
focus2
Designers
Shawn Freeman, Todd Hart,
Cort Langworthy, Brad Walton
Illustrators
Shawn Freeman, Cort Langworthy
Photographers
Dick Patrick, Jake Dean, Richard
Seagraves
Programmers
David Adams, Walker Hale IV

Even when limited by the Web's 216-color, browser-safe palette, it's tempting to throw as much color as possible at a Web site—like having the jumbo set of Legos rather than one of the little kits. However, the designers here know the value of reining in excessive color, and the duotoned title images prove it.

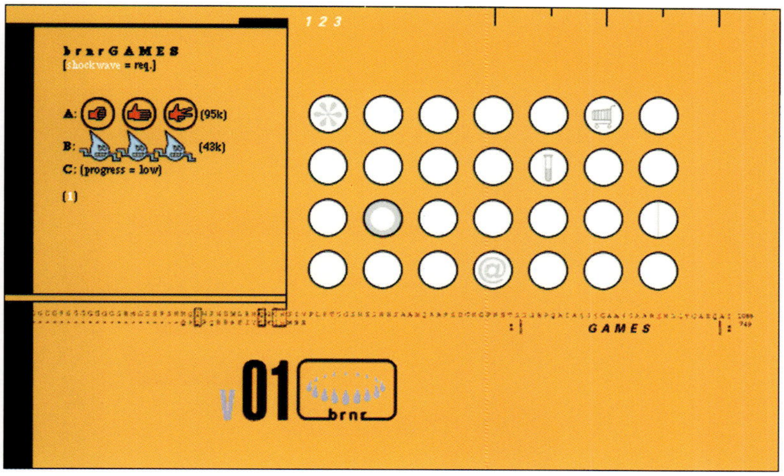

Title
BRNR Labs
URL
http://www.brnr.com/
Designer
Michael French

The first noticeable color element here is, of course, the bright background; second are the white circles. Tying the two together are the gray icons and accents (notice the BRNR logo, gray against the background instead of white) that are the featured elements of the main page. These objects get noticed not because of their color, but because of the disparity between the other two.

Title
qaswa
URL
http://www.qaswa.com/
Design Firm
qaswa communications
Designer
Ammon Haggerty

The designers here seem to have done more with white than other sites do with fully loaded color palettes. Using white as a base, they've carved out sections that push the brightly colored icon elements forward. Photoshop users will recognize the pale checkerboard background pattern as that program's default transparency indicator.

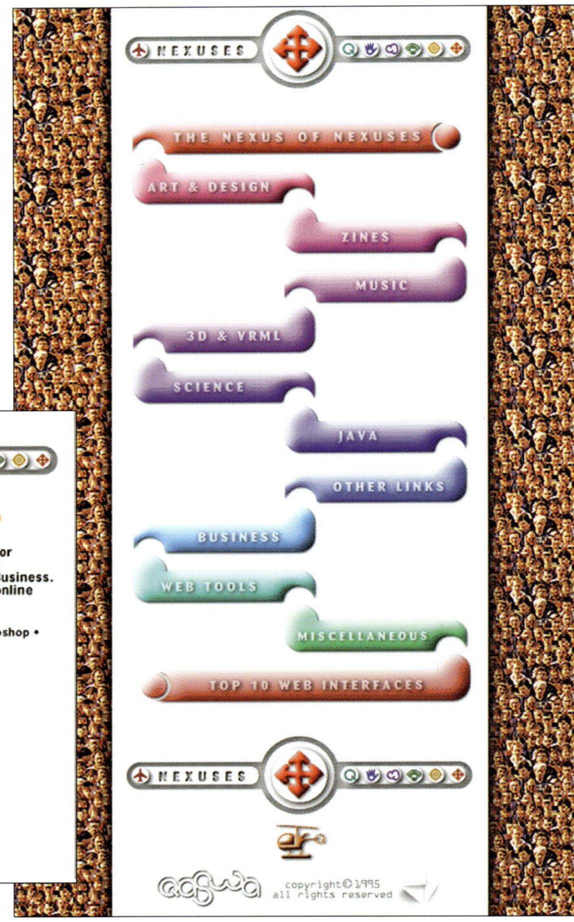

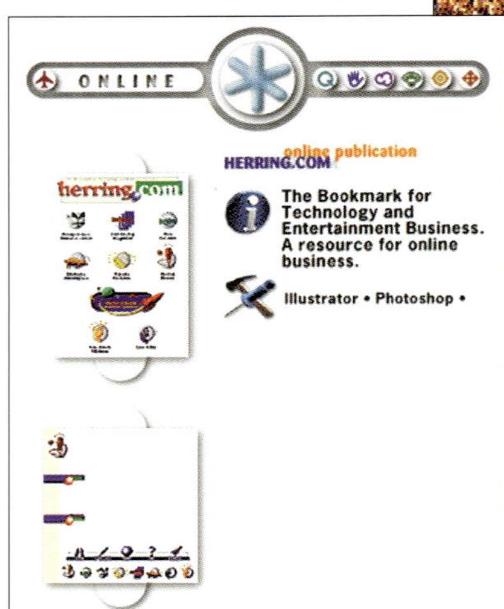

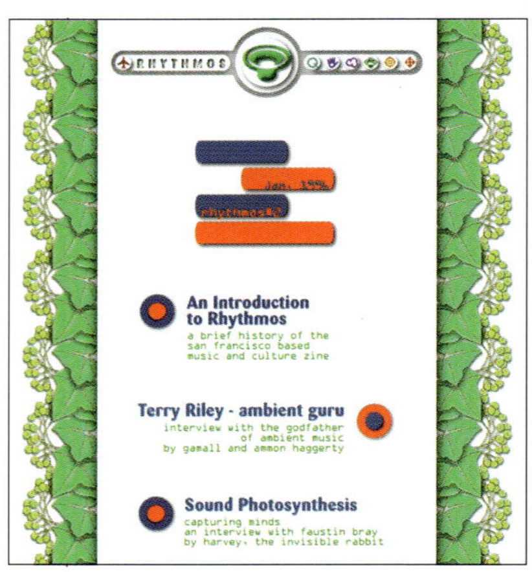

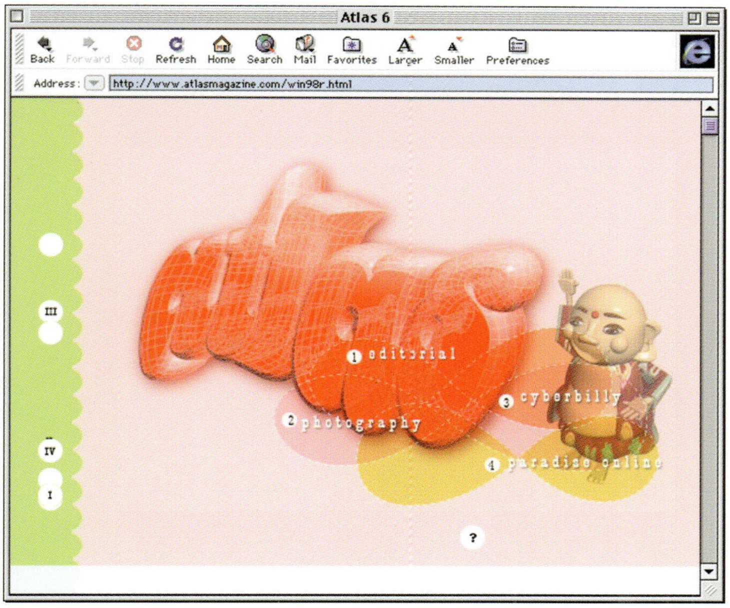

Title
Atlas Magazine
URL
http://www.atlasmagazine.com/win98r.html
Design Firm
Atlas
Designer/Illustrator
Amy Franceschini
Photographers
Olivier Laude,
Catherine Karnow,
Bob Sacha,
Adam Kufeld, et al.
Programmer
Michael Macrone
Authoring Platform
Mac, PC

A homepage that (on some browsers) flashes, reloads, and requires that you lunge to click on links, is made even more bizarre by a really eccentric color palette. There is an aesthetic to going over the top, which Atlas magazine embodies in its editorial and that they have reflected in their site's design.

Title
smallprint
URL
http://www.smallprint.net/
Designer/Illustrator/
Programmer
Miika Saksi
Authoring Platform
PC

Smallprint is a mysterious set of recursive pages that share a few basic colors across the entire tiny site. Photographs are screened back in a yellowish green, while beige and khaki show up on every page. The dithering of these colors presents strong alternating one-pixel vertical bars that add a corduroy texture to the pages.

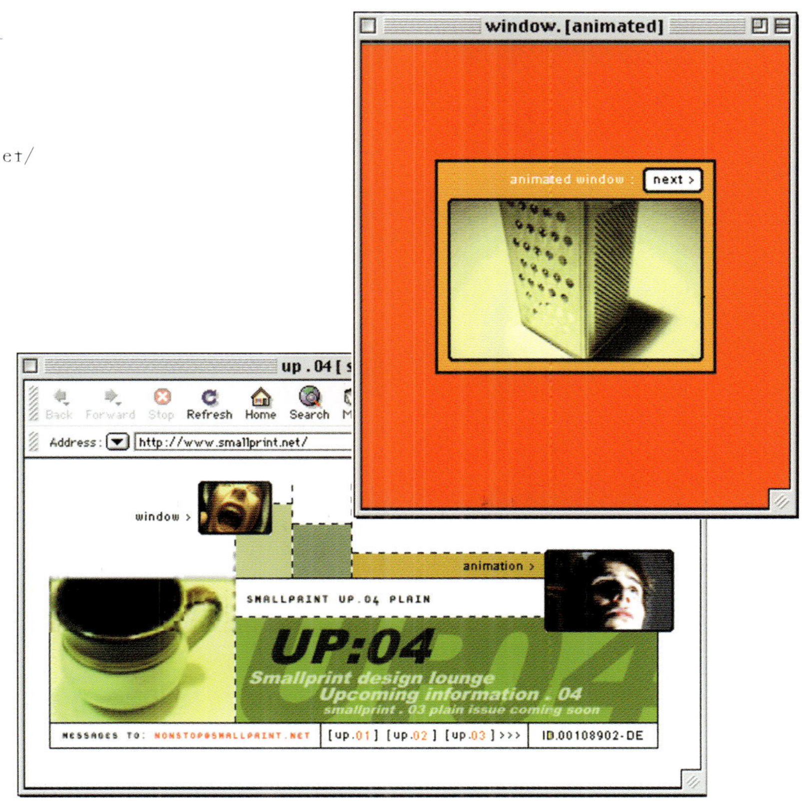

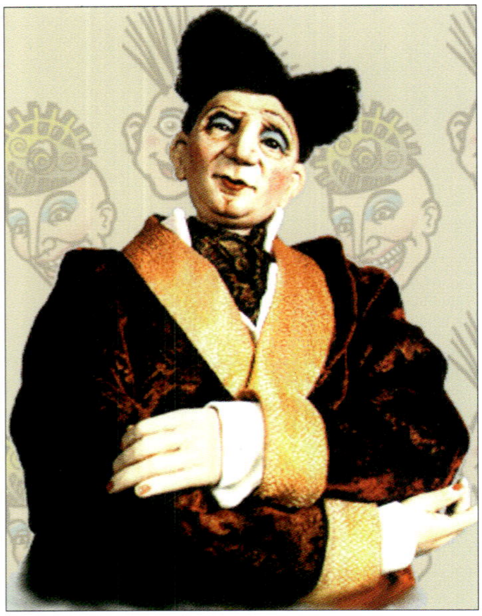

Title
We Make Art Dolls and Automata
URL
http://www.home.earthlink.net/~chomed/cmcollector.html
Designer/Illustrator/Photographer
chris chomick
Authoring platform
pc

The dolls that appear on each page are subtly cartooned (maybe caricatured) using a comic-book palette on the illustrations in the background and at the header. Each section has a pale tint in the background that plays off the tints in the both photographs and illustrations. The marvelous Roland Montague in red velvet always points home.

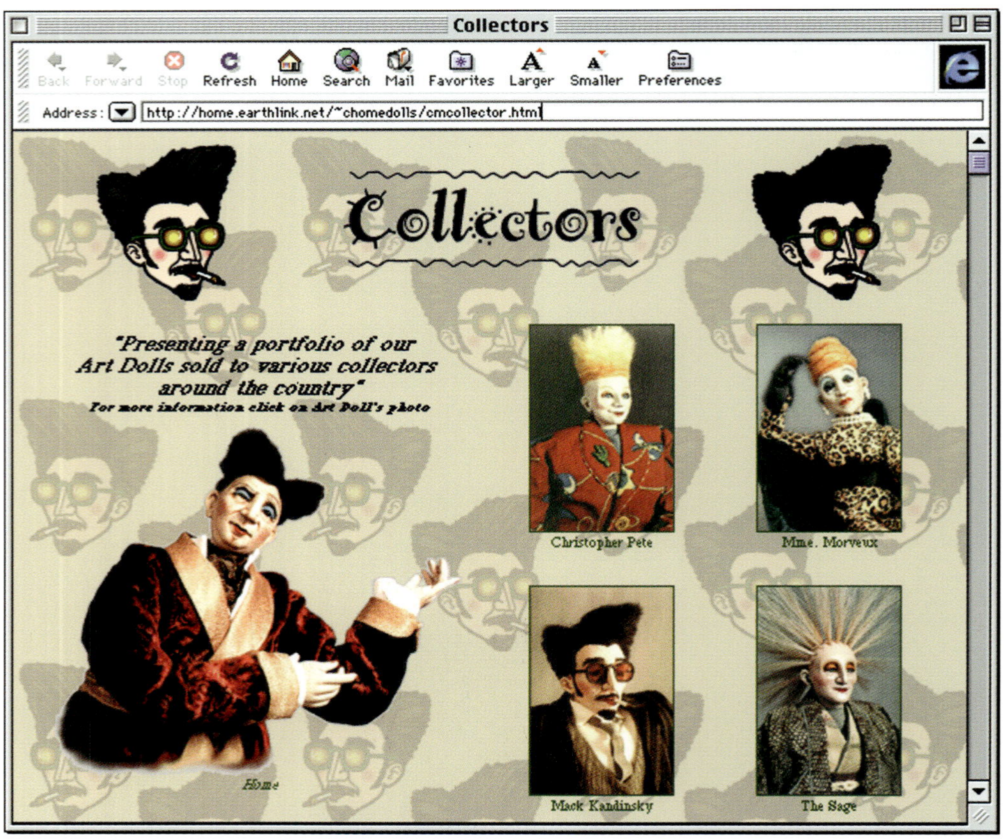

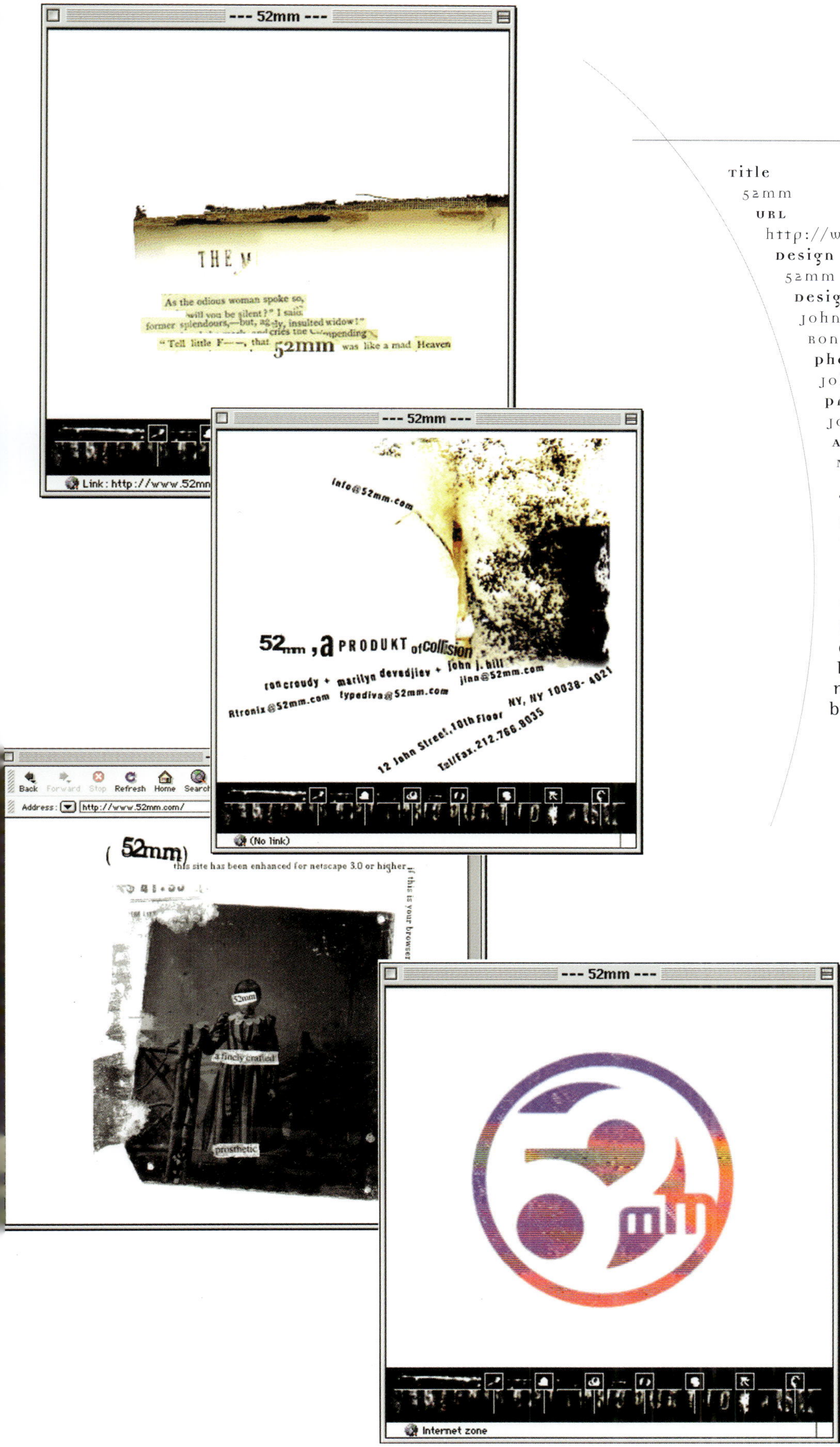

Title
52mm
URL
http://www.52mm.com/
Design Firm
52mm
Designers/Illustrators
John J. Hill, Marilyn Devedjiev,
Ron Croudy
Photographers
John J. Hill, Marilyn Devedjiev
Programmer
John J. Hill
Authoring Platform
Mac

These designers effectively bring the world of photocopier art to the Internet. Using images with just gray, faded-newspaper yellows, or rainbow-photocopy-streaked, the whole site looks like objects found in windows years later or left over in the recycling bin. It's a consistent aesthetic, made more pronounced by an occasional burst of outrageous colors.

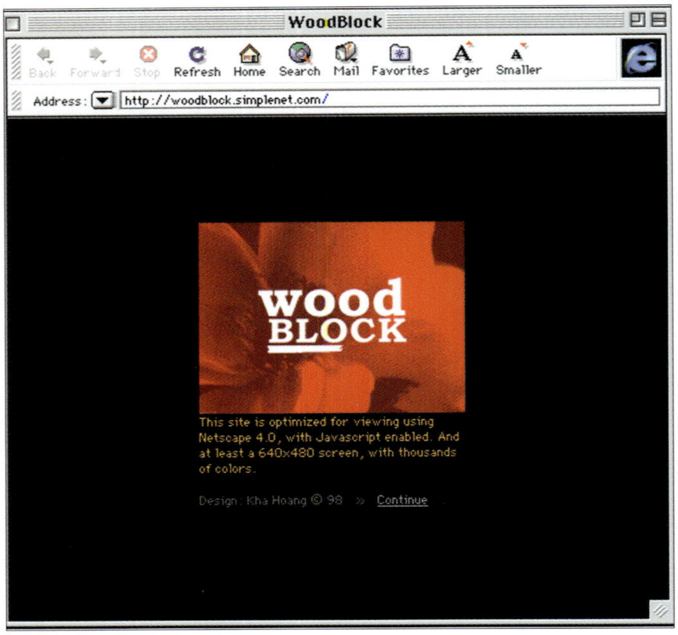

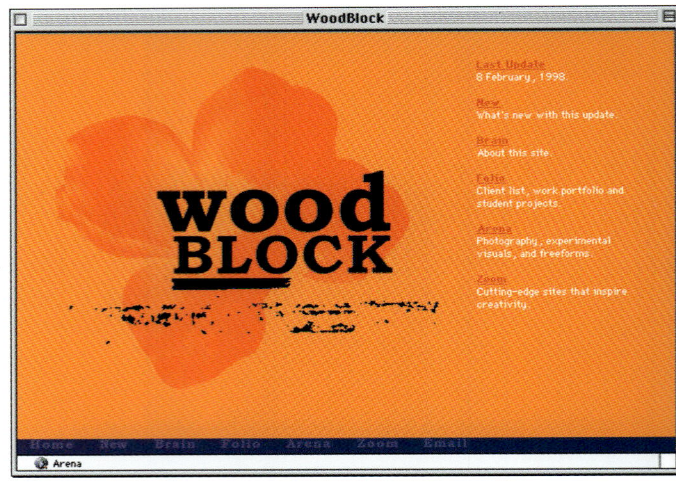

Title
woodblock
URL
http://www.woodblock.simplenet.com/
Designer/Illustrator/Programmer
Kha Hoang
Authoring platform
Mac

Look at the distinction of two grays at the bottom of the entry page to the site: the design credit and the continue link. This is the epitome of using small distinctions to indicate large differences in purpose; there's no mistaking the credit for the navigation. The homepage and subsequent pages typically use background colors to set off type, but pick up the type color in an illustration. On the homepage, this extends to the ALINK color being the same as the background, and the text color matching the flower's red.

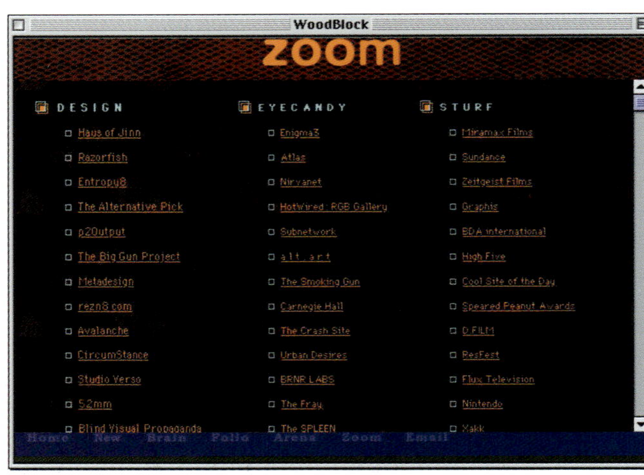

title
Los Angeles County Arts Commission
URL
http://www.lacountyarts.org/
design firm
Looking/Los Angeles
designers
Donna Fischer, David Young
programmer
David Young
authoring platform
Mac

The colors don't have an intrinsic meaning, but they do clearly differentiate one section from another. Each section carries forth its color by using multiple tints for different information areas. Type is knocked out, where necessary, for legibility. The metaphor never breaks down from the home extended out to any subpage of the site. The colors aren't all Web safe, but they're used sparingly enough to avoid real conflicts. Table cells are filled with colors for a quick display.

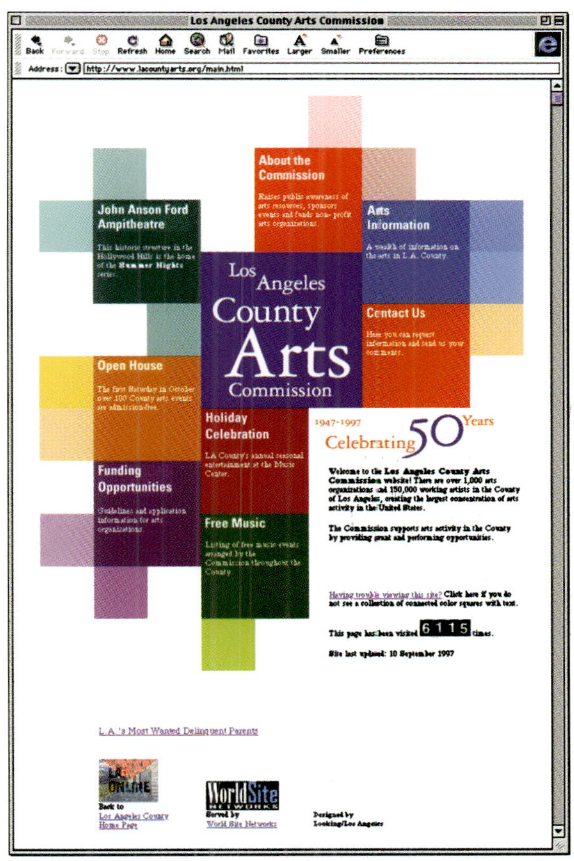

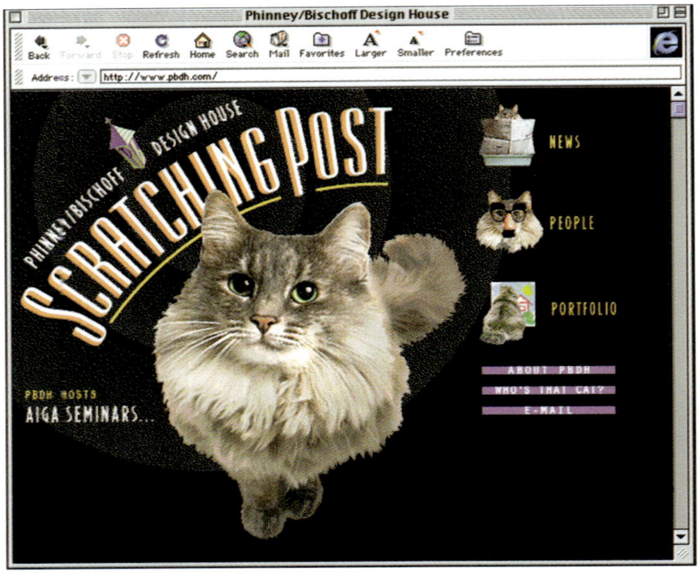

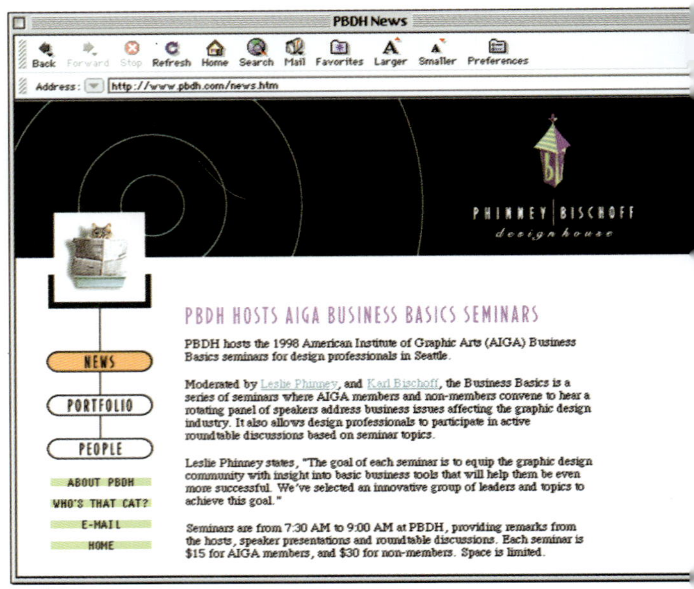

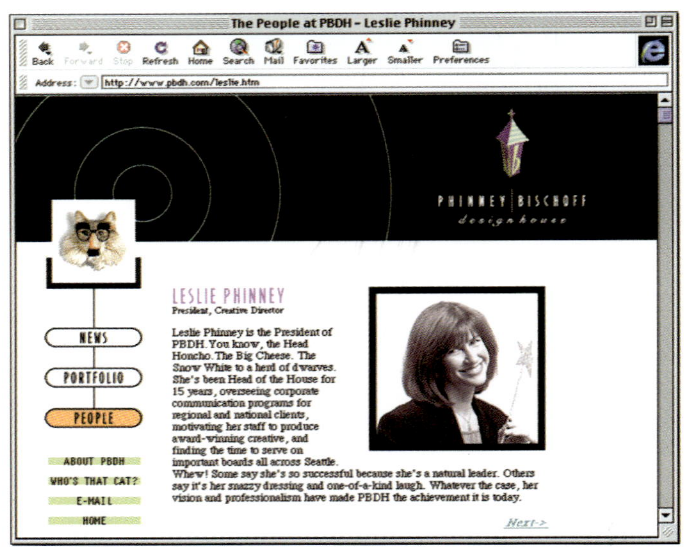

Title
Phinney/Bischoff Design House, Inc.
URL
http://www.pbdh.com/
Design Firm
Phinney/Bischoff Design House, Inc.
Designer/Illustrator
Neil Robertson
Photographer
Karl Bischoff
Programmers
Neil Robertson, Scotty Carreiro
Creative Directors
Leslie Phinney, Karl Bischoff
Authoring Platform
Mac

With a cat as a mascot, the colors of fur seem to predominate the site, along with the corporate identity colors. Using some clever dithering, the Phinney/Bischoff Design House site is able to incorporate photos (of their top cat, Ruby) as well as solid colors for interface elements. Rather than use excessive gradations and leave the color display to the vagaries of a browser, the green, concentric waves on the homepage were rendered as a one-color bitmap image.

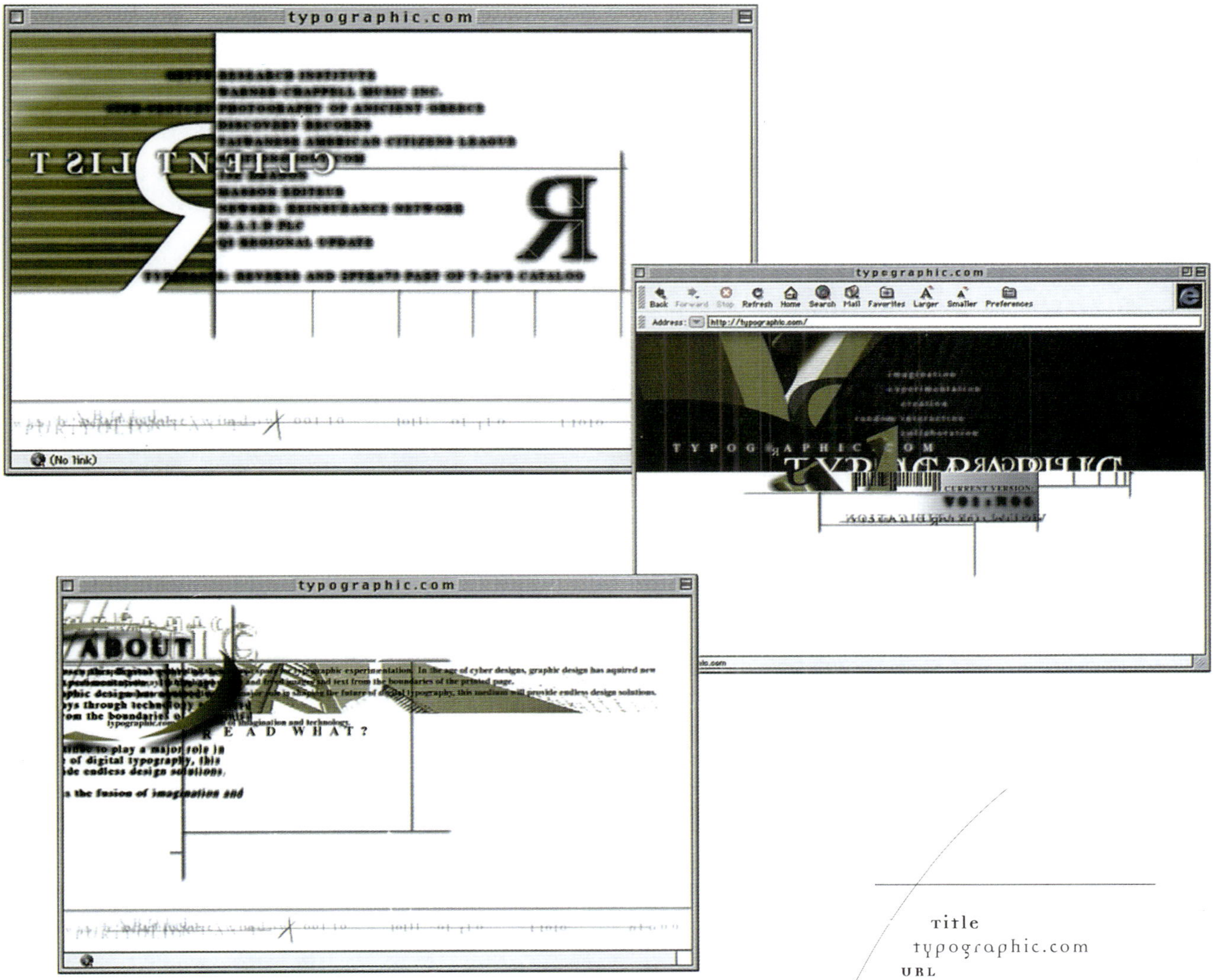

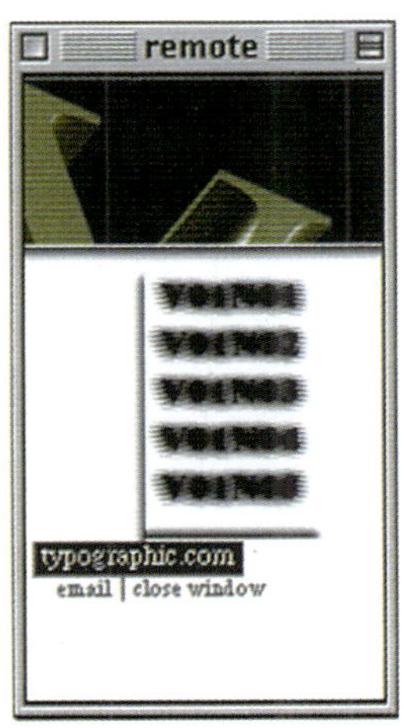

Title
typographic.com
URL
http://www.typographic.com/
Design Firm
typographic.com
Designer/Illustrator/
Programmer
Jimmy Chen
Authoring Platform
Mac

This typographic site demonstrates the color of white as well as any print counterpart. White is used effectively to knock-out letters, to fuzz edges, and to emphasize space, especially on the homepage. The only real color present is the beige that is so severely dithered that it creates an incredibly strong vertical motion that almost emulates a line of type.

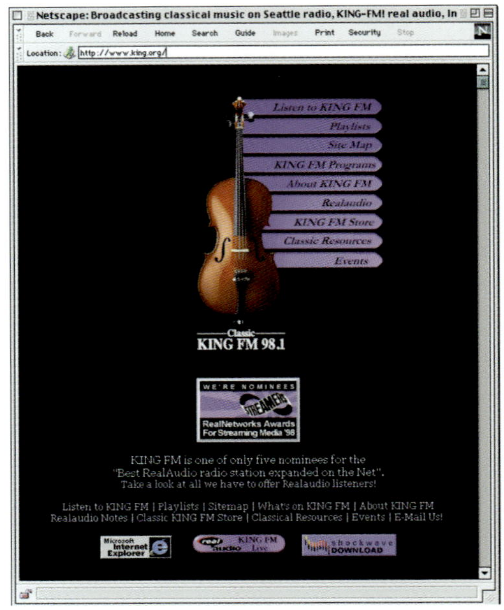

Title
KING-FM Radio
URL
http://www.king.org/
Design Firm
USWeb Seattle
Designers
Kristin Ingalls, Mark Fromson,
David McKeague, Dan Riley
Programmers
Bob Cotrell, Dan Riley
Authoring Platform
Mac, Unix, PC

As the Web site for a music station featuring classical music, the design needs to portray an environment as classic—and classy—as the symphonies that are played. The photos of instruments are rich in color against the black background, counterbalanced by navigational buttons in royal-violet gradations.

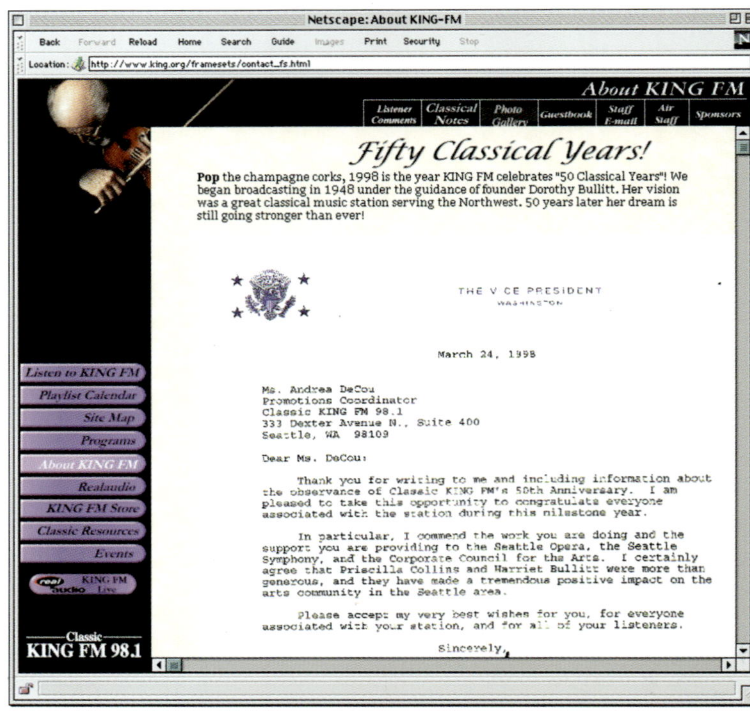

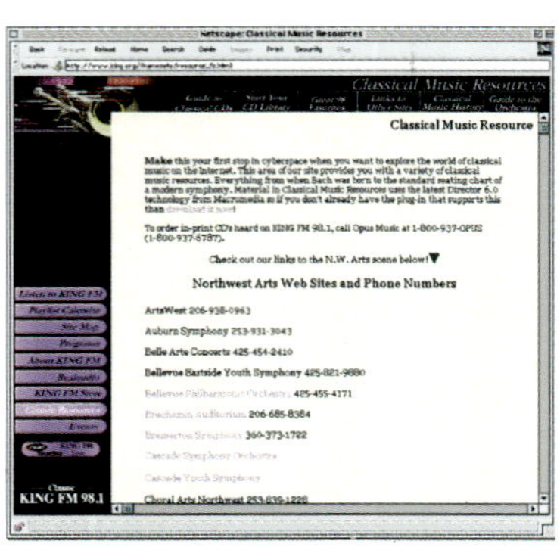

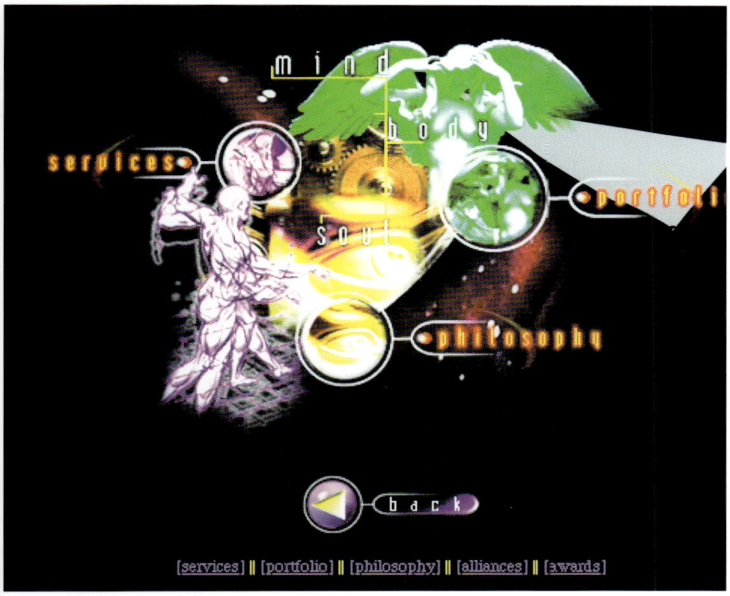

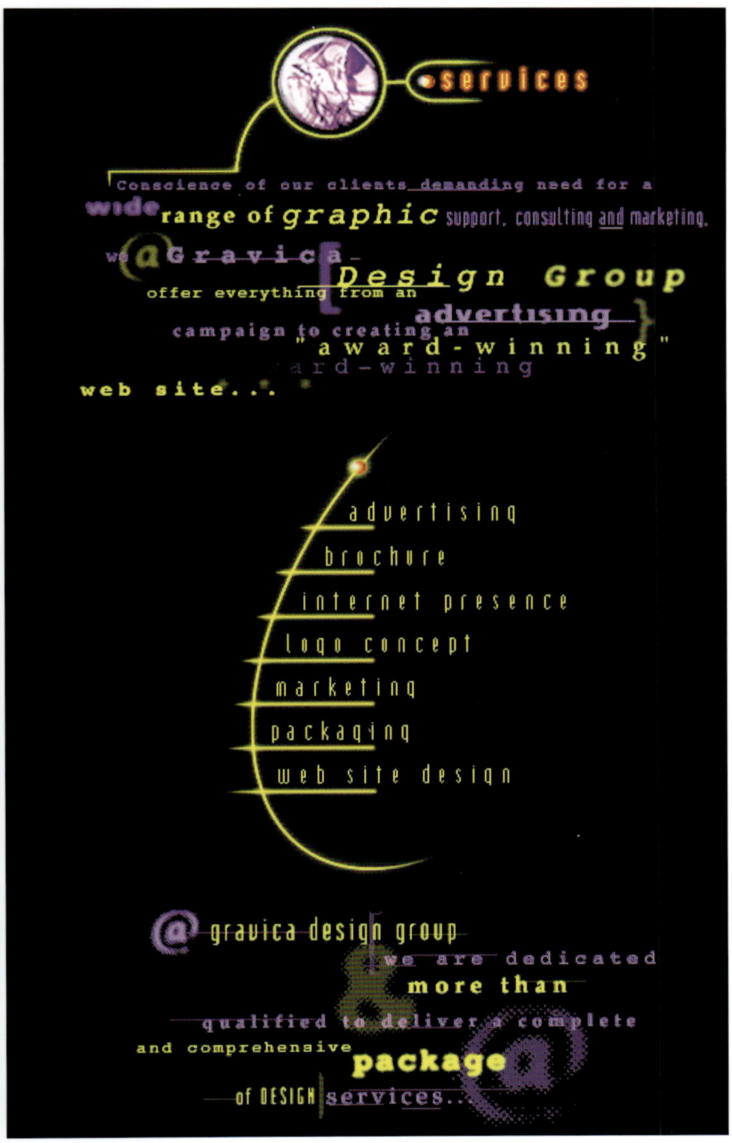

Title
Gravica Design Group
URL
http://www.iliad.com/gravicadesign/
Design Firm
Gravica Design Group
Designers
Michael McDonald,
Charles Molloy
Programmers
Michael McDonald,
Seth I. Rich
Authoring Platform
HTML

Black is often overused on the Web, but the designers at Gravica have lightened up the screen with superb accompanying colors. The reds and oranges combine to produce warm section titles, while the lavender cloud of space dust transitions evenly into the green angel's wings and yellow, swirling nebulae. The black background becomes what it should be: incidental, not overpowering.

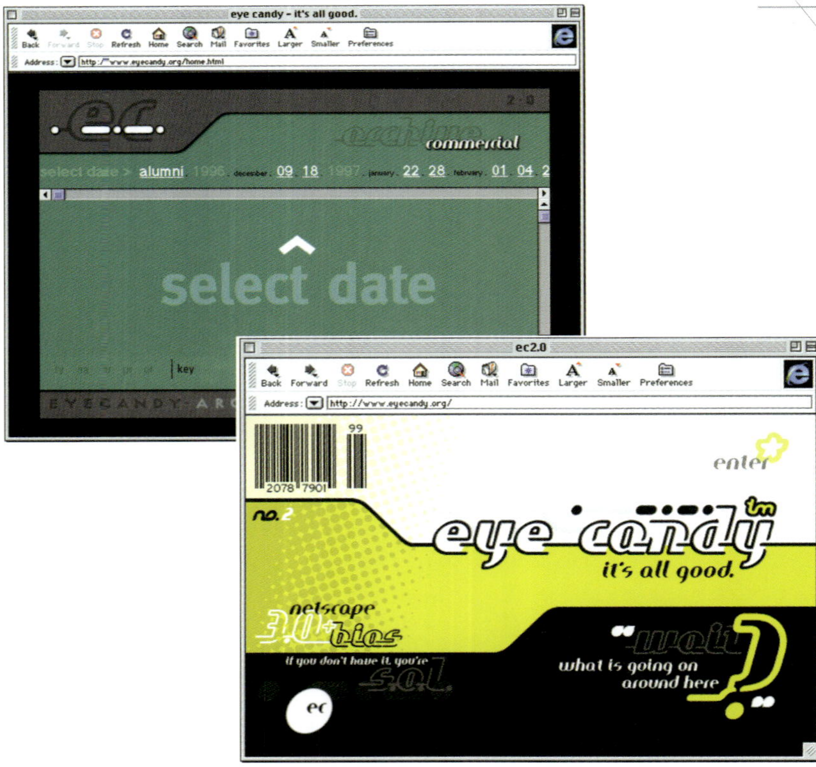

Title
eye candy
URL
http://www.eyecandy.com/
Designer/Programmer
Josh Ulm
Authoring platform
Mac

Being jarring without annoying is a tough balance, but eye candy uses a combination of bright colors, fake halftones, and smooth gradations to create visual interest that helps move the browser along and identifies different sections. Most of the type and graphics are in a slightly brighter color than the overall background.

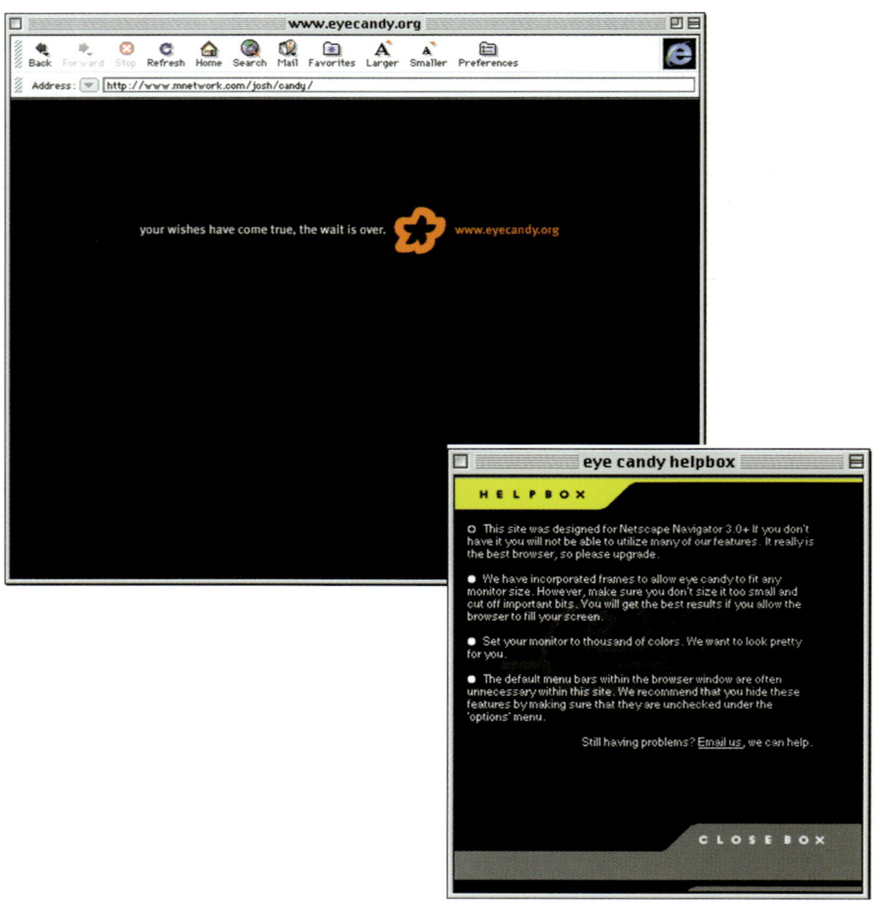

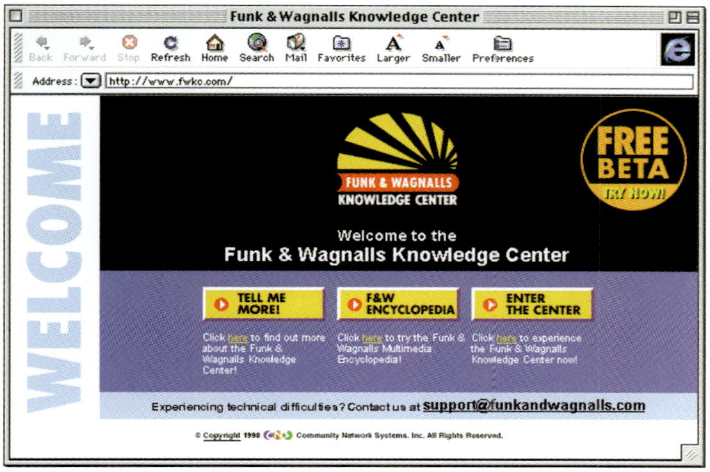

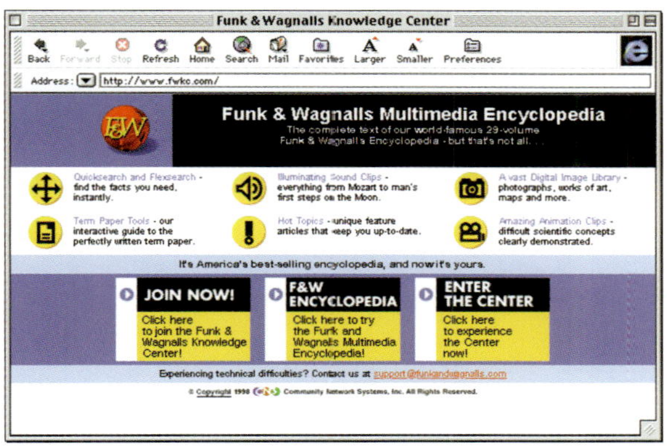

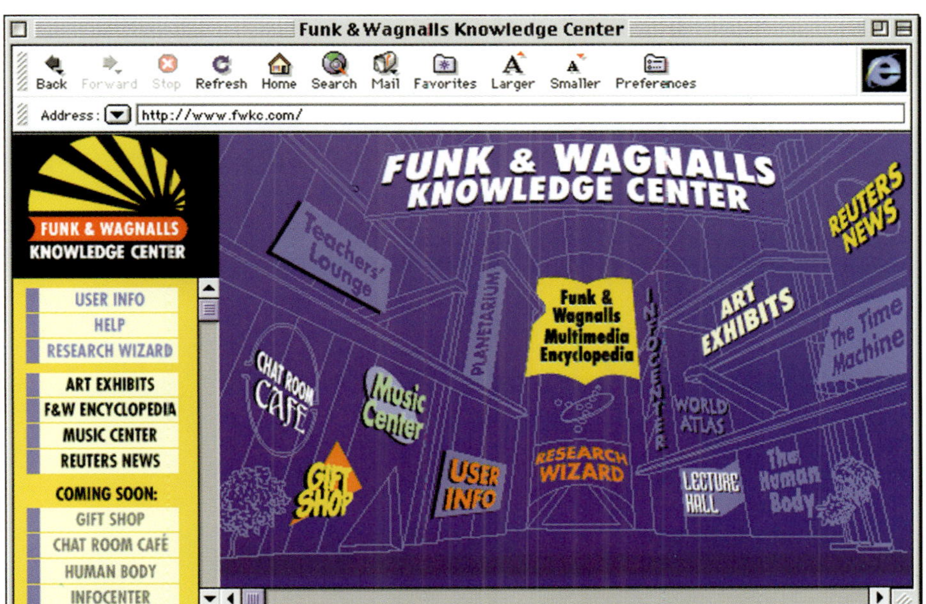

title
virtual community of tomorrow
URL
http://www.fwkc.com/
design firm
community Network systems
designers
vadim kapridov, Matvey shapiro, Ephraim Tabackman
illustrators
vadim kapridov, Alexei kazantsev
programmers
Havi goodman, Yisrael Naiman, Harry cohen
project management
galen karten, kenny zwiebel
authoring platform
Mac, PC

Using a minimum of colors that clearly define functions, sections, and even areas of a page, the Funk & Wagnalls Knowledge Center makes it easy to identify features and the current location on the well-structured site. The colors are repeated effectively, too: the blue in the navigation bar is the same used to knock-out the headline and the caption type. The red in the Funk & Wagnalls logo is repeated as the link color in the text.

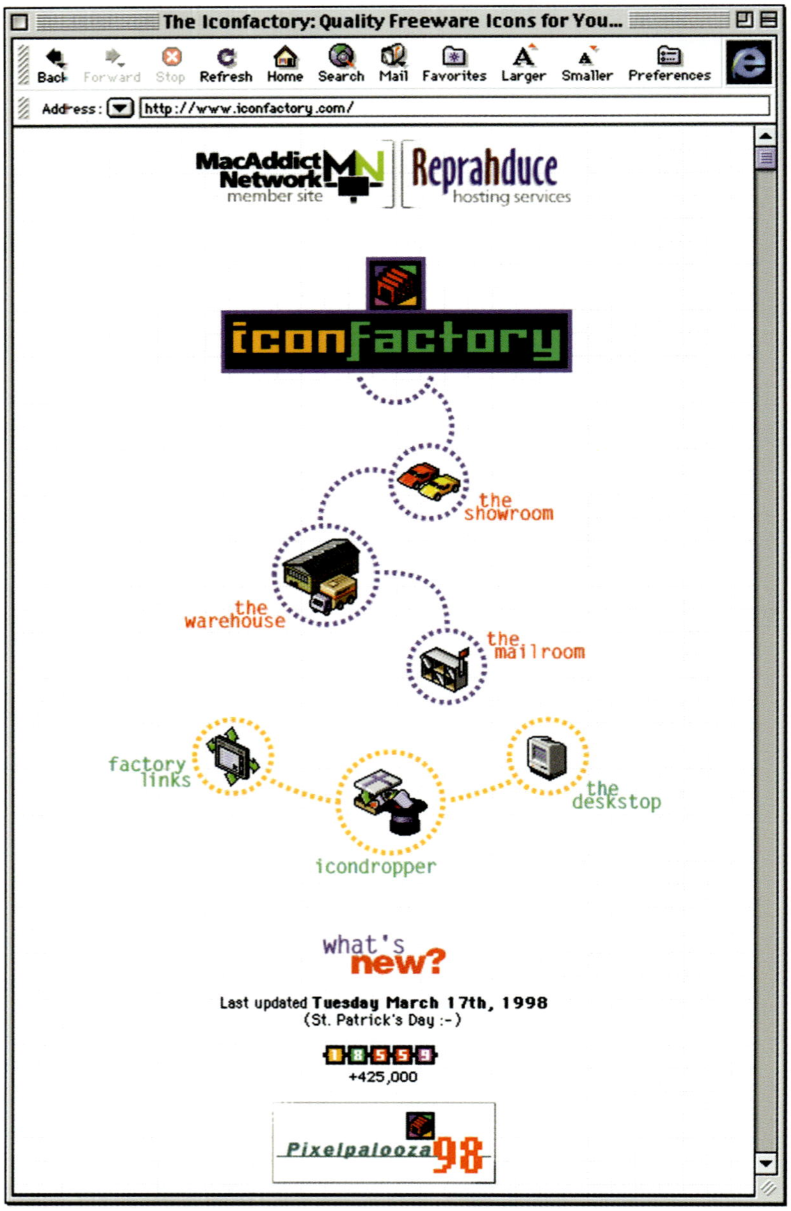

Title
The Iconfactory
URL
http://www.iconfactory.com/
Design Firm
The Iconfactory
Designers/Illustrators
Corey Marion,
Talos Tsui, Gedeon Maheux
Programmer
Craig Hockenberry
Authoring Platform
Mac

Icon Factory has two distinct areas, one for downloads and another for related information, which the colors help divide. As Macintosh icon designers, the colors are all used as solid tints to illustrate simple, but evocative, forms. Although primary and secondary colors are used to call out details—like the arrows on the factory-links icon—less vivid shades of gray and other colors are used to add a slightly more-than-two-dimensional effect.

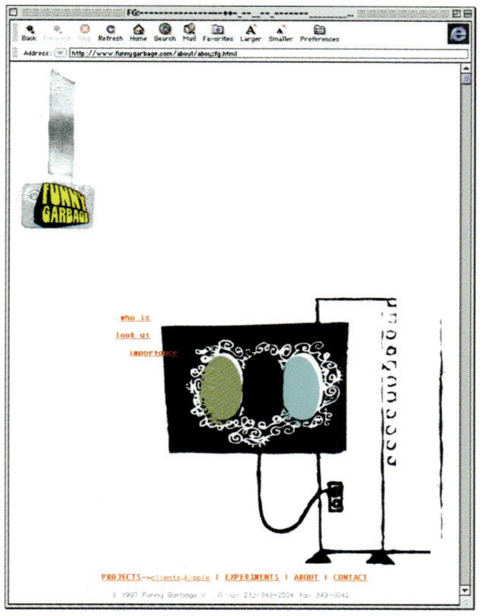

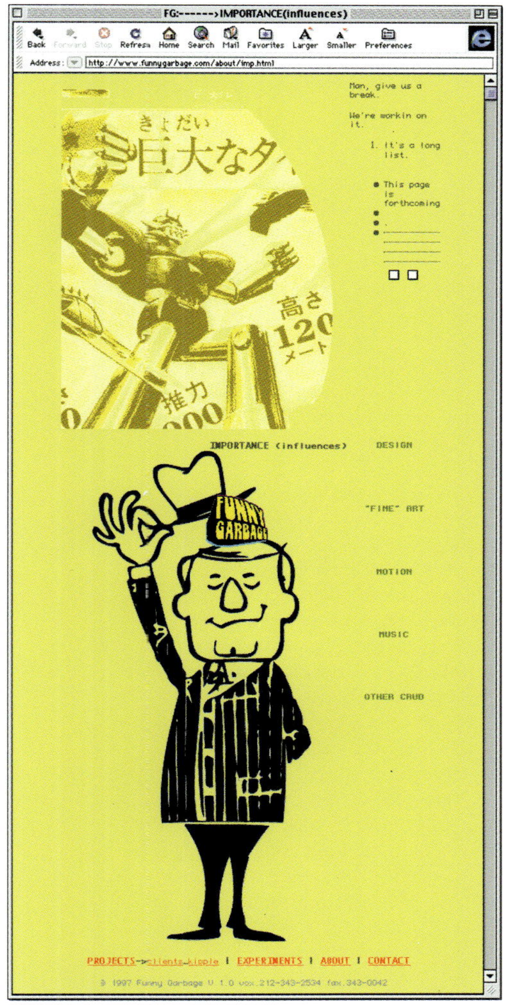

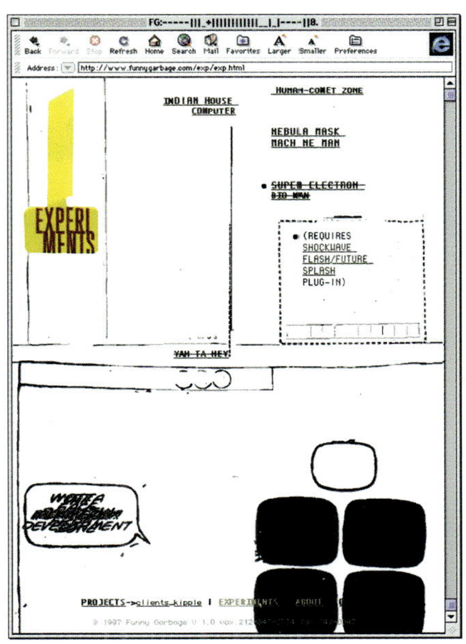

Title
funny garbage
URL
http://www.funnygarbage.com/about/aboutfg.html
Design firm
funny garbage
Designers
peter girardi, chris capuozzo
Illustrators
Todd James, Devin flynn
Programmers
fred Kahl, Dan wyszynski, Nina ong
Producers
fred Kahl, Kristin ellington, Esther Robinson
Authoring platform
Mac, pc

Funny Garbage tries to throw you off the scent of their real content by using backgrounds that look like bad photocopies, sporadic and bright color, and large fields of white. But careful perusal of the site shows repeating themes: jagged borders, thin, wavy lines that shake through GIF animation, big, strange shapes, and flashing colors.

Title
Yale-New Haven Medical Center
URL
http://info.med.yale.edu/index.html
Design firm
Center for Advanced Instructional Media, Yale University
Designer/Illustrator
Patrick J. Lynch
Photographer
Yale University Biomedical Communications
Programmer
Sean Jackson
Authoring platform
Mac

One of the few sites to use photography of their own events, Yale-New Haven Medical Center presents a calm, easy-to-navigate interface—as it needs to be. The navigation bars use the same gray to knock-out white type (for other, related organizations) and as positive space for choices that navigate within the site. The photographs pick up hospital colors without making that into a negative experience: the light and baby blues of hospital gowns and scrubs contrast with warmer wood tones and grays. They're not afraid to show a little excitement, either: a yellow bar marks noteworthy events.

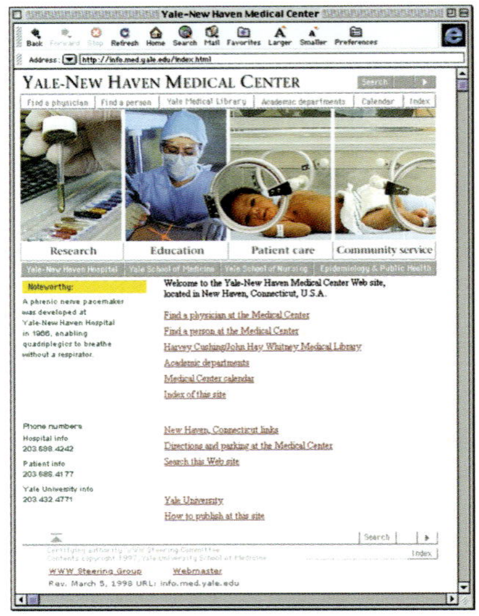

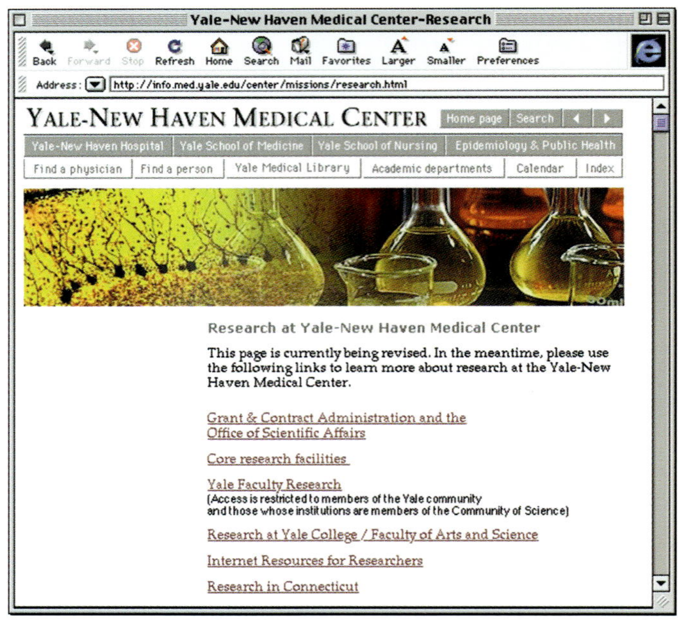

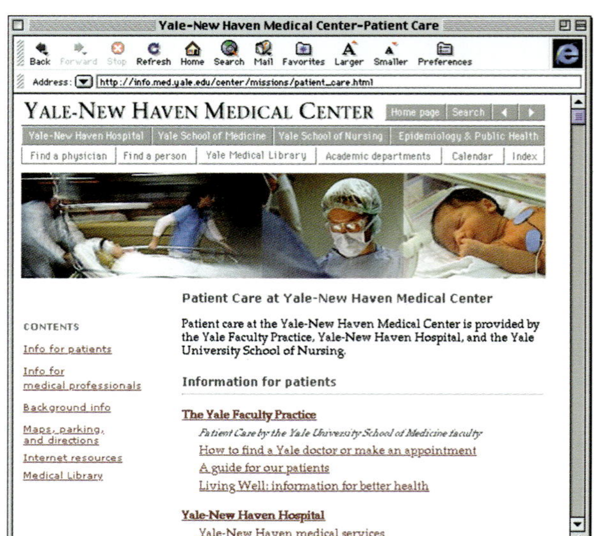

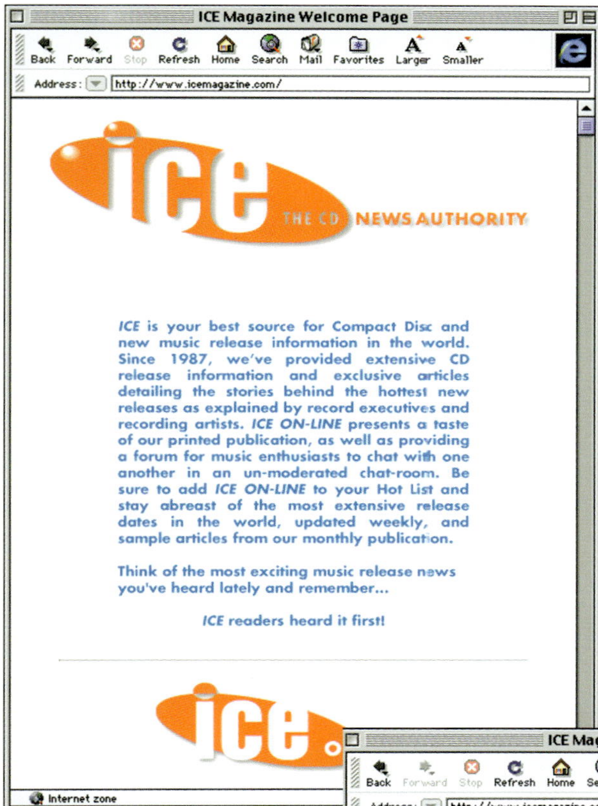

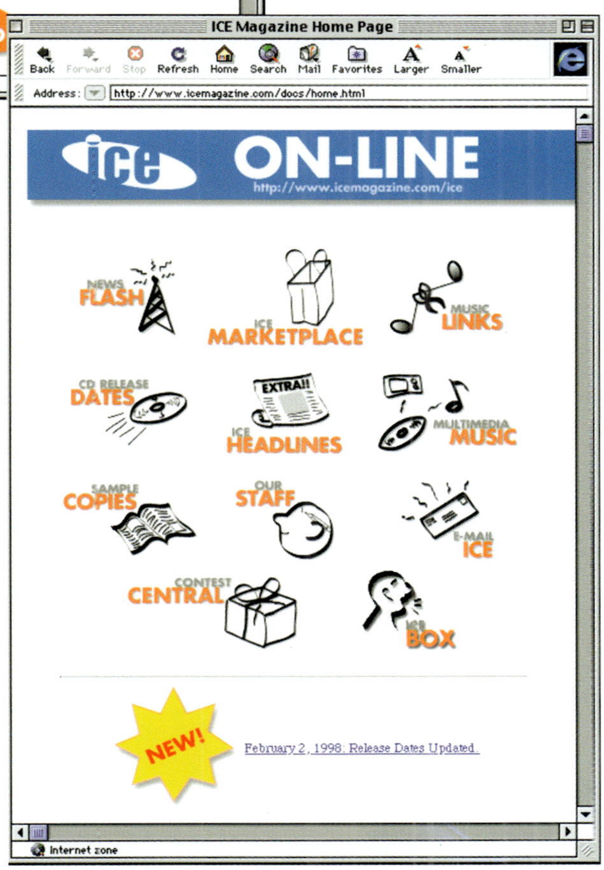

Title
ICE Magazine
URL
http://www.icemagazine.com/
Design firm
ICE Magazine
Designer/Illustrator
Henry Rael Jr.
Programmers
Henry Rael Jr., Jacob Rael
Authoring platform
Mac

Simplicity can often seem profound, and by those standards, Ice On-Line seems very deep. The introductory page uses just a couple of colors (plus some shading and highlights). The icons on the main page of the site pick up the same colors to use for links to other sections.

Title
curricular computing
URL
http://www.dartmouth.edu/~cc/
Design firm
Dartmouth College Curricular Computing
Designer/Illustrator/Photographer/Programmer
Sarah Horton
Authoring platform
Mac
Images courtesy of PhotoDisc, Inc.,
the copyright holder

Five images are used on the home page to this section at Dartmouth College and the details from these colorful images, which evoke the sylvan setting of the school, are repeated as part of the top menu bar on each page. The color of the top of the page is drawn from one of the images as well. Text color on secondary pages isn't overlooked: soft grays are used in less-important textual details and as a backdrop to a text menu appearing on the left of each page of the section.

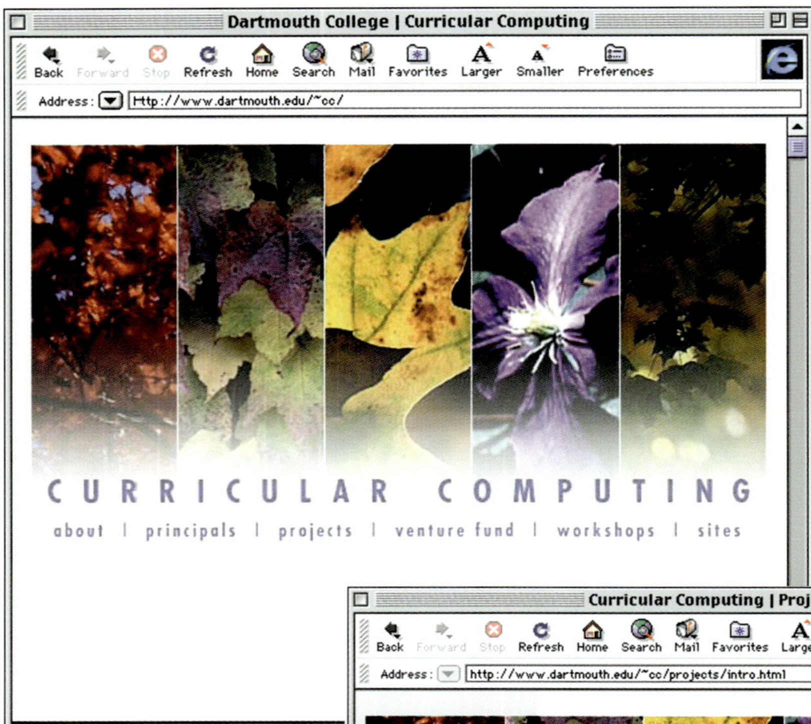

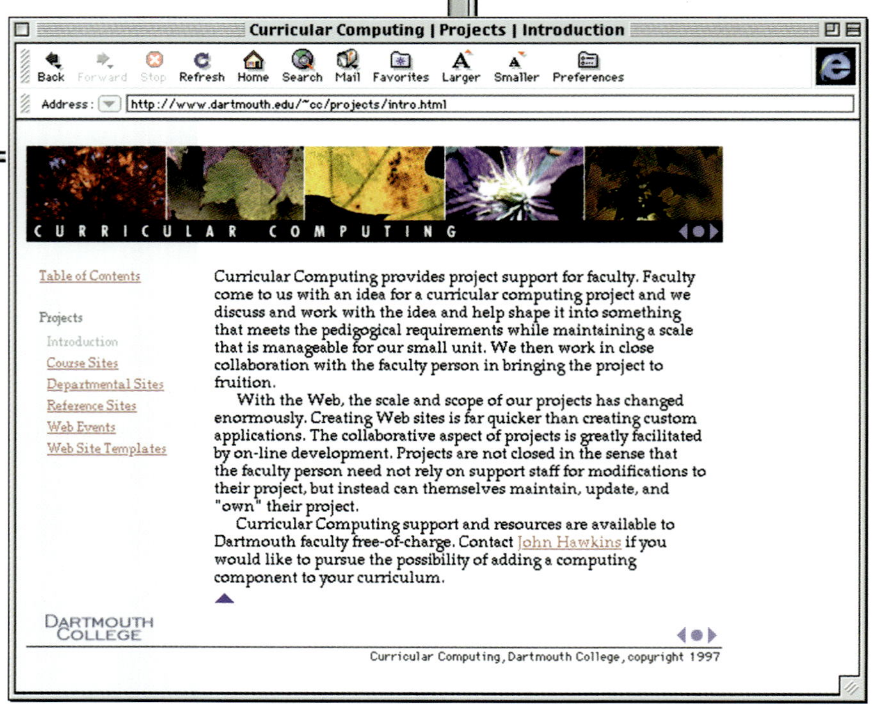

Title
parent soup
URL
http://www.parentsoup.com/
Design firm
parent soup
Designer/Illustrator
christina fredericks
Programmers
fay ku, tom simpson
Authoring platform
mac

Aimed at parents, not children, the site tries to have visual sophistication while alluding to children's art. The color fields behind navigation elements look like finger painting—but with clean edges. The lines on the site are drawn to look like crayon marks (but are a little straighter than the real thing). The designers chose to go outside the Web-safe palette to achieve these richer effects, but they don't suffer much at eight bits.

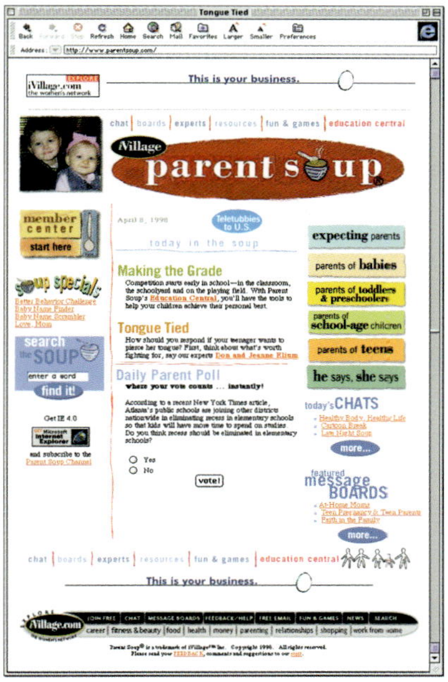

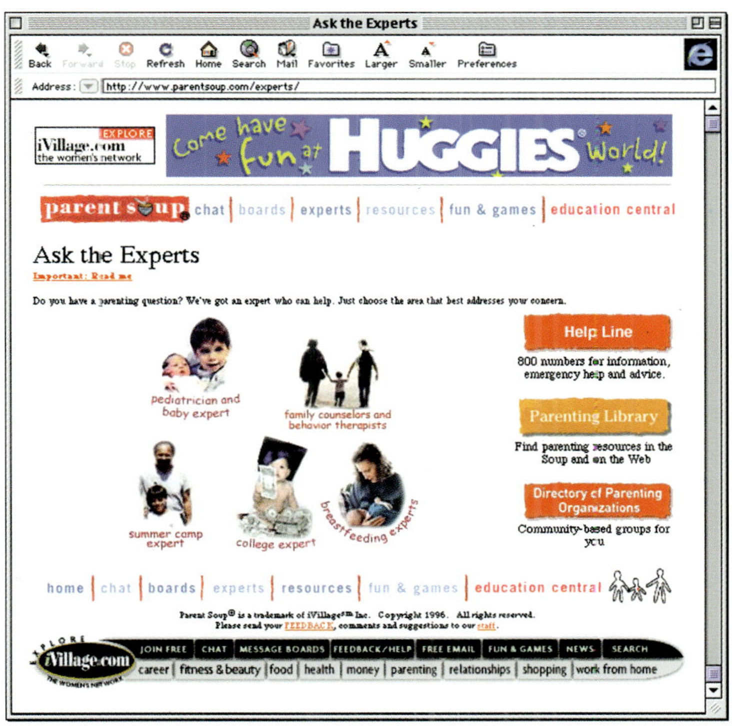

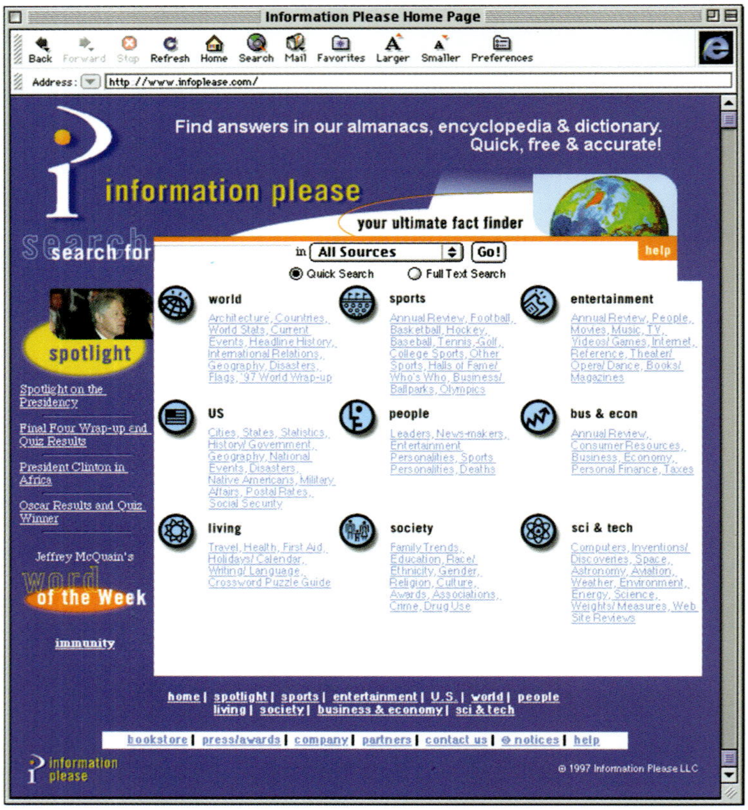

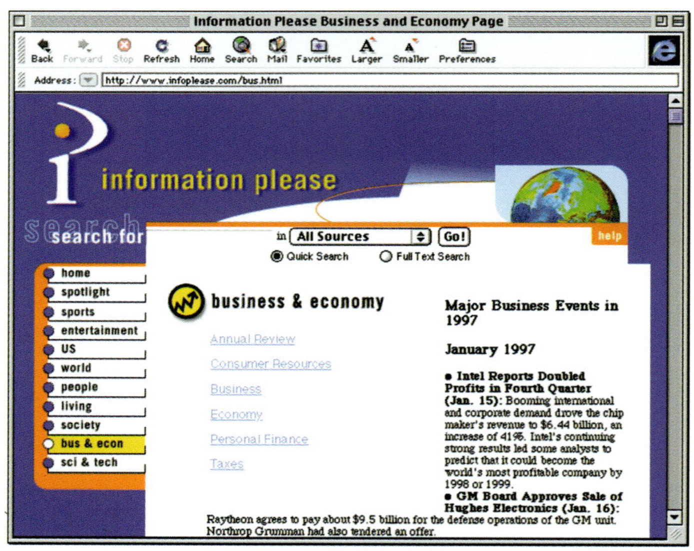

Title
information please
URL
http://www.infoplease.com/
Design firm
Stoltze Design
Designers
Clifford Stoltze, Susanne Hefel, Cynthia Patten, Rebecca Fagan
Illustrator
James Kraus
Programmers
Boris Goldowsky, Paul Evenson
Authoring platform
Mac, PC, Unix

It's hard to say why a dark blue makes one think of an information desk, but there's a definite association that the designers of this site play off. The palette is limited to the information blue, a spotlight yellow, a text/icon navigation light blue, a top-bar orange, and very few colors on the globe.

Title
Jetpack Online Magazine
URL
http //www.jetpack.com/
Design Firm
Jetpack Digital Media
Designer
Mike Levin
Programmer
Marc Brown
Authoring Platform
Mac

Jetpack uses flashy, bright colors to remind you of a future that never happened. It's a combo-1950s/retro-chic-of-tomorrow, where cars with fins recede into the distance on a vibrant dark-blue field, almost like they're flying. The icons are all of the atomic age: spacemen, portable record players, bowling pins, and jet planes. Bright colors or semi-psychedelic, concentric circles of contrasting hues sit behind the links.

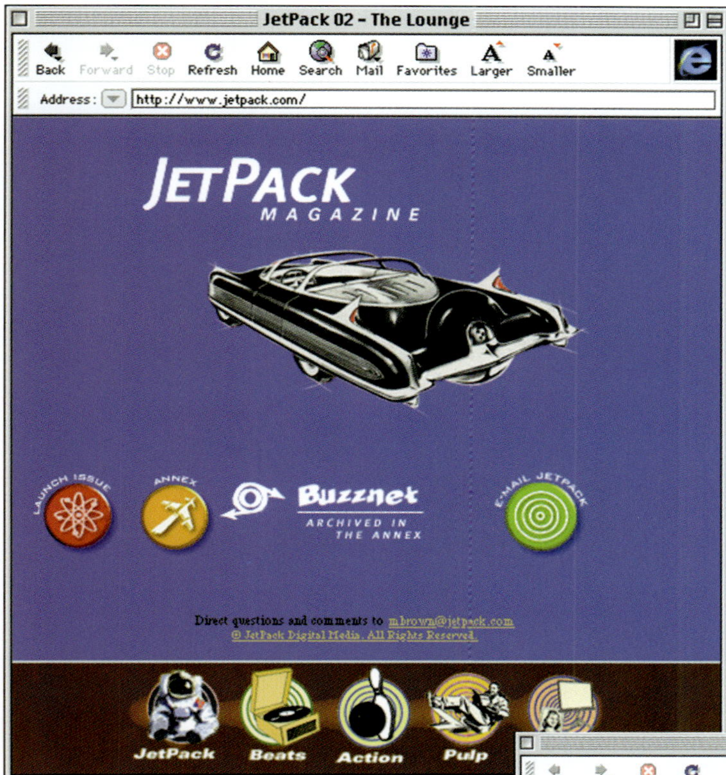

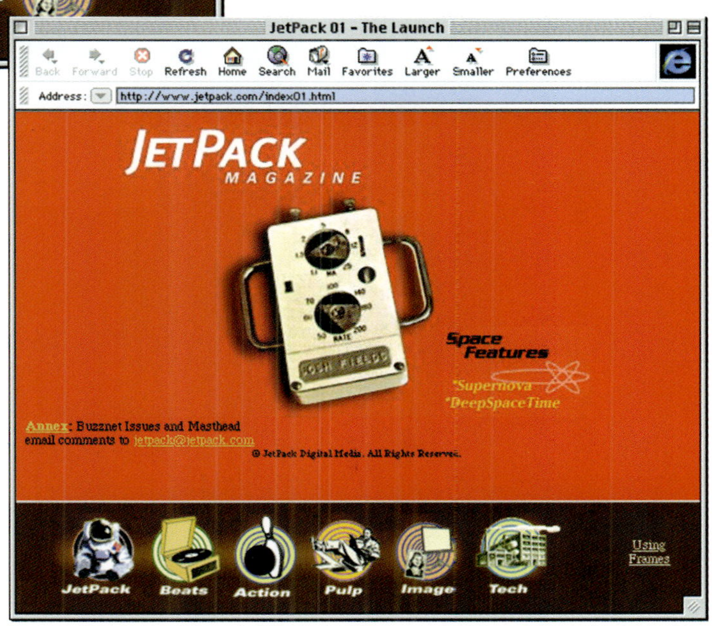

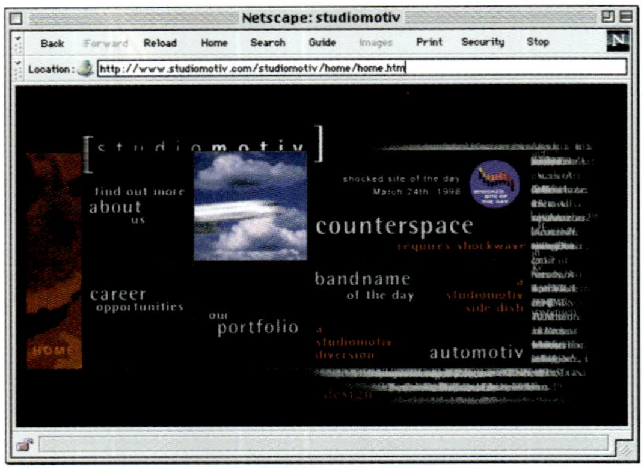

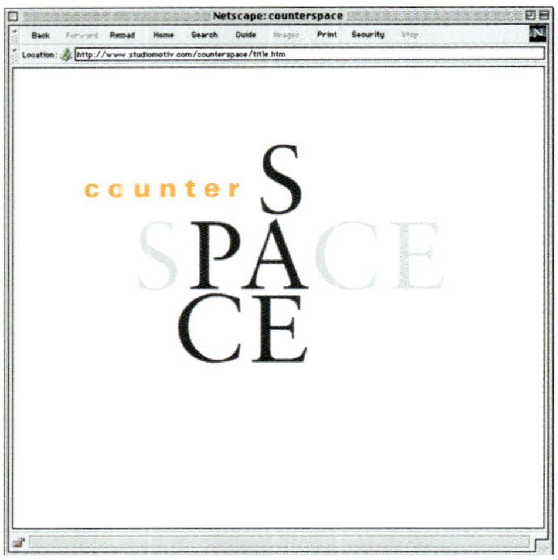

Title
studiomotiv
URL
http://www.studiomotiv.com/studiomotiv/home/home.htm
Design firm
studiomotiv
Designers
Brett collins, Ed stull, Robert Abbott
Illustrator
Brett collins
Programmers
Bill Litfin, paul Rothrock
Authoring platform
pc

Another black background, but this time the burnt orange of the text and the illustration, combined with white titles and layered typographic texture, constrain the black as only the page's backdrop. Once past the opening, white dominates, with gray and a lighter orange for highlights.

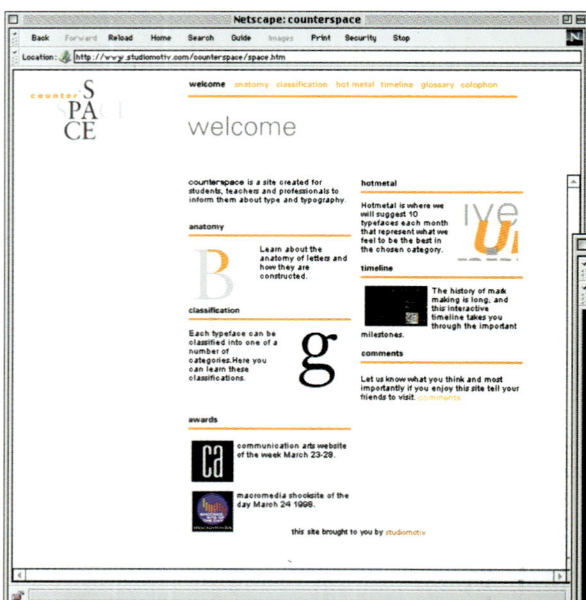

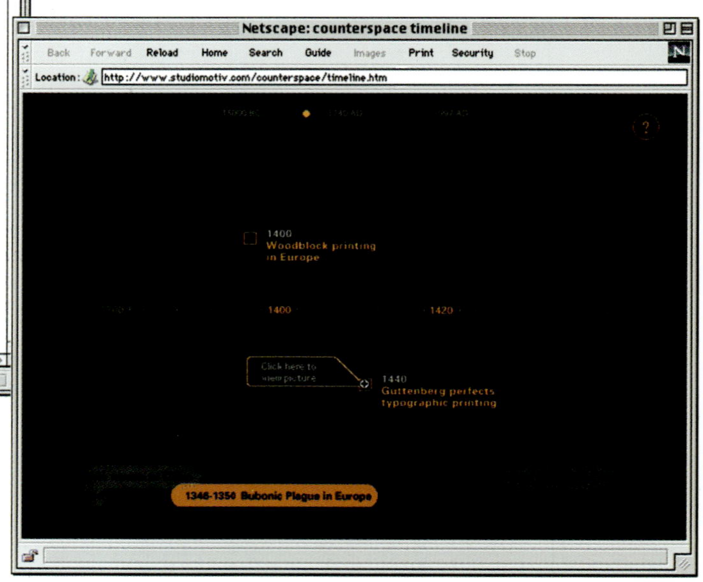

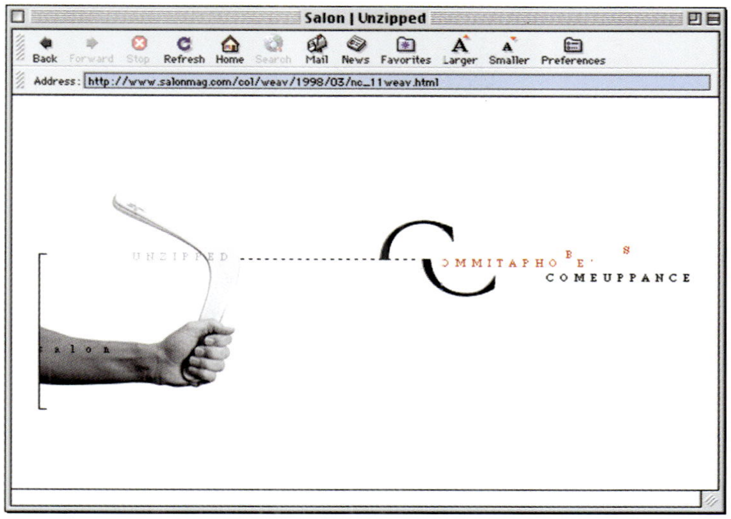

title
salon magazine
URL
http://www.salonmagazine.com/
design firm
salon magazine
designer
Mignon Khargie ("Girl in Landscape", "Commitaphobe's Comeuppance"); Karen Templer ("Mutiny on the Net")
illustrator
Adam Mcauly ("Mutiny on the Net")
writer
Jonathan Lethem ("Girl in Landscape")
authoring platform
Mac

Salon has established itself as one of the best-designed sites on the Web, and for good reason. The generous use of white space tends to highlight everything, especially the ever-changing opening screens for different sections (such as Unzipped, shown here). Link highlight colors regularly adapt to the site's title illustrations, subtly forcing a consistency that isn't often encountered.

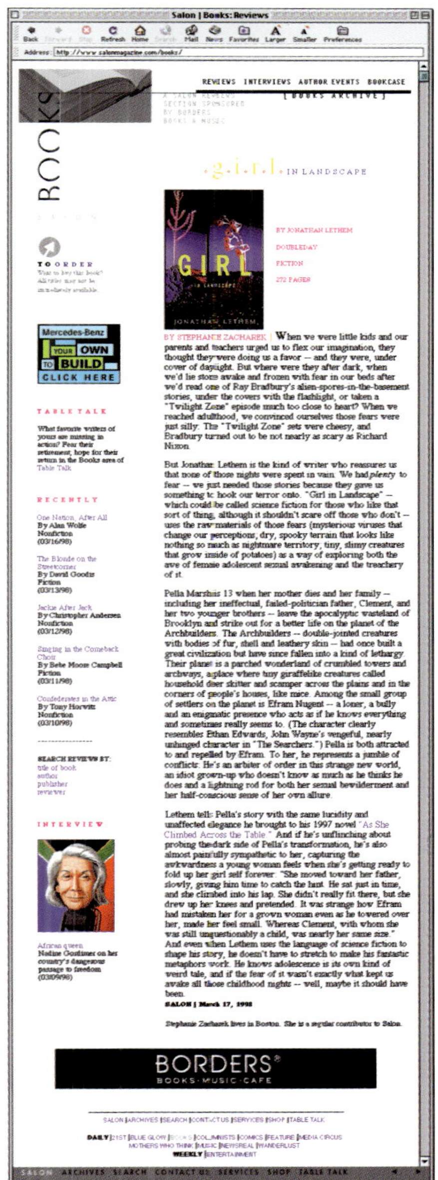

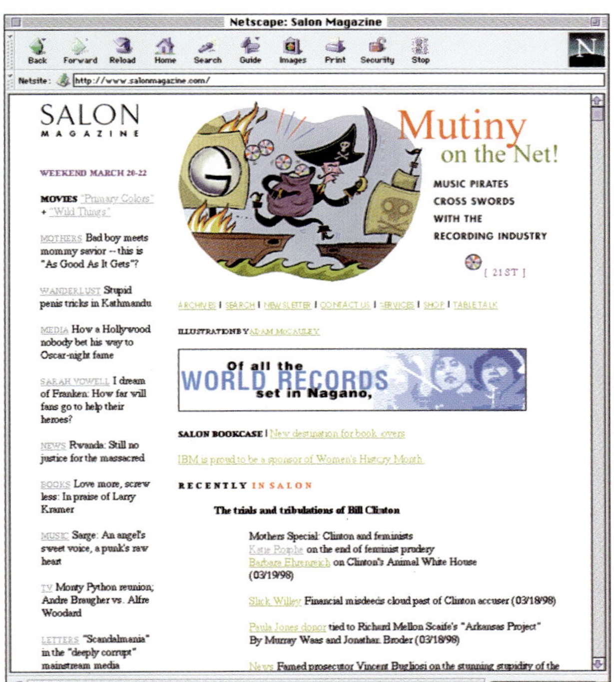

title
urban Desires
URL
http://www.desires.com/
Design firm
Agency.com
Designer/Illustrator
Jean Esquivel
Programmer
Mike parker
Authoring platform
Mac

The creators of this site don't want to use urban to reflect anything vaguely reminiscent of a typical real-life city. No, here you get the feeling of being in a crowded, steamy metropolis: red, black, gray, and mustard colors have the gritty tone brought on by lack of direct sunlight. At the same time, however, you're likely to encounter white, blue, and purple hues—an ever-surprising paradise nestled deep within the city.

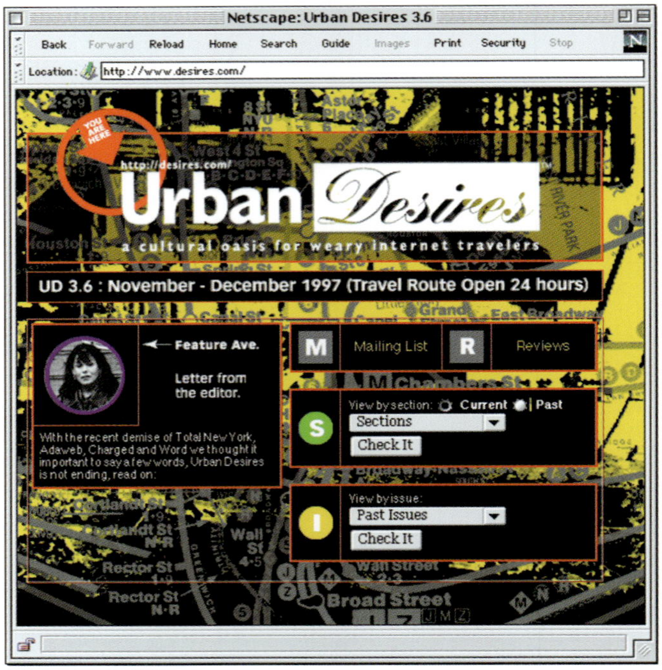

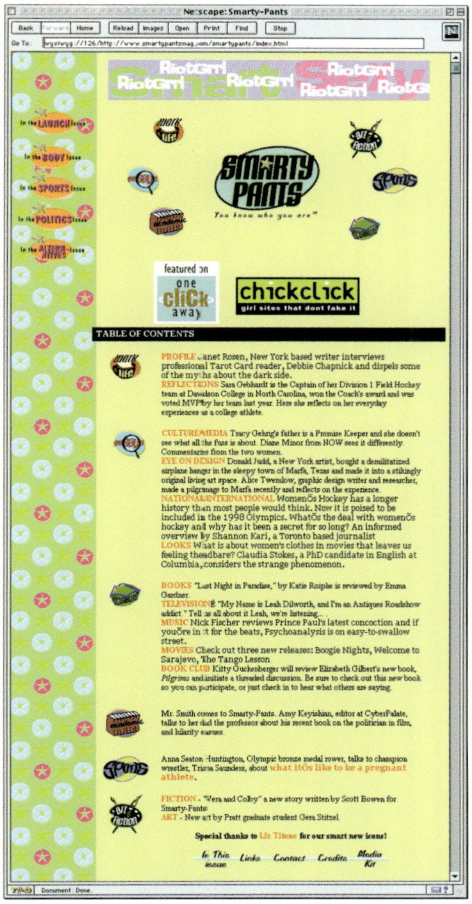

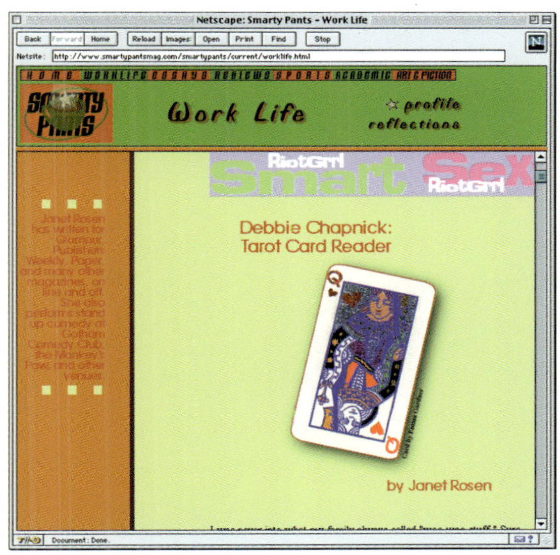

title
smarty pants magazine
URL
http://www.smartypantsmag.com/smartypants/index.html
design firm
gotham interactive
designer/illustrator
emma gardner
logo
susan sears
icons
Liz Titone
programmer
paul sullivan
Authoring platform
Mac, pc

With its lime-green accents and maroon stars, this late 1990s site with its 1970s color scheme practically oozes culture. The multicolored navigation bar on the left side of the main page establishes this site's mood; solid swatches of pastels and earthy hues framing internal pages make them both appealing and readable.

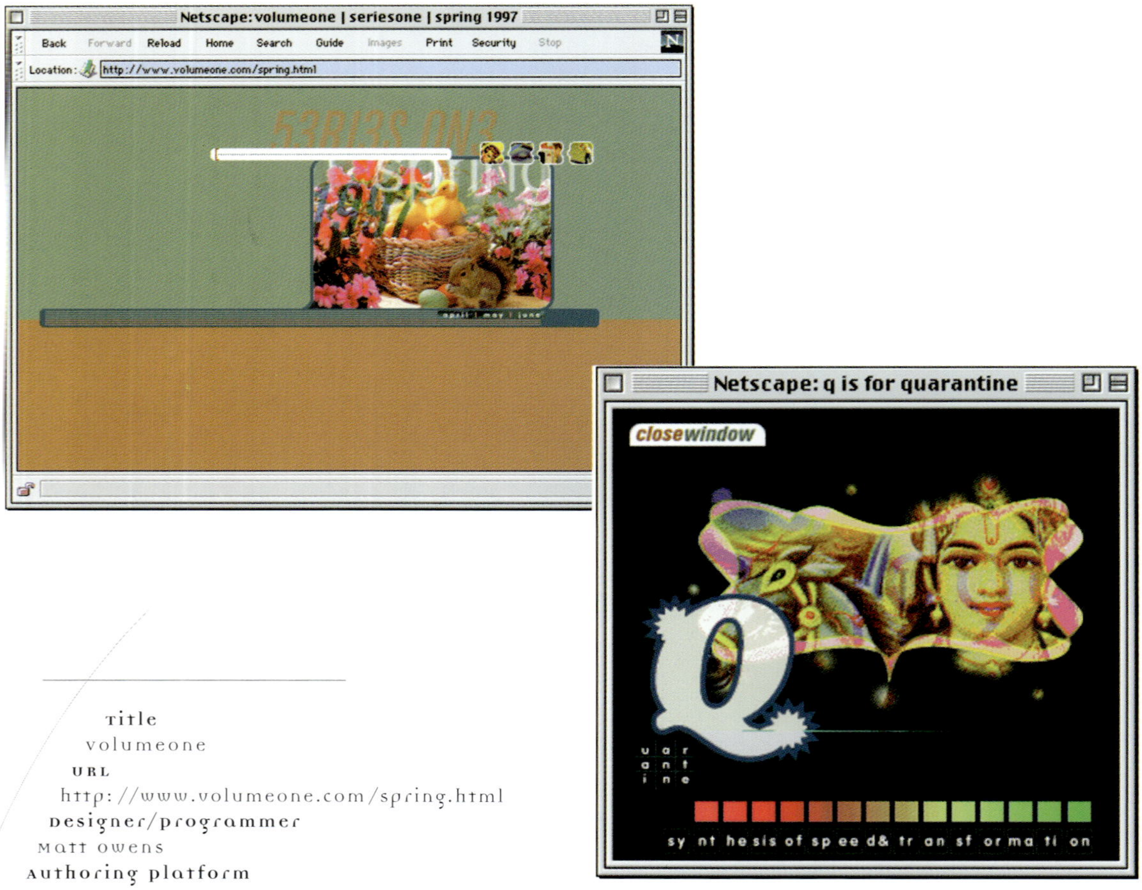

Title
volumeone
URL
http://www.volumeone.com/spring.html
Designer/programmer
Matt owens
Authoring platform
Mac

Many sites that use color well tend to select a limited palette and stick to it, ensuring consistency among their pages. But it's also perfectly acceptable to use a broad set of colors, such as the flat-green and tan background of this spring page. Clicking the icons brings up small windows that use color schemes specifically tailored to each window's content.

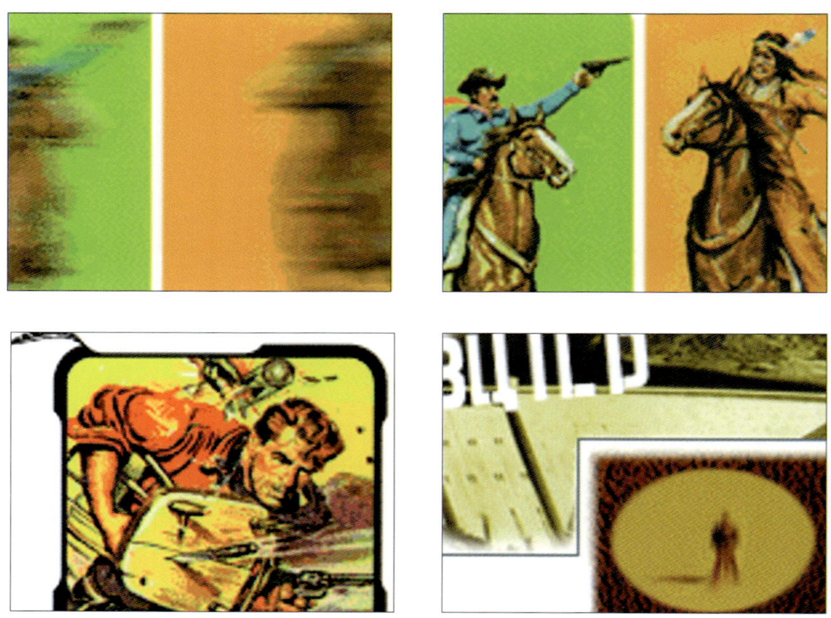

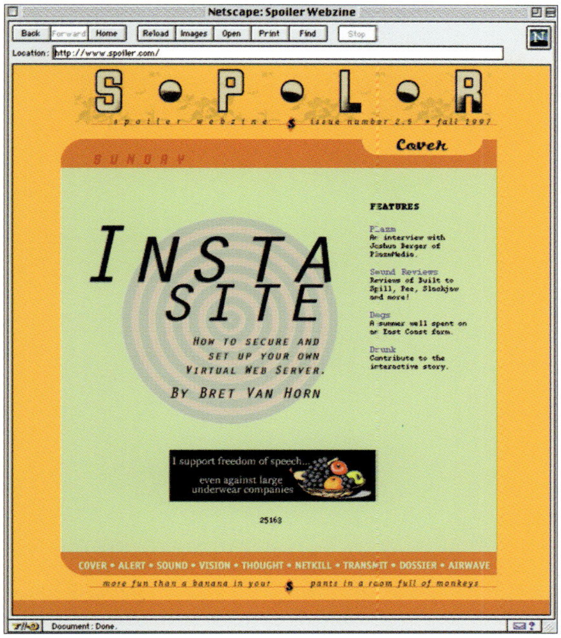

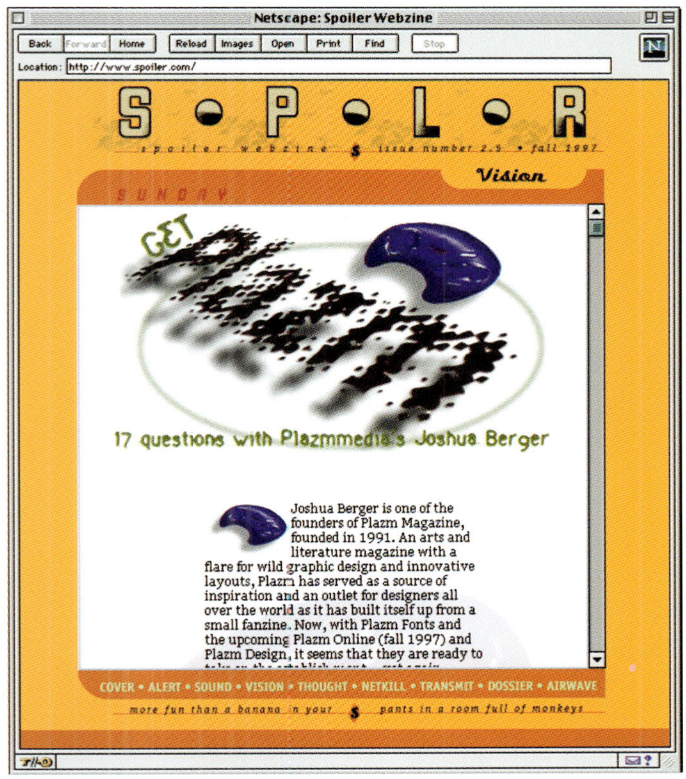

Title
spoiler webzine
URL
http://www.spoiler.com/
Design firm
spoiler Media
Designer/programmer
Bret Van Horn
Authoring platform
Mac, unix

Webzines have been able to get away with color schemes that would normally make print publishers cringe. Without the pressure of visual competition on a newsstand, Webzines like this can use a combination like dark mustard and brownish-orange to quickly establish a tone before the reader even gets to the site's content.

Title
souldanse: Art for the soul
URL
http://www.souldanse.com/melanie/
Designer
Melanie A. Ceraso
Illustrator
Paul Pearson
Photographer
Dave Siekaniec
Programmers
John M. Carlin, Melanie A. Ceraso
Authoring platform
PC

Transparency isn't normally regarded as a compelling Web feature, but this site's use of transparency accents an already beautiful design. The way in which the figures in the upper-right corner of the screen cross at least four levels of color gives the page depth in an unexpected manner.

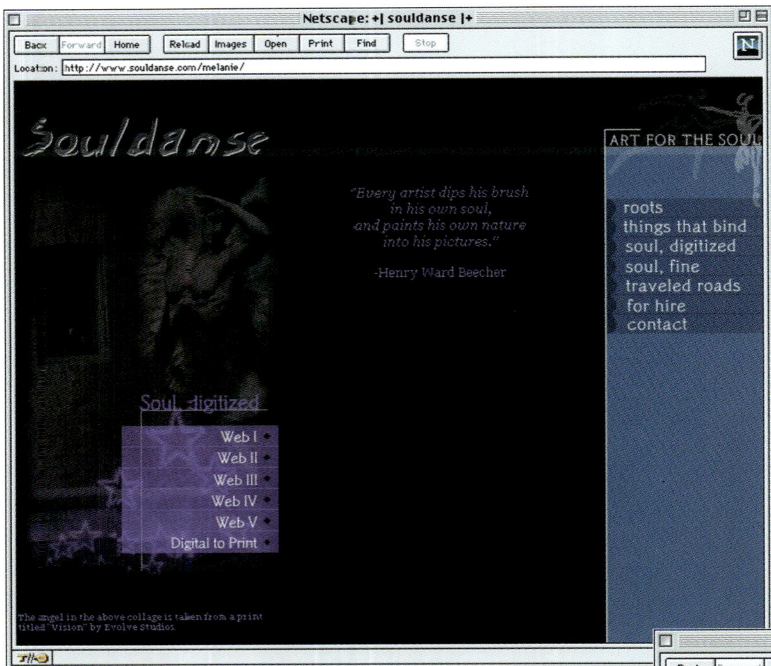

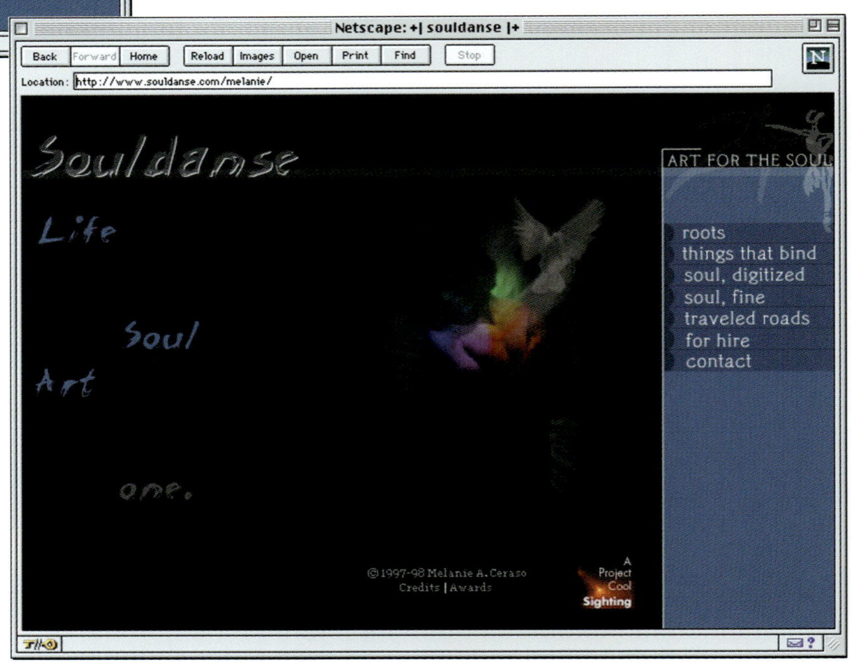

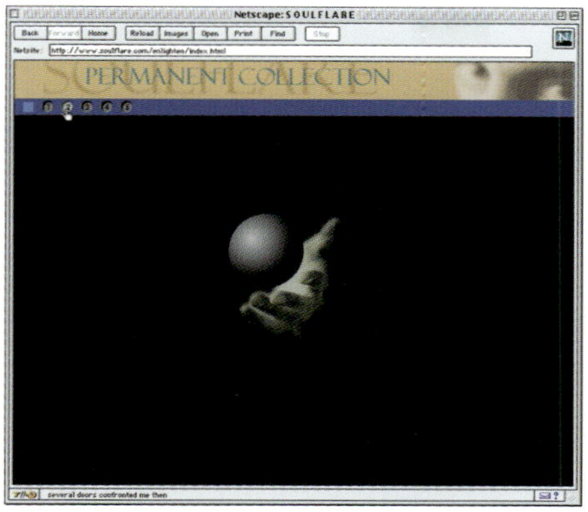

Title
soulflare
URL
http://www.soulflare.com/classic/
Designer/programmer
Lance Arthur
Authoring platform
PC

Without even entering the site, the use of color here is impressive. To gain access requires clicking the circle below the figure's extended hand; when the mouse pointer contacts it, the page lights up with color. Inside, the tan-and-blue color scheme holds the black frame in place in an almost reassuring manner.

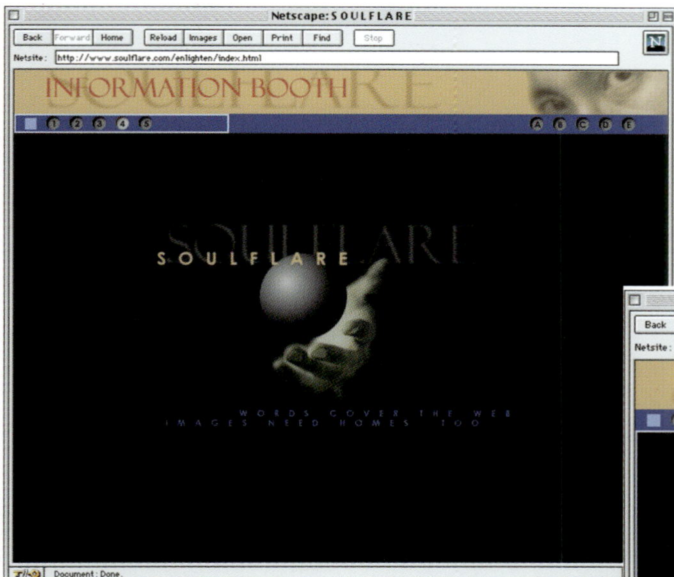

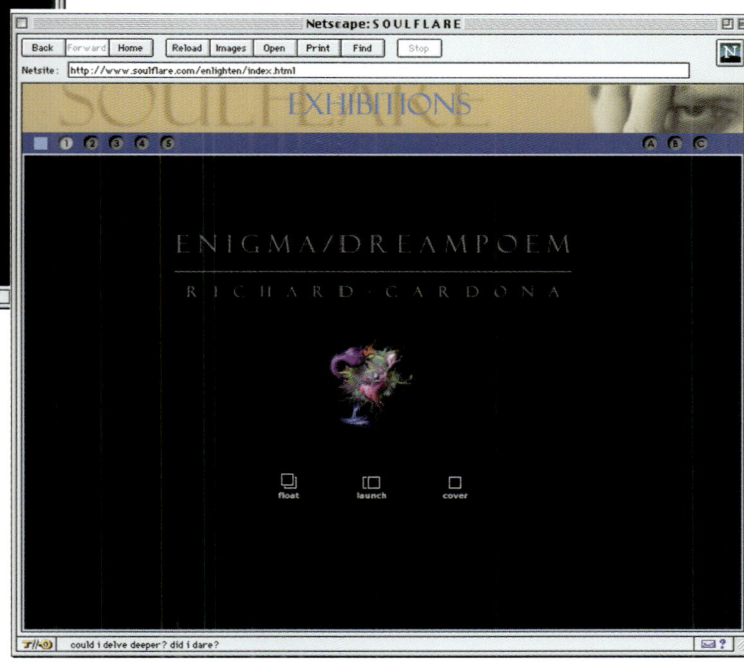

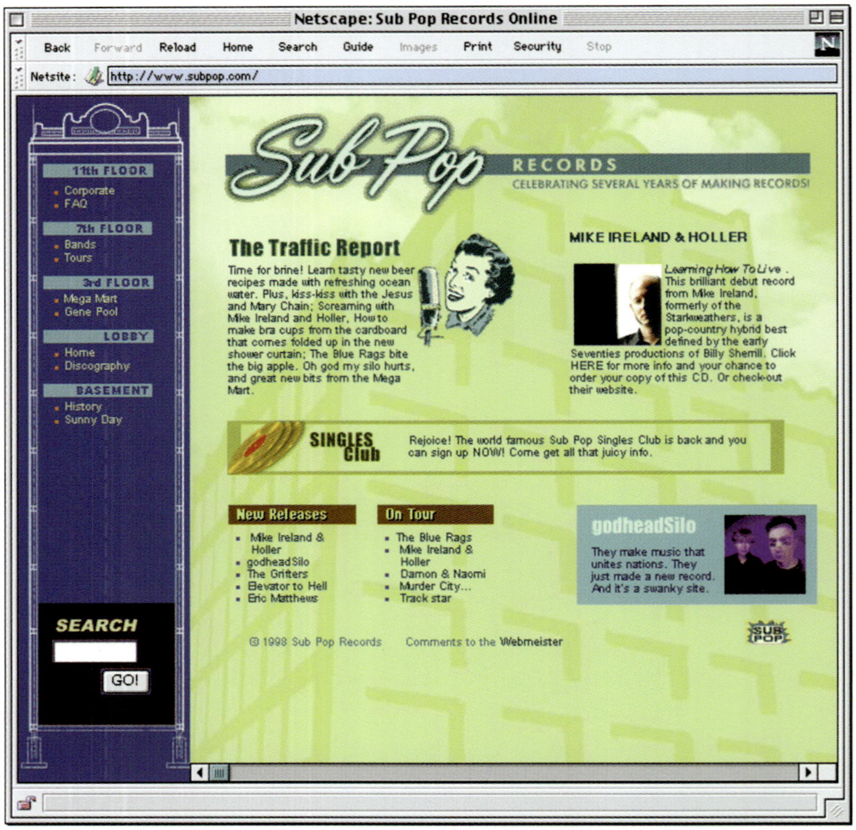

Netscape: Sub Pop Records Online
Back Forward Reload Home Search Guide Images Print Security Stop
Netsite: http://www.subpop.com/
11th FLOOR
Corporate
FAQ
7th FLOOR
Bands
Tours
3rd FLOOR
Mega Mart
Gene Pool
LOBBY
Home
Discography
BASEMENT
History
Sunny Day
SEARCH
GO!
Sub Pop
RECORDS
CELEBRATING SEVERAL YEARS OF MAKING RECORDS!
The Traffic Report
Time for brine! Learn tasty new beer recipes made with refreshing ocean water. Plus, kiss-kiss with the Jesus and Mary Chain; Screaming with Mike Ireland and Holler. How to make bra cups from the cardboard that comes folded up in the new shower curtain; The Blue Rags bite the big apple. Oh god my silo hurts, and great new bits from the Mega Mart.
MIKE IRELAND & HOLLER
Learning How To Live . This brilliant debut record from Mike Ireland, formerly of the Starkweathers, is a pop-country hybrid best defined by the early Seventies productions of Billy Sherrill. Click HERE for more info and your chance to order your copy of this CD. Or check-out their website.
SINGLES Club
Rejoice! The world famous Sub Pop Singles Club is back and you can sign up NOW! Come get all that juicy info.
New Releases
Mike Ireland & Holler
godheadSilo
The Grifters
Elevator to Hell
Eric Matthews
On Tour
The Blue Rags
Mike Ireland & Holler
Damon & Naomi
Murder City...
Track star
godheadSilo
They make music that unites nations. They just made a new record. And it's a swanky site.
© 1998 Sub Pop Records Comments to the Webmeister

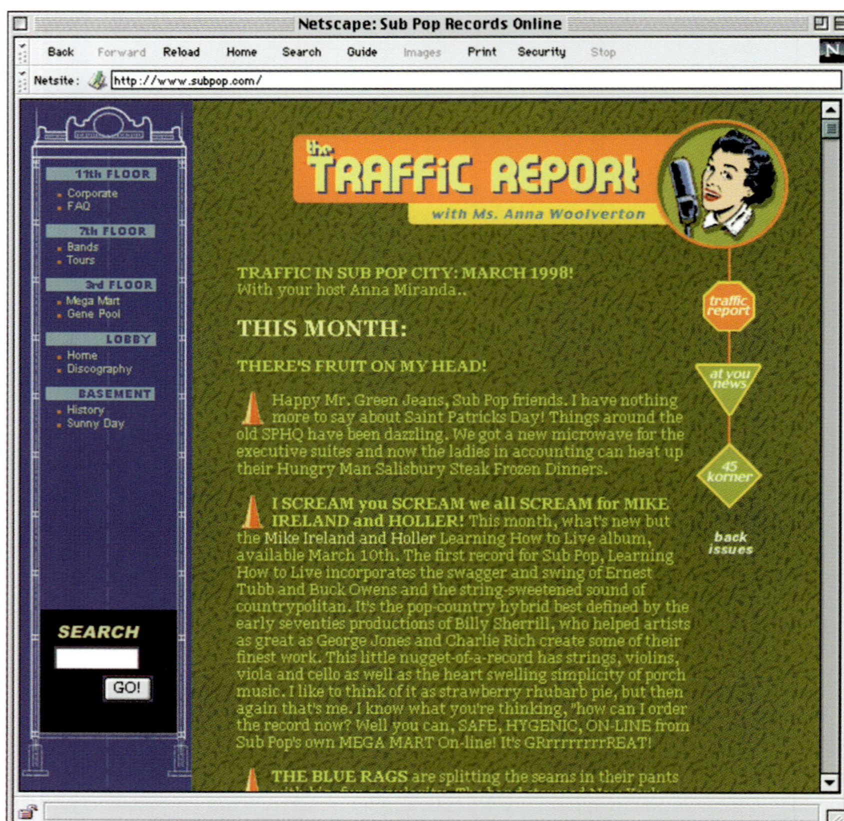

Netscape: Sub Pop Records Online
Back Forward Reload Home Search Guide Images Print Security Stop
Netsite: http://www.subpop.com/
11th FLOOR
Corporate
FAQ
7th FLOOR
Bands
Tours
3rd FLOOR
Mega Mart
Gene Pool
LOBBY
Home
Discography
BASEMENT
History
Sunny Day
SEARCH
GO!
the TRAFFIC REPORT
with Ms. Anna Woolverton
TRAFFIC IN SUB POP CITY: MARCH 1998!
With your host Anna Miranda..
THIS MONTH:
THERE'S FRUIT ON MY HEAD!
Happy Mr. Green Jeans, Sub Pop friends. I have nothing more to say about Saint Patricks Day! Things around the old SPHQ have been dazzling. We got a new microwave for the executive suites and now the ladies in accounting can heat up their Hungry Man Salisbury Steak Frozen Dinners.
I SCREAM you SCREAM we all SCREAM for MIKE IRELAND and HOLLER! This month, what's new but the Mike Ireland and Holler Learning How to Live album, available March 10th. The first record for Sub Pop, Learning How to Live incorporates the swagger and swing of Ernest Tubb and Buck Owens and the string-sweetened sound of countrypolitan. It's the pop-country hybrid best defined by the early seventies productions of Billy Sherrill, who helped artists as great as George Jones and Charlie Rich create some of their finest work. This little nugget-of-a-record has strings, violins, viola and cello as well as the heart swelling simplicity of porch music. I like to think of it as strawberry rhubarb pie, but then again that's me. I know what you're thinking, "how can I order the record now? Well you can, SAFE, HYGENIC, ON-LINE from Sub Pop's own MEGA MART On-line! It's GRrrrrrrrrREAT!
THE BLUE RAGS are splitting the seams in their pants
traffic report
at you news
45 korner
back issues

Title
sub pop Records
URL
http://www.subpop.com/
Designer
Joe Walker
Programmers
Ian Dickson, Ed Slocomb, Joe Walker

Variations of green dominate this site, though you won't find any forest or hunter shades. The colors, combined with 1950s-era-inspired typography, give the site a vintage feel while featuring up-and-coming bands.

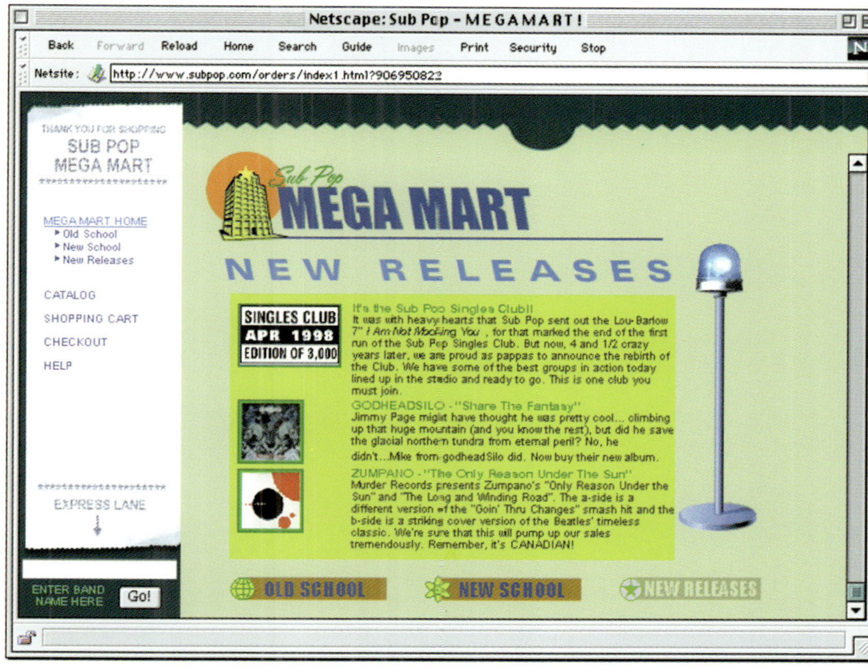

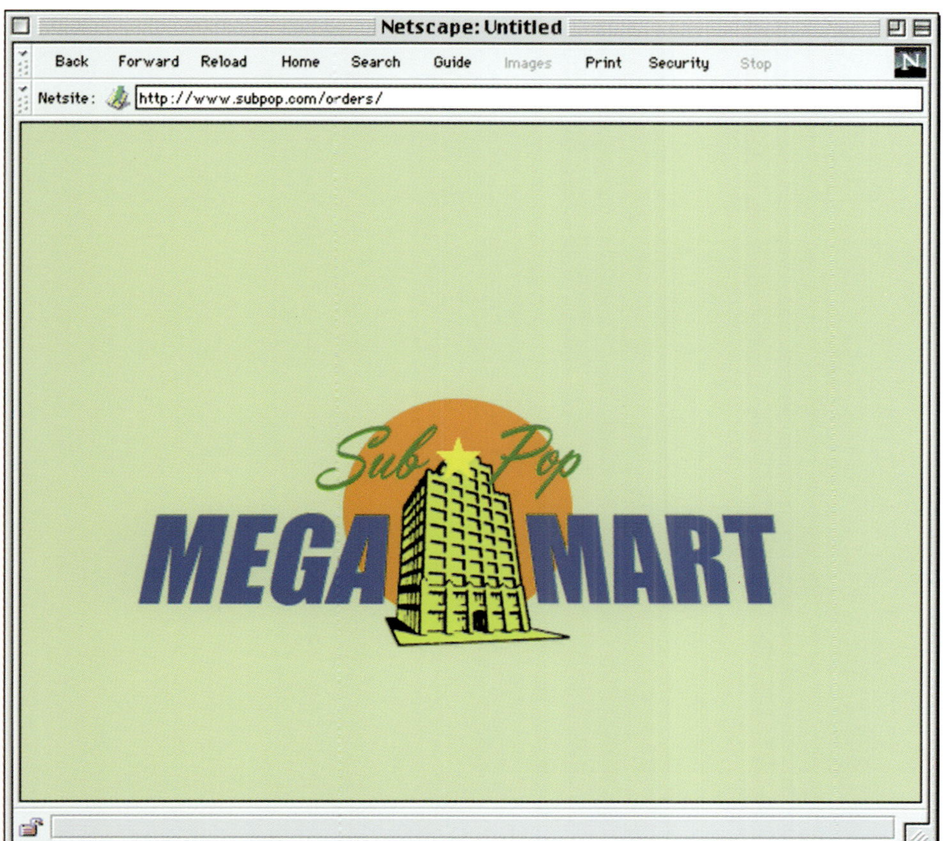

Title
web page Design for Designers
URL
http://www.wpdfd.com/
Design firm
pixel productions UK
Designer/Illustrator/photographer/programmer
Joe Gillespie
Authoring platform
Mac

There are hundreds of how-to sites geared toward Web designers, but surprisingly few that cover design theory instead of HTML tutorials. This site establishes its professional feel with its minimal—but highly effective—use of bright colors in the main title and as accents. The horizontal pinstriped background subtly enhances the readability of the site's white content without straining the reader's eyes.

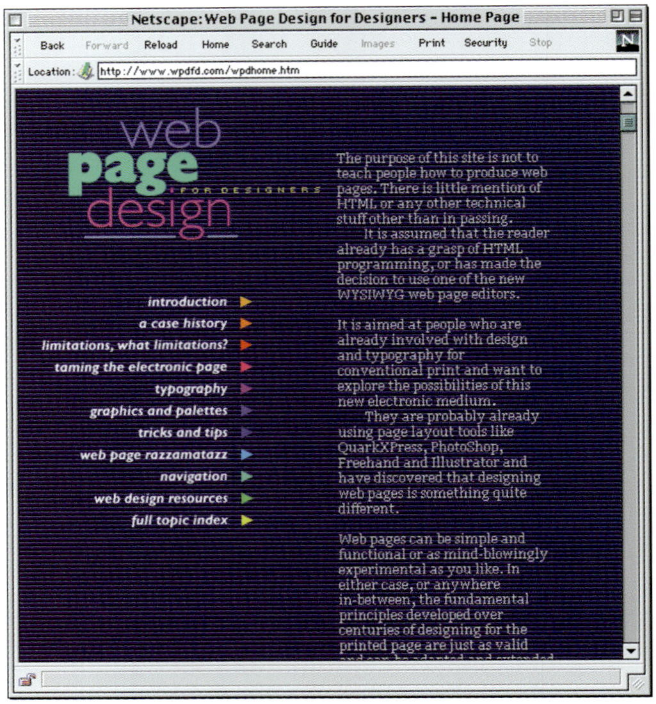

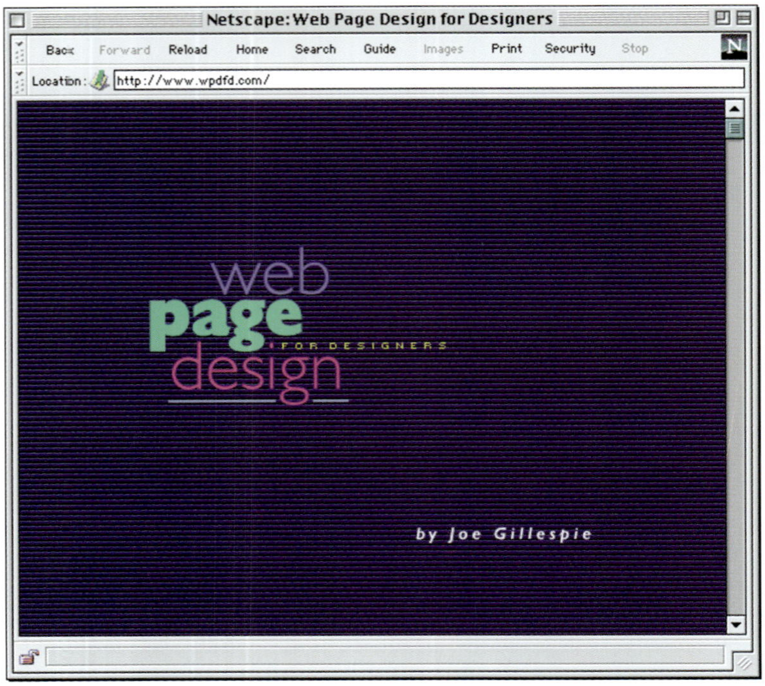

Title
zark
URL
http://www.zark.com/
Designer/Illustrator/Programmer
charley parker
Authoring platform
Mac

It was only a matter of time before comics built a home for themselves on the Web; this site has contented itself with building a small mansion. The colors are vibrant and obviously computer-generated, lacking the halftoning problems inherent in printed comic books; color gradations, especially on monitors with higher than 8-bit color, are smooth and refined.

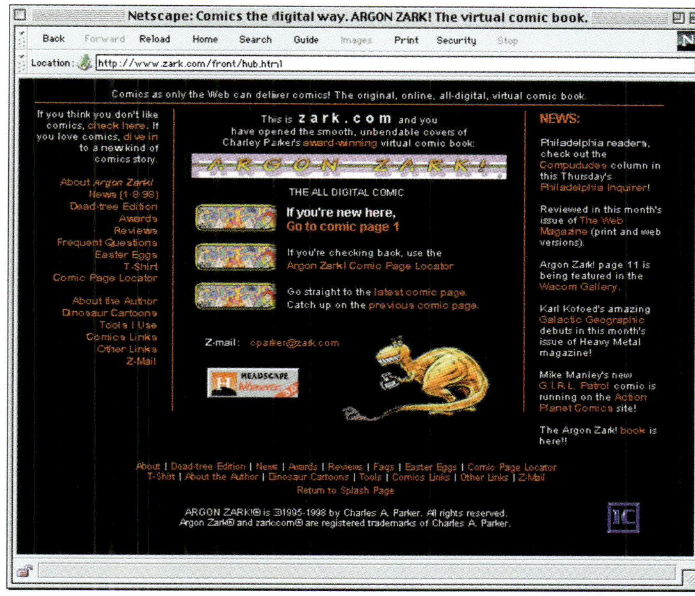

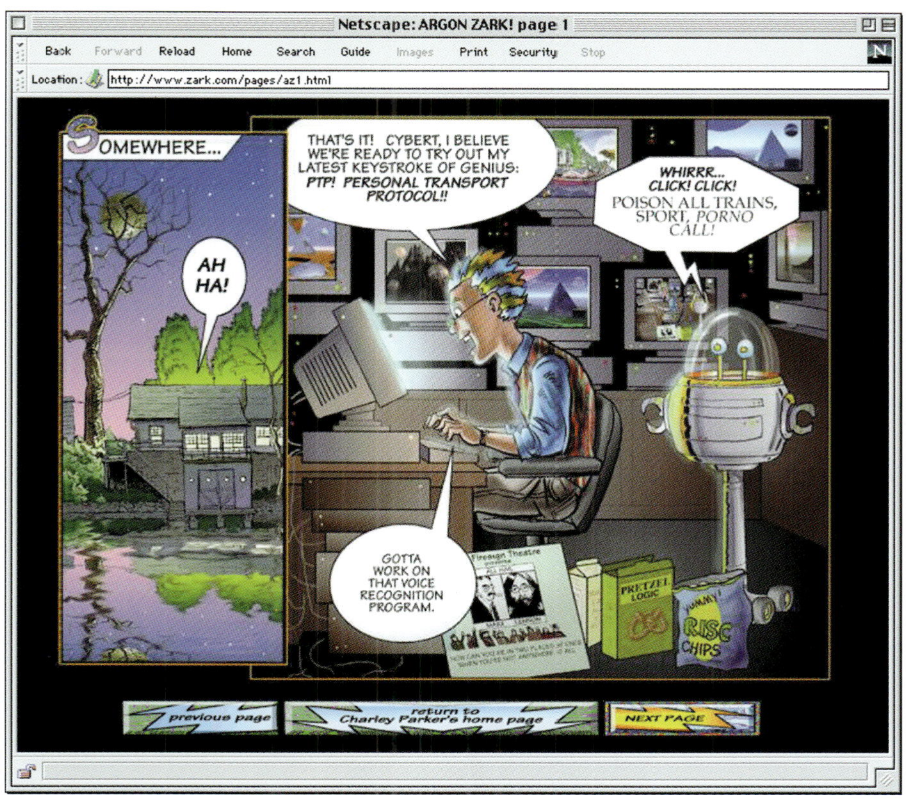

Title
212
URL
http://www.212.net/
Design Firm
madisonavenue.com
Illustrators
David Haadler, Sue Ann Kim, Marianna Trofimova
Photographers
Emilie Wilson, David Haadler, J. Michael Seyfert
Programmers
Kevin Toye, David Haadler, John Northrop, Jill Penning, J. Michael Seyfert
Creative Director
J. Michael Seyfert
Authoring Platform
PC

The multicolored background serves to separate and reiterate the skyscraper-esque bars of information in this New York-based e-zine. The effect is immediately striking and intentionally places the viewer into a world of density and variation.

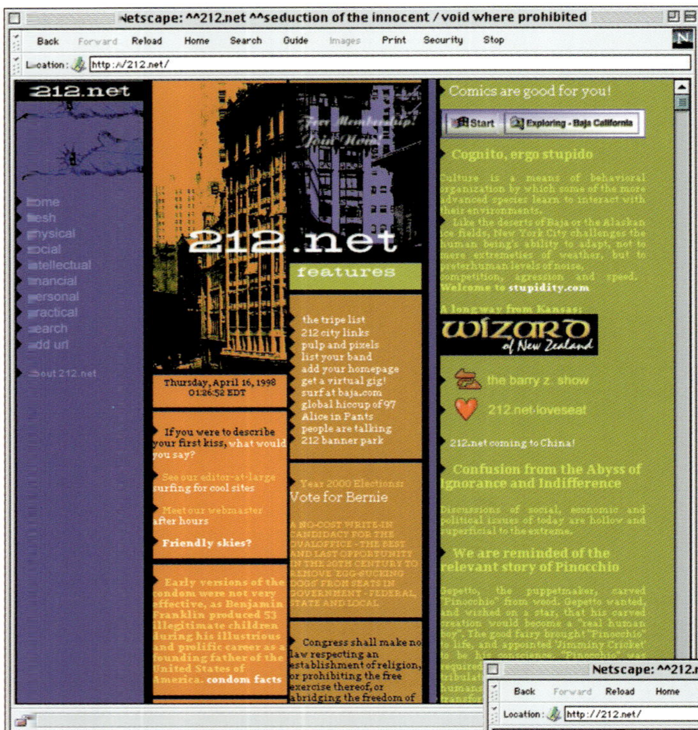

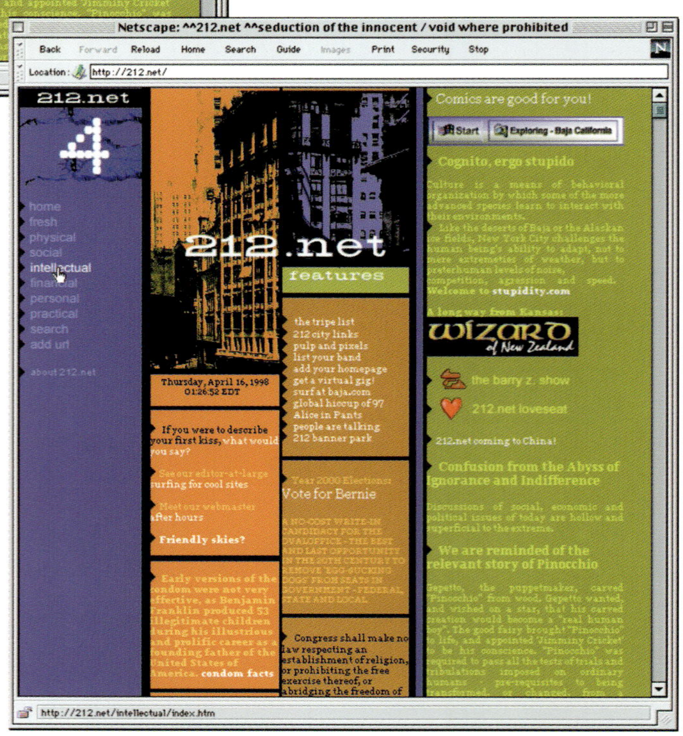

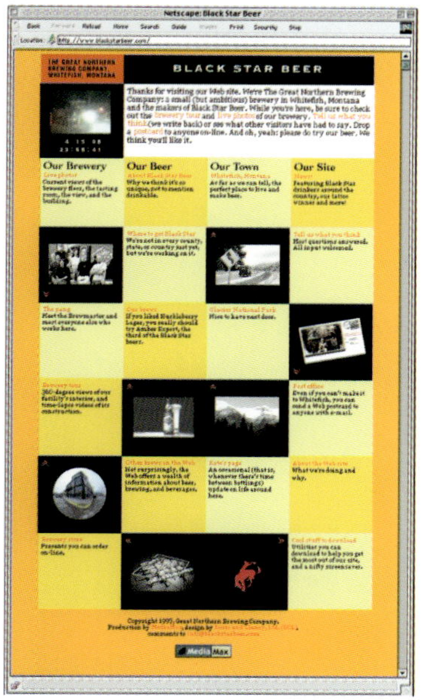

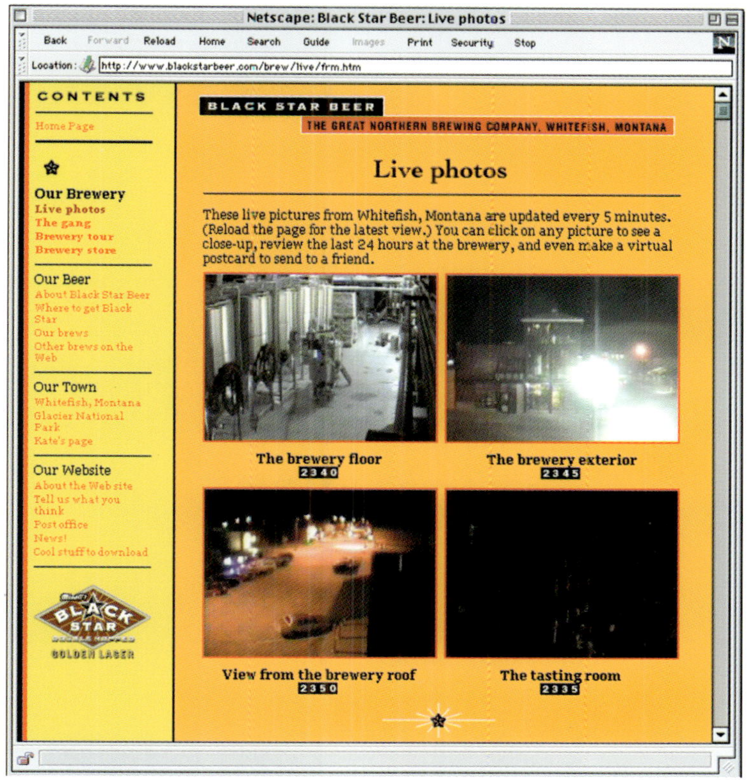

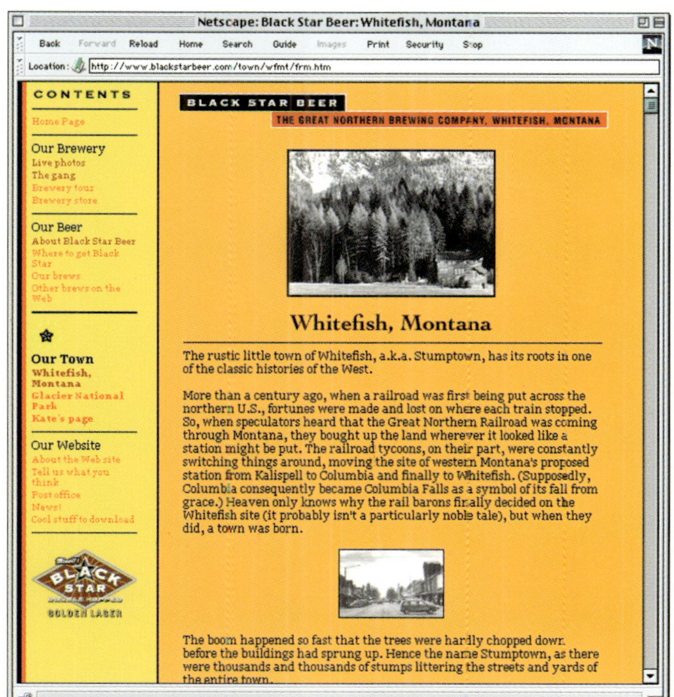

Title
Black Star Beer
URL
http://www.blackstarbeer.com/
Design Firm
DCL (Doris and Clancy, Ltd.)
Designers
Doris Mitsch, Clancy Nolan
Photographers
Doug Menuez, Mike Calabro, Amy R. Colson
Programmer
MediaMax
Writers
Toby Barlow, Doris Mitsch, Kate Greenlee
Authoring Platform
Mac, PC

Cleverly hidden in full view on this site is the fact that there is a lot of information being pushed on the homepage. Rather than offer multiple boring lists of links, the designers have spread out across a two-toned checkerboard. The golden colors evoke the lager offered by the brewery, and make the photos in the black boxes pop off the screen.

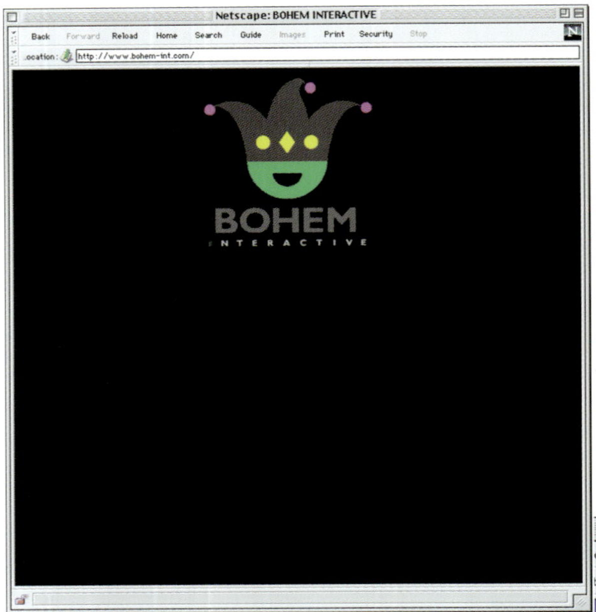

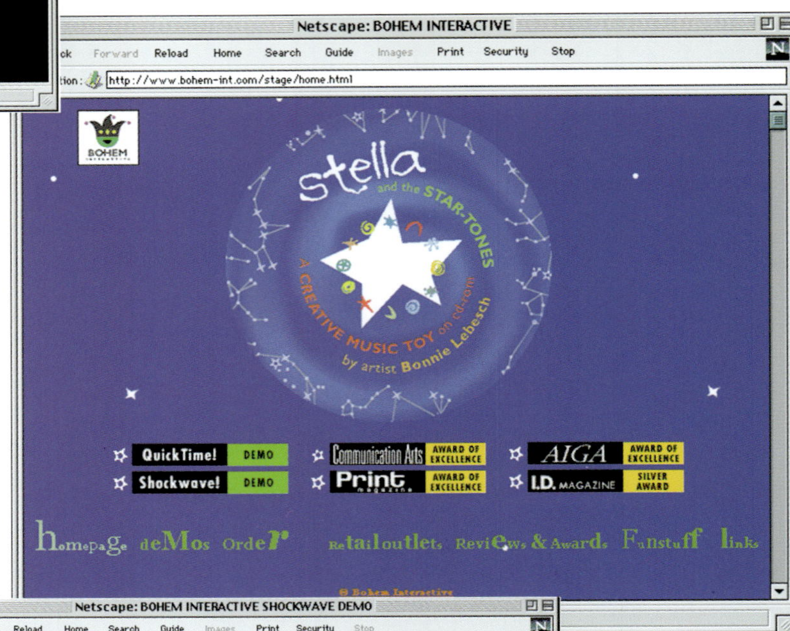

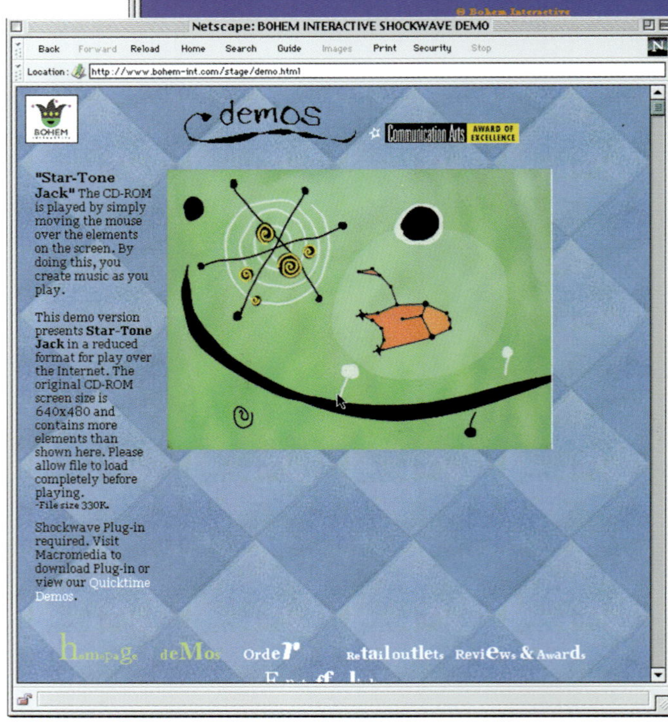

Title
Bohem Interactive
URL
http://www.bohem-int.com/
Design Firm
Bohem Interactive
Designer/Photographer
Bonnie Lebesch
Illustrators/Programmers
Bonnie Lebesch, Don Barnett
Authoring Platform
Mac

This site for an award-winning multimedia CD-ROM remains true to its source, keeping text to a minimum and showcasing the program's quirky colors and artwork. The blue background tile provides a perfect bedspread on which to lay out the CD's musical demos.

title
Lunar Prospector
URL
http://www.lunar.arc.nasa.gov/index.html
design firm
NASA Ames Research Center
designers
Ken Bollinger, Glenn Deardorf, Jeffrey Ma
illustrators
Jeffrey Ma, Justin Hafford, Lisa Chu-Thielbar,
Alison Davis
programmers
Larry Kellogg, Jonathan Yee
authoring platform
Mac, PC, Unix

Much of the space imagery we see has turned into visual clichés, which is why the unexpected arc of the Earth on the right side of this homepage is refreshing to view. The designers at NASA have tapped images that transcend what is normally seen: the Earth, with its cloud-swept blue oceans, and the Moon, containing multiple layers of detail not usually seen with the naked eye.

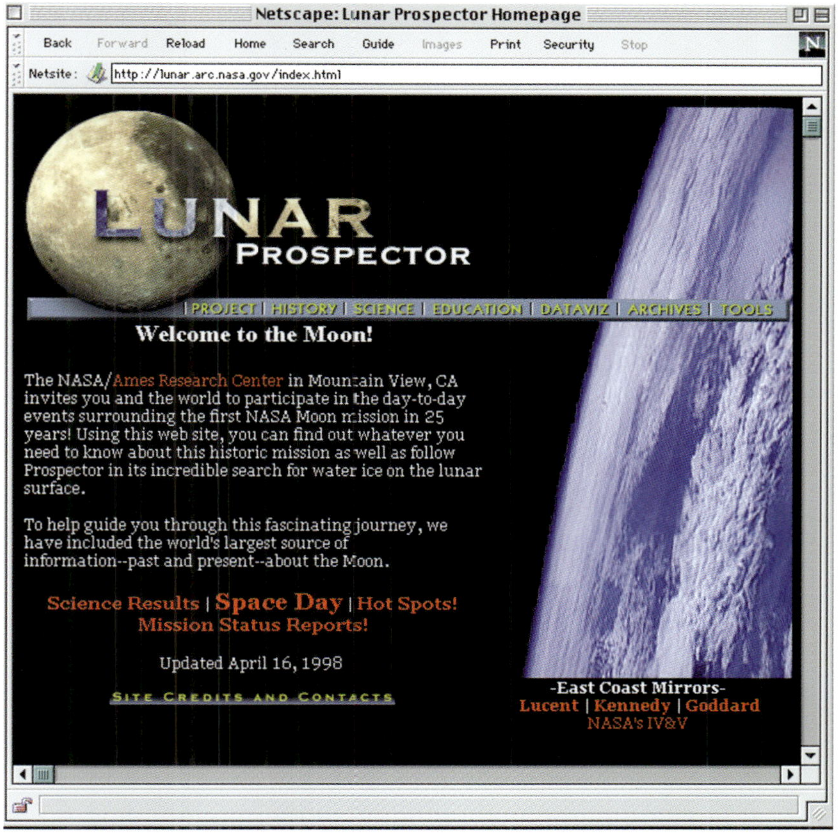

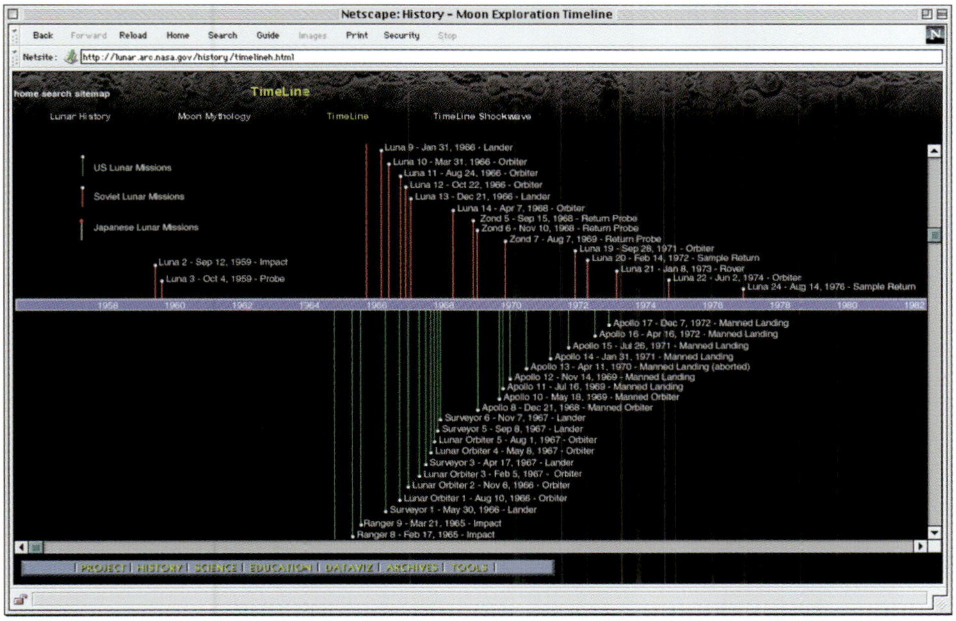

title
Meany Theater-UW World Series
URL
http://www.meany.org/
design firm
Accelerated Web Development/Hinton and Steel
designers
Jeff DeRoshia, Judy Simpson, Jesse Damm
photographer
KAN Photography
programmer
Accelerated Web Development
authoring platform
PC

The main image on this site isn't remarkable for a broad use of colors, but rather for the smoothness of the blends and fades, both in the water-map and the blue-green strip at the top of the page. On a pixel-by-pixel basis, this page fills up the Web's limited 256-color palette with similar hues, retaining its smoothness, even on 8-bit displays.

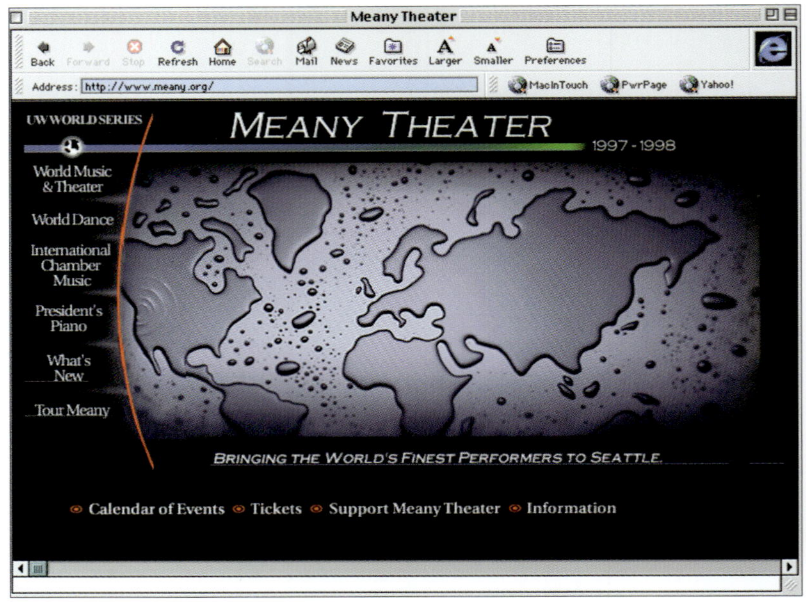

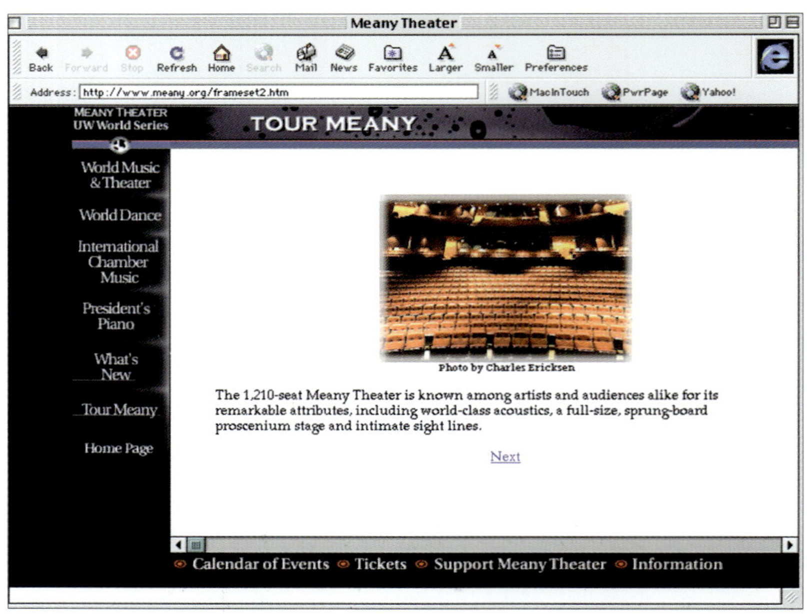

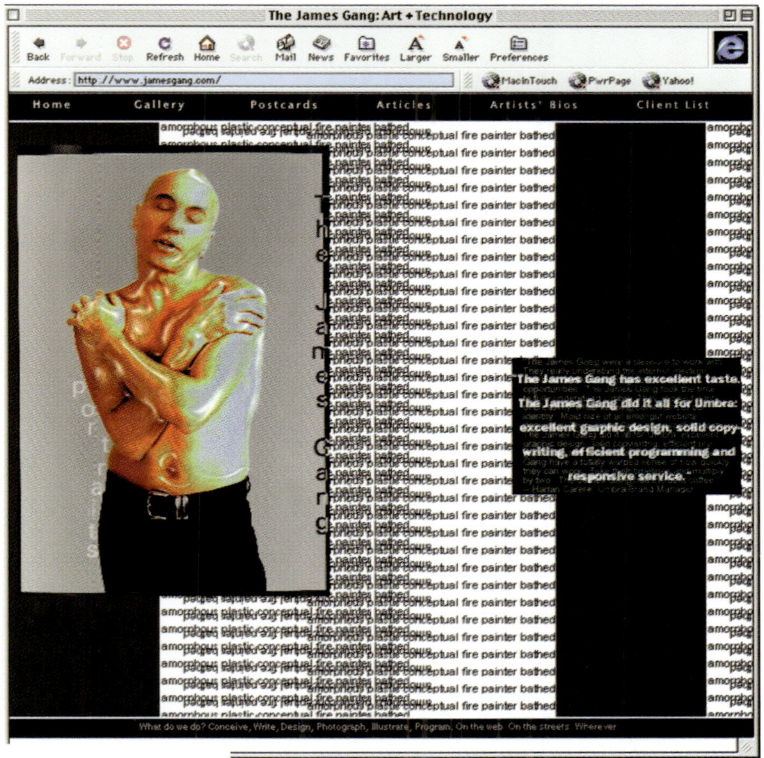

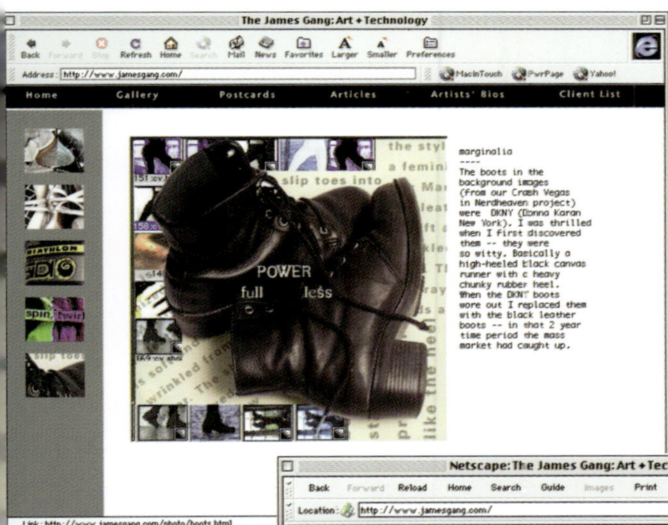

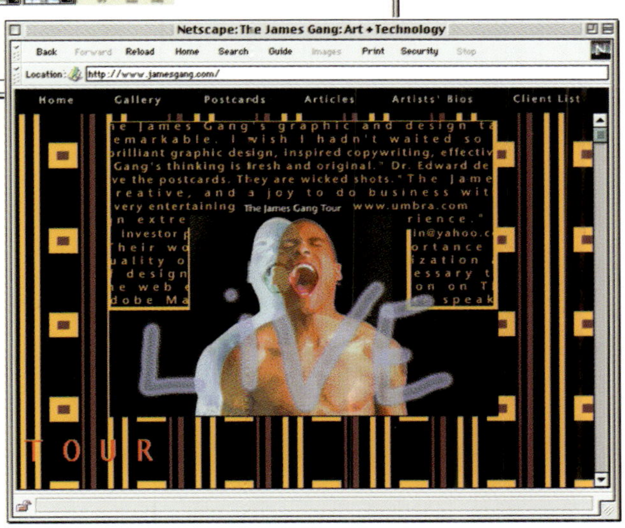

Title
The James Gang
URL
http://www.jamesgang.com/
Design Firm
The James Gang: Art + Technology
Designers
Franke James, MFA; Bill James
Illustrator/Photographer
Franke James, MFA
Programmer
Bill James
Models
Ronnae (Ford Models)
Authoring Platform
Mac

Many sites that use color successfully prefer to maintain visual consistency and control. The James Gang, however, uses color as an explosion, often letting it fall where it may. Whether added for dramatic emphasis, as on the figure on the main page, or as a patterned background, color on this site remains unbound.

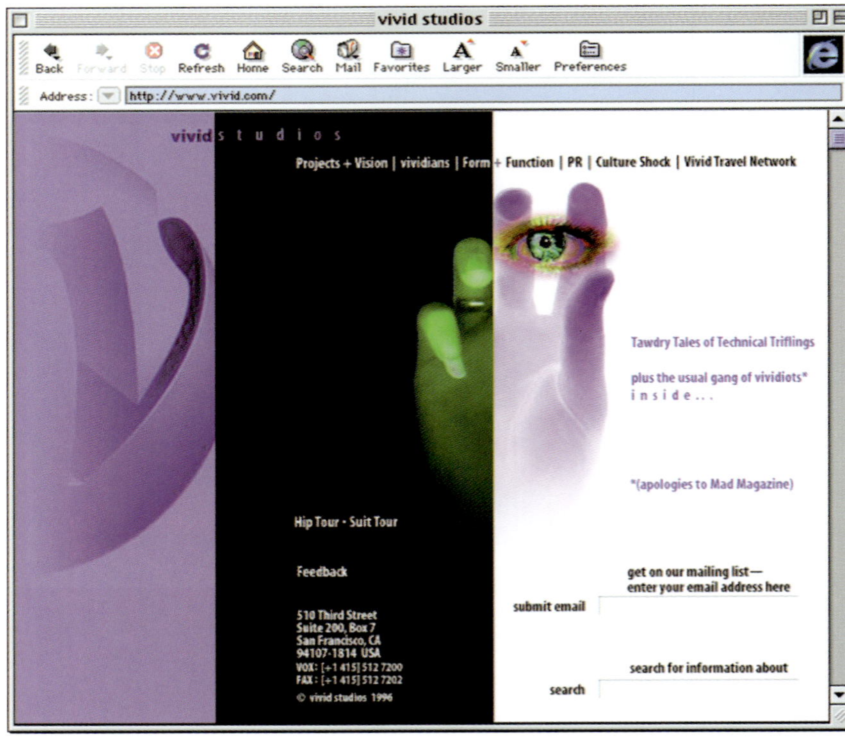

Title
vivid studios
URL
http://www.vivid.com/
Design Firm
vivid studios
Photographers
Brian Bell, Chuck Gathard, Marsha Plat
Programmers
Paul Guth, Nat Johnson
Creative Director
Nathan Shedroff
Information Designer
Drue Miller
Visual Designers
Jeff Davis, Nathan Shedroff, Maurice Tani
Writer
Drue Miller
Authoring Platform
Mac, Unix

This studio is selling itself to an elite clientele, and the royal purple on the homepage feels sophisticated. Mostly shades of purple and green are used, but the reversed-out center vertical panel—reversing the purple hand to green—creates three distinct areas from left to right that don't interfere with separate navigation and link actions from top to bottom.

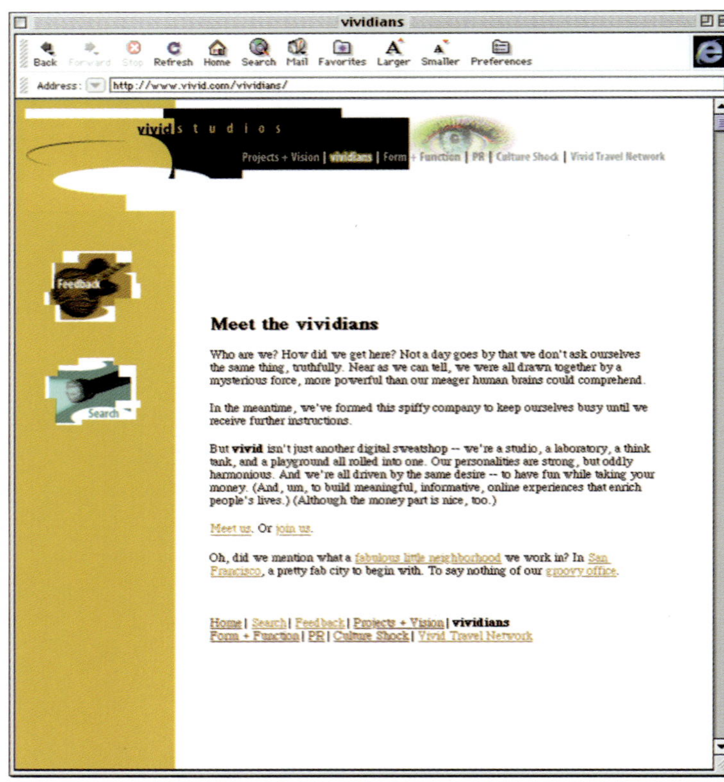

Title
Mike Motz: promotional portfolio
URL
http://www.cal.shaw.wave.ca/~mmotz/
Design Firm
Mike Motz
Designer/Illustrator/Programmer
Mike Motz

An artist who is promoting, in part, his cartoon style, the colors come from the TV animation palette. Although it seems to be more active, the color palette is surprisingly small: a light, medium, and dark pastel green; plus red, blue, and yellow. Almost everything else uses shadowed versions of those six. In a nice, small touch, his red signature has a green shadow, which changes to the contrasting green for whichever area the signature covers.

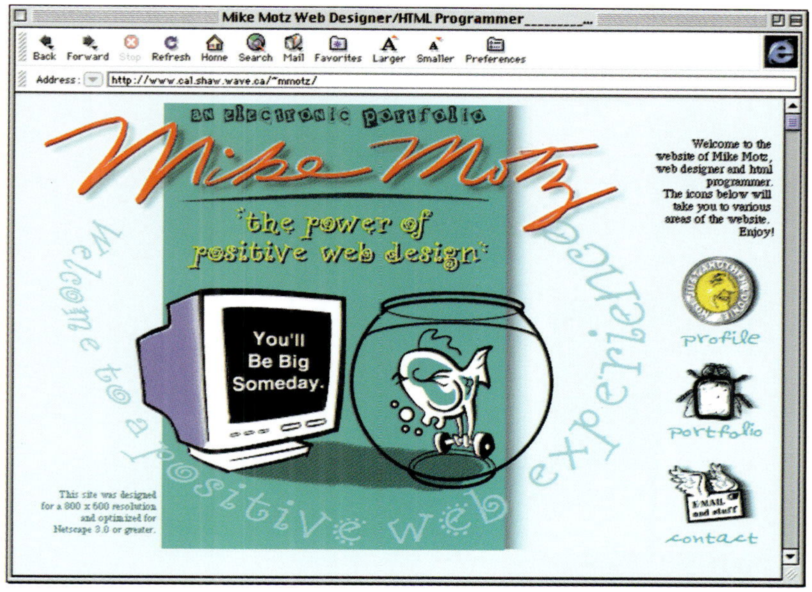

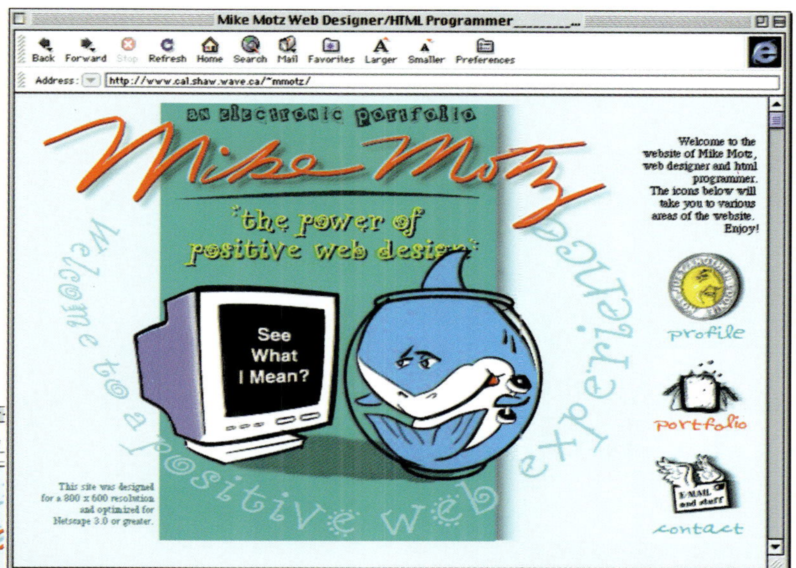

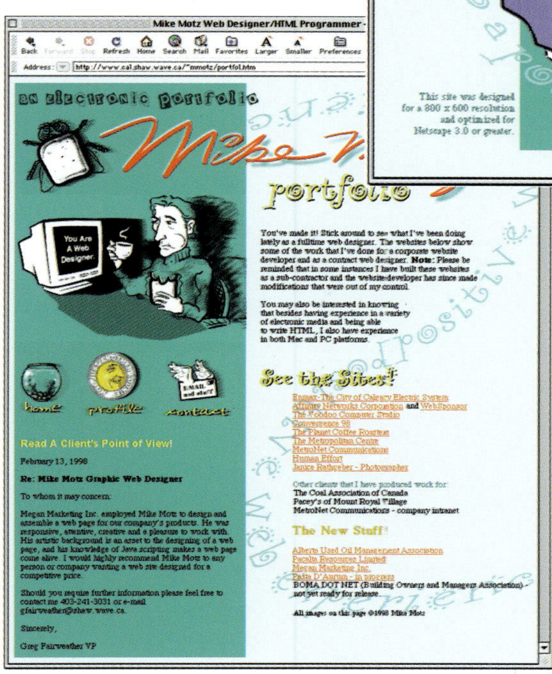

typography

It took a while to convince typographers that electronic publishing was a good idea. The amount of control that a designer could exercise over the spacing, kerning, and leading of type was poor, at best, during the first years of desktop publishing.

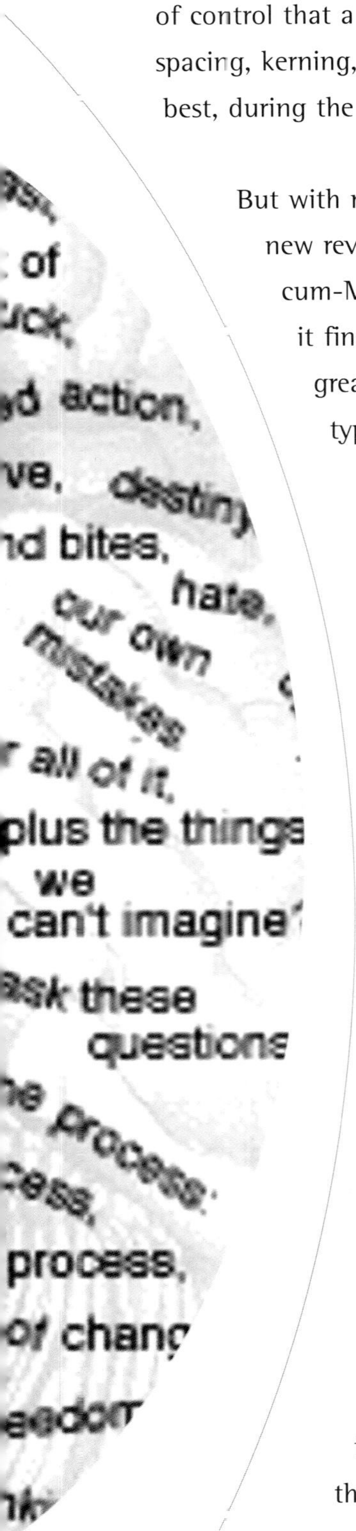

But with maturity came precision. Each new revision of QuarkXPress or Aldus-cum-Macromedia FreeHand brought with it finer controls, better options, and a greater sense that you could really make type do whatever you wanted it to.

Then along came the World Wide Web, and years of progress appeared to be thrown out the window. Fortunately, it was a temporary setback.

As with desktop publishing, it took some time to regain balance, and four years after the real introduction of the graphical World Wide Web, typography has reasserted itself in the design process.

The examples you'll find in this book are drawn from sites we found that had gone beyond simply creating images out of printed pages. Each site draws some advantage from or is designed for the Web, and takes into account the special requirements needed to render or display type in a small, scrollable, and live window.

Some sites actively fight legibility with a purpose: ironically enough, typographic.com is one of them; but others also push the aesthetic line, but not so far that we're repelled.

The competing innovations incorporated in Cascading Style Sheets (CSS), OpenType, and TrueDoc haven't yet trickled down to every designer or every user. Most sites that use type well have worked either with rendered type—type turned into an image—or have used a few standard font adjustments (like increasing or decreasing size with the <FONT SIZE=X> tag) to achieve more variety.

There's a lot of ingenuity in these pages from designers who have had to struggle to meet their own standards for typography in a limiting medium. However, the future promises to offer as much flexibility as desktop publishing now affords.

“There’s a lot of ingenuity in these pages from designers who have had to struggle to meet their own standards for typography in a limiting medium. However, the future promises to offer as much flexibility as desktop publishing now affords.”

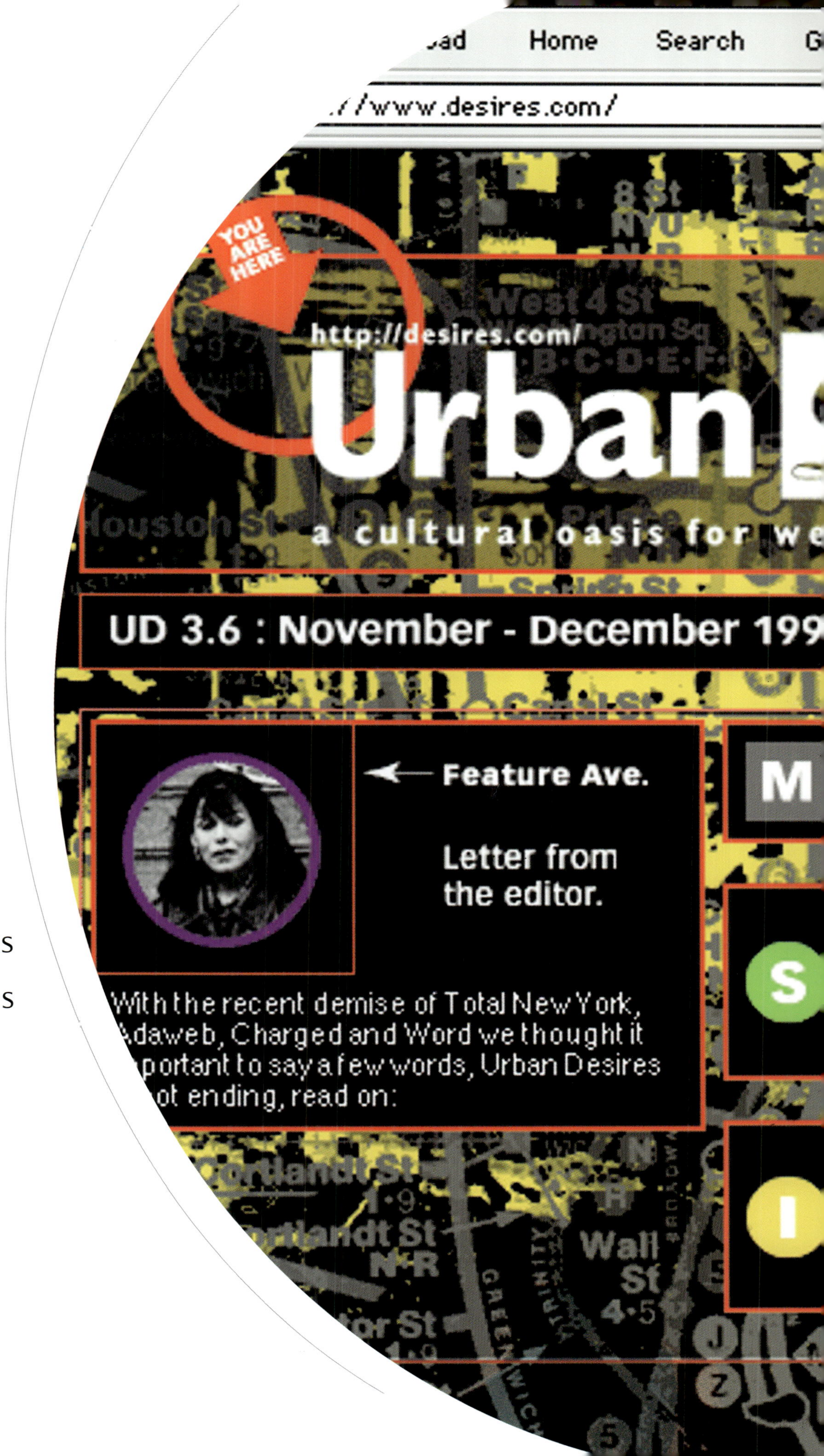

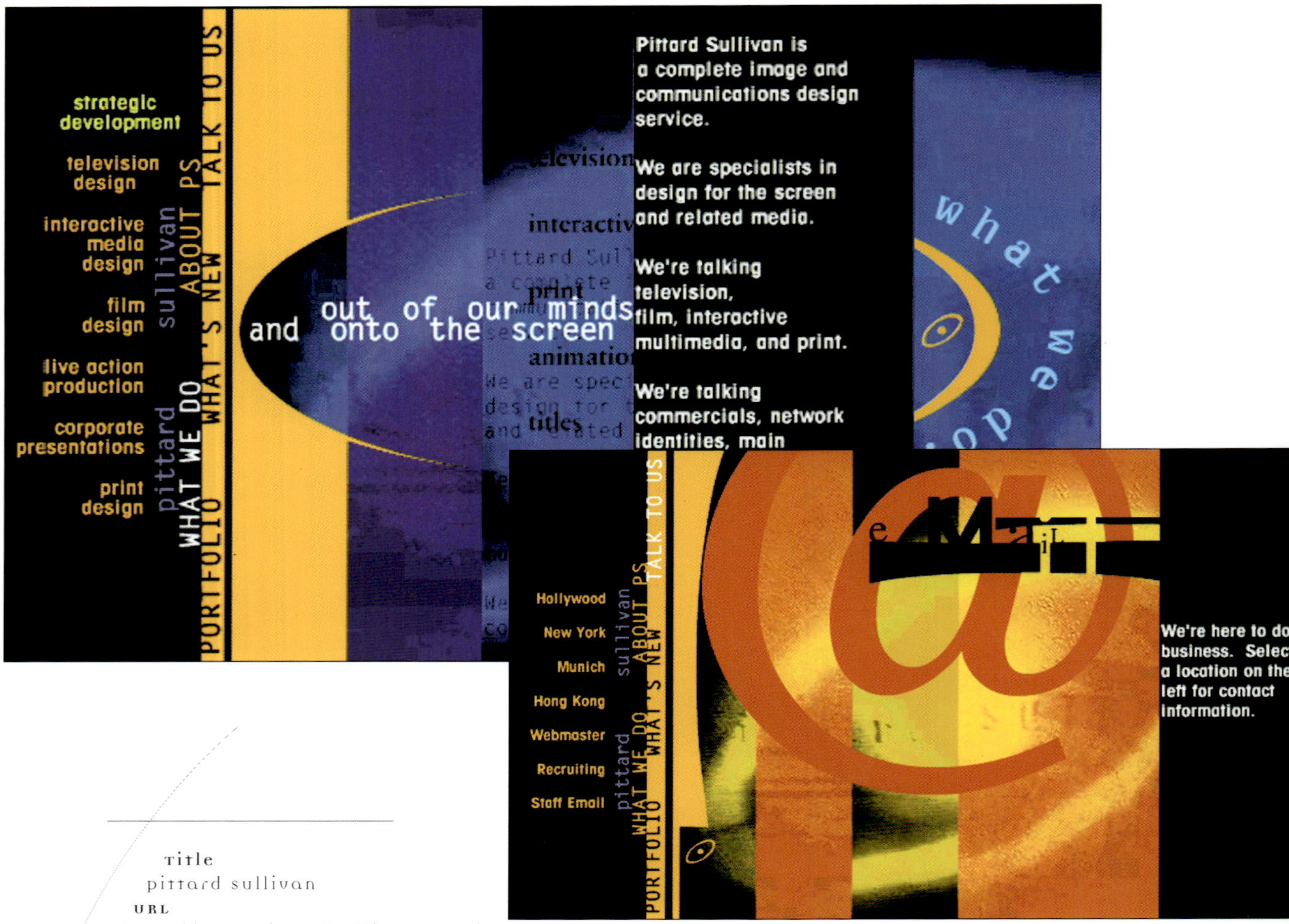

Title
pittard sullivan
URL
http://www.pittardsullivan.com/
Design Firm
pittard sullivan
Designers
Aaron King, Soo Chyun, Ron Romero
Programmers
Bryan Keeling, Marvin Price

It's impossible to ignore the typography on these pages. Using primarily sans-serif fonts, text is the basis for the site's navigation and graphic elements, which are made interactive with the use of JavaScript rollovers and Shockwave Flash technology.

Title
Goblin Design
URL
http://www.goblindesign.com/
Design Firm
Goblin Design
Designer/Illustrator/Programmer
Silas Tobal

The gothic font chosen for Goblin's name isn't unexpected, but creating the appearance of being cast in metal makes the title of this page decidedly modern. In the navigation bar, raised metallic-looking letters seem to be set behind rounded glass, giving the site a professional feel without resorting to Photoshop filter excesses.

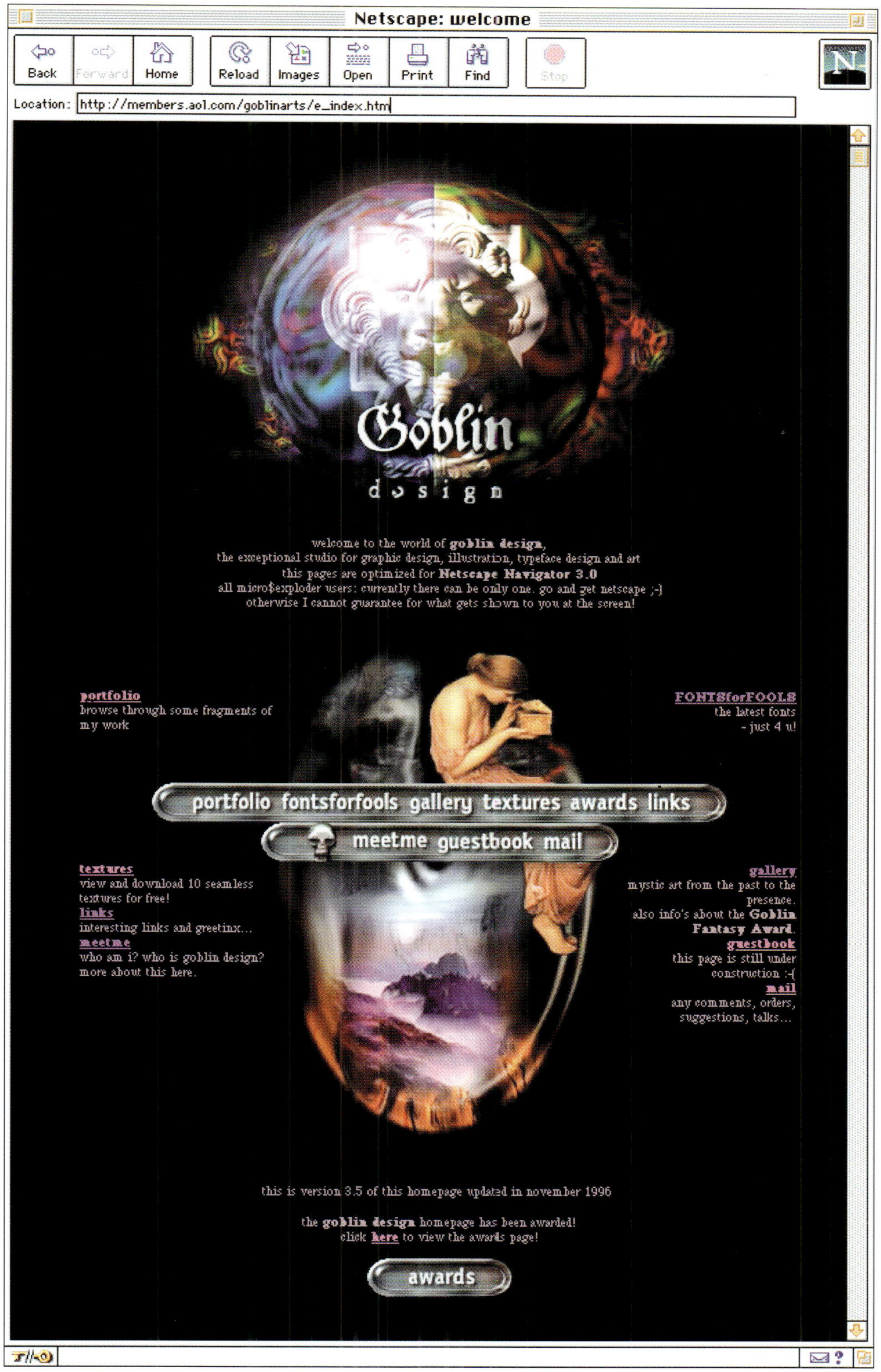

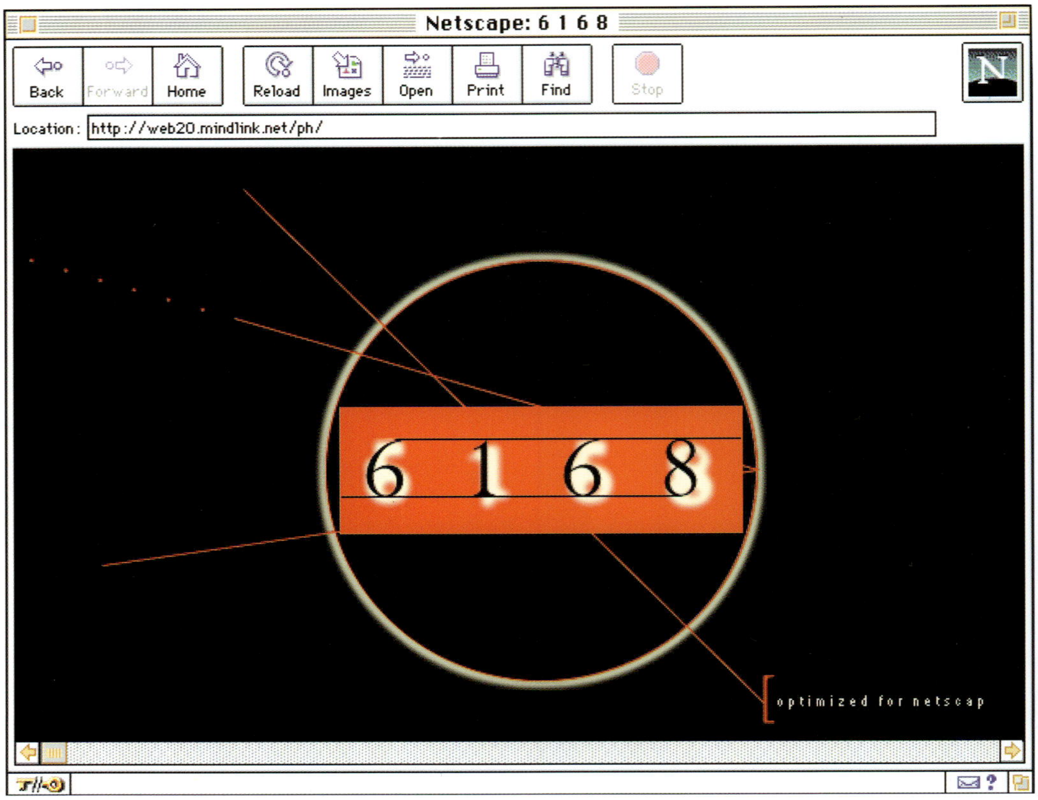

Title
6168
URL
http://www.6168.org/
Design Firm
MCO Digital productions
Designers
Peter Horvath, Sharon Matarazzo

Most Web typography involves creating graphics of text in a variety of fonts, so it's refreshing to find a site that focuses its design on plain old browser-generated text. Expanded letterspacing and extra leading add atmosphere to the 6168 art exhibit. The surprise here, however, is that the same plain text blocks are actually animated GIFs!

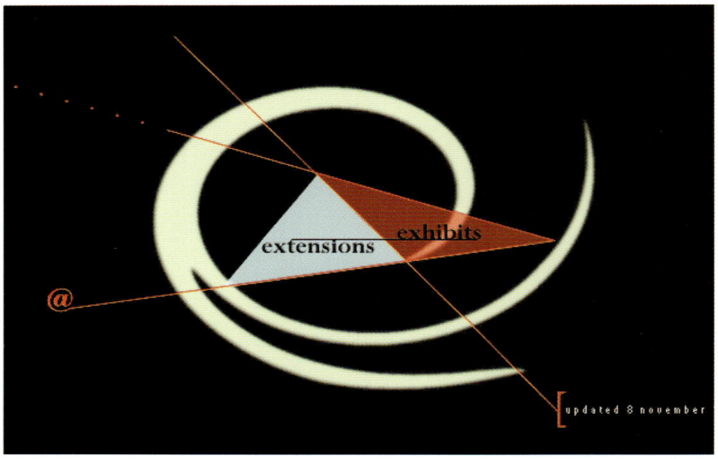

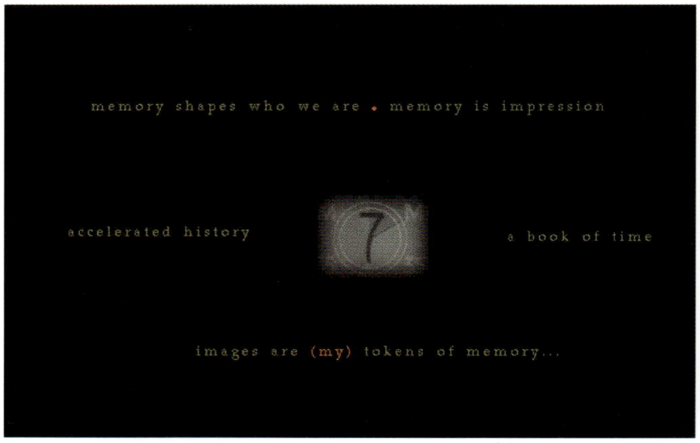

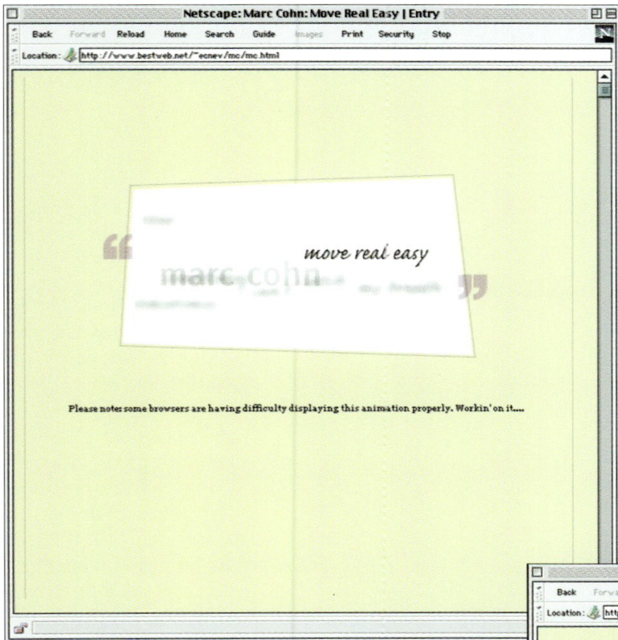

Title

Marc cohn: Move Real Easy

URL

http://www.bestweb.net/~ecnev/mc/mc.html

Design firm

One Art Design

Designer/Illustrator/programmer

Eric C. Nevin

Authoring platform

Mac

The casual script employed on the opening animation and the album title reflects the easy motion of its subject matter; used sparsely, the unique typeface works as a counterbalance to the loose, open lettering of *marc cohn* and the formal caps that appear in the navigation.

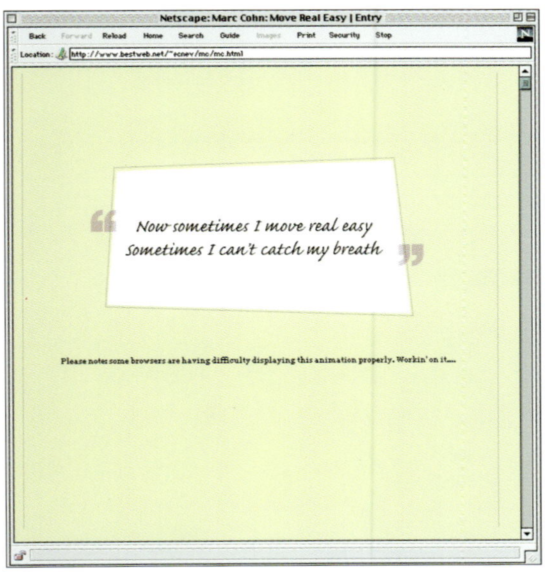

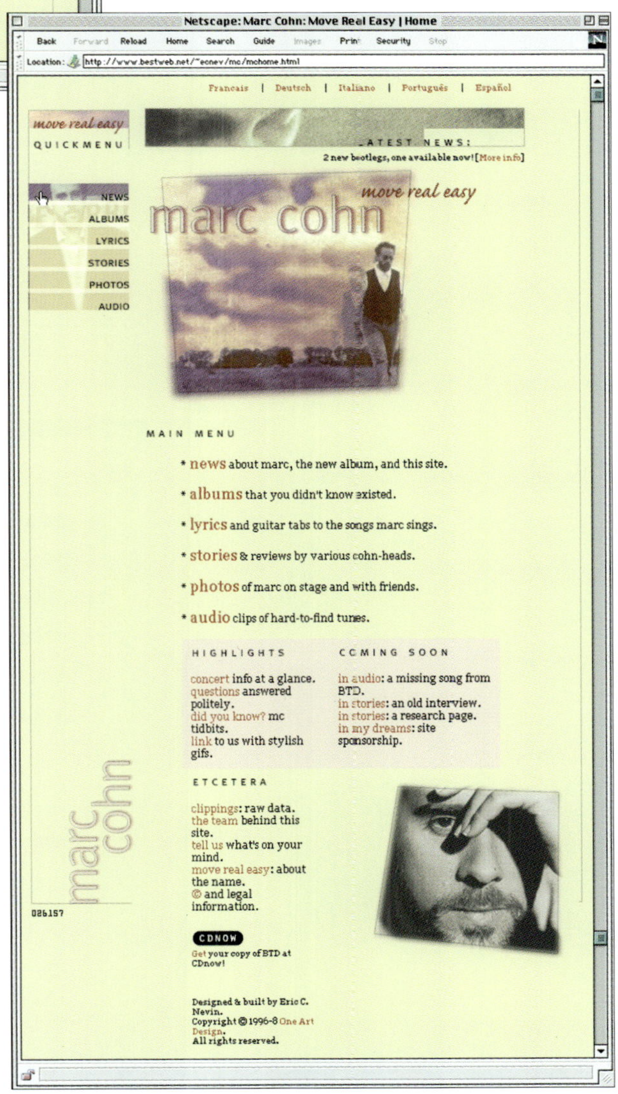

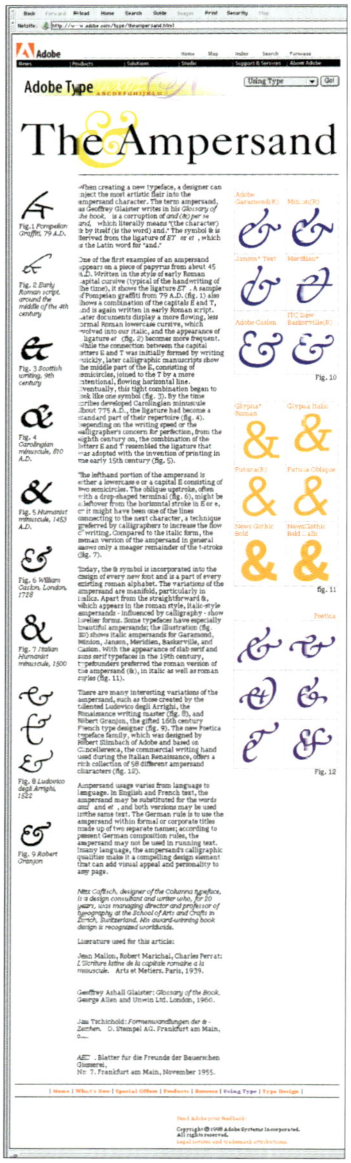

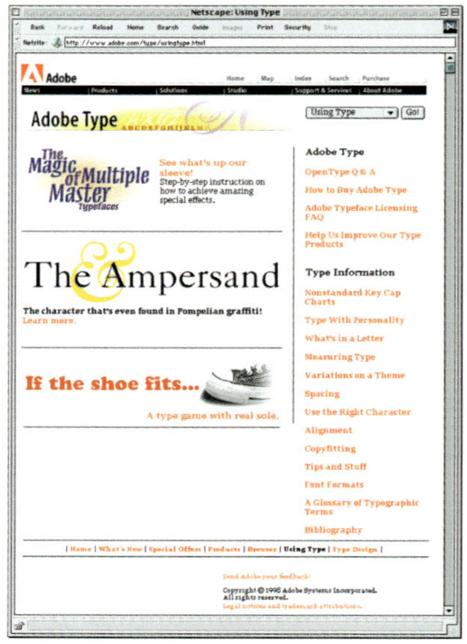

Title
Adobe Systems
URL
http://www.adobe.com/type/main.shtml
Design firm
Adobe Systems Web Department
Authoring platform
Mac, PC, Sun Sparc

Adobe has been at the forefront of digital type for years, and their pages devoted to typography reflect this. The title image on the opening page manages to demonstrate the breadth of the company's offerings without falling into the trap of cramming multiple faces on one page. Credit the generous amount of white space throughout the site for providing balance and allowing the typefaces to draw attention to themselves.

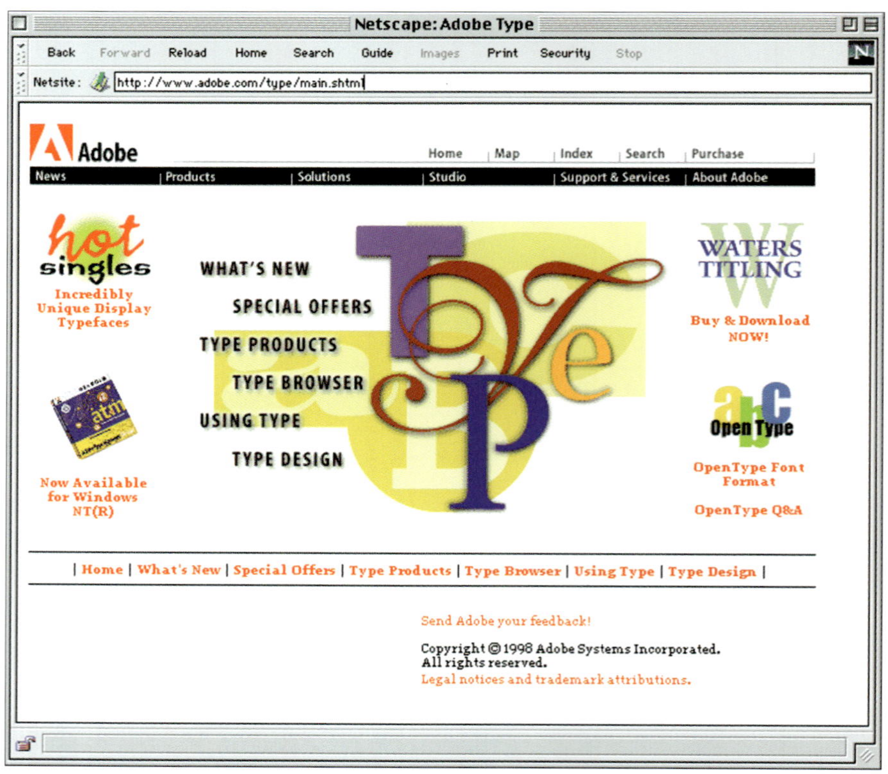

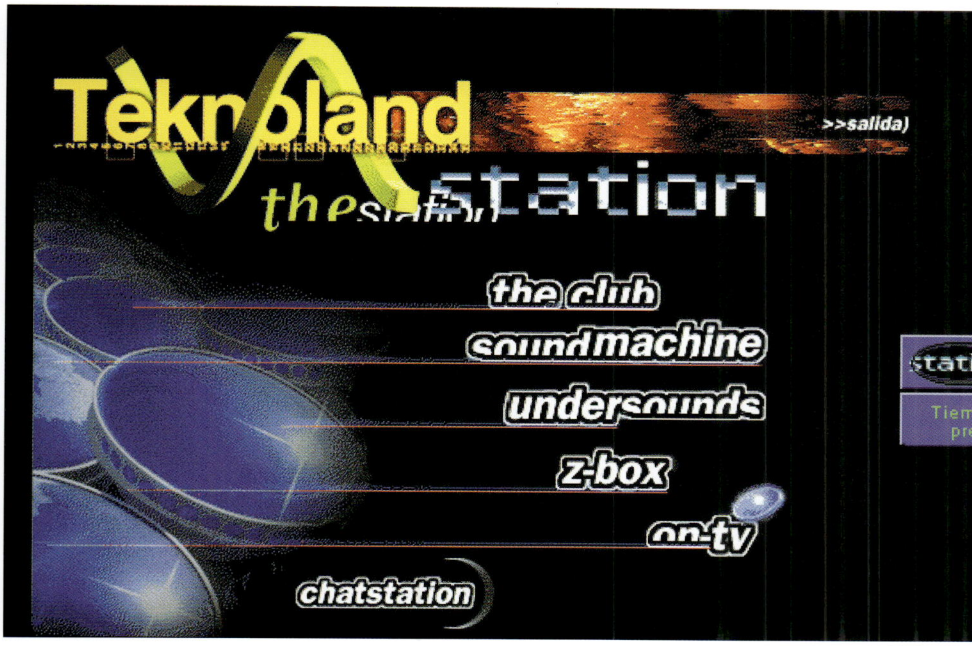

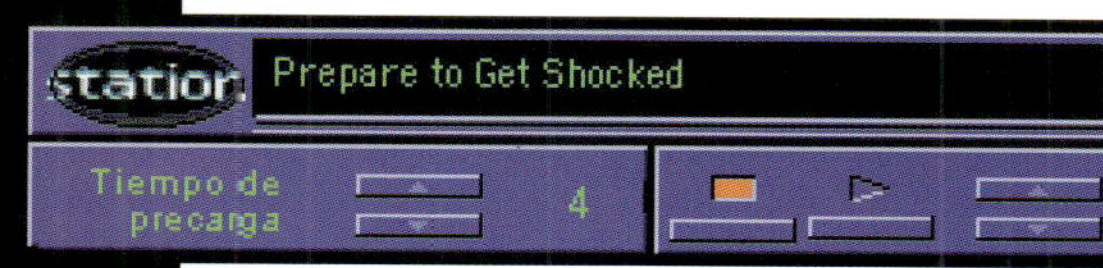

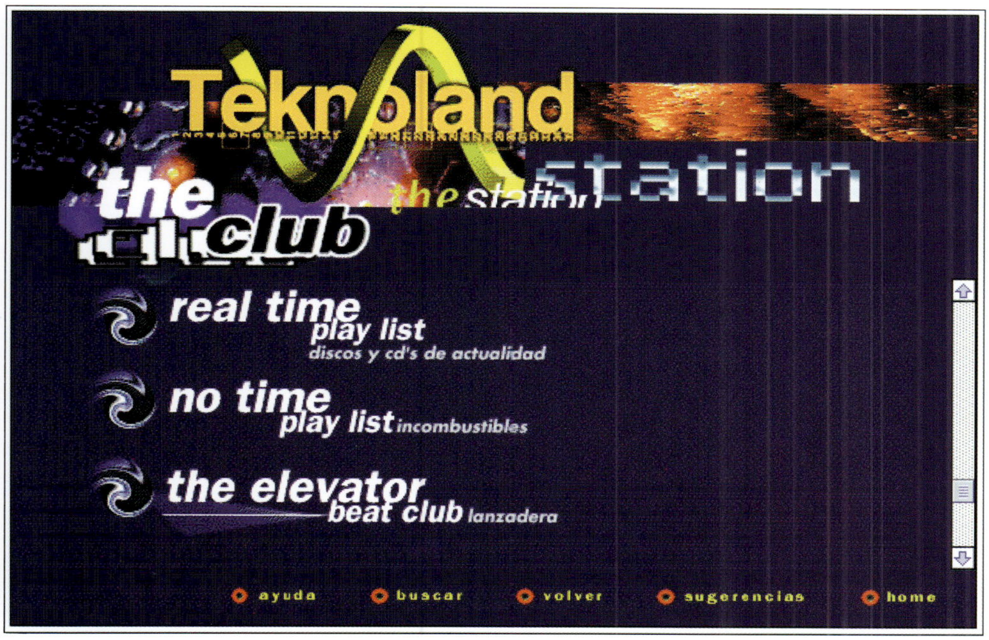

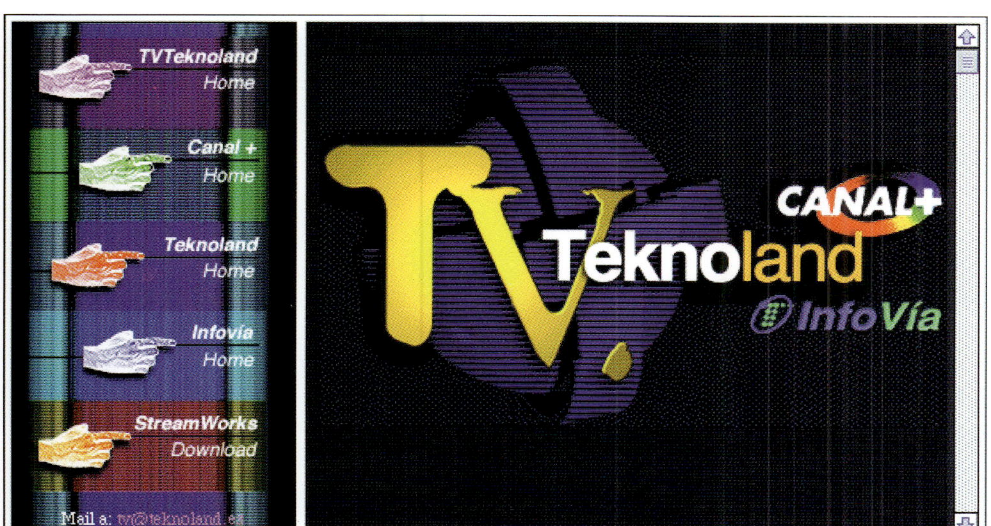

Title
Teknoland
URL
http://www.teknoland.es/arte/fura/
Design Firm
Teknoland
Art Director
David L. Cantolla
Designer
Joe Luis Garcia
Programmers
Colman Lopez, Jesus Suarez
Authoring
Nestor Matas, Michael Mangicotti
Authoring Platform
Mac, PC

To emphasize the eclectic nature of La Fura dels Baus, an artistic performance company, the Teknoland designers have taken standard sans-serif type and assembled it at various sizes without regard for baselines. After dirtying-up the letters a bit, the resulting text is simultaneously descriptive and contextually expressive.

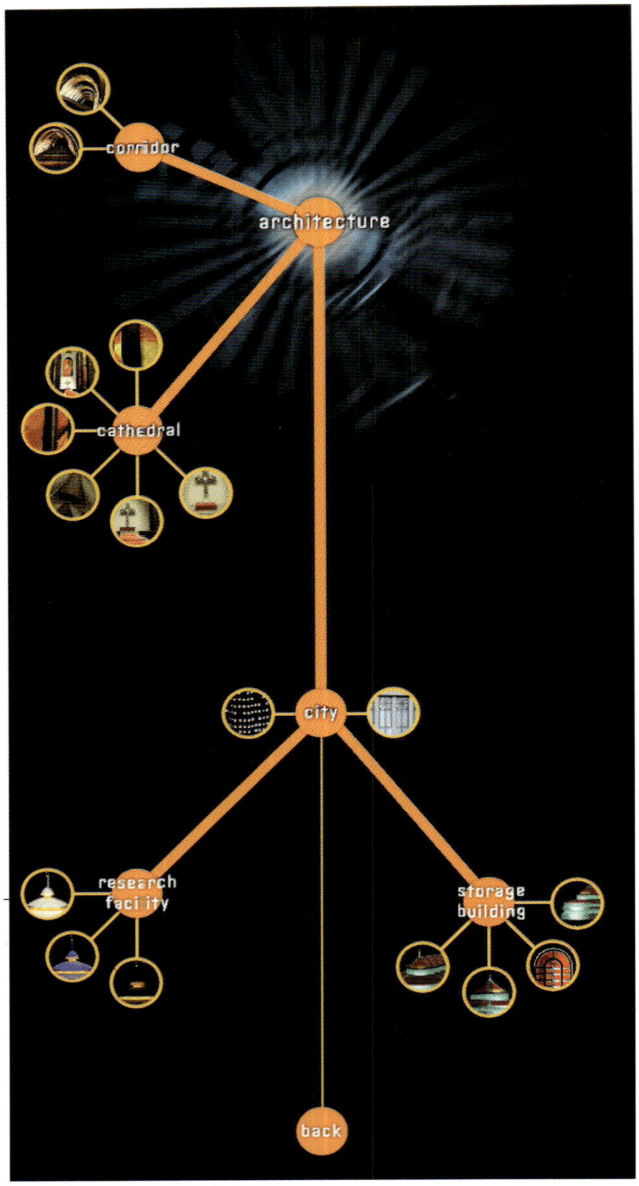

title
kjetil vatne graphics + design
URL
http://www.prodat.no/personer/kjetil_vatne/
design firm
kjetil vatne graphics + design
designer
kjetil vatne

The rounded sans-serif face used here possesses enough weight to justify its use as navigational titles, while softening the edge of the pages' bold colors. Expanding the table of contents title past the point of visibility suggests that a single screen can't hold everything the viewer is about to see.

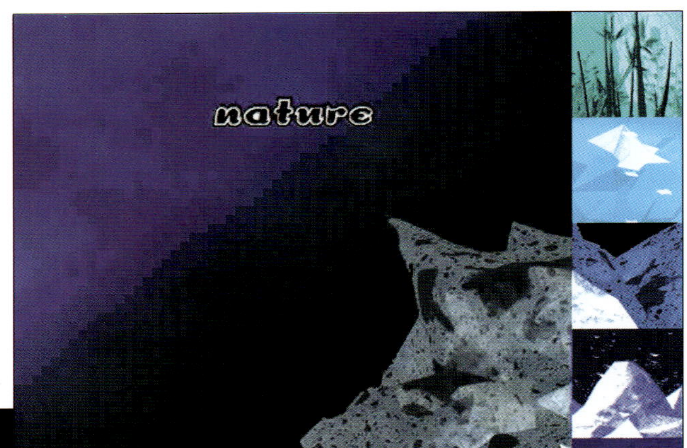

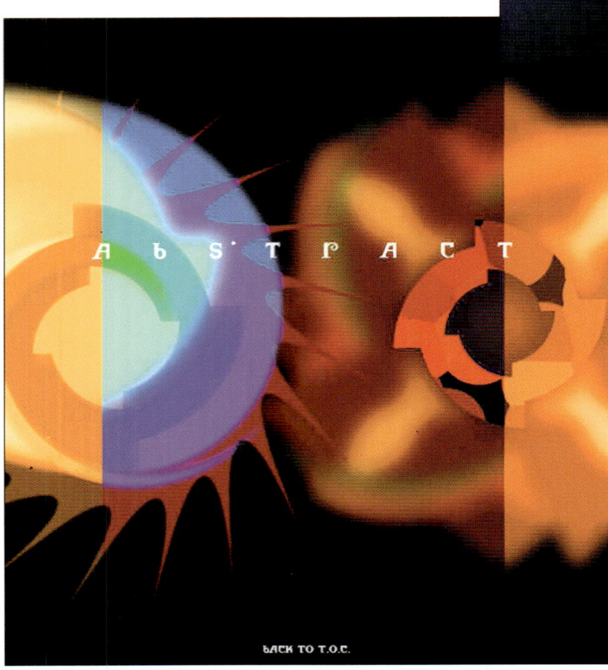

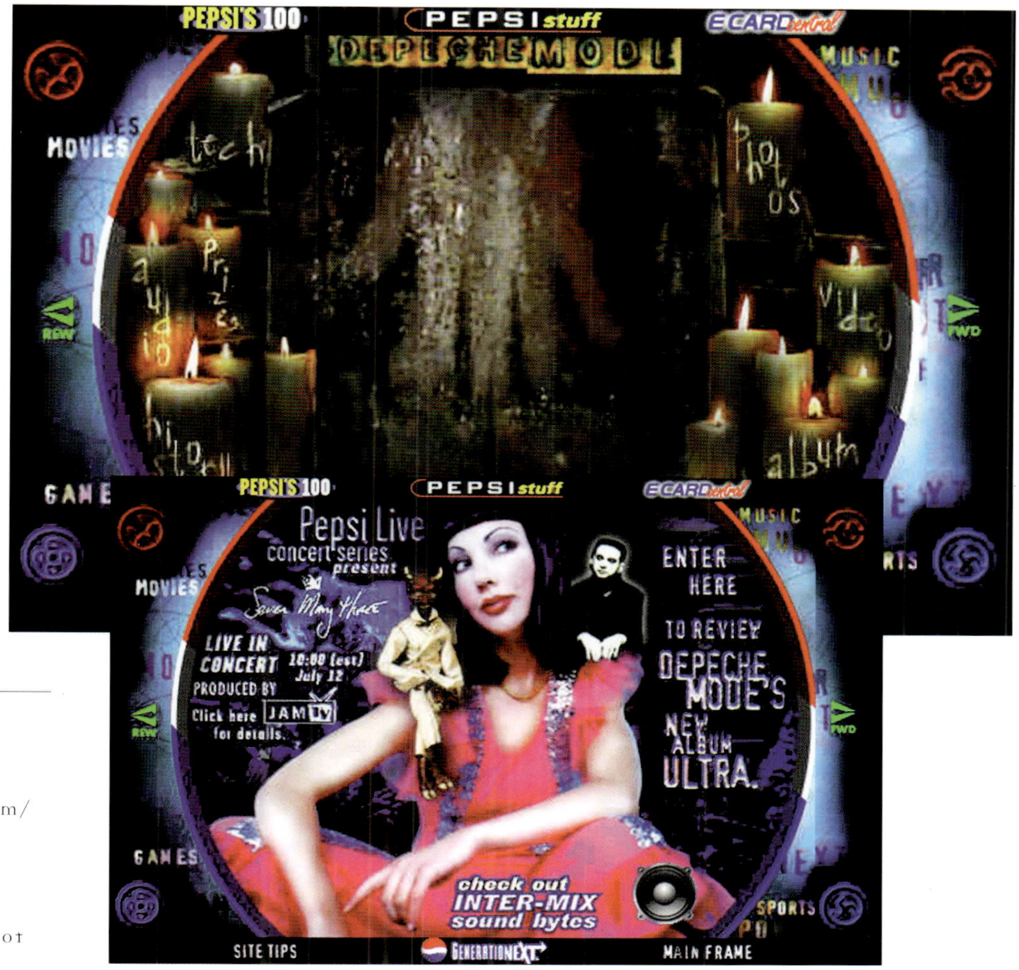

Title
pepsi world
URL
http://www.pepsi.com/
design firm
DDB Interactive
designers
Chris Hess, Frances Ko,
Mike Gonzales, Tricia Elliot
photographer
Jill Green
programmers
Thomas Jeffry, Shelley Shay,
Sal Torneo

Pepsi wants to show the diversity of its world, and here you'll find the gamut of typographic styles and layouts. That does not necessarily mean a mess of overturned alphabet soup; the carved letters in candle wax of the Depeche Mode screen proves that effective typography does not have to come from a keyboard.

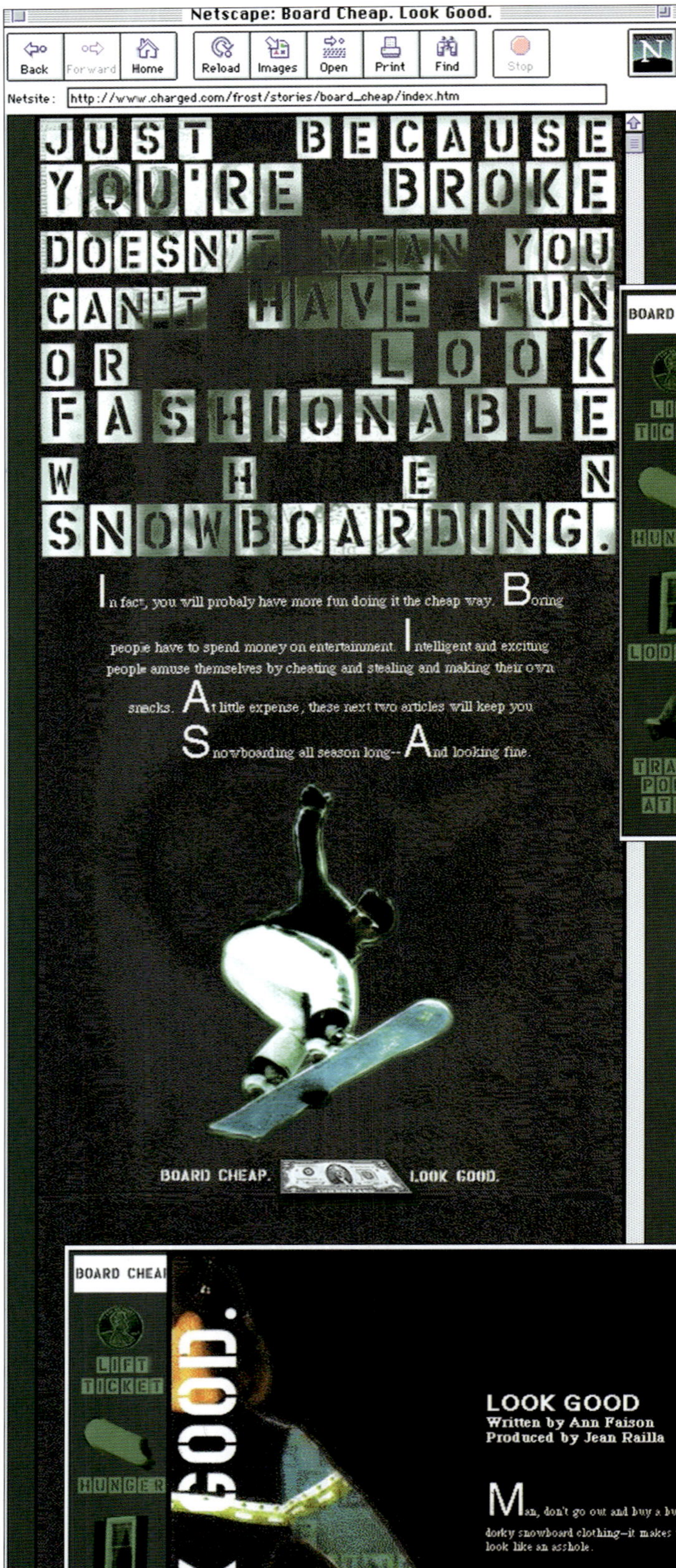
Netscape: Board Cheap. Look Good.
Back
Forward
Home
Reload
Images
Open
Print
Find
Stop
Netsite: http://www.charged.com/frost/stories/board_cheap/index.htm
JUST BECAUSE YOU'RE BROKE DOESN'T MEAN YOU CAN'T HAVE FUN OR LOOK FASHIONABLE WHEN SNOWBOARDING.
In fact, you will probaly have more fun doing it the cheap way. Boring people have to spend money on entertainment. Intelligent and exciting people amuse themselves by cheating and stealing and making their own snacks. At little expense, these next two articles will keep you Snowboarding all season long--And looking fine.
BOARD CHEAP.
LOOK GOOD.

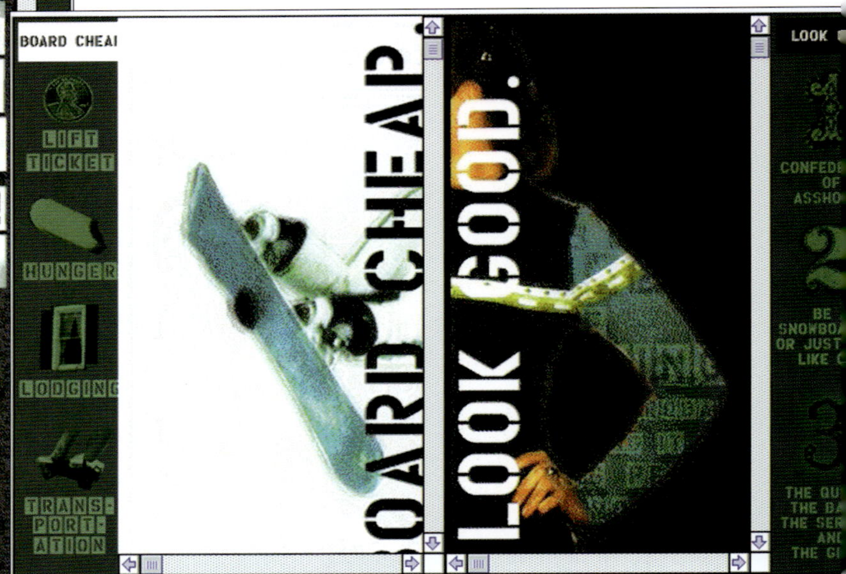
BOARD CHEA
LIFT TICKET
HUNGER
LODGING
TRANS-PORT-ATION
BOARD CHEAP.
LOOK GOOD.
LOOK
CONFEDE OF ASSHO
BE SNOWBOA OR JUST LIKE O
THE QU THE BA THE SER AND THE GI

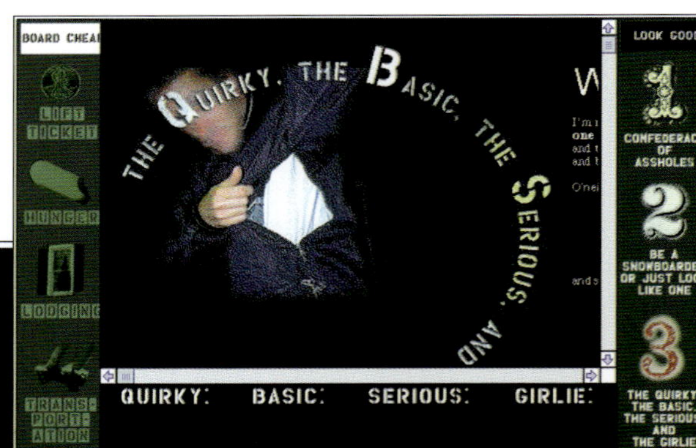
BOARD CHEA
LIFT TICKET
HUNGER
LODGING
TRANS-PORT-ATION
THE QUIRKY, THE BASIC, THE SERIOUS, AND
QUIRKY:
BASIC:
SERIOUS:
GIRLIE:
LOOK GOOD
CONFEDERACY OF ASSHOLES
BE A SNOWBOARDER OR JUST LOOK LIKE ONE
THE QUIRKY, THE BASIC, THE SERIOUS, AND THE GIRLIE

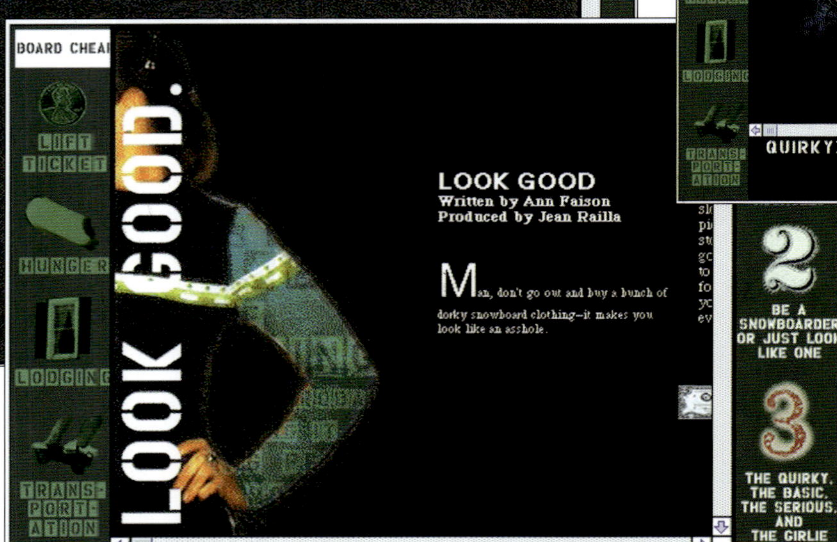
BOARD CHEA
LIFT TICKET
HUNGER
LODGING
TRANS-PORT-ATION
LOOK GOOD.
LOOK GOOD
Written by Ann Faison
Produced by Jean Railla
Man, don't go out and buy a bunch of dorky snowboard clothing--it makes you look like an asshole.
BE A SNOWBOARDER OR JUST LOOK LIKE ONE
THE QUIRKY, THE BASIC, THE SERIOUS, AND THE GIRLIE

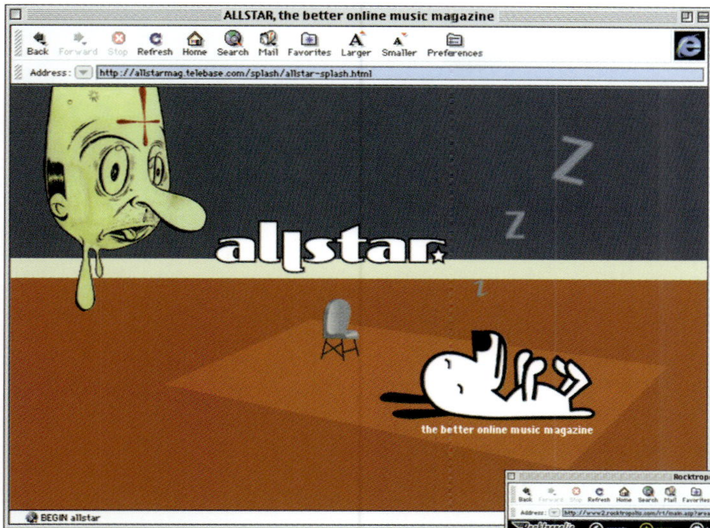

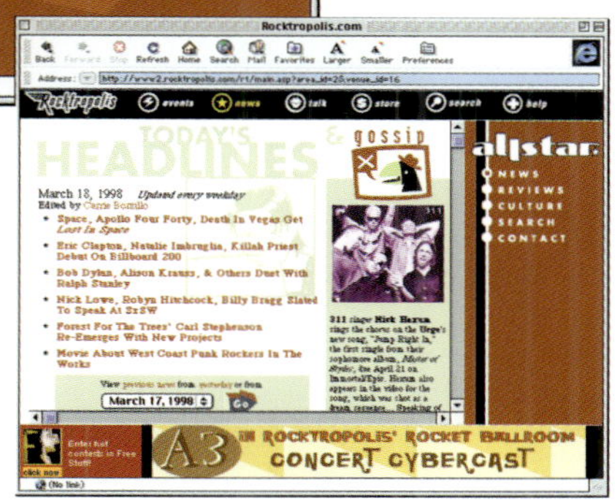

Title
Allstar Magazine
URL
http://www.allstarmag.com/
Design Firm
N2K Entertainment
Designers
Robert Lord, Trevor Gilchrist,
Michelle Comas, Victor Bornia
Illustrators
Adriane Tomine, J. Otto Seybold
Programmers
Robert Lord, Victor Bornia
Authoring Platform
Mac, PC

The logo for the site picks up on the retro theme, giving the site a 1950s feel. The main navigation bar (for Rocktropolis, the site under which Allstar lives) uses a sans-serif italic face that has the same weight as the circles surrounding the icons for each area on the site.

Title
Board Cheap/Look Good
URL
http://www.charged.com/frost/stories/board_cheap/index.html
Design Firm
Entropy8 Digital Arts
Designer
Auriea Harvey

The appeal of this page is clearly focused toward the snowboard enthusiast with little or no income, which makes the stencil-pattern typeface an attractive draw. Custom-coloring the letters takes an otherwise standard font variation (especially with its perfectly aligned baselines) and gives it a bit of rebel-in-the-snow character.

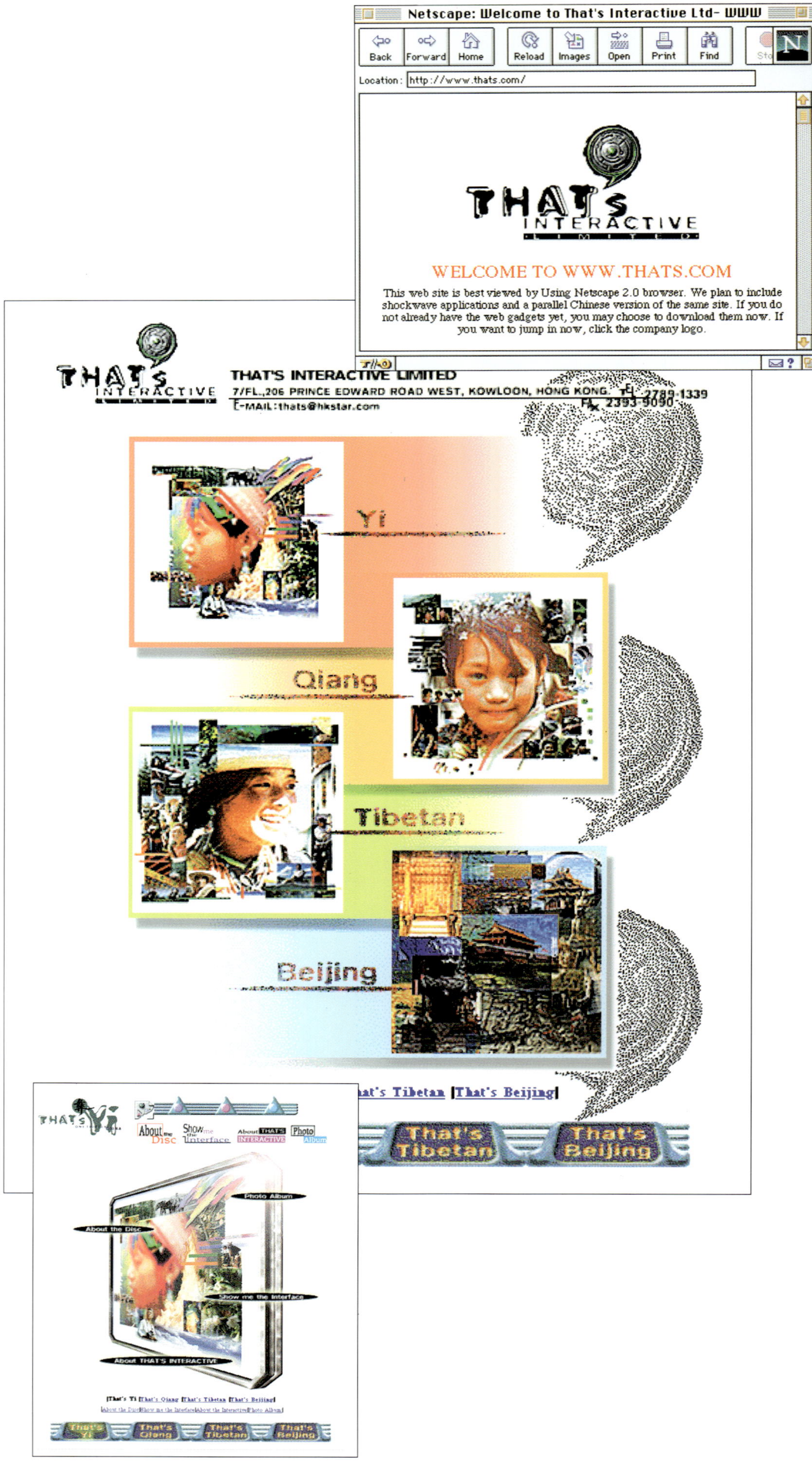

Title
That's Interactive

URL
http://www.thats.com/

Design Firm
That's Interactive Limited

Designers
Foley Kwok, Joey Pun

Producer
Stephen Kam

Programmer
Canty Lee

Authoring Platform
HTML

Designers have been trying to get away from bitmapped typefaces since the early days of desktop publishing (even bitmapped "computer-locking" fonts are in smooth PostScript format now). Here, however, much of the text is not only bitmapped, but multicolored and highly dithered. The resulting grainy text accentuates the digital nature of the company's CD-ROM products.

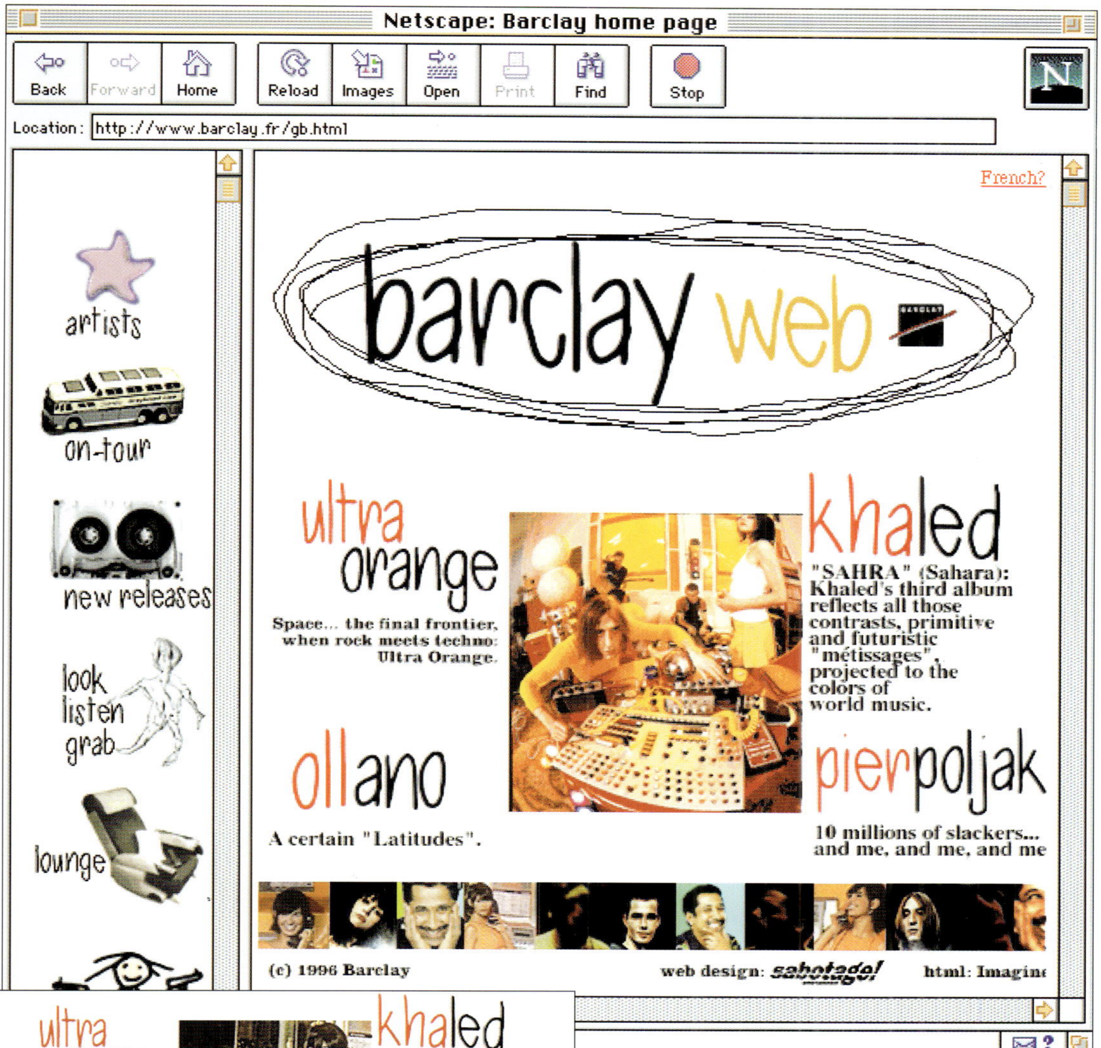

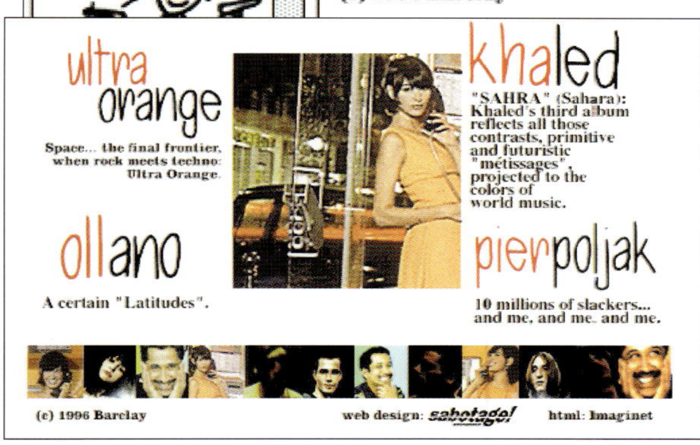

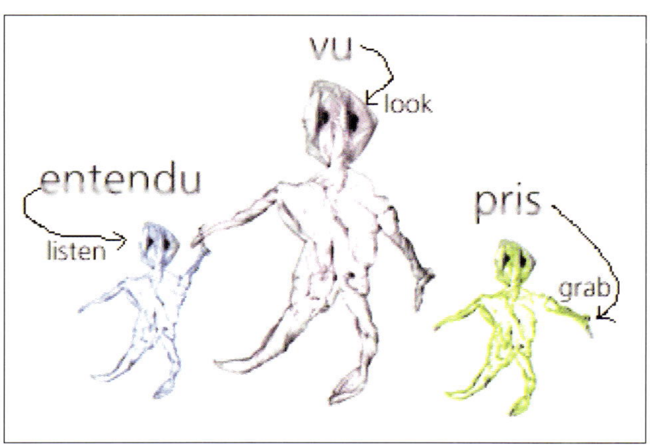

Title
Barclay Web
URL
http://www.barclay.fr/gb.html
Design Firm
Sabotage! Entertainment
Designers
Guillaume Wolf, Amaziane Hammouche

Many music publications strive for glossy, streamlined looks that reflect the cutting edge of the industry. Barclay Web takes a different approach, using a handwritten font and sketches to suggest that the editors are sharing their personal picks with the reader; it almost feels like swapping notes in the back of a high-school classroom.

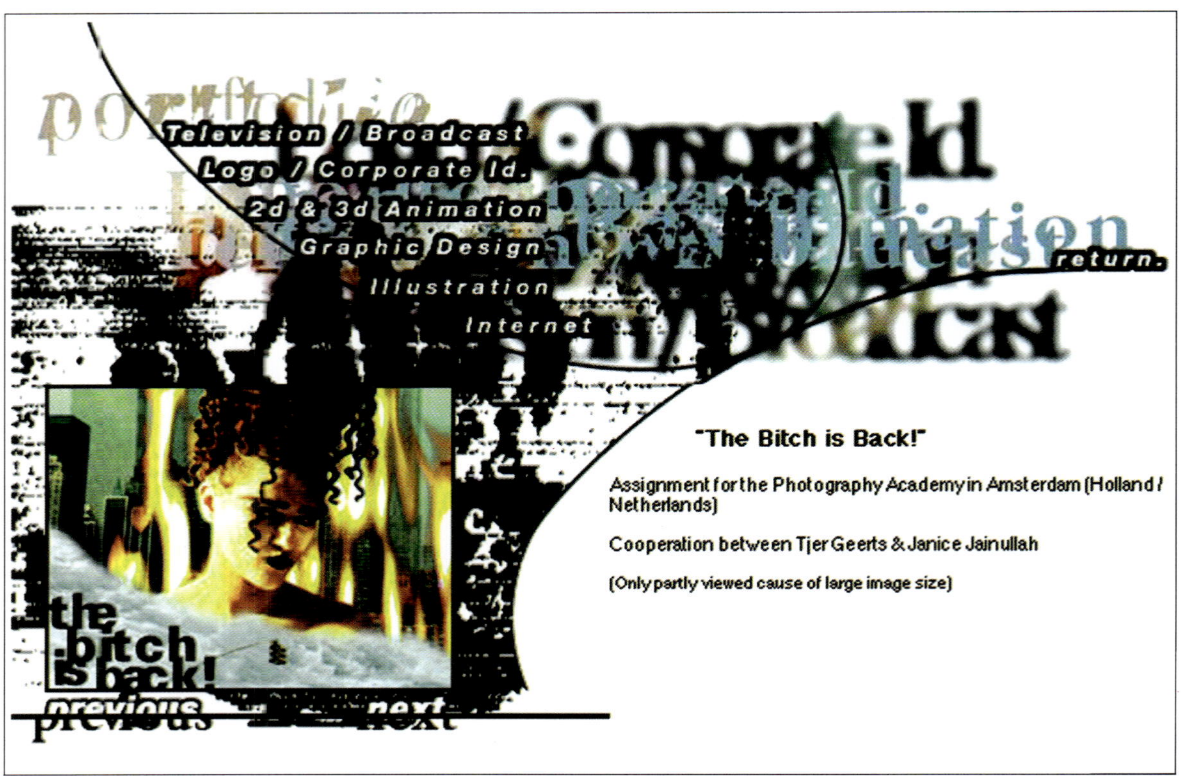
portfolio
Television / Broadcast
Logo / Corporate Id.
2d & 3d Animation
Graphic Design
Illustration
Internet
return.
the bitch is back!
previous
next
"The Bitch is Back!"
Assignment for the Photography Academy in Amsterdam (Holland / Netherlands)
Cooperation between Tjer Geerts & Janice Jainullah
(Only partly viewed cause of large image size)

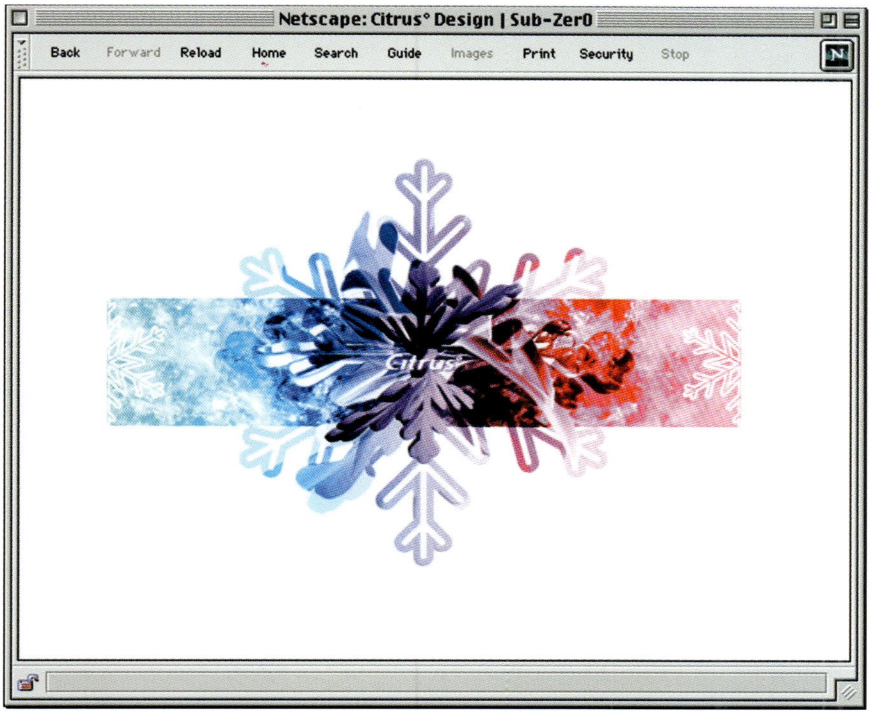

Title
citrus°
URL
http://www.citrus.co.uk/
Design firm
citrus°
Designers/Illustrators/photographers/programmers
Jim Cooper, Steve Meades
Authoring platform
Mac

Possibly the most perfect site on the Internet, Citrus conforms to all the best principles of Web design—and all in just two pages of a placeholder site. The first page uses a simple, black background combined with elegant typography and elements that are used in a typographic fashion: the snowflake and small grids of pixels on either side of an animated GIF. The second page explodes the snowflake into the primary graphic element (now in color), while the company's name is neatly placed in the center.

Title
Jetset
URL
http://www.bedrijfsnet.nl/~jetset
Design firm
Jetset Design
Designer
Tjer Geerts

Much has been said about grunge typography in the last few years—enough to warrant its own category. What's interesting about this site is that it's creating a grunge look, but with classic typefaces. By layering, slicing, rearranging, and reversing characters, the viewer is treated to controlled chaos rooted in traditional typography.

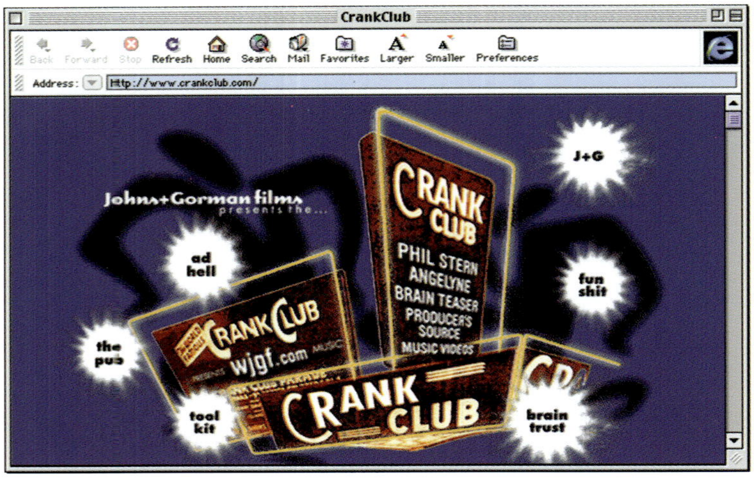

Title
crankclub
URL
http://www.crankclub.com/
Design firm
Johns+Gorman/Interactive
Designer/Illustrator
Rick Moris
Programmers
Glenn Morrissey, Ed Gildred
Creative Director
Gary Johns
Producer
Sylvia Kahn
Authoring platform
Mac, PC

The typefaces chosen for this site are consciously ironic and backwards-hearkening. Although there's a lot of flash and color, only three display faces are used: a cursive in the top navigation bar, Futura (mostly in all caps) for navigation on a page, and a funky face with a lowercase *e* like a sickle moon that has a distinctly different uppercase and lowercase.

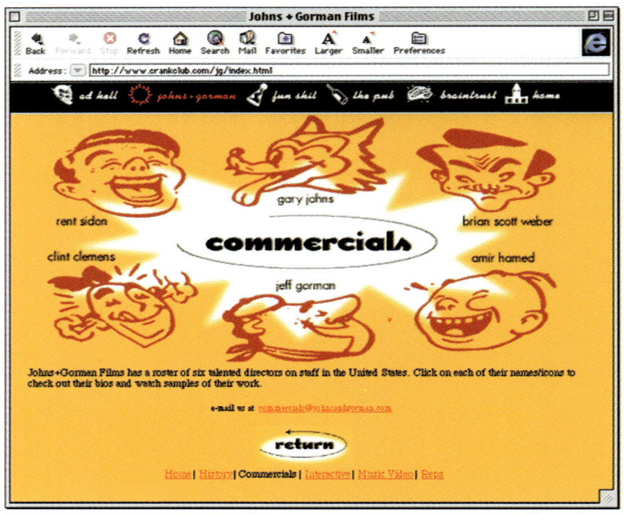

Title
Iconoclast: Where Have All the Designers Gone?
URL
http://www.prophetcomm.com/iconoclast/
Design firm
Prophet Communications
Designer
Josh Feldman

It's interesting that in creating a page that tries to differentiate digital design from print design, the designer of this page uses fonts that approximate the often variable quality of paper-and-ink publishing. The text appears layered and uneven, which accentuates the digitally-created background image in the upper-right corner.

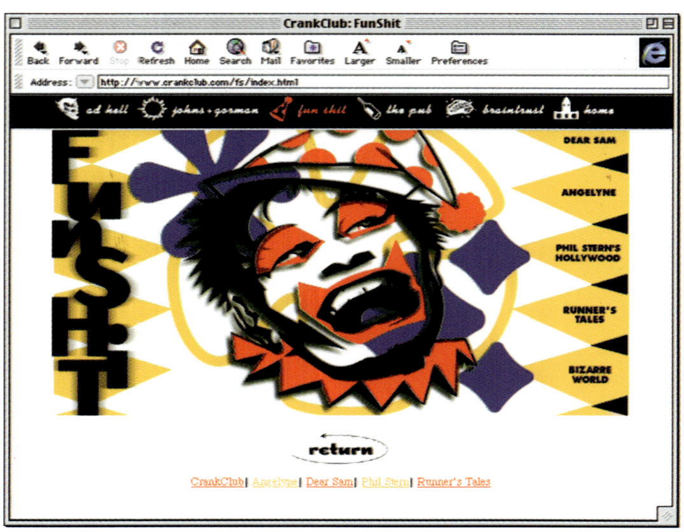

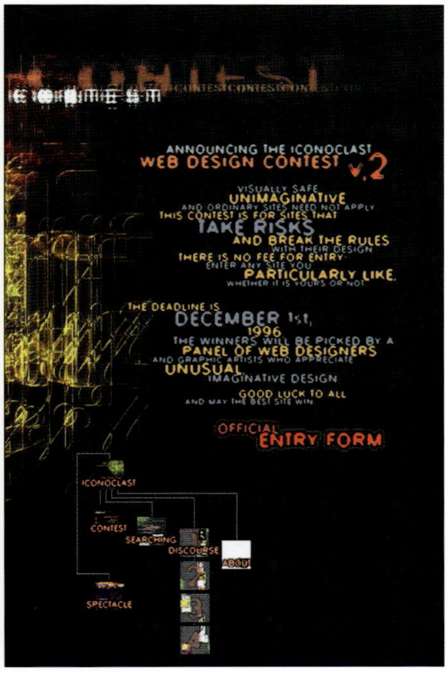
ANNOUNCING THE ICONOCLAST
WEB DESIGN CONTEST v.2
VISUALLY SAFE
UNIMAGINATIVE
AND ORDINARY SITES NEED NOT APPLY
THIS CONTEST IS FOR SITES THAT
TAKE RISKS
AND BREAK THE RULES
WITH THEIR DESIGN
THERE IS NO FEE FOR ENTRY
ENTER ANY SITE YOU
PARTICULARLY LIKE.
WHETHER IT IS YOURS OR NOT.
THE DEADLINE IS
DECEMBER 1st,
1996
THE WINNERS WILL BE PICKED BY A
PANEL OF WEB DESIGNERS
AND GRAPHIC ARTISTS WHO APPRECIATE
UNUSUAL
IMAGINATIVE DESIGN.
GOOD LUCK TO ALL
AND MAY THE BEST SITE WIN.
OFFICIAL
ENTRY FORM
ICONOCLAST
CONTEST
SEARCHING
DISCOURSE
ABOUT
SPECTACLE

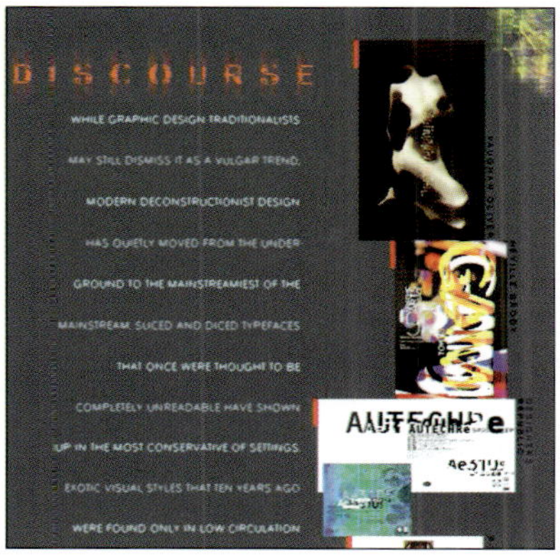
DISCOURSE
WHILE GRAPHIC DESIGN TRADITIONALISTS
MAY STILL DISMISS IT AS A VULGAR TREND,
MODERN DECONSTRUCTIONIST DESIGN
HAS QUIETLY MOVED FROM THE UNDER
GROUND TO THE MAINSTREAMIEST OF THE
MAINSTREAM. SLICED AND DICED TYPEFACES
THAT ONCE WERE THOUGHT TO BE
COMPLETELY UNREADABLE HAVE SHOWN
UP IN THE MOST CONSERVATIVE OF SETTINGS.
EXOTIC VISUAL STYLES THAT TEN YEARS AGO
WERE FOUND ONLY IN LOW CIRCULATION
NEVILLE BRODY

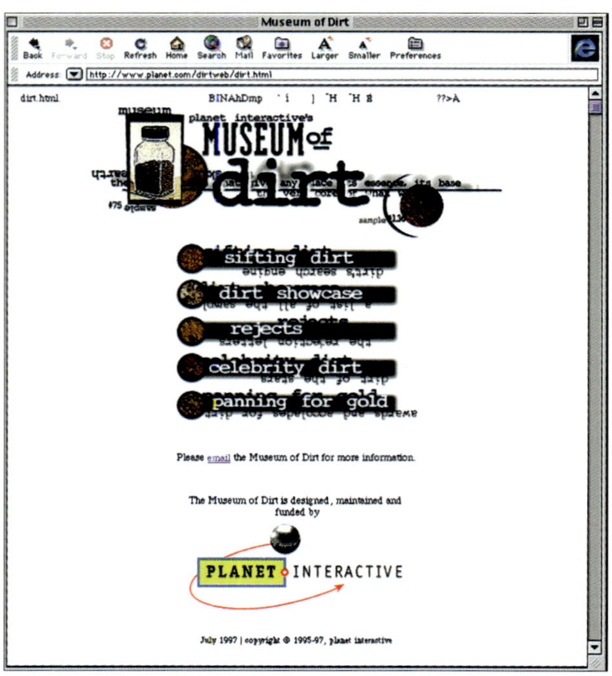

Title
Museum of Dirt web site

URL
http://www.planet.com/dirtweb/dirt.html

Design Firm
Planet Interactive, Inc.

Designer
Brian Cook

Photographer
Chris Mascio

Programmer
Rich Martin

Art Direction
Glenn Johanson

Authoring Platform
Mac

It is in fact a museum of dirt, and the designers have played on that theme in the Web site. The museum-label-like type is a big, closely spaced typewriter font. The explanation of each category on the home page is upside down and partially obscured, but still entirely legible.

title
contempt productions
URL
http://www.contempt.net/
design firm
contempt productions
design
sung h. chang

The striking background color here surrounds the customized title lettering—clearly English, but styled and spaced to resemble futuristic Chinese characters. That combination, along with the bold sans-serif body text, imparts the sense of command and control required to boast of "revolutioniz[ing] design." It's also worth noting the activity generated by the wrapped text on the Faye Wong and This Mortal Coil pages.

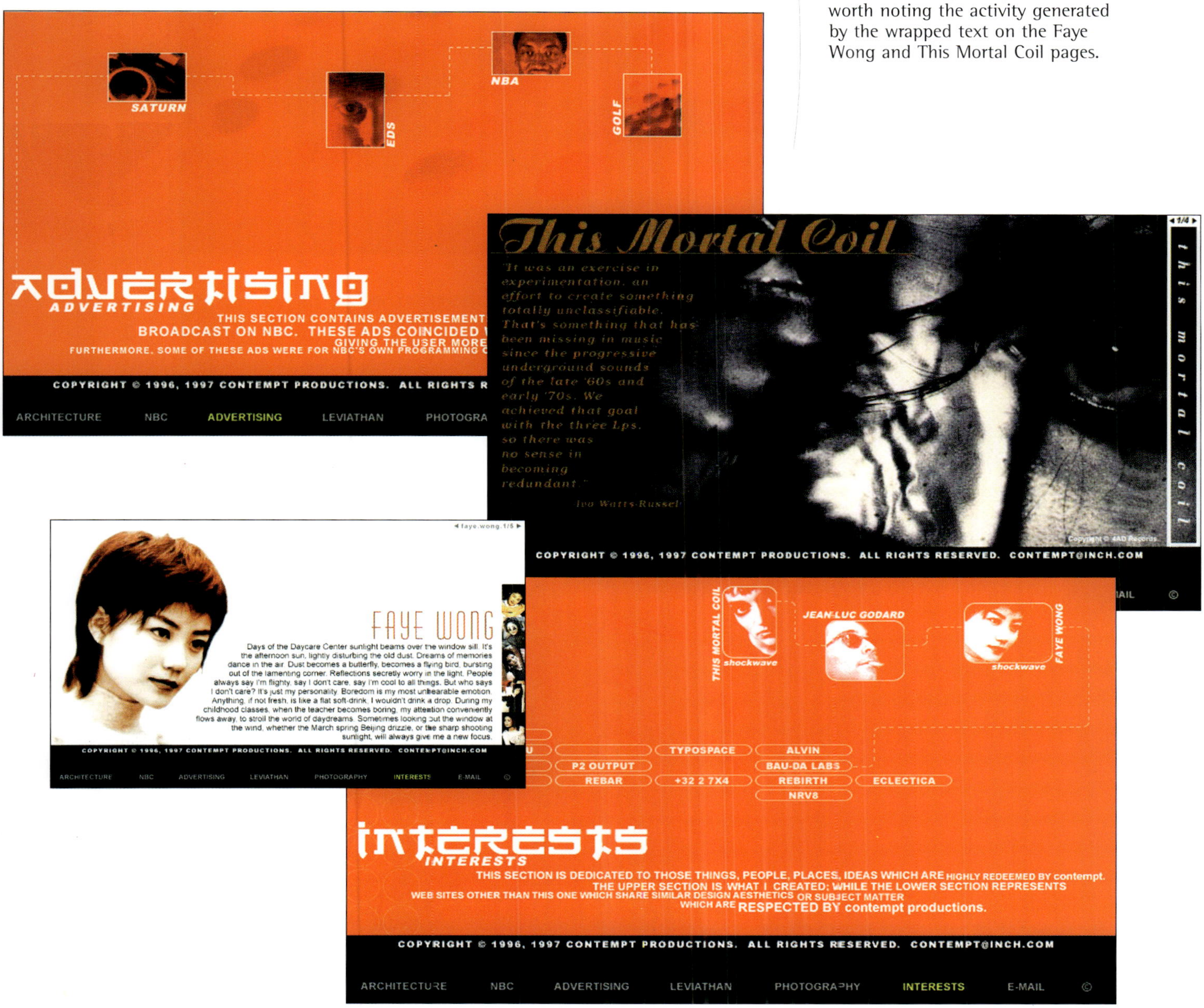

Title
Dreamless Studios
URL
http://www.dreamless.com/
Design firm
Dreamless Studios
Designer/programmer
David Decheser
Illustrator/photographer
Eric Dinyer

By itself, the term *dreamless* evokes empty darkness. Expressed in the morphing and often decaying typography of the Dreamless Studios site, however, the word becomes as fitful as any night consumed by mental images. The type here can be characterized as modern medieval, a mixture of traditional calligraphic letterforms and stylized scripts that blur, distort, burn, and glow.

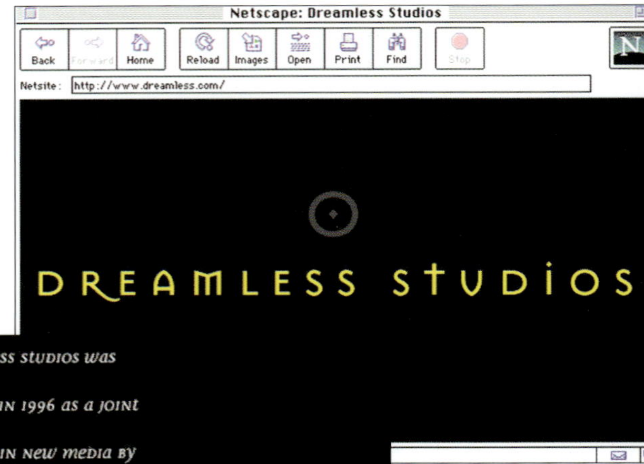

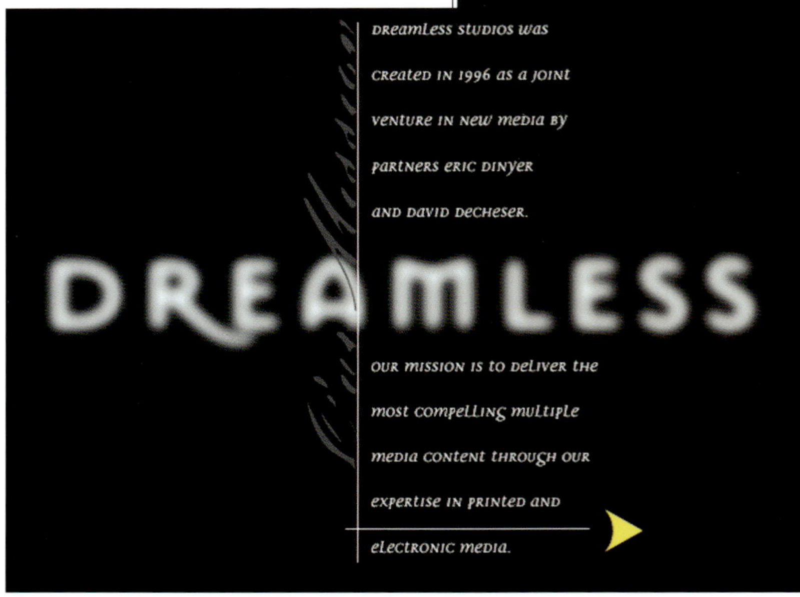

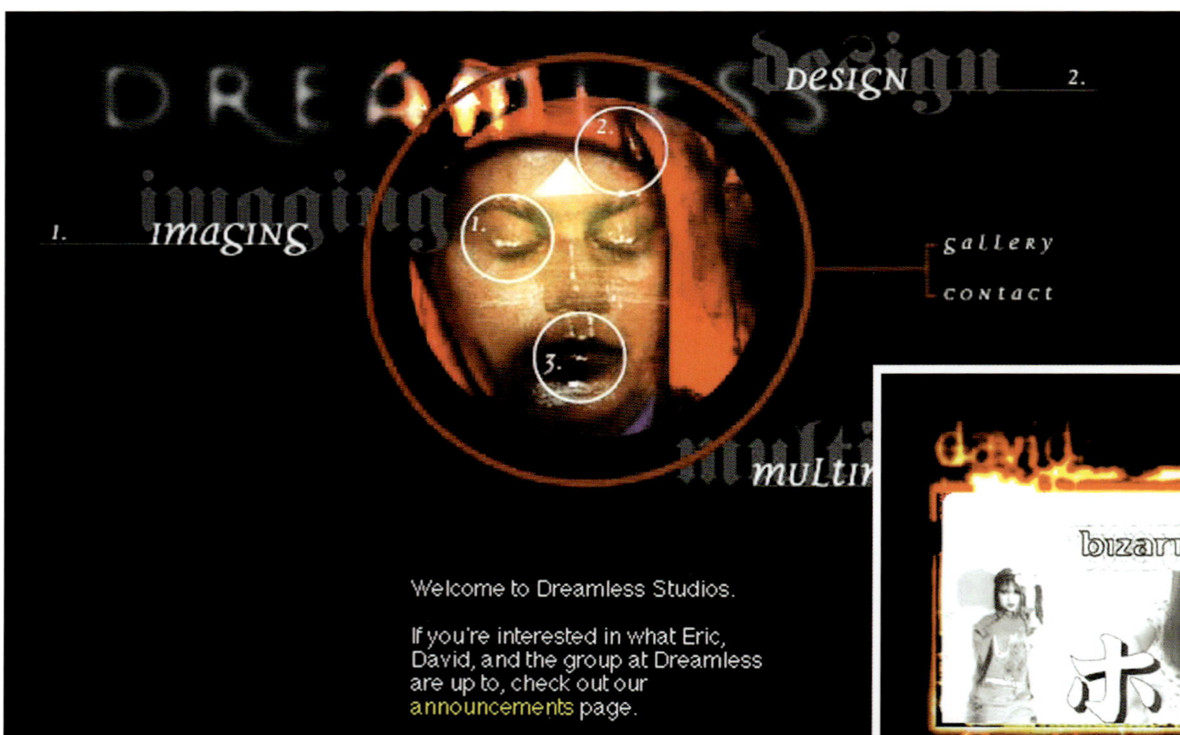

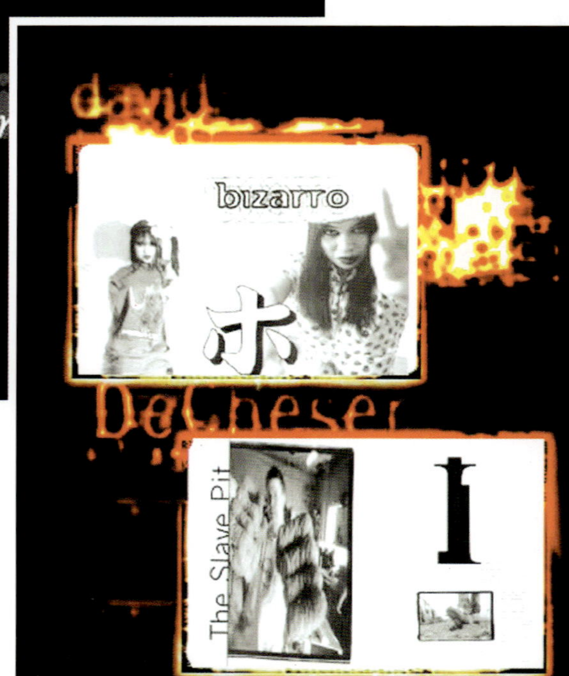

Title
Dreamless Studios Multimedia
URL
http://www.dreamless.com/multimed.htm
Design Firm
Dreamless Studios
Designer/Programmer
David Decheser
Illustrator/Photographer
Eric Dinyer

Without directly employing effects such as GIF89a animation or Shockwave files, the manipulation of the type puts the words and the pages in motion. Instead of looking like a page where each element has been measured and placed with precision, the word *media* appears as if it's been frozen mid-frame from a movie or animation.

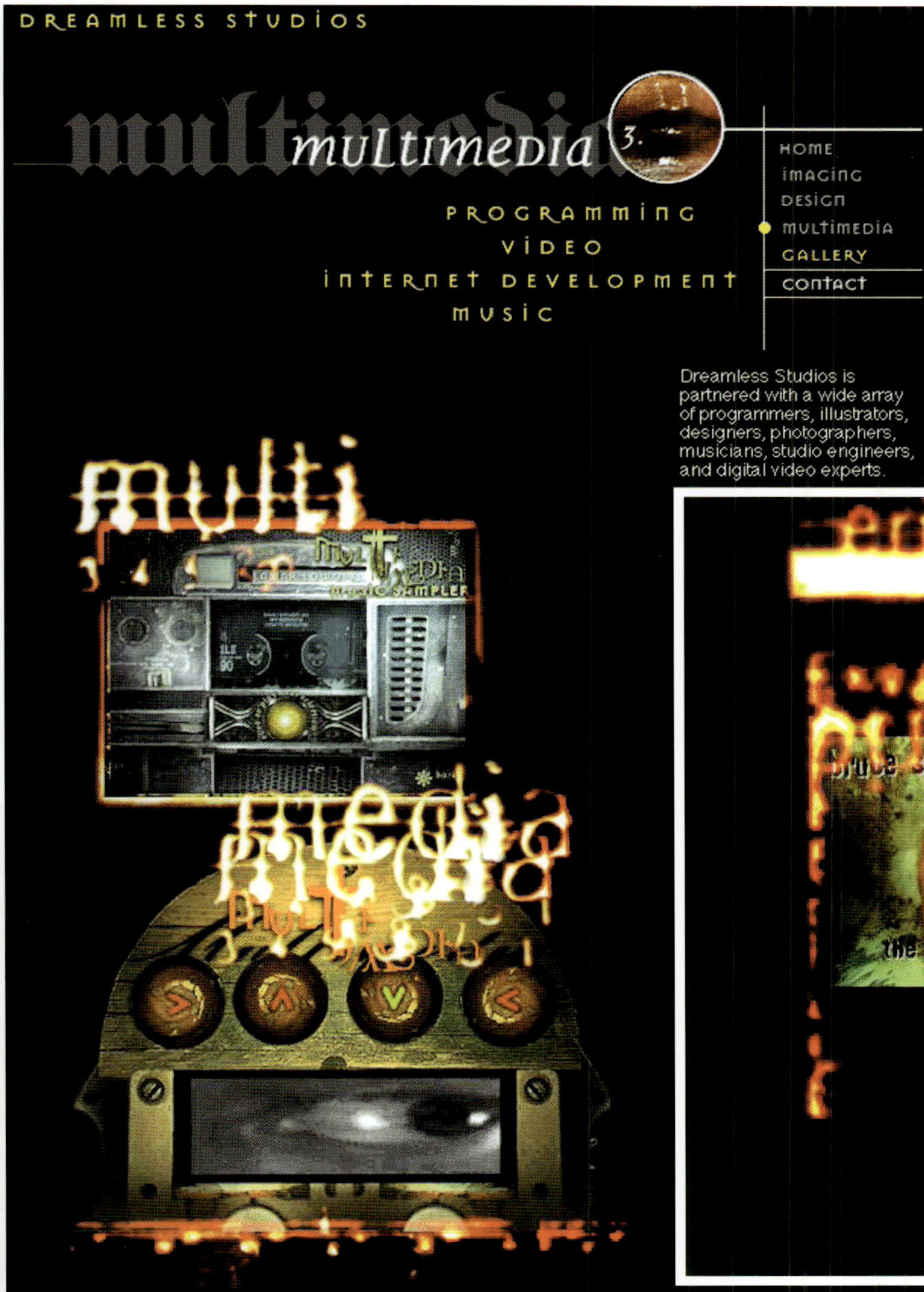

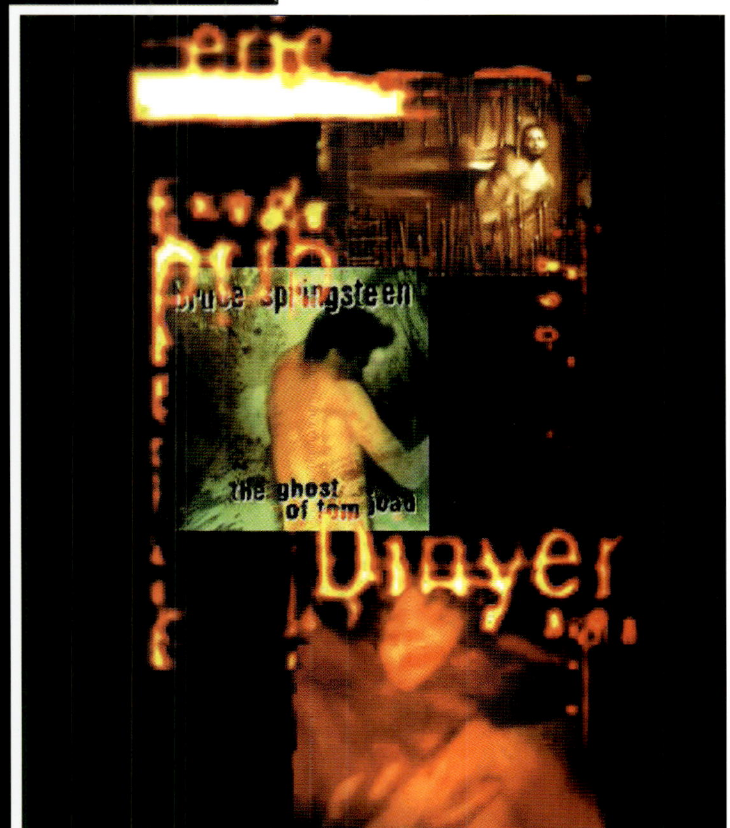

title
giant robot
URL
http://www.giantrobot.com/
designer/programmer
David Yu
illustrator/photographer
staff of giant robot magazine
authoring platform
Mac

It's hard to argue with a bold font. In order to quickly make an impact, the title here is big, bold, and painted an attention-grabbing red and black. Its heaviness allows the all-capped subtitle to be letterspaced cleanly, while italicized variations point you into the site.

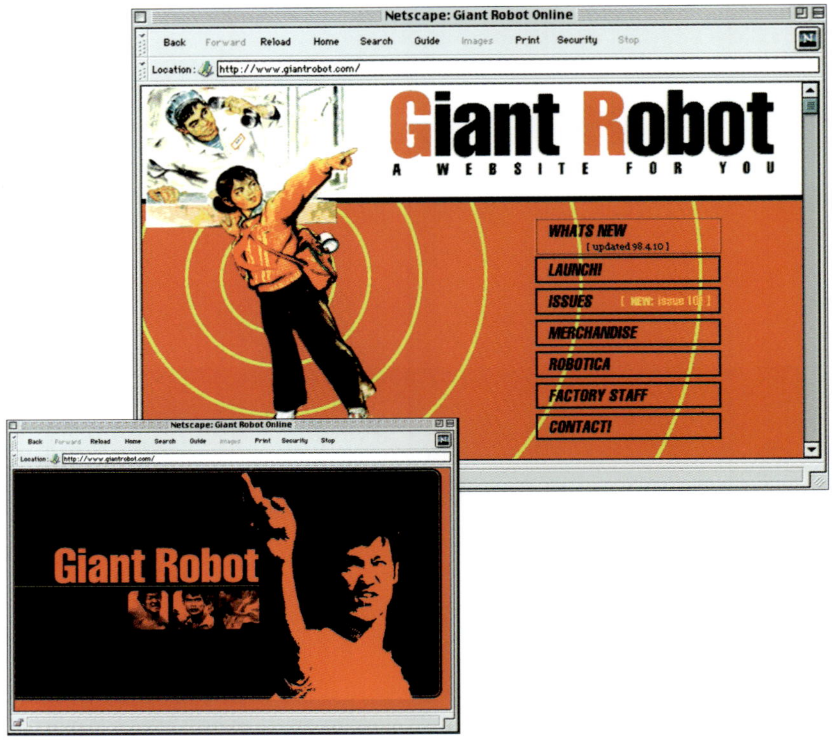

Title
skate I-95
URL
http://www.charged.com/tar/stories/i95/
Design firm
Entropy8 Digital Arts
Designer
Auriea Harvey

Yes, you can mix typefaces and not get your creative license revoked. The combination of stylized sans-serif and grunge-written title faces presents the attitude expected to draw in this site's skateboarding audience.

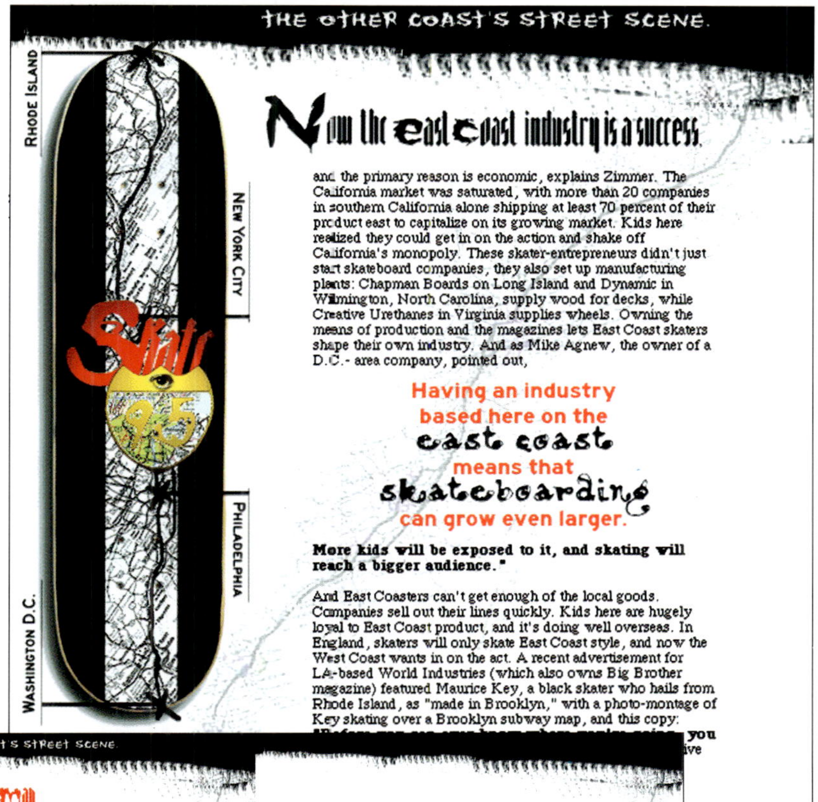

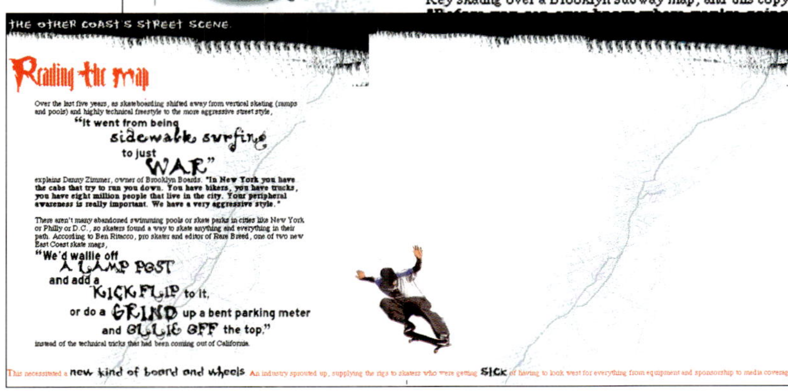

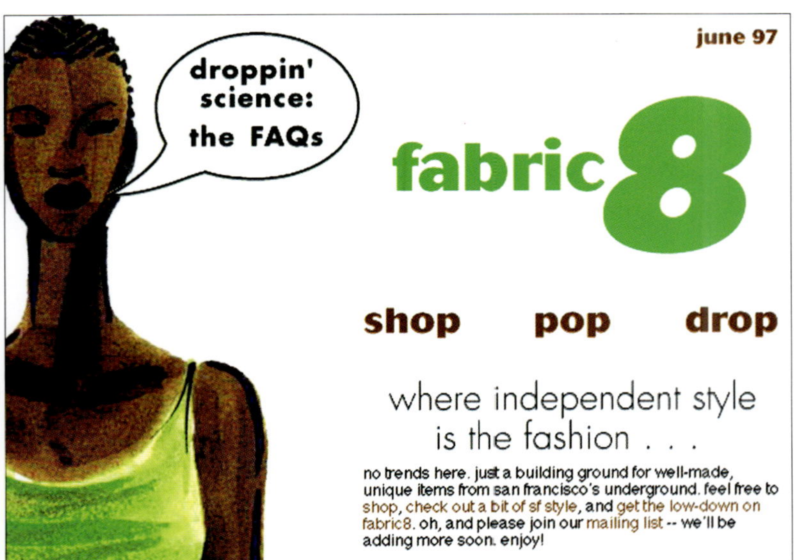

Title
fabric8 online boutique
URL
http://www.fabric8.com/
Design firm
fabric8 productions
Designers
olivia ongpin, Antony Quintal
Photographers
Drea Donio, Keith Ross, Jackie Way
Programmers
Antony Quintal, olivia ongpin, Joe Emenaker

The variety of vendors and designers sharing space at Fabric8 leads to a mix of typographic styles, customized to fit the mood of the intended customers.

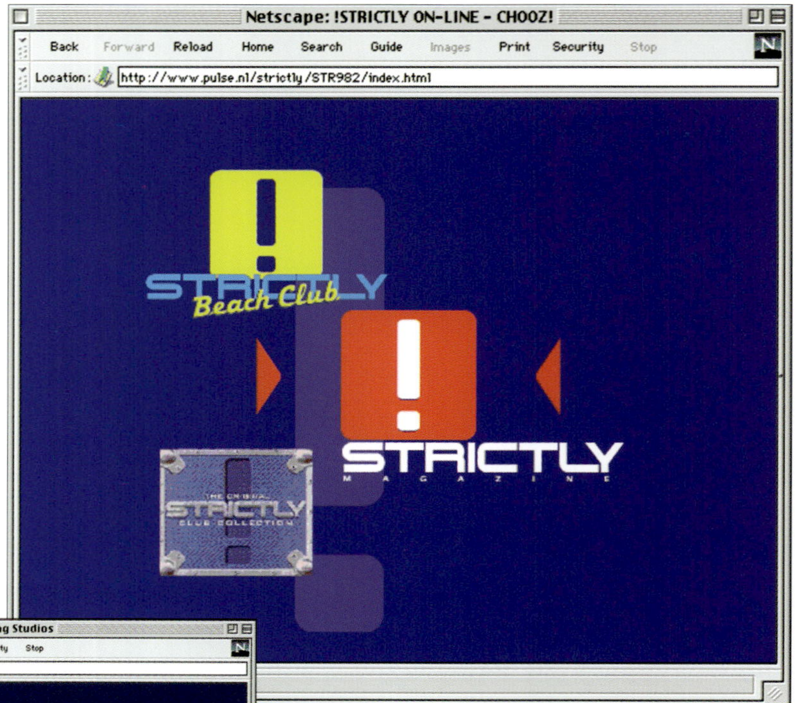

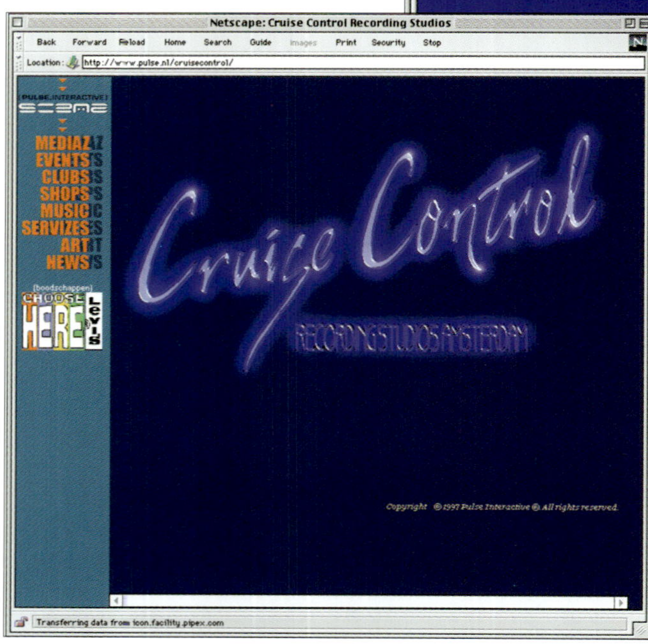

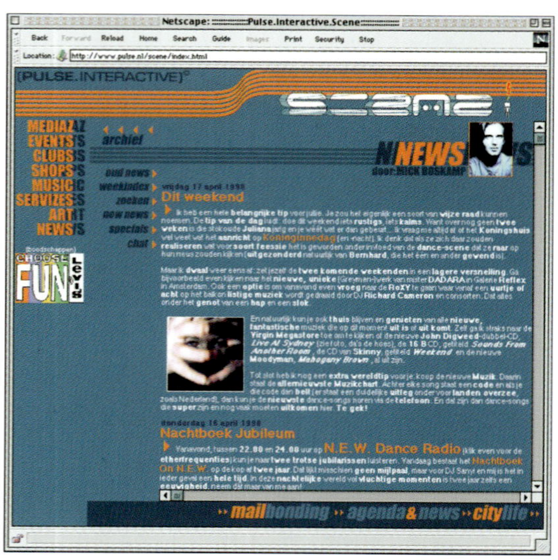

Title
pulse.interactive scene Magazine
URL
http://www.pulse.nl/scene/index.html
Design firm
pulse.interactive
Designer
Tino Nooten
Editors
Mick Boskamp, Marthijn Klopper
Authoring platform
Mac

Bold, rounded, and oblique, much of the typography on this site reflects its hyper-hip content. This is not a destination for brooding commentary, but for reports on the best of new music, art, and events. The fonts here help propel the reader into this mindset.

Title
Millicent
URL
http://www.millicent.digital.com/
Design Firm
Organic Online Inc.
Designer
Jennifer Martinez
Information Architect
Bjorn Heinrichs
Account Manager
Meghan O'Leary
Producer
John Bagby
Associate Producer
Greg Black
Engineer
Orion Letizi
Content Engineer
Rocky Mullin
Strategic Planner
Polly Arenberg

The typeface Helvetica, and sans-serif fonts akin to it, are often derided because of their outright simplicity. (As one of the Macintosh's default fonts, Helvetica has found its way onto more materials than one would like to count.) Here, however, the power of its clarity works to full effect: The type is professional, easy to read, and able to hold unusual colors (sea-green and pale orange) against a dark blue background.

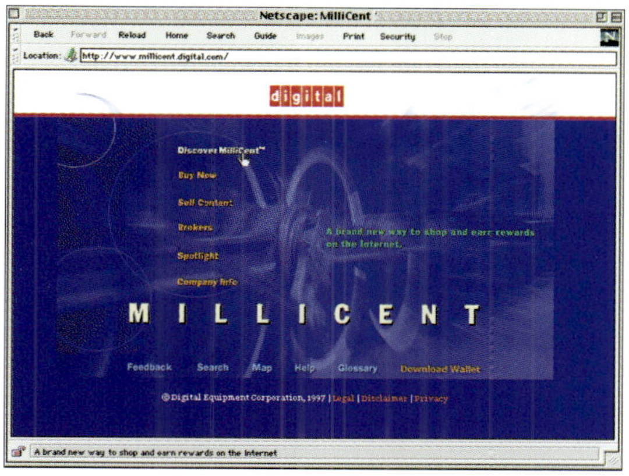

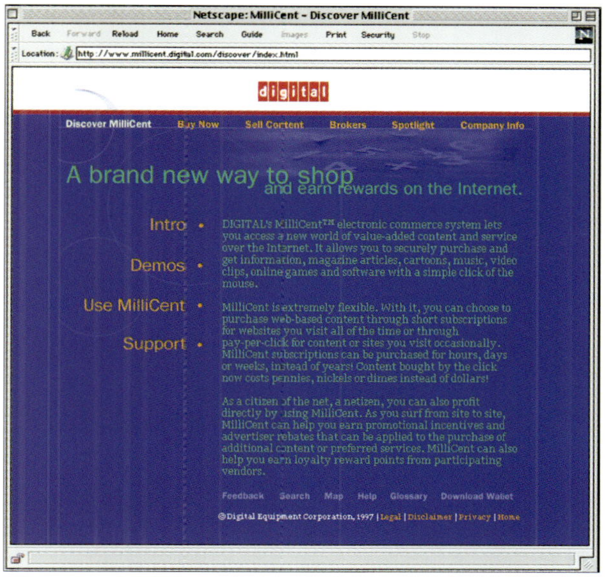

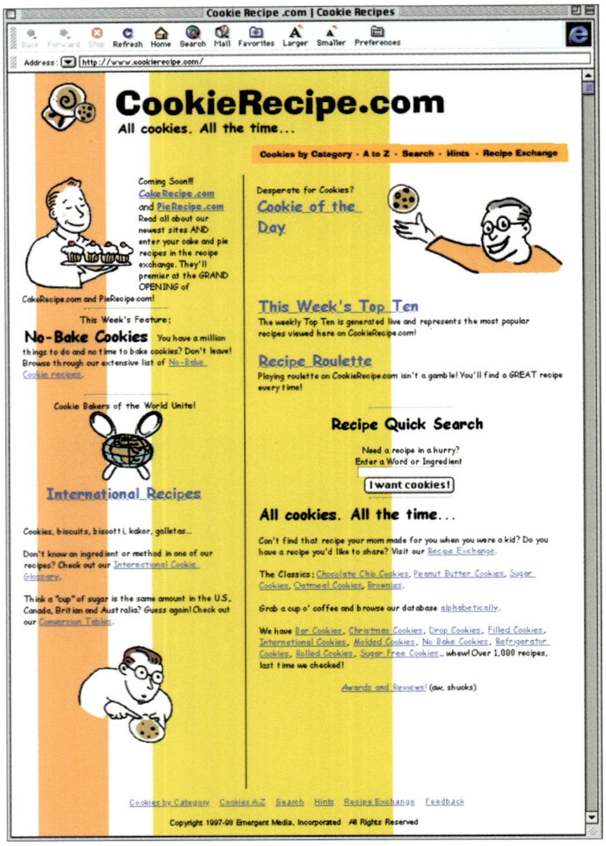

Title
cookierecipe.com
URL
http://www.cookierecipe.com/
Design Firm
Emergent Media, Inc.
Designer/Illustrator
Yann Oehl
Programmers
Tim Hunt, Kala Anderson, Dan Shepherd
Authoring Platform
PC

A site about cookies should feel childlike but not childish (to paraphrase *The Fantastiks*). Cookierecipe.com requires that the Microsoft-supplied (and free) Comic Sans face be installed to fully benefit from the whimsy, but the lighthearted and practical site doesn't need anything more to emphasize its nature.

Title
Blind Visual Propaganda
URL
http://www.blind.com/
Design Firm
Blind Visual Propaganda
Designer/Illustrator
Christopher T. Do
Programmer
Arthur Do

Designers often aim for clarity, but at the Blind site, clarity is intentionally elusive. Mocking the familiar look of a doctor's eye-exam chart, the opening page features a Shockwave-based sliding focus bar that sharpens a swath of text while blurring the rest of the title.

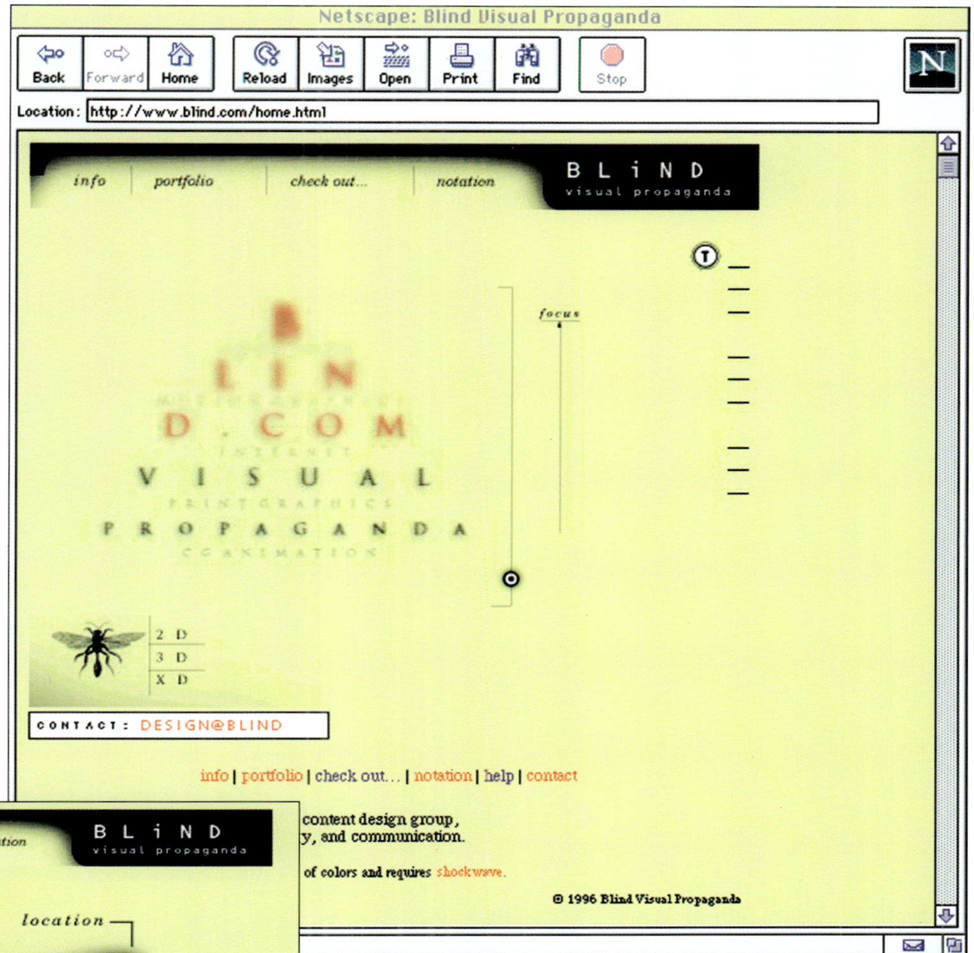

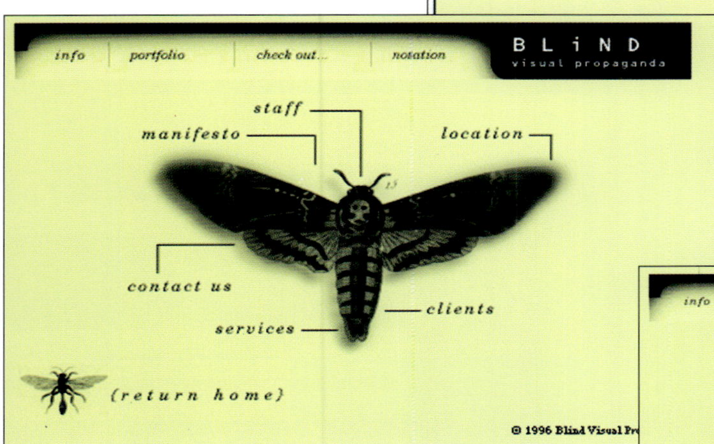

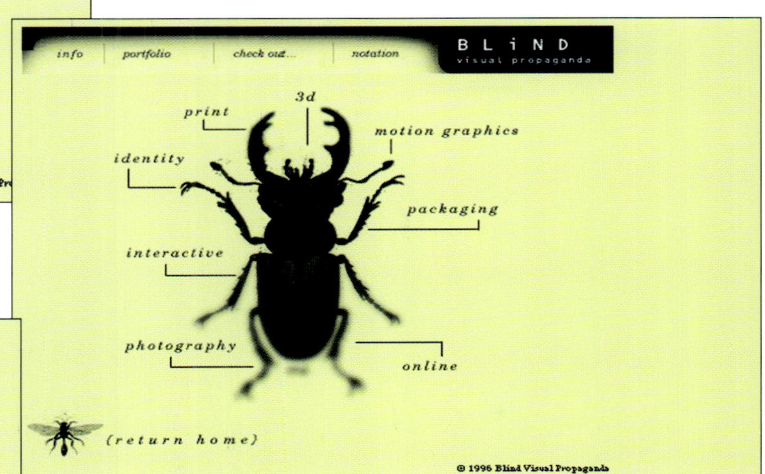

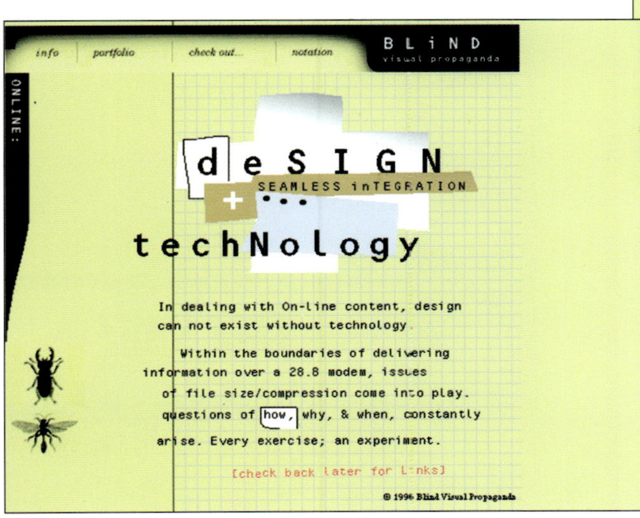

Title

popi Music Magazine

URL

http://www.popi.com/

Design firm

HyperHead New Media

Designer/programmer

Ross Teasley

Authoring platform

Mac, PC

Can too much typographical variety sabotage good design? Definitely. However, thanks to the subject matter of this site (a music magazine), combining exaggerated typefaces enhances the pages' character. Uneven, layered, illuminated—these are musical concepts rendered in letter form.

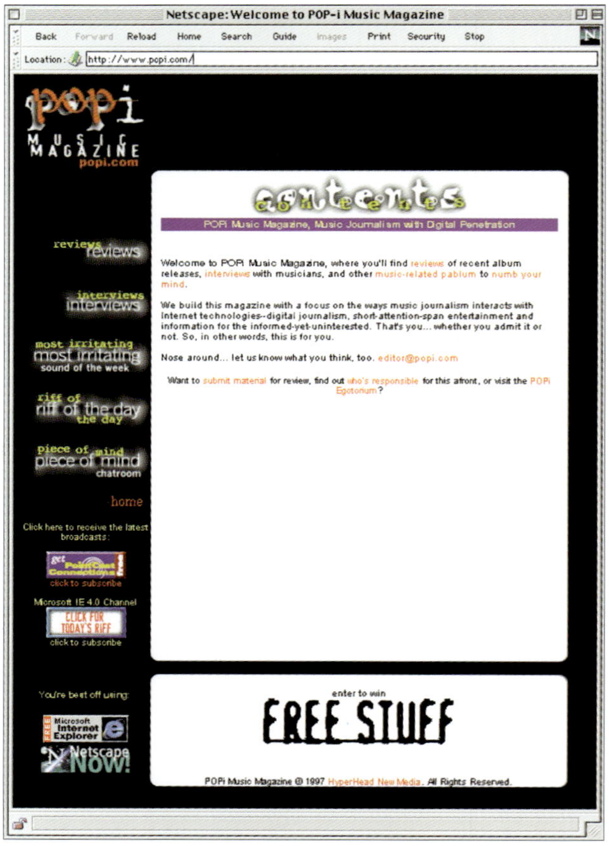

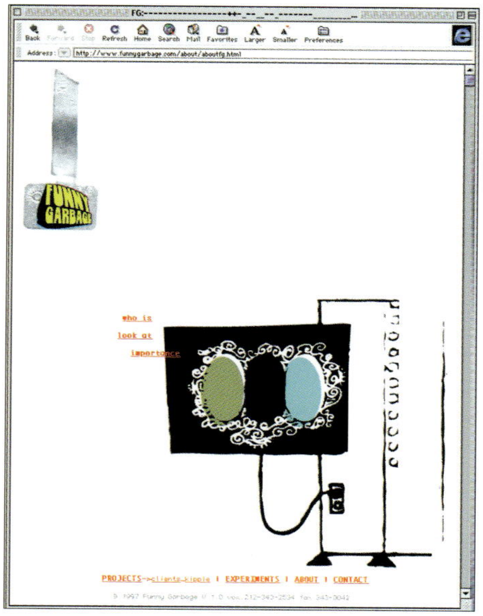
Back
Refresh
Home
Search
Mail
Favorites
Larger
Smaller
Preferences
Address:
http://www.funnygarbage.com/about/aboutfg.html
FUNNY GARBAGE
who is
look at
importance
PROJECTS-->clients-kipple | EXPERIMENTS | ABOUT | CONTACT

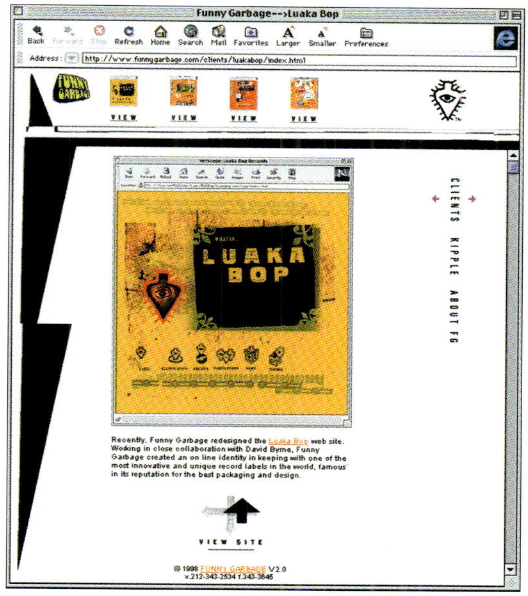
Funny Garbage-->Luaka Bop
Back
Forward
Stop
Refresh
Home
Search
Mail
Favorites
Larger
Smaller
Preferences
Address:
http://www.funnygarbage.com/clients/luakabop/index.html
VIEW
VIEW
VIEW
VIEW
LUAKA BOP
CLIENTS
KIPPLE
ABOUT FG
Recently, Funny Garbage redesigned the Luaka Bop web site. Working in close collaboration with David Byrne, Funny Garbage created an on line identity in keeping with one of the most innovative and unique record labels in the world, famous in its reputation for the best packaging and design.
VIEW SITE
© 1998 FUNNY GARBAGE V2.0
v.212-343-2534 f.343-3646

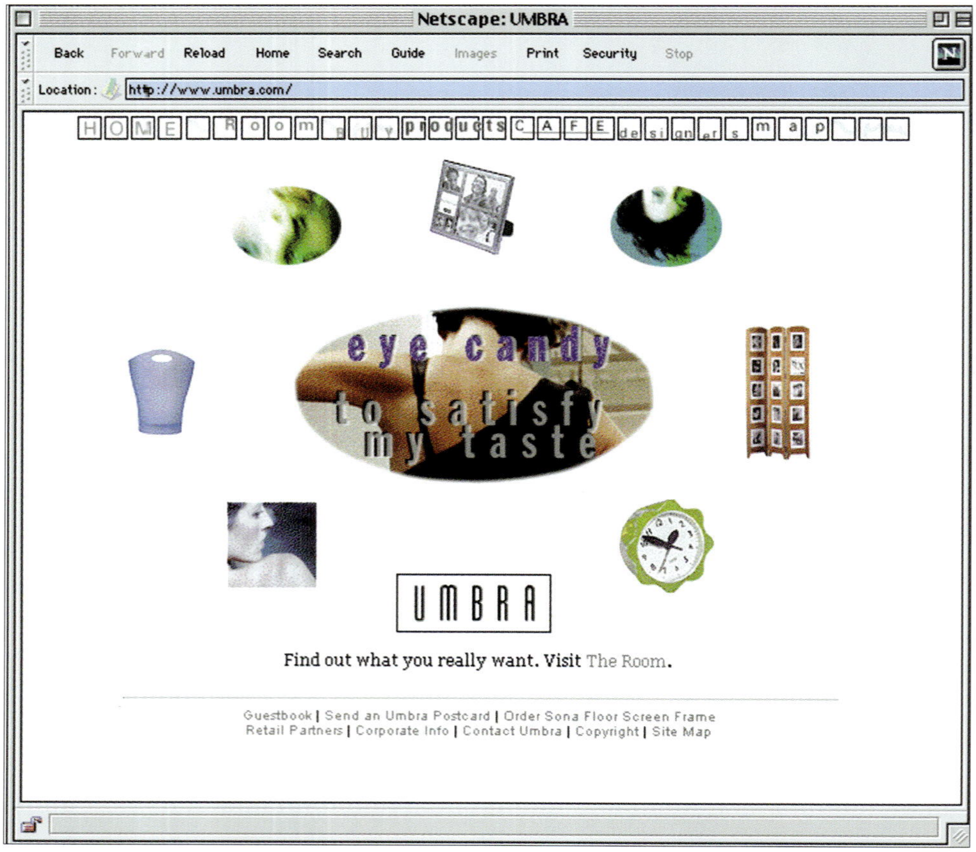

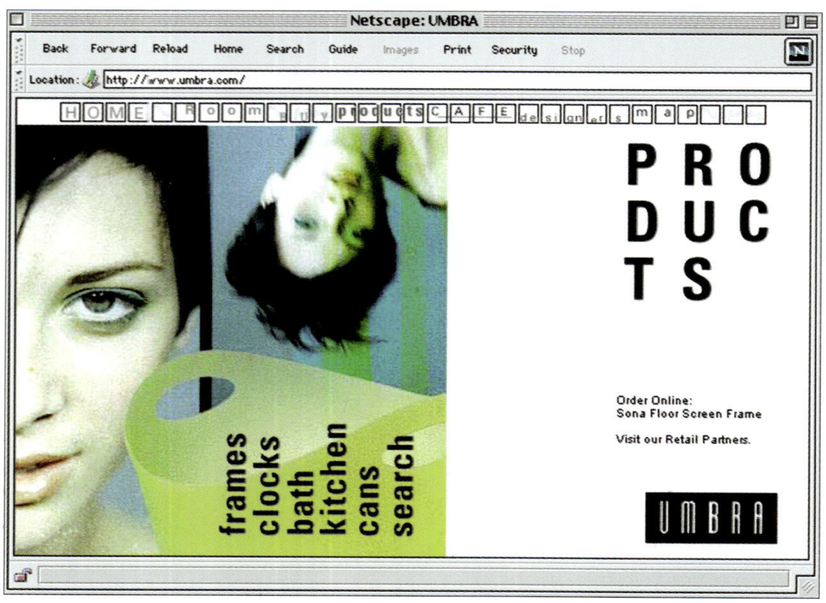

Title
umbra
URL
http://www.umbra.com/
Design firm
The James Gang
Designers
Bill James, Franke James
Illustrator/photographer
Franke James
Programmer
Bill James
Authoring platform
Mac

Discussions of typography invariably revolve around fonts, but that doesn't cover the field. Equally important, in some cases, is the placement of the type. Here, a horizontal navigation bar stands apart because the text labels for each link vary in size, don't share a common baseline, and occasionally get truncated or spaced unusually.

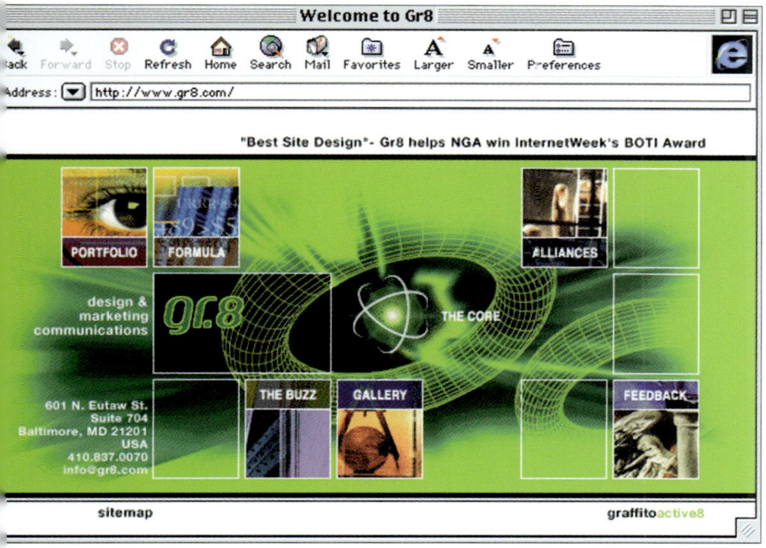

title
gr8
URL
http://www.gr8.com/
Design firm
gr8
Designers
Morton Jackson, Heath Flohre,
Becky Bochatey, Chuck Gates,
Matt Agro, Chuck Seeley
programmers
Chris Walsh, Heath Flohre,
Becky Bochatey
Authoring platform
Mac, PC

The site map exactly matches the home page substituting large numbers for the illustrations. The numbers correspond typographically (and navigationally) to the subdivisions of the site. The numbers, wherever they appear, are always the largest element, whether in the graphic site map, the more text-oriented one, or in the section headings.

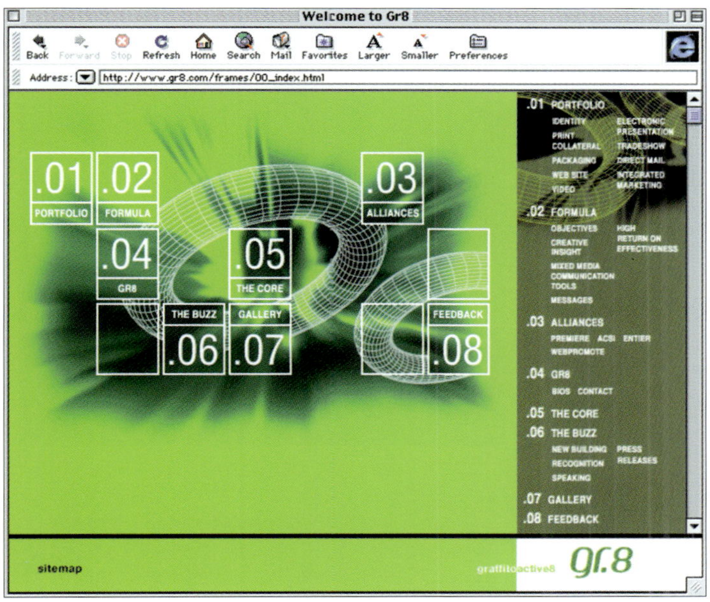

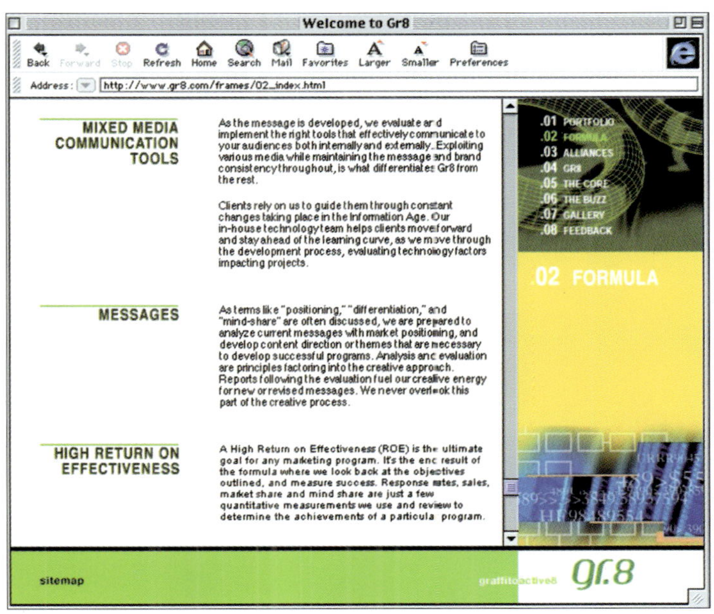

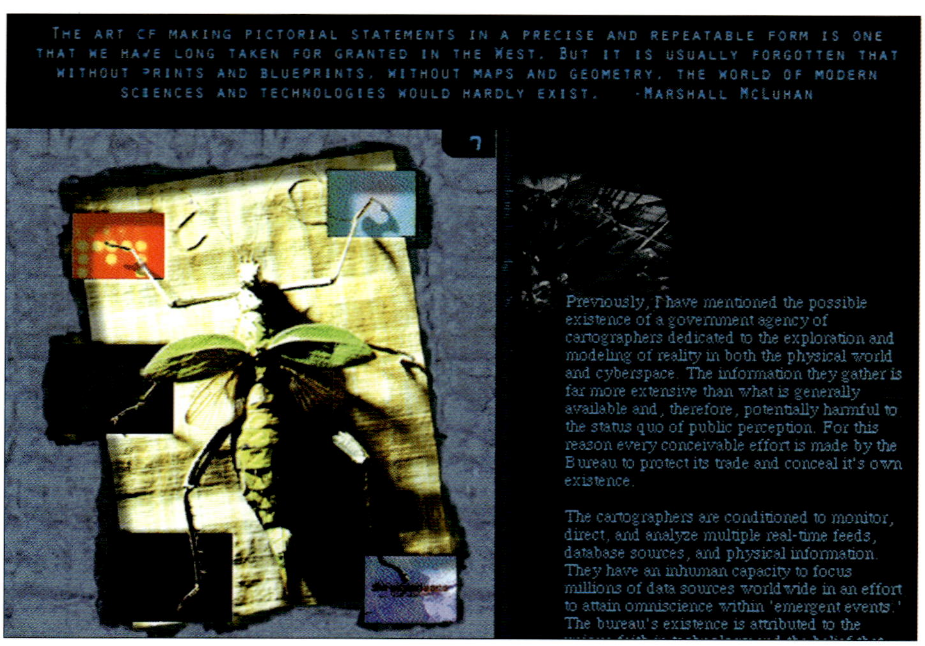

Title
circumstance Design
URL
http://www.circumstance.com/
Design Firm
circumstance Design
Designers/Illustrators
Tim Barber, David Bliss
Programmer
David Bliss

Despite the multimedia capabilities afforded by the Internet, the Web is still largely flat. Although you can make text move with JavaScript and other technologies, not every browser will display them. The solution is to create motion in motionless imagery, like the layered titles here, where the relevant title comes to the front on its page.

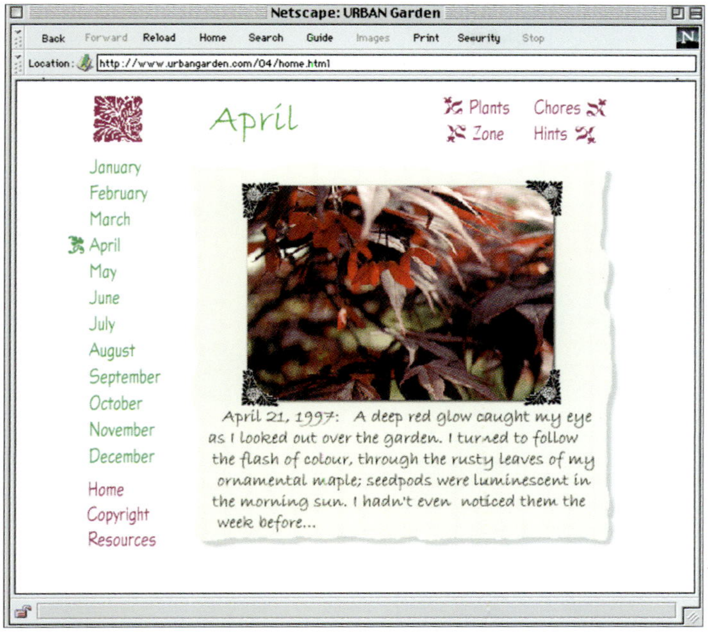

title
urban garden
URL
http://www.urbangarden.com/index.html
design firm
Buzz solutions
designer/illustrator/
photographer/programmer
Deanna Beat
authoring platform
pc

This sparsely designed site relies almost entirely on its typography. Built using images instead of actual text, the body typeface here suggests carefully handwritten journal entries; the relatively tall X-height makes the words particularly readable. Flowery dingbat characters, used as navigation aids, do not detract from the botanical content of the site.

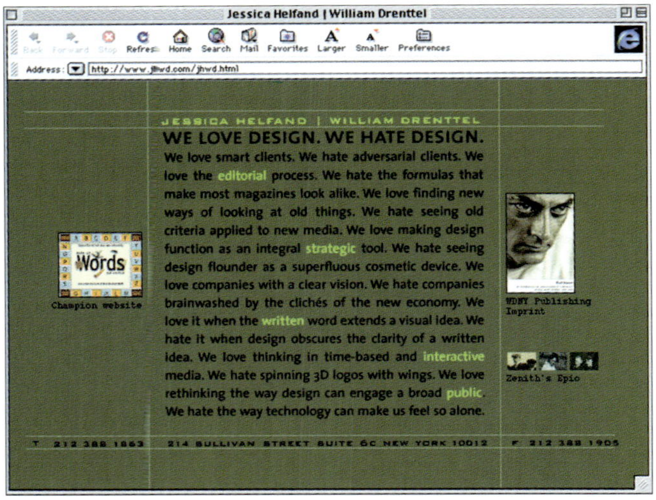

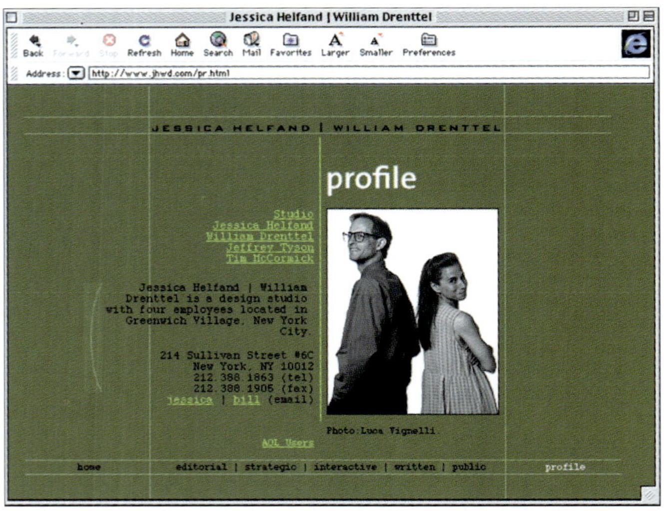

title
jessica Helfand | william Drenttel
URL
http://www.jhwd.com/jhwd.html
design firm
jessica Helfand | william Drenttel
designers
jessica Helfand, william Drenttel, jeffrey Tyson
programmers
jeffrey Tyson, steve Bull (java)
editor
Timothy Mccormick
authoring platform
Mac

Without using much but Courier, the site manages to look elegant. The type is carefully placed and sized, yet remains somewhat unpredictable. Courier is used in a few sizes: one for text, another for navigation links, and a third for captions (where italic is thrown in). Section headings and the firm name are the only rendered type on lower-level pages; the home page is a carefully set block of text.

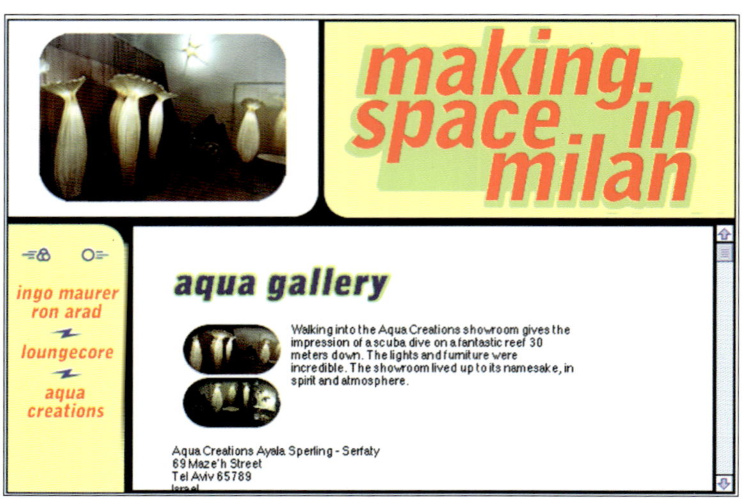

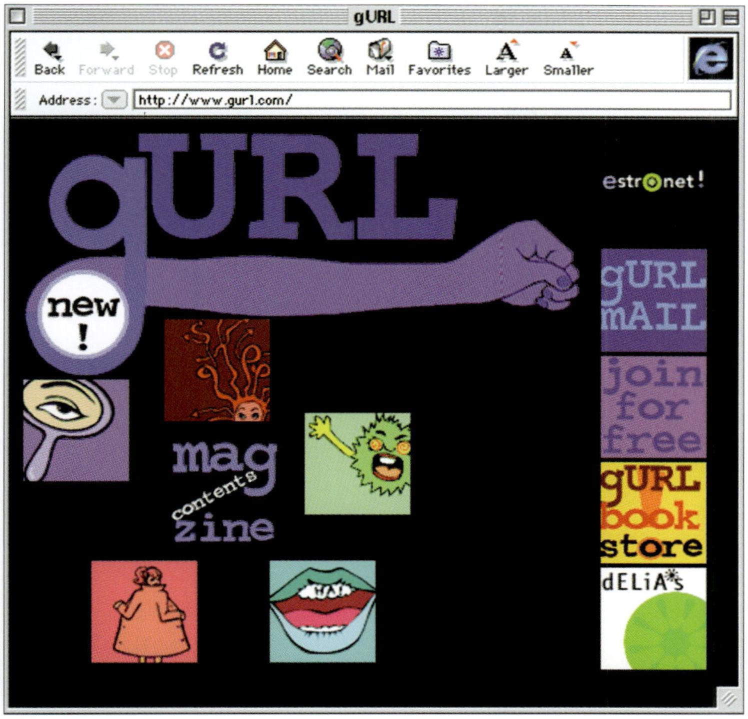

Title
gURL
URL
http://www.gurl.com/
Design Firm
gURL
Designer/Illustrator
Rebecca Odes
Programmers
Sonya Allin, Esther Drill
Authoring Platform
Mac

With its many hand-drawn illustrations and spot colors, this site pushes a fun, down-to-earth atmosphere that invites exploration. The blocky typeface almost looks as if it's been cut from construction paper, making it ideal for placement anywhere in the layout and flexible when applying different colors.

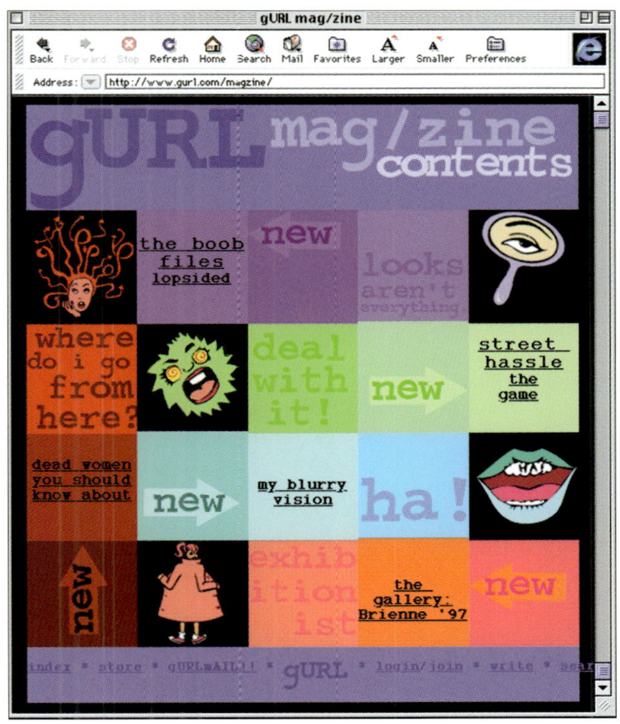

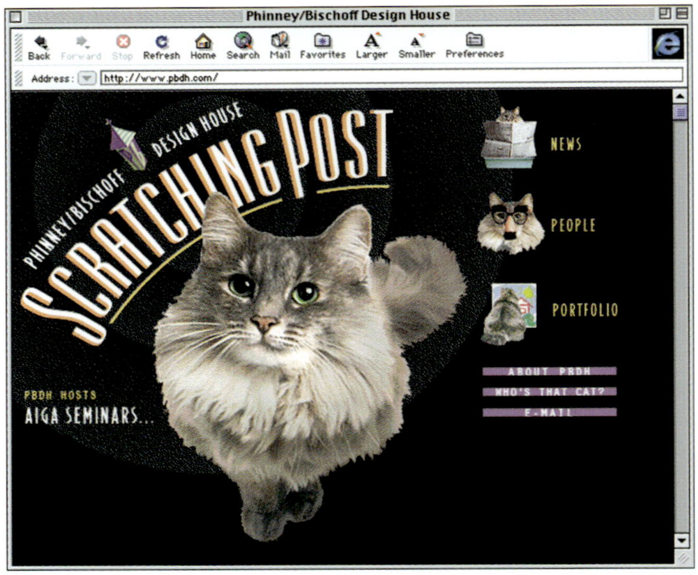

Title
phinney/bischoff design house, inc.
URL
http://www.pbdh.com/
design firm
phinney/bischoff design house, inc.
designer/illustrator
neil robertson
photographer
karl bischoff
programmers
neil robertson, scotty carreiro
creative directors
leslie phinney, karl bischoff
authoring platform
mac

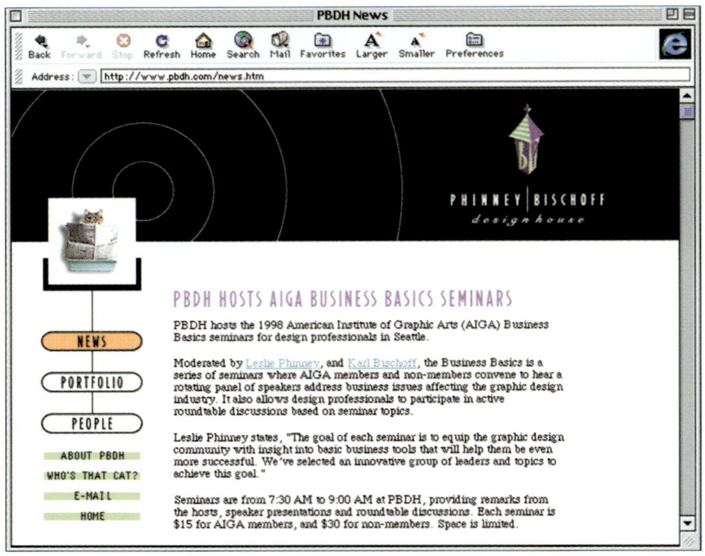

The narrow stylized sans-serif font found throughout this site does more than just stand out from the Web browser's default text font. Reminiscent of 1930s cinema and theater lettering, the typeface (especially curved and layered on the main screen) suggests that clients will receive work worthy of performance, not just standard viewing fare.

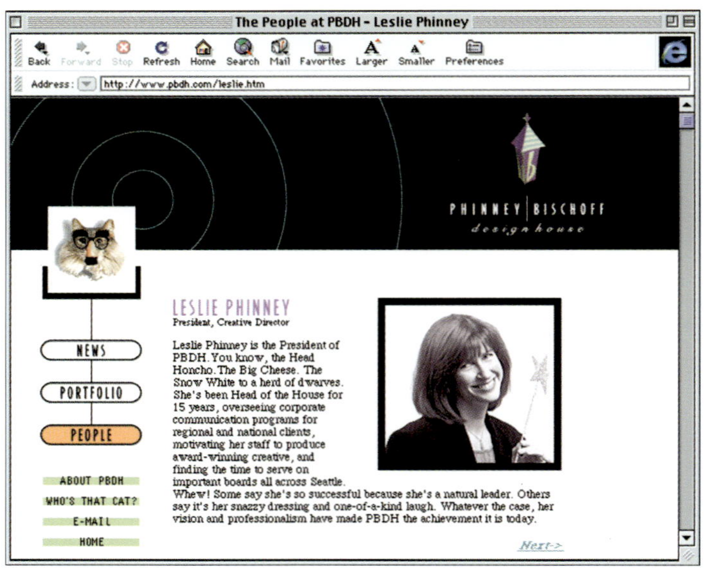

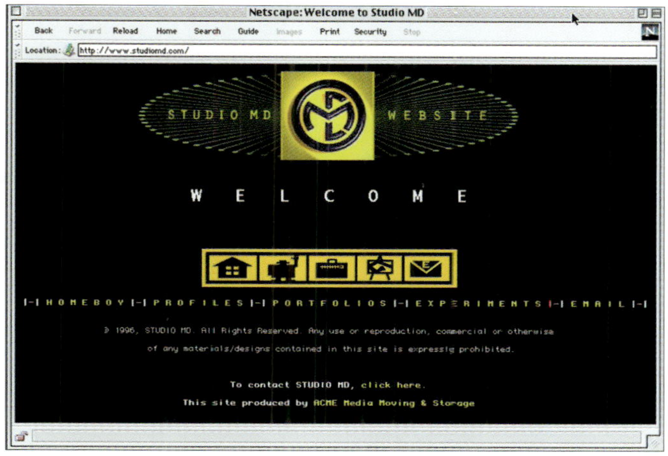

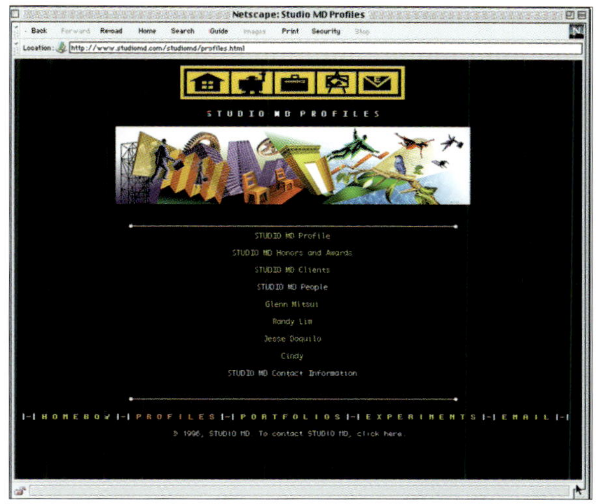

Title
studio M D
URL
http://www.studiomd.com/
Design firm
studio M D
Designers
Glenn Mitsui, Randy Lim,
Jesse Doquilo
Illustrators
Glenn Mitsui, Jesse Doquilo
Programmer
Tim Celeski
Authoring platform
Mac

In HTML, the <CODE> and <TT> tags are usually reserved for displaying programming examples or similar information using a fixed-width font such as Courier or Monaco. Here, the designers have chosen to run with this style for all body copy, which makes it very readable and a subtle change from most other sites.

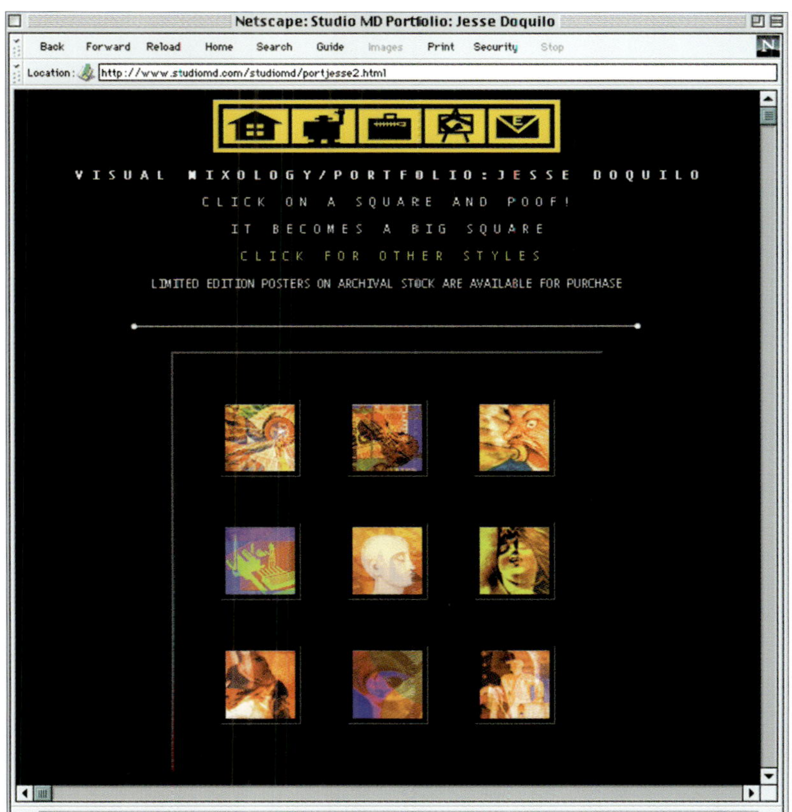

title
Bau-Da Design Lab, Inc.
URL
http://www.bauda.com/
design firm
Bau-Da Design Lab, Inc.
designer/illustrator
P.B. Brown
programmer
Eric Brown
authoring platform
Mac

Bau-Da takes a fairly traditional approach combined with a pseudo-scientific whimsy. They use a heavy san-serif type in all caps coupled with lowercase, italic serif. This gives the site a certain solidity that doesn't take itself too seriously. Bau-Da favors rendering type to ensure exact placement, such as the list of album cover portfolio pieces, where each name is a separate graphic to allow navigation even without images loading.

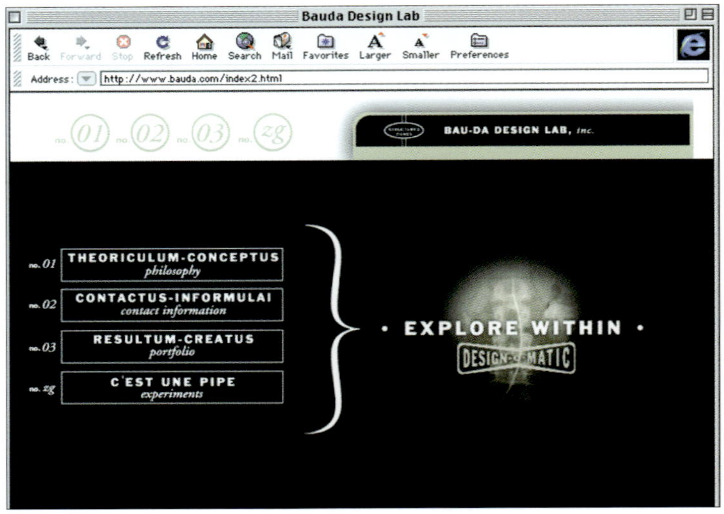

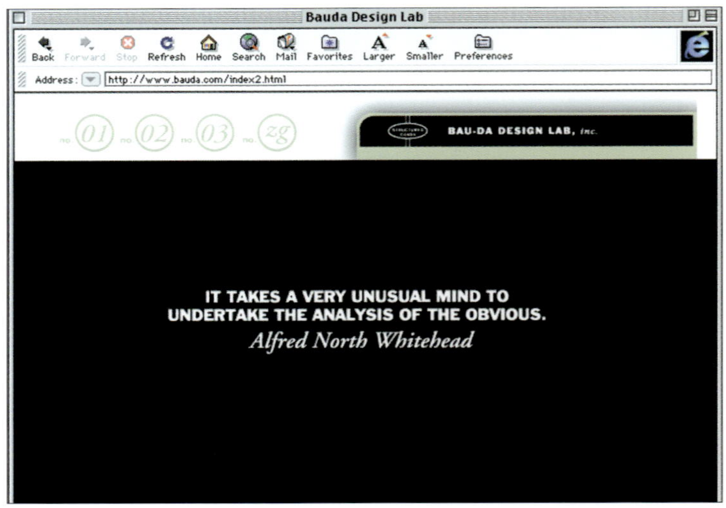

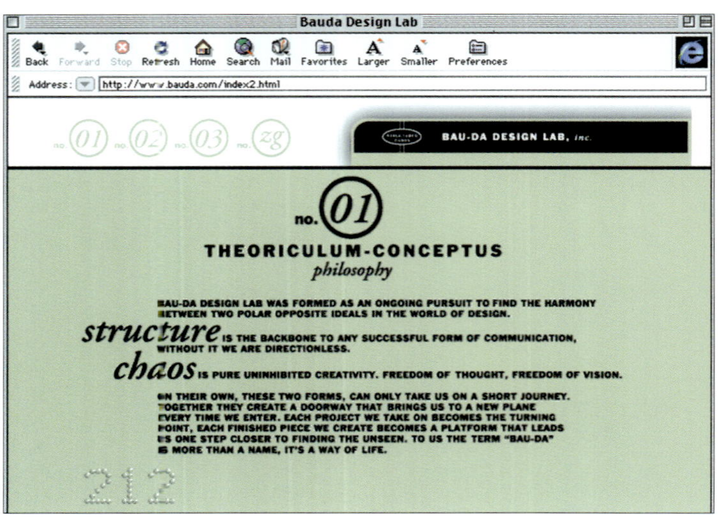

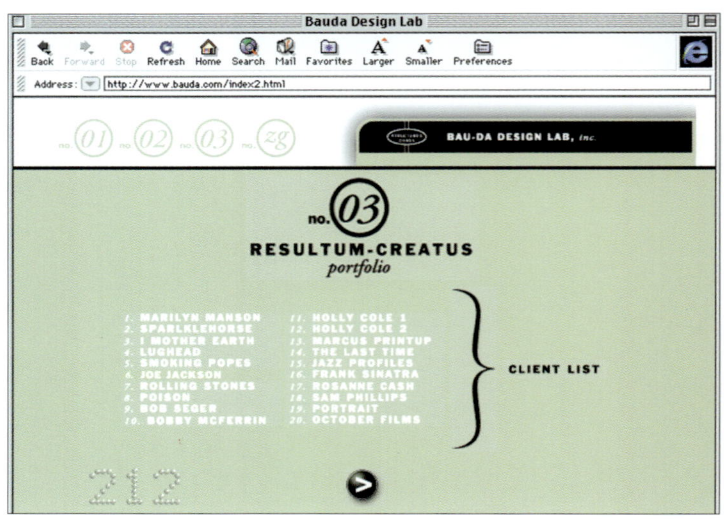

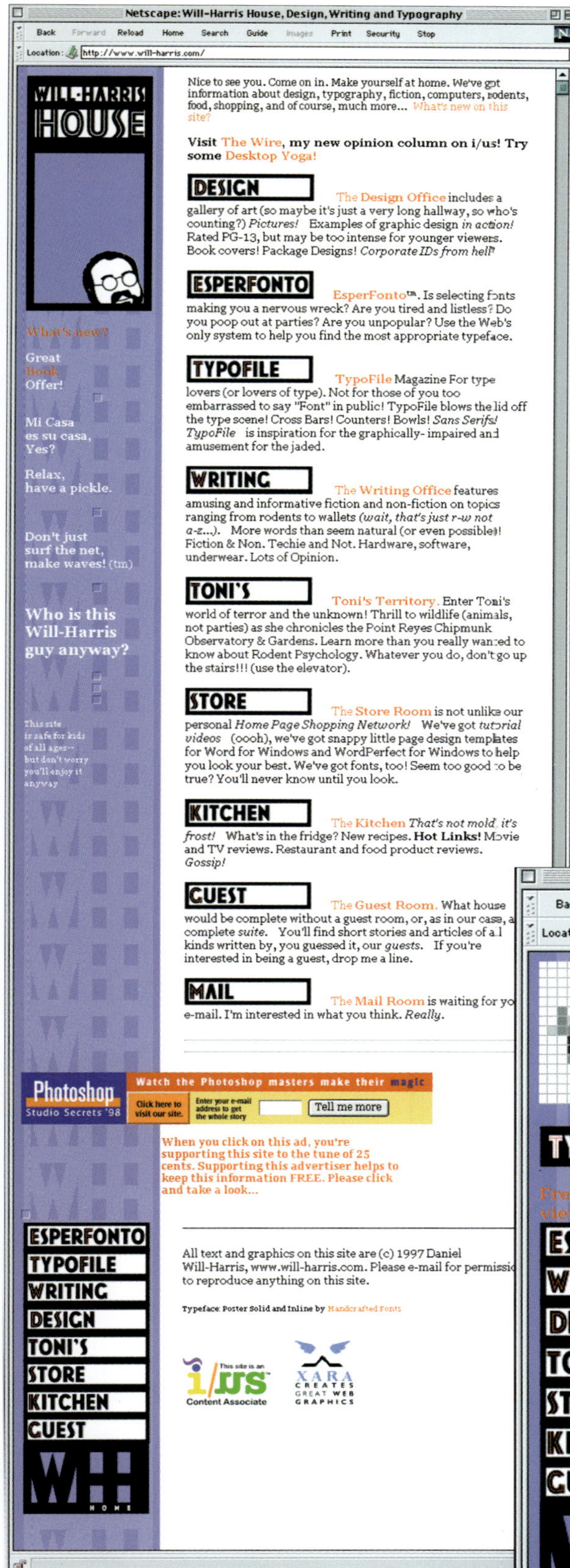

Title
Will-Harris House
URL
http://www.will-harris.com/
Design Firm
Will-Harris House
Designer/Illustrator/Programmer
Daniel Will-Harris
Authoring Platform
PC

One of the interesting aspects of this site's typography is not the unique fonts that are used, but their technical setup: for increased flexibility, each letter is rendered as its own file—words are constructed by placing the letter images side-by-side. This way, if the words or the fonts change, only the HTML has to be modified, instead of recreating new graphics from scratch.

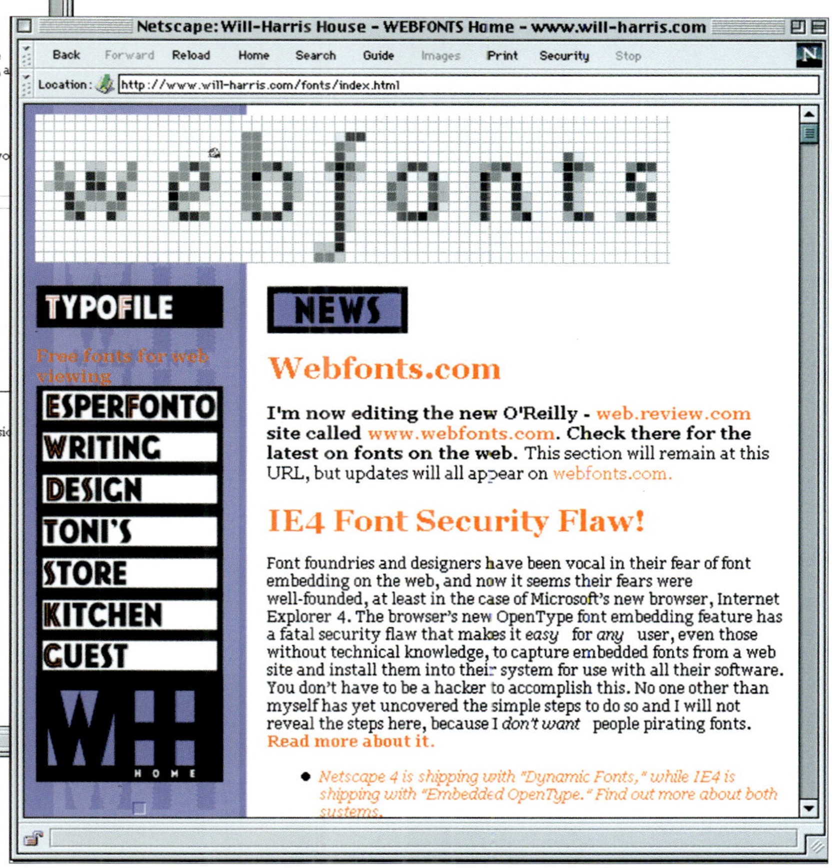

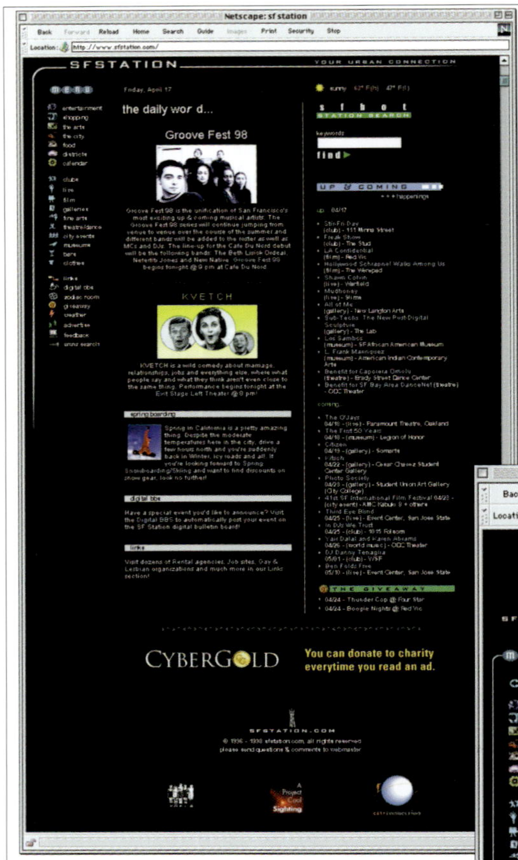

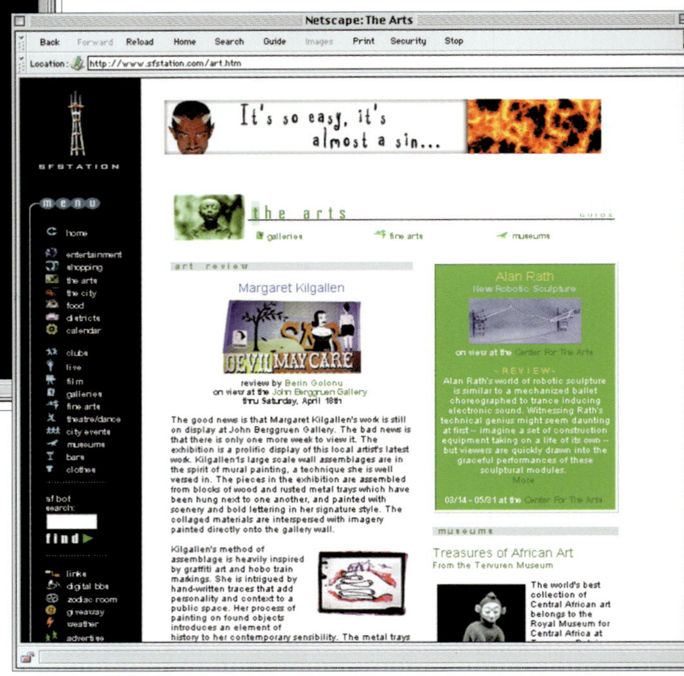

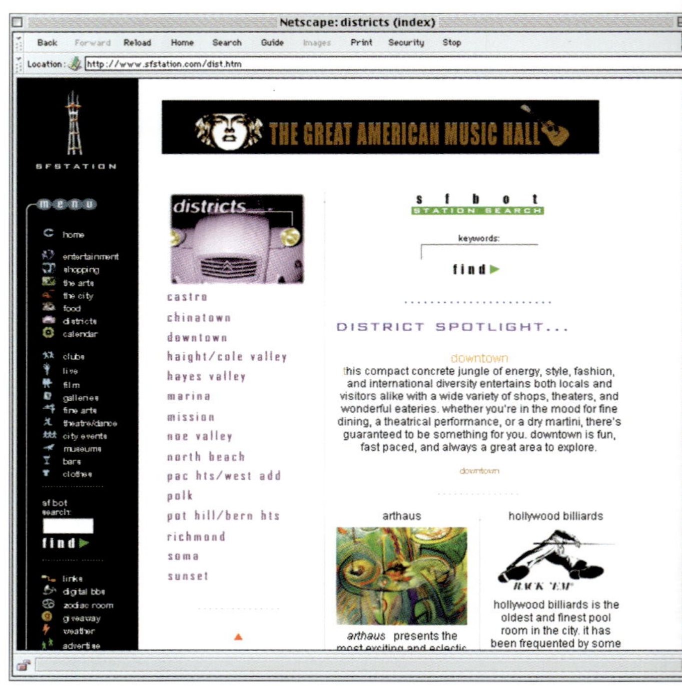

Title
sfstation
URL
http://www.sfstation.com/
Design Firm
sfstation
Designers
Mike Richards, Kyu Kyung
Illustrator
Kyu Kyung
Photographer
Curtis Christophersen
Programmers
Vincent Archuleta, Kyu Kyung, Mike Richards
Authoring Platform
Mac, PC

The visual importance in this text-heavy site is weighted toward making a great deal of information as readable as possible. The designers have chosen to force the body text to display in a sans-serif font: The text is streamlined and meant to be skimmed by the reader, who is likely looking for a few nuggets of information, not the page as a whole. The sans-serif typography, even in title graphics, also adds to the site's modern feel.

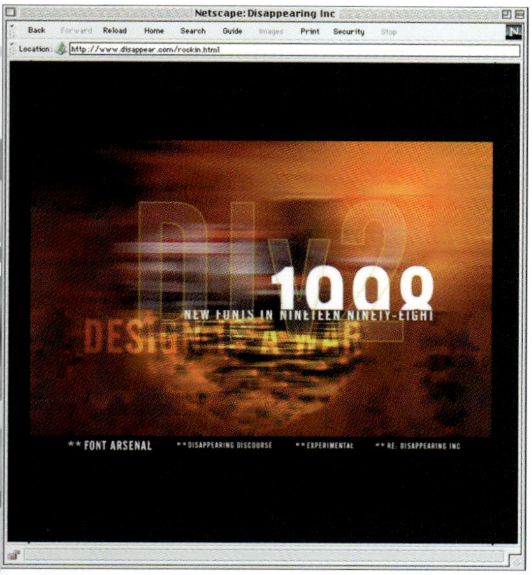

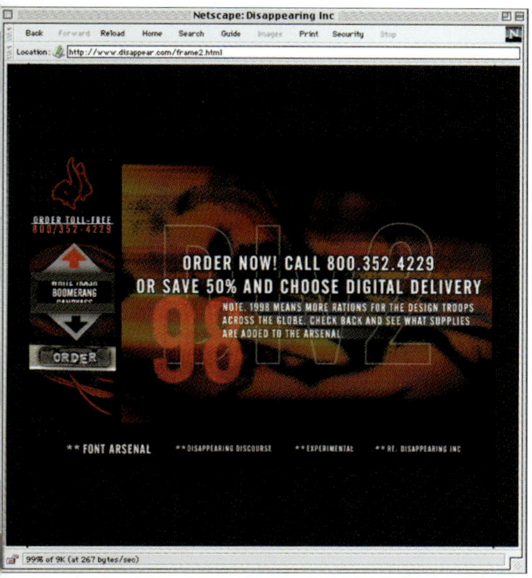

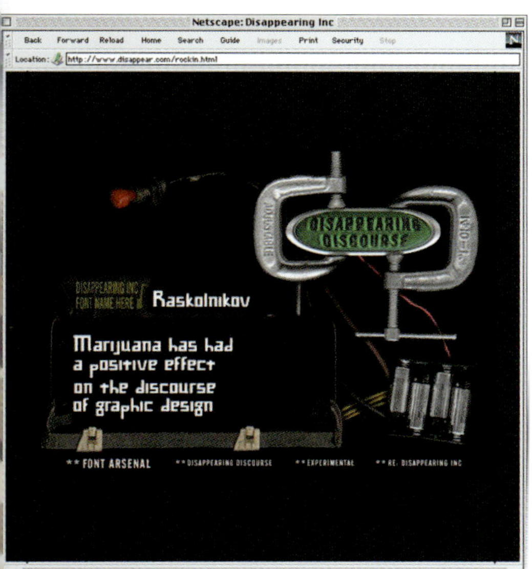

Title

The Disappearing Inc Font Arsenal

URL

http://www.disappear.com/rockin.html

Design firm

Disappearing Inc

Designers/Illustrators/Photographers

Jason Lucas, Jeff Prybolsky

Programmer

Al McElrath

Authoring platform

Mac

Many inexperienced designers tend to look past plain fonts such as the condensed sans-serifs used here. Typefaces with solid fills are great for slicing, fading, blurring, outlining, layering, and applying other effects that do not obscure the words themselves but add to the design.

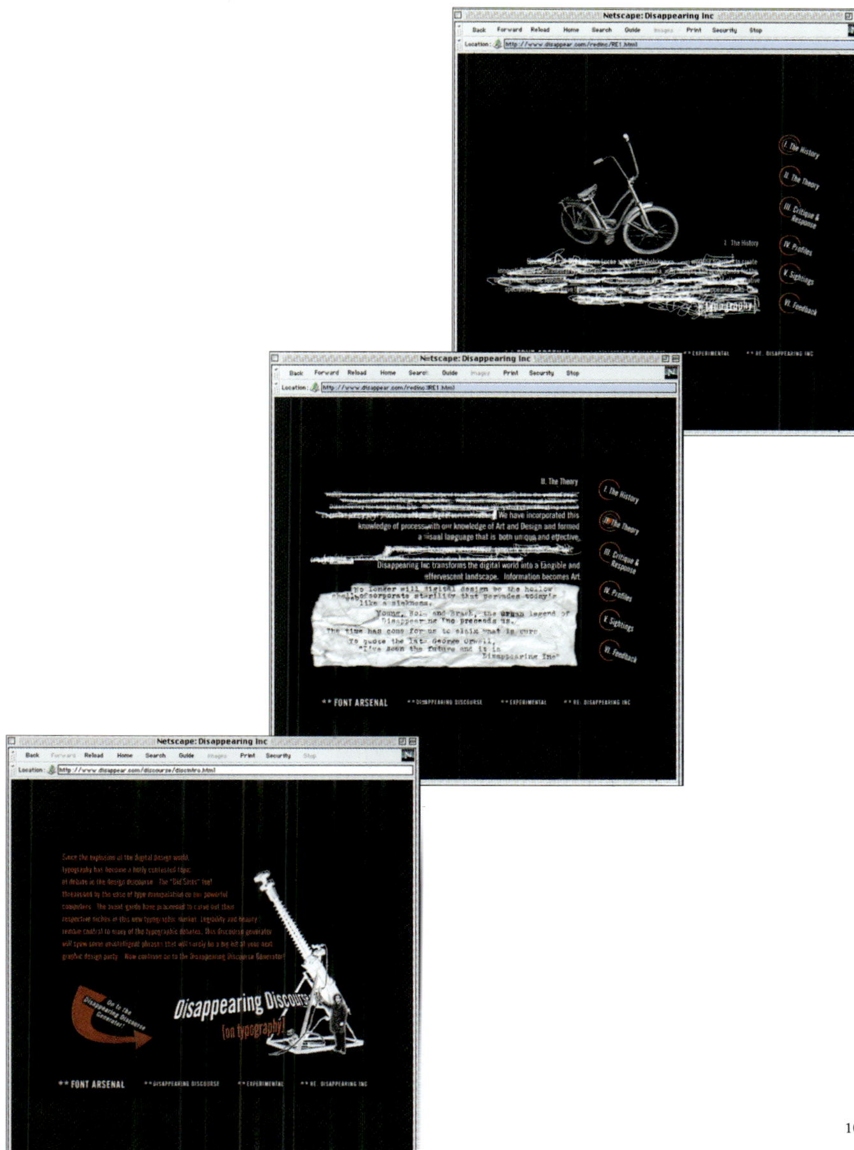

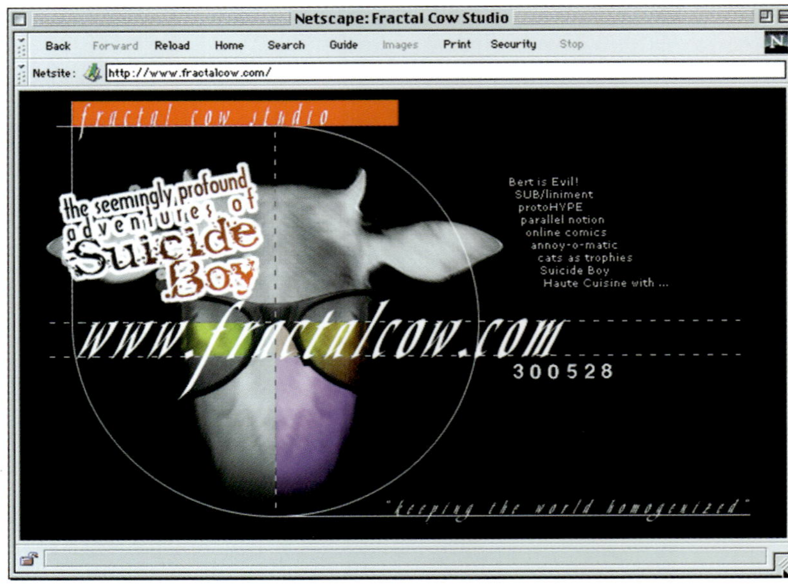

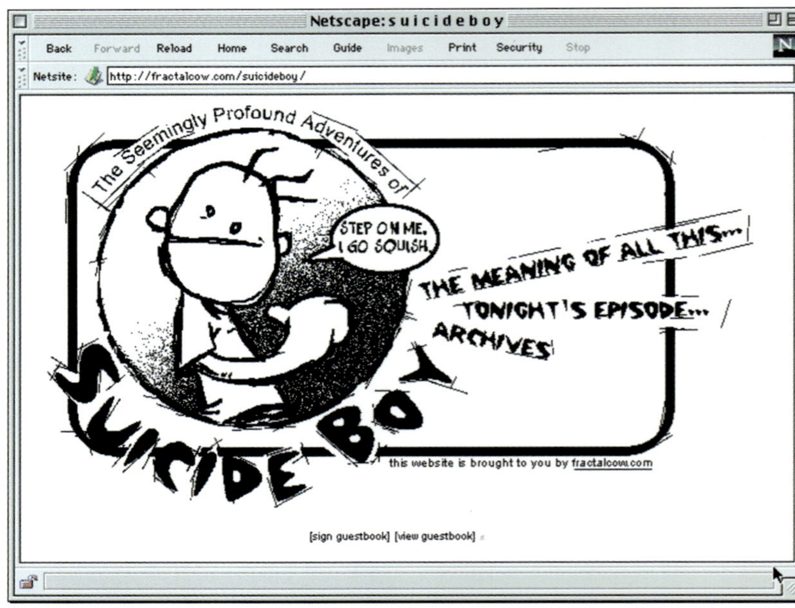

Title
fractal cow studio
URL
http://www.fractalcow.com/
Design Firm
http://www.binary-soup.com and fractal cow studio
Designer/Illustrator/Photographer/Programmer
Dino Ignacio
Authoring Platform
PC

There are a number of typographic elements at work at this site. The teaser for Suicide Boy is striking partly because of its splattered serif font, and partly due to the red-to-black blended fill. The titles are variations of the same font, a stylized script that appears in two angles of italicization to denote a sense of cutting-edge, forward momentum.

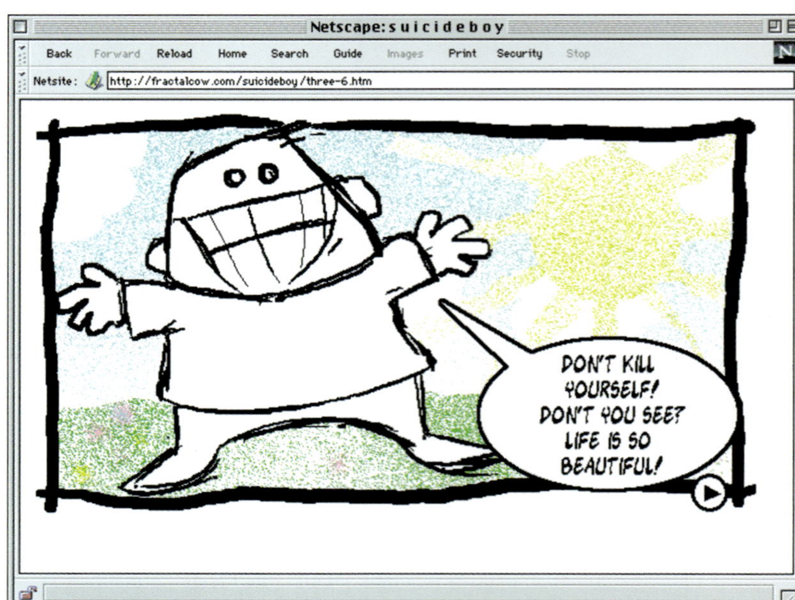

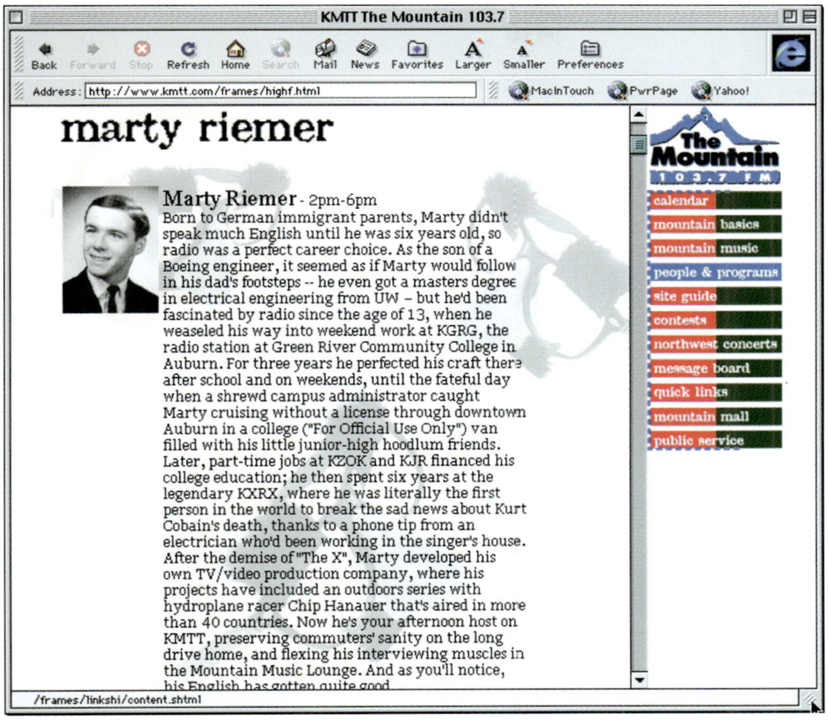

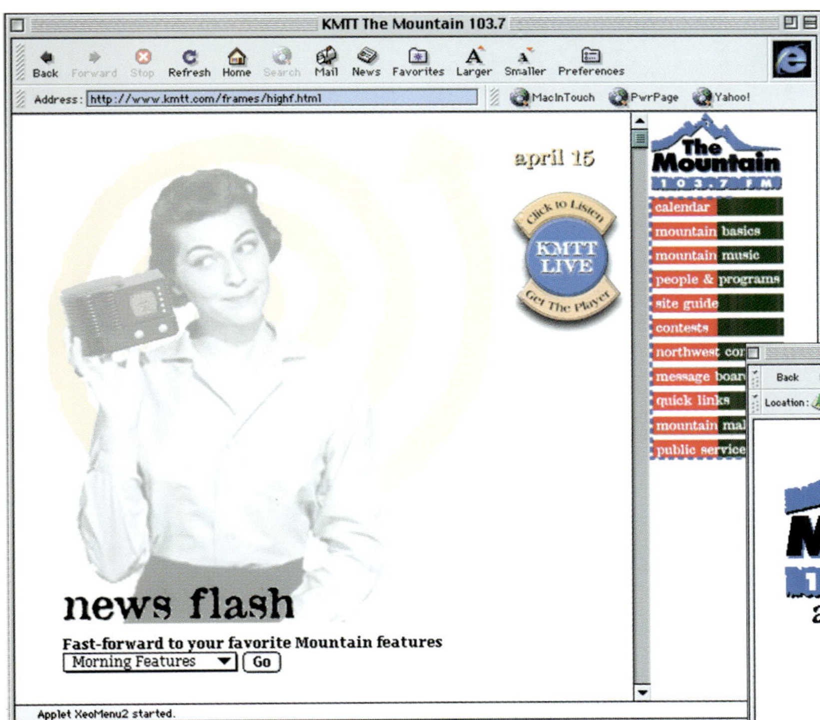

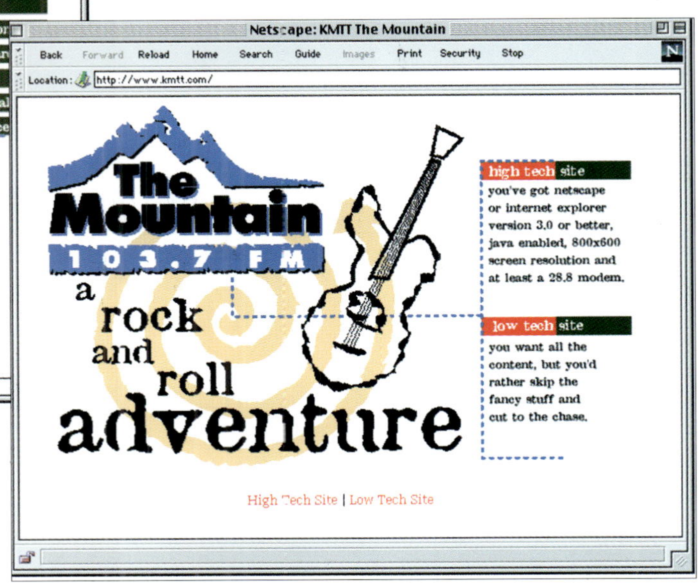

Title
KMTT-FM
URL
http://www.kmtt.com/
Design Firm
US Web
Designers
Kristin Ingalls, Mark Fromson
Programmer
Bob Cottrell
Authoring Platform
Mac, PC

The radio station featured in this Web site caters to a broad middle spectrum of listeners between the ages of 20 to 70+. As a result, it's no surprise to see that the feel generated by the typefaces used here straddles the line between old-fashioned (manual typewriters with slightly uneven hammers) and progressive.

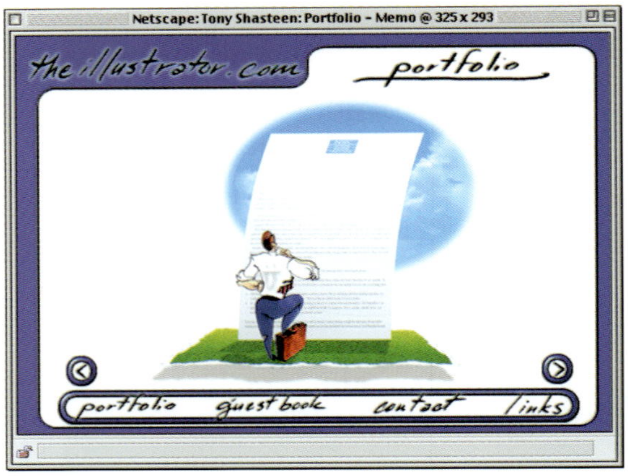

Title
The Illustrator
URL
http://www.theillustrator.com/
Design Firm
Tony Shasteen Illustration & Design
Designer/Illustrator
Tony Shasteen
Programmers
Digital Positions
David Taylor-Klaus, Beth Cooper
Authoring Platform
Mac

There are many typefaces out there that are based on personal handwriting, but sometimes it's better just to go with someone's original scrawls than try to force a font to achieve the same effect. These pages echo the designer's profession of illustrator, giving viewers a peek into a virtual sketch pad.

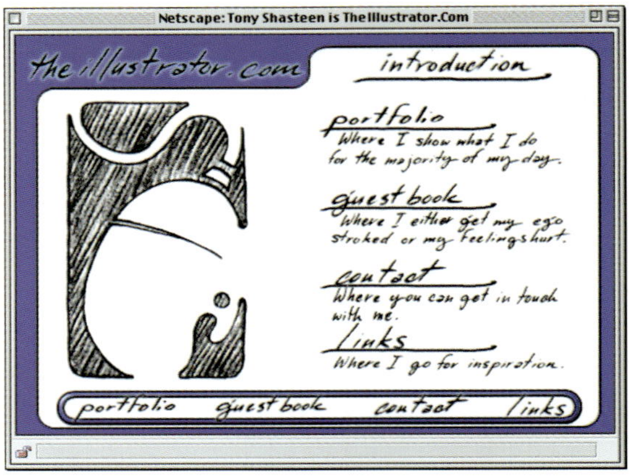

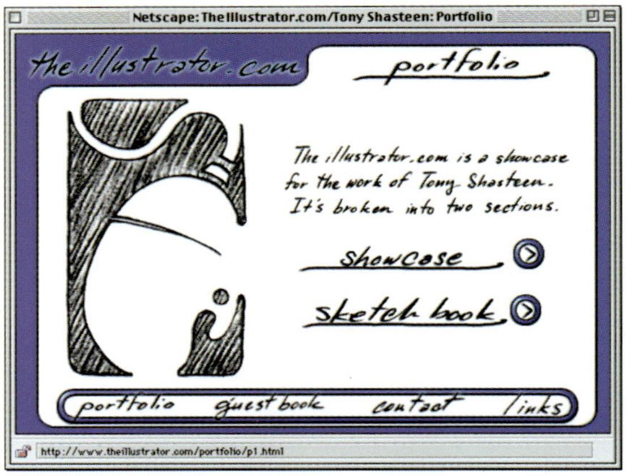

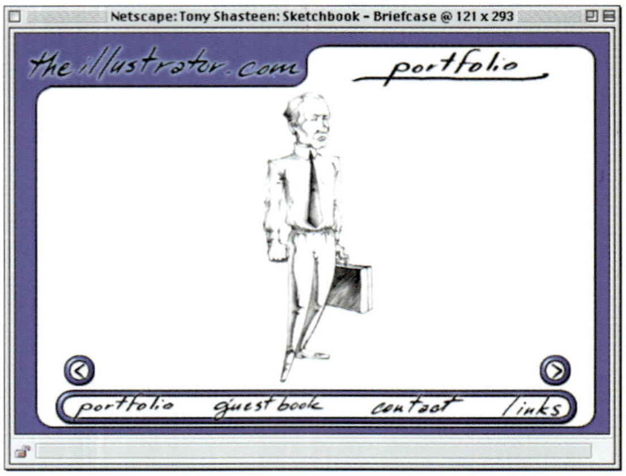

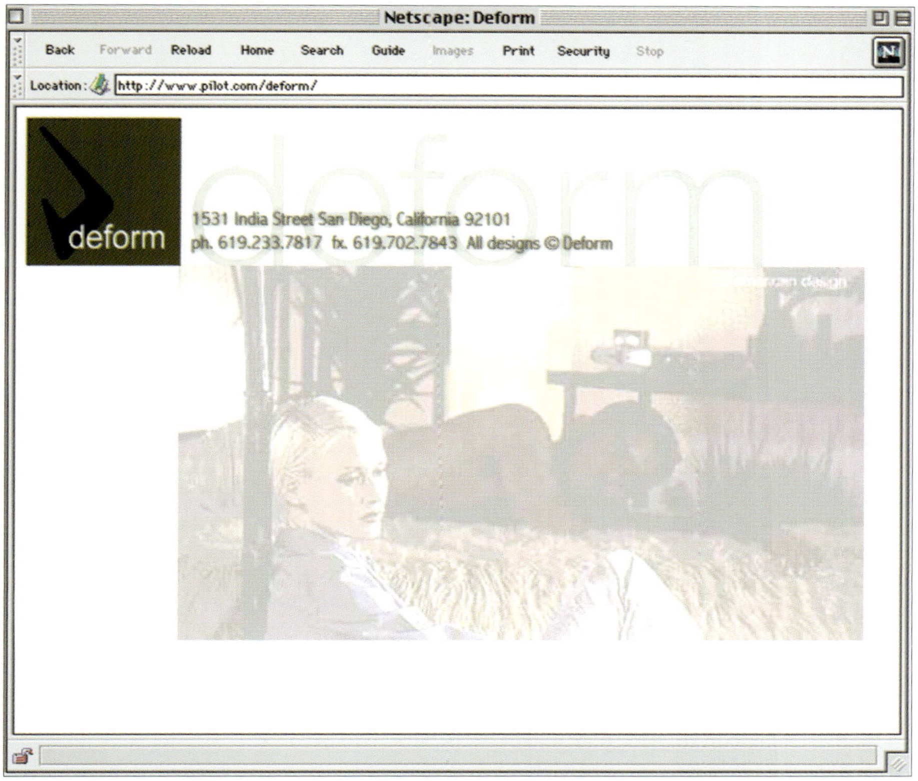

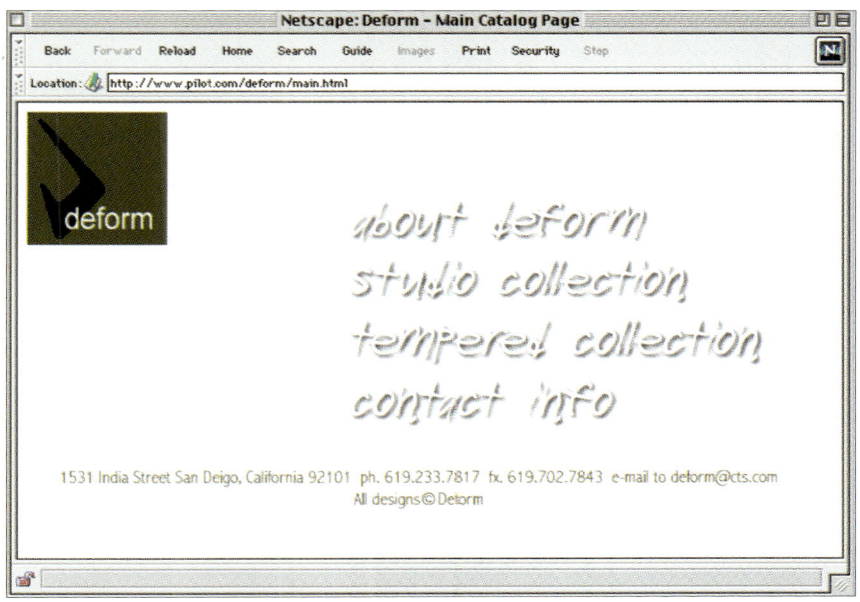

Title
deform
URL
http://www.pilot.com/deform
Design Firm
Computer Diversion
Designer/Illustrator/Programmer
Randal Antler
Photographer
David Harrison
Authoring Platform
PC

If you look into the area of text readability, you'll find that many experts believe that dark text placed on a light background (black on white, at the extreme) is easier to read. Here, however, you find white text on a white background, offset by a moderately dark drop shadow, along with pale green contact information and the word *deform* as further background texture.

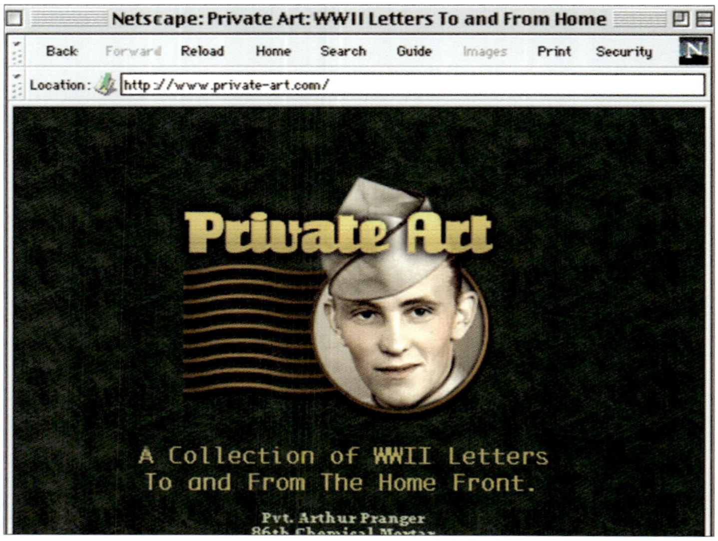

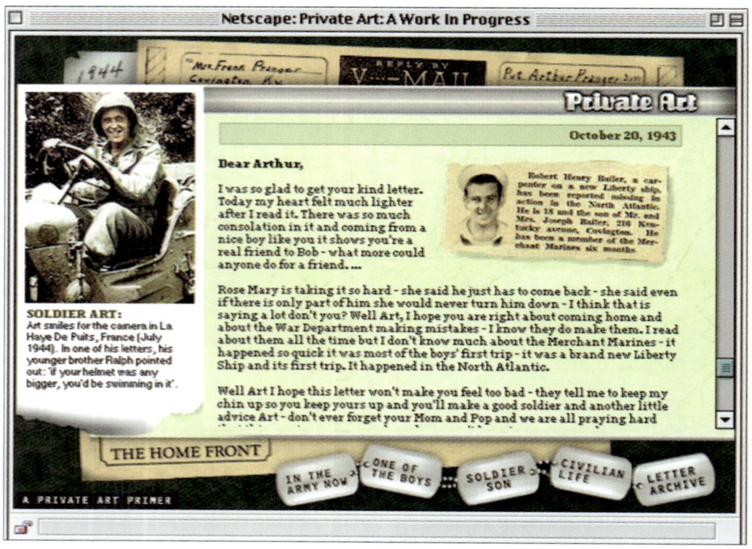

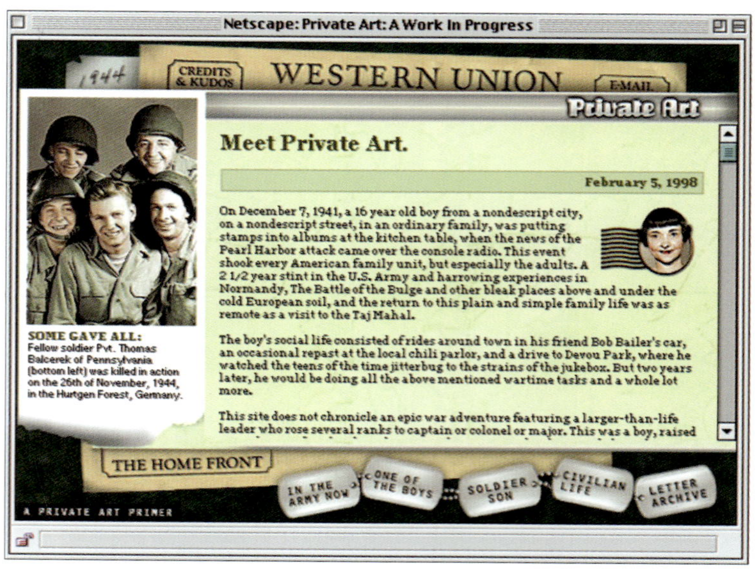

Title
Private Art: A Collection of WWII Letters To and From the Home Front
URL
http://www.private-art.com/
Design Firm
Enviromedia, Inc.
Designer/Illustrator
Rebecca Pranger
Programmer
Larry Pranger
Authoring Platform
Mac

For the most part, the typography here isn't meant to suggest a certain mood, but rather to replicate the look of items in the United States during World War II—the combination of which serves to provide the site's atmosphere. For example, the equally spaced capital letters of dog tags rest near the rich serifs of Western Union stationery.

Title
JASON project
URL
http://www.jasonproject.org/expedition.html
Design firm
Stolte Design (homepage); JASON Foundation (all other pages)
Designers/Illustrators/Programmers
Christian Stolte (homepage); Patrick Shea, Todd Viola (all other pages)
Authoring platform
PC (all except homepage)

A research into history and the world around us, this site features a classical serif font for the quote adorning the front page, stylized capitals for the Jason Project logo text, and bolder sans-serif type for interior elements. The journal is coded in HTML to display a more informal typeface (Comic Sans, which appears if the user has it pre-installed) resembling handwriting.

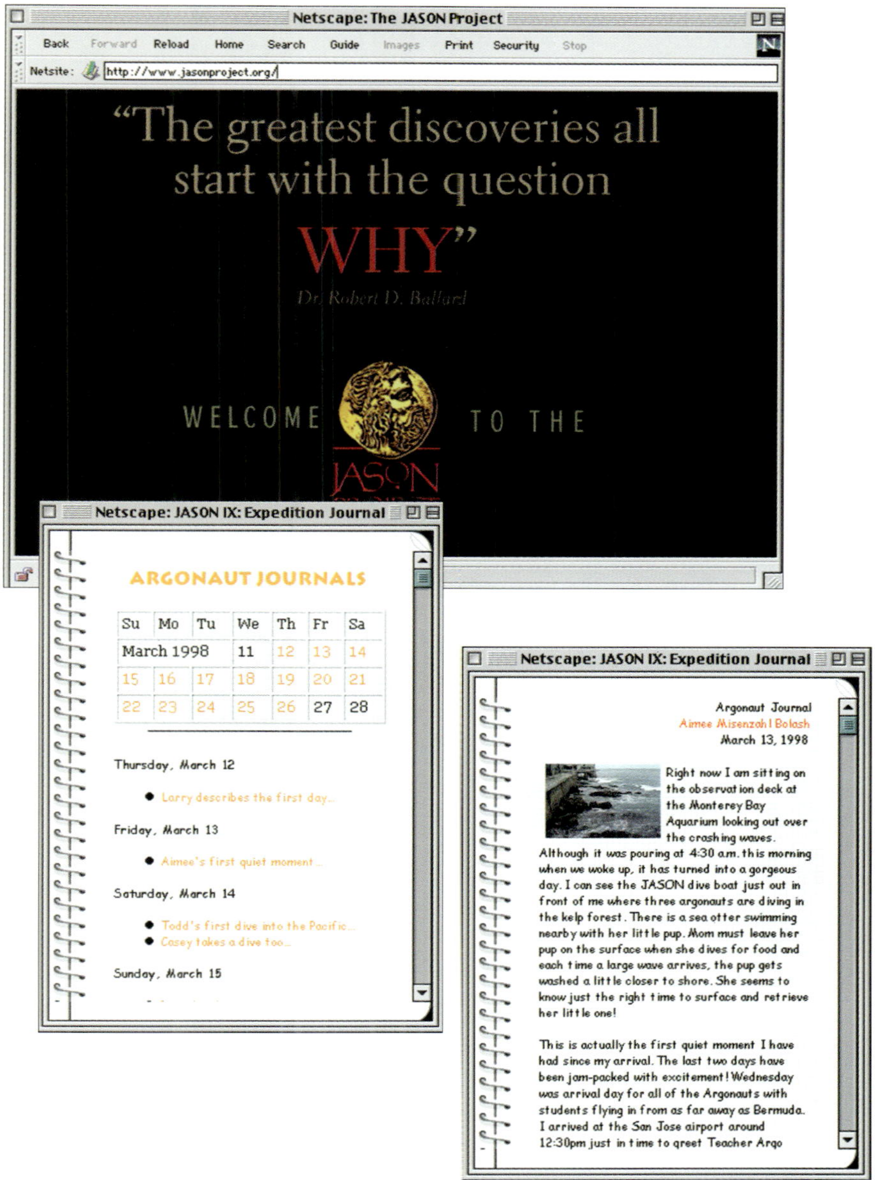

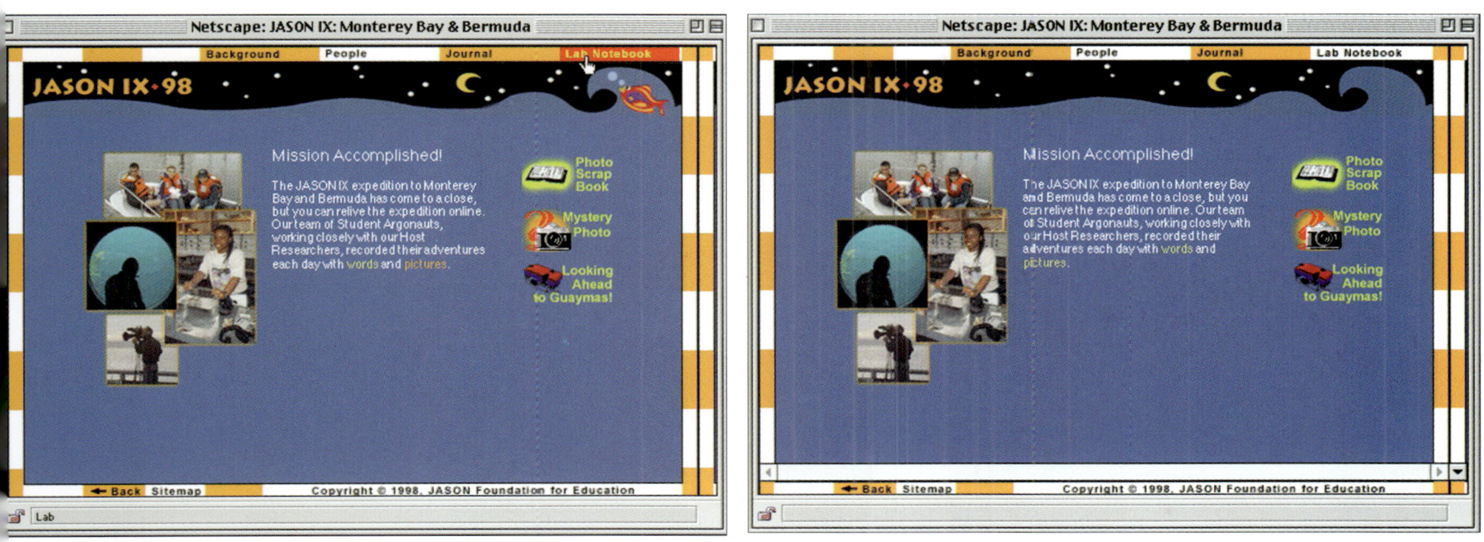

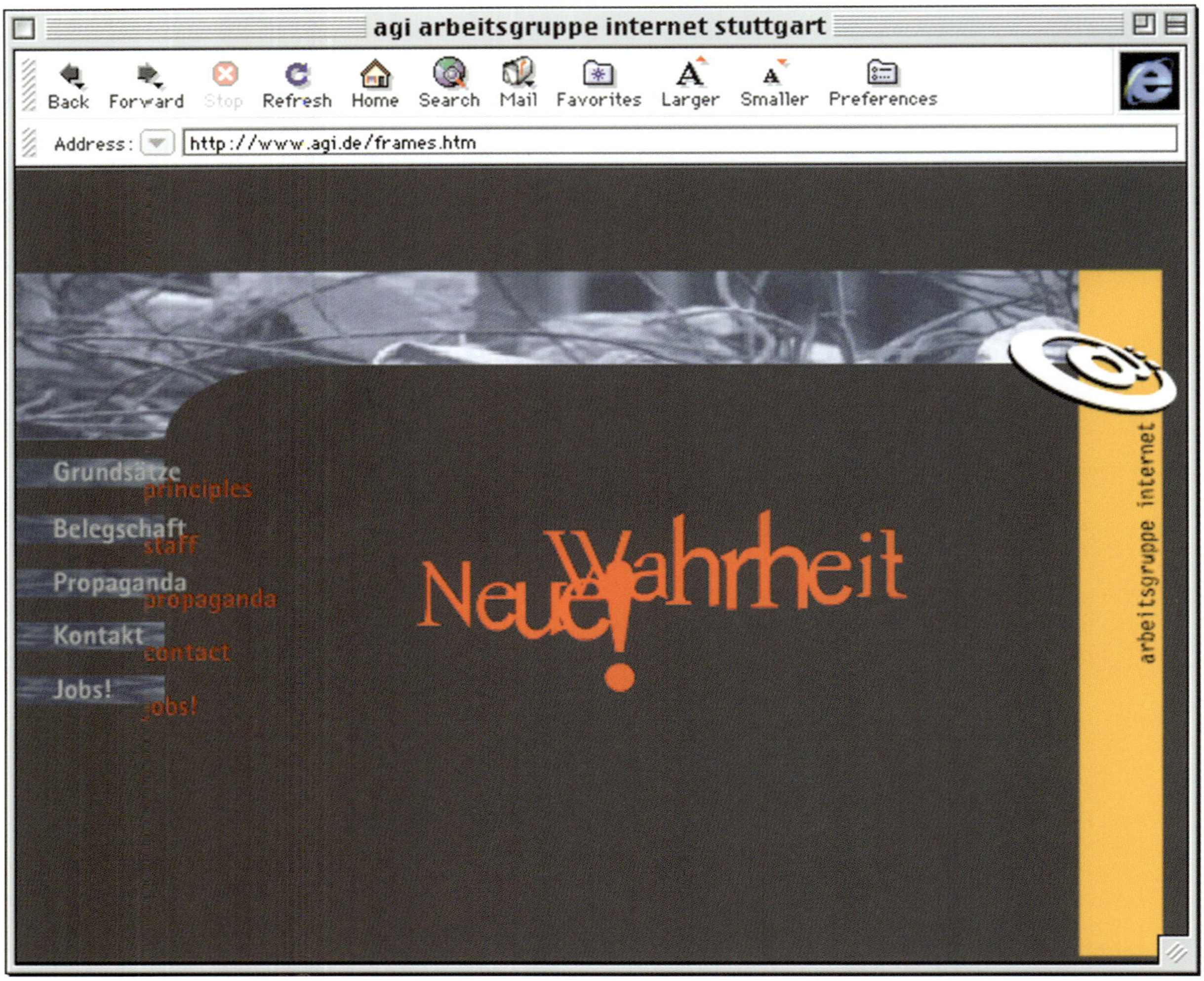

title
agi business media productions gmbh
URL
http://www.agi.de/frames.htm
design firm
agi business media productions
designers
Tim Buetz, Bernd Fessler, Arwin Hambasic
photographer
Thomas Möller
programmers
agi technology—Gaylord Aulke, Oliver Schmid, Tim Buetz
authoring platform
Mac, PC

The Arbeitsgruppe Internet (or Internet Workgroup) has an entirely bilingual site. They emphasize German slightly over English, making the German navigation elements and blocks of text in white; the navigation links are also capitalized. English text is slightly less legible, appearing in a dark red, smaller, and below the German. In each section, the section name appears on top of the list in a different, more irregular typeface.

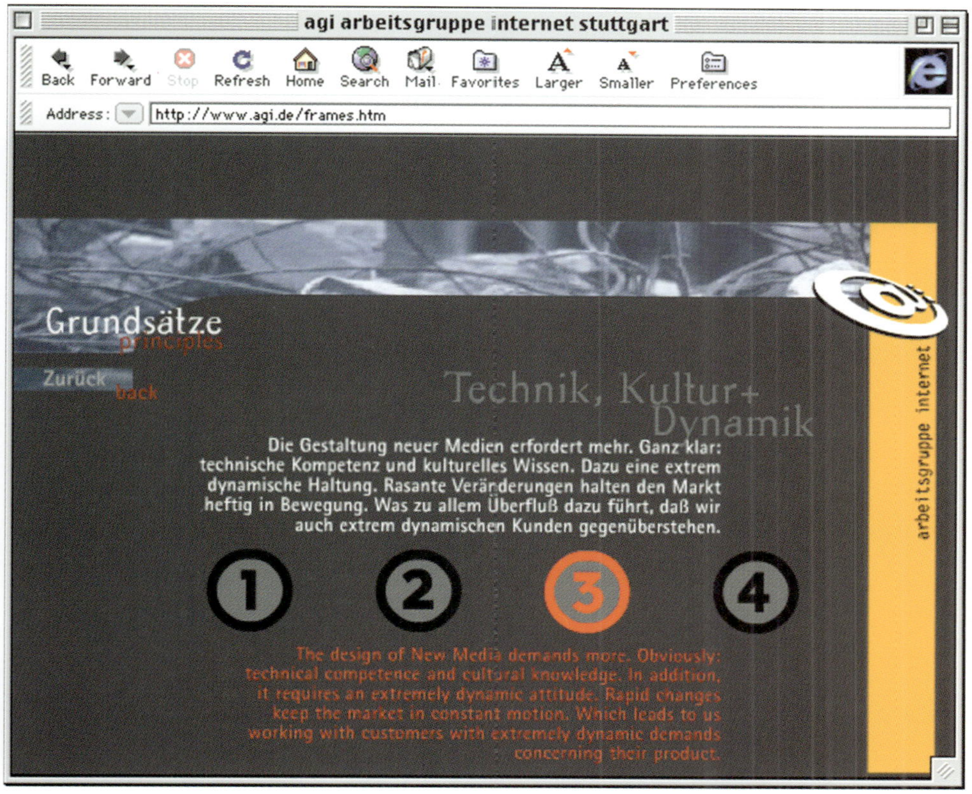
agi arbeitsgruppe internet stuttgart
Back Forward Stop Refresh Home Search Mail Favorites Larger Smaller Preferences
Address: http://www.agi.de/frames.htm
Grundsätze
principles
Zurück
back
Technik, Kultur+ Dynamik
Die Gestaltung neuer Medien erfordert mehr. Ganz klar: technische Kompetenz und kulturelles Wissen. Dazu eine extrem dynamische Haltung. Rasante Veränderungen halten den Markt heftig in Bewegung. Was zu allem Überfluß dazu führt, daß wir auch extrem dynamischen Kunden gegenüberstehen.
1 2 3 4
The design of New Media demands more. Obviously: technical competence and cultural knowledge. In addition, it requires an extremely dynamic attitude. Rapid changes keep the market in constant motion. Which leads to us working with customers with extremely dynamic demands concerning their product.
arbeitsgruppe internet

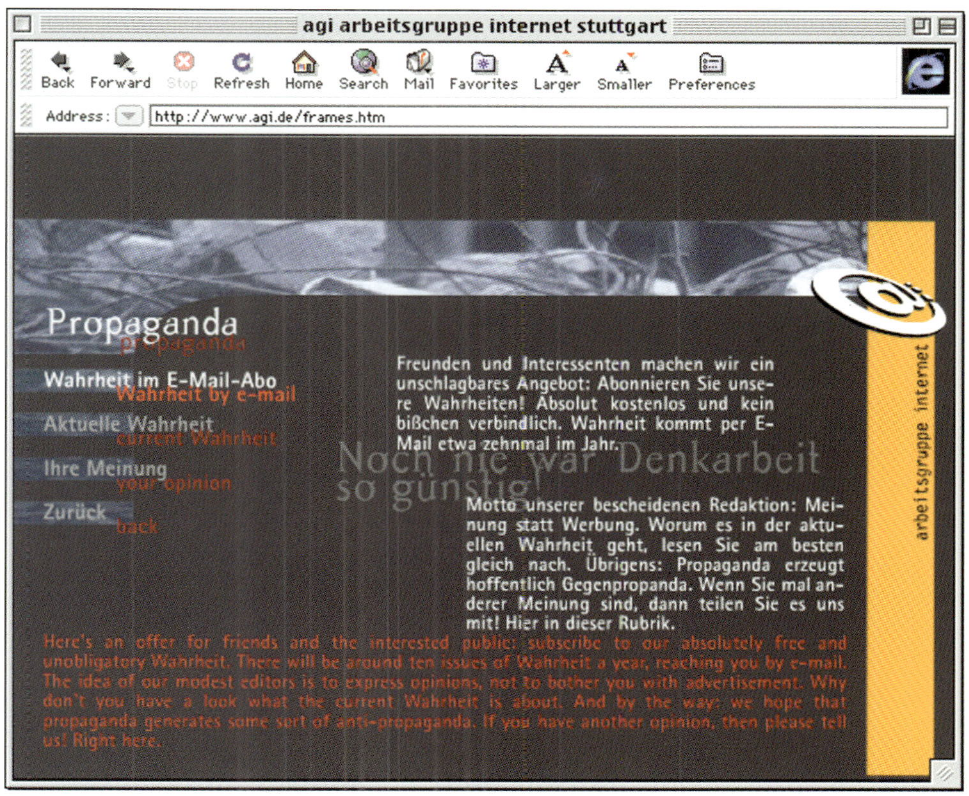
agi arbeitsgruppe internet stuttgart
Back Forward Stop Refresh Home Search Mail Favorites Larger Smaller Preferences
Address: http://www.agi.de/frames.htm
Propaganda
propaganda
Wahrheit im E-Mail-Abo
Wahrheit by e-mail
Aktuelle Wahrheit
current Wahrheit
Ihre Meinung
your opinion
Zurück
back
Freunden und Interessenten machen wir ein unschlagbares Angebot: Abonnieren Sie unsere Wahrheiten! Absolut kostenlos und kein bißchen verbindlich. Wahrheit kommt per E-Mail etwa zehnmal im Jahr.
Noch nie war Denkarbeit so günstig!
Motto unserer bescheidenen Redaktion: Meinung statt Werbung. Worum es in der aktuellen Wahrheit geht, lesen Sie am besten gleich nach. Übrigens: Propaganda erzeugt hoffentlich Gegenpropanda. Wenn Sie mal anderer Meinung sind, dann teilen Sie es uns mit! Hier in dieser Rubrik.
Here's an offer for friends and the interested public: subscribe to our absolutely free and unobligatory Wahrheit. There will be around ten issues of Wahrheit a year, reaching you by e-mail. The idea of our modest editors is to express opinions, not to bother you with advertisement. Why don't you have a look what the current Wahrheit is about. And by the way: we hope that propaganda generates some sort of anti-propaganda. If you have another opinion, then please tell us! Right here.
arbeitsgruppe internet

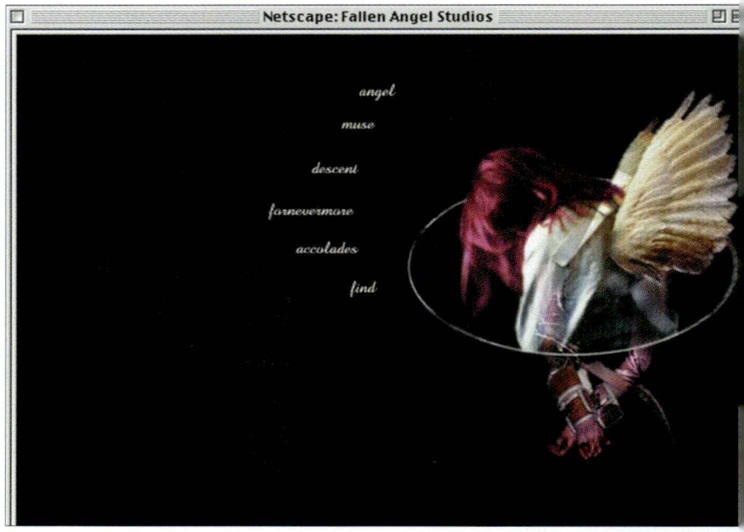

Title
fallen Angel studios
URL
http://www.fallenangelstudio.com/
Design firm
knight errant design
Designer/Illustrator/Photographer
Bob Libby
Authoring platform
pc

Darkness encroaches most of this site, with murky photos and dimly lit accents, like the tarnished-copper button marked *fin.* The typography appears equally in conflict with darkness: the white text looks almost overly anti-aliased, so the letters' edges drift into the surrounding black.

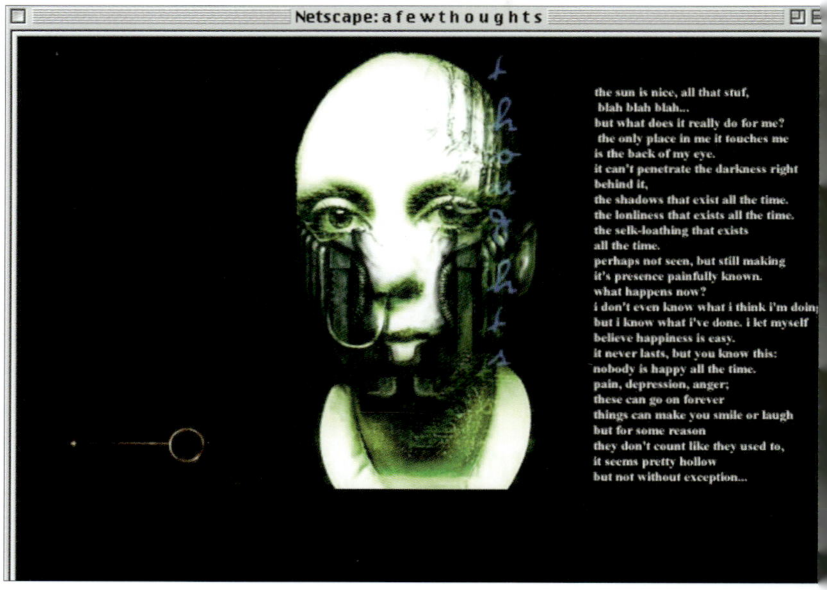

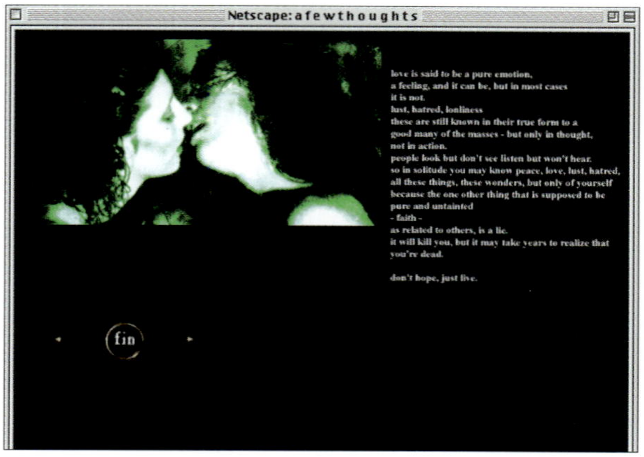

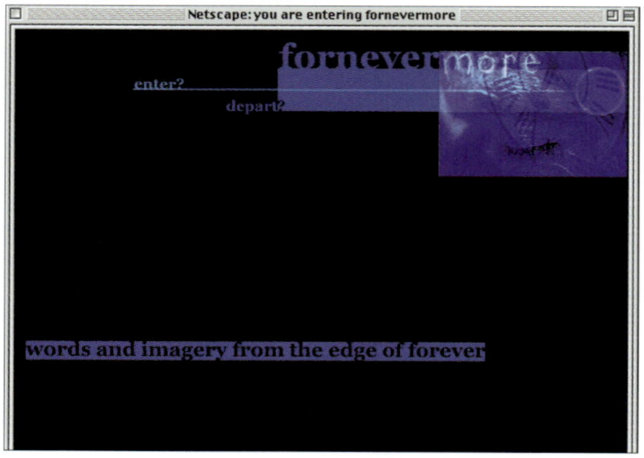

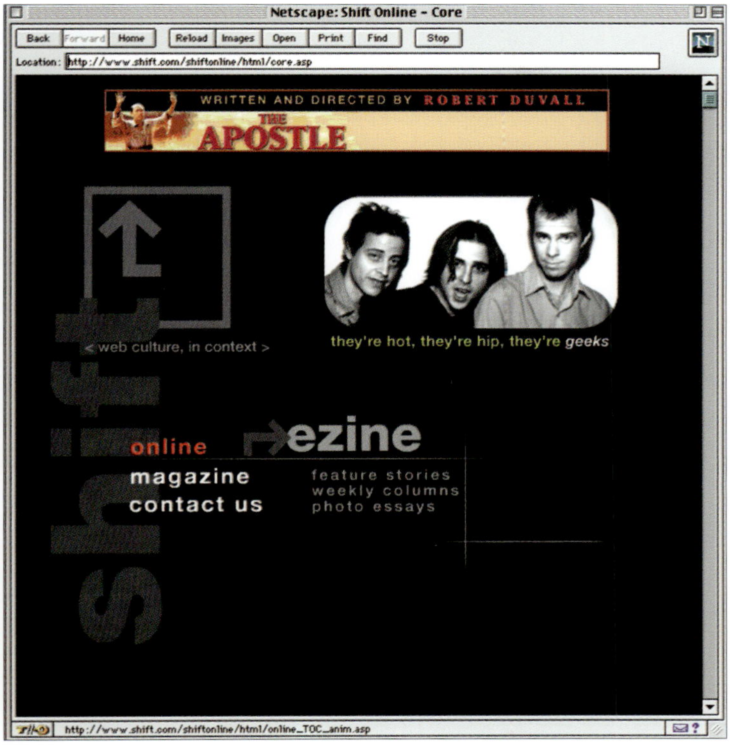

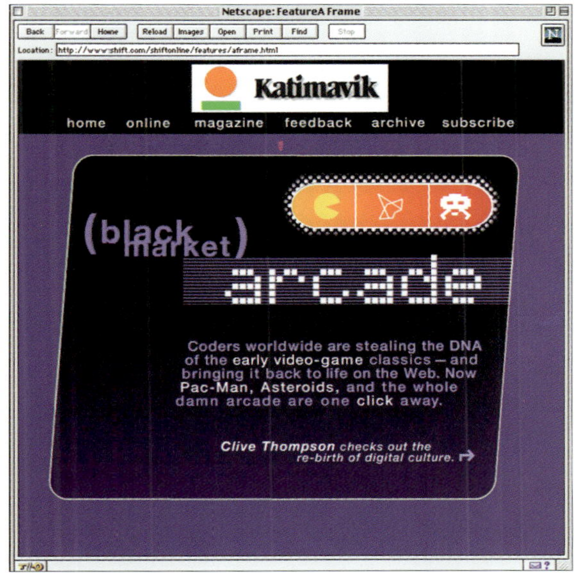

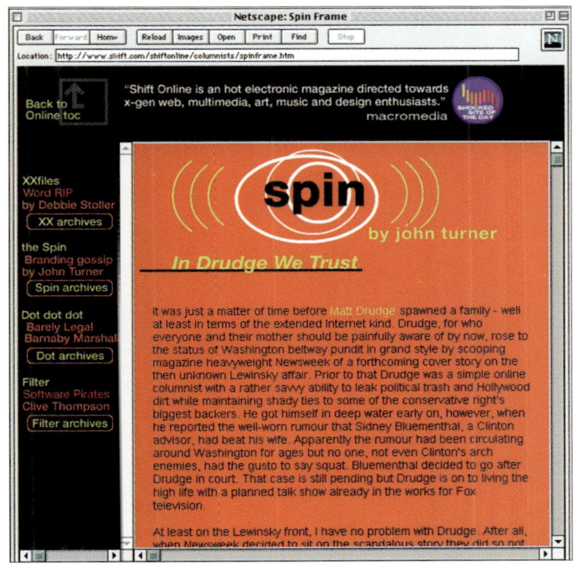

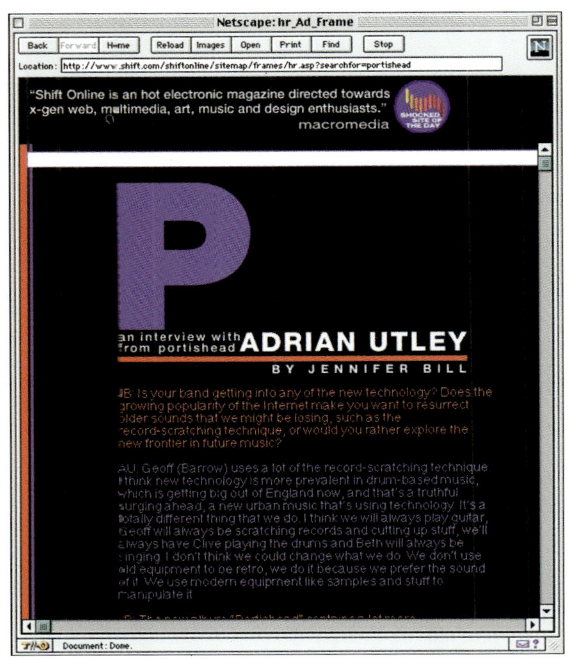

title
shift online
URL
http://www.shift.com/shiftonline/htm/core.asp
designers
Barnaby Marshall, Dave Sylvestre
programmer
Al Baghal
authoring platform
Mac

Another example of rendering type with Flash technology, the heavy sans-serifs of the title page do not try to be clever; the larger sizes and reserved color usage works to point you into the site. Once inside, animated titles are customized according to the articles' subject matter.

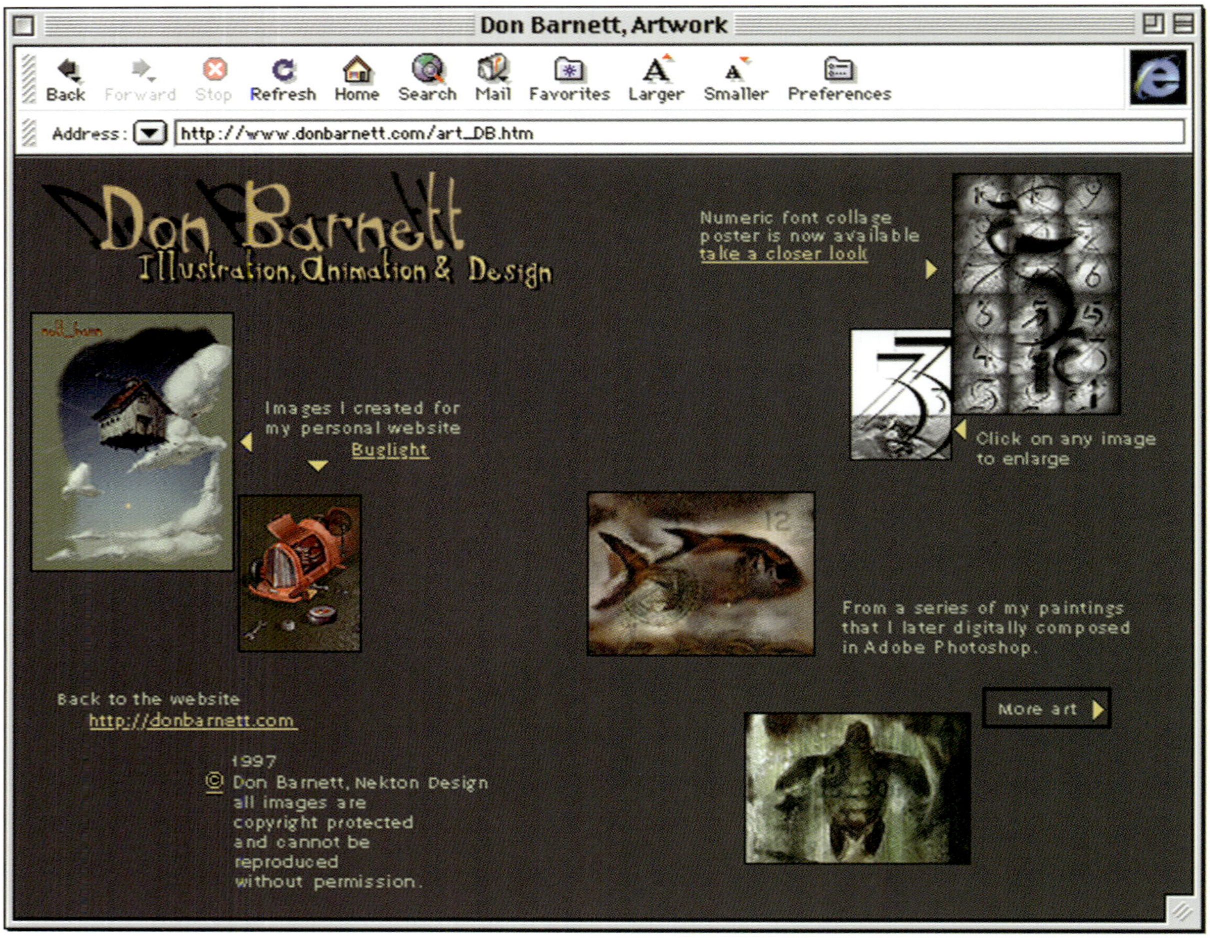

Title
Don Barnett
URL
http://www.donbarnett.com/
Design firm
Nekton Design
Designer/Illustrator/Programmer
Don Barnett
Authoring platform
Mac

Not everyone can design their own typefaces to use on a Web site, but you can draw a few lessons from how Don Barnett uses them. His site, Bug Light, plays with notions of light and shadow; there's usually an extra shading or extended shadow behind his name. He also plays with regular type to give it a quality of motion that matches his drawings and type as in the Gaudi tribute.

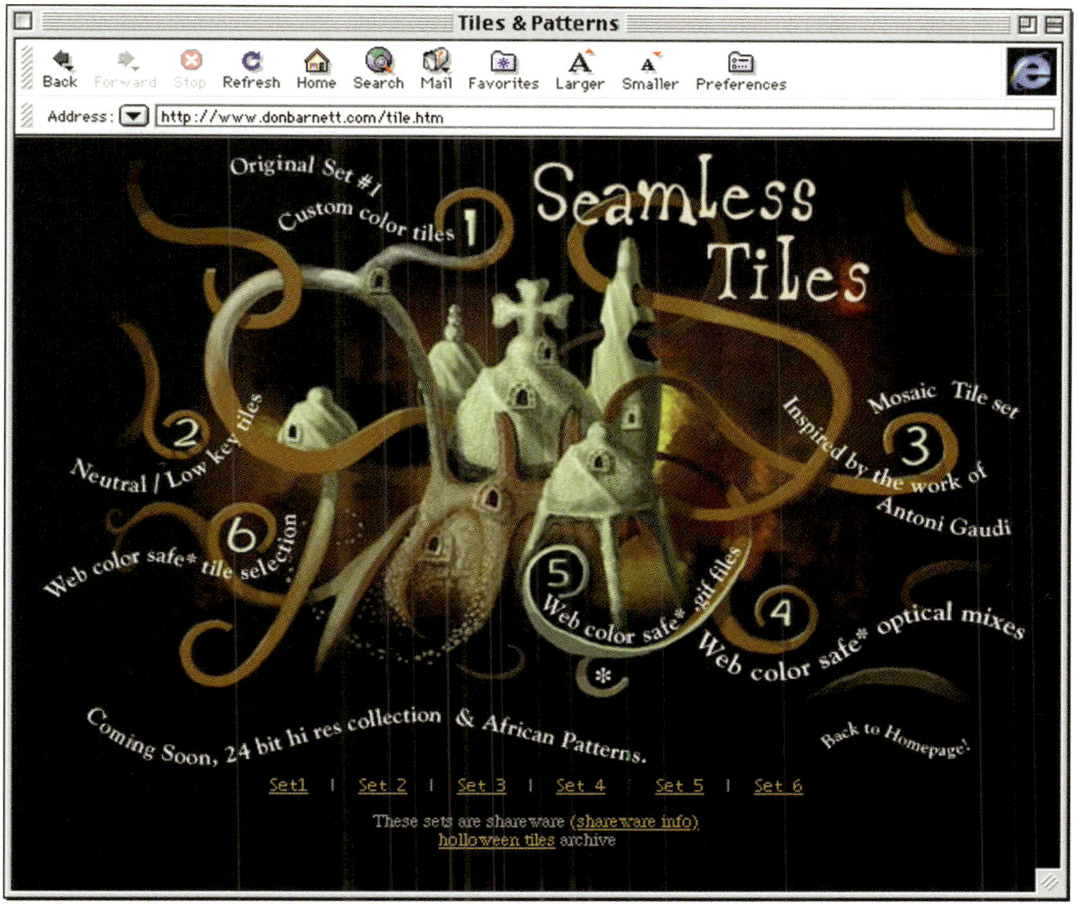
Tiles & Patterns
Back
Forward
Stop
Refresh
Home
Search
Mail
Favorites
Larger
Smaller
Preferences
Address:
http://www.donbarnett.com/tile.htm
Seamless Tiles
Original Set #1
Custom color tiles 1
2 Neutral / Low key tiles
Mosaic Tile set
3 Inspired by the work of Antoni Gaudi
6 Web color safe* tile selection
5 Web color safe* gif files
4 Web color safe* optical mixes
*
Coming Soon, 24 bit hi res collection & African Patterns.
Back to Homepage!
Set1 | Set 2 | Set 3 | Set 4 | Set 5 | Set 6
These sets are shareware (shareware info)
holloween tiles archive

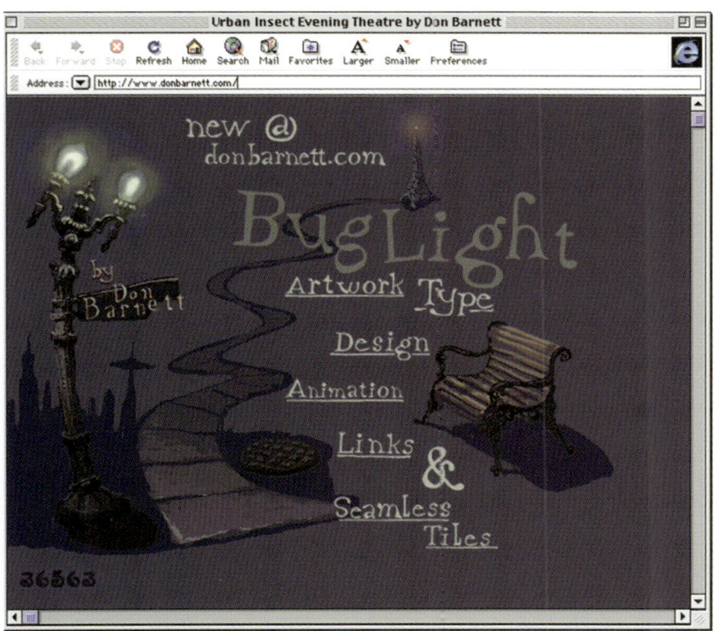
Urban Insect Evening Theatre by Don Barnett
Back
Forward
Stop
Refresh
Home
Search
Mail
Favorites
Larger
Smaller
Preferences
Address:
http://www.donbarnett.com/
new @
donbarnett.com
BugLight
by Don Barnett
Artwork
Type
Design
Animation
Links
&
Seamless Tiles
36563

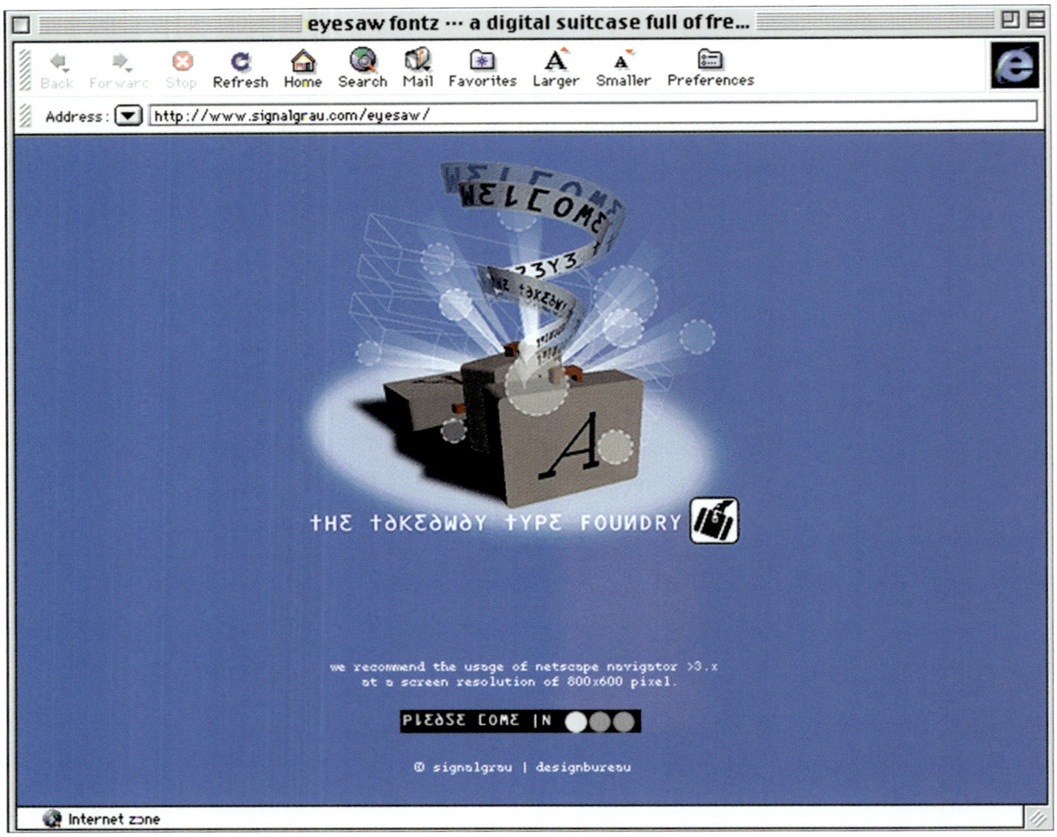
eyesaw fontz ··· a digital suitcase full of fre...
Back Forward Stop Refresh Home Search Mail Favorites Larger Smaller Preferences
Address: http://www.signalgrau.com/eyesaw/
WELCOME
THE TAKEAWAY TYPE FOUNDRY
we recommend the usage of netscape navigator >3.x
at a screen resolution of 800x600 pixel.
PLEASE COME IN
© signalgrau | designbureau
Internet zone

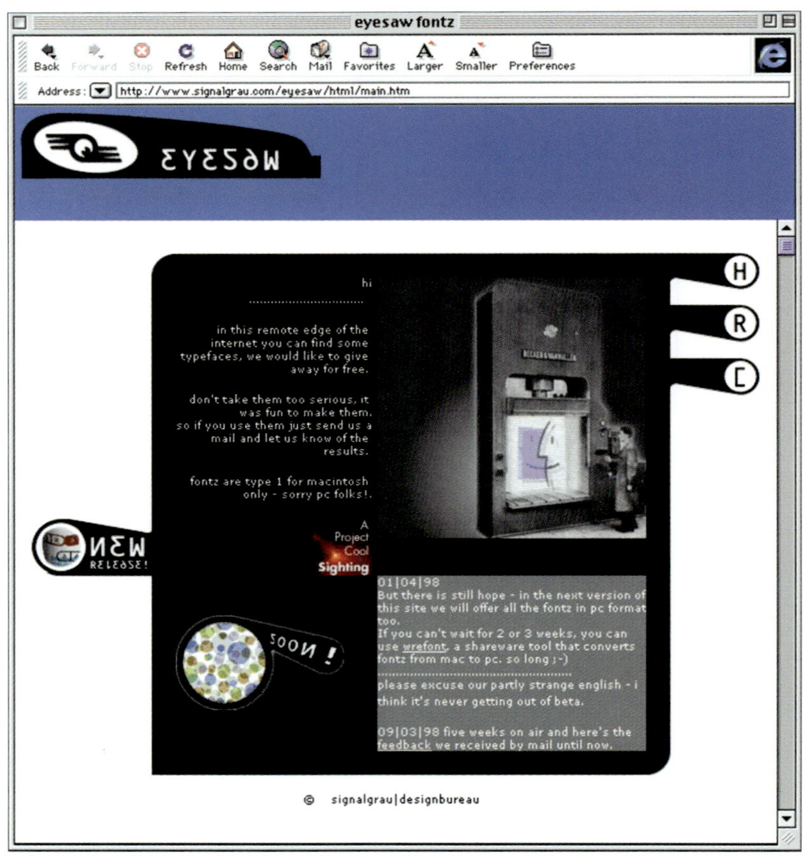
eyesaw fontz
Back Forward Stop Refresh Home Search Mail Favorites Larger Smaller Preferences
Address: http://www.signalgrau.com/eyesaw/html/main.htm
EYESAW
hi
in this remote edge of the internet you can find some typefaces, we would like to give away for free.
don't take them too serious, it was fun to make them. so if you use them just send us a mail and let us know of the results.
fontz are type 1 for macintosh only - sorry pc folks!.
A Project Cool Sighting
NEW RELEASE!
SOON!
01|04|98
But there is still hope - in the next version of this site we will offer all the fontz in pc format too.
If you can't wait for 2 or 3 weeks, you can use wrefont, a shareware tool that converts fontz from mac to pc. so long ;-)
please excuse our partly strange english - i think it's never getting out of beta.
09|03|98 five weeks on air and here's the feedback we received by mail until now.
H
R
C
© signalgrau|designbureau

title
eyesaw fontz
URL
http://www.signalgrau.com/eyesaw/
design firm
signalgrau design bureau
designer/illustrator/
photographer/programmer
Dirk Uhlenbrock
authoring platform
Mac

Like many sites devoted to type, Eyesaw takes a minimal approach to type on the site, using a total of three faces in about four sizes: the standard Courier (used for navigation), a small sans serif (used for body copy), and their display font for rendered heads. The main display face turns typographic conventions on their head—literally. Every character in the font is a transposed, reversed, upside down, or rotated version of a real letter; many letters are made up of numerals that have been flipped.

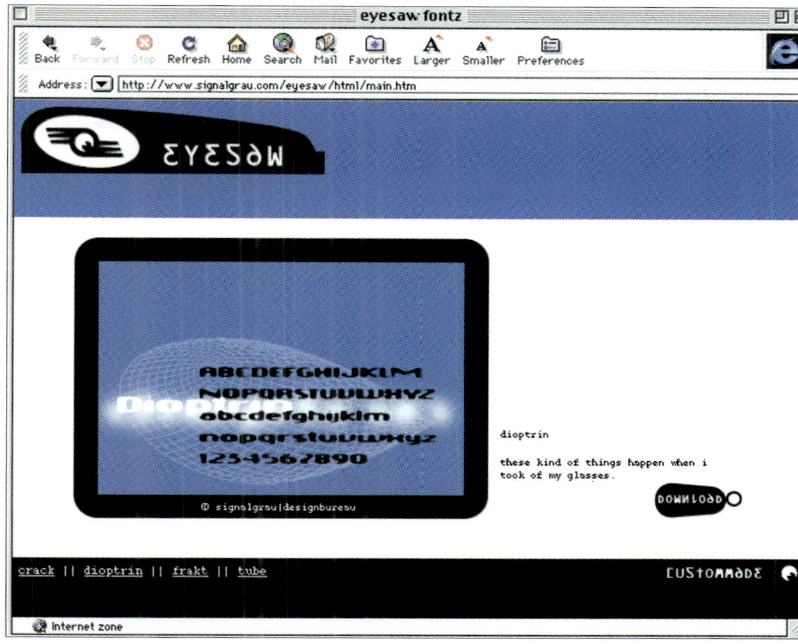

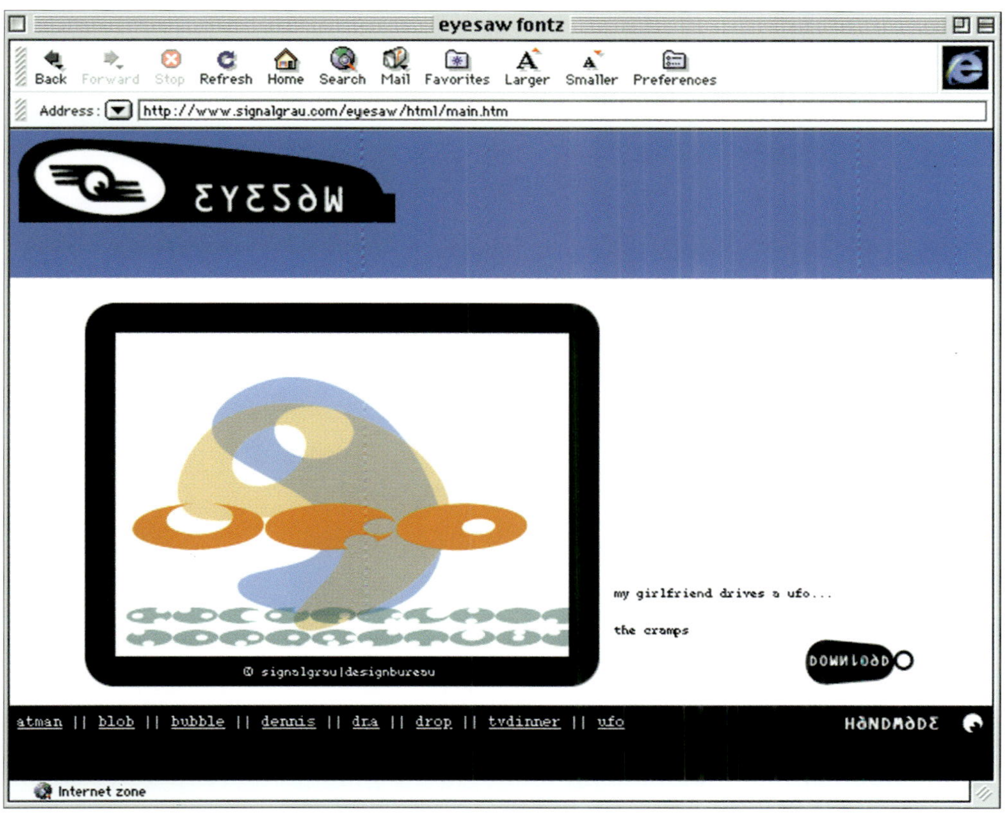

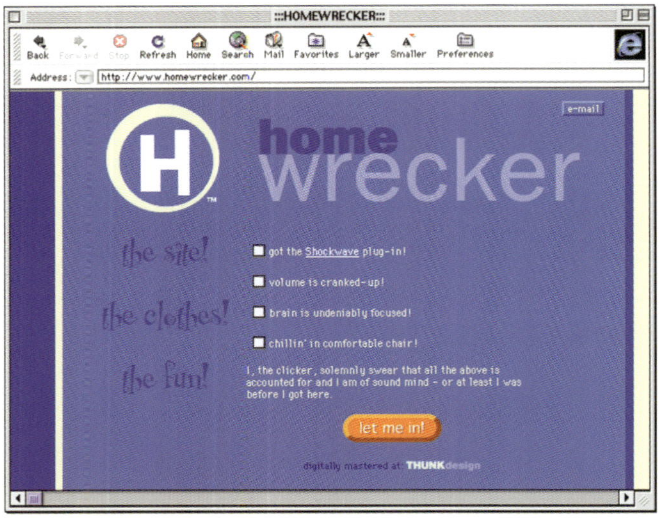

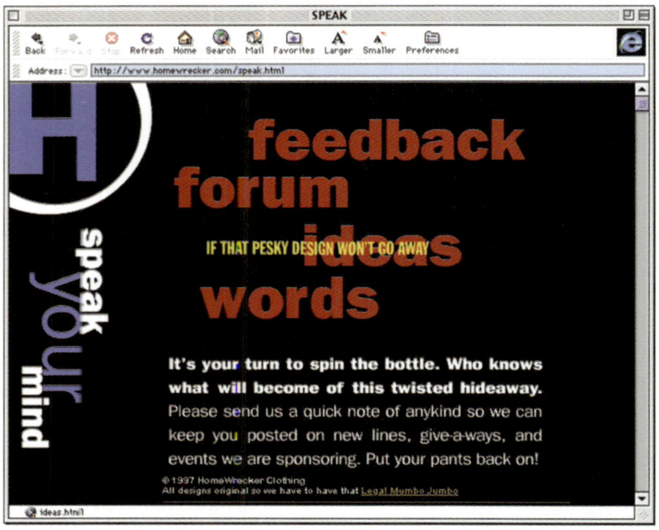

Title
Homewrecker
URL
http://www.homewrecker.com/
Design Firm
THUNKdesign
Designer/Illustrator/
Photographer/Programmer
James Tucker
Authoring Platform
Mac, PC

Homewrecker echoes earlier Microsoft advertising campaigns in type and color, ricocheting off a world-domination theme by playing with the typographic elements. A small Shockwave movie uses only Helvetica to get the point across. Nice touches permeate the site; there's not a page that doesn't create some visual interest by overlapping, coloring, or rotating type.

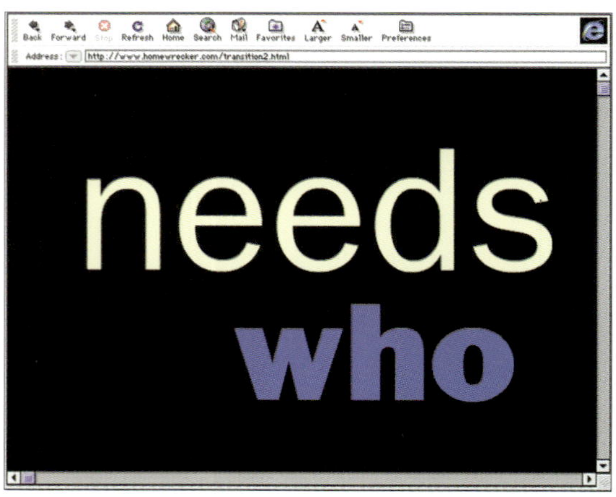

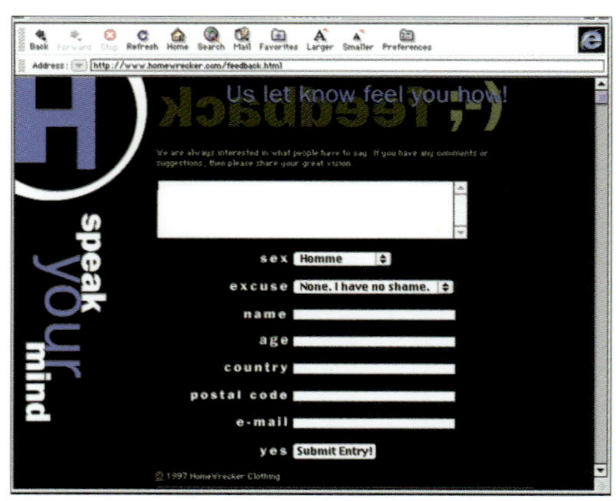

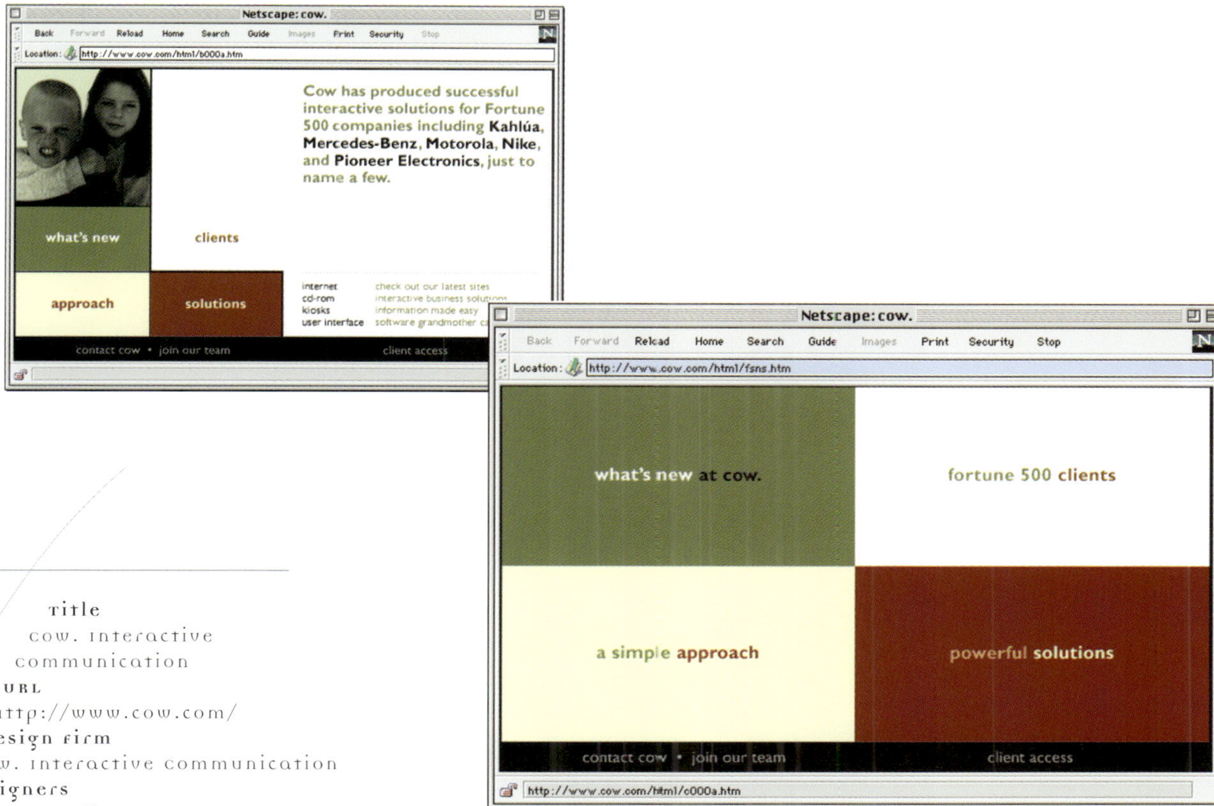

Title
cow. Interactive communication

URL
http://www.cow.com/

Design Firm
cow. Interactive communication

Designers
Bryan Powell, Tex Otto

Programmers
Jonathan Santos, Thierry Benichou

Account Director
Drew Sievers

Creative Directors
Bryan Dorsey, Mateo Neri

Technical Director
Jonathan Santos

Content Manager
Steven Lovy

Backend Engineer
Tammy McKean

Copywriters
Bryan Dorsey, Steven Lovy, Tom Pope, Brian Higa

This just may be the best example of clear, simple, and clever navigation you'll find in this book, a geometric beauty. Sections are organized according to color in a two-by-two grid, with the active section occupying most of the browser window; the grid is tucked into the corner opposite the page's content. So, depending on which page you're on, the navigation shifts among the window's four corners. Supporting details are numbered and appear in the active frame when clicked, or open up a new window.

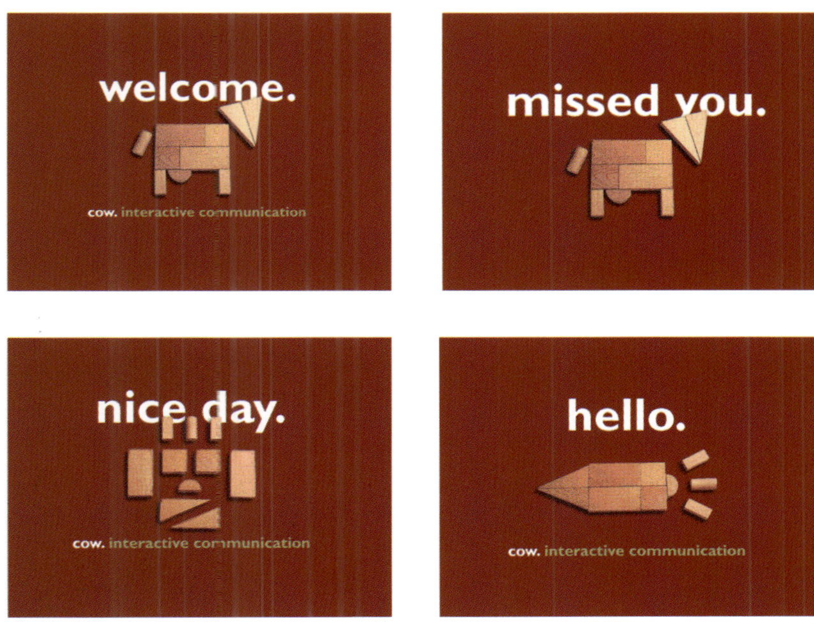

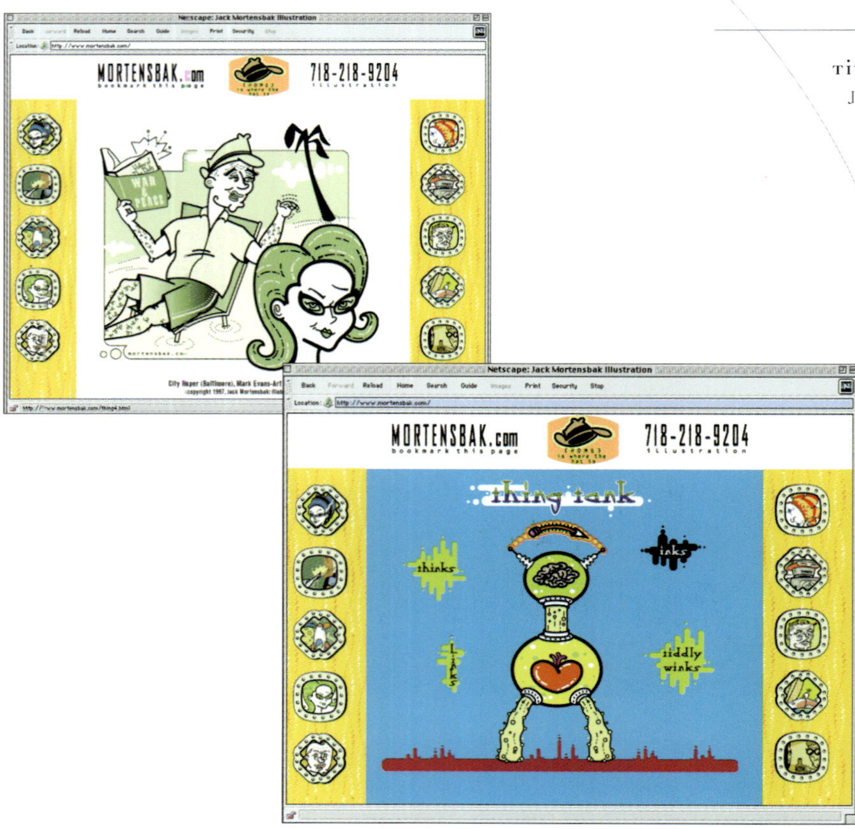

Title
Jack Mortensbak: illoboy!
URL
http://www.mortensbak.com/
Designer/Illustrator
Jack Mortensbak
Programmer
Ben Malloway
Authoring platform
Mac

Although the text on this site is minimal, the few words rendered still manage to accentuate the pages' attitude. Navigational links are set in a cartoonish serif with odd sharp angles, adding to the eccentric feeling created by the artwork.

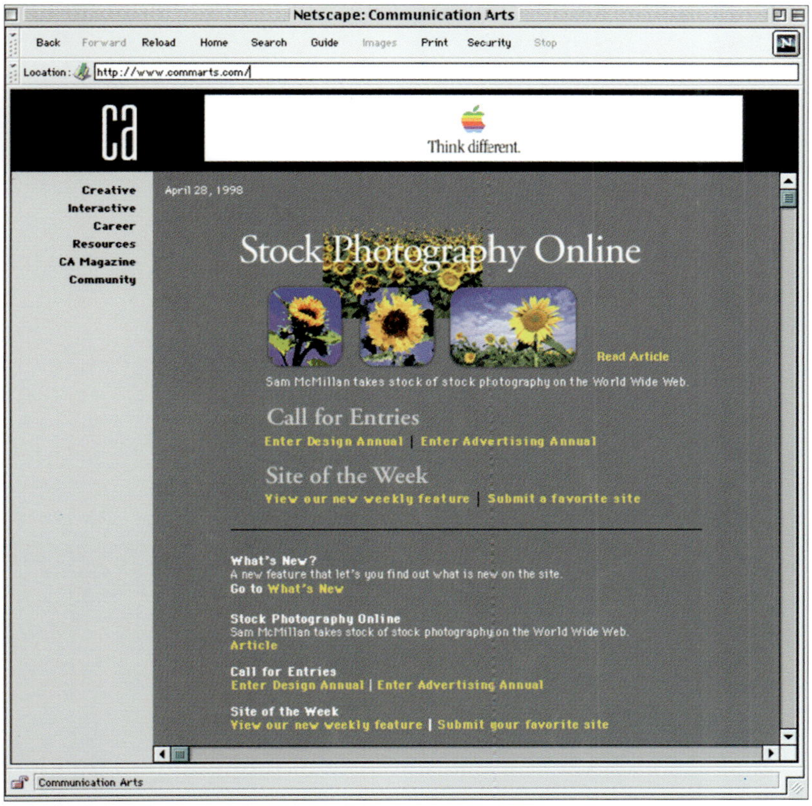

Title
Communication Arts
URL
http://www.commarts.com/
Interactive Media Designer
Bonnie Smetts
Interactive Media Developer
Gary Wium
Technology Director
Jeff Stafford
Stock Photography
PhotoDisc, Inc.
Editors/Creative Directors
Patrick Coyne, Jeff Stafford
Authoring Platform
Mac, PC

At first glance, the type on these pages looks bland and featureless, especially if you are used to viewing text on a computer monitor. Closer inspection reveals a deliberate use of fonts designed for onscreen readability, such as the bold Geneva used for the left-hand navigation (note that the words are rendered as graphics, not HTML-based text, for compatibility among various operating systems).

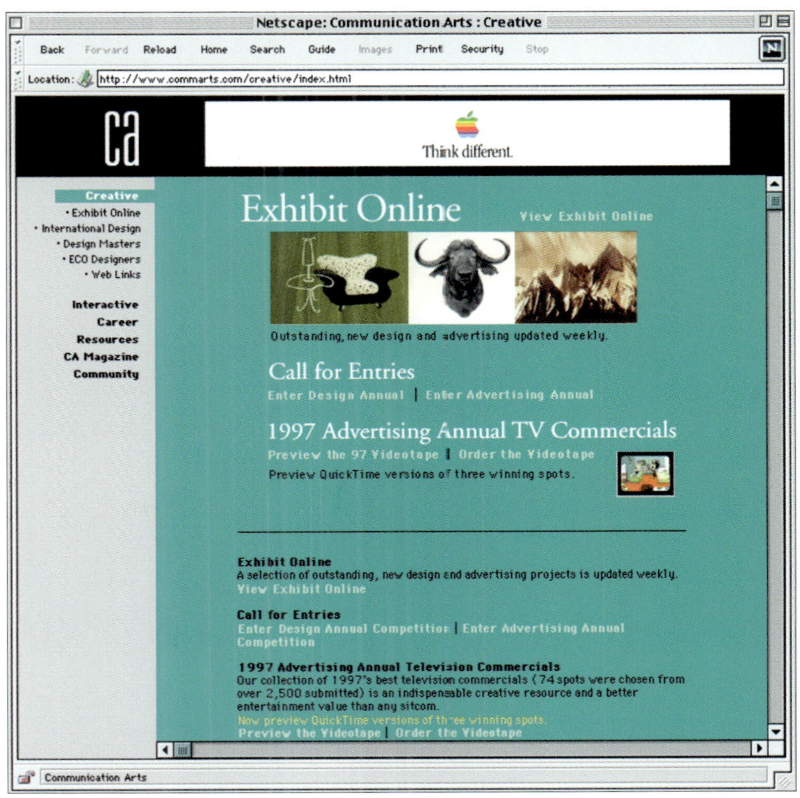

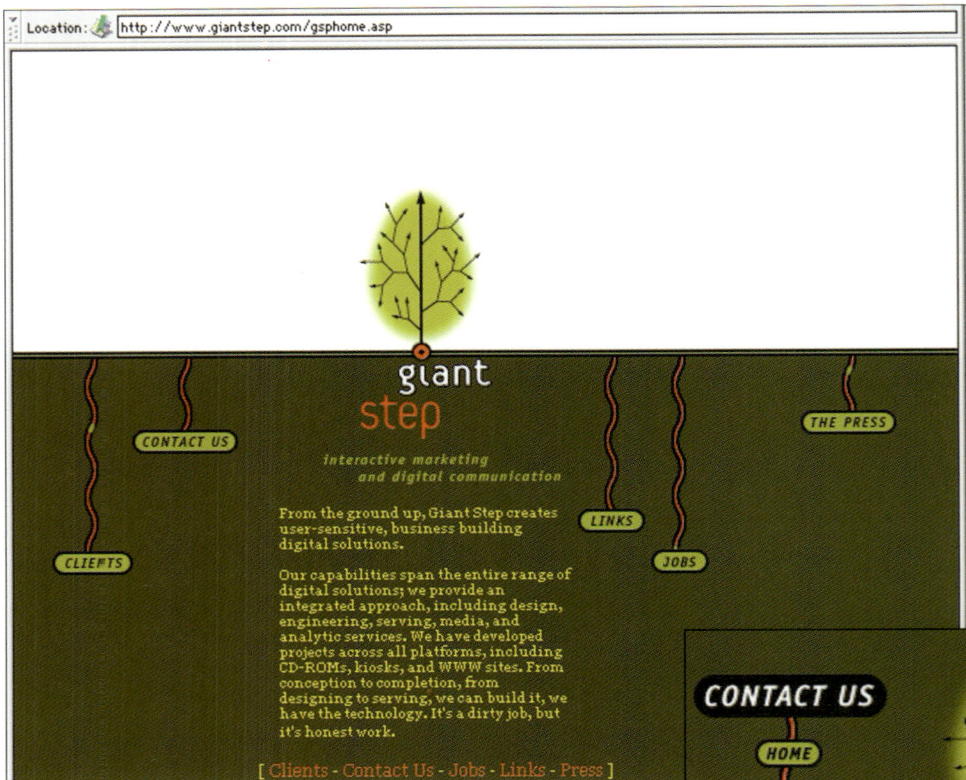

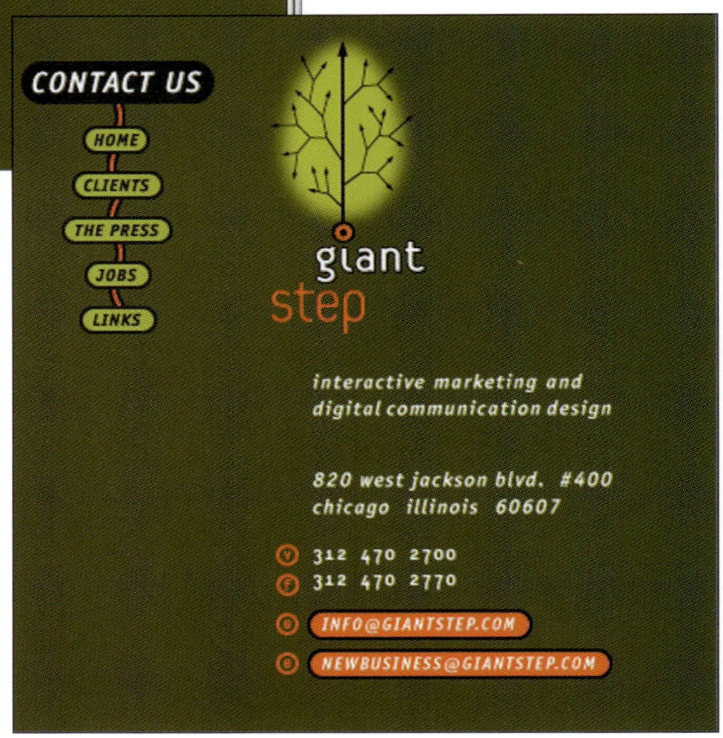

title
giant step
URL
http://www.giantstep.com/gsphome.asp
designers
Xavier Wynn, Sheau Hui Ching, Sean Moran
engineer
Kerry O'Donnell
project managers
Gregory Galloway, Melisa Vazquez

A good typeface can benefit a design, but too often the type just floats on the page or screen. Here, the designers have incorporated the *i* in *giant* to represent the seed of the company's growing-tree logo. Note also that *giant* isn't very giant at all, though its size and placement suggest larger things for the future.

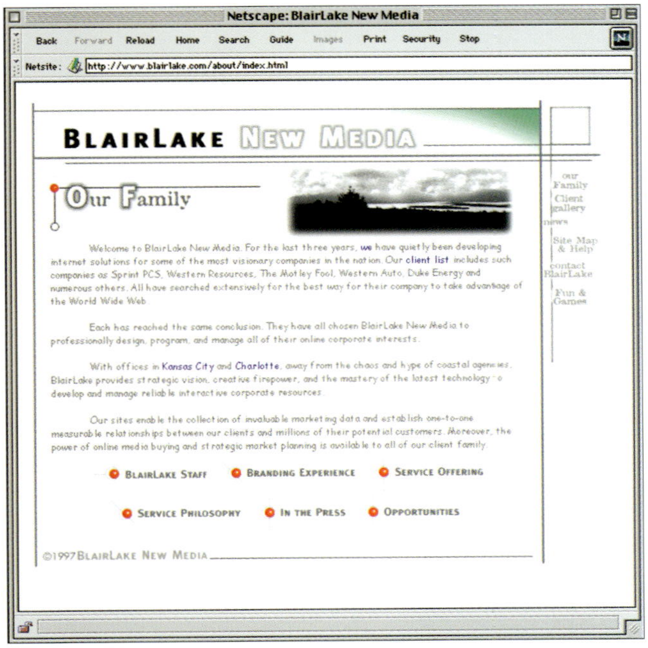

Title
BlairLake New Media

URL
http://www.blairlake.com/features/index.html

Design firm
BlairLake New Media

Designer
Jeremy Walla

Programmer
Ken Wilson

Authoring platform
Mac

Although many design firms like to think of themselves as families, the BlairLake site tries to extend the concept of a small, friendly design house throughout their site. One method of reinforcing that idea is by using the Web-friendly font Comic Sans for body text; while remaining legible, it also carries a slightly informal attitude with it.

Navigation

Developments in browsers and Web-publishing tools notwithstanding, the one constant in most Web sites appears to be the colored navigation bar running down the left side of the page.

We set out with this book to unshackle ourselves from this standard by finding examples of sites that were both richly navigable and (as often as possible) used other techniques to lead the user through the site. There's nothing wrong with the left-side, colored navigation bar per se, but with countless pages to look at already—starting with c|net's mustard yellow—we thought we'd break with this new "tradition."

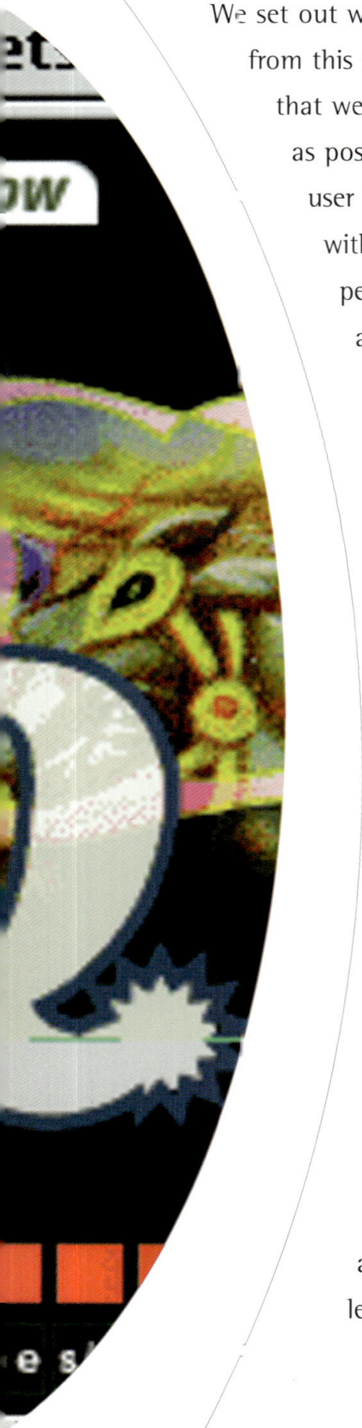

The left-side navigation bar became a feature of the Web landscape because of the idea that every page should, by its nature, lead you to every other page on a site. It's a common desire on the part of marketing folks who want to make sure that the valuable investment made in the Web site isn't lost on the user.

But most designers featured in this book have chosen a different tack, using context to provide navigational aids. In some cases, sites are deliberately unnavigable—but it's still useful to learn from these positive examples of contrary design. Some of the most obscurely engineered sites, like Eye Candy and Funny Garbage, are incredibly compelling—much more so than expensive commercial sites where you would rarely venture deeper than the home page.

What might seem contradictory, however, is that many of our favorite sites include excellent site maps, a number of which you'll find here. Good site design should make navigation seem self-evident. However, assuming the principle that every page doesn't necessarily lead you to every other, a site map can, in the best cases we present here, short-circuit the clicking process, propelling you in a hyperspace leap from deep in one part of the site, through the site map, to the depths of a different level.

This is thinking both inside and outside of the box: the structure is still hierarchical and navigable through navigation bars, text links, or other elements (inside the box), but the site map jumps you into a super-observer position (outside the box) where you can decide exactly where you want to go today.

Navigation is not just a set of links: it is a way of thinking about and structuring a site so that information, illustrations, or documents always feel like they are within reach, not buried far away or impossible to find. Even when you may have to click four or five times, a good design keeps you interested while you're navigating, and keeps the prize (the page you're trying to get to) within your grasp.

"Most designers featured in this book have chosen a different tack, using context to provide navigational aids. In some cases, sites are deliberately unnavigable—but it's still useful to learn from these positive examples of contrary design."

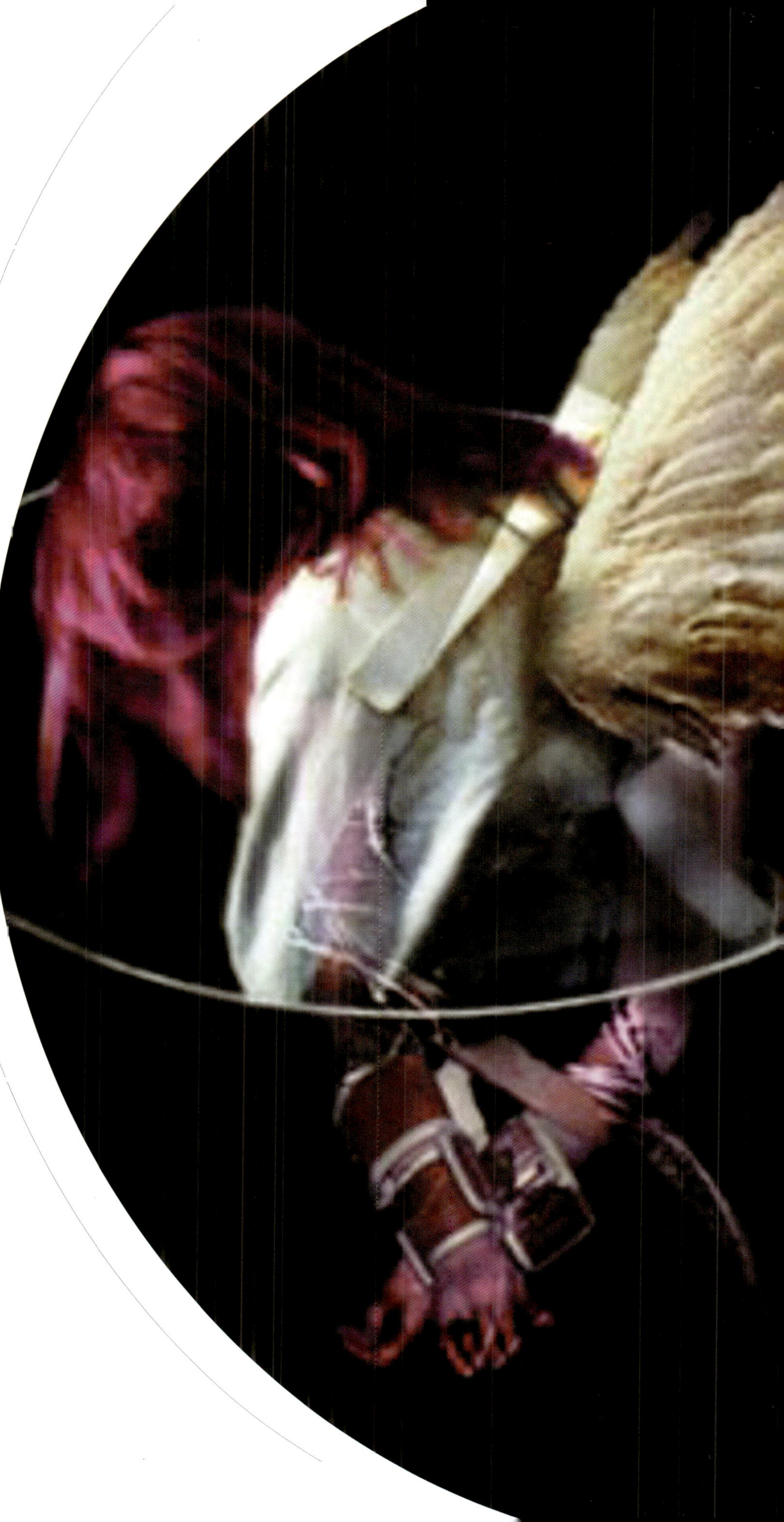

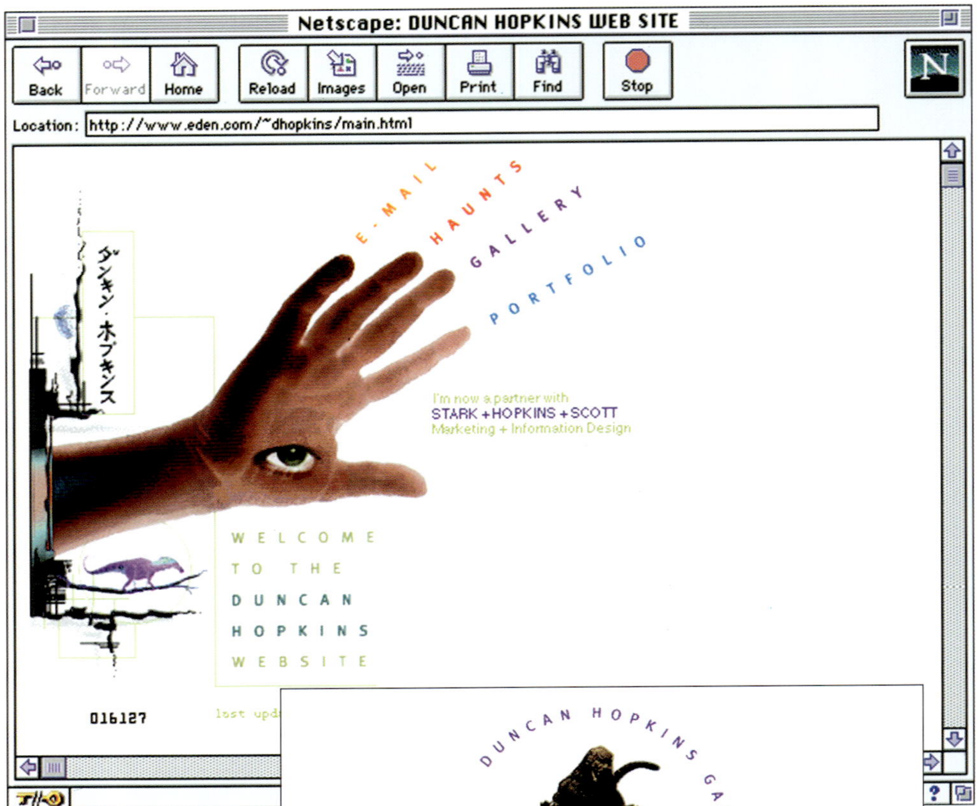

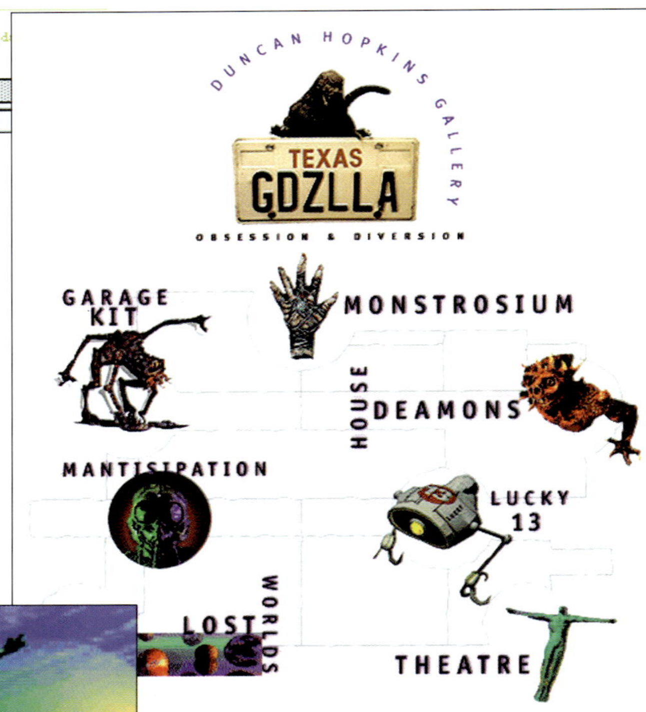

Title
Duncan Hopkins web site and gallery
URL
http://www.syndeticdesign.com/dhopkins/main.html
Design firm
Syndetic Design
Designer
Duncan Hopkins

Around the world, the best method for getting and receiving directions is by pointing. Duncan Hopkin's is outstretched hand of links takes that familiar gesture and uses it as a clean, slightly skewed way of pointing to the inside of his site. You'll notice, however, that on subsequent pages he uses whichever navigation method is most appropriate (or clever) for each section.

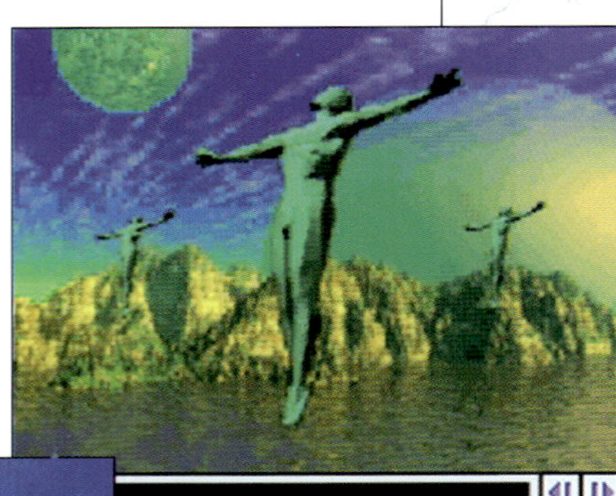

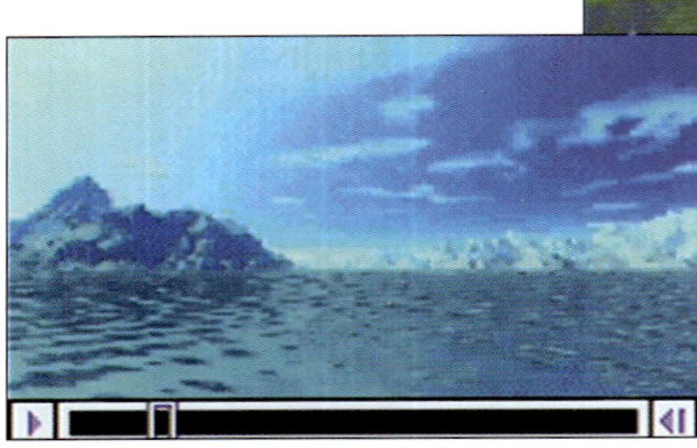

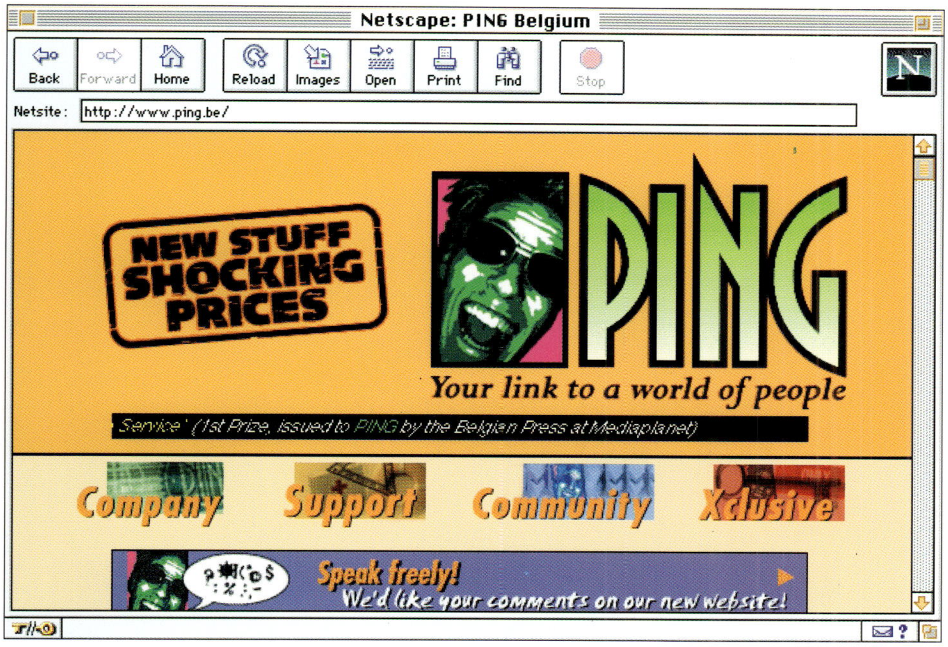

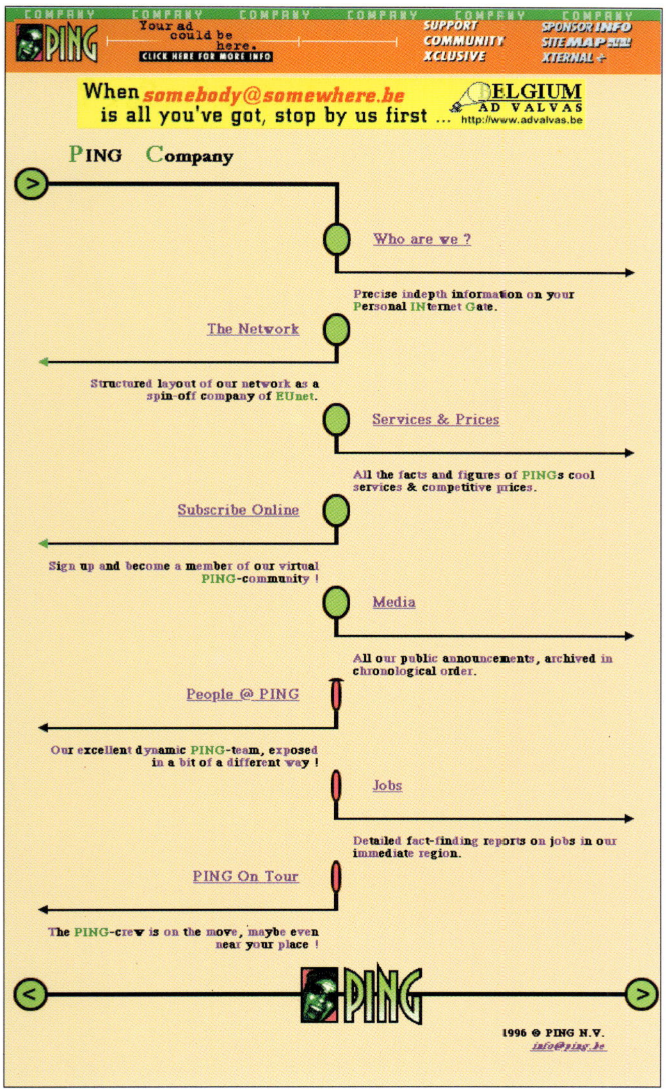

Title
PING Belgium
URL
http://www.ping.be/
design firm
PING Belgium
designers
Dirk Zurngenter, Peter Van Hees, Bernard Gillbrecht
illustrator
Bart De Neve
photographer
Peter Van Hees
programmers
Mark Van Hemme, Peter Van Hees, Marchteet Garrels

One of the main difficulties in site navigation is expressing many directions in a compressed, easy-to-understand format. The designers at Ping chose to use frames to build trees of subdirectories that are always on screen; going back a level does not require reloading and redrawing a page.

Title
beyondexpress.com
URL
http://www.beyondexpress.com/index.html
Design firm
pageworks
Designer/Illustrator/Programmer
Kip Shaw
Photographer
Chris Jones
Authoring platform
Mac

Beyondexpress.com shows one of the best examples of a good left-side navigation bar. The items are organized with little hierarchy and differentiation, but serve two different purposes: the top half takes you to subsections; the bottom half lists downloads. On subsidiary pages, a clever iconography takes you home, to the top of the page, to the previous page, or lets you leave a comment. Text labels are added to icons in the first occurrence at the top, but the icons (and their purpose) are repeated for the depth of the page.

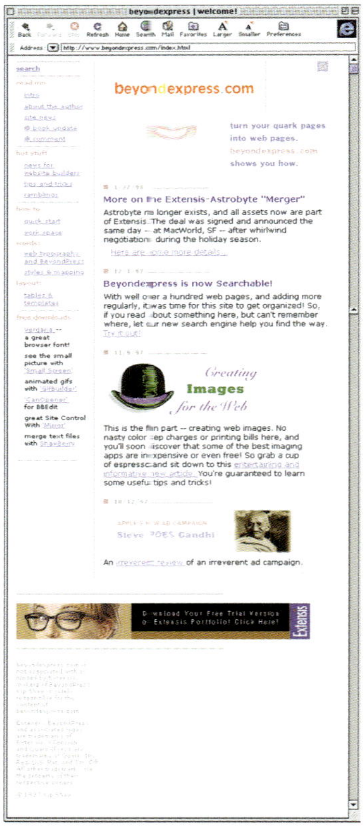

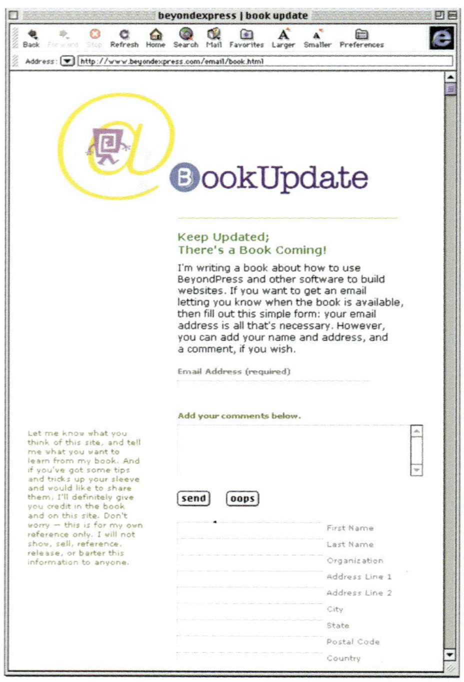

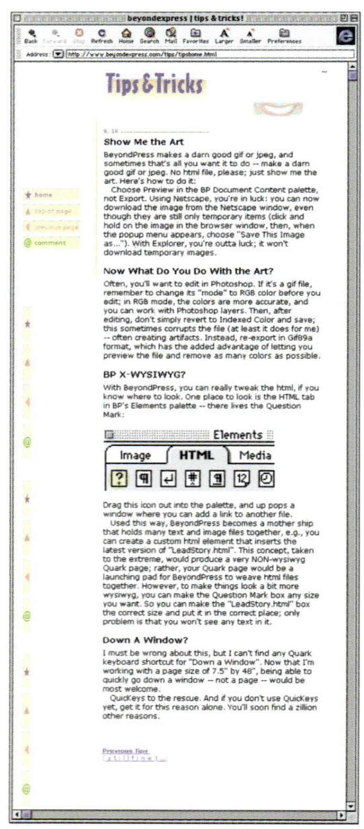

Title
Internet Underground Music Archive
URL
http://www.iuma.com/
Designers
Brandee Selck, David Beach
Programmer
Jeff Patterson

Although it can be tempting to devise new and intricate navigation methods, sometimes you just need a few links to do the trick. To spice things up a bit, the IUMA designers chose to create a number of different button bars that reflect the character of a particular page's content. Changing the look is easy—if you use the same file names for the new images, you may not have to adjust each page's HTML code.

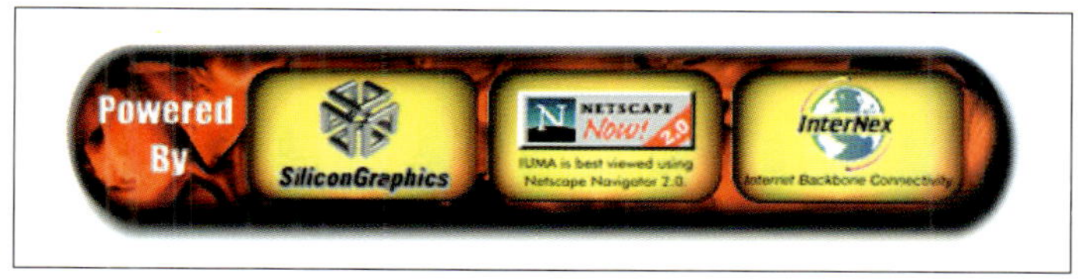

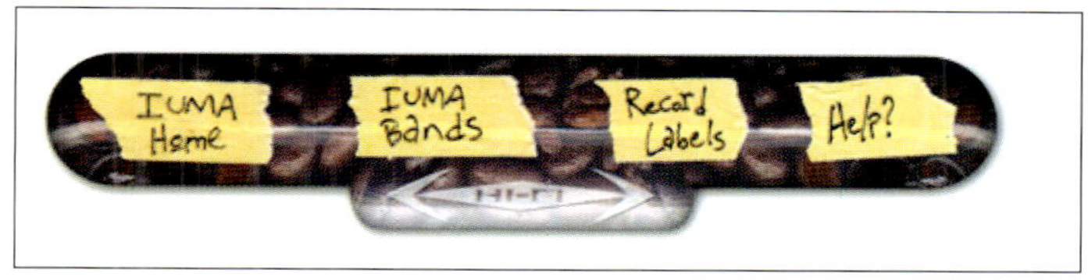

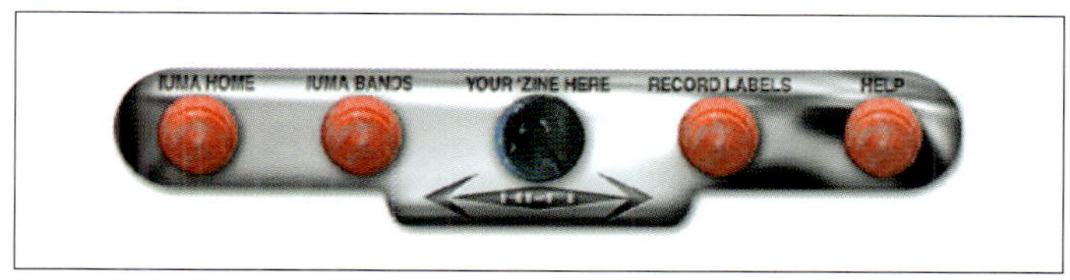

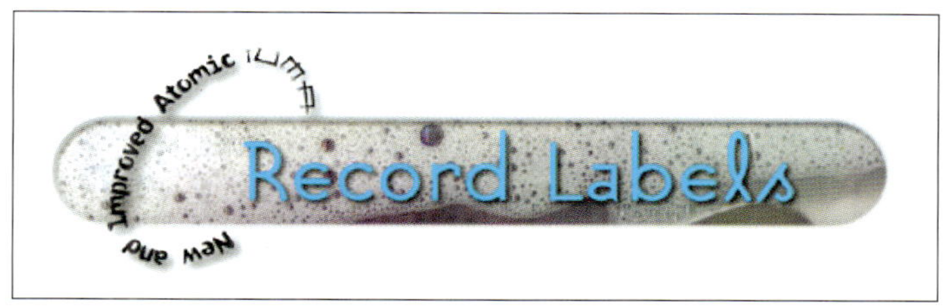

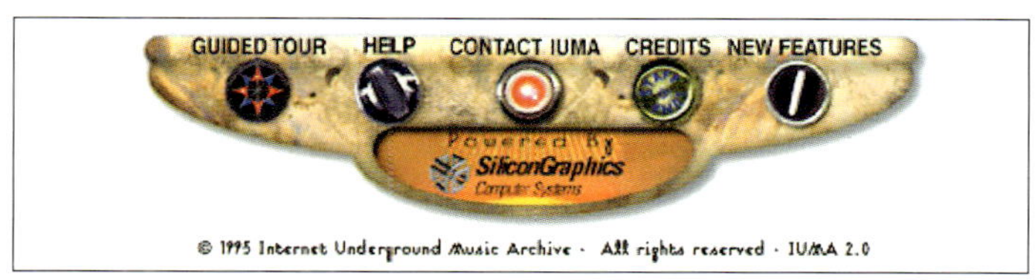

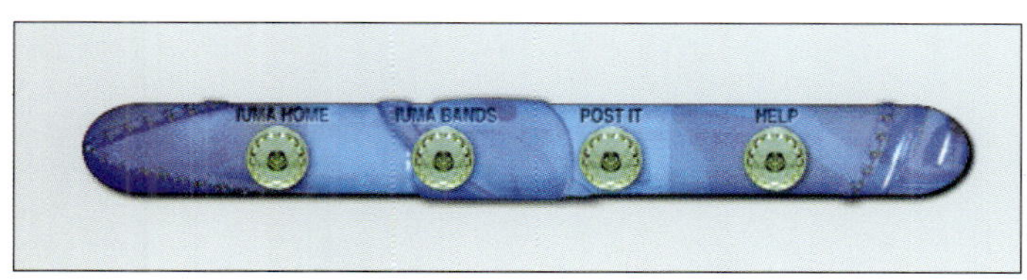

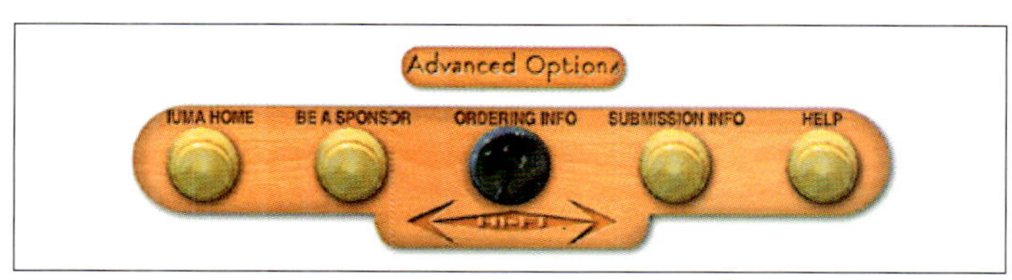

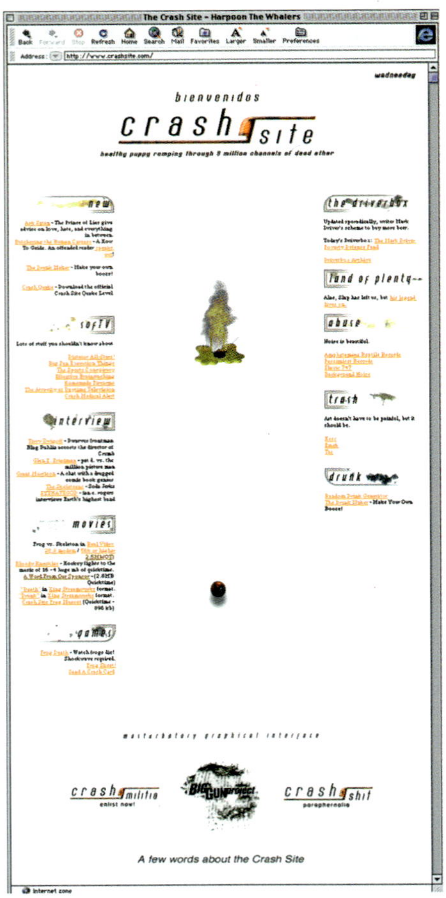

Title
crash site
URL
http://www.crashsite.com/
Design firm
rvision/Big gun project
Designers
Jim Evans, Gibran Evans
Illustrator
Gibran Evans
Programmers
Ian Rogers, Mark Thompson
Authoring platform
Mac

Crash site somehow makes effective use of flush-right type, a long page, small type, and lots of white space—kind of a tour de force of items that designers are usually encouraged to avoid. But the simple text links divided into categories explain enough about every section and subsection to avoid deep linking. The page, though deep, loads fast because of the focus on text.

Title
core77
URL
http://www.core77.com/
Designers
Eric Ludlum,
Stuart Constantine

Sometimes it's hard enough dealing with one tree of links, but what about when you have two or more? The Core77 site covers industrial-design issues, but also provides resources such as articles, employment resources, and more. The solution for tackling it all was this combination of circular and hierarchical navigation systems.

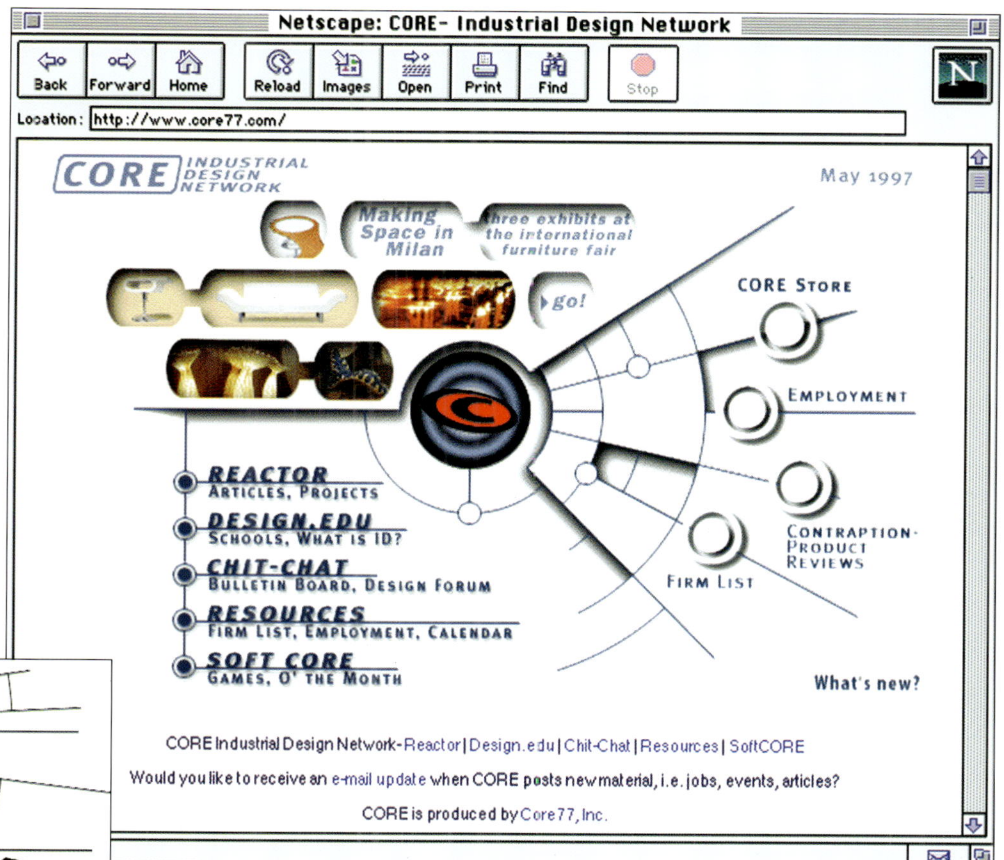

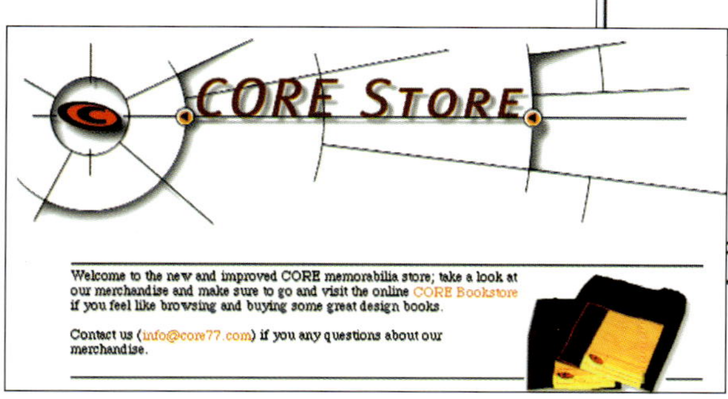

Title
AIGA (American Institute of Graphic Arts)
URL
http://www.aiga.org/
Design Firm
Graffito/Active8
Designers
Tim Thompson, Jon Majerik
Photographer
Morton Jackson
Programmer
Jon Majerik

You do not have to rely on just one navigation method. Without hogging precious screen real estate, this site uses both circular and block navigation to quickly point visitors deep into the site. The slanted elliptical grouping to the right leads to main categories, while the blocked-out subsection titles are displayed to the left.

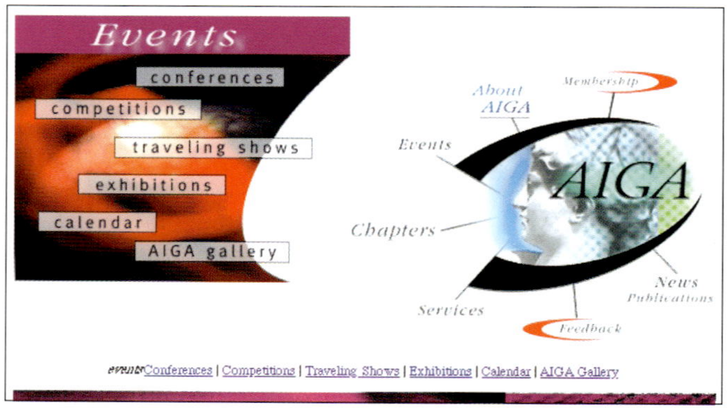

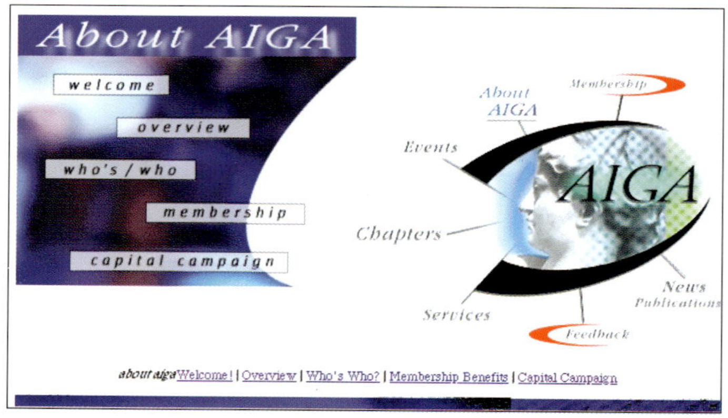

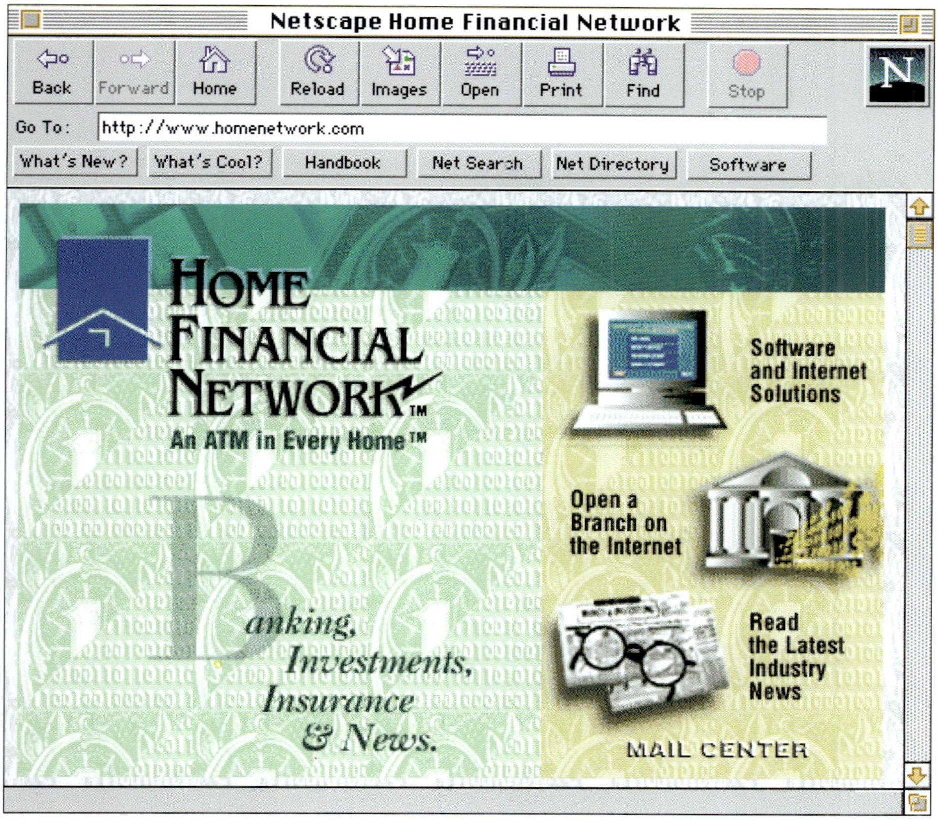

Title
Home Financial Network
URL
http://www.homenetwork.com/
Design Firm
The Design Office Inc.
Designers
Yung Beck, Dave Green, Andrea Flamini, Joe Feigenbaum
Programmer
Andrea Flamini

Although this site primarily uses money-related icons to denote features and sections, the beauty of its navigation lies in its consistent use of repeating visual elements. All pages include the top bar that varies only in color, retaining its image and placement.

Title
Bau-Da Design Lab, Inc.
URL
http://www.bauda.com/
Design Firm
Bau-Da Design Lab, Inc.
Programmers
Eric Brown/Readynetgo
Authoring platform
HTML, Javascript

Why be content with just one set of navigation elements on a given Web page? As you can see here, the site's main page opens with the square buttons on the left, as well as the grayed-out corresponding numbers above. JavaScript rollover effects help to give the reader a sense of where they are in the site.

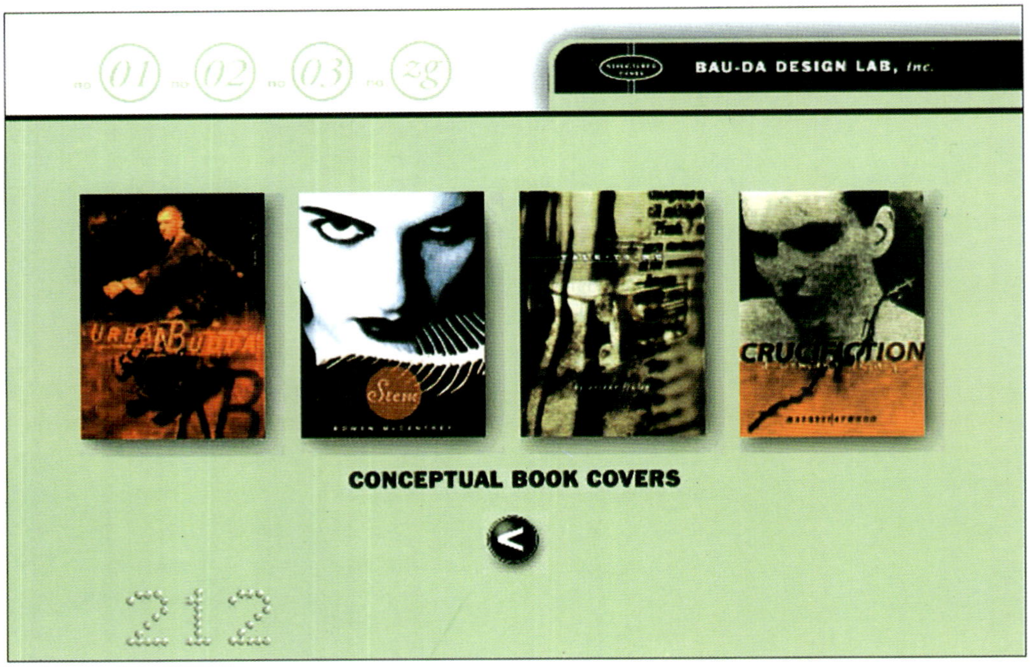

Title
frank ford
URL
http://www.frank-ford.com/
Designer
frank ford

Web design may be a cutting-edge field, but its two-dimensional medium limits it to something one still can't touch. As if reaching out to the viewer, the hand-shaped navigation (and the similarly-shaped portfolio-page graphic resembling a wind-blown inkblot) offers clear navigation using a form familiar to any viewer.

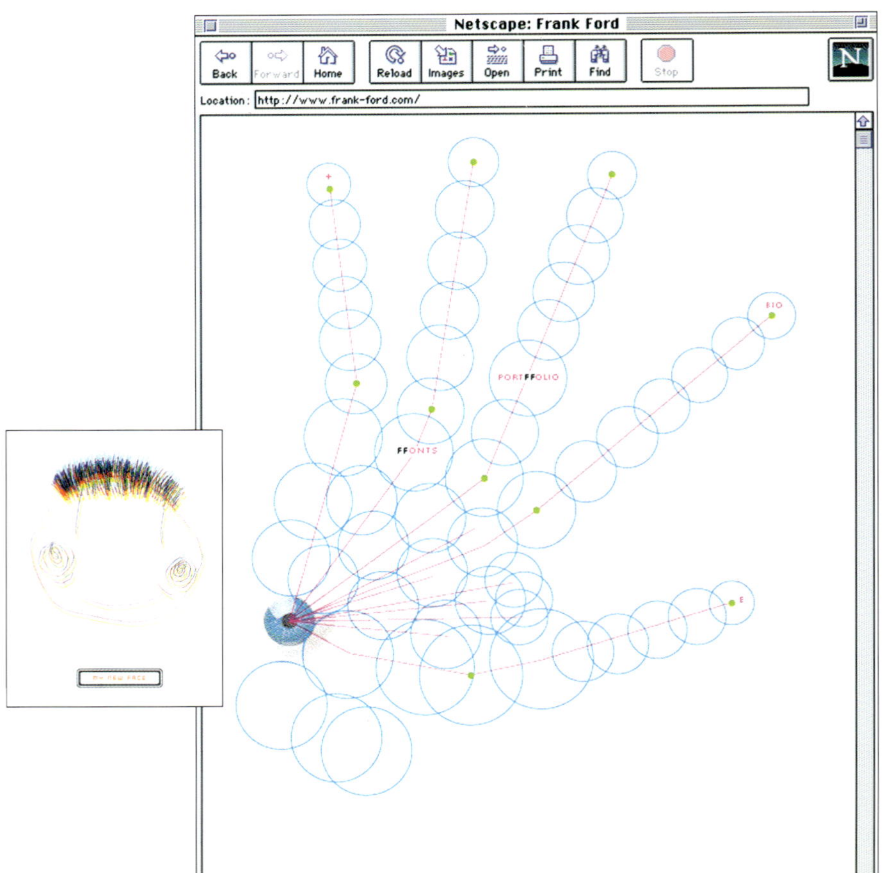

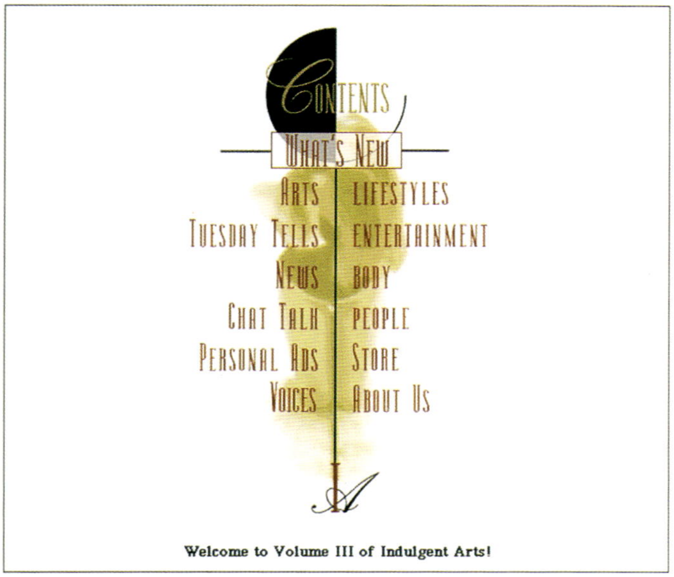

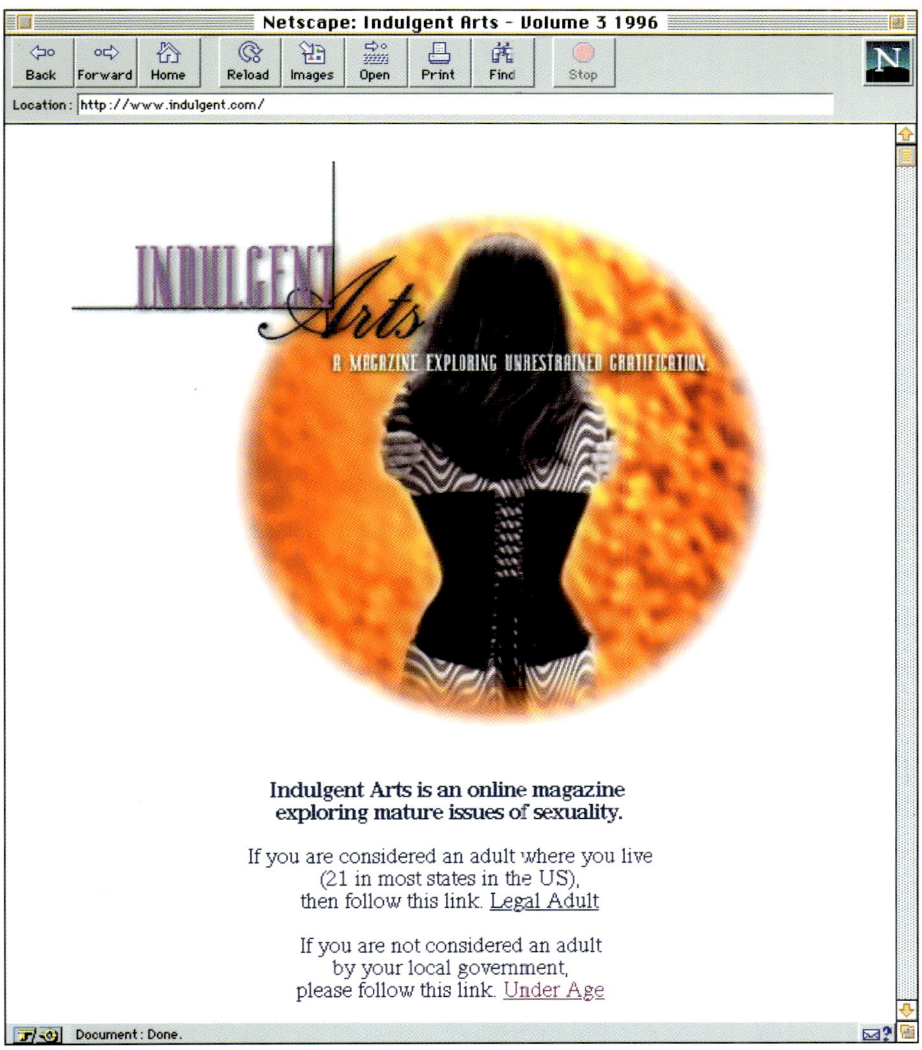

Title
Indulgent Arts Magazine
URL
http://www.indulgent.com/
Design Firm
C.A.P.
Designer/Illustrator
Rhonda Anton
Photographer/Programmer
Craig Bramscher

Even without the provocative cover image of a woman's back, the contents page for Indulgent Arts suggests a view of a person's back, with links running up and down the spine. Access to all main areas of the site is expressed in a conservative amount of space, which leaves room for content and breathing room.

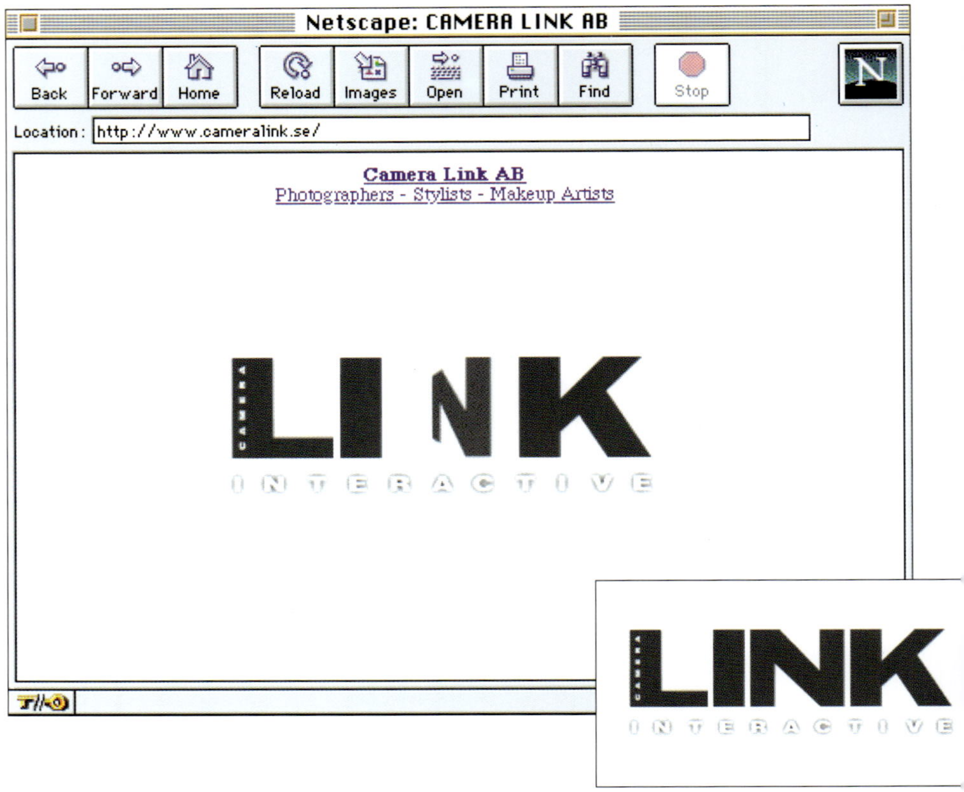

Title
camera link AB
URL
http://www.cameralink.se/
design firm
Robot
designer
Raket/Robot
programmer
Jesper Weissglas

Providing direction to a Web site does not mean that you have to give people "dumb" buttons and still pictures. Real people ask questions and offer advice, which the designers here have emulated.

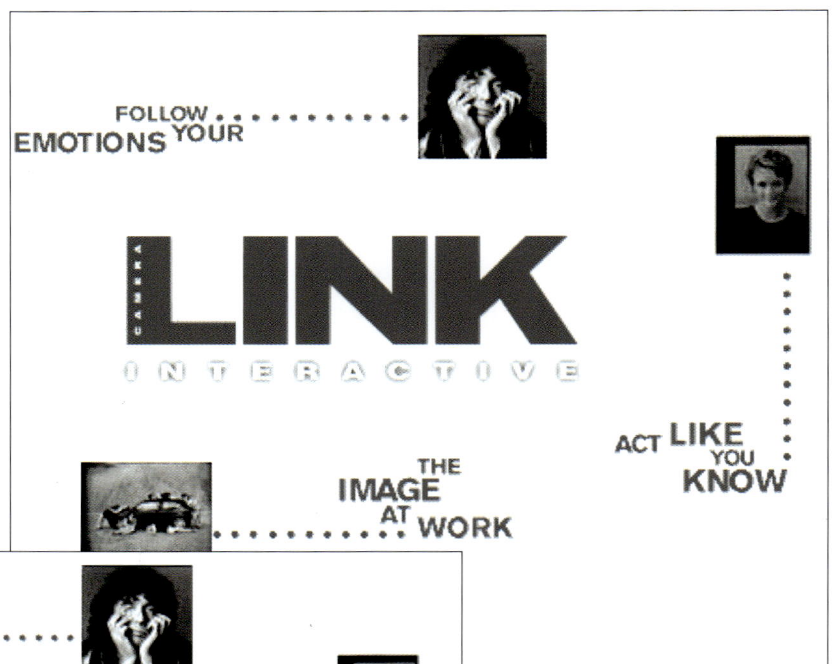

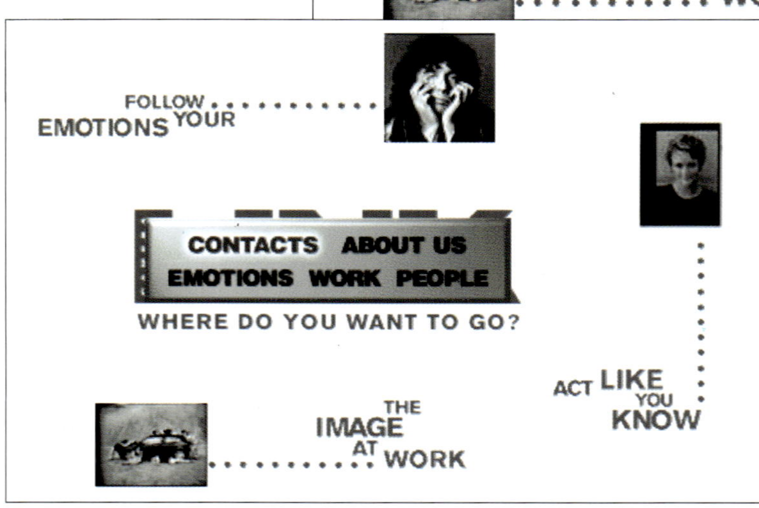

Title
Radio Real World
URL
http://realworld.on.net/
Design Firm
Real World Multimedia
Designer/Illustrator/
Photographer/Programmer
York Tillyer
Authoring Platform
Mac

Good navigation often means that the viewer must always know where she's headed before committing to a direction. This approach, however, takes away a lot of the fun of exploration. On this site's home page, you're presented only with colored bands (for the text-inclined, positioning one's cursor over a color displays the link's destination at the bottom of the browser window). Consistent use of color quickly makes an initially enigmatic navigation system understandable and familiar.

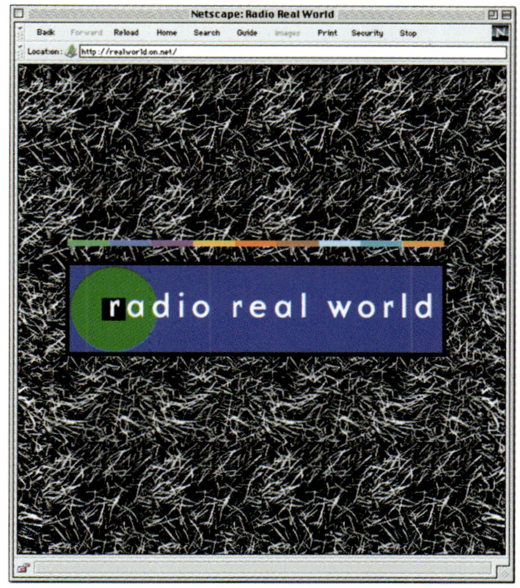

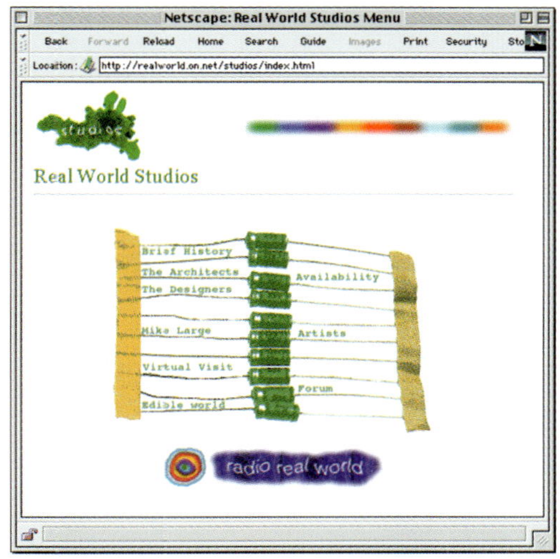

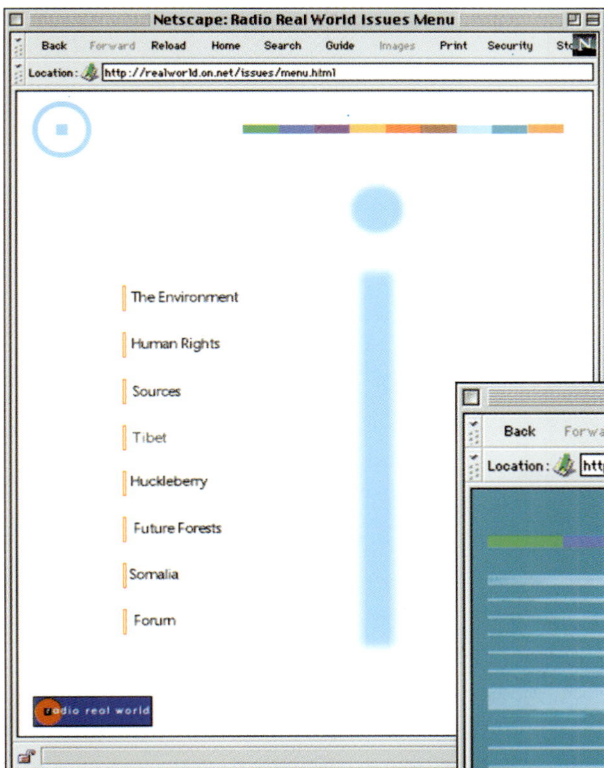

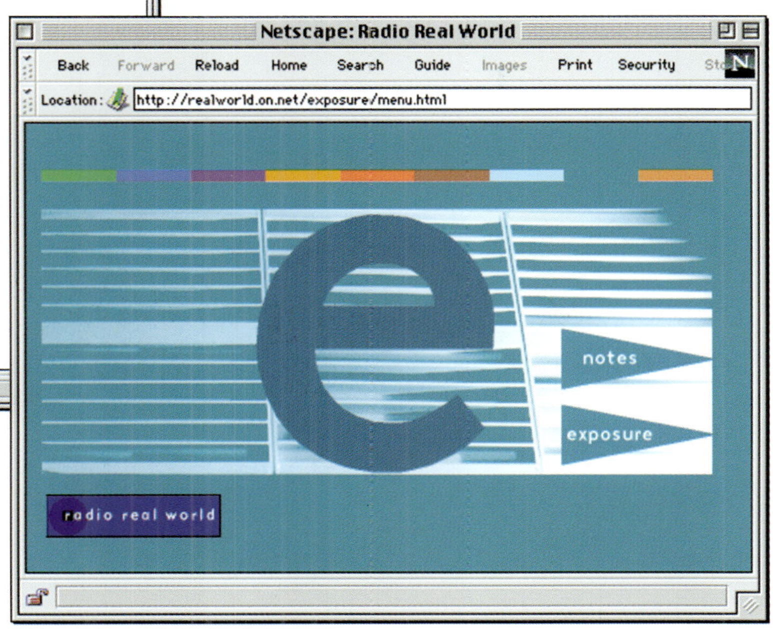

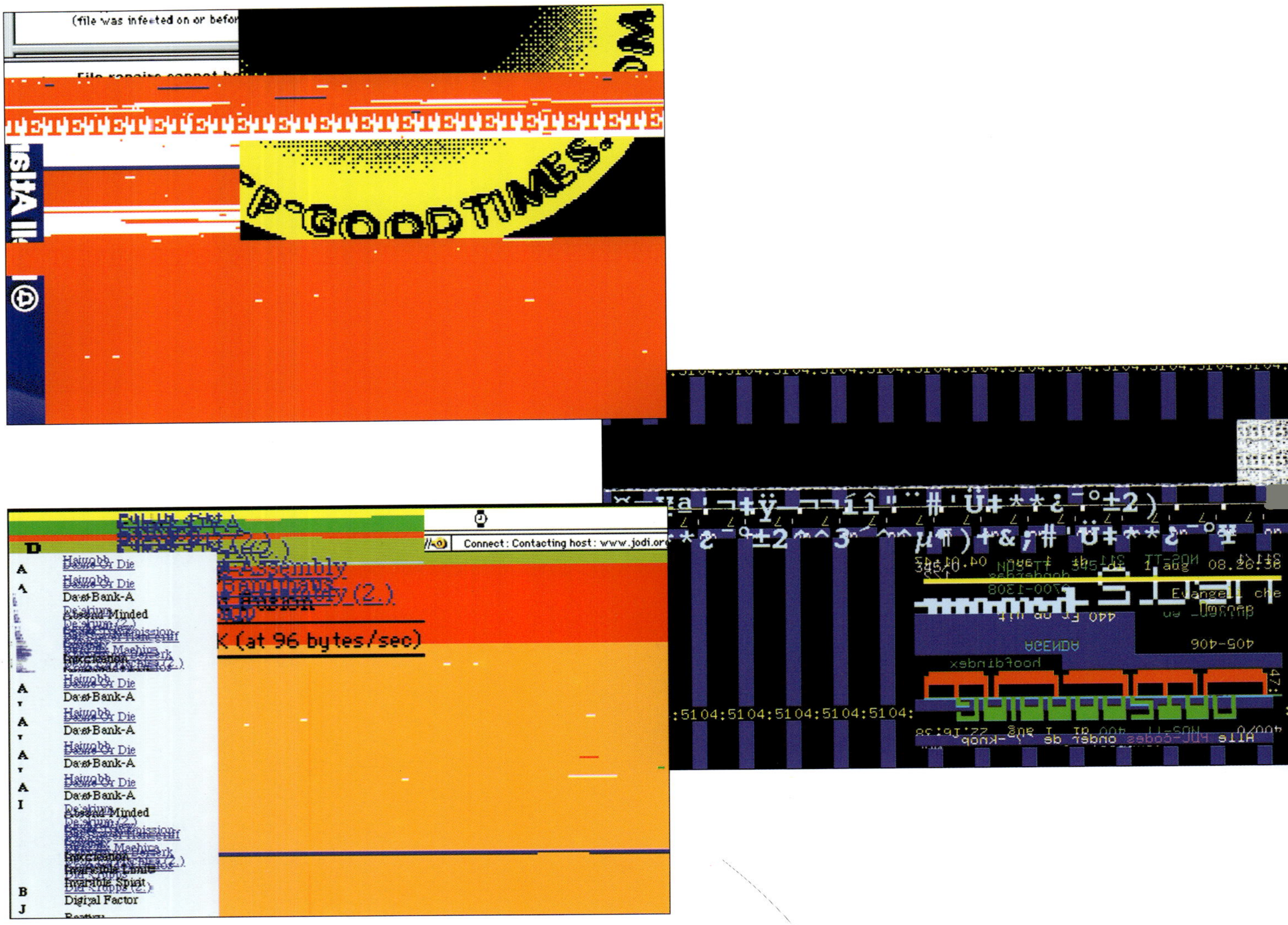

Title
Jodi.org
URL
http://www.jodi.org/
Designers
Joan Heemskerk, Dirk Paesmans

There are times when a visitor wants to stumble onto a new site, then explore it for all it's worth. Then there is Jodi.org, a Web site that seems to throw all the rules about site navigation out the window. Clicking on links (or random URLs) takes you to another aspect of the simulated machine that appears on screen.

title

Nerve° Magazine

URL

http://www.nervemag.com/

designer/illustrator/programmer

joey cavella

photographer

walt chrynwski

authoring platform

mac

Navigation depends on direction, and to establish direction, you need to create a sense of place. The opening page of Nerve° presents a cluttered living room whose objects lead to other parts of the site. What's unique here, though, is the drop-down highlights window shade, which obscures the setting with some context, instead of a list of links off to one side. The animated dangling pull-cord just begs to be clicked.

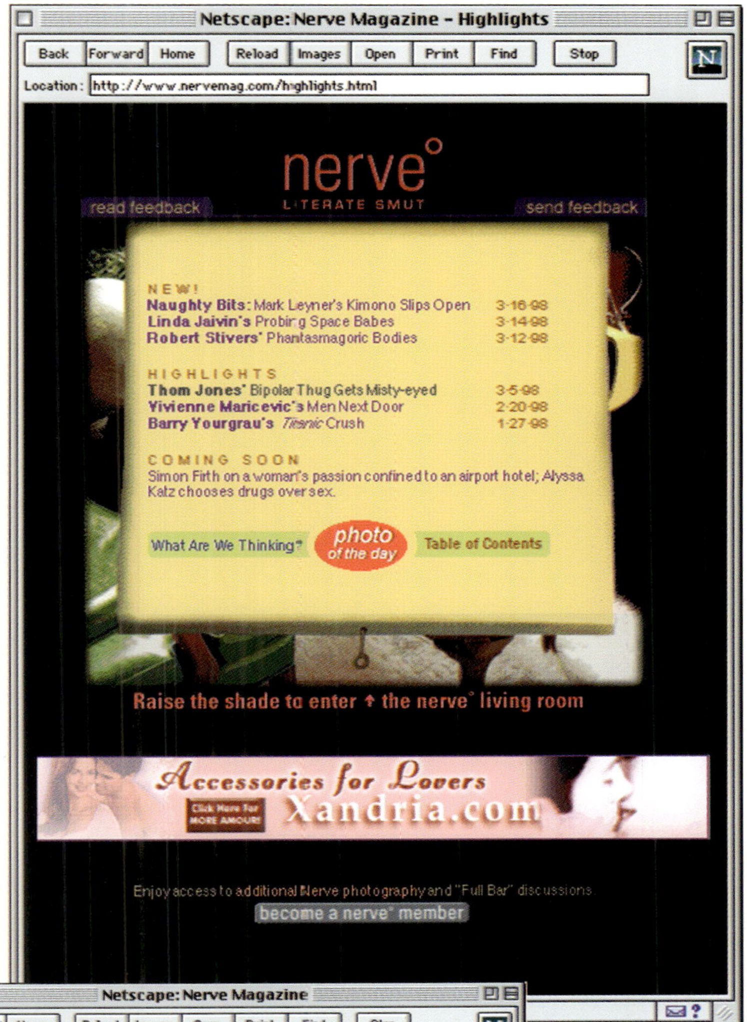

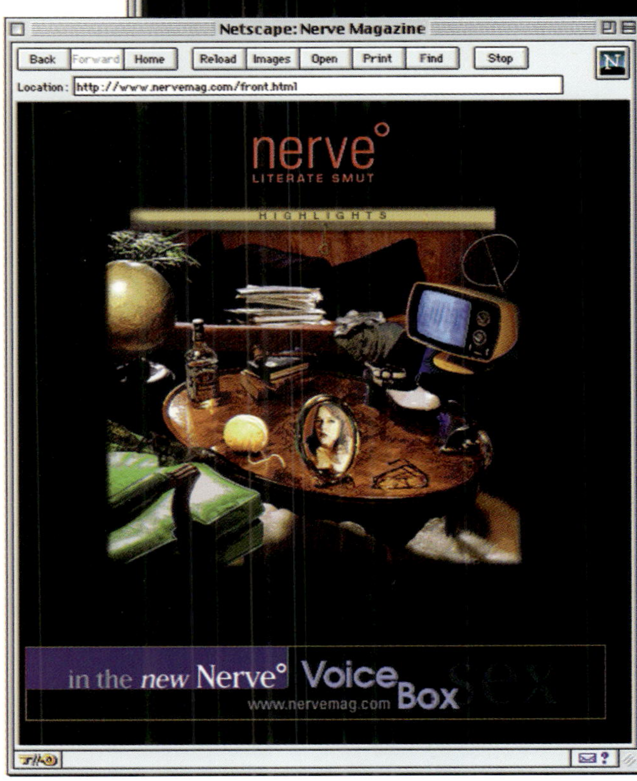

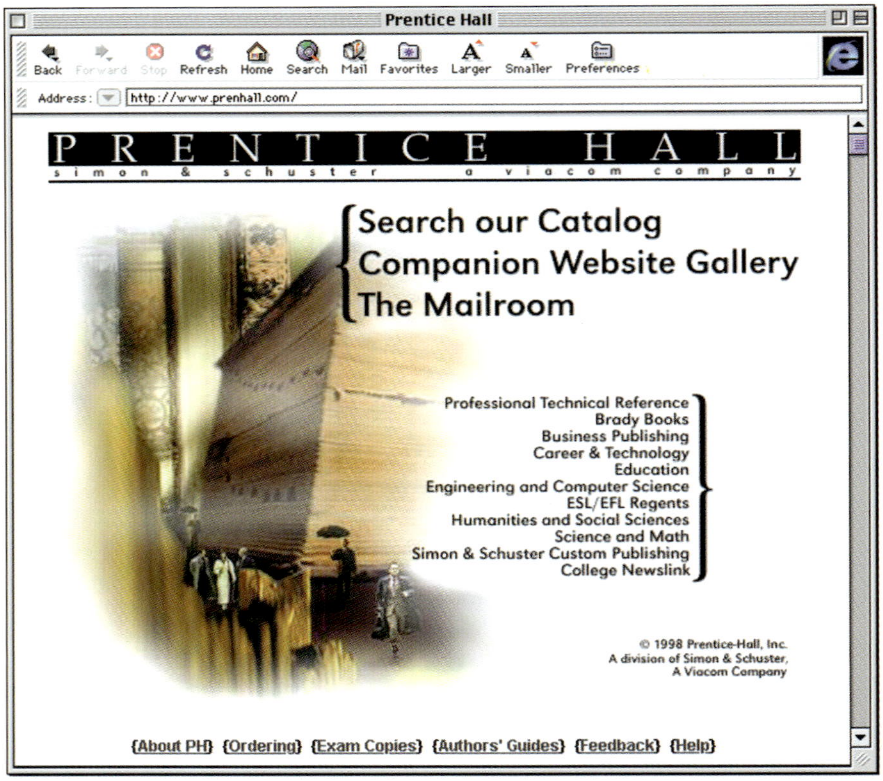

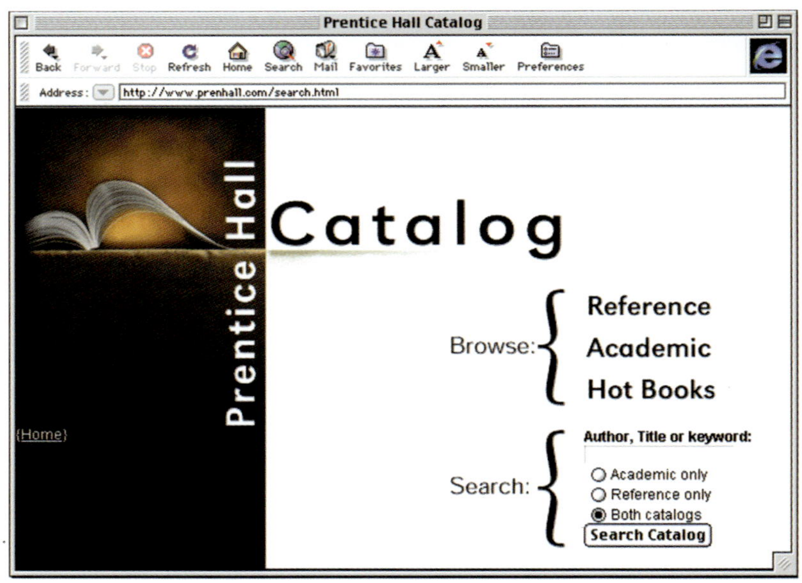

Title
Prentice Hall Higher Education website
URL
http://www.prenhall.com/
Design Firm
Media Technology Group, Simon & Schuster Higher Education
Designers
Ray Henderson, Daniel Beck
Illustrators
Daniel Beck, Carolyn Wagner
Programmers
Daniel Beck, Paul Pekar, Carolyn Wagner
Authoring Platform
Mac, Unix, PC

Braces are used as an organizing principle for items in the same category in this site. It helps these items hang together without requiring colors or other visual cues. Larger categories are placed higher on the page and in a larger type size, but it's surprisingly effective to stick a big brace to the left or right as a method of defining categories. This theme is picked up by using braces in text on the bottom navigation bar.

Title
Entropy8
URL
http://www.entropy8.com/
Design Firm
Entropy8 Digital Arts
Designer
Auriea Harvey
Programmers
Auriea Harvey, Marc Antony Vose
Authoring Platform
Mac, PC

With such a graphics-intensive site as this one, screen real estate is a valuable commodity. To provide navigation without distraction, a separate floating window pops up containing gateways to the rest of the site.

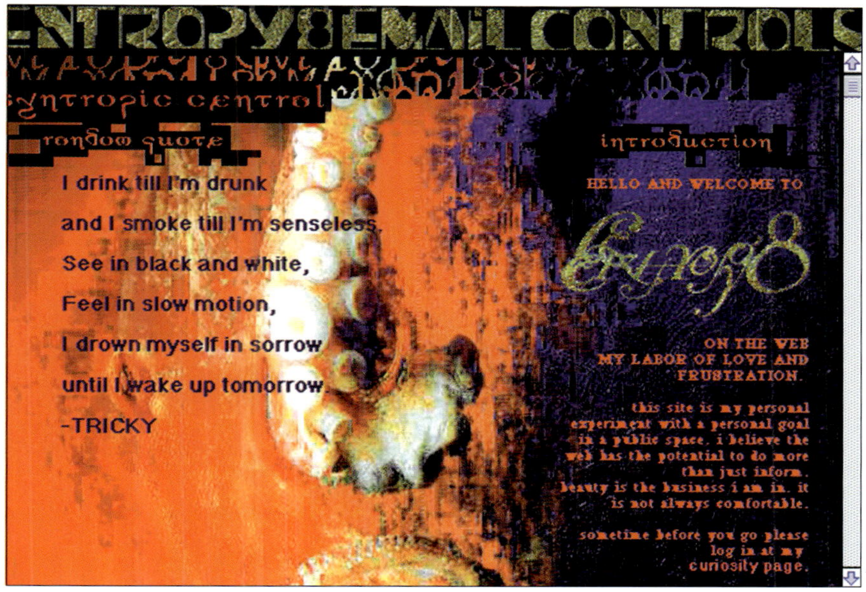

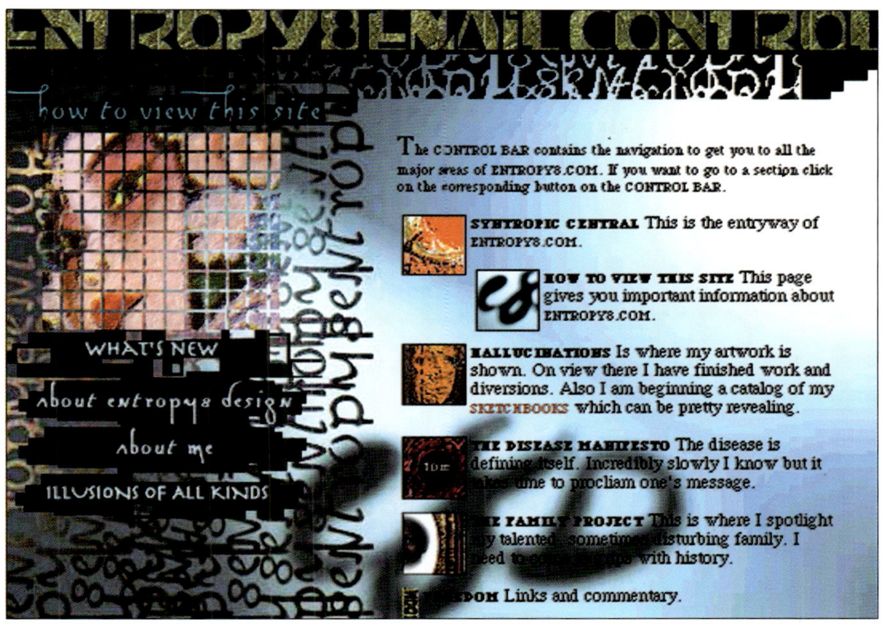

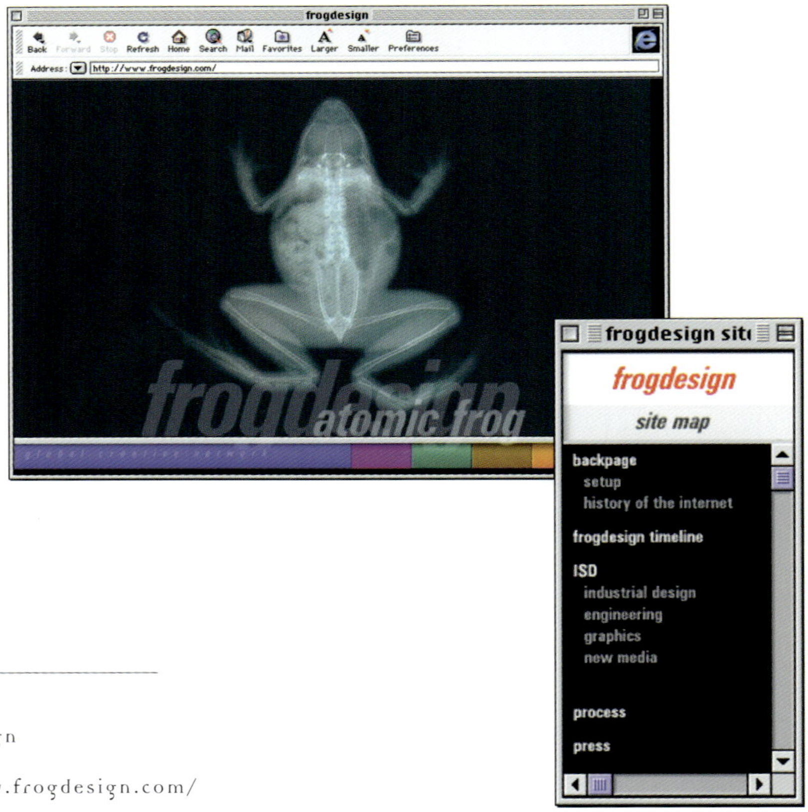

Title
frogdesign
URL
http://www.frogdesign.com/
Design firm
frogdesign
Designer/Illustrator/Programmer
frogdesign team
Authoring platform
Mac, PC

frogdesign pulls out the stops with a scrolling Shockwave presentation showing the history of the firm. A small slider at the top allows you to zoom back and forth across the years; dragging on it moves it at a variable speed. The site is built like a machine, as the company designs industrial products, like the Macintosh. Dragging the mouse over the buttons at lower right swaps in images that light up, like plastic lit from the inside. A pop-up window provides a map of the main areas of the site.

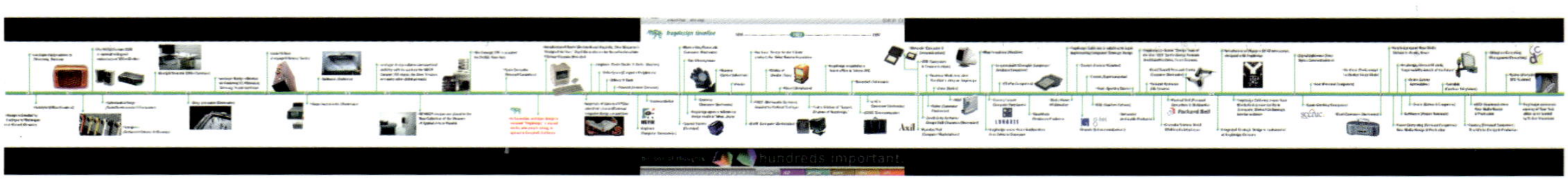

Title
Artseensoho
URL
http://www.artseensoho.com/
Designer/Illustrator
Tim Trompeter
Photographers
Peter Cunningham, Tim Trompeter
Authoring Platform
Mac

The site is geographically centered, and each map page is as long as the street or section of it. Crosstown blocks, not very long when you get to Soho, take up pages by themselves, but downtown blocks run as deep as they need to. Clicking on directional text, like "Turn West on Prince St." takes you to the appropriate page.

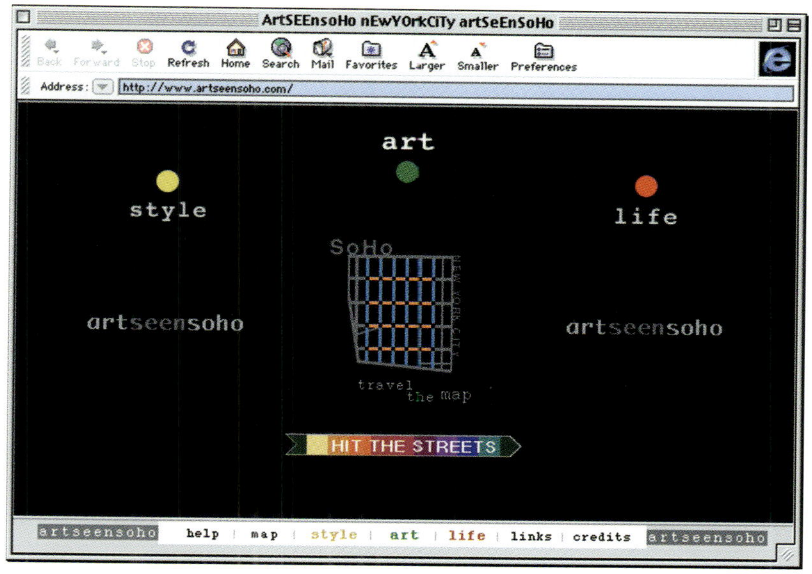

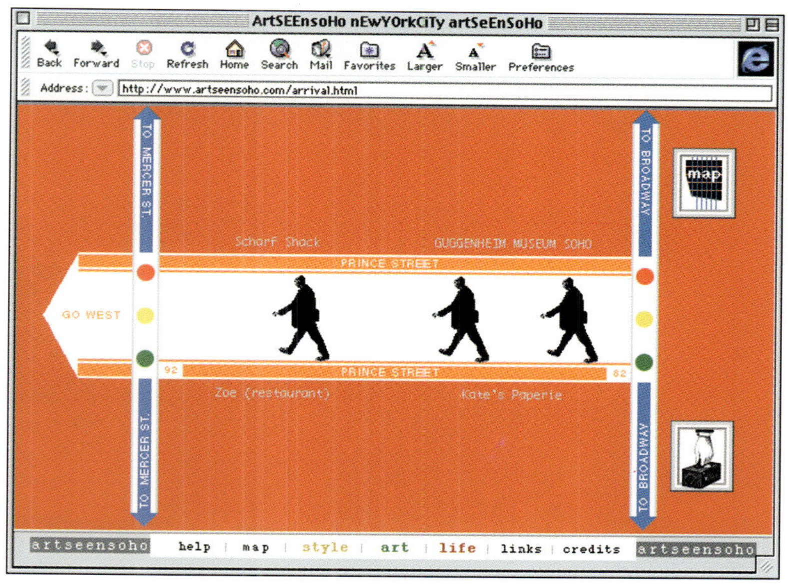

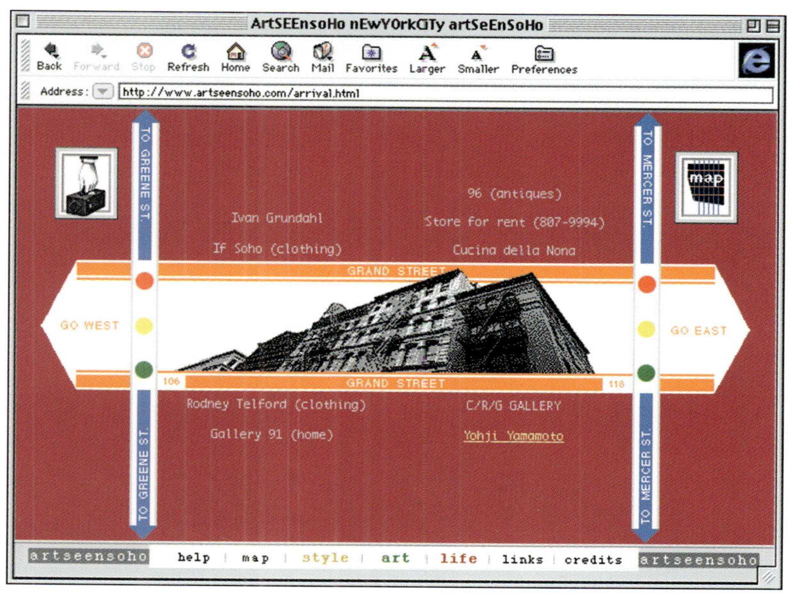

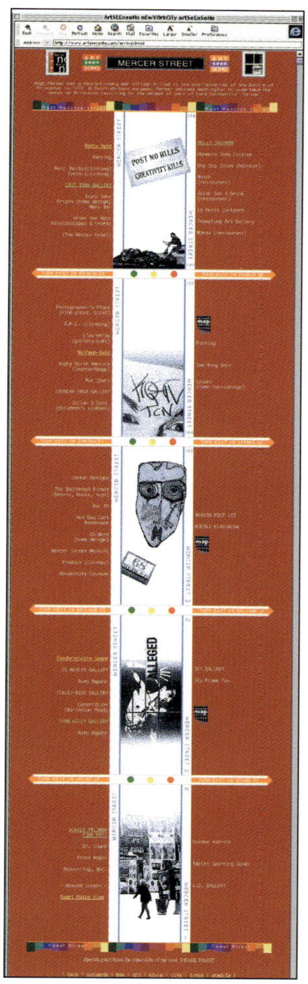

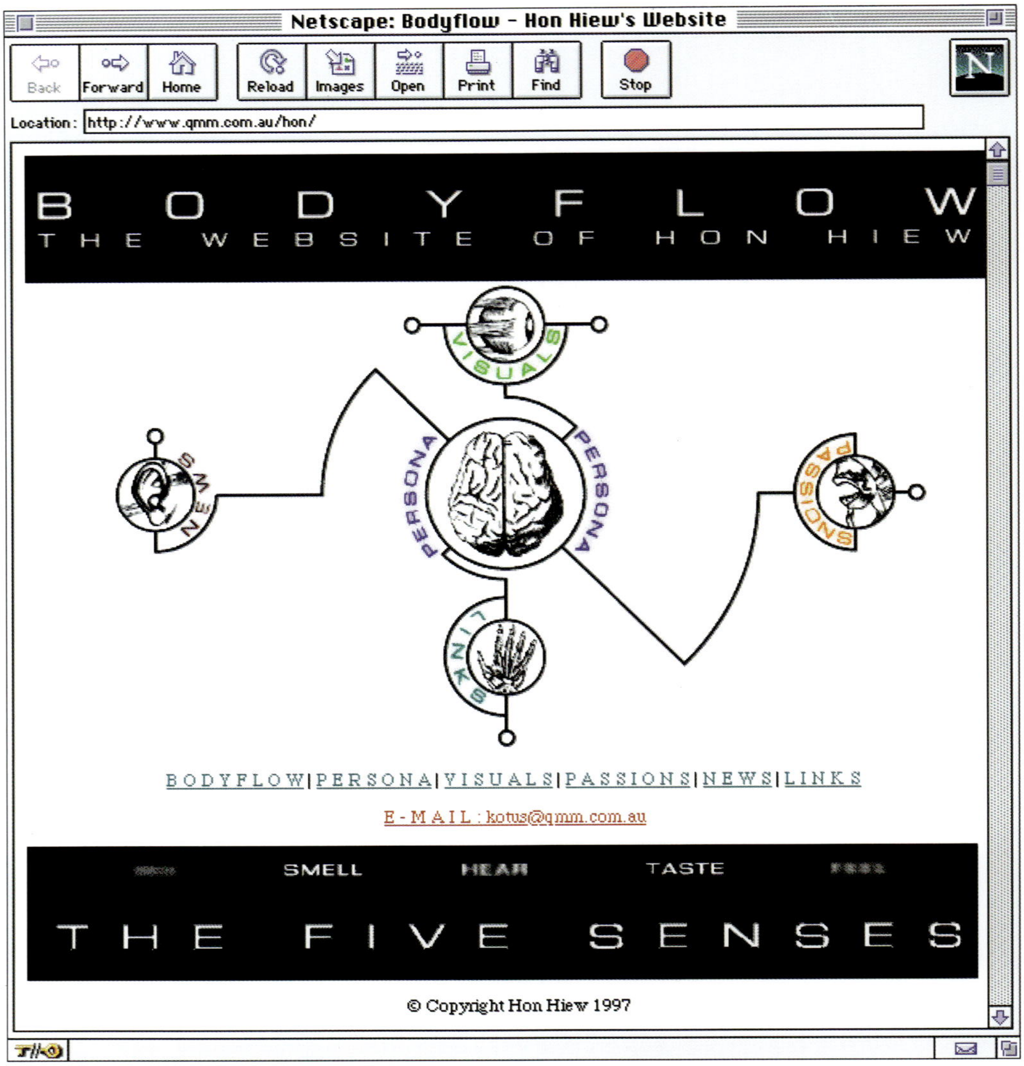

Title
Bodyflow portfolio
URL
http://www.qmm.com.au/hon
Designer
Hon Hiew

The navigational elements here are not notable for their originality—essentially just icons with text labels—but the geometric fragments that tie them together make for a striking design. They reinforce the atmosphere of scientific cleanliness introduced by medical drawings, which add to the spirit of examination and exploration.

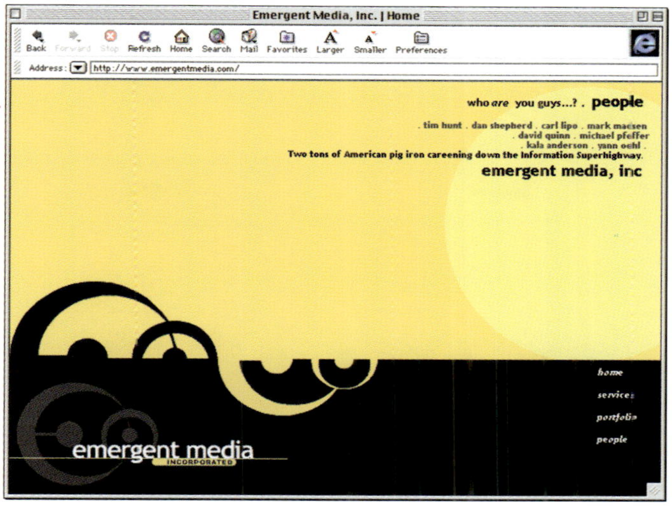

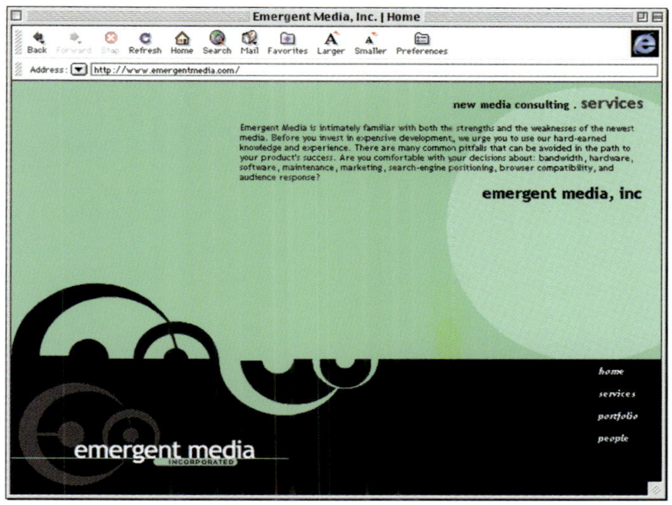

Title
Emergent Media, Inc.
URL
http://www.emergentmedia.com/
Design Firm
Emergent Media, Inc.
Designer
Yann Oehl
Programmers
Tim Hunt, Kala Anderson, Dan Shepherd
Authoring platform
PC

A color scheme for each section emphasizes location, while a tiny number of options clearly lets you move around the site. Four items in the lower right take you to main topics; each topic uses text links in the upper right for subcategories. The section is identified by color and by somewhat larger type firmly lodged in the extreme upper right.

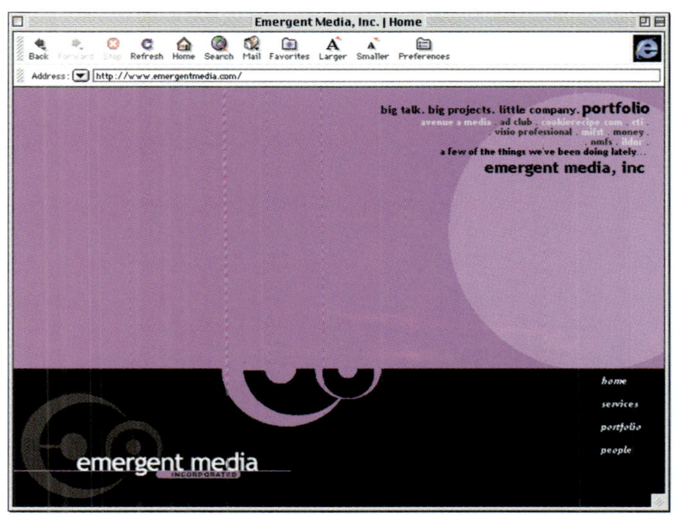

title
BoxTop Software, Inc.
URL
http://www.boxtopsoft.com/
design firm
MWB Interactive/invisible, ink
designer
Ed Sultan, invisible, ink.
illustrators
Daniel Thomas, MWB Interactive; Ed Sultan, invisible, ink; Travis Anton, BoxTop Software, Inc.
photographer
Travis Anton, BoxTop Software, Inc.
programmers
HTML—Ed Sultan, invisible, ink/Travis Anton, BoxTop Software, Inc.; CGI—Danny Lowe, BoxTop Software, Inc./Travis Anton, BoxTop Software, Inc.; Java—Open Cube Technologies
producer/writer
Travis Anton, BoxTop Software, Inc.
authoring platform
Mac

Each product is separately color coded and associated with a funky, fantastic machine on this site. Arriving at a product page shows you a highlighted and enlarged version of the machine graphic along with a horizontal banner with the product's color. The side navigation panel is contextual by product; the bottom text navigation bar shows departments, just as they do in text on the upper right on the home page.

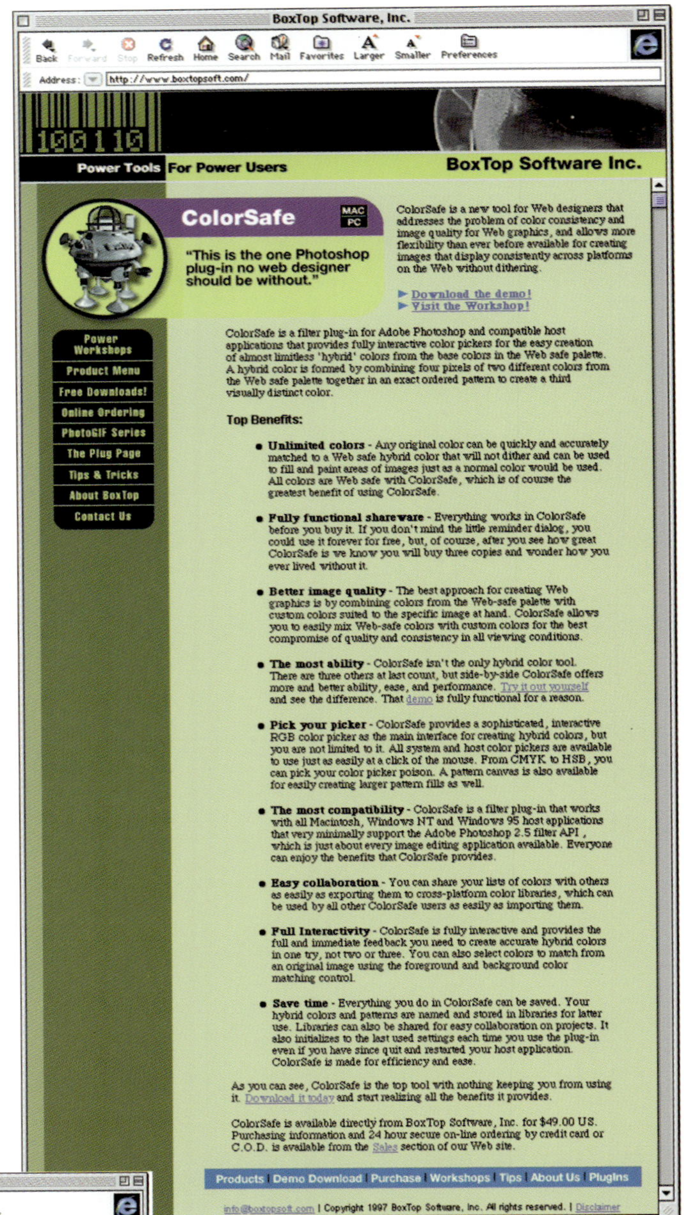

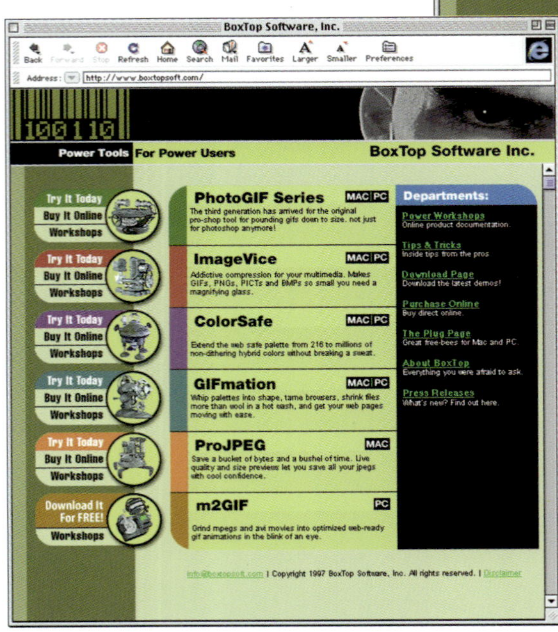

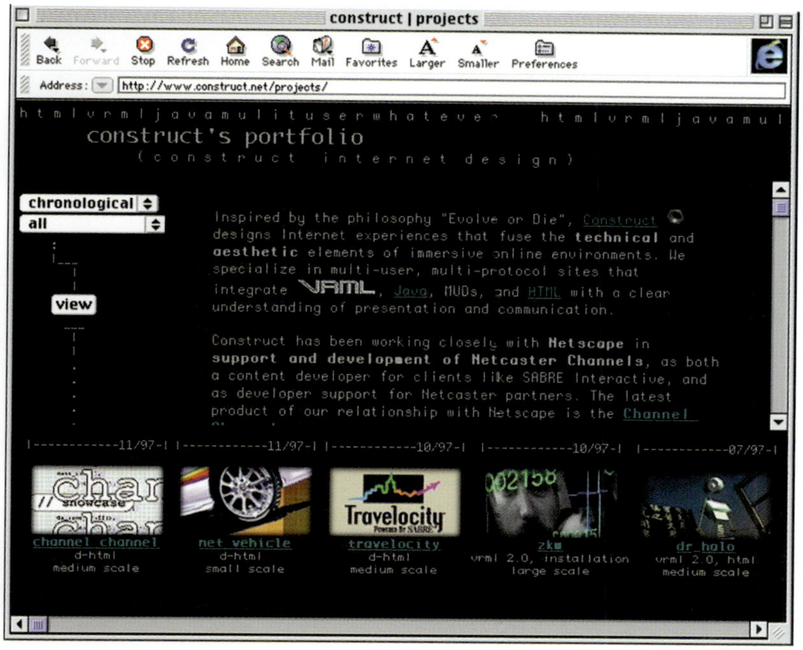

Title
construct internet design
URL
http://www.construct.net/projects/
Design firm
construct internet design
Designer/Illustrator
Annette Loudon
Programmer
Cynsa Bonorris
Authoring platform
Mac, SGI

An interesting use of a long, scrolling horizontal window, the site presents its portfolio as a series of ever-rightward scrolling actions. The form at the left lets you select what you are seeing in that window, and in what order.

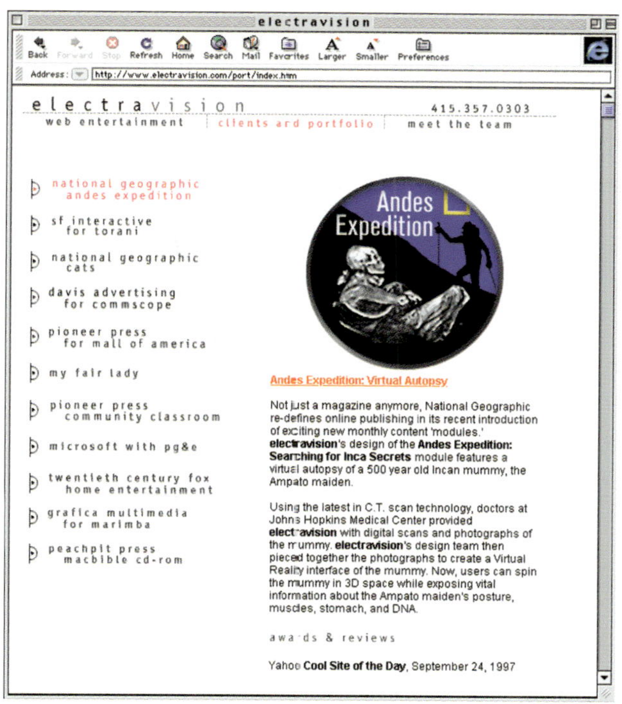

Title
electravision
URL
http://www.electravision.com/
Design firm
electravision
Designer
Rattakorn potharam
Illustrators
Lisa Lopuck, Rattakorn potharam
Programmer
Landon Bouma
Authoring platform
Mac, BBEdit

The site is cleanly divided into three sections; the current section is highlighted in red. Each set of subsections shows up at the left with the current location also highlighted; it's a visual two-dimensional coordination of where you're at. Every item in the subcategory is similar enough to allow equal presentation without any confusion.

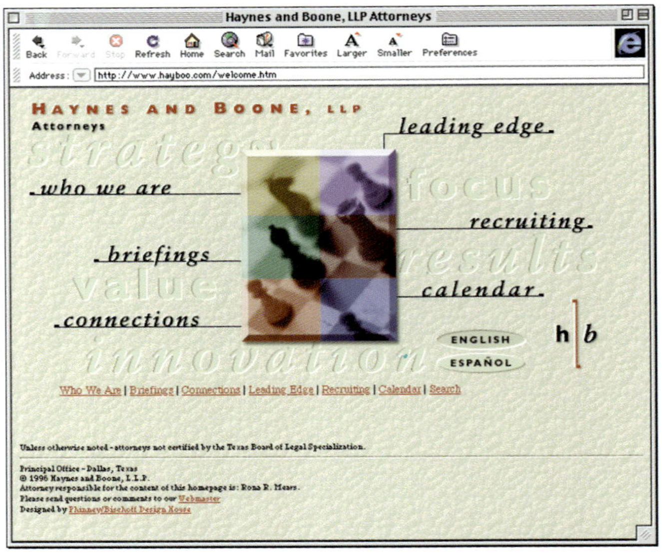

Title
Haynes and Boone web site
URL
http://www.hayboo.com/
Design firm
Phinney/Bischoff Design House, Inc.
Designers
Neil Robertson, Dean Hart
Illustrator
Dean Hart
Programmers
Glenn Fleishman, Neil Robertson
Creative Directors
Karl Bischoff, Leslie Phinney
Responsible Attorney
Rona Mears
Authoring platform
Mac

This information-rich site has to be careful to avoid presenting too many options at each level, but it nicely balances the number of screens you have to drill down before reaching content with the number of links on each page. All links are echoed in bottom text bars. The home page uses embossed, sandy type to present concepts, while the concrete items are black type with lines drawn to the particular piece of the graphic that represents each section. The home page allows a switch between English and Spanish through an embossed button that echoes other type on the page.

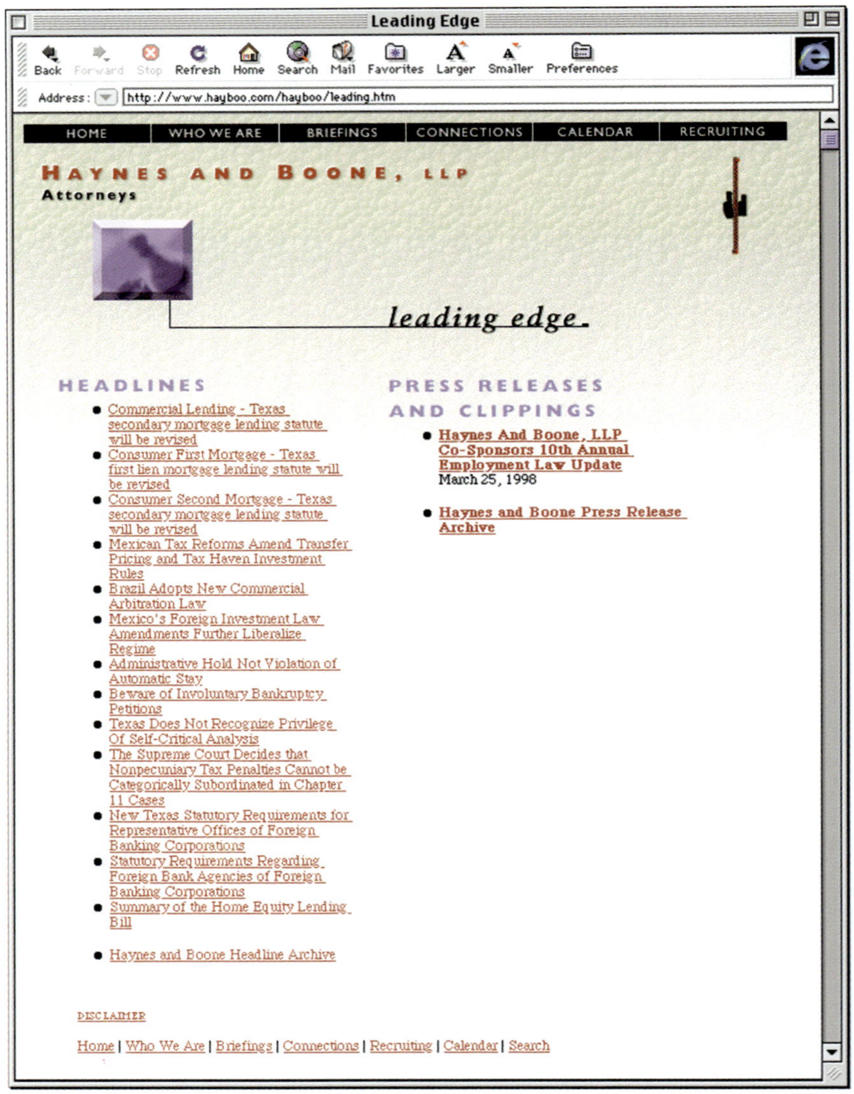

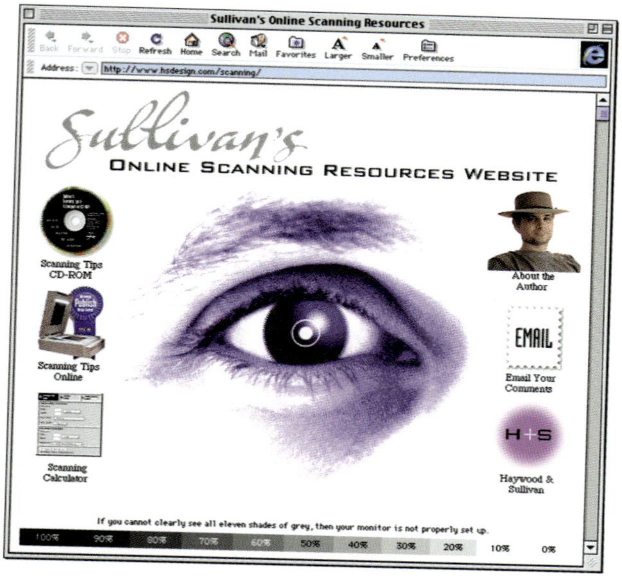

Title
sullivan's online scanning Resources

URL
http://www.hsdesign.com/scanning/

Design firm
Haywood + sullivan, inc.

Designer
Michael J. sullivan

photographer
Liz Haywood

programmer
Michael J. sullivan

calligraphy
Dianna stetson

Authoring platform
Mac

A rare example, this site's links or items on the home page represent almost exactly what you're being taken to. The CD-ROM takes you to a CD-ROM page, the author's photo to a bio, and so on. It bypasses metaphor except for the stamp taking you to e-mail—close enough to not quibble.

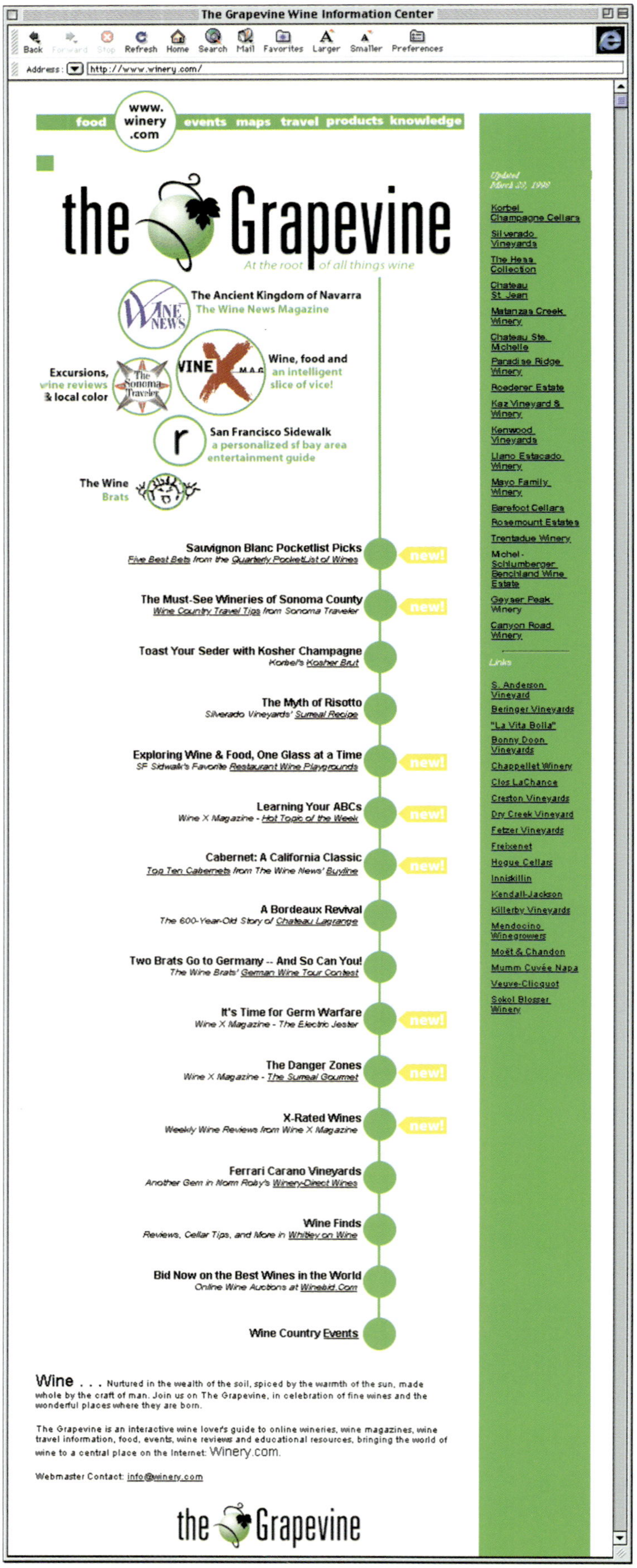

Title
winery.com
URL
http://www.winery.com/
Design Firm
The Grapevine
Designer/Illustrator
Christopher Slye
Programmer
Joe Naujokas
Authoring Platform
Mac

Grapes are the form, the content, and the means of getting around. Subsequent pages may lead elsewhere, but the home page provides a cluster of options at the top followed by a long and deep list of specifics. The vertical grape line is used to call out articles, while a navigation bar at right has a similarly long list of wines and vineyards. The home page is dense, with information presented everywhere you look, but highly accessible.

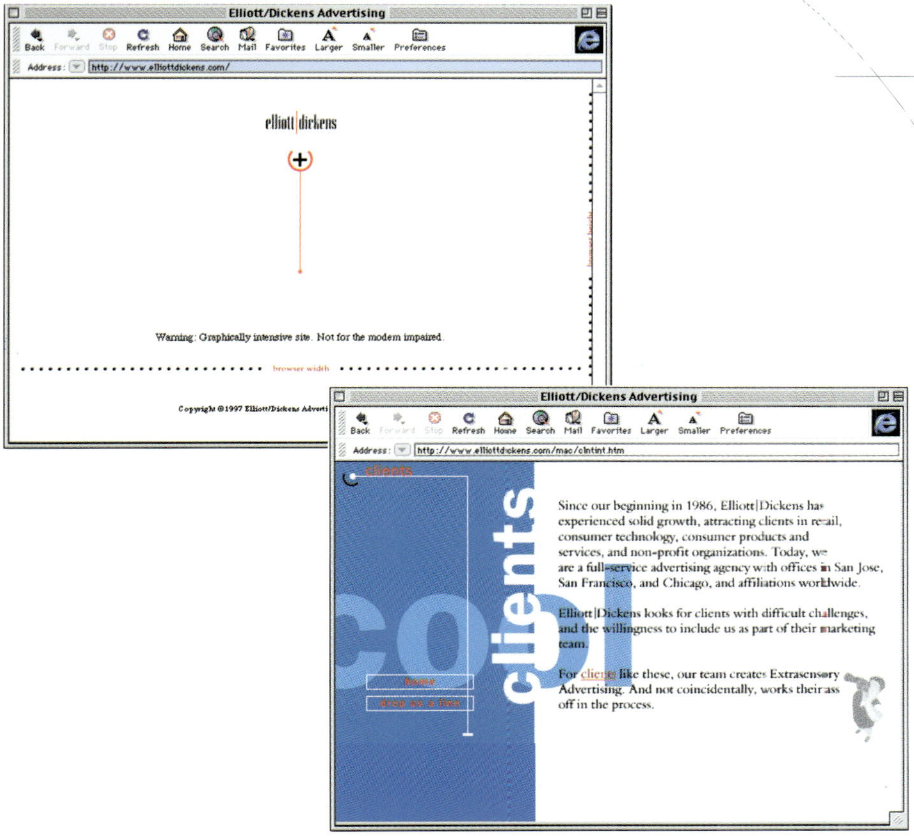

Title
elliott/dickens
URL
http://www.elliottdickens.com
Design firm
elliott/dickens
Designers
percy wang, Dave cook, cardinal o'neill, chris Tiernan
photographer
Jack christiansen
producers
Ted ganchiff, Andy Laing
Authoring platform
Mac, pc

The designers take an interesting approach to navigation by advising browser height and width on the home page, and then immediately violating the horizontal direction by making pages about twice that width. They turn the horizontal scrollbar into a page flip control: when you click on the scrollbar area, you get the other half of the page instantly.

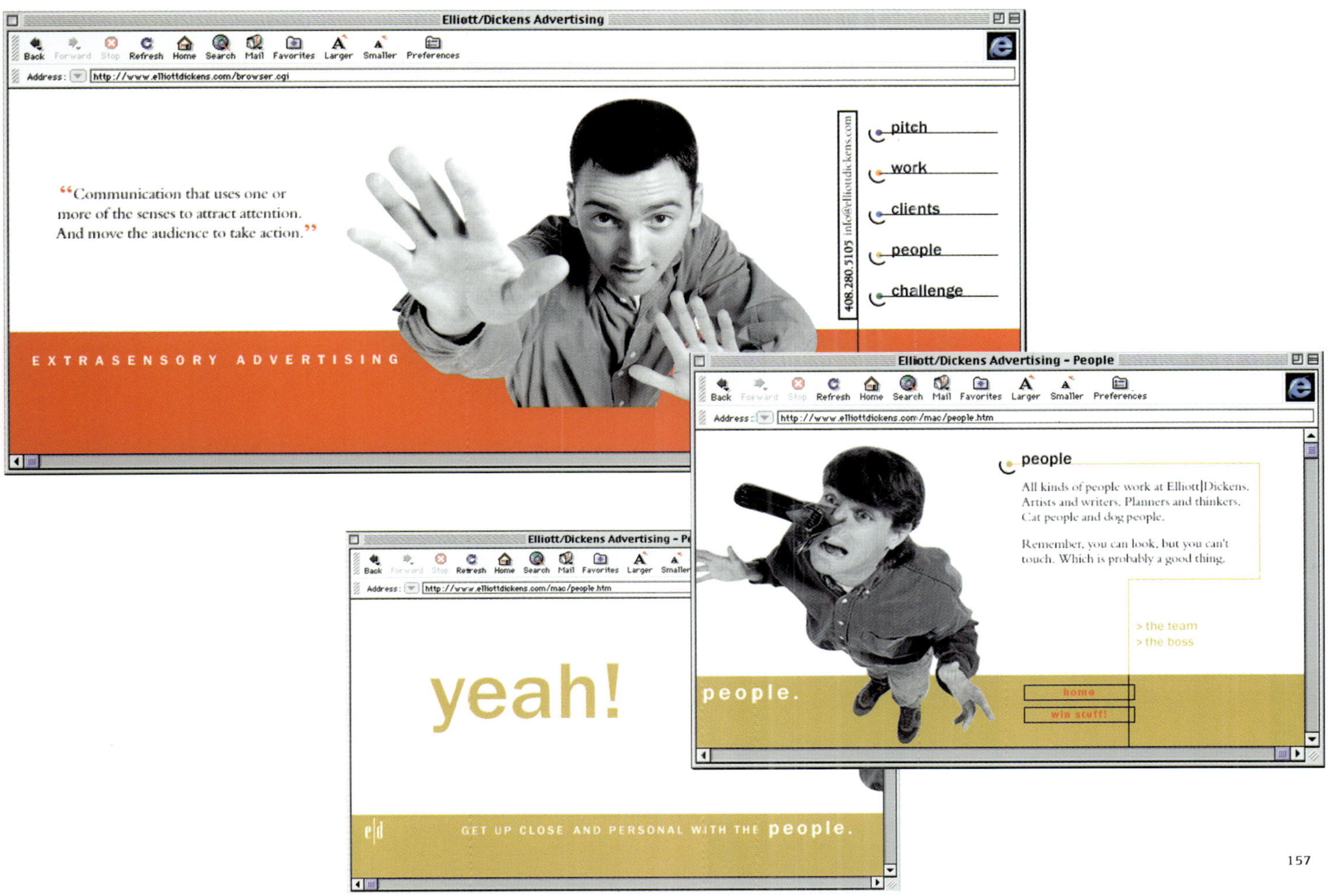

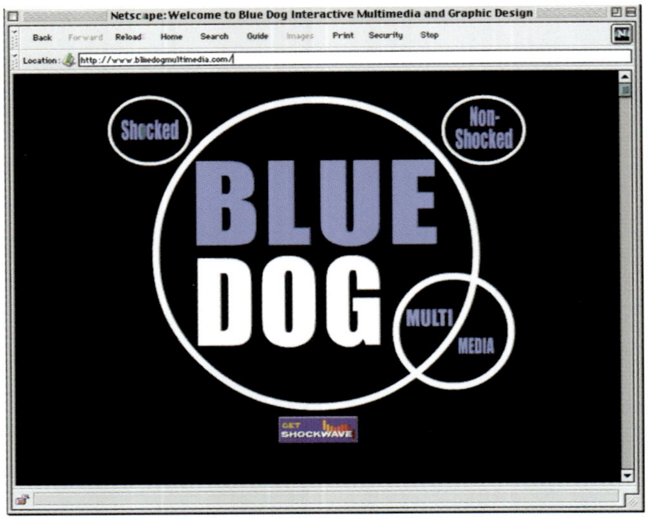

Title
Blue Dog Multimedia
URL
http://www.bluedogmultimedia.com/
Design Firm
Blue Dog Multimedia
Designer/Illustrator/
Photographer/Programmer
Mark Underhill
Authoring Platform
Mac

One of the strengths of the Macromedia Flash format is that it does a great job of scaling vector artwork for animations. Since much of the best vector artwork comprises the letters A through Z, it's no wonder that many Flash-based sites, such as this one, heavily employ animated type. The navigation here leaves nothing hidden, and adds audio touches to your choices.

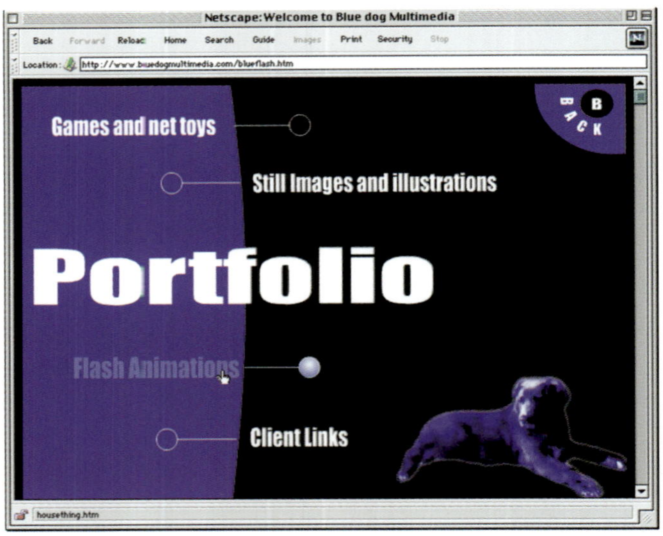

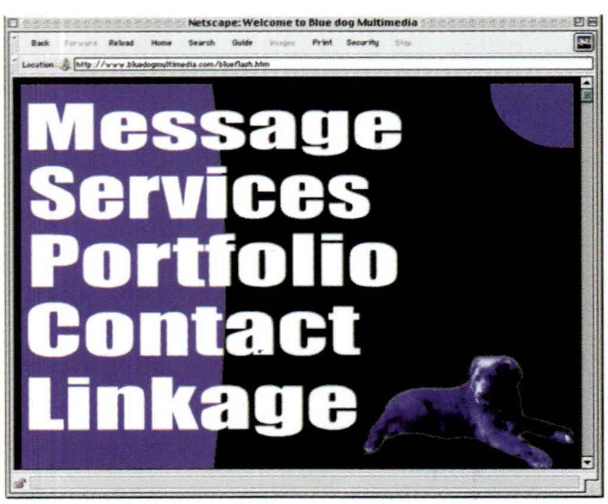

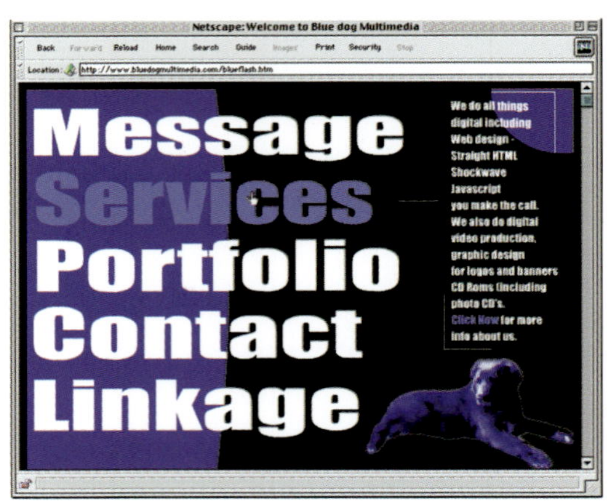

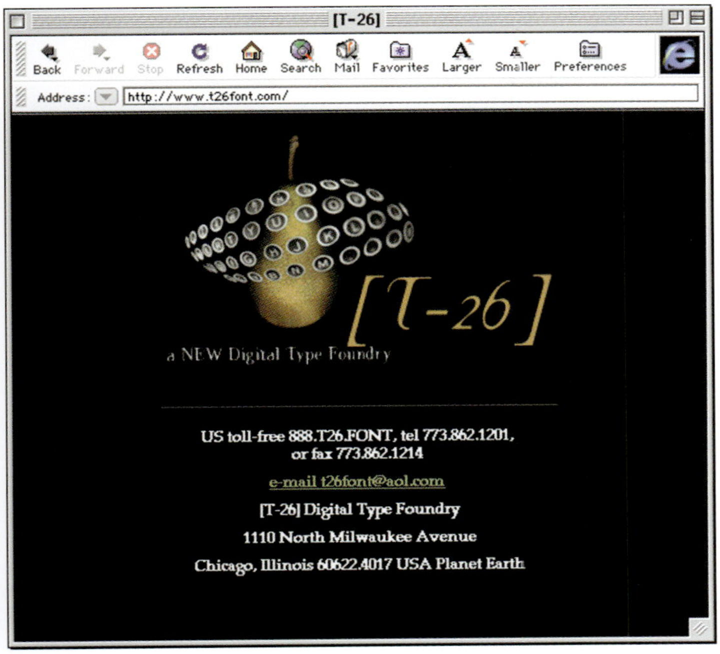

Title
[T-26] Digital Type Foundry
URL
http://www.t26font.com/
Design firm
Segura Inc.
Designer/Illustrator/Programmer
Jim Marcus
Photographers
Jim Marcus, Sandy Sager
Authoring platform
Mac

The left-side navigation bar uses triangles to expand and collapse a site map. You can be in a section and click expand or collapse, or click on the triangle to blow out the section. Whatever section you're in has its subcategories displayed in a top frame in a more artistic fashion than the utilitarian (and useful) side bar.

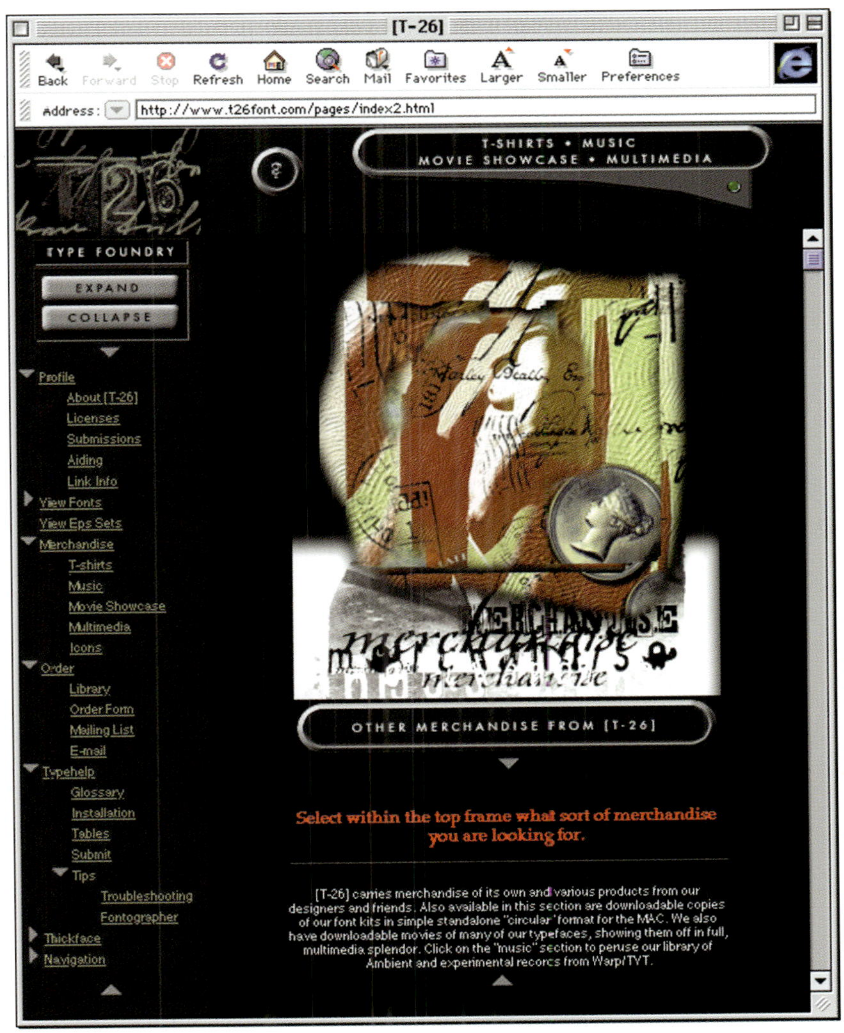

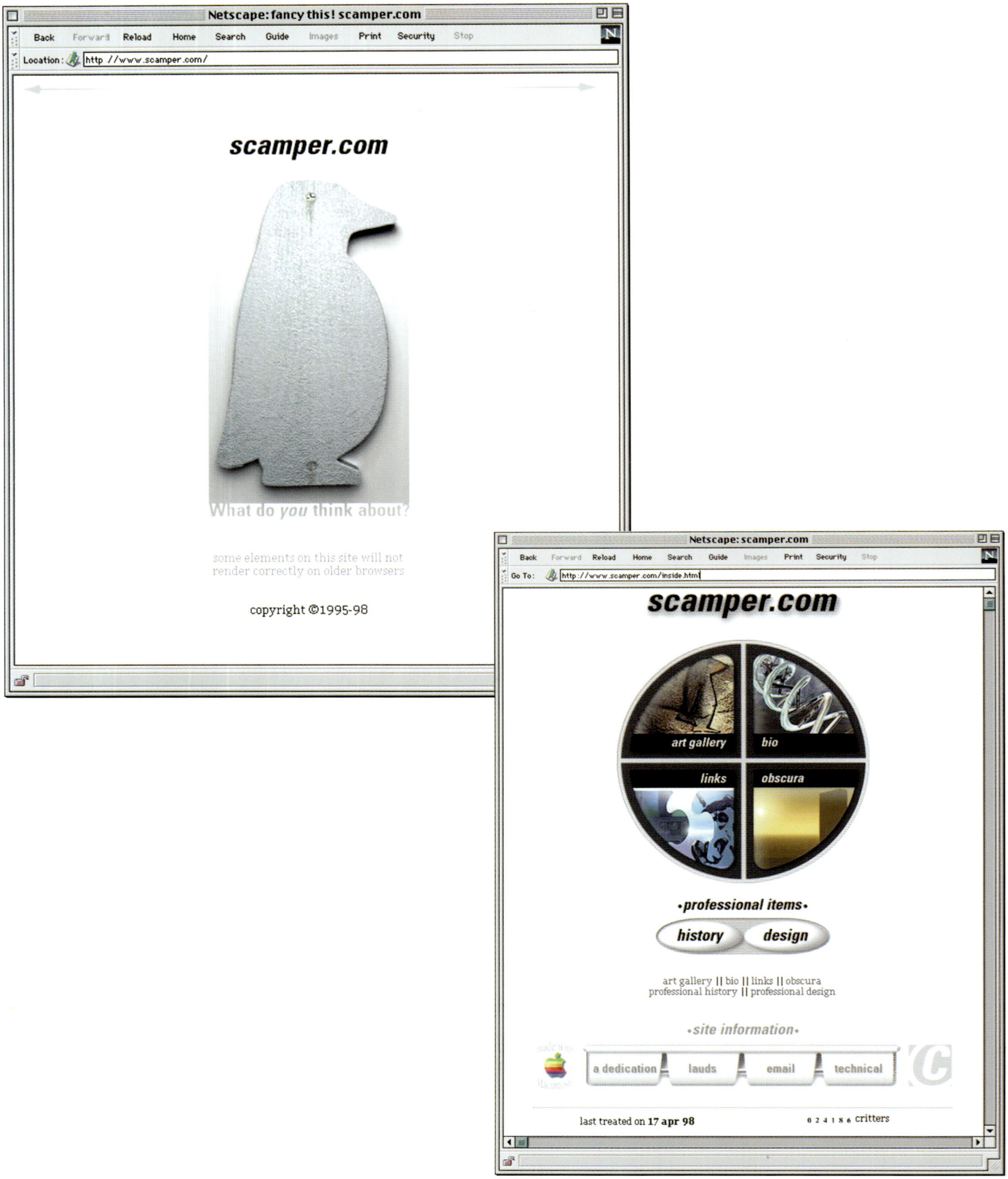
Netscape: fancy this! scamper.com
Back Forward Reload Home Search Guide Images Print Security Stop
Location: http //www.scamper.com/
scamper.com
What do you think about?
some elements on this site will not
render correctly on older browsers
copyright ©1995-98
Netscape: scamper.com
Back Forward Reload Home Search Guide Images Print Security Stop
Go To: http://www.scamper.com/inside.html
scamper.com
art gallery
bio
links
obscura
•professional items•
history
design
art gallery || bio || links || obscura
professional history || professional design
•site information•
a dedication
lauds
email
technical
last treated on 17 apr 98
critters

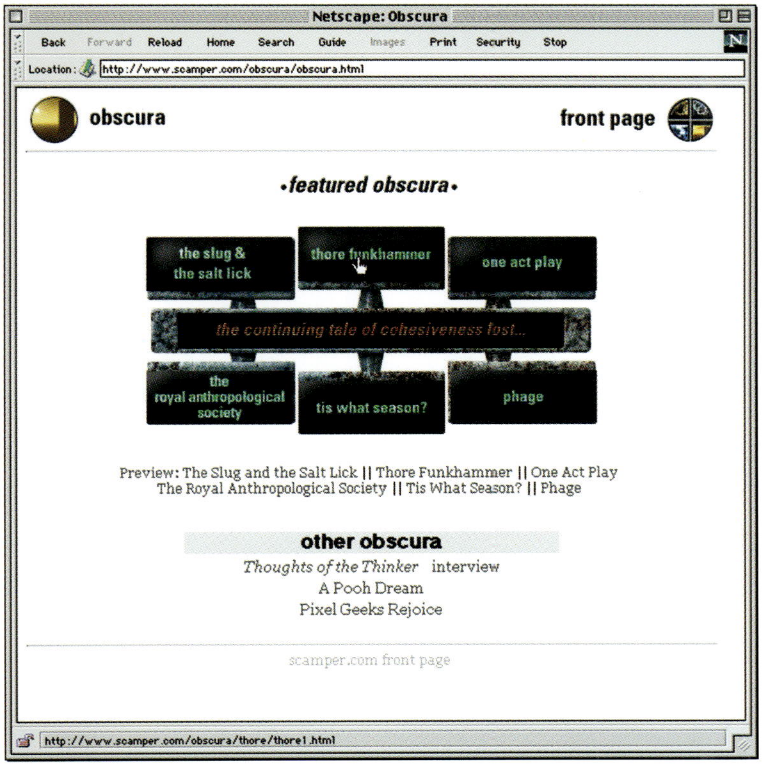

Title
scamper
URL
http://www.scamper.com/inside.html
Design firm
scamper.com
Designer/programmer
Jeff Robinson
Authoring platform
Mac

Initially, the navigation here appears rather standard. With the exception of some nice JavaScript rollover effects on the main graphics, the page is pretty straightforward. But its standard appearance is a testament to the fact that there are three levels of information being presented (the main buttons, professional items, and site details). That's twelve possible directions on a page whose clean design suggests 6.

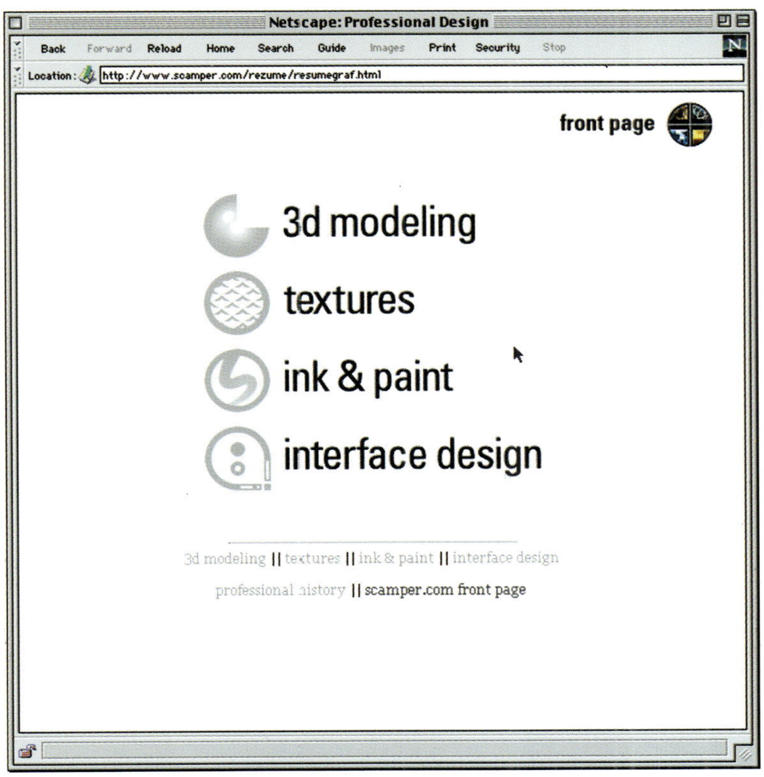

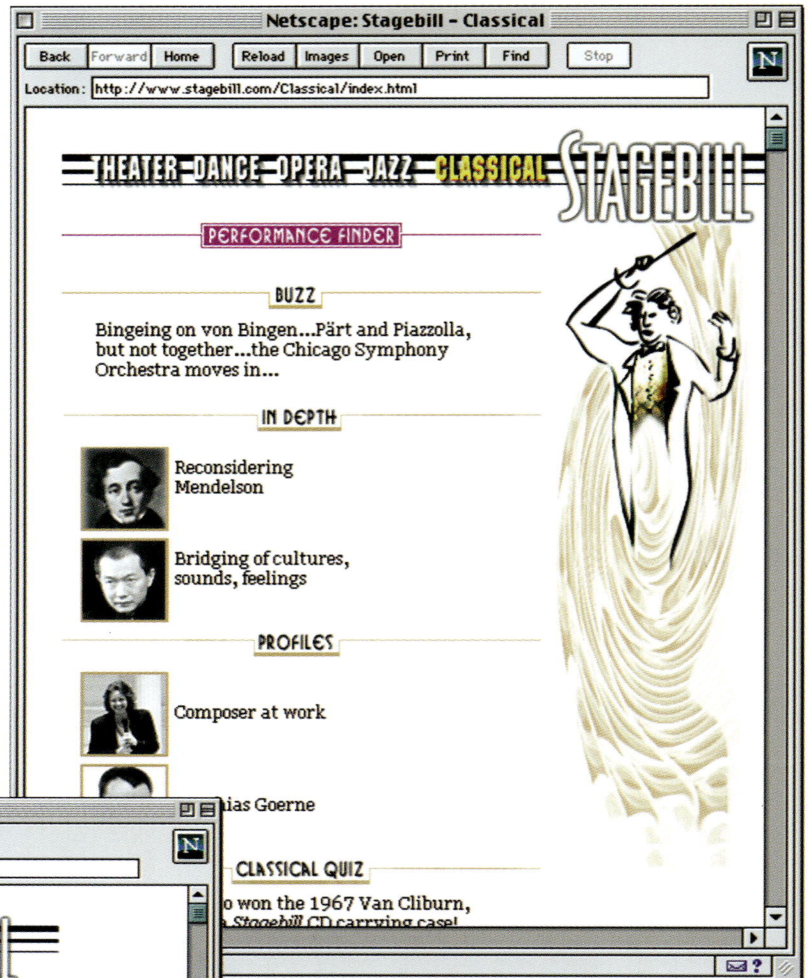
Netscape: Stagebill - Classical
Back Forward Home Reload Images Open Print Find Stop
Location: http://www.stagebill.com/Classical/index.html
THEATER DANCE OPERA JAZZ CLASSICAL STAGEBILL
PERFORMANCE FINDER
BUZZ
Bingeing on von Bingen...Pärt and Piazzolla, but not together...the Chicago Symphony Orchestra moves in...
IN DEPTH
Reconsidering Mendelson
Bridging of cultures, sounds, feelings
PROFILES
Composer at work
CLASSICAL QUIZ

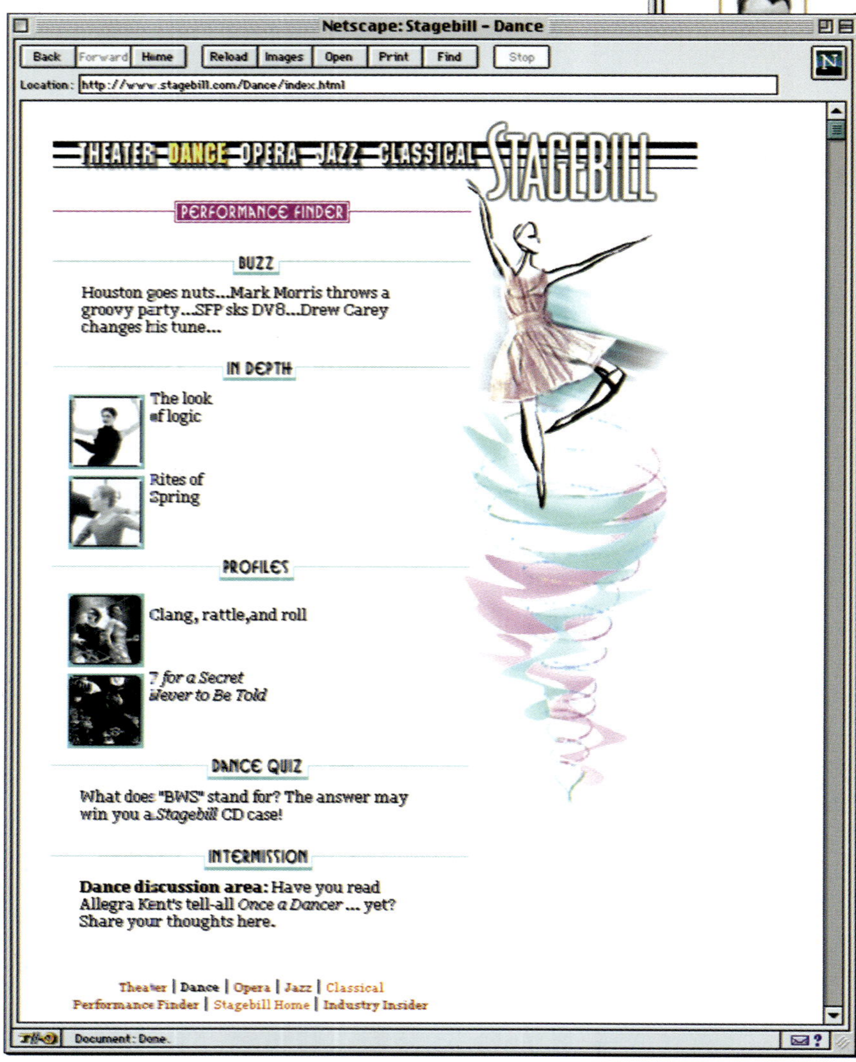
Netscape: Stagebill - Dance
Back Forward Home Reload Images Open Print Find Stop
Location: http://www.stagebill.com/Dance/index.html
THEATER DANCE OPERA JAZZ CLASSICAL STAGEBILL
PERFORMANCE FINDER
BUZZ
Houston goes nuts...Mark Morris throws a groovy party...SFP sks DV8...Drew Carey changes his tune...
IN DEPTH
The look of logic
Rites of Spring
PROFILES
Clang, rattle, and roll
7 for a Secret Never to Be Told
DANCE QUIZ
What does "BWS" stand for? The answer may win you a Stagebill CD case!
INTERMISSION
Dance discussion area: Have you read Allegra Kent's tell-all Once a Dancer ... yet? Share your thoughts here.
Theater | Dance | Opera | Jazz | Classical
Performance Finder | Stagebill Home | Industry Insider
Document: Done.

Title
Stagebill
URL
http://www.stagebill.com/
Design Firm
T3 Media
Designers/Illustrators/Programmers
Chris Bryant, Michael Diamant
Producer
Shira Kalish

The designers of this site have done a good job of enlivening the pages while keeping the overall design clean and professional. JavaScript rollovers highlight the section your cursor points at, with a little razzle-dazzle added to the site's logo on subsequent pages. Inside, each main section is split into subsections, where the navigation appears within the contents of the page, rather than awkwardly grouped in a corner or side of the screen.

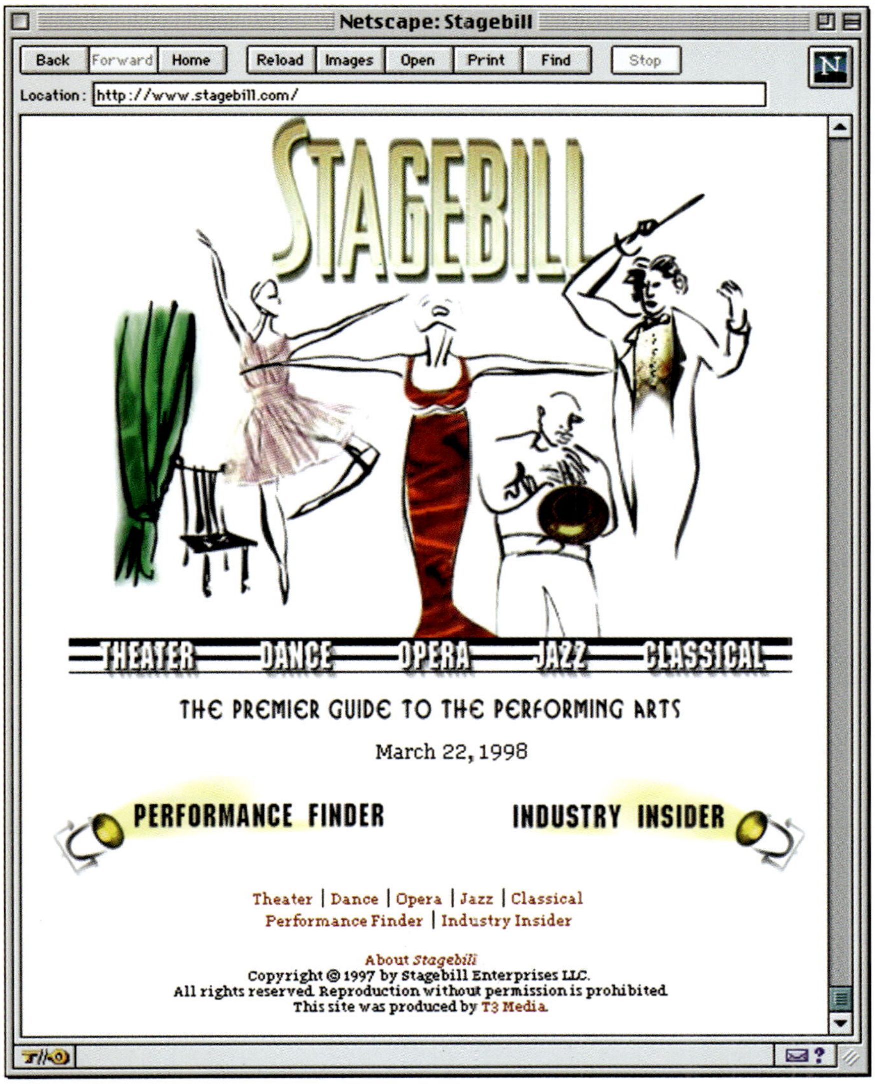

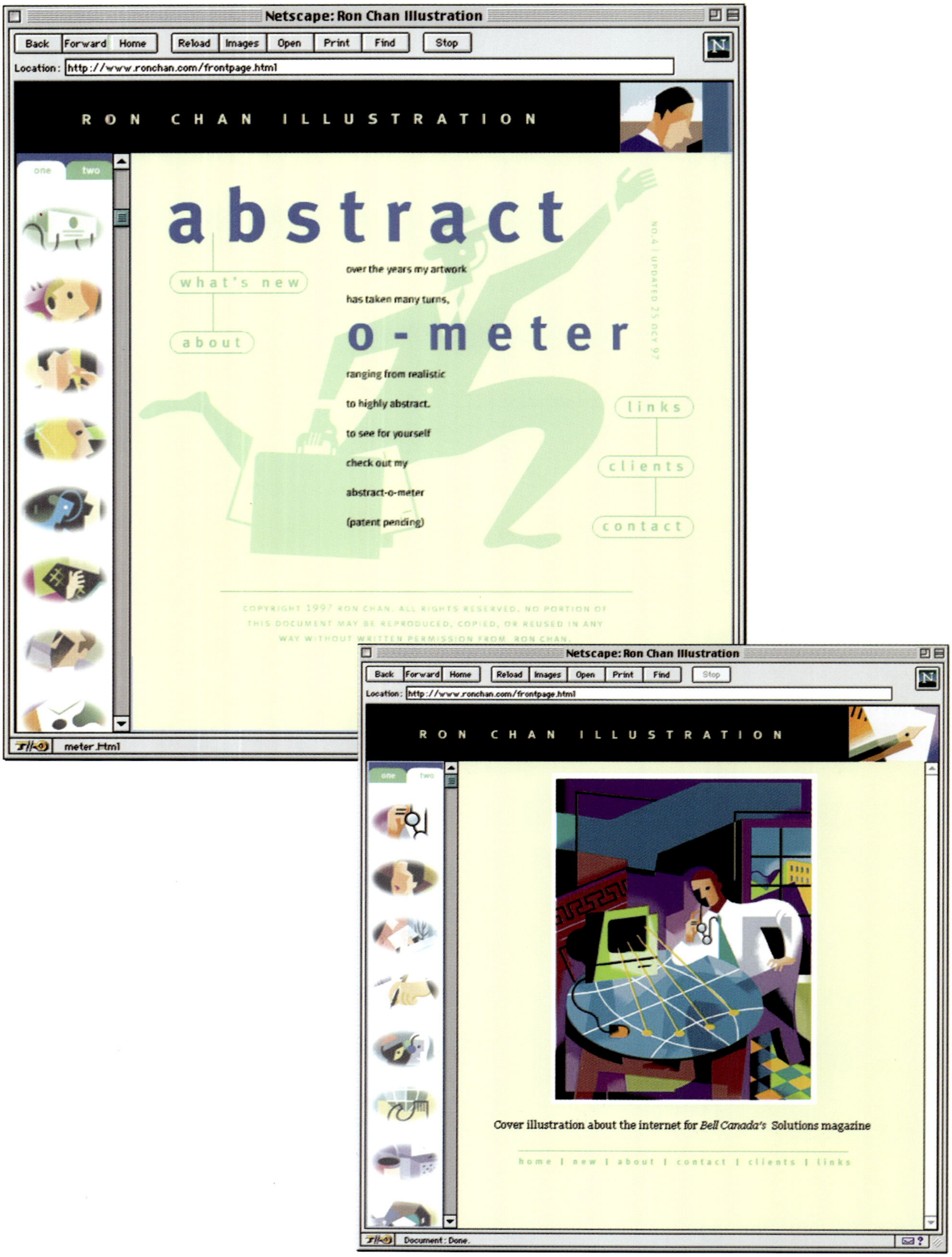

Netscape: Ron Chan Illustration
Back Forward Home Reload Images Open Print Find Stop
Location: http://www.ronchan.com/frontpage.html
RON CHAN ILLUSTRATION
one two
abstract
what's new
about
over the years my artwork
has taken many turns,
o-meter
ranging from realistic
to highly abstract.
to see for yourself
check out my
abstract-o-meter
(patent pending)
links
clients
contact
NO.4 | UPDATED 25 OCT 97
COPYRIGHT 1997 RON CHAN. ALL RIGHTS RESERVED. NO PORTION OF THIS DOCUMENT MAY BE REPRODUCED, COPIED, OR REUSED IN ANY WAY WITHOUT WRITTEN PERMISSION FROM RON CHAN.
meter.Html
Netscape: Ron Chan Illustration
Back Forward Home Reload Images Open Print Find Stop
Location: http://www.ronchan.com/frontpage.html
RON CHAN ILLUSTRATION
one two
Cover illustration about the internet for Bell Canada's Solutions magazine
home | new | about | contact | clients | links
Document: Done.

Title
Ron Chan: Portfolio
URL
http://www.ronchan.com/
Designer/Illustrator/Programmer
Ron Chan
Authoring Platform
Mac

The Web has become a useful medium for artists to open up their portfolios to prospective clients. Using a simple frame layout, illustrator Ron Chan offers small vignettes containing pieces of his artwork in place of full thumbnails to tempt the viewer; clicking a sample brings up the artwork in the main frame. Clicking one of the tabs in the left panel brings up another set of artworks, minimizing the need to scroll down several screens to see the rest of what's being offered.

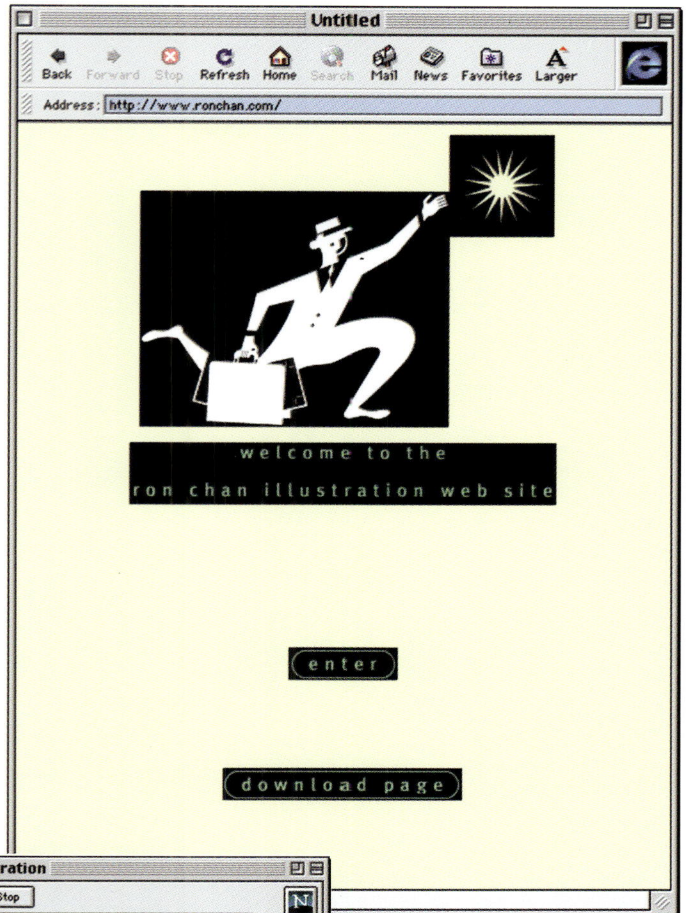

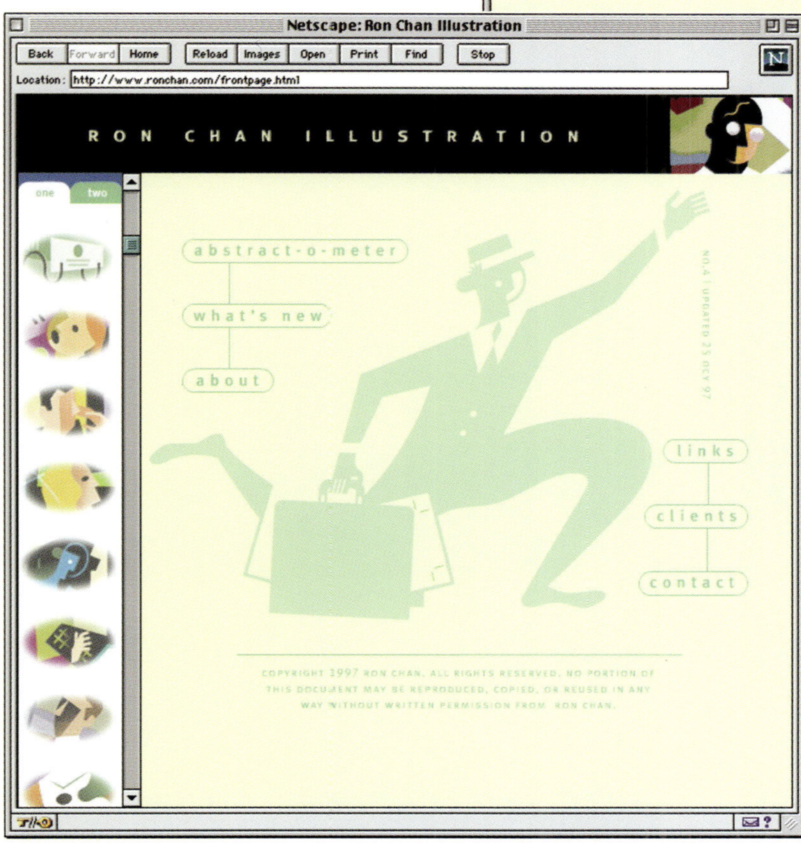

Title
4 guys interactive
URL
www.4guys.com/
Design firm
4 guys interactive

4 Guys has created a unique blend of styles to make an impressive, clear interface. Using a Macromedia Flash pop-up window, 4 Guys combined the pop-up window with traditional frames for impressive usability. 4 Guys used good design to make clear what could have been a confusing amount of information, including as many as eight frames within the window.

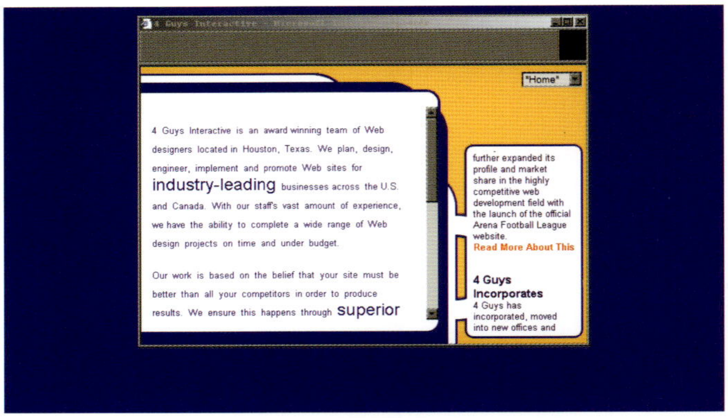

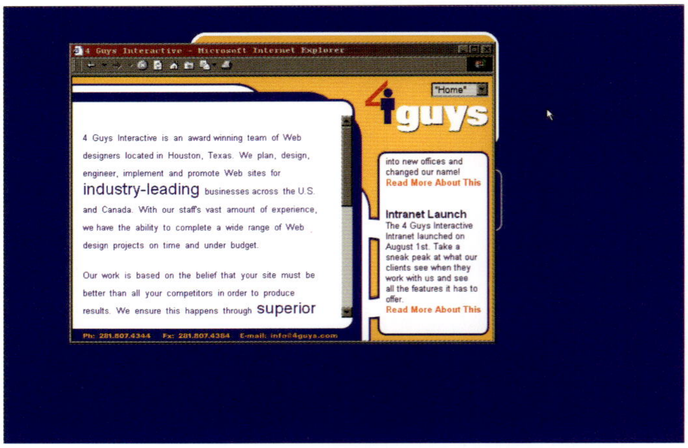

"Portfolio"

4guys

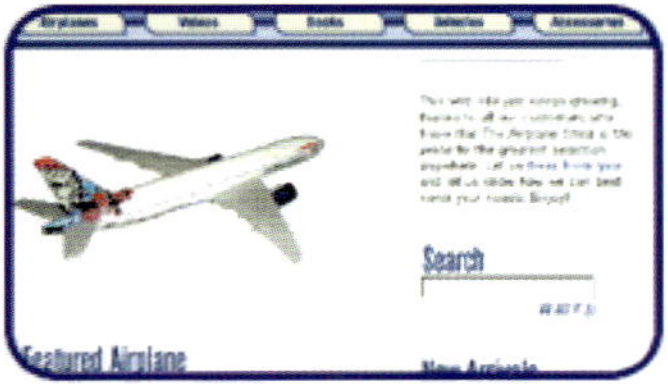

http://www.airplaneshop.com

The Airplane Shop is the Web's largest online model plane shop. This fully functional E-commerce site boasts such features as zoomable images, recommendation based on past purchases, a monthly newsletter, user updateable pricing and quantities and dynamic best sellers. The site has over 7000 items for sale and is extremely easy to make an order.

PREVIOUS | NEXT

Client List

- The Airplane Shop
- Mitsubishi
- Northside Realty
- Caterpillar
- Litton
- Arena Football
- Flip2it
- Intermat
- SCOC
- NGC
- Others...

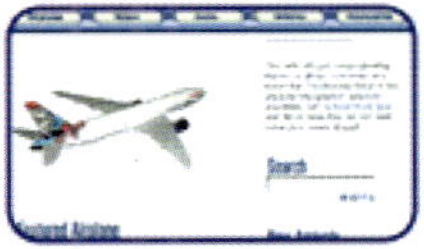

Ph: 281.807.4344 Fx: 281.807.4384 E-mail: info@4guys.com

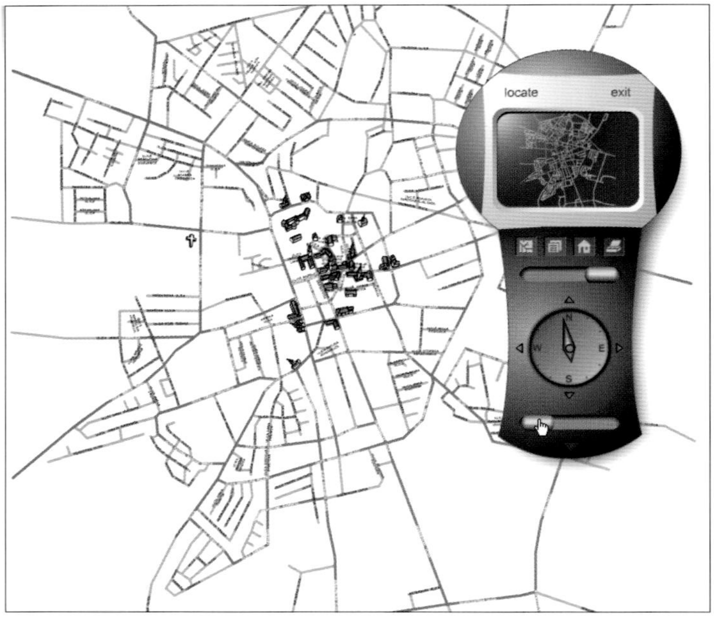

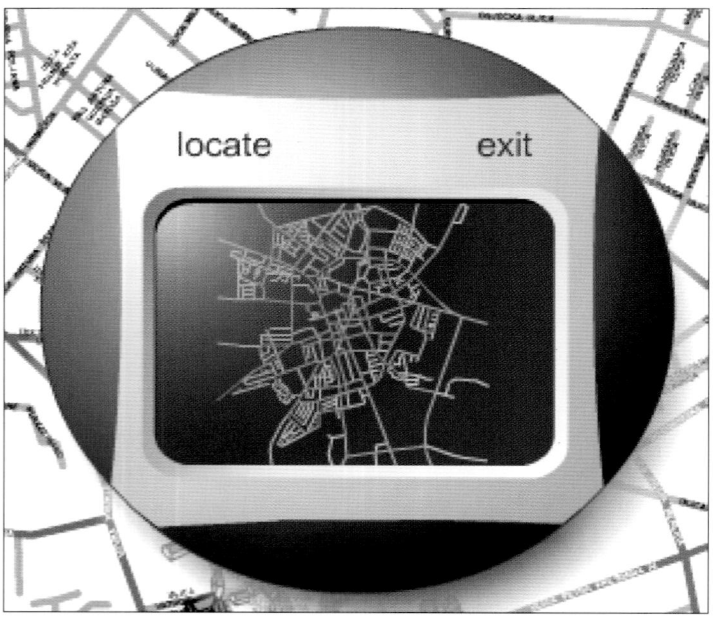

Title
varazdin
URL
www.2000.varazdin.com/
Design firm
varazdin 2000
Designer
Rajko sekelj

Rajko Sekelj has created a map of his hometown—Varazdin, Croatia—completely in Flash. Varazdin uses an elegant, simple interface for navigation in one of the few purely Flash sites on the Internet. A single console contains all the controls that you need to look at street names and buildings, zoom in and out, and move north and south around the map. This site is truly unique.

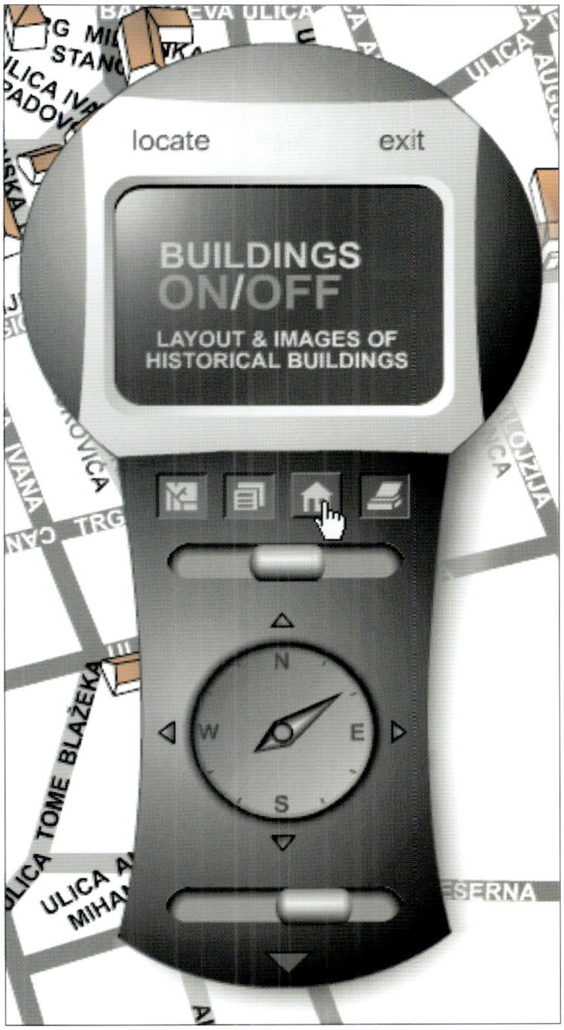
locate
exit
BUILDINGS
ON/OFF
LAYOUT & IMAGES OF
HISTORICAL BUILDINGS
N
W
E
S
ULICA TOME BLAŽEKA

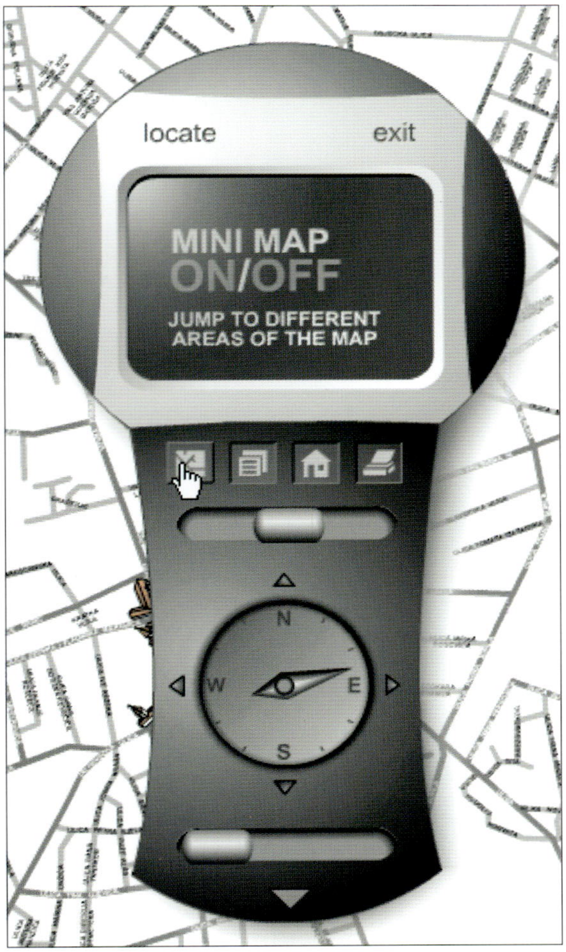
locate
exit
MINI MAP
ON/OFF
JUMP TO DIFFERENT
AREAS OF THE MAP
N
W
E
S

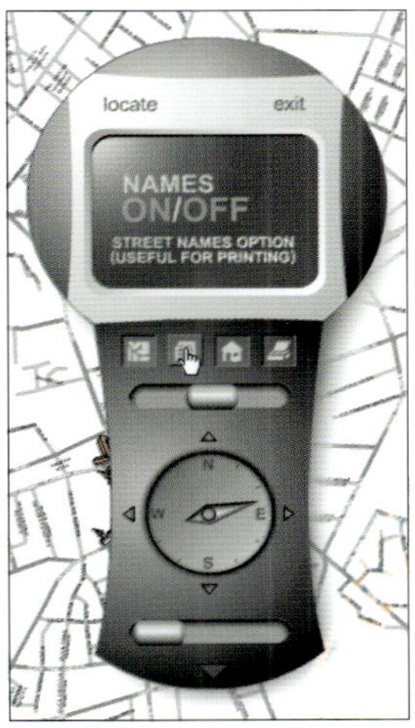
locate
exit
NAMES
ON/OFF
STREET NAMES OPTION
(USEFUL FOR PRINTING)

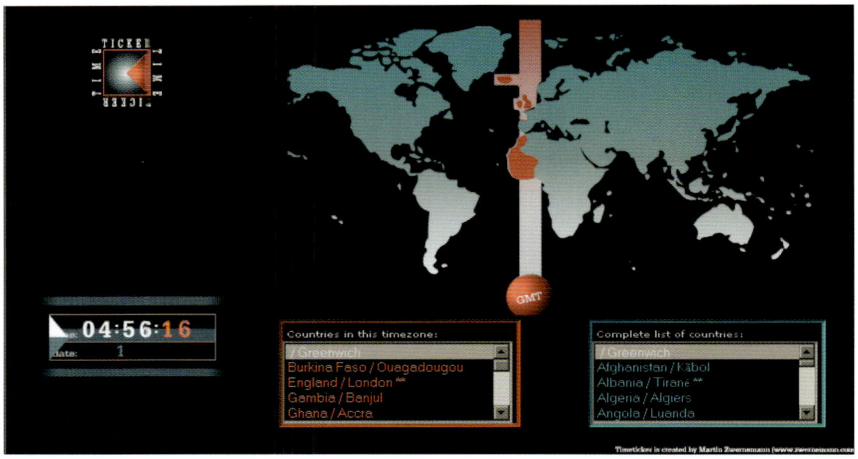

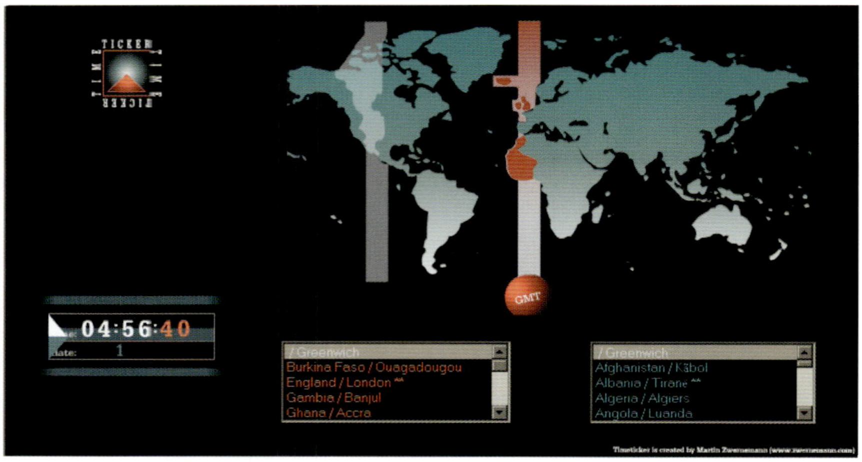

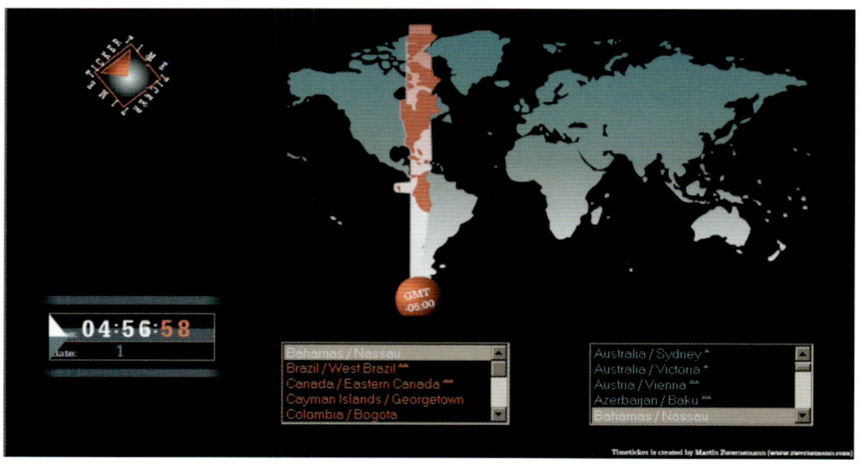

Title
Timeticker
URL
www.timeticker.com/
Design Firm
Timeticker
Zwernemann
Designer
Martin Zwernemann

Here is another Flash-implemented site. Timeticker simply tells you the time anywhere in the world, using a beautiful navigation system. Just mouse-over the time zones until you find the one you're interested in, then click on it to find out what time it is and which countries are in that time zone.

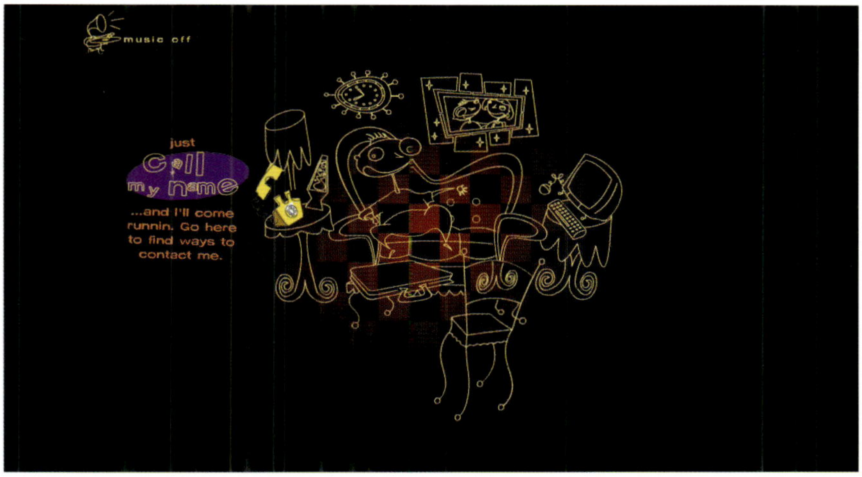

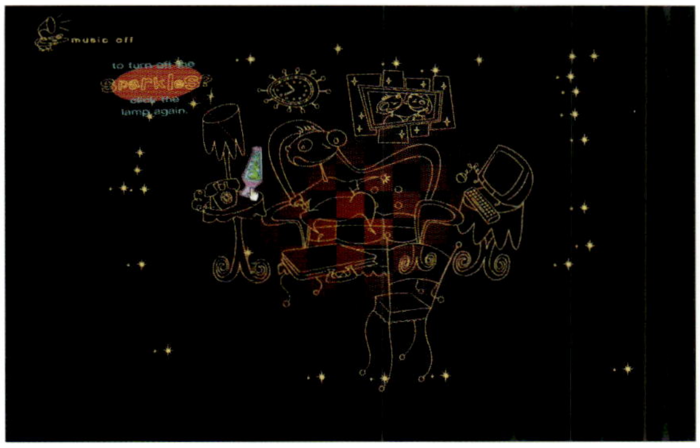

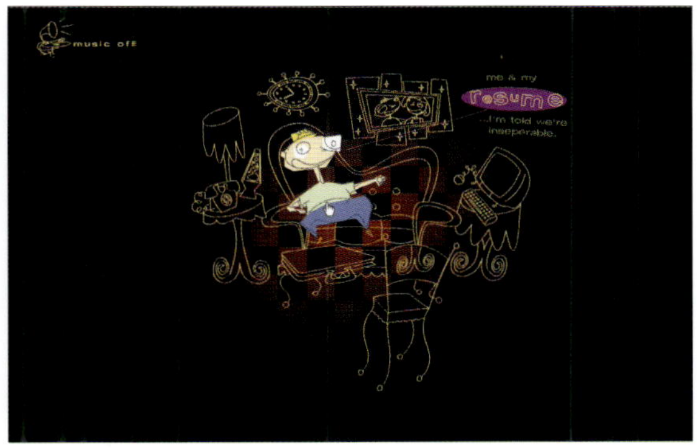

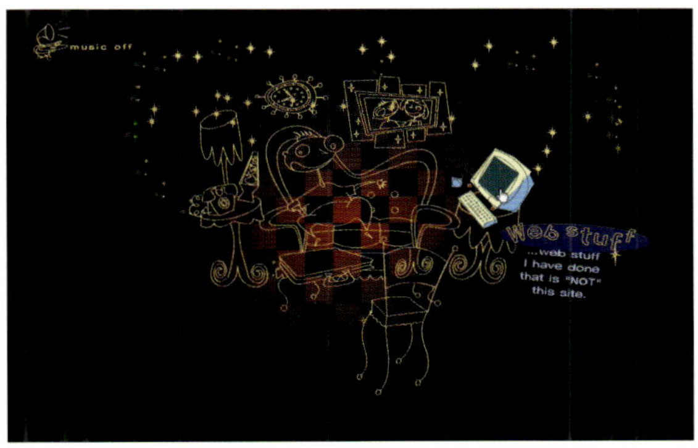

Title
online interview with Randall Larson
URL
people.mn.mediaone.net/gonzoz
Design Firm
online interview with Randall Larson
Designer
Randall Larson

"I can't draw very well, so I make everything move," Randall says. Each drawing is a button leading to a different section of the site. Randall's site features more than the typical resumé and bio; it has a real-time question-and answer-screen and lots of little touches that make the site completely interactive.

Title
Yster
URL
yster.just.nu
Design firm
SLB Interactive

Yster uses Flash to create a simple interface that moves on the mouse-over to reveal th three buttons' functions. The tabs slide down the side of the center circle.

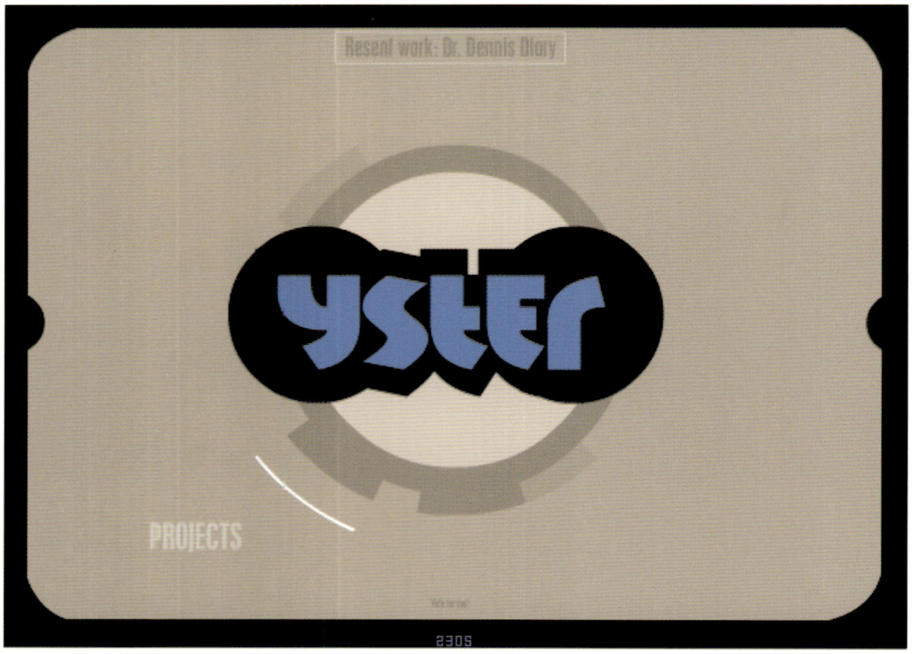

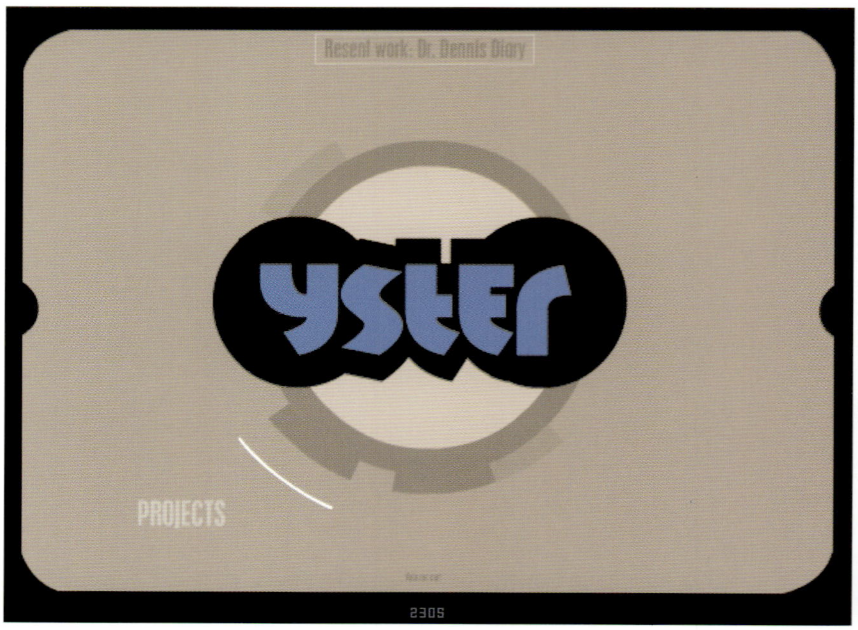

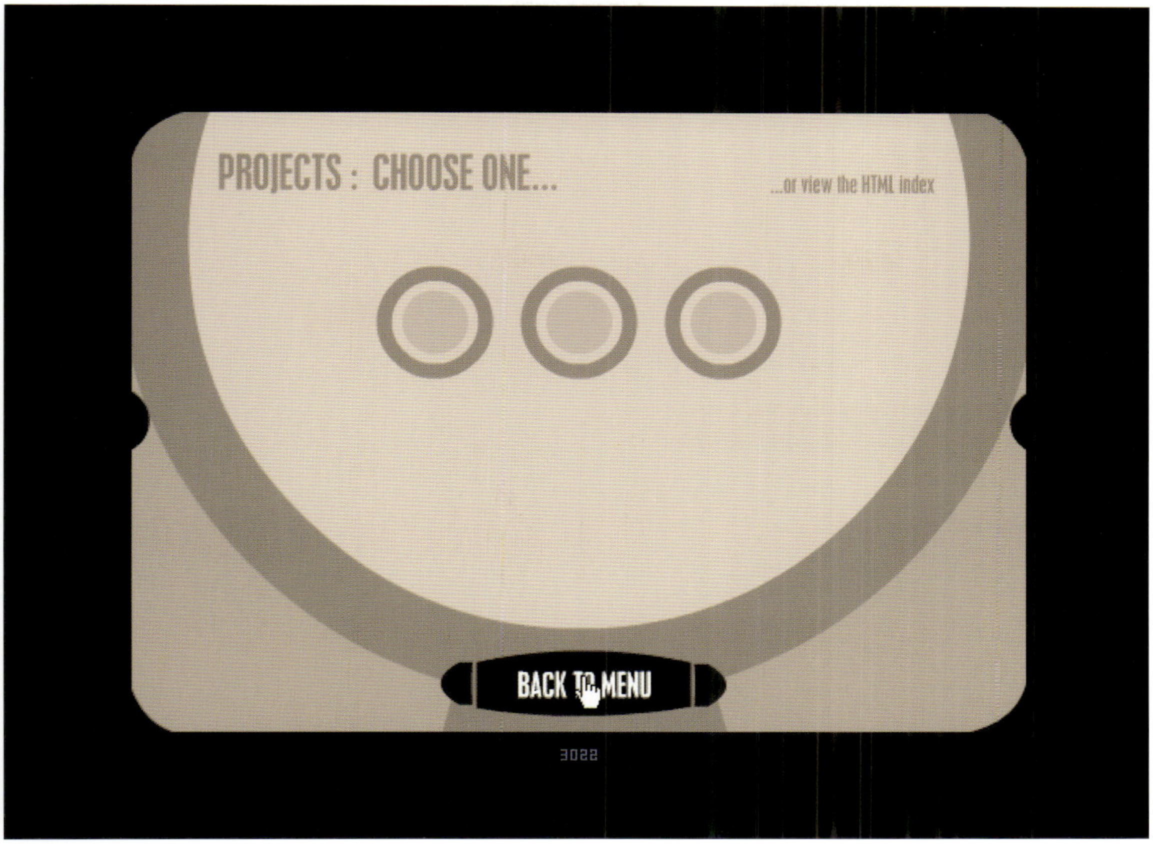
PROJECTS : CHOOSE ONE...
...or view the HTML index
BACK TO MENU
3022

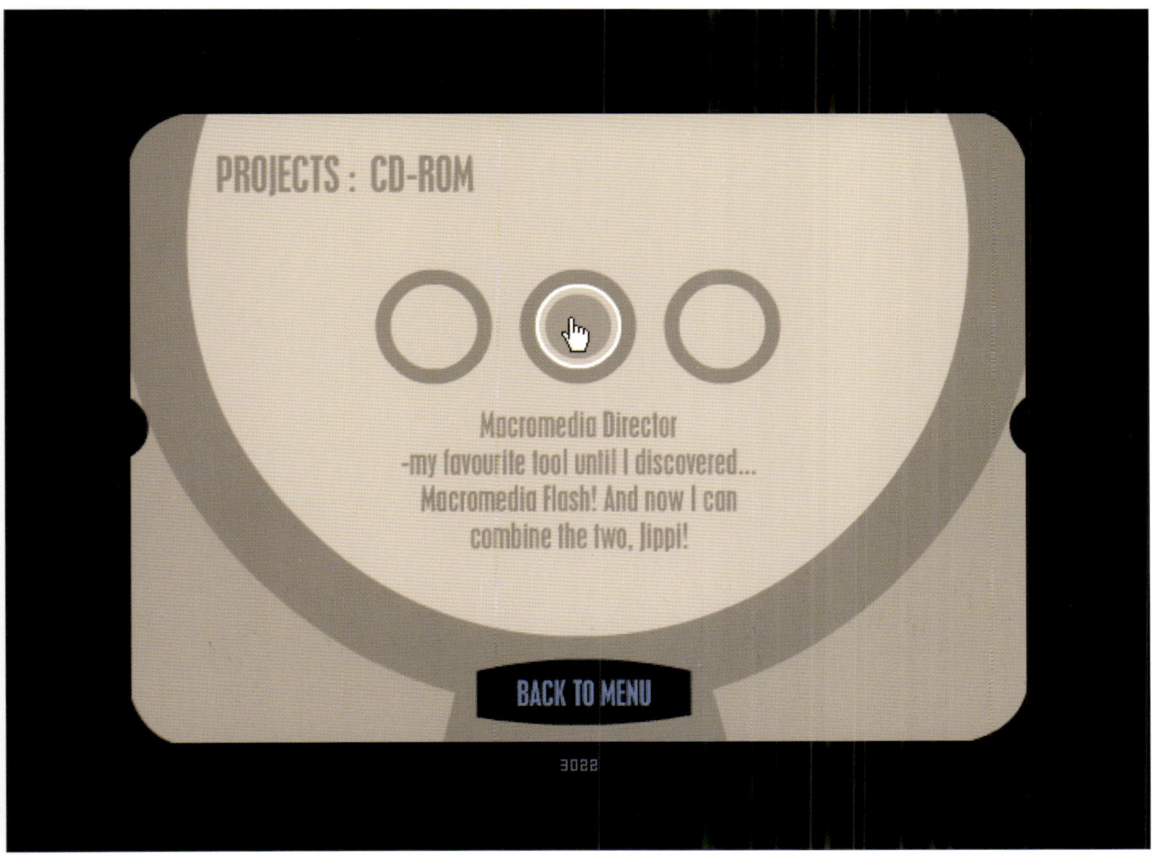
PROJECTS : CD-ROM
Macromedia Director
-my favourite tool until I discovered...
Macromedia Flash! And now I can
combine the two, jippi!
BACK TO MENU
3022

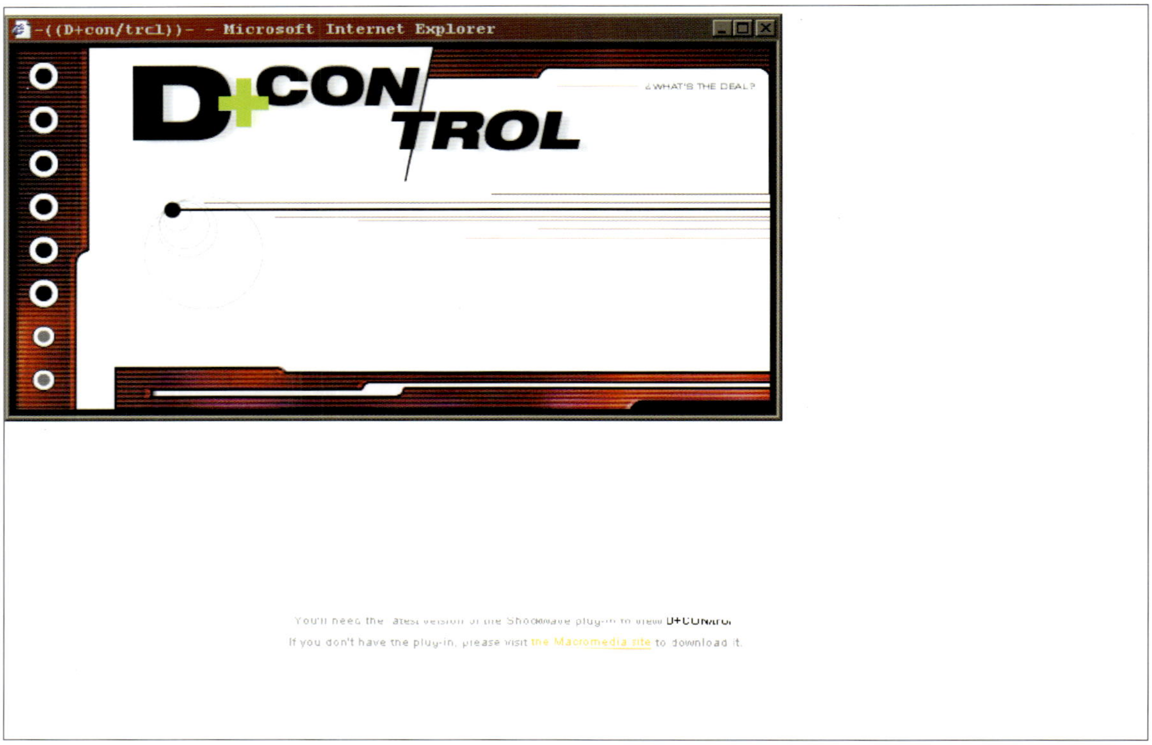

Title
D+CON/trol
URL
www.decontrol.com/deconvi/
Design Firm
One Ten Design Inc.

As the name implies, D+CON/trol is intentionally confusing to navigate. The buttons are marked with ambiguous labels. Sit back and explore; give up some of that control!

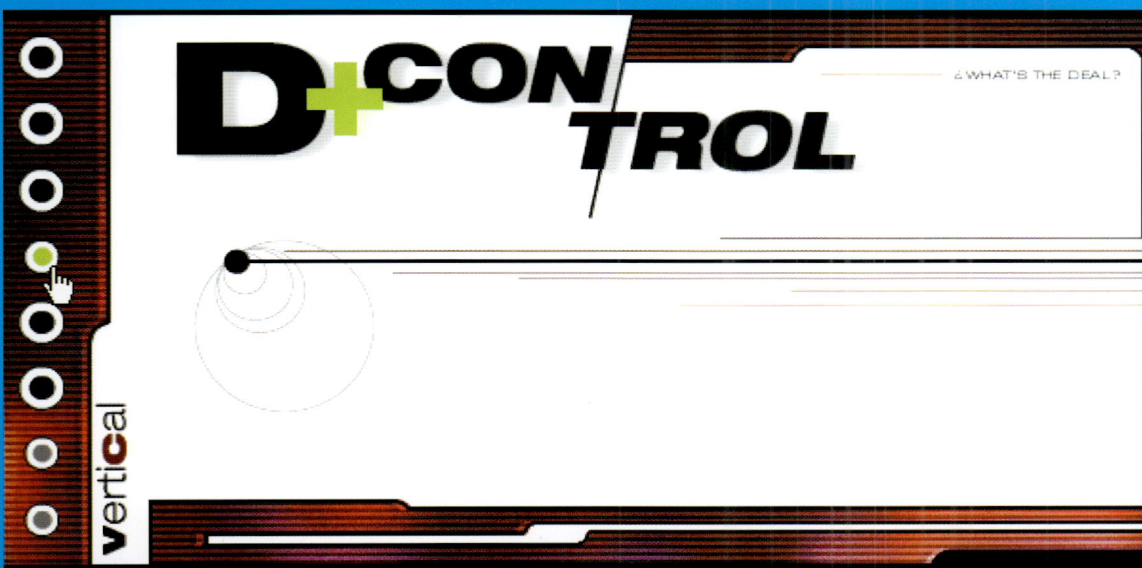
D+CON
TROL
¿WHAT'S THE DEAL?
vertical

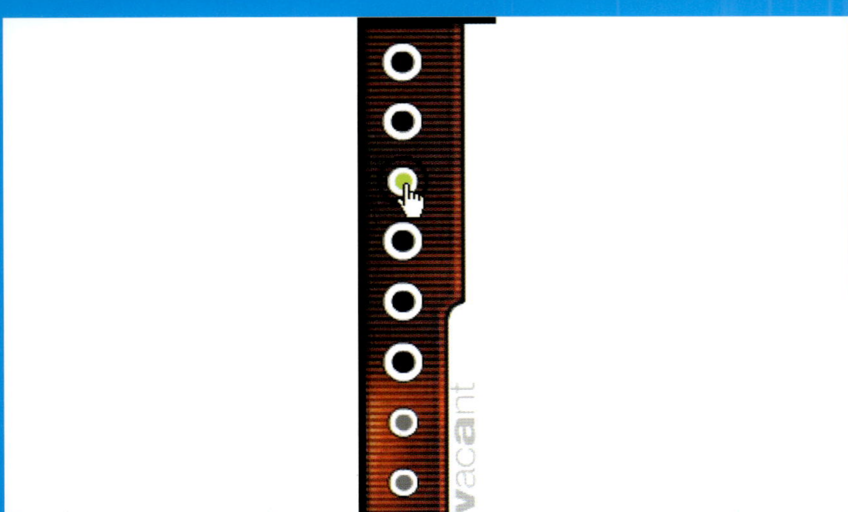
vacant

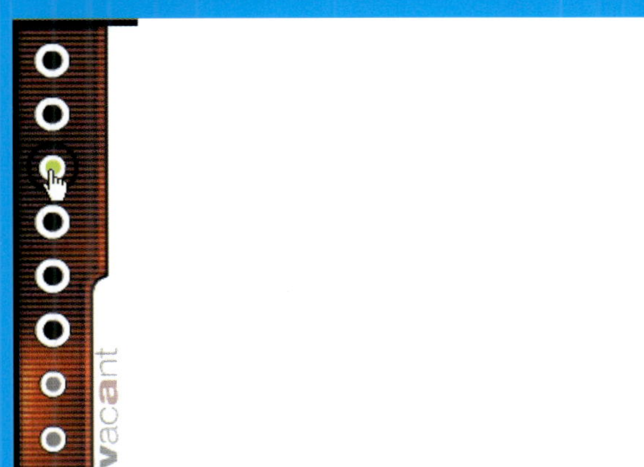
vacant

Title
Clint Baker's Portfolio Viewing Machine
URL
www.clintbaker.com
Design Firm
Clint Baker
Designer
Clint Baker
Icon Illustrator
Clint Baker

"The amazing viewing machine" is a creative, one-step navigation system invented by Clint Baker to showcase his artwork. Just scroll over the picture viewer until you find an image you would like to see and then click on it...the next evolution in thumbnails.

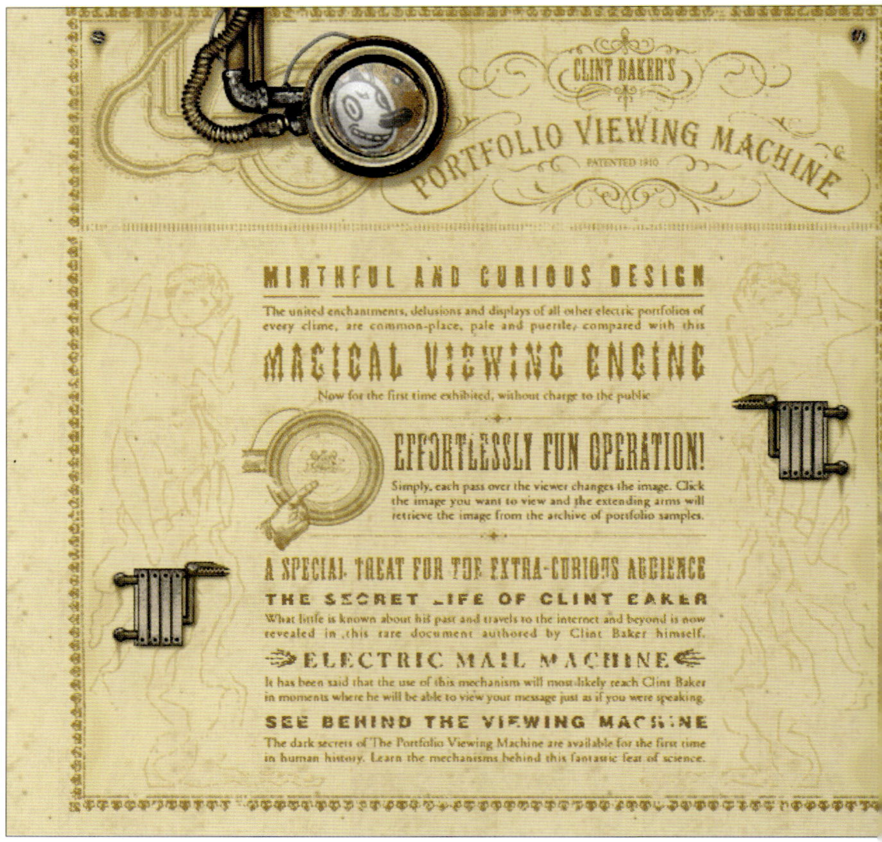

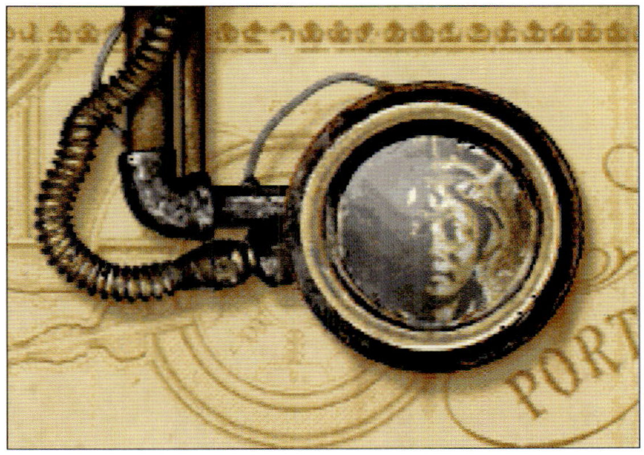

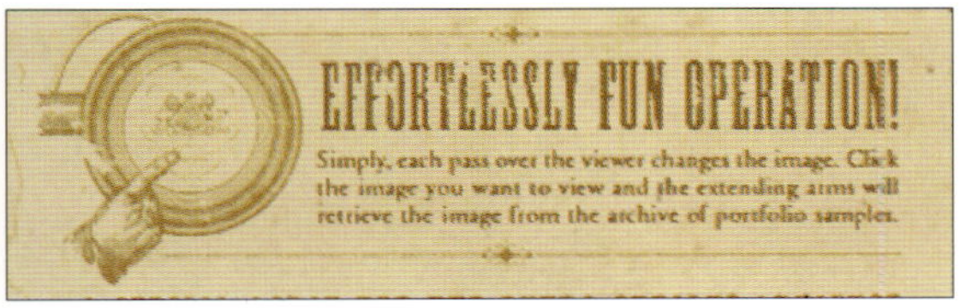
EFFORTLESSLY FUN OPERATION!
Simply, each pass over the viewer changes the image. Click the image you want to view and the extending arms will retrieve the image from the archive of portfolio samples.

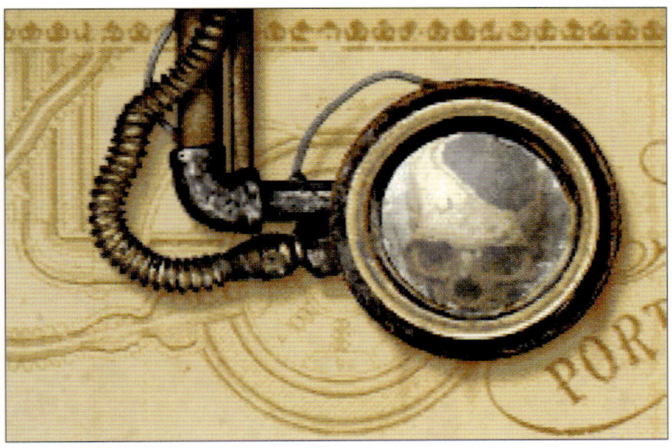

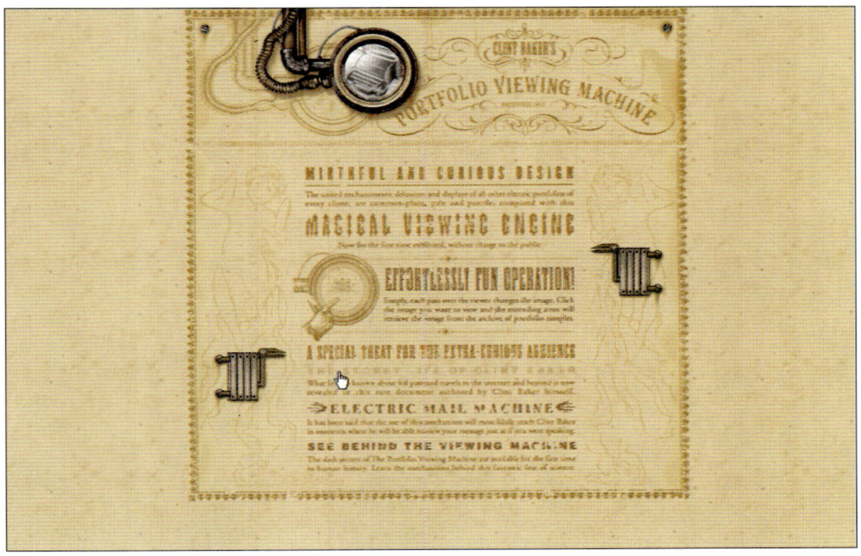
CLINT BAKER'S
PORTFOLIO VIEWING MACHINE
MIRTHFUL AND CURIOUS DESIGN
MAGICAL VIEWING ENGINE
EFFORTLESSLY FUN OPERATION!
A SPECIAL TREAT FOR THE EXTRA-CURIOUS AUDIENCE
ELECTRIC MAIL MACHINE
SEE BEHIND THE VIEWING MACHINE

Title
Human Evolution

URL
www.sscf.ucsb.edu/~hagen/crania/

Designers
Phillip L. Walker, Edward H. Hagen, Dirk Brandts
University of California, Santa Barbara/Department of Anthropology

The homepage of the Human Evolution site features a timeline navigation bar. Just pick an epoch and view the Flash-animated skulls. The animations load in the window above the navigation bar. This page offers a nice combination of frames and Flash.

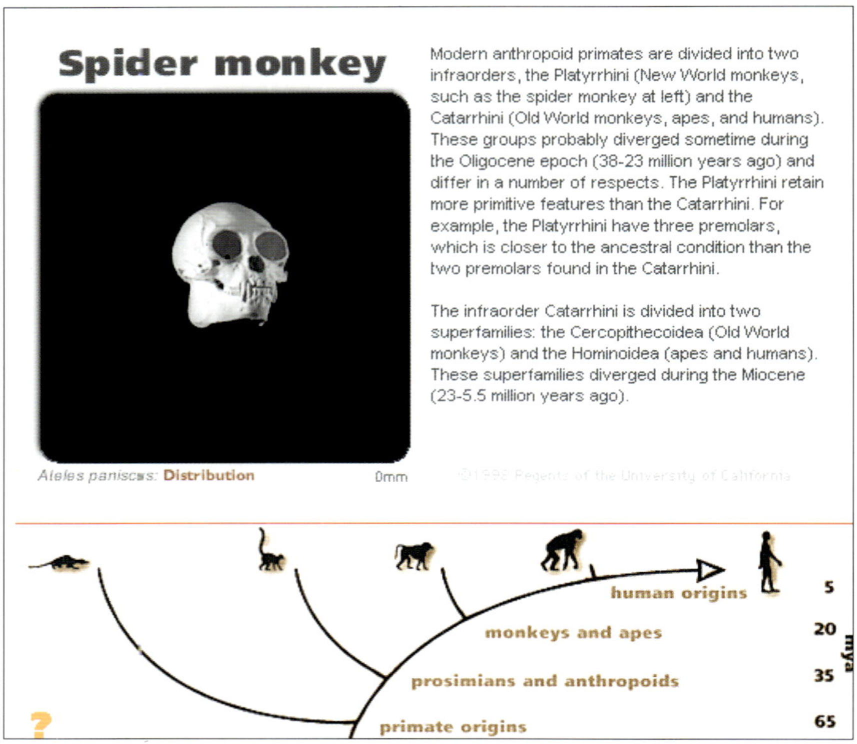

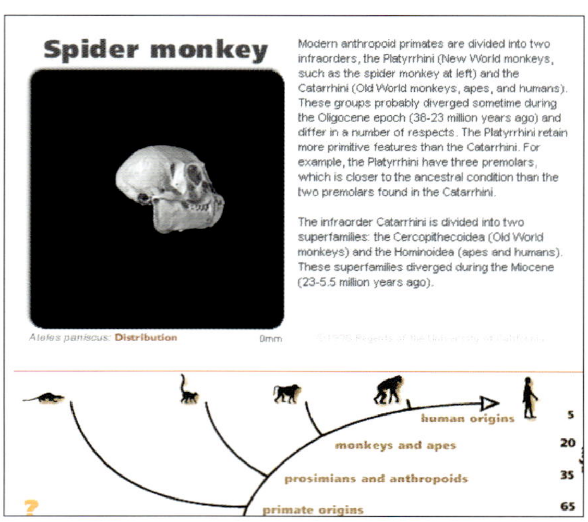

Homo sapiens

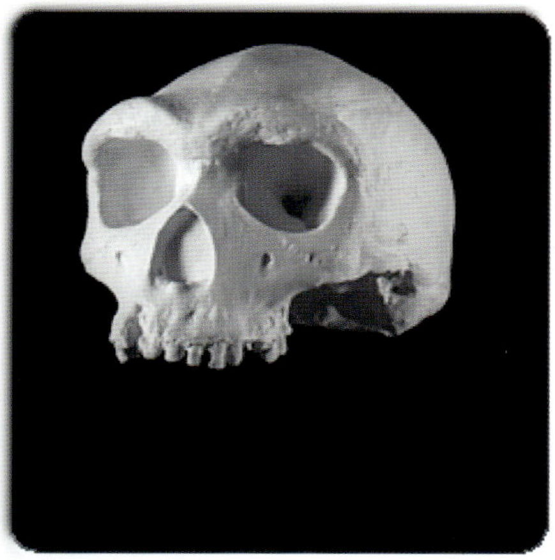

Broken Hill 1: **Site** 0mm

Modern-looking humans, differing sufficiently from Homo erectus to be recognized as a new species, began to appear in Africa and Europe about 400,000 years ago. These advanced hominids contrasted with H. erectus mainly in their large cranial capacities of 1100 to 1400 cubic centimeters, which fall within the lower end of the modern human range. Because they retained some primitive traits not found in modern people, such specimens are often referred to as "archaic" Homo sapiens. Some paleoanthropologists believe that, as a group, the archaic H. sapiens were distinctive enough to be placed in their own species, Homo heidelbergensis.

Many archaic H. sapiens, like Broken Hill 1 at left, had massive browridges that superficially resembled those of Homo erectus. However, instead of forming a continuous bar of bone, the browridges of archaic Homo sapiens had an arched, wing-like configuration that was low in the center and followed the contours of the orbits.

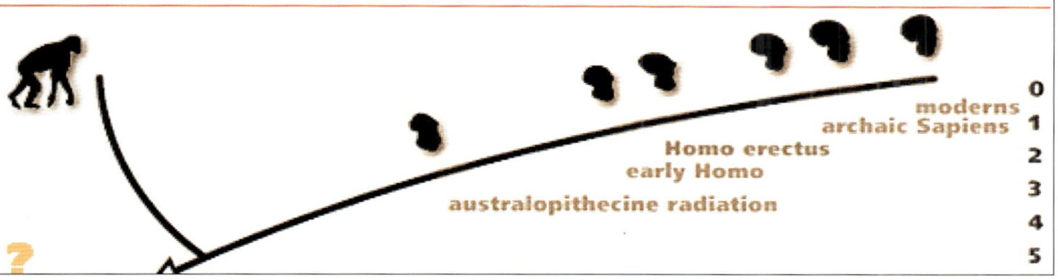

Homo sapiens

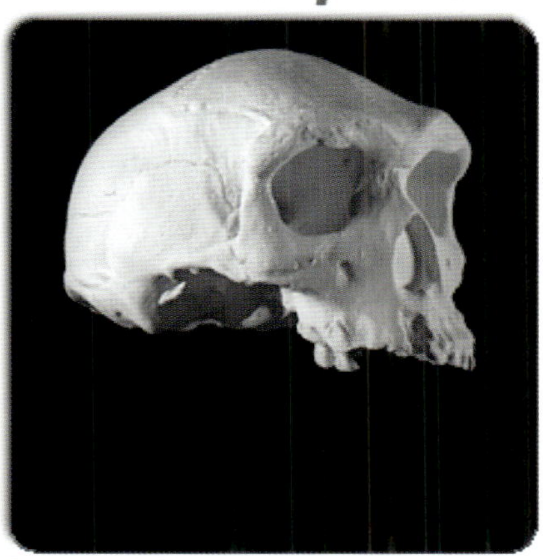

Broken Hill 1: **Site** 0mm

Modern-looking humans, differing sufficiently from Homo erectus to be recognized as a new species, began to appear in Africa and Europe about 400,000 years ago. These advanced hominids contrasted with H. erectus mainly in their large cranial capacities of 1100 to 1400 cubic centimeters, which fall within the lower end of the modern human range. Because they retained some primitive traits not found in modern people, such specimens are often referred to as "archaic" Homo sapiens. Some paleoanthropologists believe that, as a group, the archaic H. sapiens were distinctive enough to be placed in their own species, Homo heidelbergensis.

Many archaic H. sapiens, like Broken Hill 1 at left, had massive browridges that superficially resembled those of Homo erectus. However, instead of forming a continuous bar of bone, the browridges of archaic Homo sapiens had an arched, wing-like configuration that was low in the center and followed the contours of the orbits.

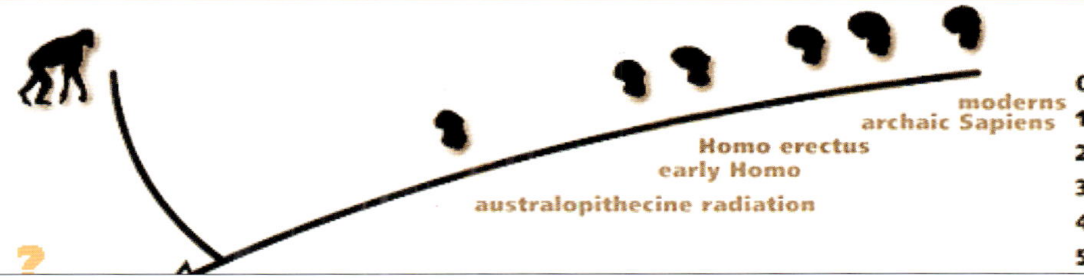

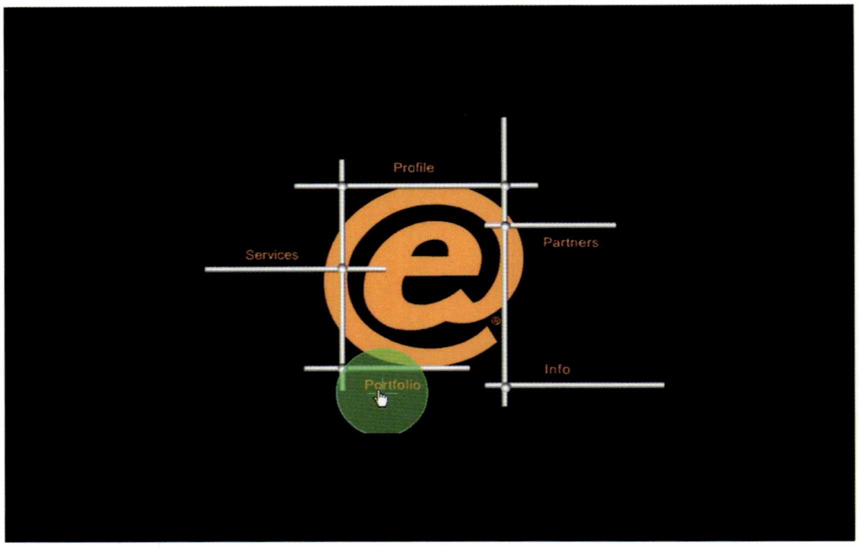

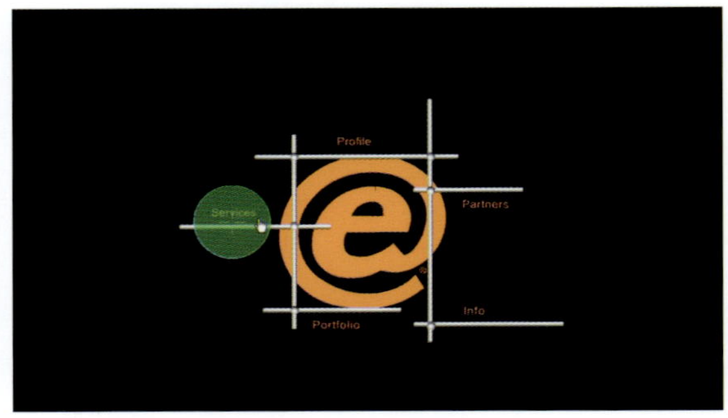

Title
Eurorunner
URL
www.eurorunner.com/
Design Firm
Euro.runner srl
Designers
Jacopo Deyla/flash, Giuseppe Covino/Art Director, Franco Milazzo/Technical

On mouse-over, the links are captured in a sight like a rifle scope. The four buttons make navigation unambiguous and simple.

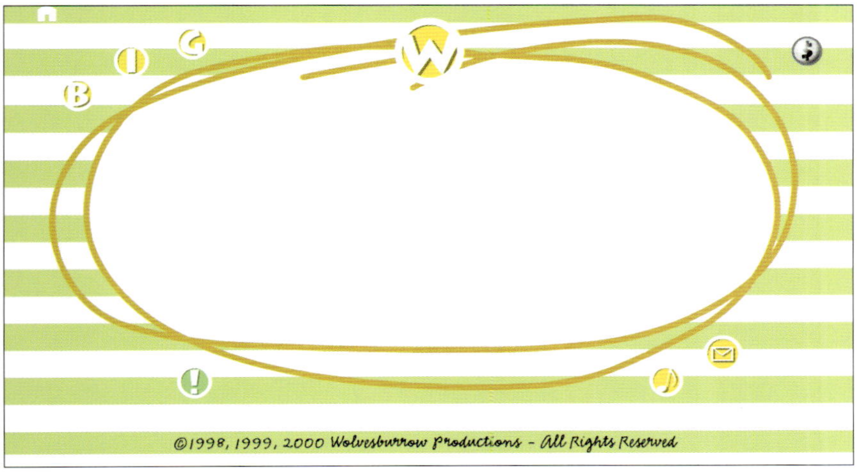

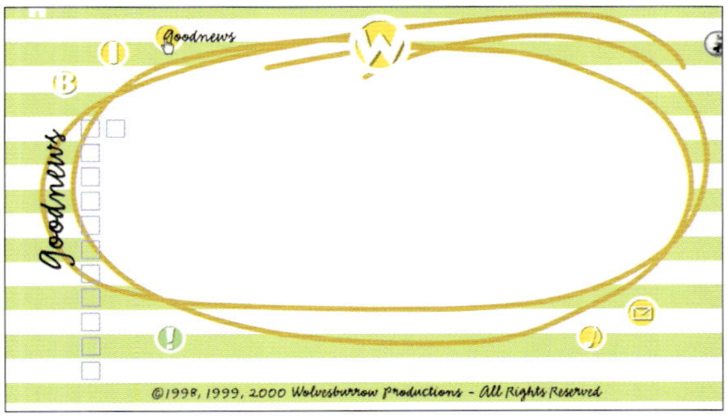

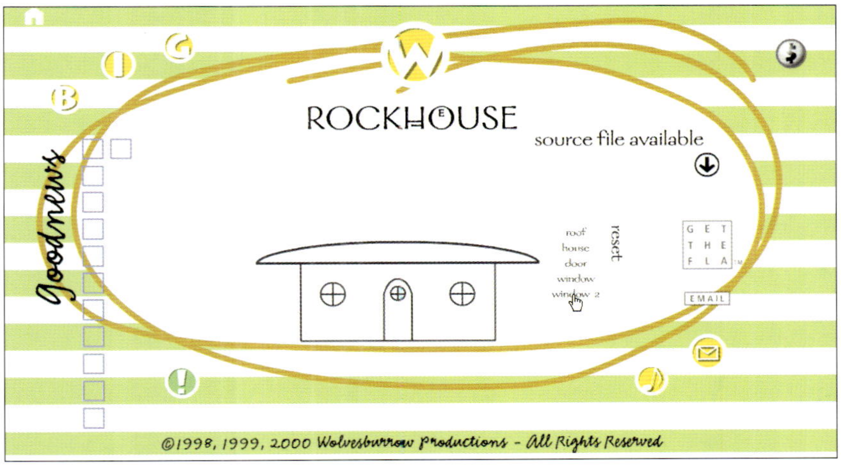

Title
wolvesburrow
URL
www.
wolvesburrow.com/
Design firm
wolvesburrow
productions

Take a look at another great Flash site. The buttons all become agreeable cursive text that point in the direction of the many exhibits on this fun site.

Title
The Multimedia Group
URL
www.themmgroup.com/
Design Firm
The Multimedia Group

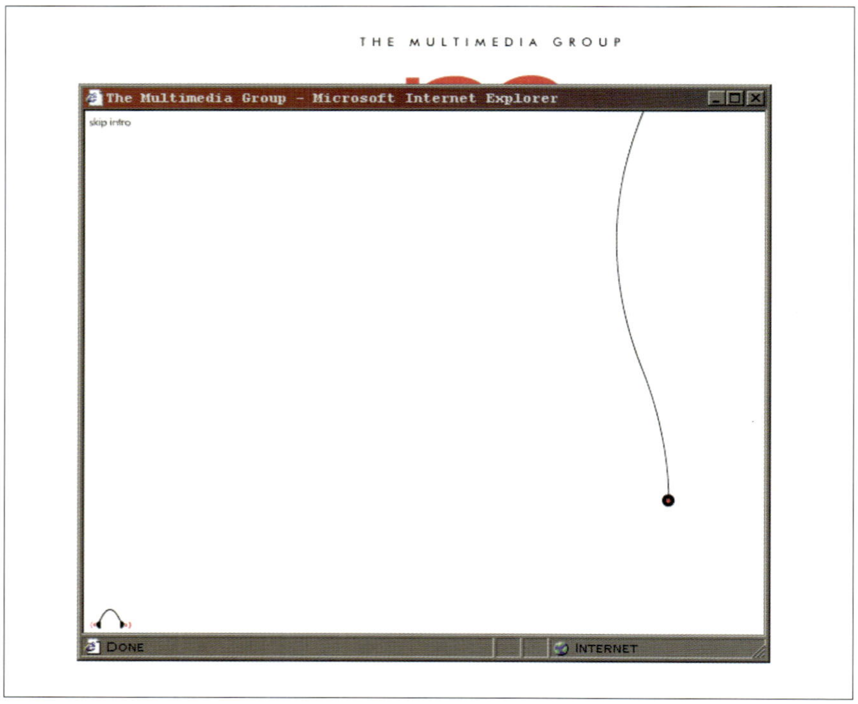

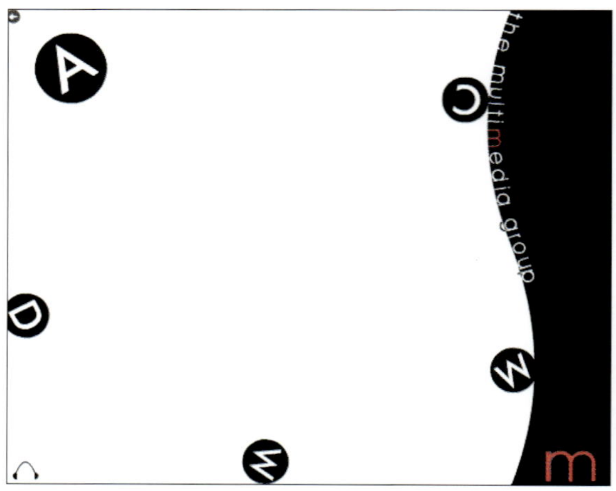

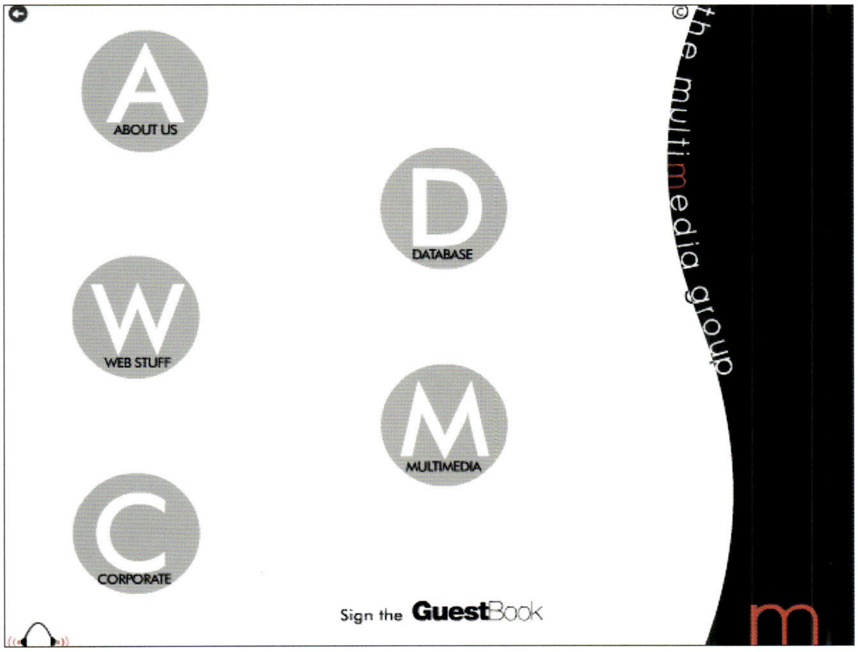

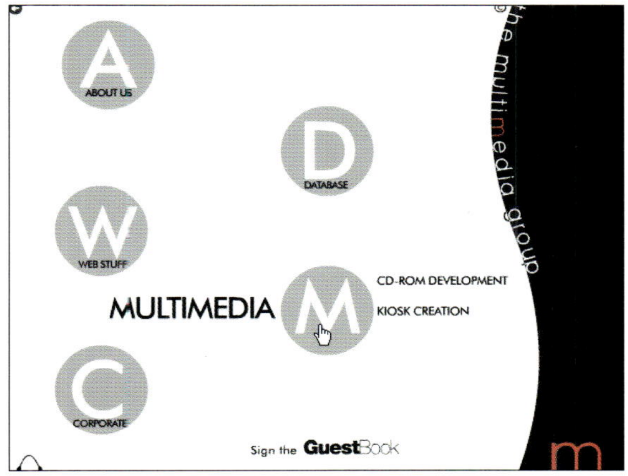

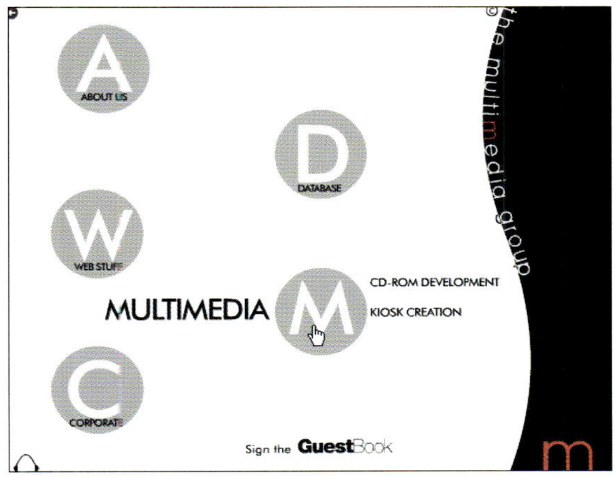

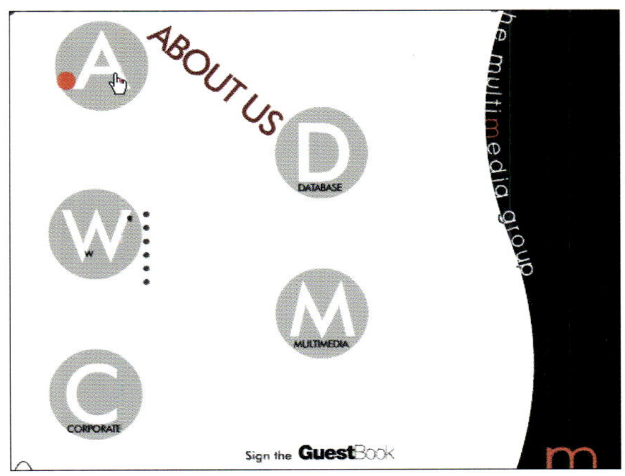

Every button on this site has its own unique movement, making the page fun and easy to navigate. Scroll over the links to pull up sub-folders that further explain where each link goes.

Title
wireless Knowledge
URL
www.wirelessknowledge.com/
Design firm
wireless Knowledge

A simple, round interface features photos of the product scrolling by in the middle. Three buttons keep it simple and clear.

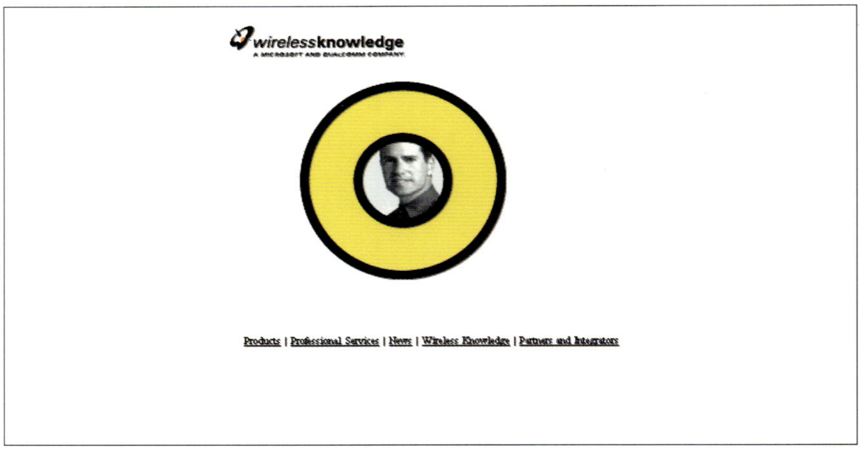

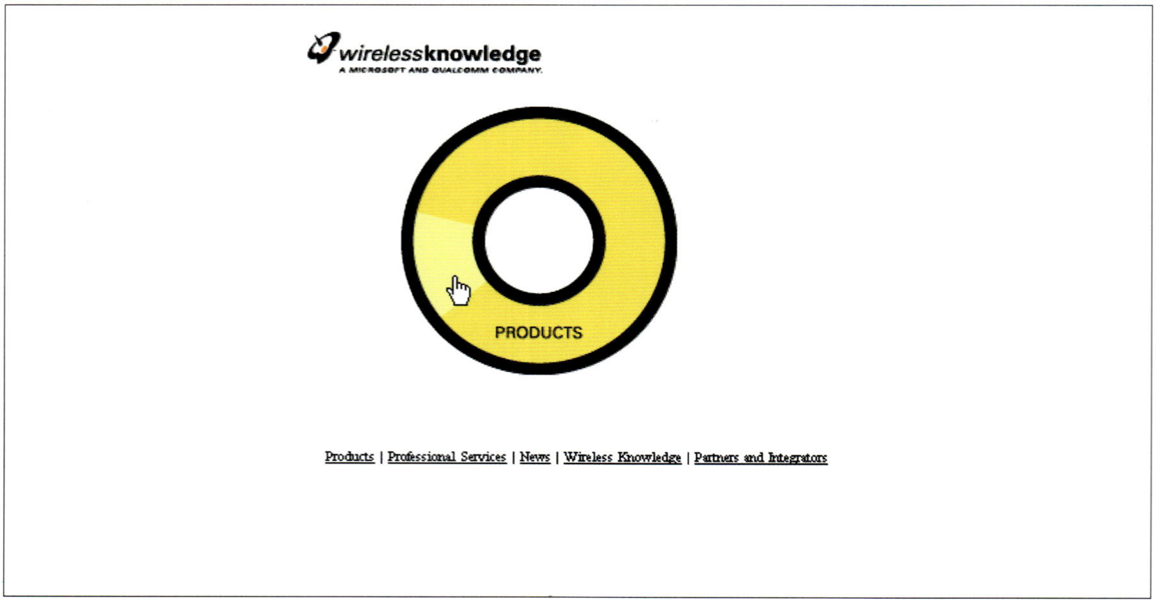

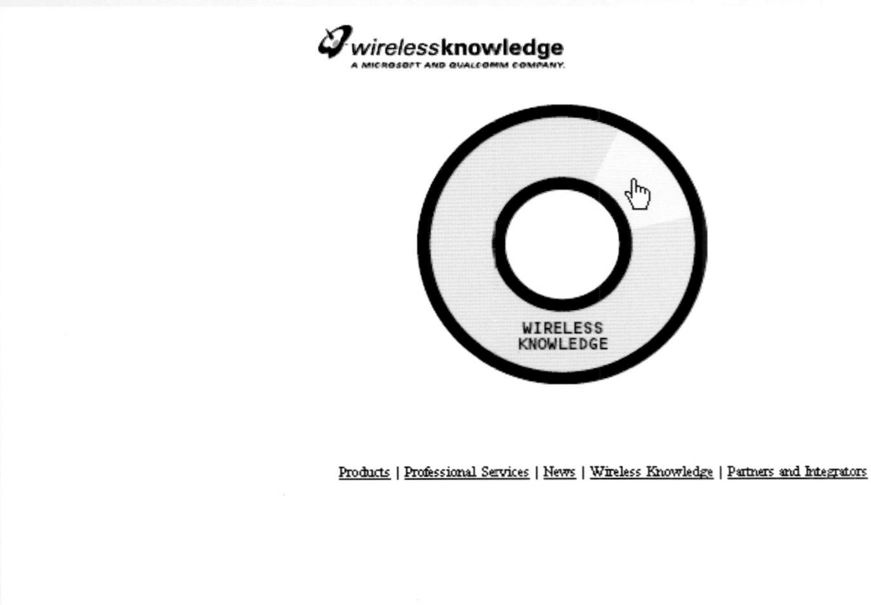
wirelessknowledge
A MICROSOFT AND QUALCOMM COMPANY.
WIRELESS KNOWLEDGE
Products | Professional Services | News | Wireless Knowledge | Partners and Integrators

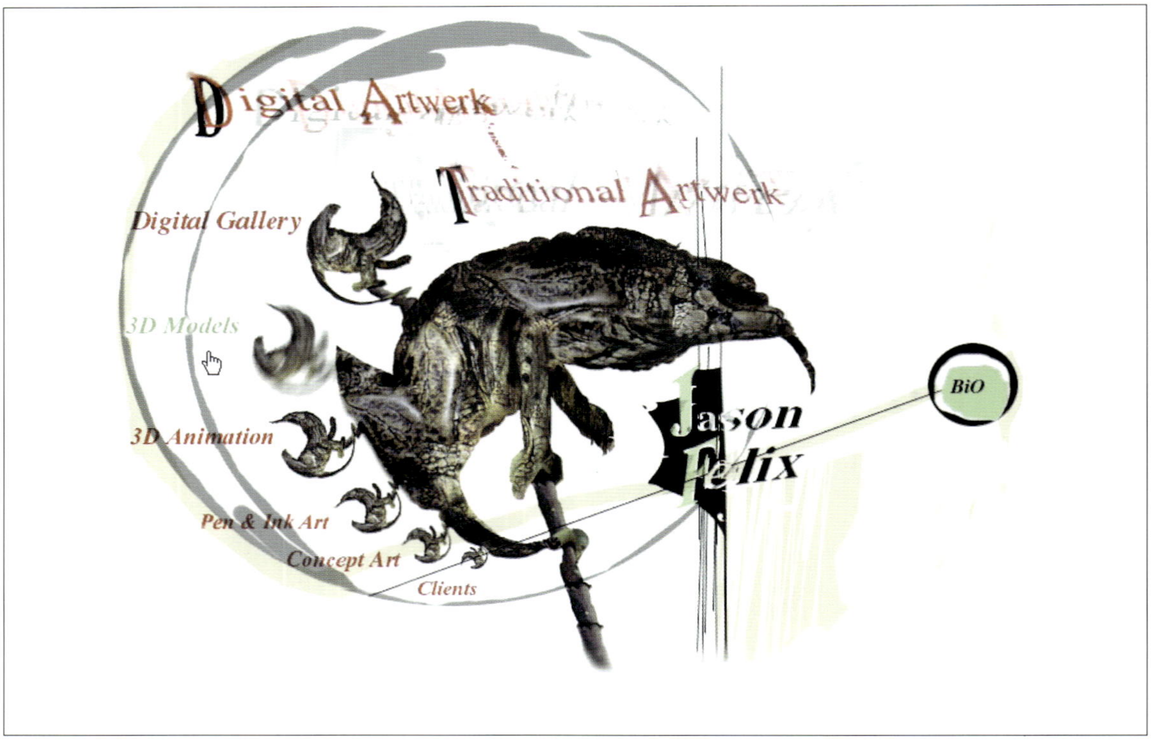

Title
Jason Felix
URL
www.jasonfelix.com/newinterface.html
Design firm
Jason Felix

A striking image is repeated to great effect on this site. The buttons fade as you scroll over, which helps you remember where you are.

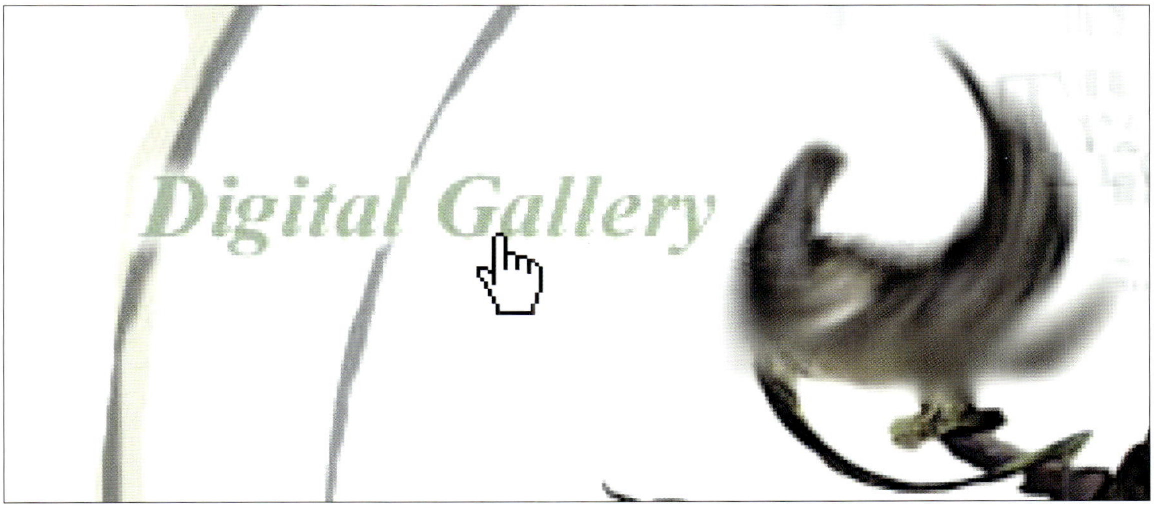
Digital Gallery

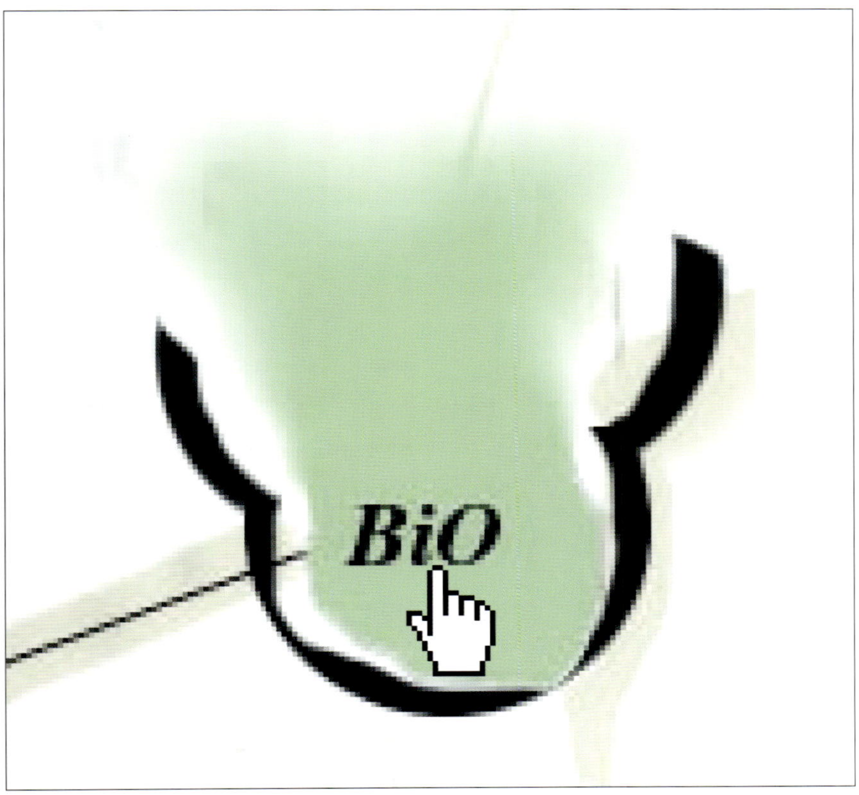
BiO

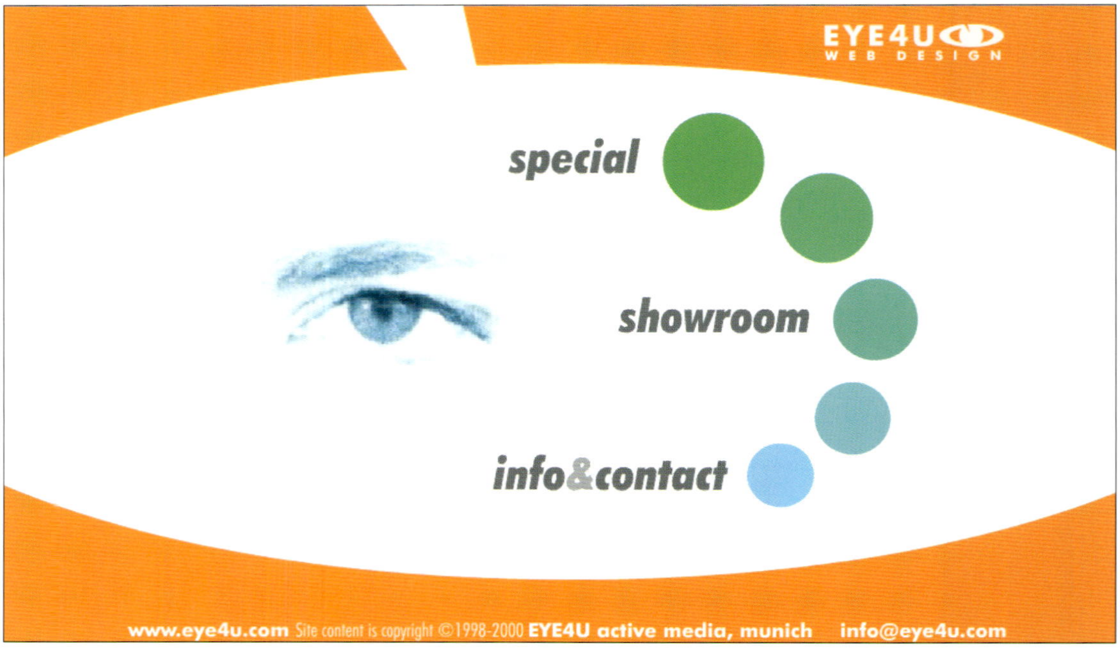
EYE4U
WEB DESIGN
special
showroom
info&contact
www.eye4u.com Site content is copyright ©1998-2000 EYE4U active media, munich info@eye4u.com

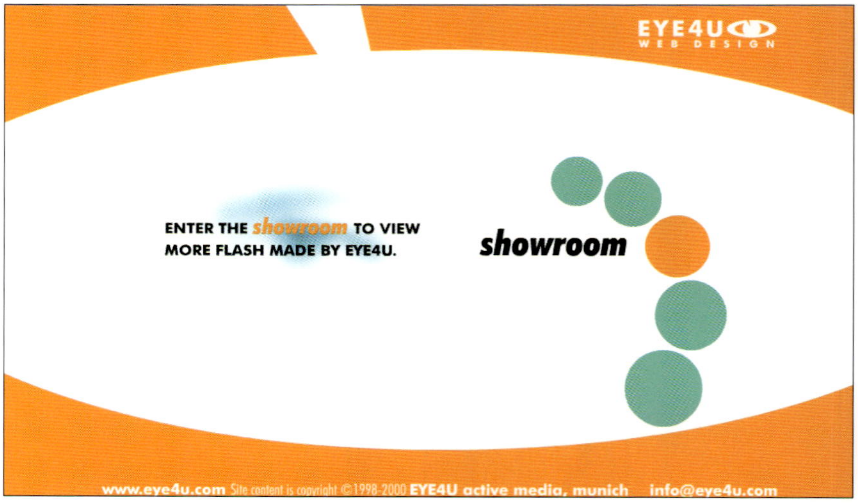
EYE4U
WEB DESIGN
ENTER THE showroom TO VIEW
MORE FLASH MADE BY EYE4U.
showroom
www.eye4u.com Site content is copyright ©1998-2000 EYE4U active media, munich info@eye4u.com

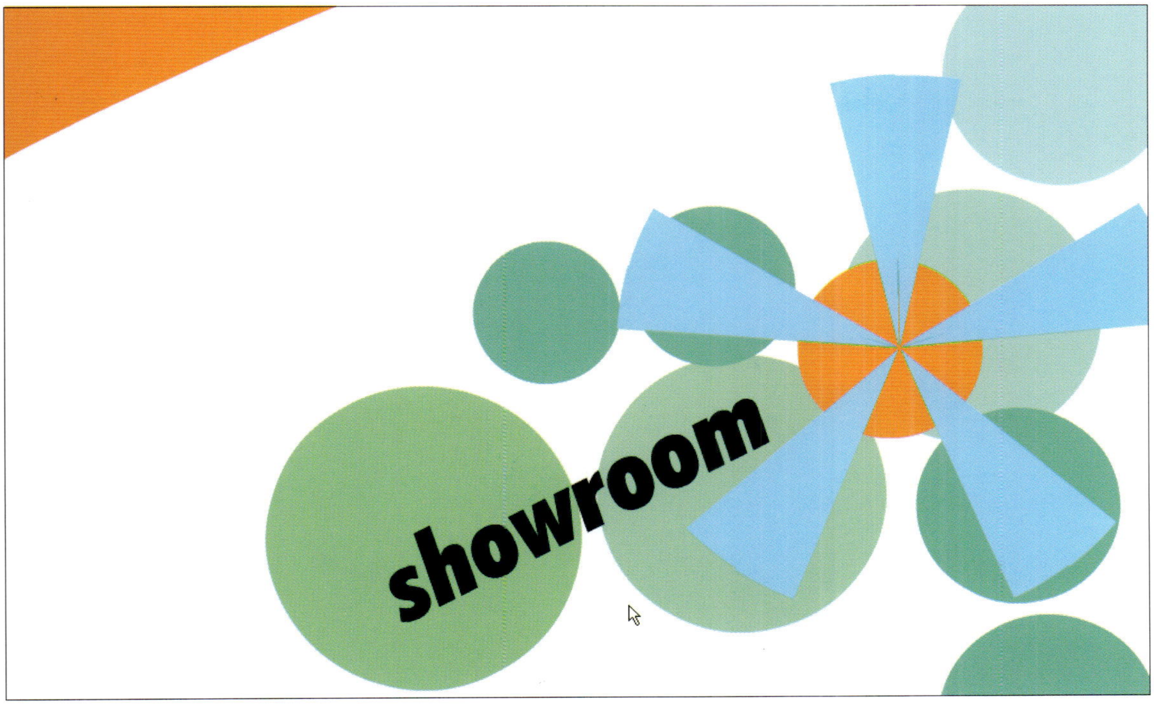

Title
Eye4U
URL
eye4u.com/home/index.htm
Design firm
Eye 4 U Active Media

Designers used Flash on this striking page to keep bandwidth down and animation at its peak. The three main buttons move and reveal iconic images on mouse-over. When clicked, the music seamlessly adds a beat.

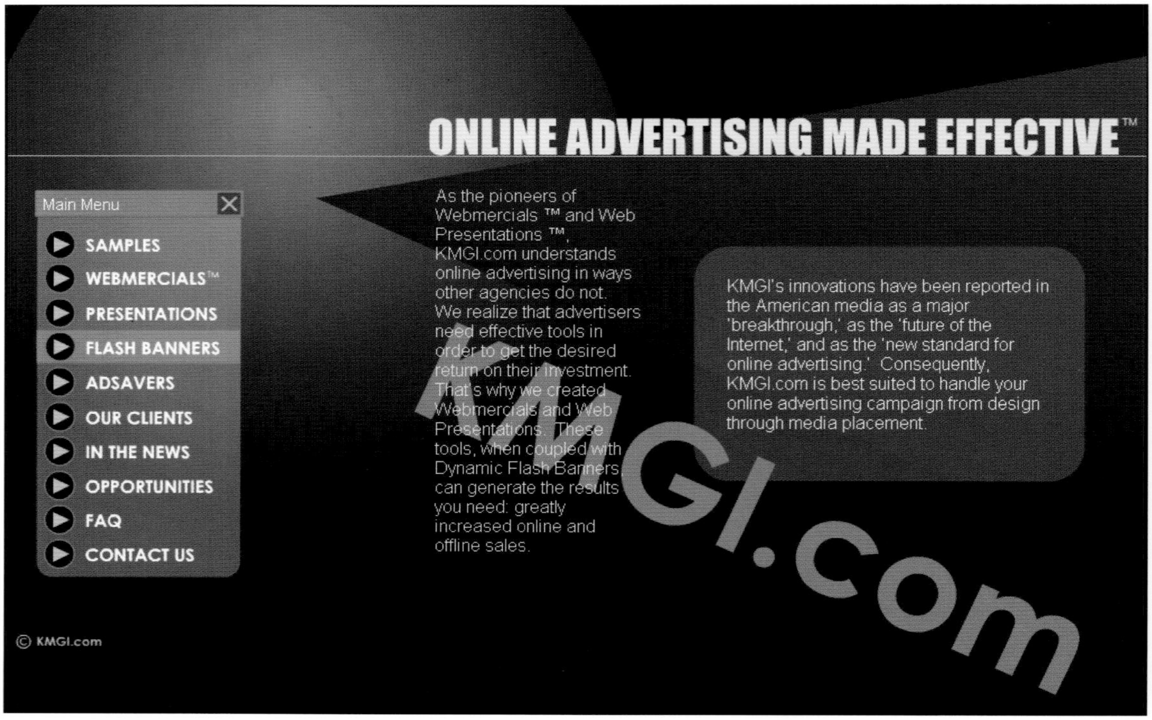

Title
KMGI
URL
www.kmgi.com/
Design Firm
KMBI.com Inc.

The Flash interface on the KMGI site is remarkably easy to use. One interface serves as both navigation bar and map. The KMGI site is one of the first—if not the first—site created totally in Flash Lingo.

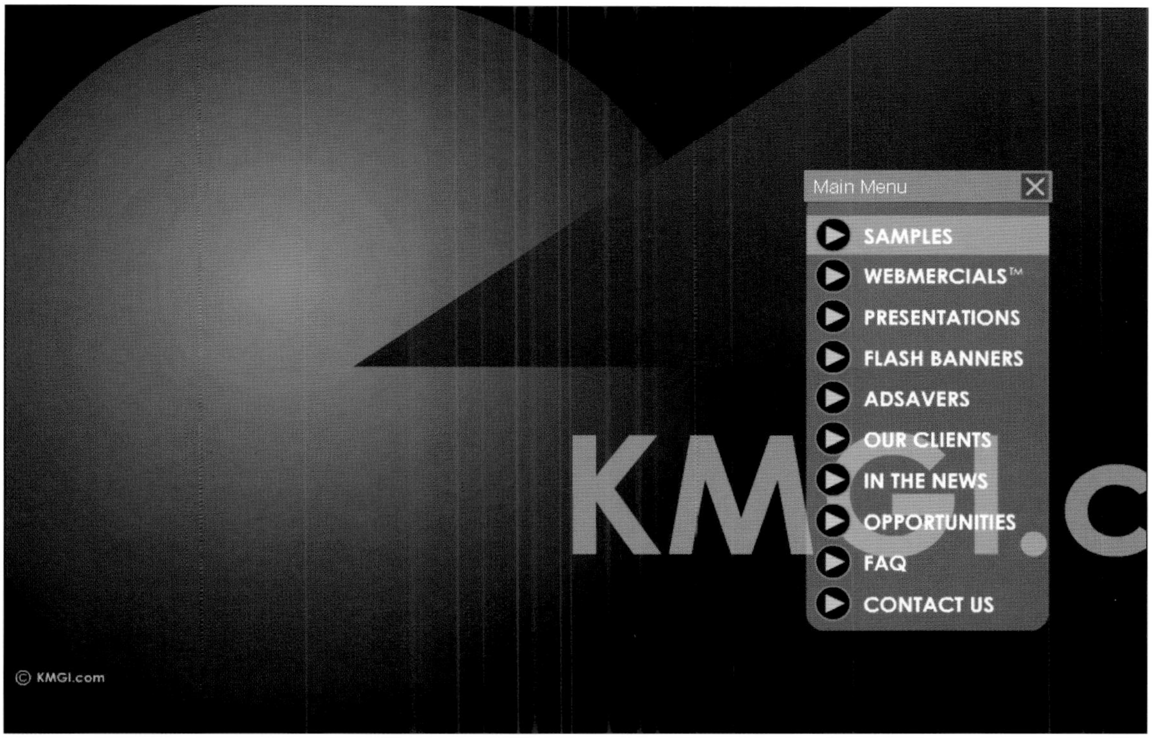
Main Menu
SAMPLES
WEBMERCIALS™
PRESENTATIONS
FLASH BANNERS
ADSAVERS
OUR CLIENTS
IN THE NEWS
OPPORTUNITIES
FAQ
CONTACT US
KMGI.c
© KMGI.com

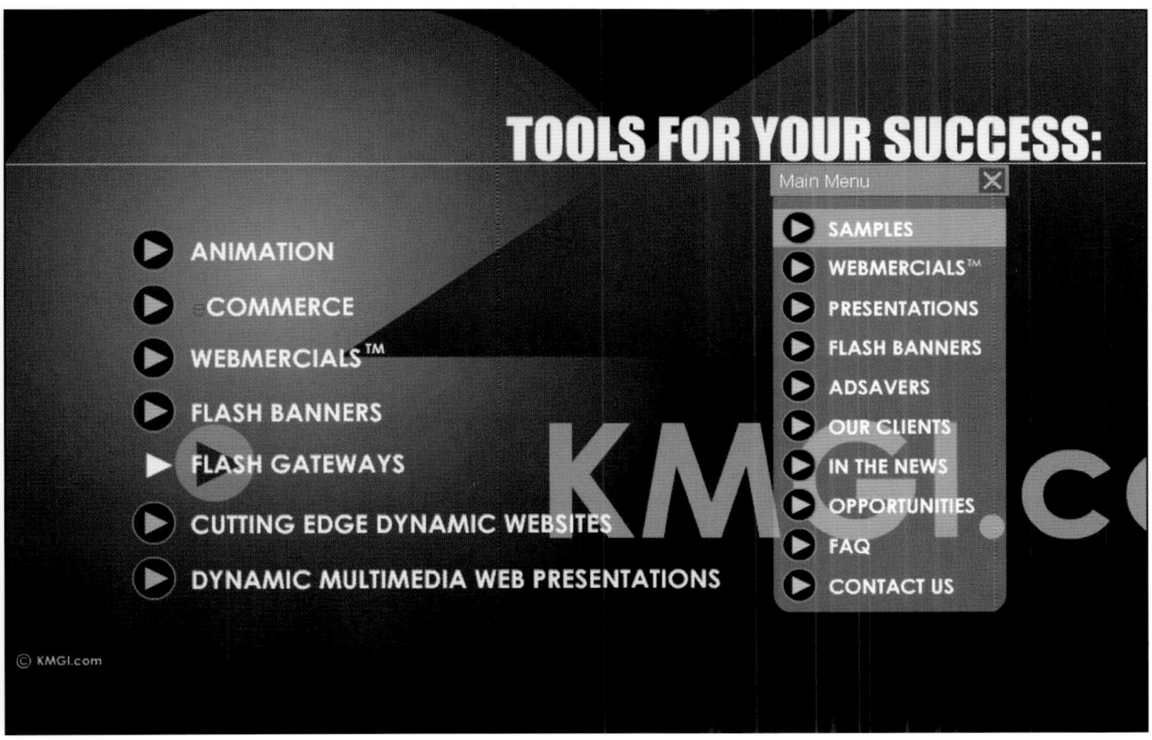
TOOLS FOR YOUR SUCCESS:
ANIMATION
eCOMMERCE
WEBMERCIALS™
FLASH BANNERS
FLASH GATEWAYS
CUTTING EDGE DYNAMIC WEBSITES
DYNAMIC MULTIMEDIA WEB PRESENTATIONS
Main Menu
SAMPLES
WEBMERCIALS™
PRESENTATIONS
FLASH BANNERS
ADSAVERS
OUR CLIENTS
IN THE NEWS
OPPORTUNITIES
FAQ
CONTACT US
KMGI.c
© KMGI.com

Title
Dennis Interactive
URL
www.dennisinter.com/di/disite.html
Design Firm
Dennis Publishing, Inc.

Dennis Interactive has included fourteen buttons on the main page without creating confusion—an impressive and professional site. The Flash-enabled buttons all are interesting animations in and of themselves. This one is possibly the best site on the Internet.

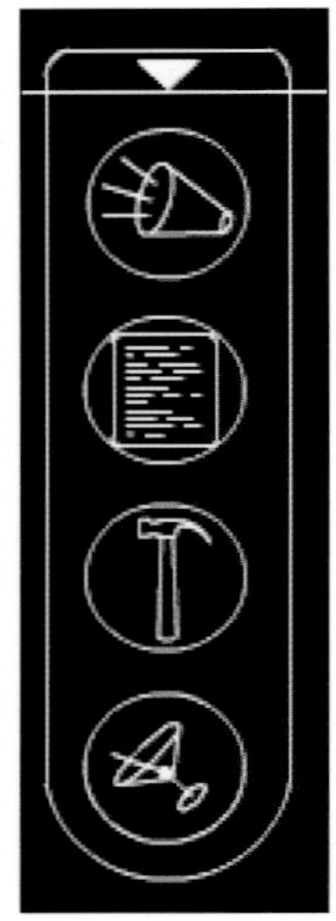

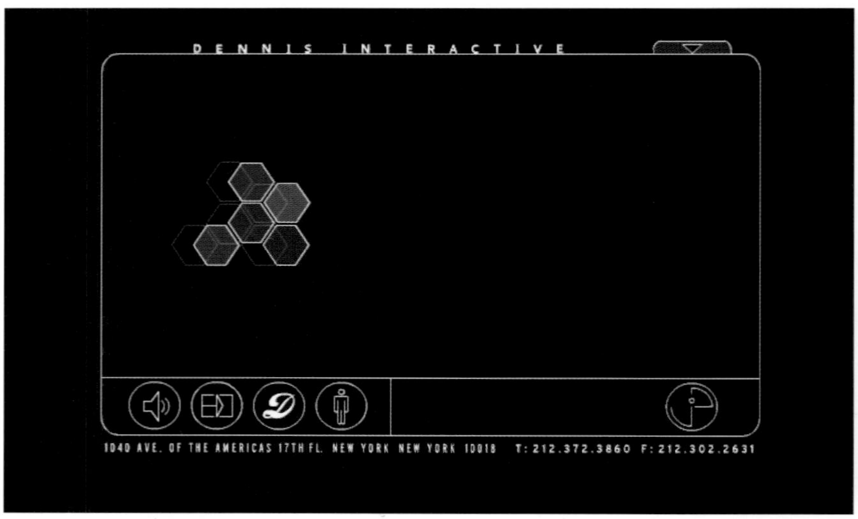

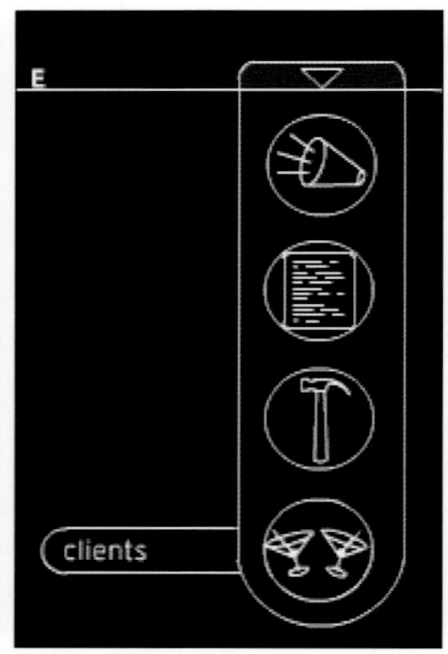

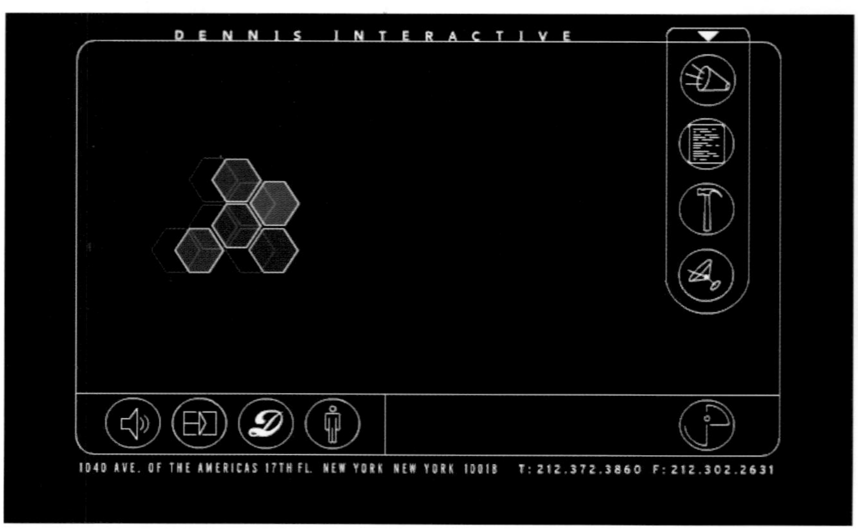

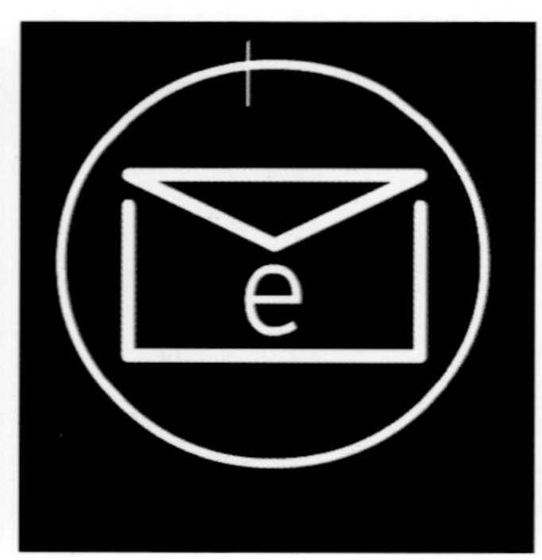

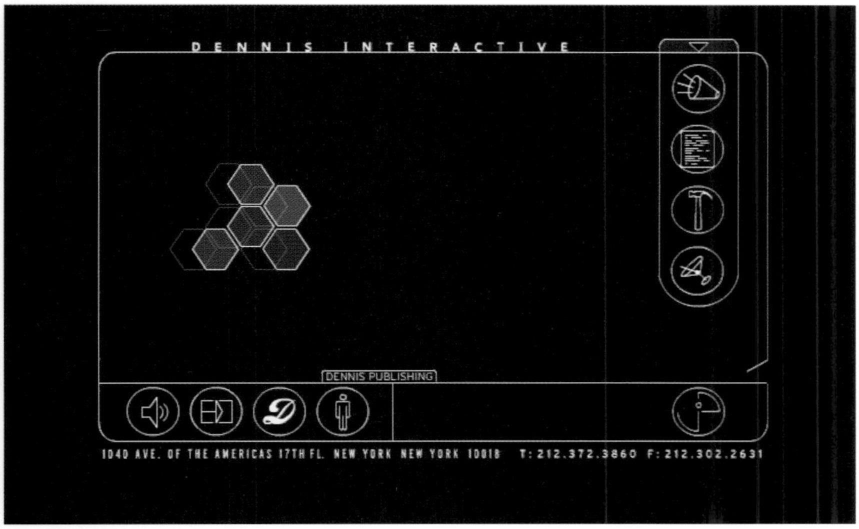
DENNIS INTERACTIVE
DENNIS PUBLISHING
1040 AVE. OF THE AMERICAS 17TH FL. NEW YORK NEW YORK 10018 T: 212.372.3860 F: 212.302.2631

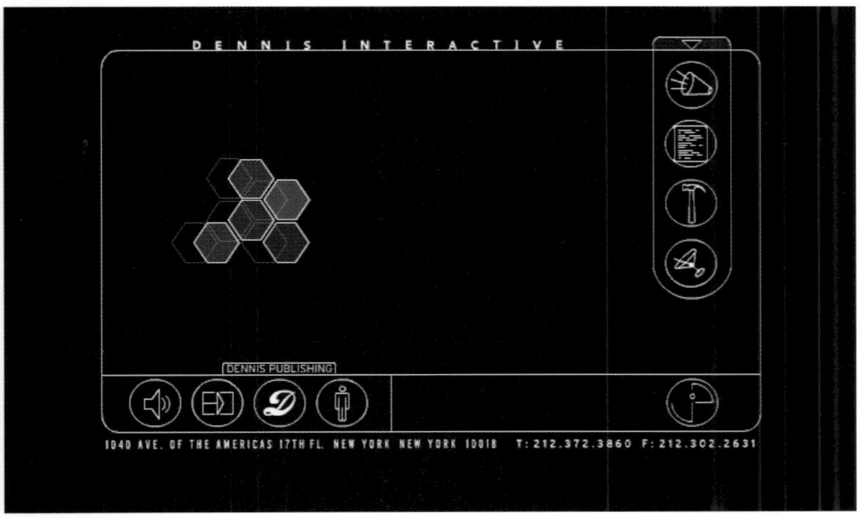
DENNIS INTERACTIVE
DENNIS PUBLISHING
1040 AVE. OF THE AMERICAS 17TH FL. NEW YORK NEW YORK 10018 T: 212.372.3860 F: 212.302.2631

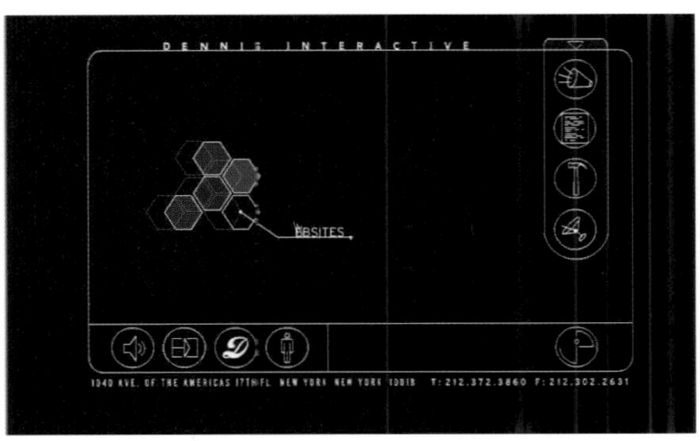
DENNIS INTERACTIVE

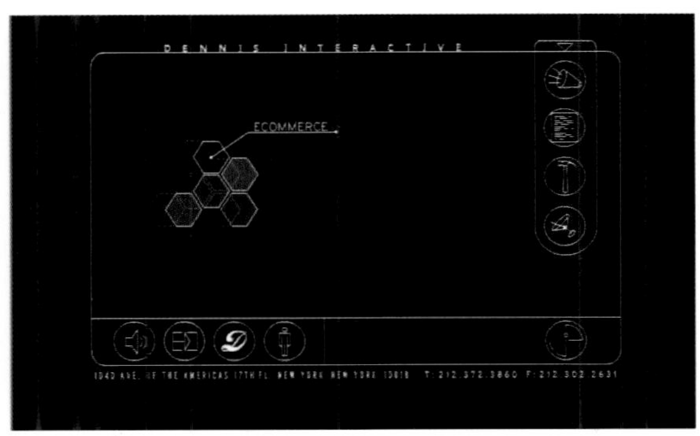
DENNIS INTERACTIVE
ECOMMERCE

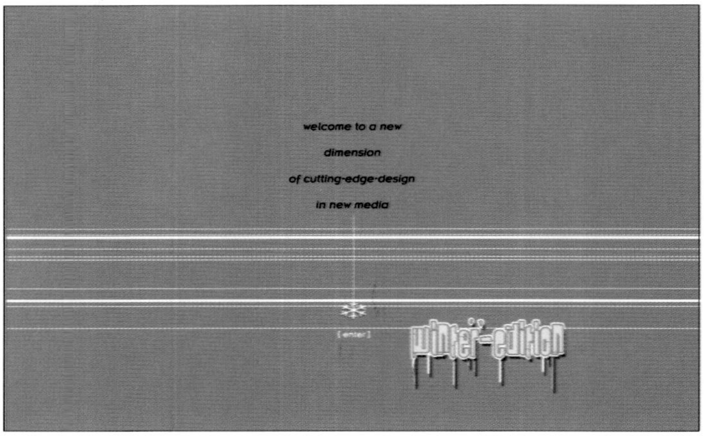

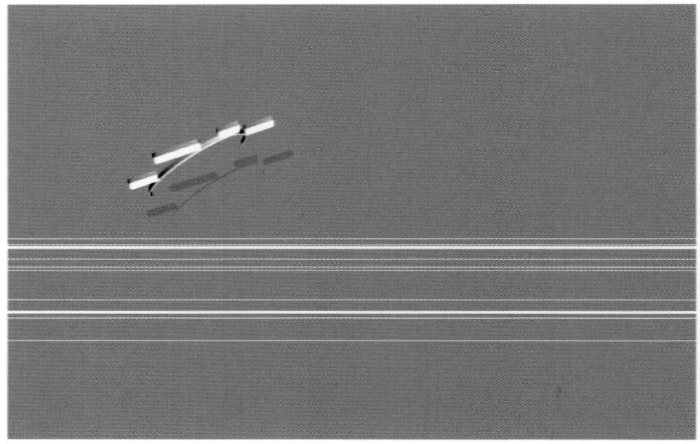

Title
Netgraphic
URL
www.netgraphic.ch/
Design Firm
Audiobox Ulanghanzepte

The interface for the Netgraphic site is clear (if you speak German) and concise. The four buttons appear to hang in midair because of the shadow Netgraphic built under the interface.

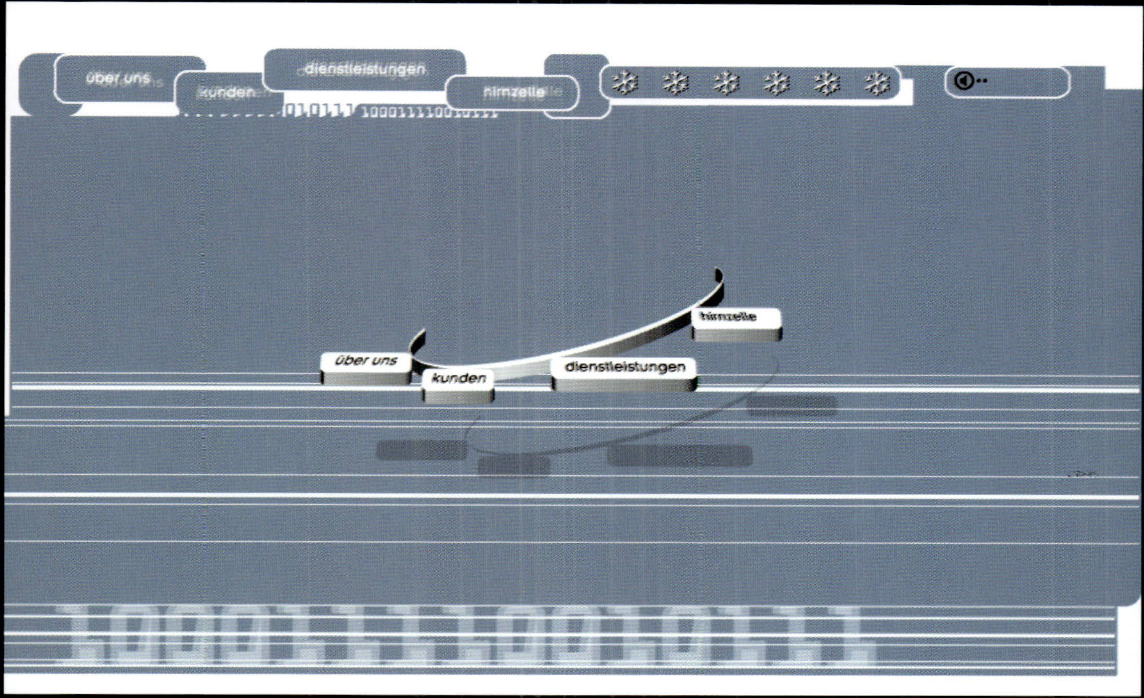
über uns
kunden
dienstleistungen
hirnzelle
über uns
kunden
dienstleistungen
hirnzelle

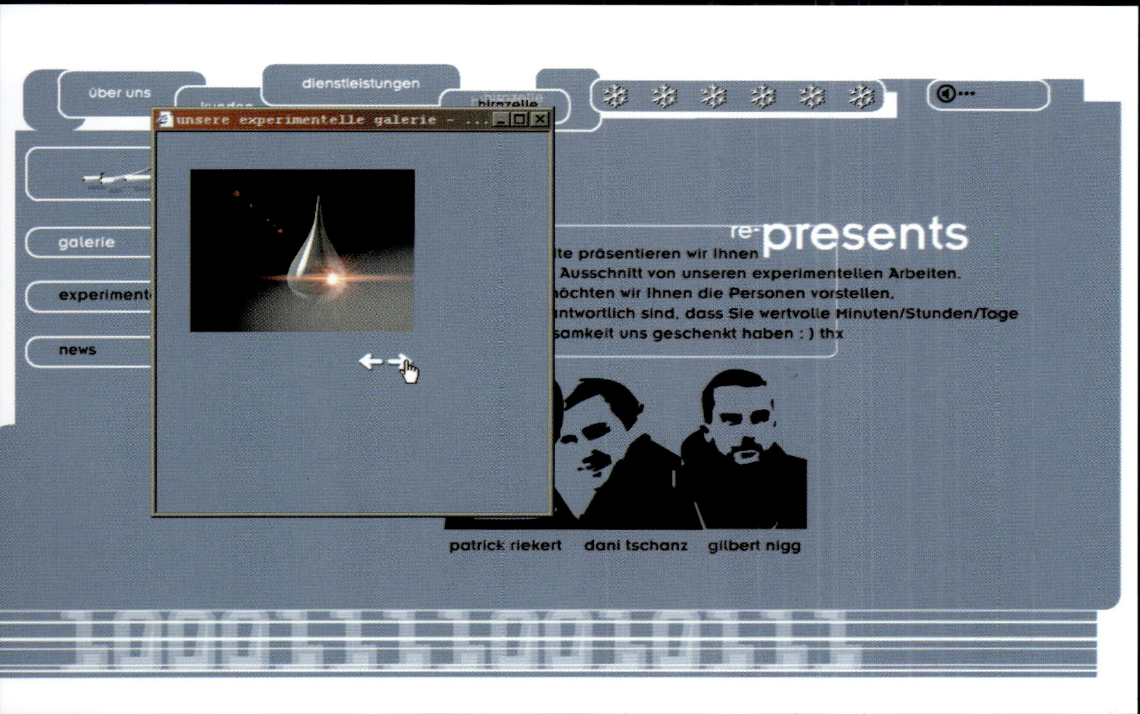
über uns
dienstleistungen
hirnzelle
unsere experimentelle galerie - ...
galerie
experiment
news
re-presents
ite präsentieren wir Ihnen
Ausschnitt von unseren experimentellen Arbeiten.
möchten wir Ihnen die Personen vorstellen,
antwortlich sind, dass Sie wertvolle Minuten/Stunden/Tage
samkeit uns geschenkt haben :) thx
patrick riekert
dani tschanz
gilbert nigg

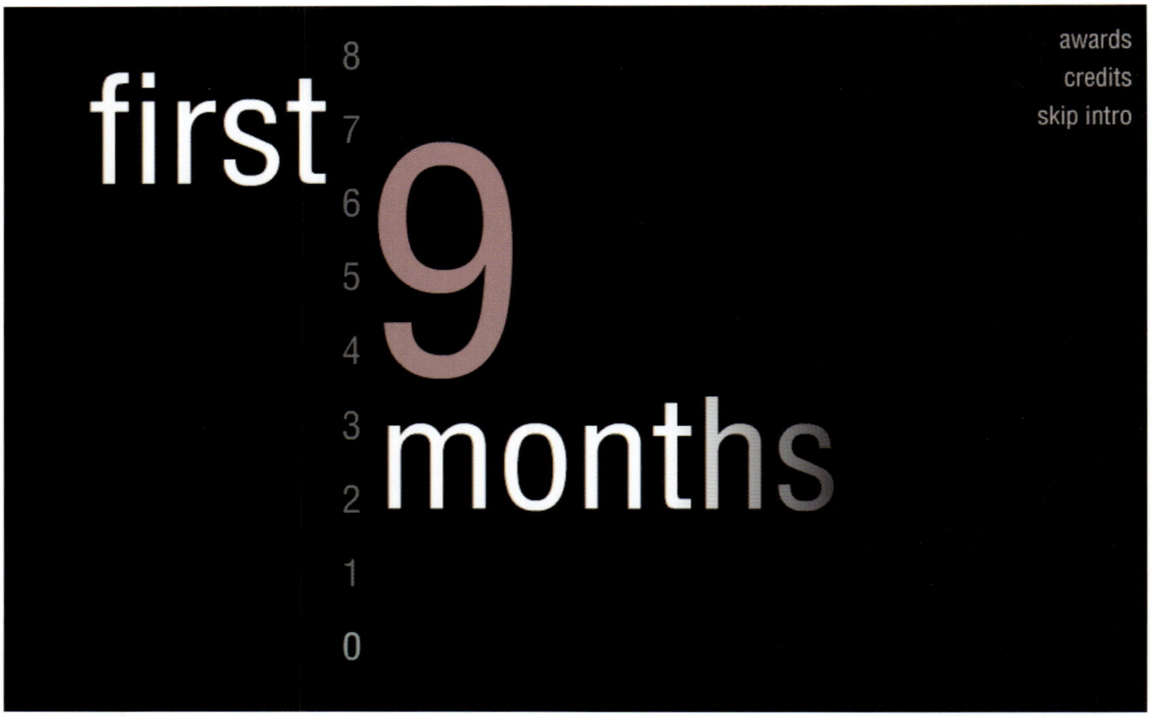

Title
First 9 Months
URL
www.first9months.com/
Design Firm
12 south.com
Designer
Joseph Moore

This site has a lot of content to sift through. The daily journal of the parents' journey through pregnancy could have been a nightmare to navigate, but First 9 Months can be broken down by day, week, or month, leaving the amount of information and speed of delivery up to you.

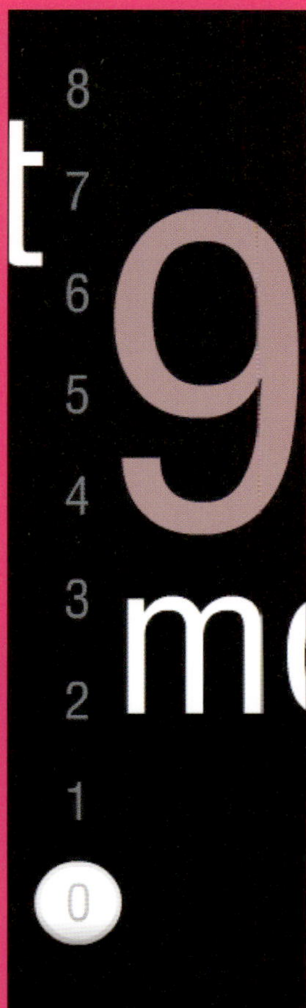
8
t
7
6
9
5
4
3
m
2
1
0

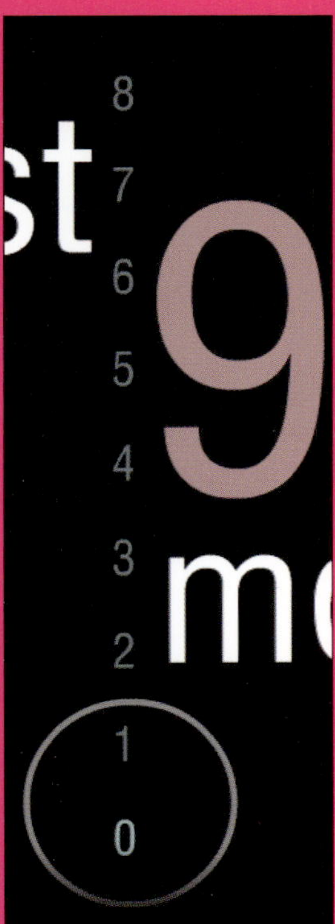
8
st
7
6
9
5
4
3
m
2
1
0

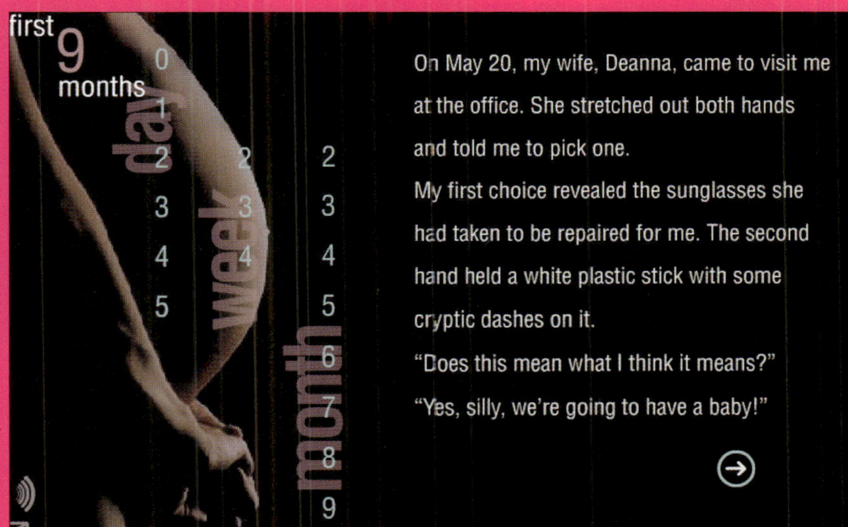
first
9
months
day
week
month
On May 20, my wife, Deanna, came to visit me at the office. She stretched out both hands and told me to pick one.
My first choice revealed the sunglasses she had taken to be repaired for me. The second hand held a white plastic stick with some cryptic dashes on it.
"Does this mean what I think it means?"
"Yes, silly, we're going to have a baby!"

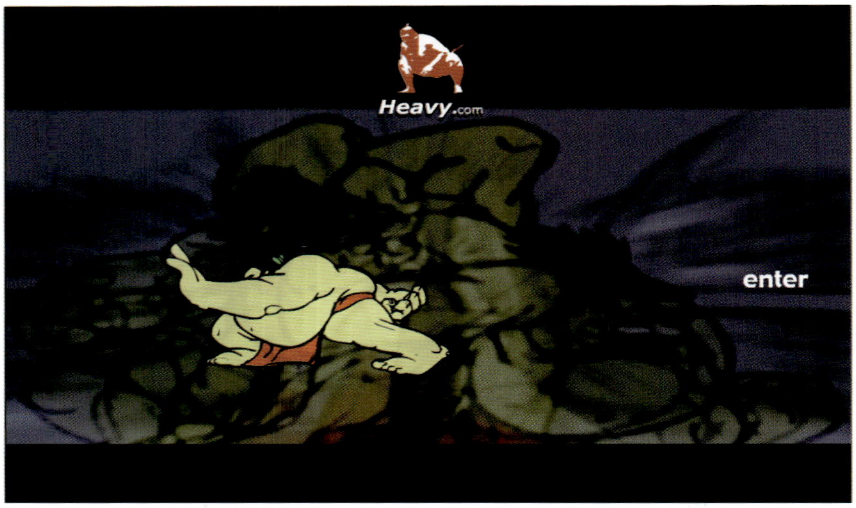

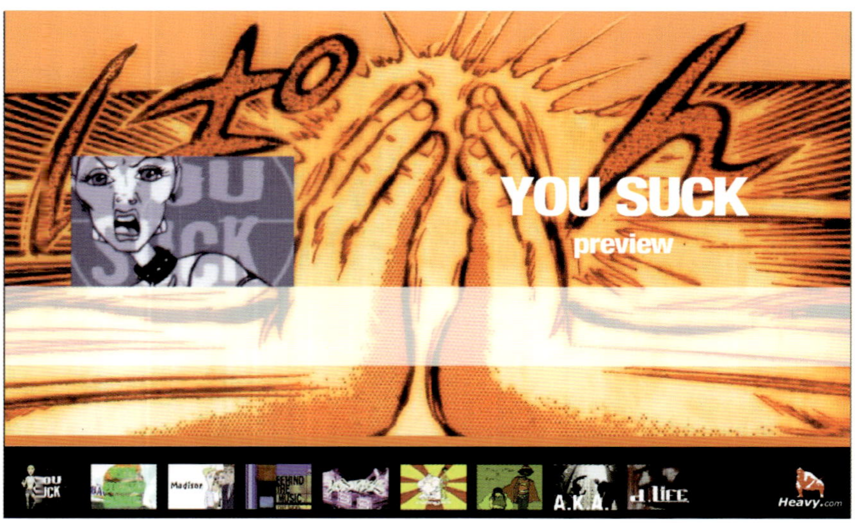

Title
Heavy.com
URL
Heavy.com
Design Firm
Heavy.com

The ability of vector graphics to take a single image and load it once into your cache allows Heavy to put buttons with screen shots along the bottom of the page, while simultaneously using the same images going by on top to add more information. The choice as to what you would like to see is thus much easier.

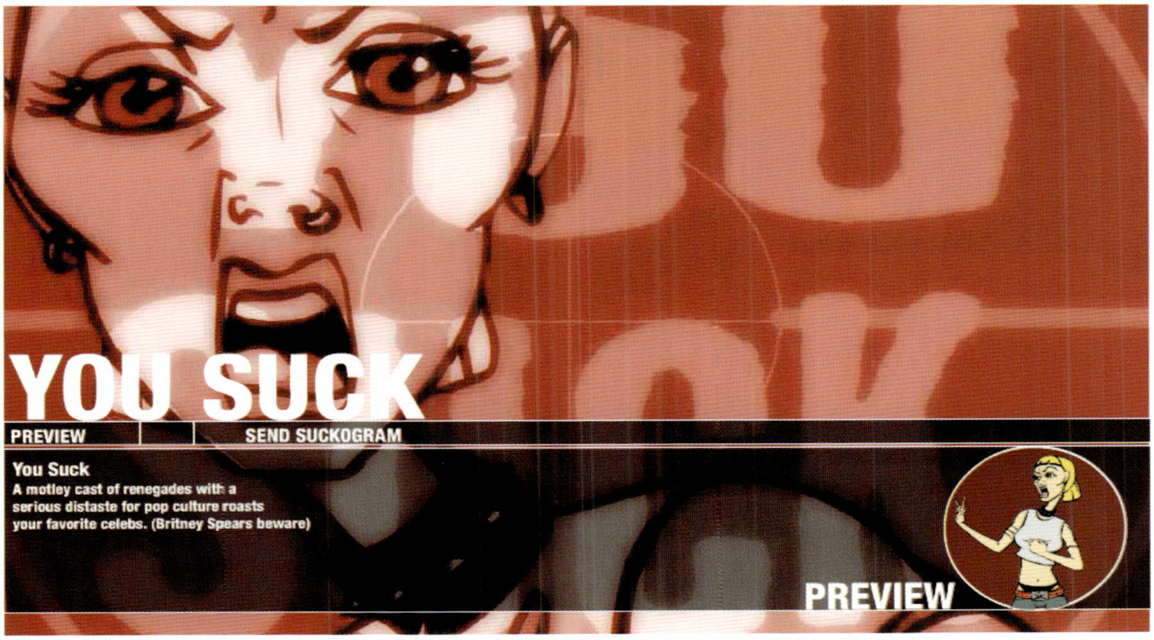
YOU SUCK
PREVIEW
SEND SUCKOGRAM
You Suck
A motley cast of renegades with a serious distaste for pop culture roasts your favorite celebs. (Britney Spears beware)
PREVIEW

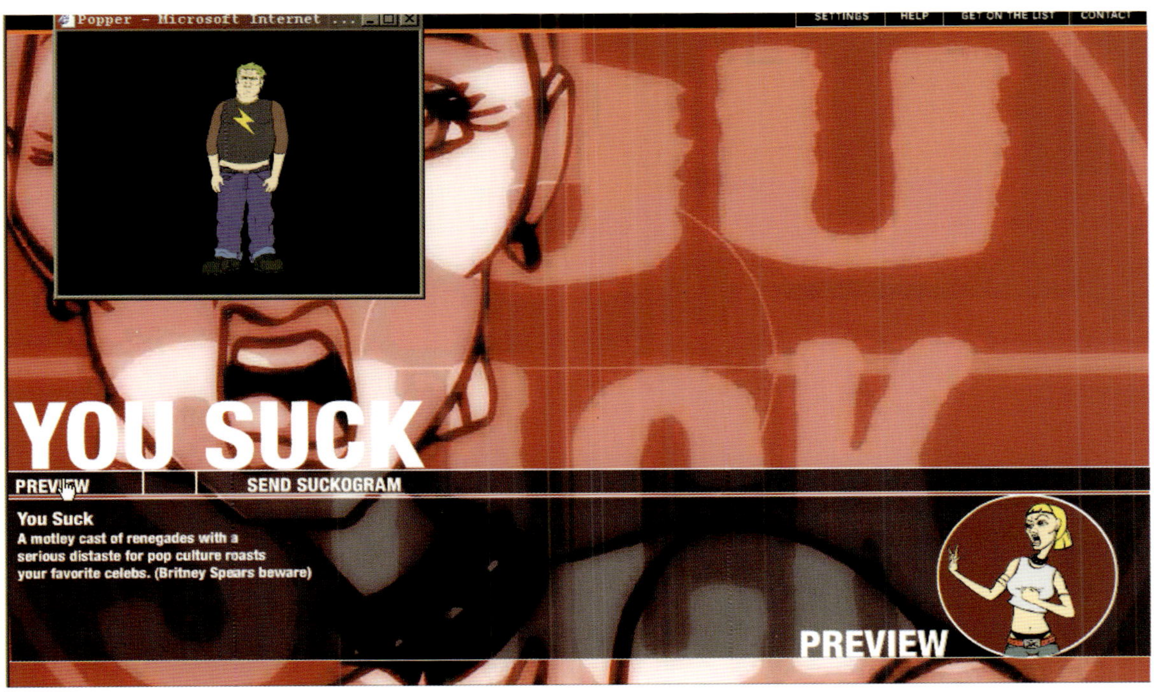
Popper - Microsoft Internet ...
SETTINGS
HELP
GET ON THE LIST
CONTACT
YOU SUCK
SEND SUCKOGRAM
You Suck
A motley cast of renegades with a serious distaste for pop culture roasts your favorite celebs. (Britney Spears beware)
PREVIEW

Title
Juxt Interactive
URL
www.juxtinteractive.com/
Design Firm
Juxt Interactive

The uses of the navigation buttons on the Juxt Interactive site are not always clear, but they do lead you into interesting places. Although this puts you at the mercy of the designers, with these guys, that's great.

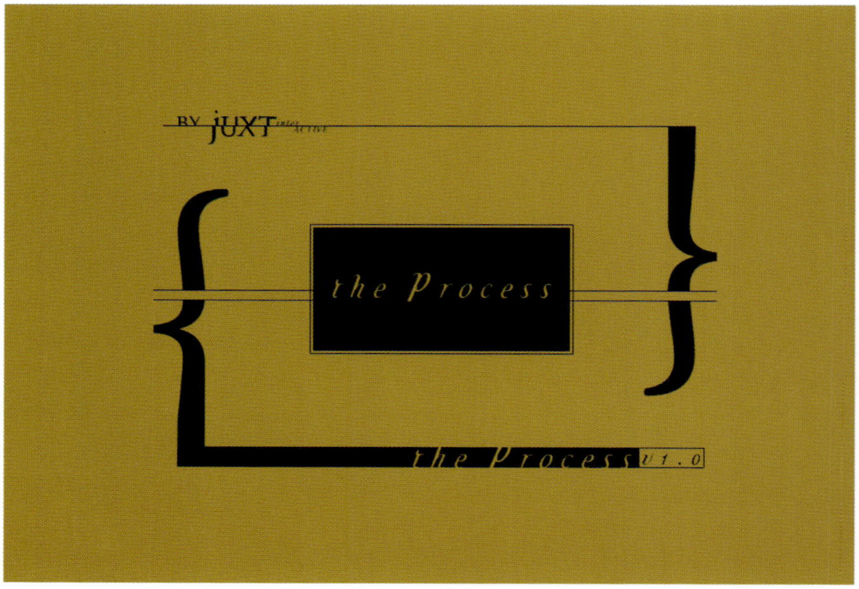

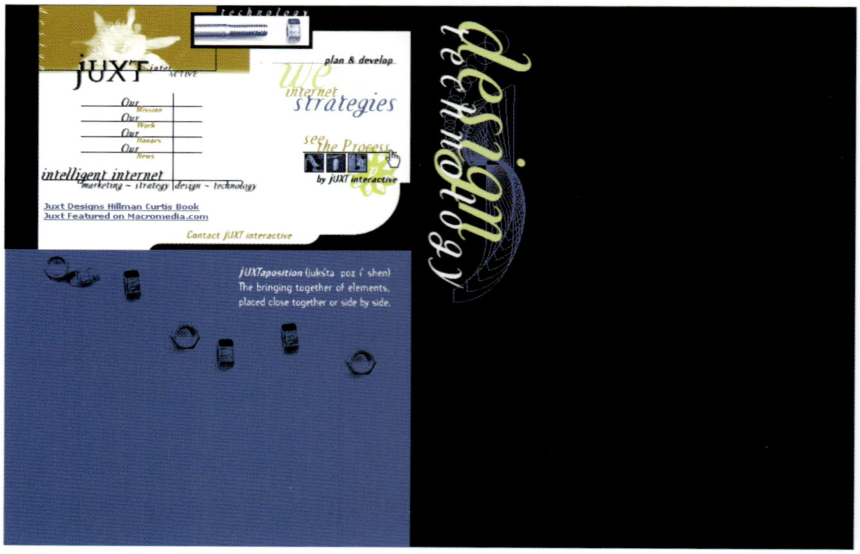

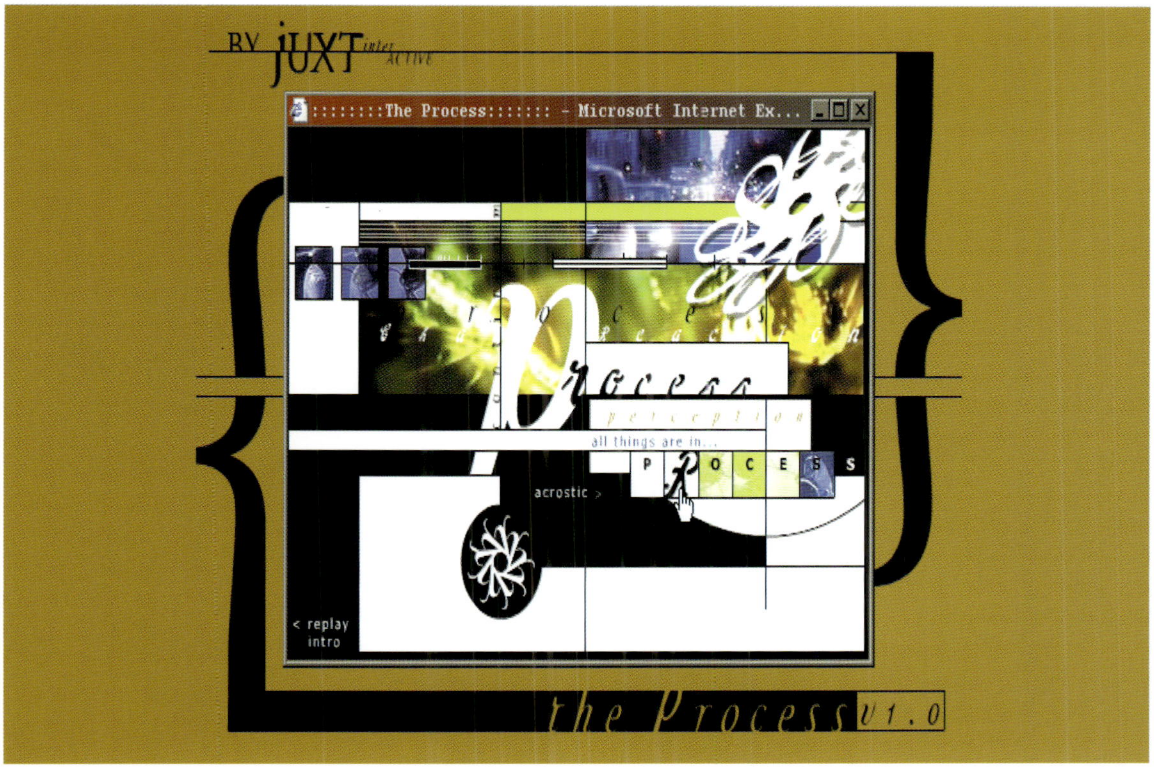
BY JUXT inter ACTIVE
::::::::The Process::::::: - Microsoft Internet Ex...
Process
perception
all things are in...
P R O C E S S
acrostic >
< replay intro
the Process v1.0

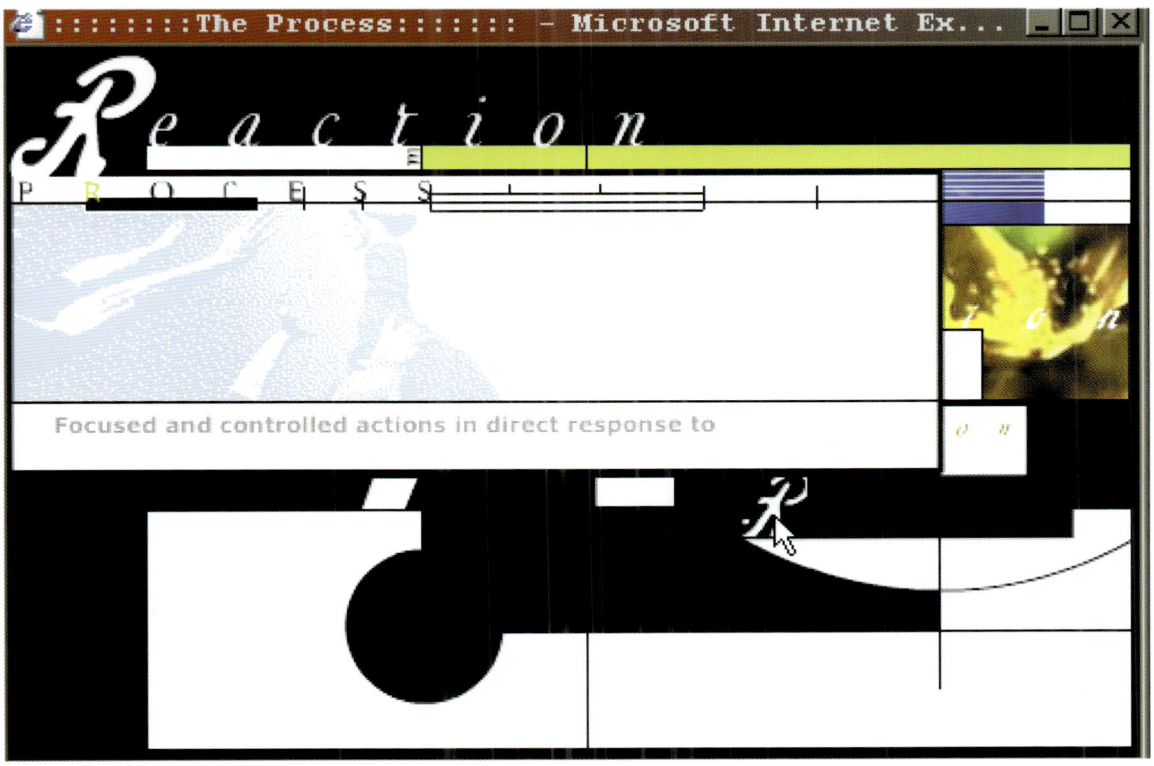
::::::::The Process::::::: - Microsoft Internet Ex...
Reaction
P R O C E S S
Focused and controlled actions in direct response to

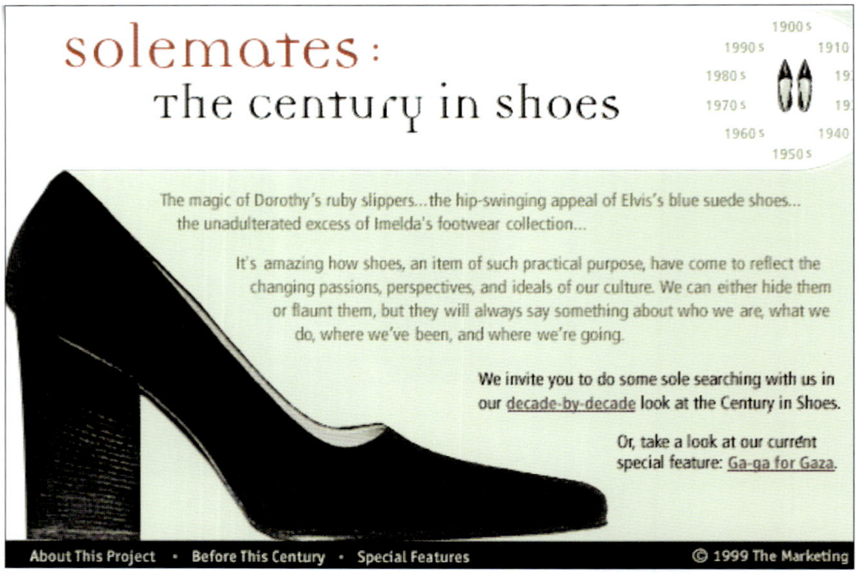

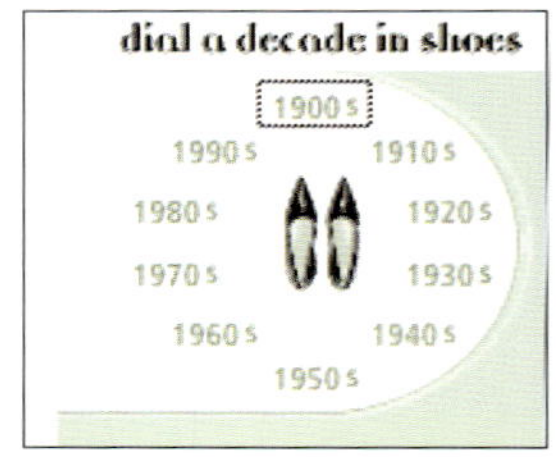

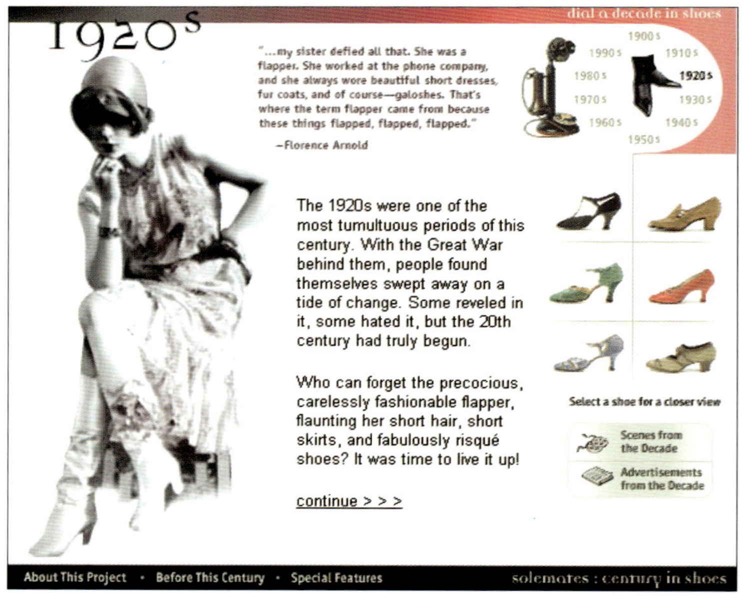

Title
solemates
URL
www.centuryinshoes.com/home.html
Design Firm
The Marketing Store

Solemates has a nice, clean, round interface that allows you to jump between decades to sample footwear in American culture. (It's more interesting than it sounds. Really!)

Title
Lambie-Nairn
URL
www.lambie-nairn.com/flash_go.html
Design Firm
Lambie-Nairn

The navigation at Laimbie-Nairn takes a moment to figure out, but once you do, you're in for a treat. The interface is incredibly elegant. The buttons on the bottom open the box on the left. The opened section holds the content.

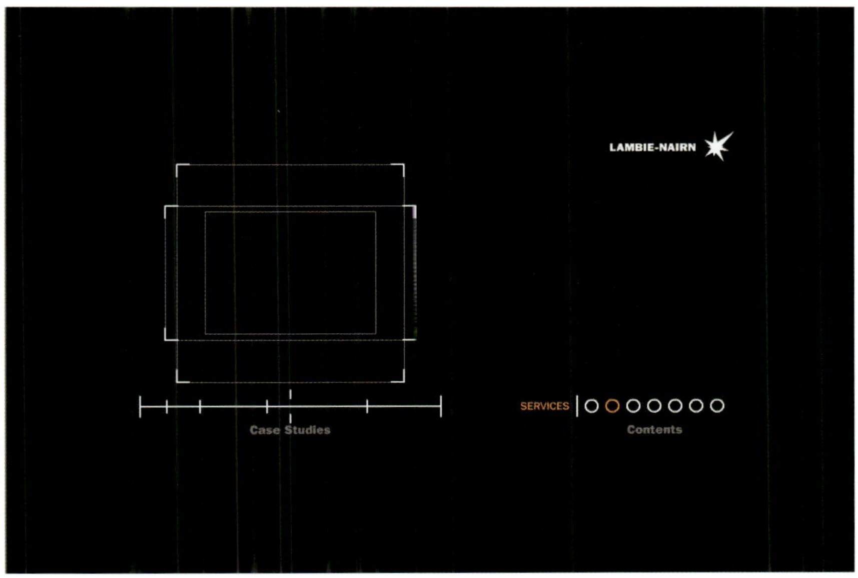

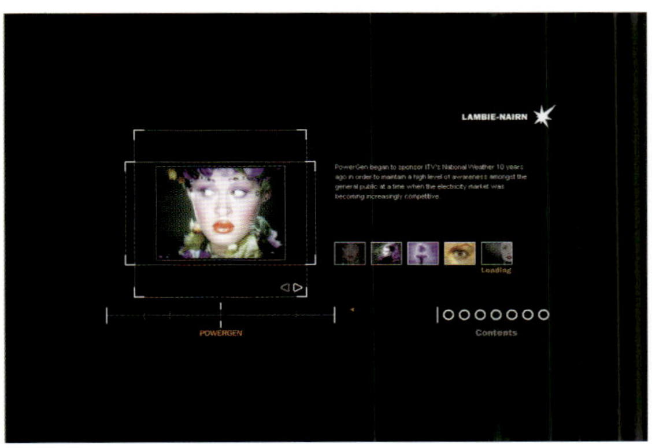

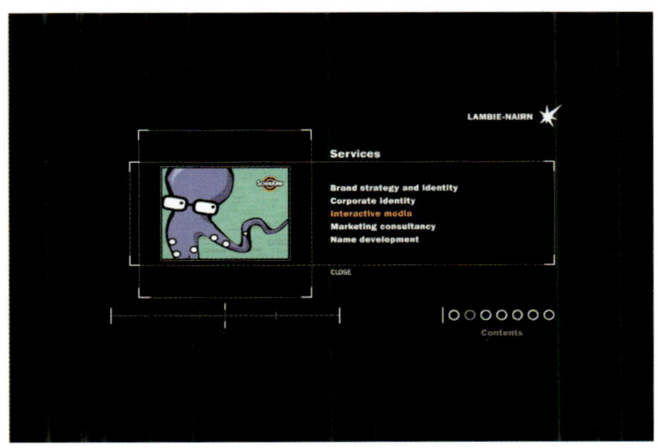

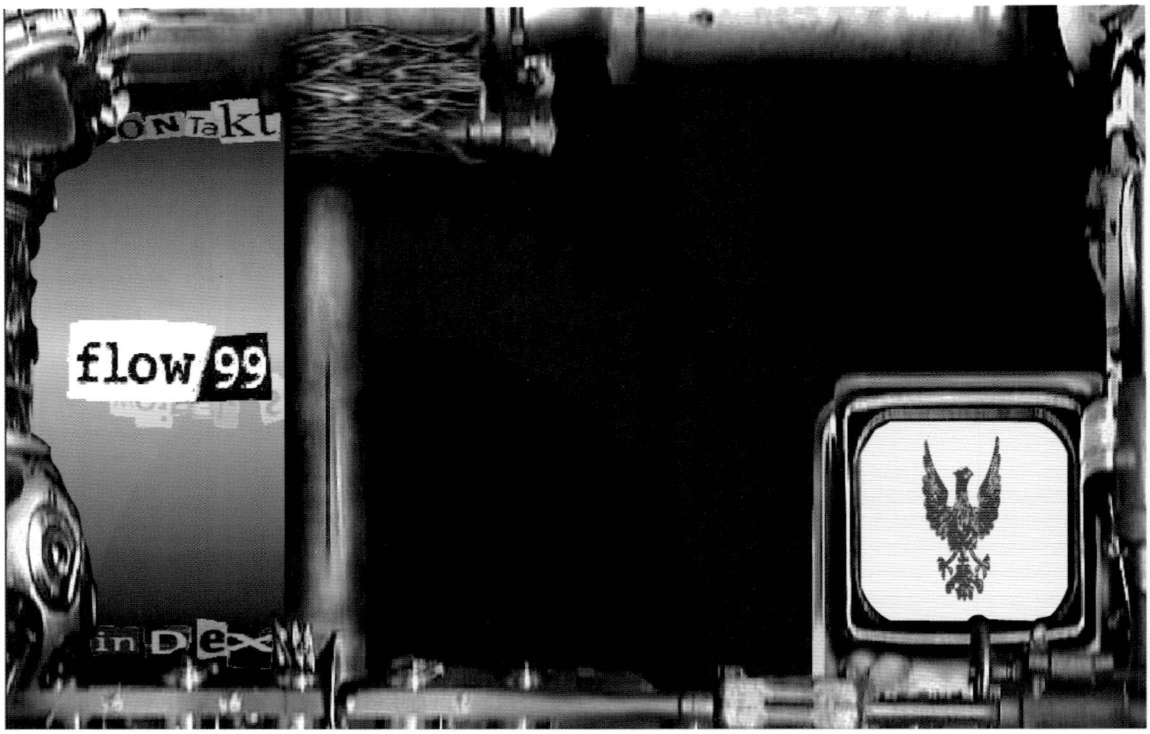

Title
wojtek
URL
www.wojtek.de/
Design firm
perplex GMBH
Designer
sal wojtek

The navigation bar is Flash enhanced. On mouse-over, the four buttons scroll through images that appear in the box in the bottom right corner of the page, making navigation easy.

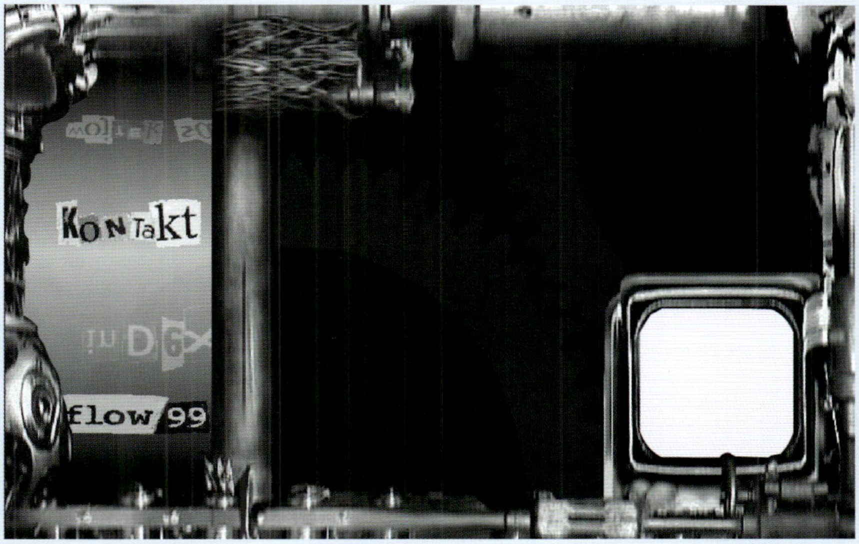
KoNTakt
flow 99

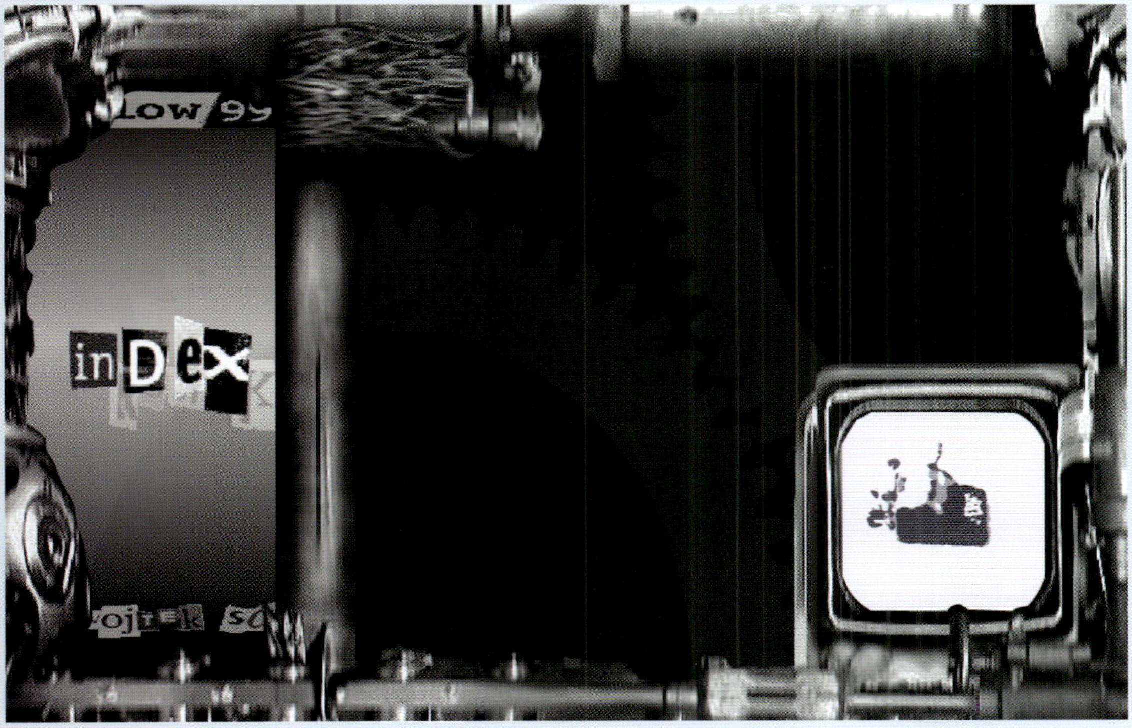
inDex

Title
petergrafik
URL
www.petergrakik.dk/
Design Firm
petergrafik

The five buttons on the Petergrafik site are useful because they evolve from iconic symbols into the text that you need in order to navigate the site.

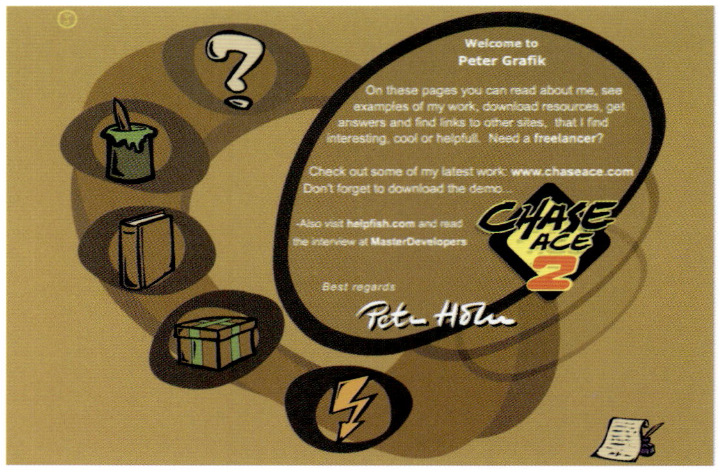

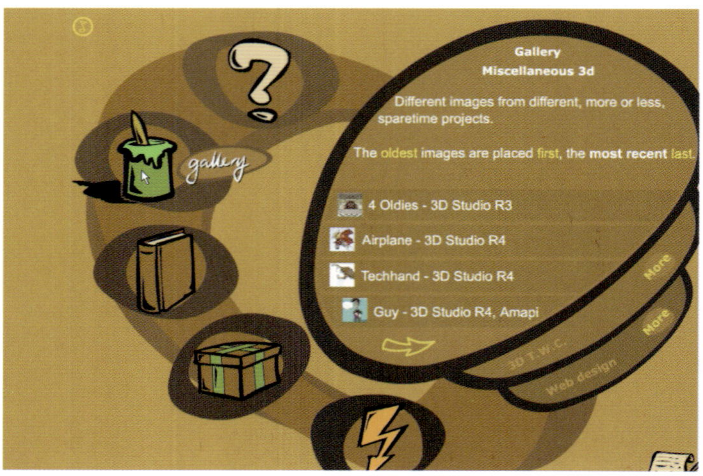

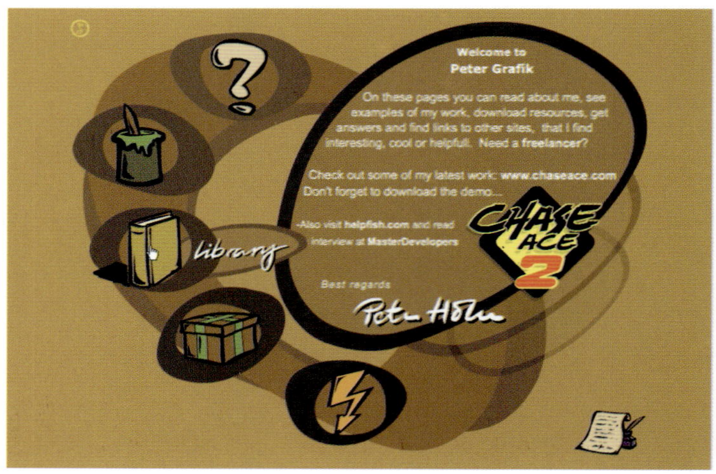

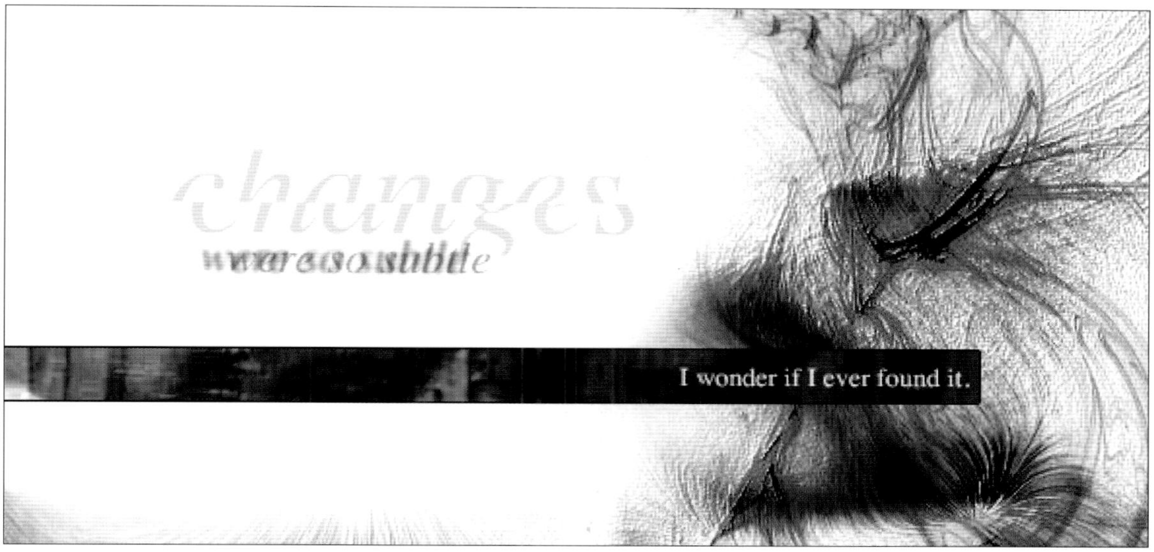

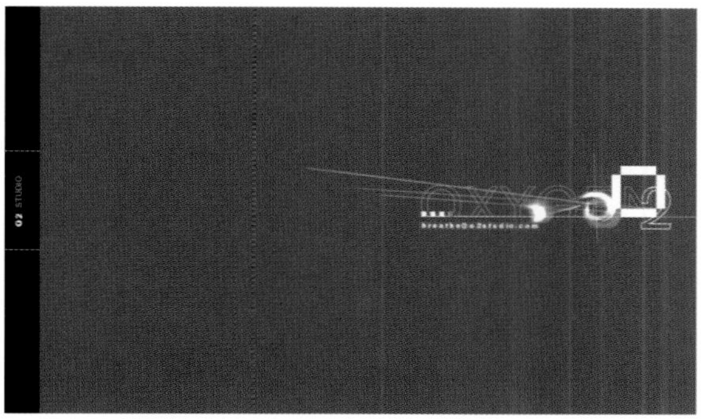

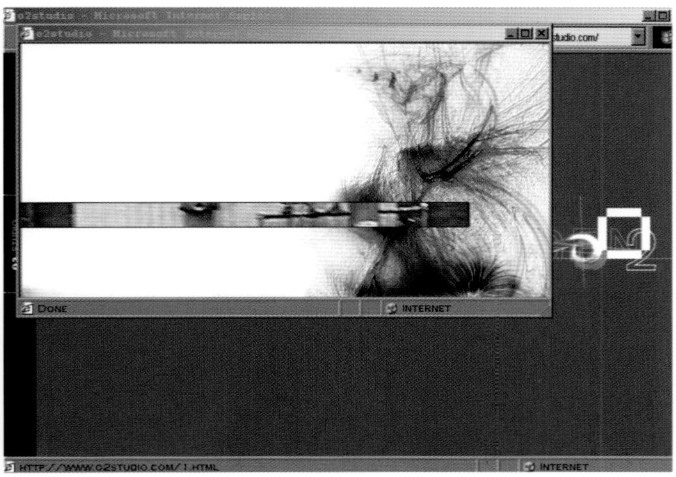

Title
o2 studio
URL
www.o2studios.com/
Design firm
o2 studios

Three buttons lead in unspecified directions on the O2 site. While this might be annoying in some cases, with this art-for-art's-sake site, it works.

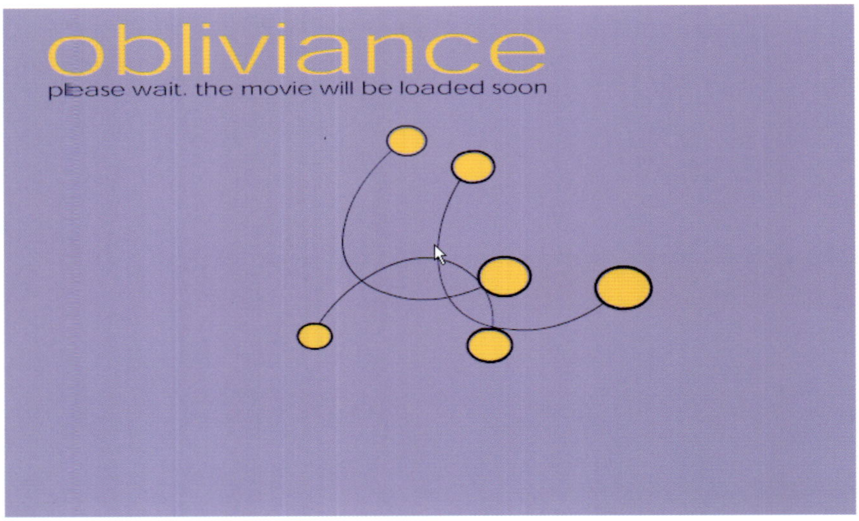

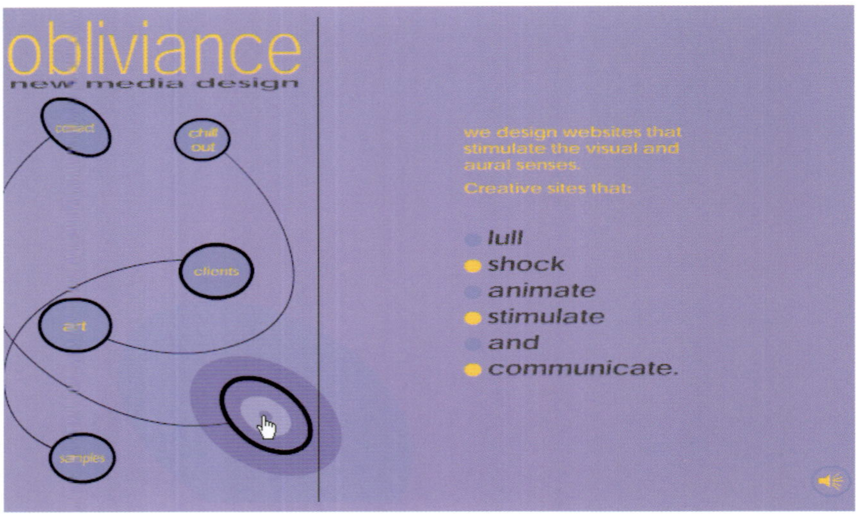

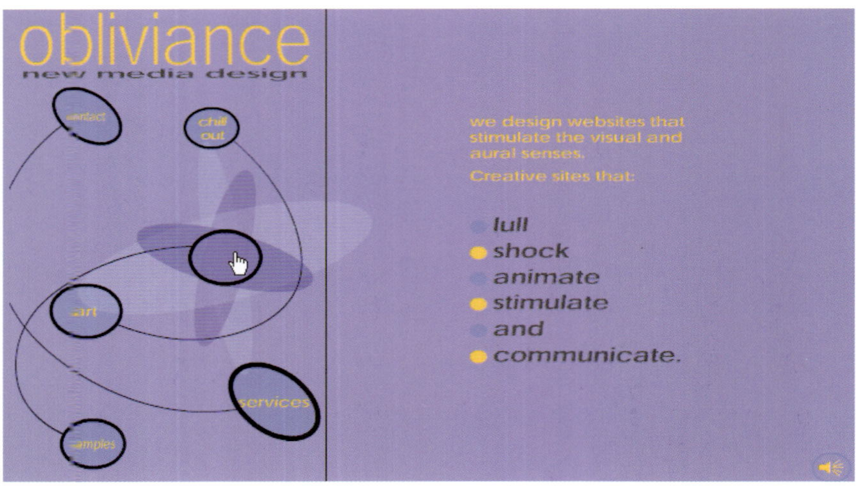

Title
obliviance
URL
www.obliviance.ndirect.co.uk/
Design Firm
obliviance
Designer
Rosalind Miller

Six simple buttons contain all the informa tion that you need in order to navigate th site. The buttons are Flash-enabled to provide interesting movement.

Title
ABI Mouldings
URL
www.abimouldings.com/
Design Firm
ABI Mouldings

An interface moves down the side of the homepage on this site, but the wonderful navigation page is the site map. Ironically, the navigation is simple enough that a site map is unnecessary. The blueprint-inspired look serves the purpose elegantly.

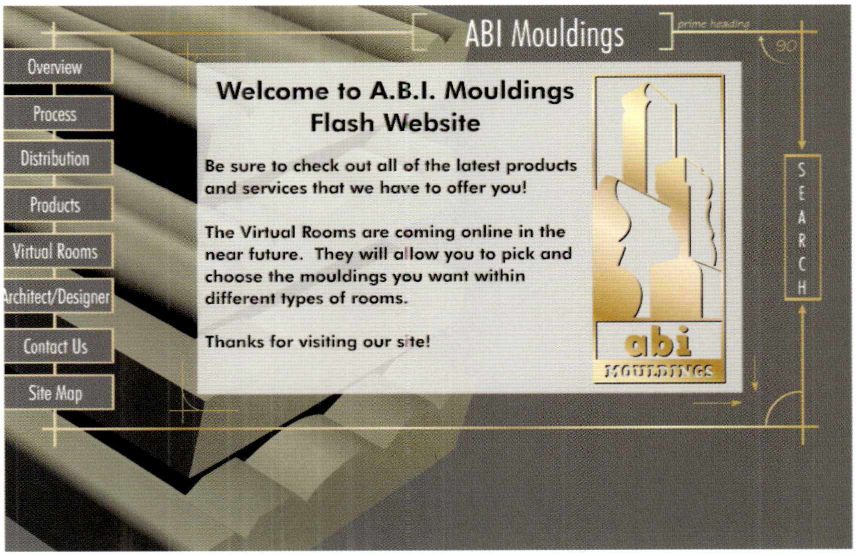

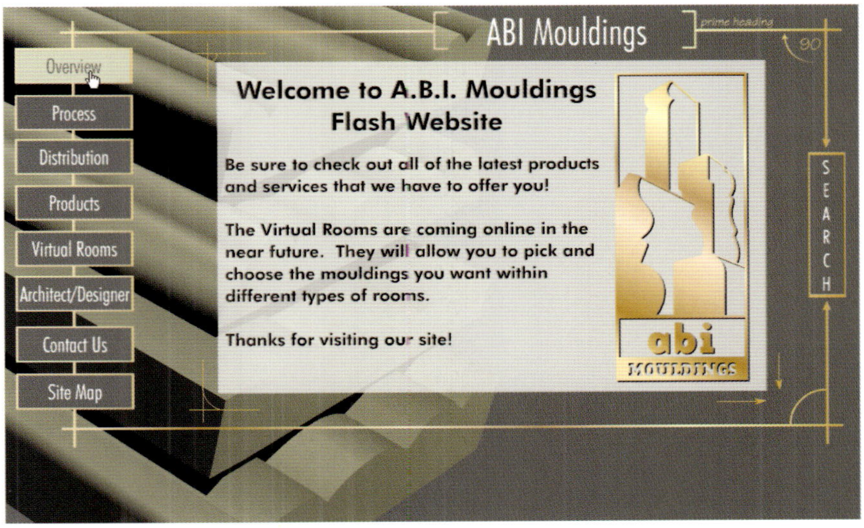

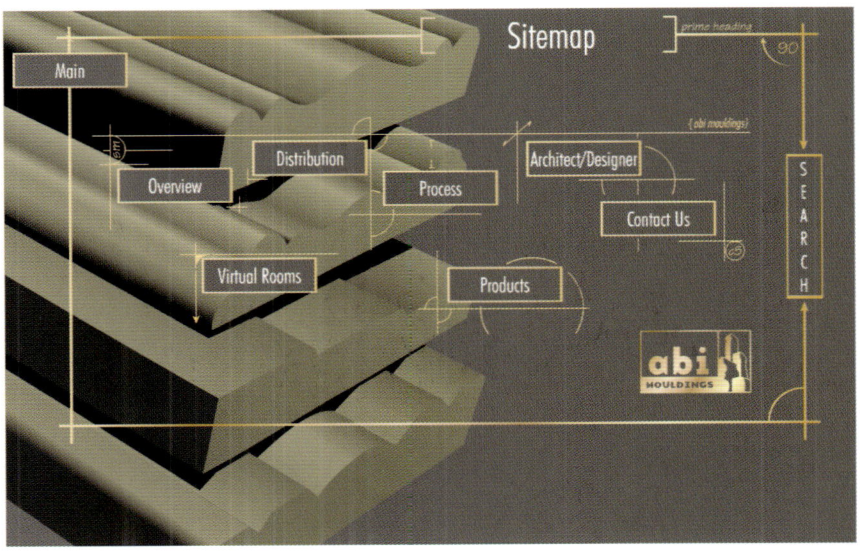

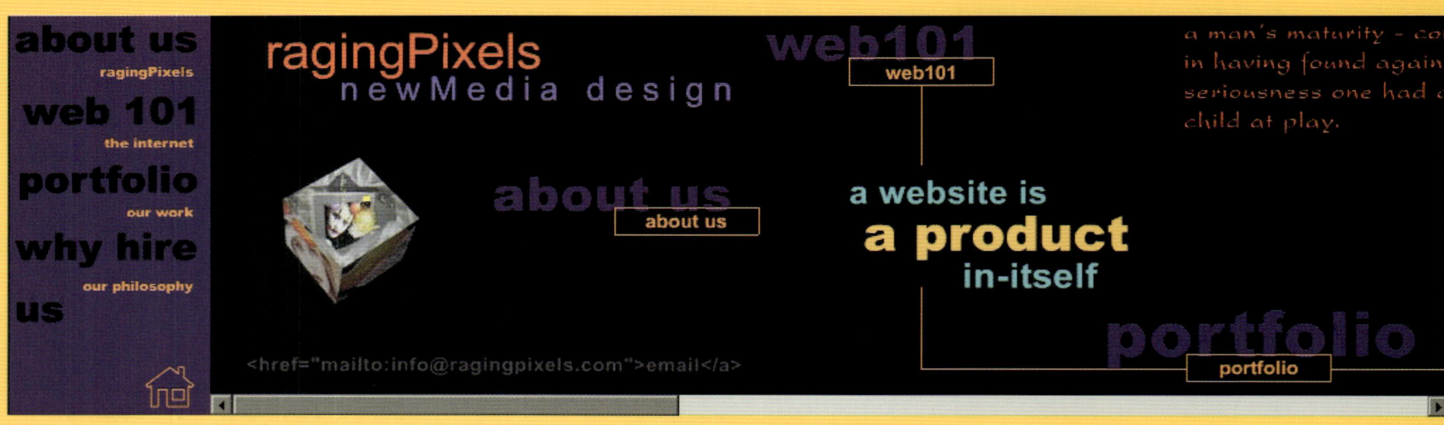

Title
ragingpixels
URL
www.ragingpixels.com/flash/ragingpixels.htm
Design firm
Raging pixels

This page scrolls horizontally, with orange buttons that run the length of the page. The buttons highlight when you scroll over them.

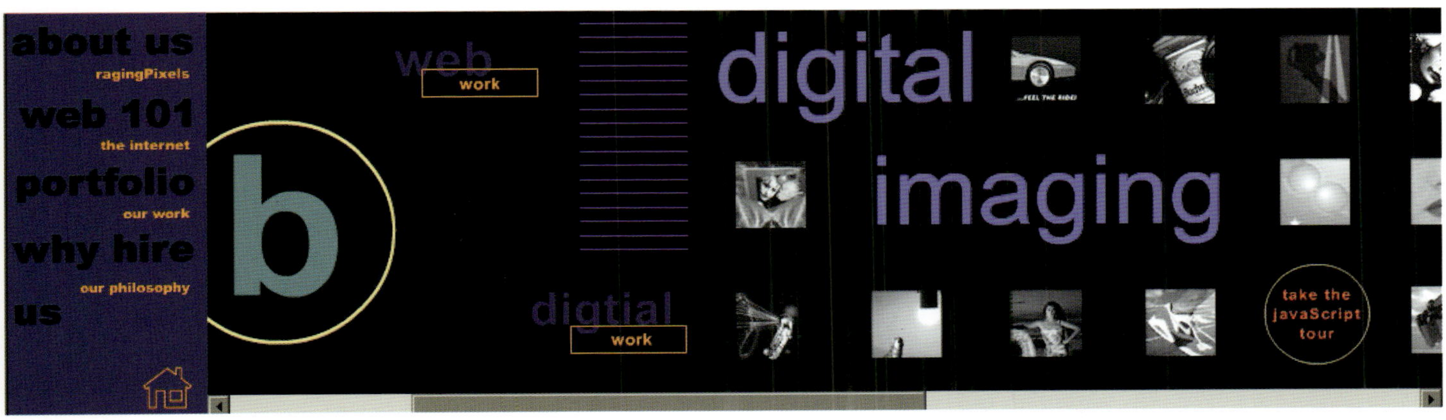
about us
ragingPixels
web 101
the internet
portfolio
our work
why hire
our philosophy
us
web
work
digital
imaging
digtial
work
take the javaScript tour

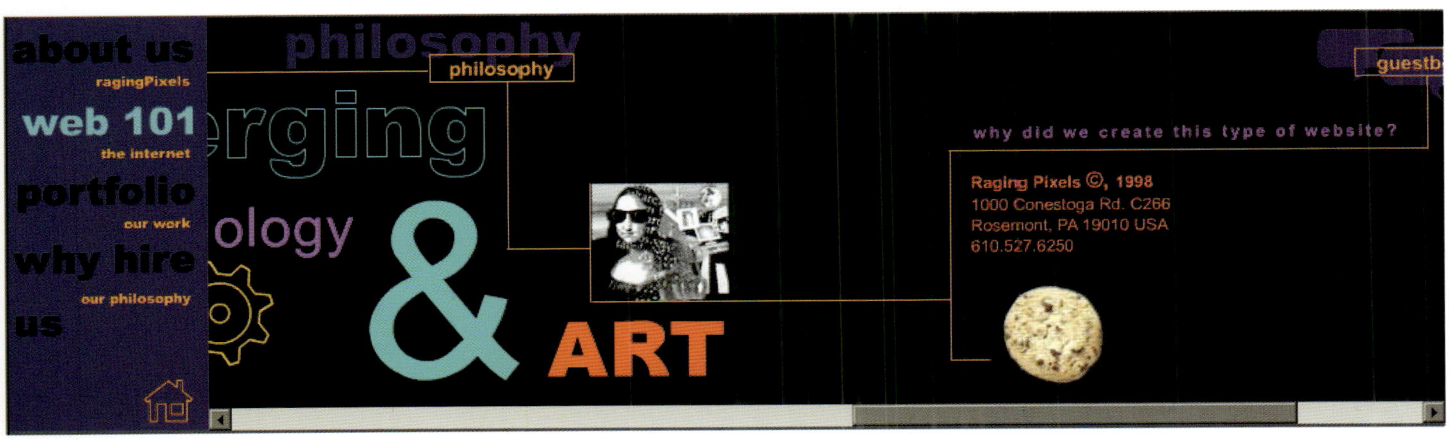
about us
ragingPixels
web 101
the internet
portfolio
our work
why hire
our philosophy
us
philosophy
philosophy
ology
& ART
why did we create this type of website?
Raging Pixels ©, 1998
1000 Conestoga Rd. C266
Rosemont, PA 19010 USA
610.527.6250

Title
Yenz
URL
www.yenz.com/
Design Firm
Yenz
Designer
kosmokrator.com

At times, Yenz is confusing, but that is not a bad thing. Navigation of the Secret Garden section requires the user to zoom in on sections in order to navigate the site.

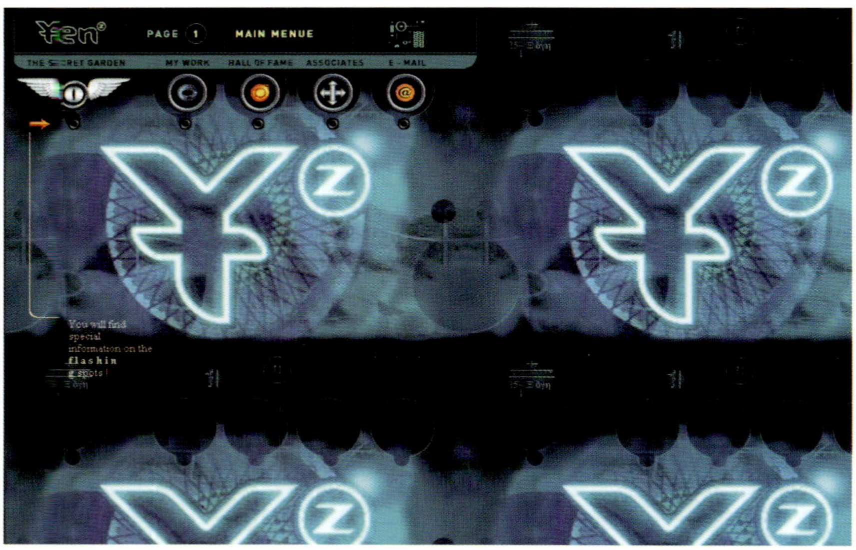

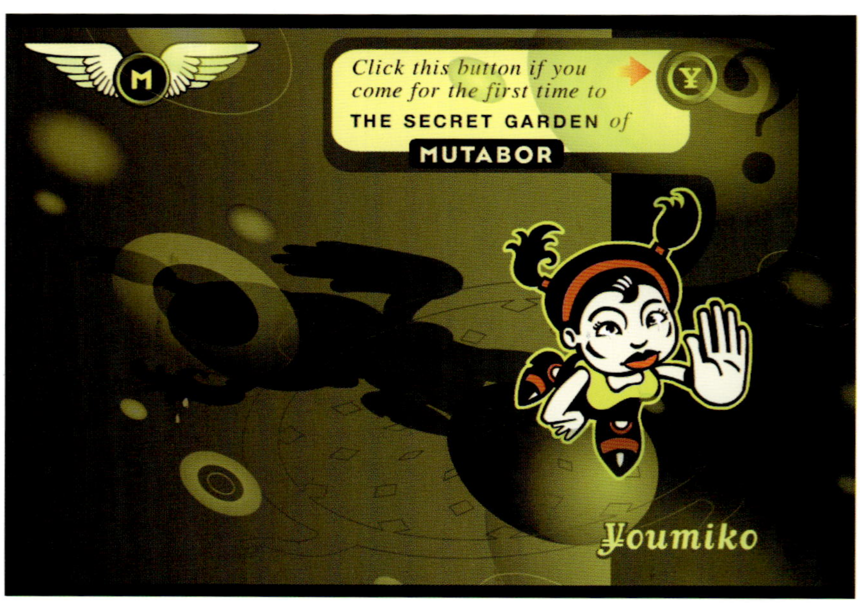

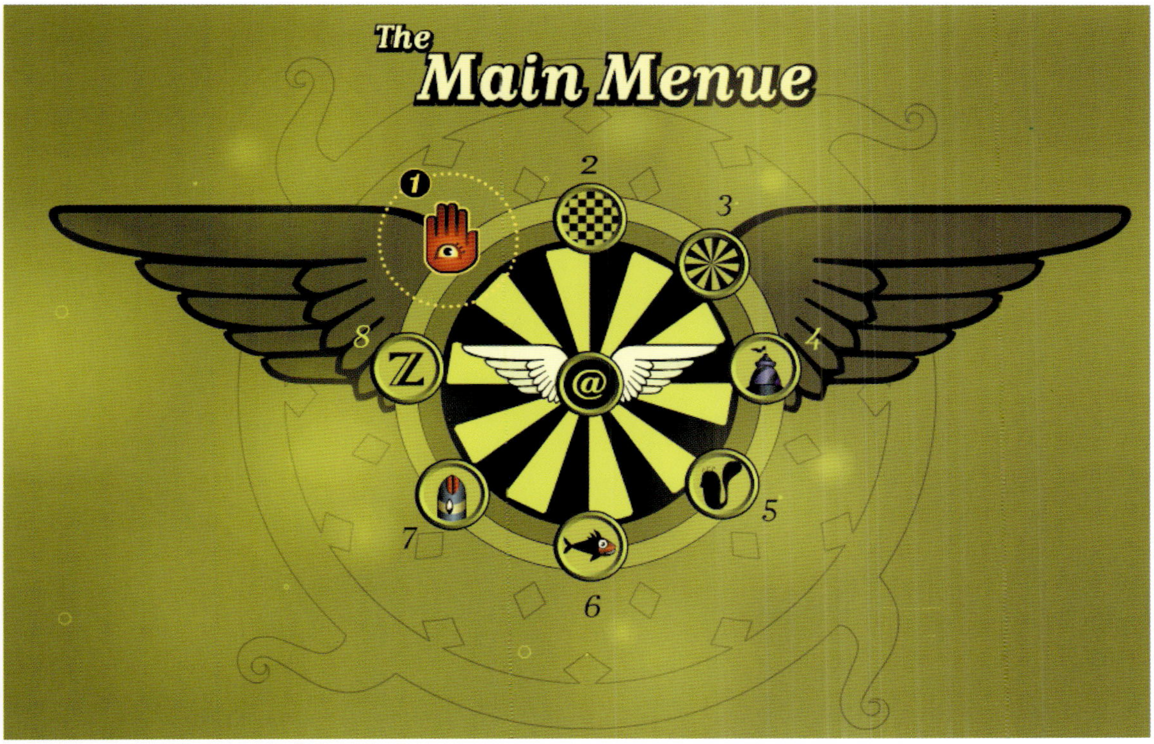
The Main Menue
1
2
3
4
5
6
7
8
Z
@

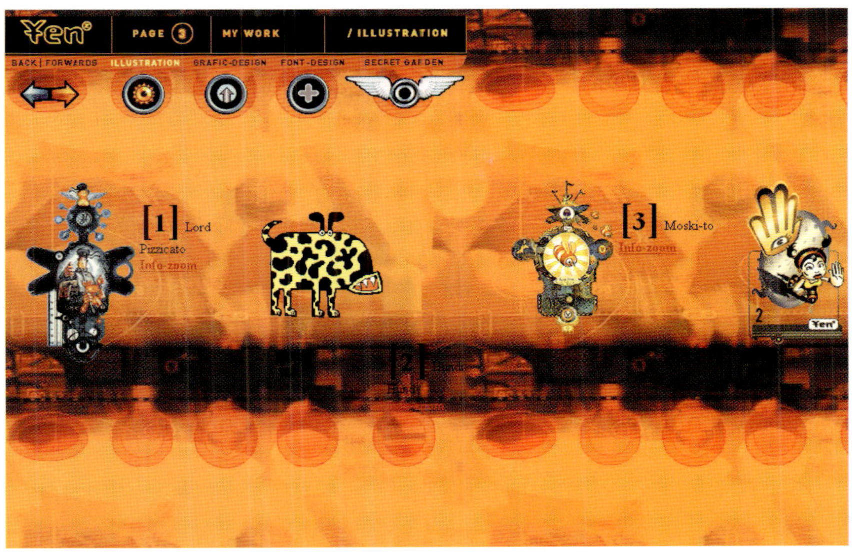
Yen
PAGE 3
MY WORK
/ ILLUSTRATION
BACK | FORWARDS
ILLUSTRATION
GRAFIC-DESIGN
FONT-DESIGN
SECRET GARDEN
[1] Lord Pizzicato
Info-zoom
[3] Moski-to
Info-zoom

Title
Typographic
URL
www.typographic.com/
Design Firm
Typographic
Designer
Jimmy Chen

The only text that is not moving or blurred is located on the four buttons along the bottom. This stability draws your eye right to them.

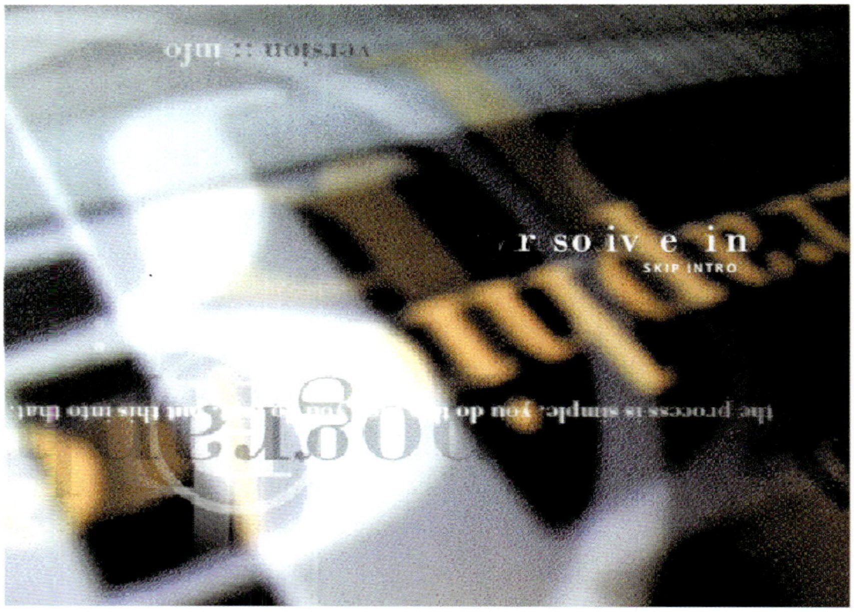

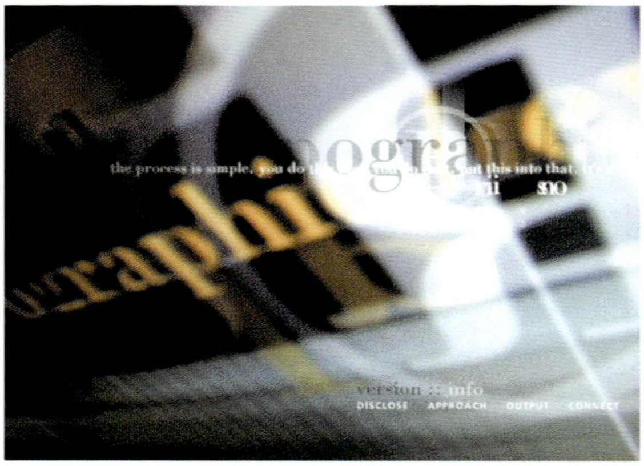

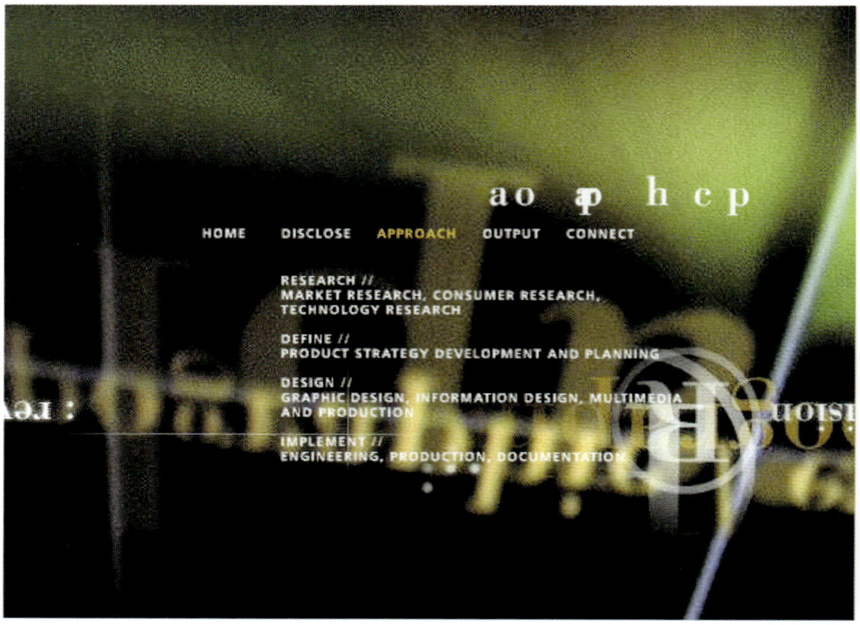

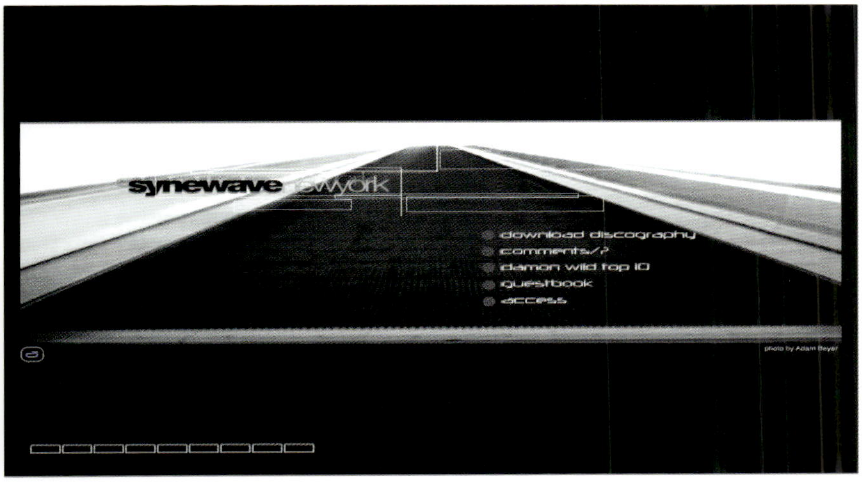

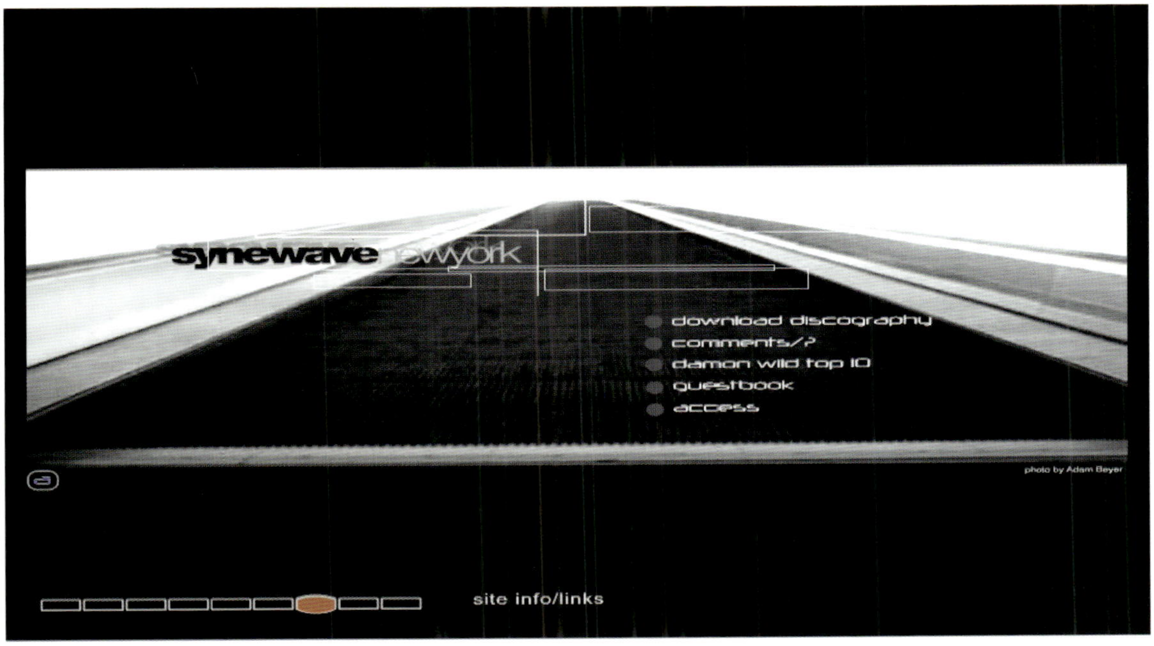

Title
synewave
URL
www.synewave.com/
Design Firm
synewave
Designer
Damon Wild

A sleek navigation ba~ runs along the bottom of this page, not revealing its purpose until mouse-over. Then, the buttons expand and light up.

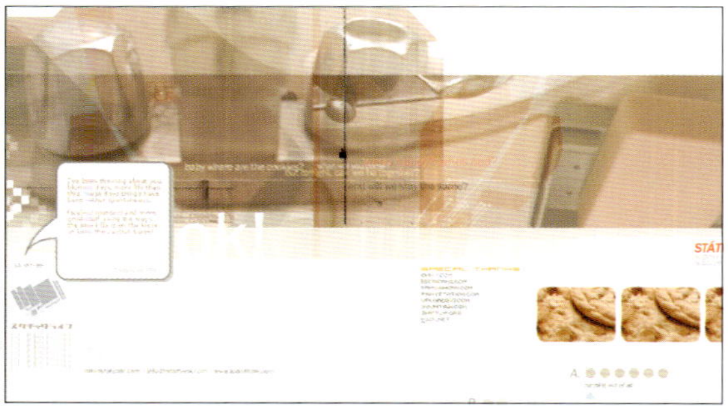

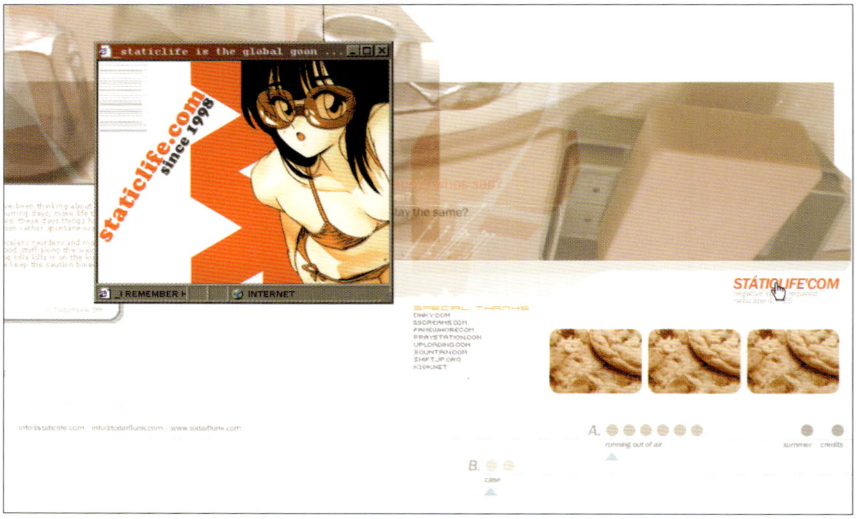

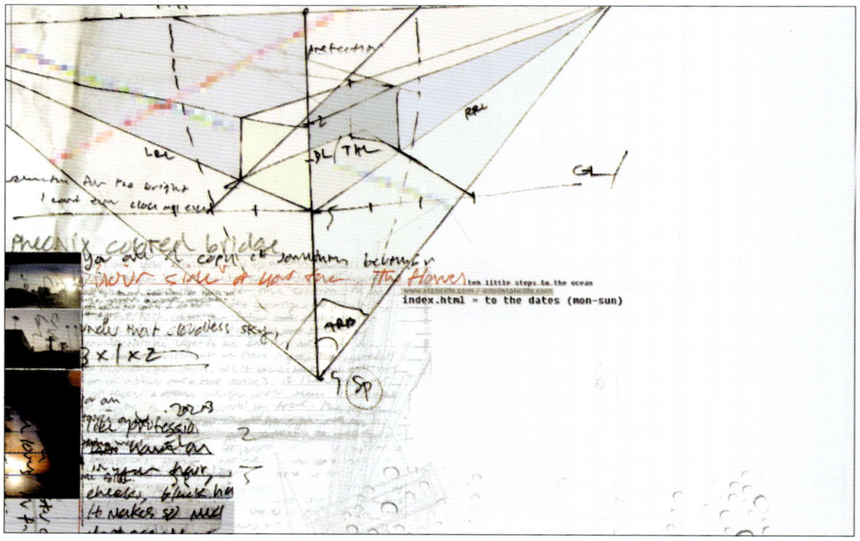

Title
staticlife
URL
www.staiclife.com/box/interface/index_ie.htm
Design Firm
Todaiflunk No-Media Network

The somewhat ambiguous navigation on this site encourages you to explore. The mixed-media images create an unsettling feeling.

Title

Dirk Rullkötter AGD

URL

www.rullkoetter.de/

Design firm

Rullkötter AGC Werbung + Design

Designer

Dirk Rullkötter

The neat thing about this site is the bee that follows your cursor around the navigation bar. The bar itself holds only four buttons, keeping navigation simple.

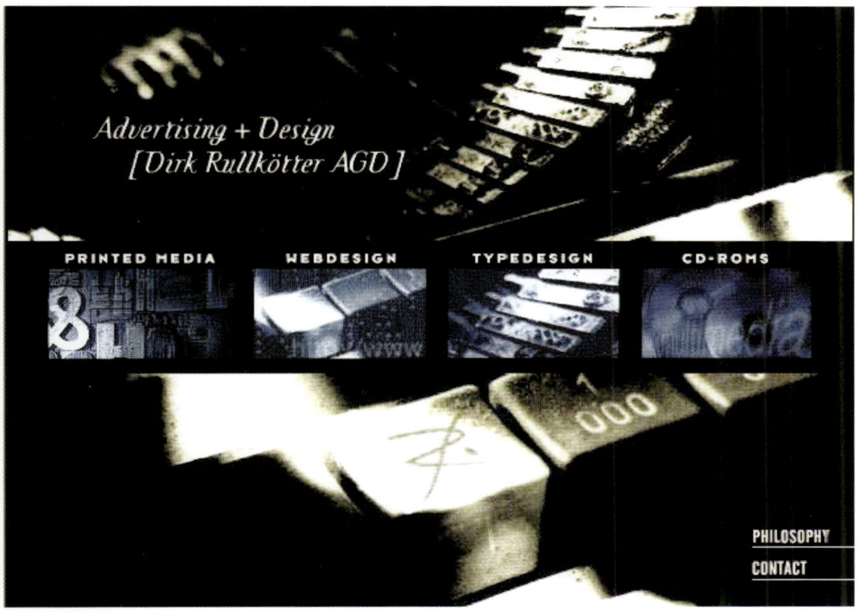

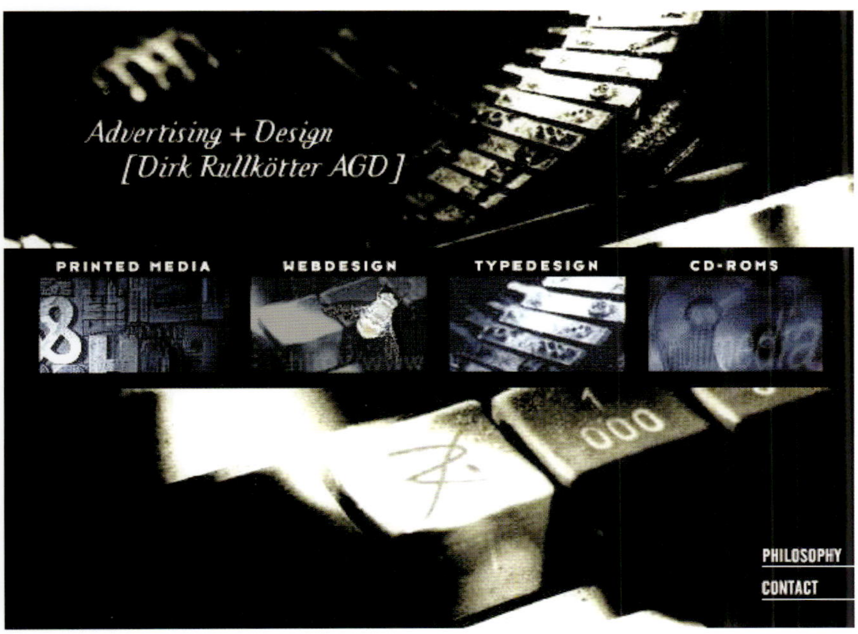

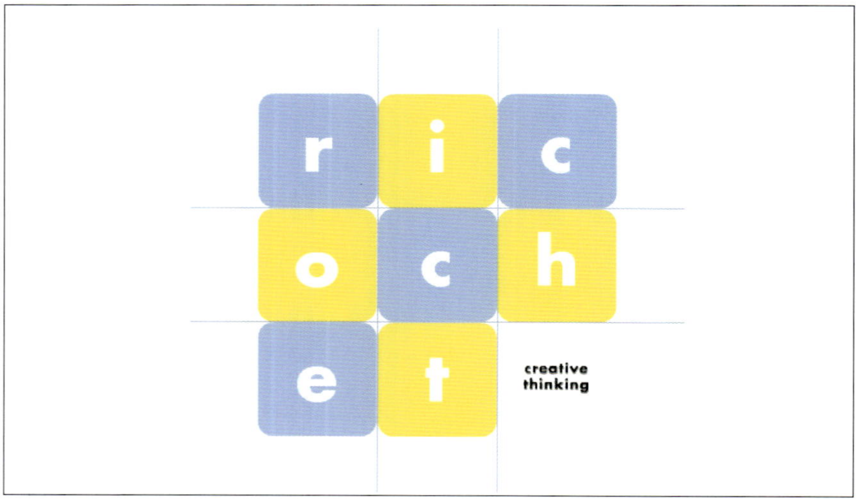

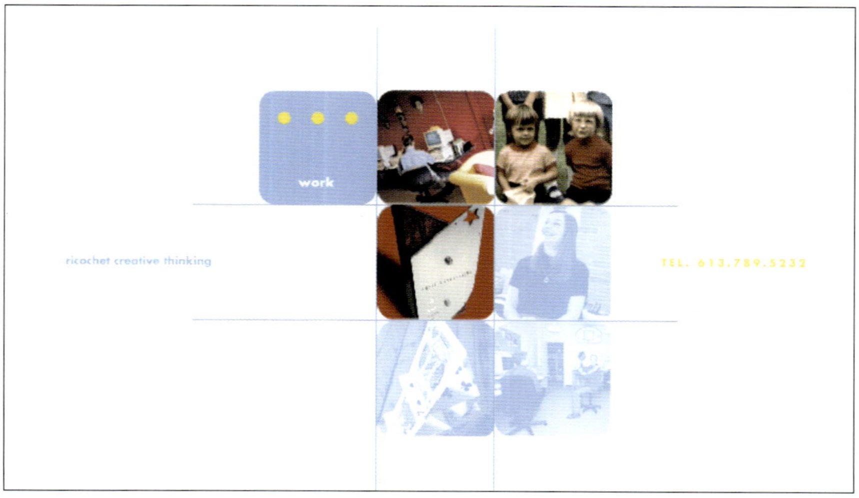

Title
Ricochet
URL
www.ricochetcreativethinking
Design Firm
Ricochet Creative Thinking
Designers
Nicholas Henry, Steve Zelle

Only a few small buttons make navigatio simple. The tiny buttons, sitting in the up corner of the main image, don't disrupt th overall design.

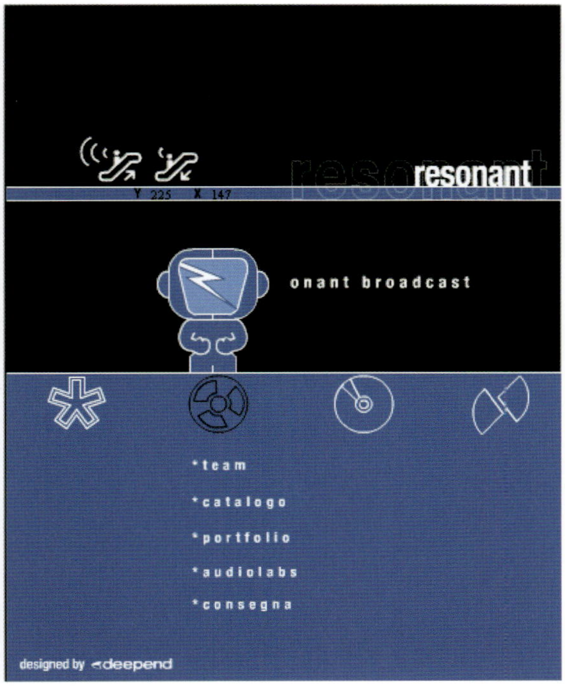

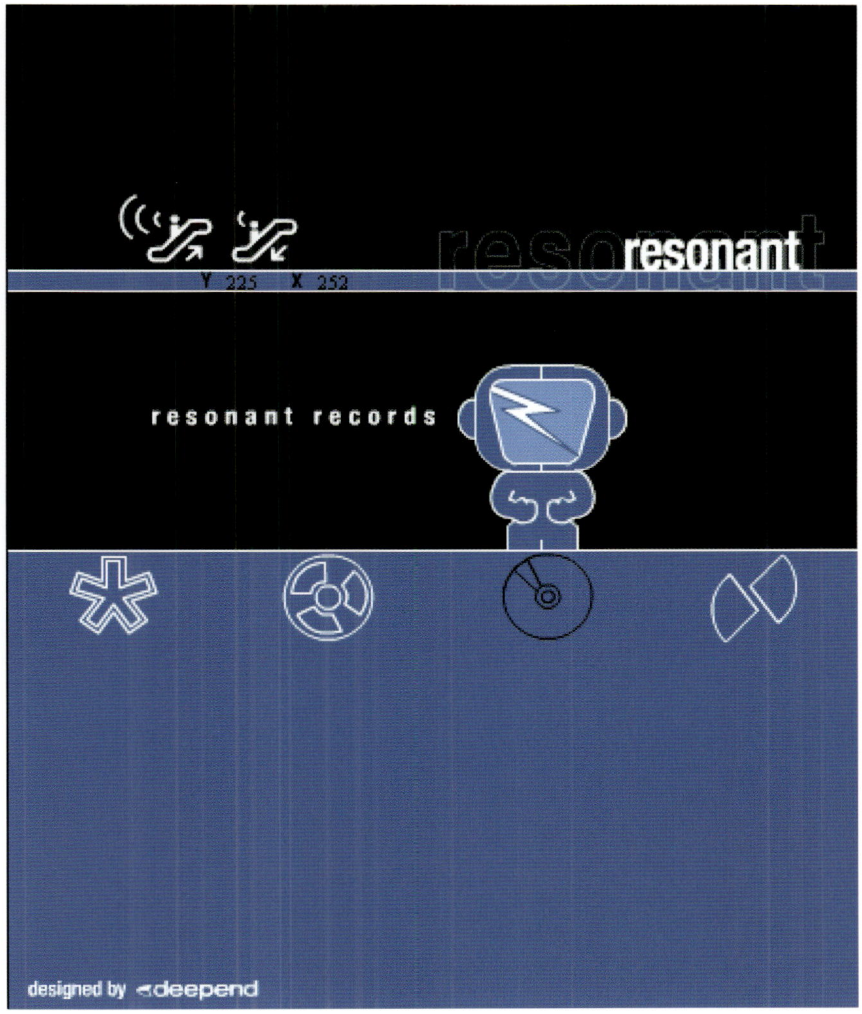

Title
Resonant
URL
www.resonant.it/
Design Firm
Resonant SRL
Designers
deepend

An alien follows the cursor back and forth across the navigation bar. This fun element makes the difference between an exciting design and every other Web page.

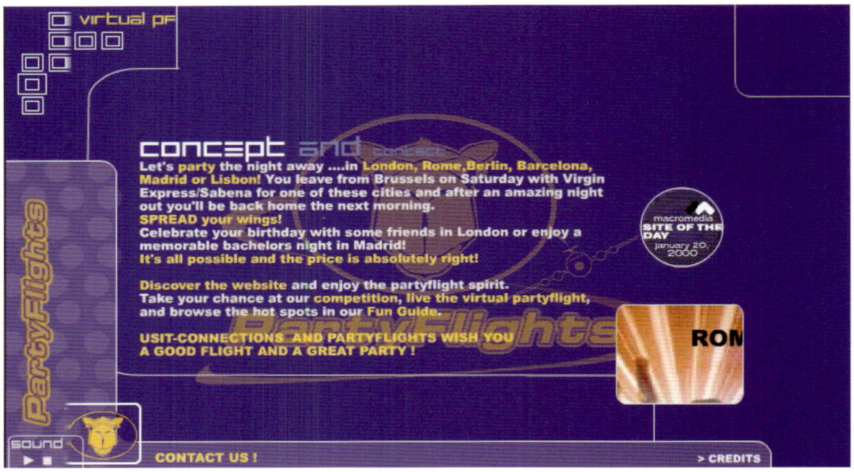

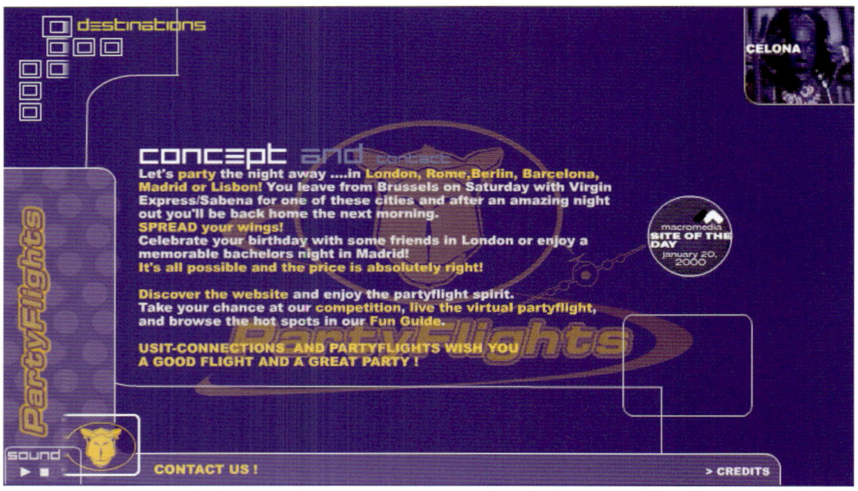

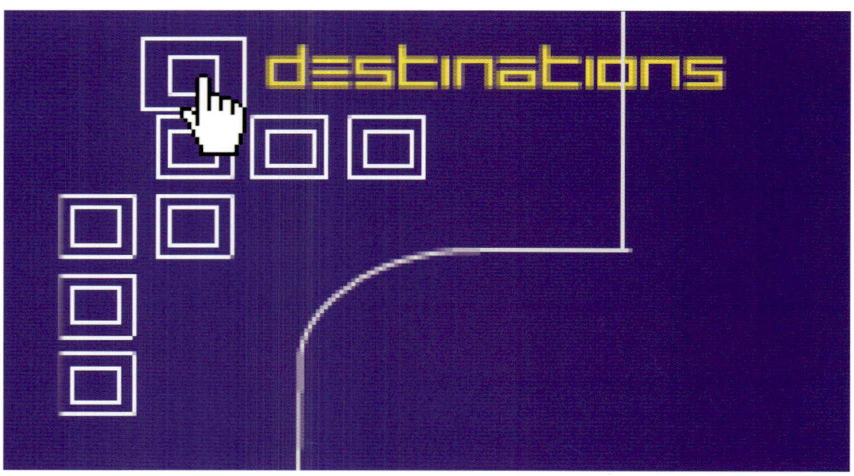

Title
partyflights
URL
www.party-flights.com/
Design Firm
Amphion Multi Media

A group of small buttons in the upper left corner can take you anywhere on the site. The destination of each button is revealed on mouse-over.

Title
ntouch
URL
ntouch.linst.ac.uk/
Design Firm
Random Media

The Chinese characters dissolve to reveal the destination of the buttons on this site. This is a design seen rarely on the Internet.

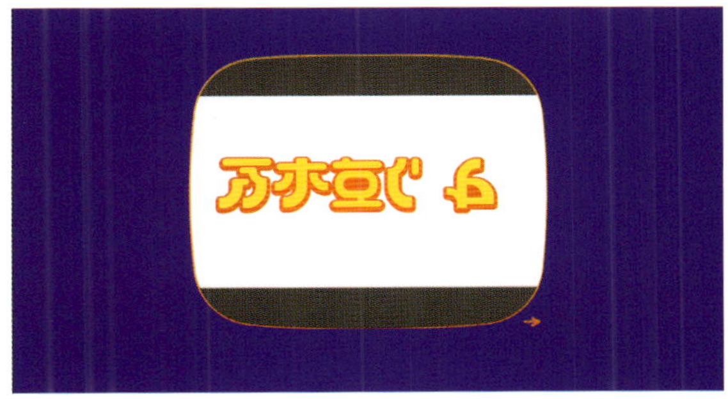

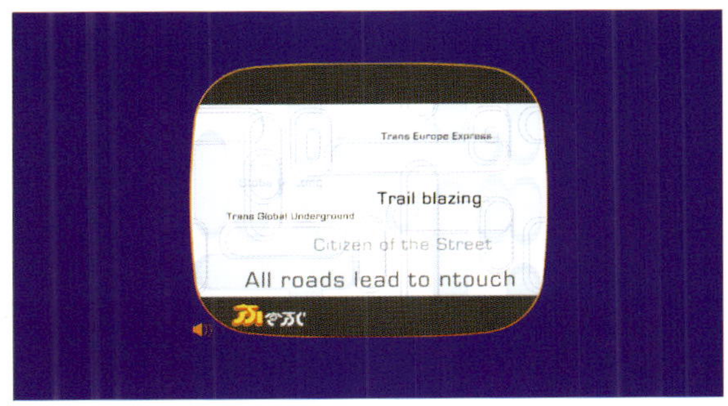

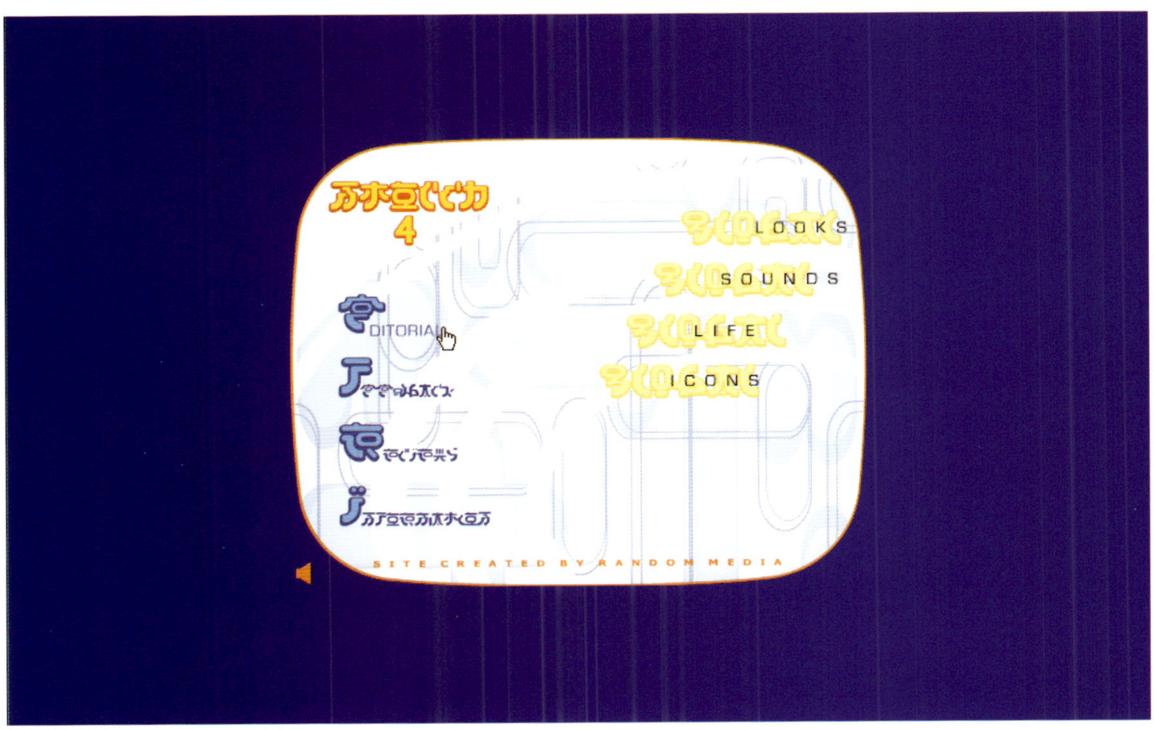

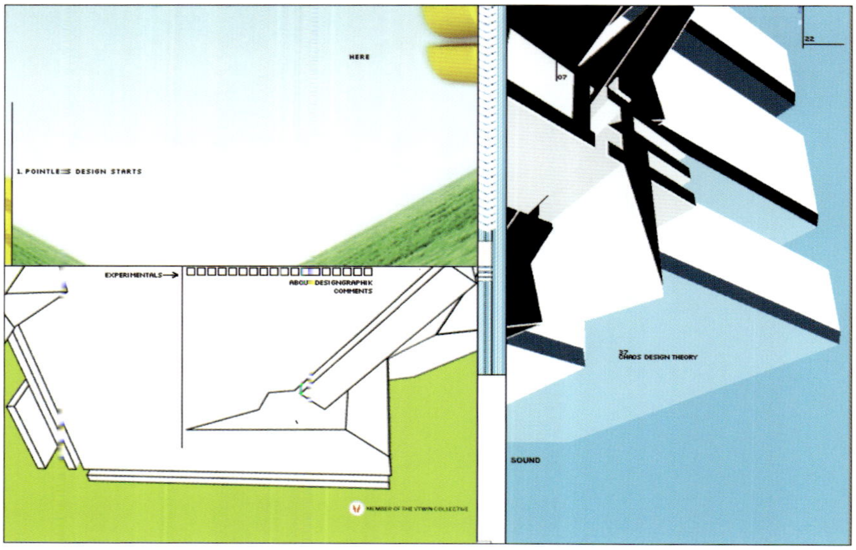
HERE
1. POINTLE≡S DESIGN STARTS
EXPERIMENTALS→
ABOU DESIGNGRAPHIK
COMMENTS
MEMBER OF THE VTWIN COLLECTIVE
22
07
37
CHAOS DESIGN THEORY
SOUND

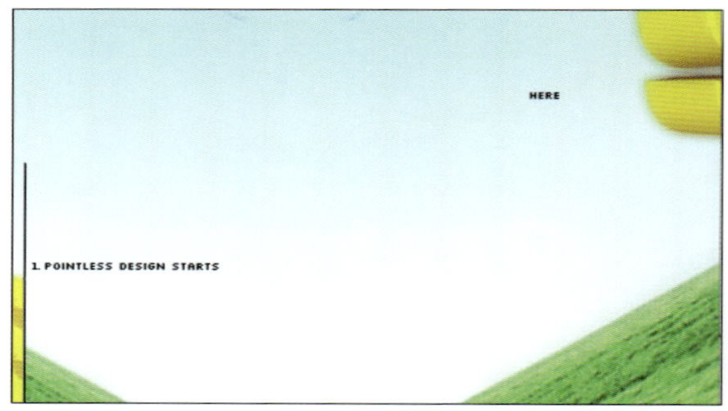
HERE
1. POINTLESS DESIGN STARTS

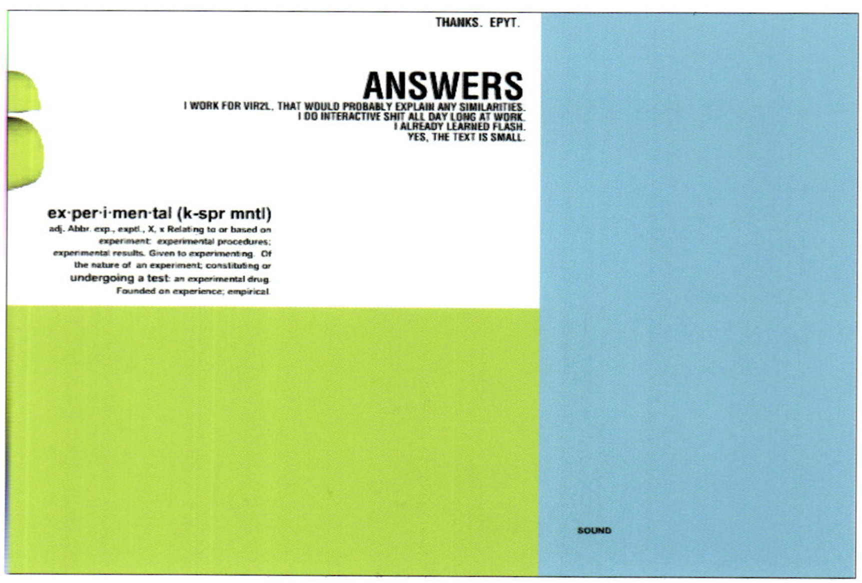
THANKS. EPYT.
ANSWERS
I WORK FOR VIR2L, THAT WOULD PROBABLY EXPLAIN ANY SIMILARITIES.
I DO INTERACTIVE SHIT ALL DAY LONG AT WORK.
I ALREADY LEARNED FLASH.
YES, THE TEXT IS SMALL.
ex·per·i·men·tal (k-spr mntl)
adj. Abbr. exp., exptl., X, x Relating to or based on experiment: experimental procedures; experimental results. Given to experimenting. Of the nature of an experiment; constituting or undergoing a test: an experimental drug. Founded on experience; empirical.
SOUND

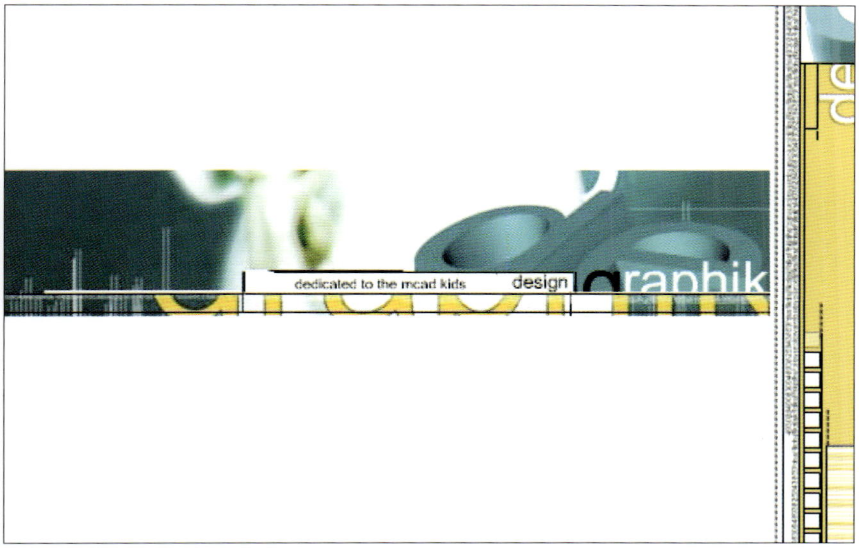

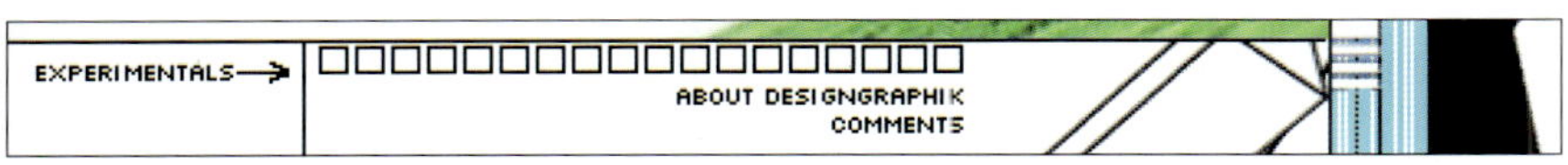

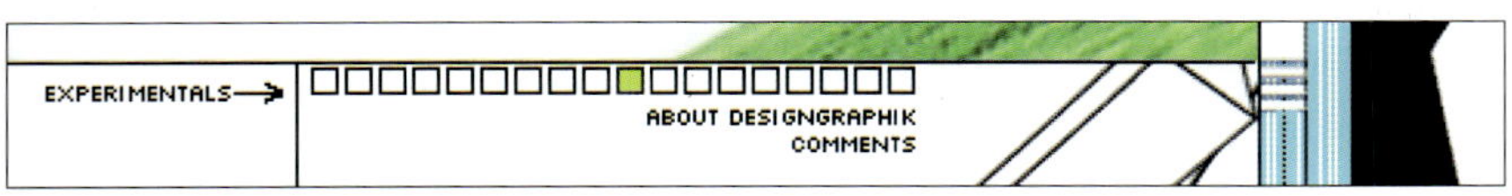

Title
DesignGraphik
URL
www.designgraphik.com/
Design Firm
DesignGraphik
Designer
Mike Young

DesignGraphik features self-described, pointless design. The navigation is somewhat confusing, but that fits into the overall concept of pointless art.

Title
Jon Duarte
URL
www.jonduarte.com/
Design Firm
Jon Duarte Communications

Jon Duarte Communications features great movement on the buttons. Letters and shapes fall towards the five simple buttons.

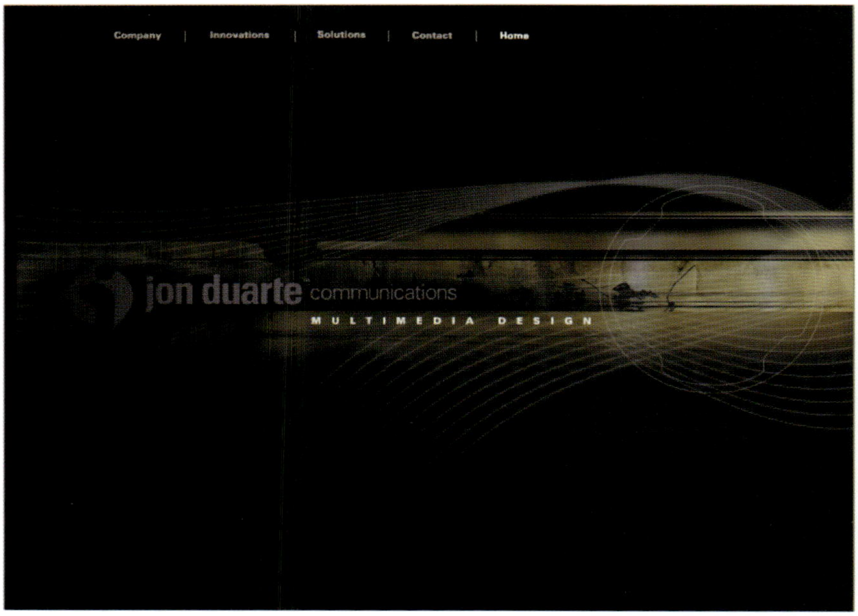

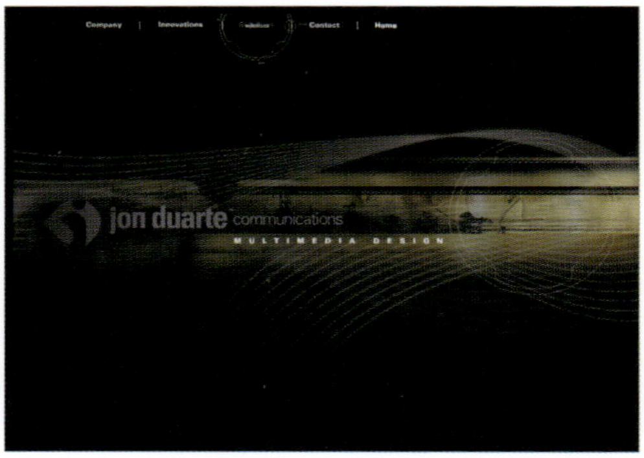

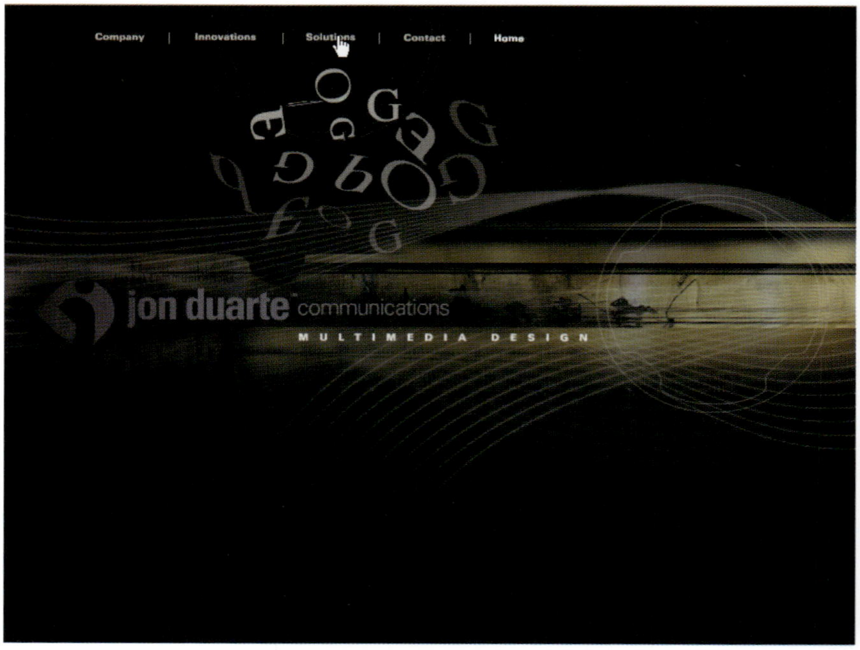

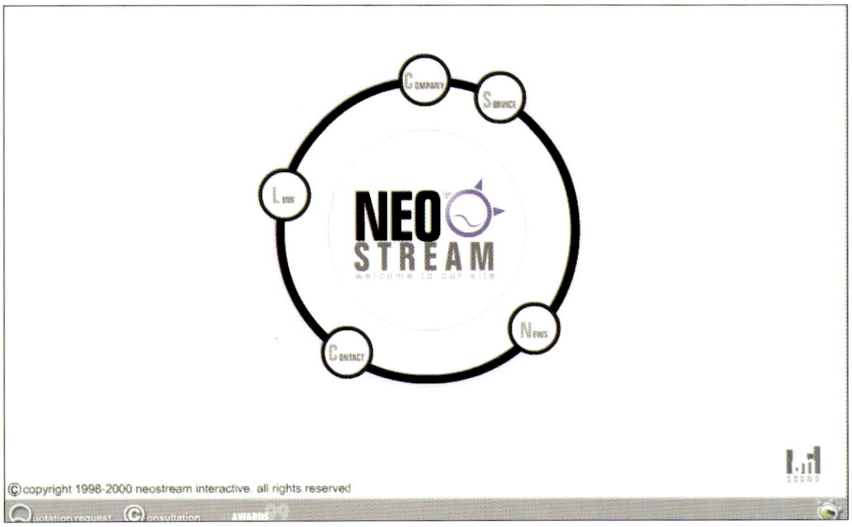

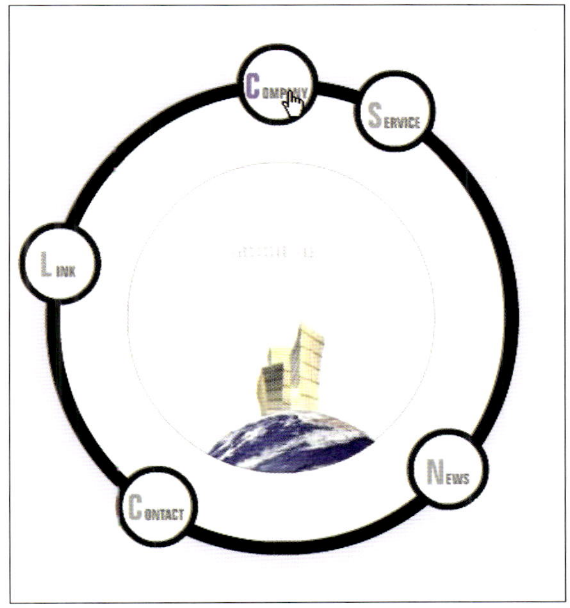

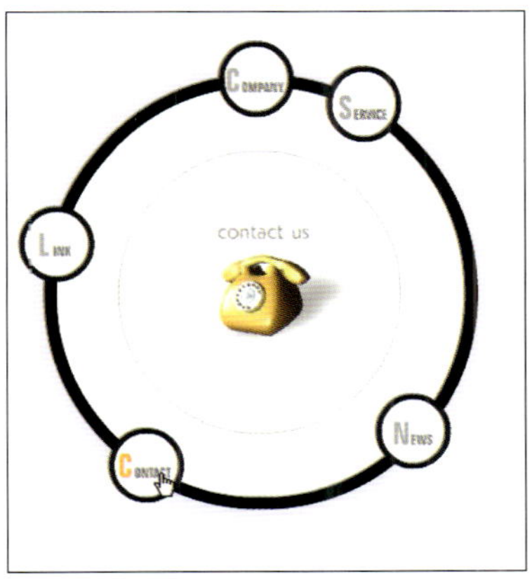

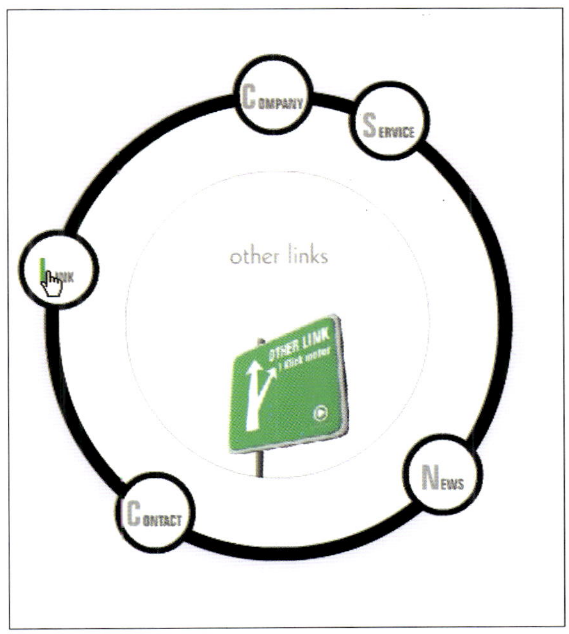

Title
Neostream
URL
www.neostream.com/
Design Firm
Neostream Interactive

One of the greatest interfaces on the Web, the Neostream site features five buttons with iconic illustrations that pop into the window on mouse-over. This is truly an international site, because the images make language unnecessary.

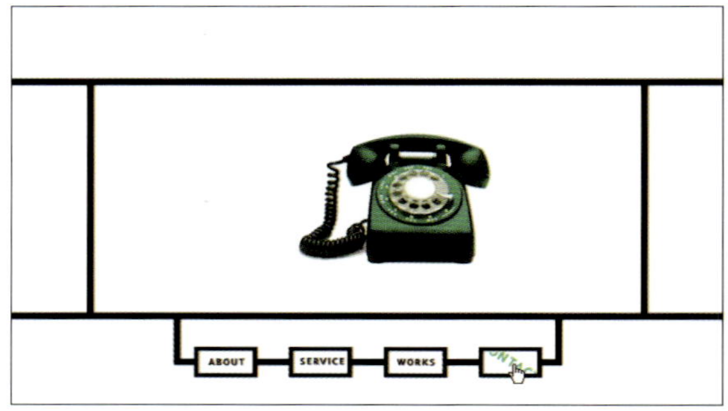

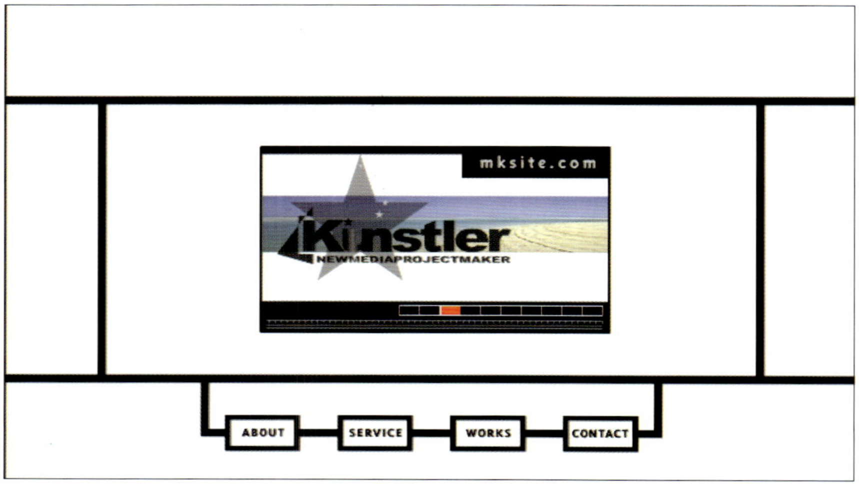

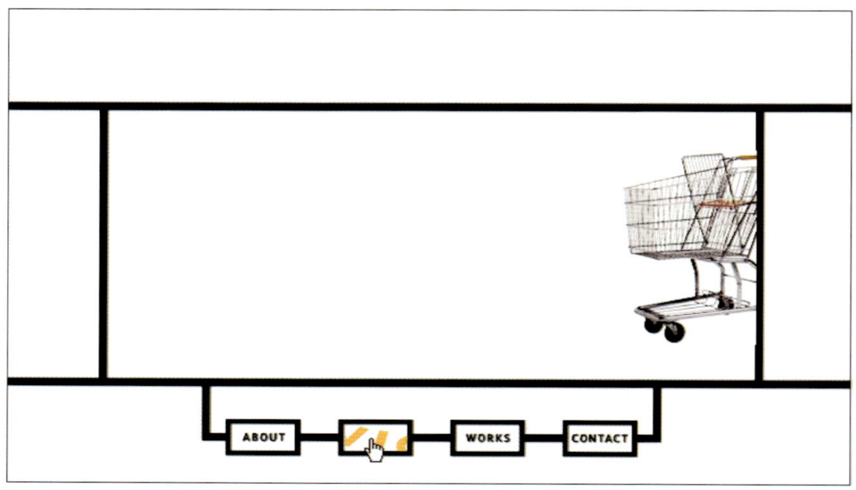

Title
MKSite
URL
mksite.com/
Design firm
MKSite
Designer
Massimo Kunstler

Like the Neostream site, MKSite features iconic images that appear on mouse-over in a great interface.

Title
Cultural Landscape Foundation
URL
www.tclf.org/
Design Firm
Coleman Design Group
Designer
Richard Benson

Five small buttons in the corner control navigation for this site. On mouse-over, the destination of each button is revealed.

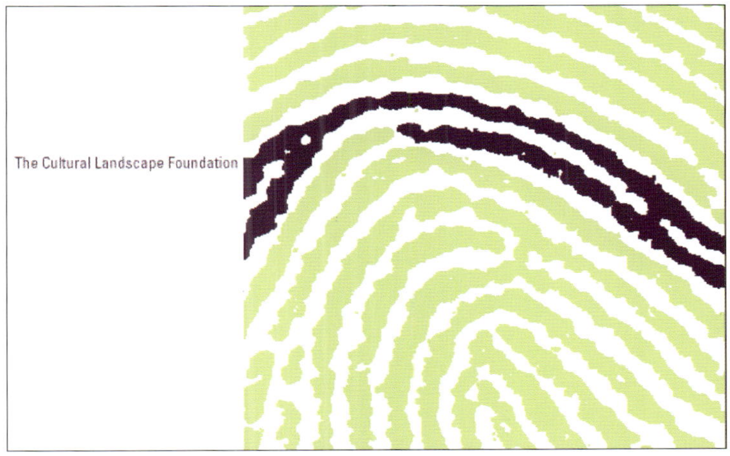

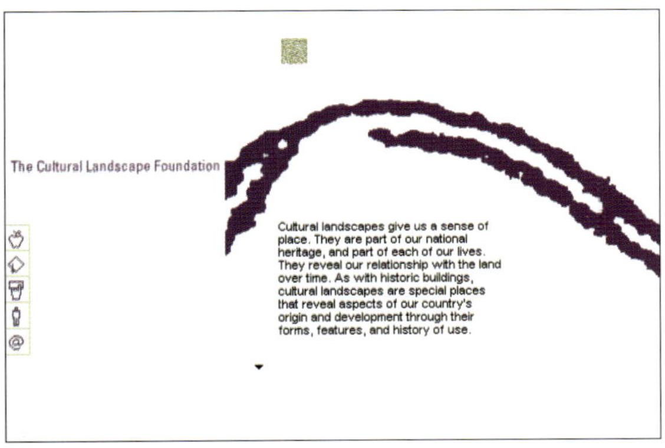

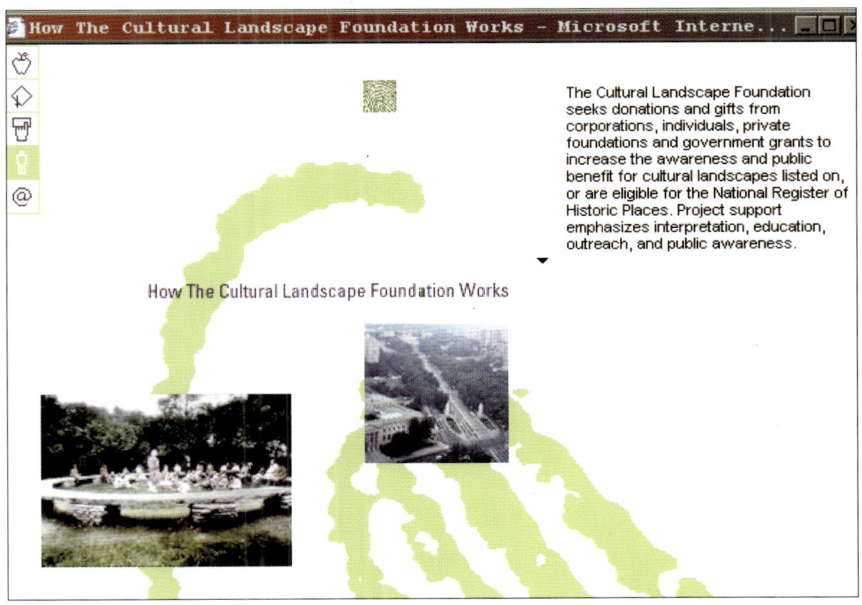

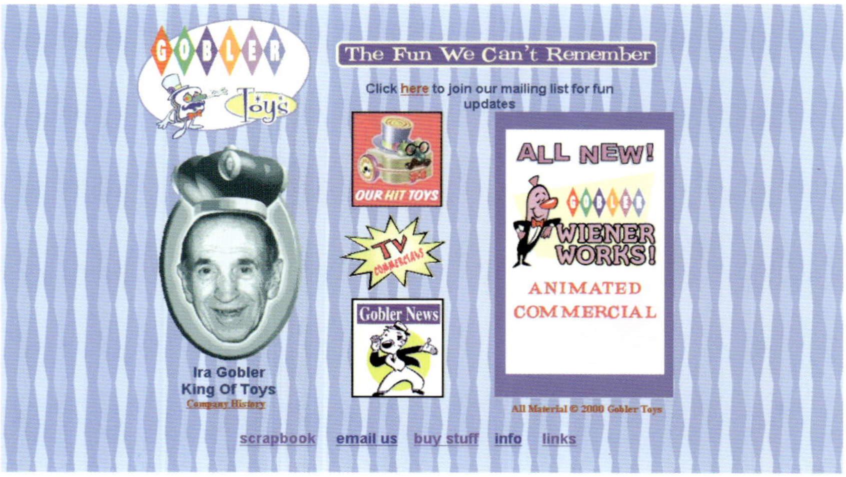

Title
gobler toys
URL
www.goblertoys.com/
Design firm
gobler toys
Designer
steve casino

Using Flash, Gobler has made every image on their homepage a button. Gobler captures a fifties kitsch look. It is one example of many sites on the Web where design has turned back on itself due to restrictions on color and speed that no longer exist in print and other media.

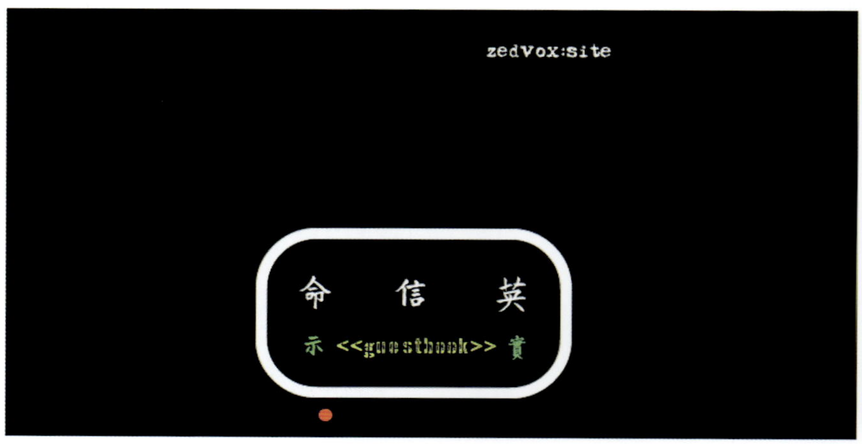

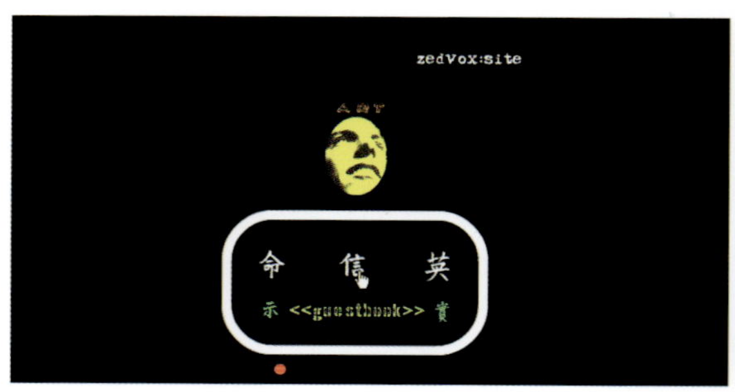

Title
zedmain
URL
members.tripod.com/zedmain.htm
Design firm
zedmain

A very simple bar reveals images on mouse-over. The three main buttons keep it clear and create some nice movement without the use of Flash.

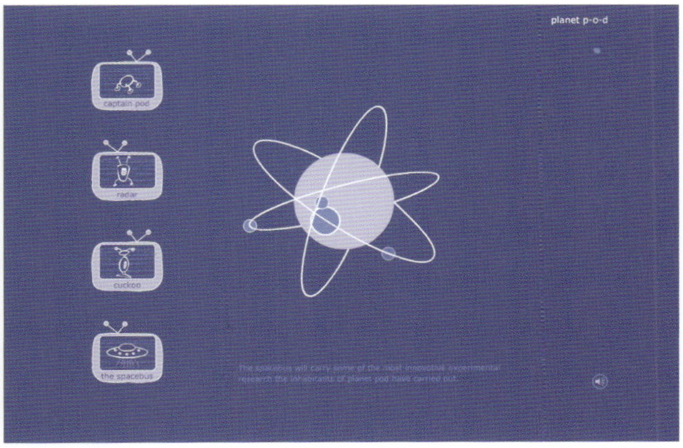

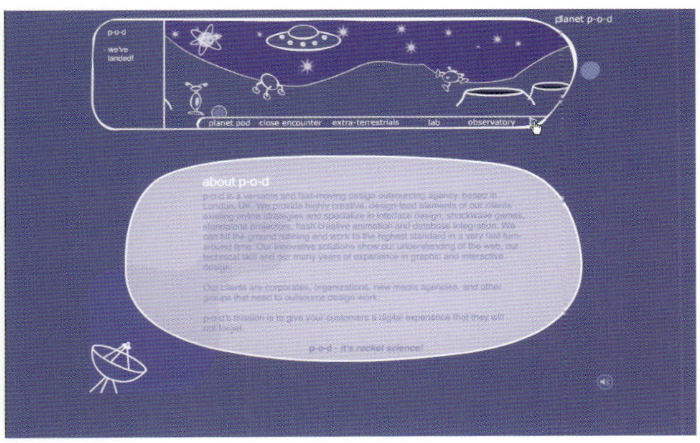

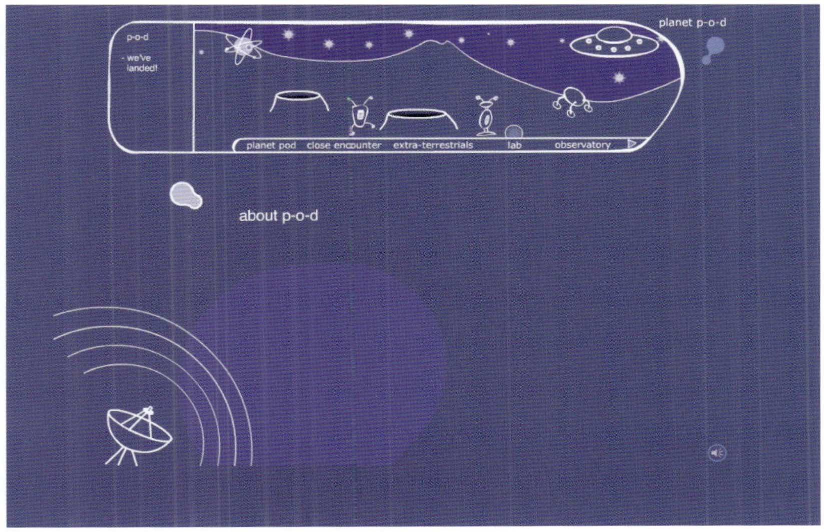

Title
planet p-o-d
URL
www.p-o-d.co.uk/
Design firm
pod New Media Ltd.

All of the cute aliens are buttons. This makes navigation easy and conforms to the overall concept. Check out the great piano soundtrack as well.

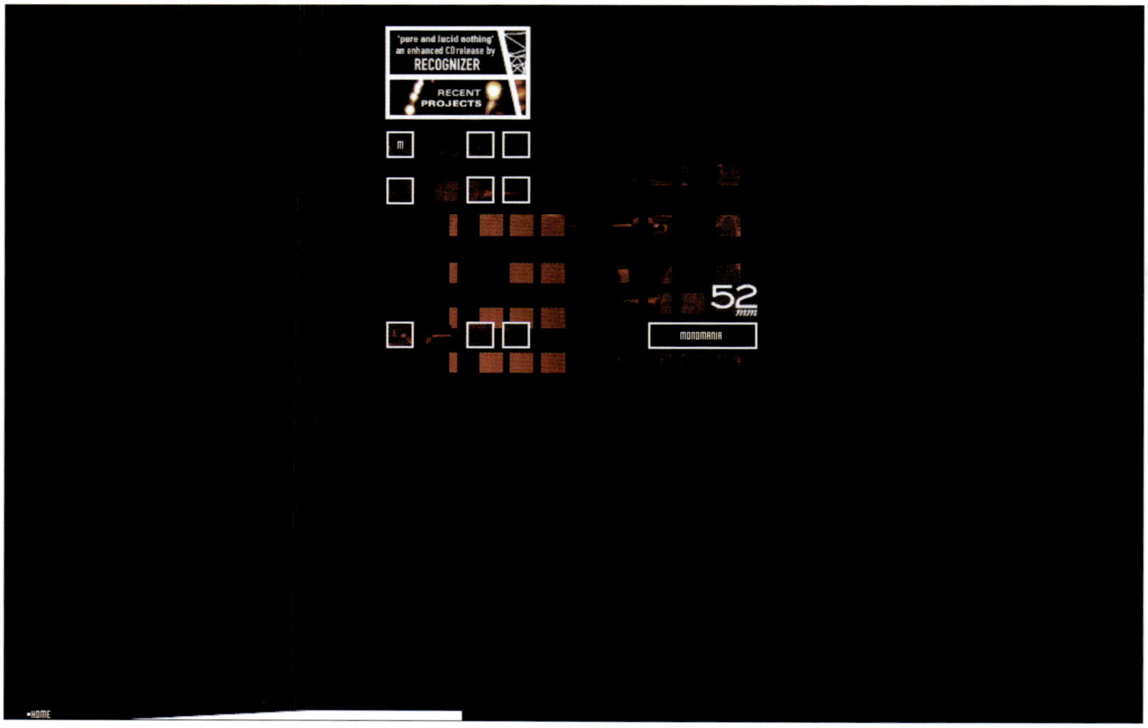
'pure and lucid nothing'
an enhanced CDrelease by
RECOGNIZER
RECENT
PROJECTS
52
mm
MONOMANIA
HOME

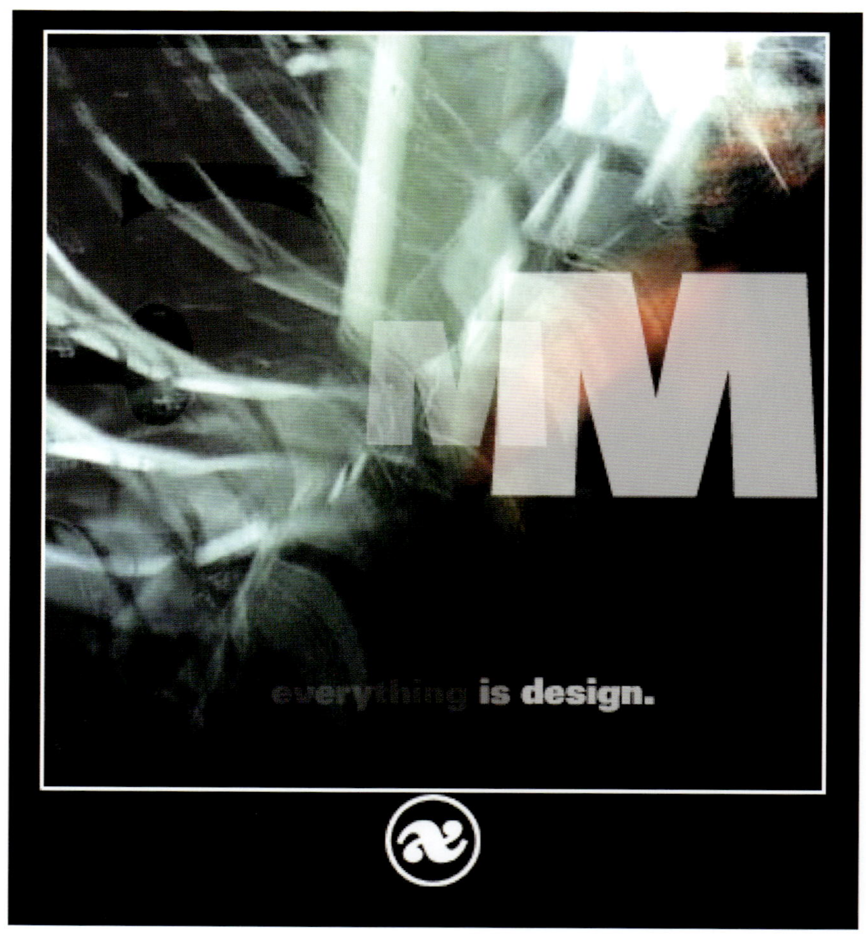
MM
everything is design.

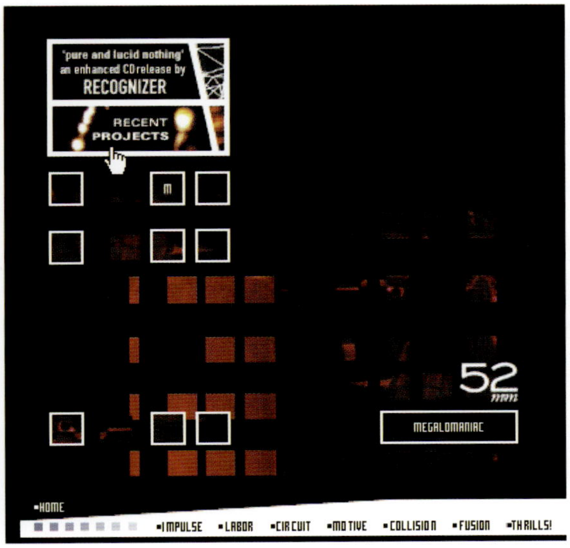

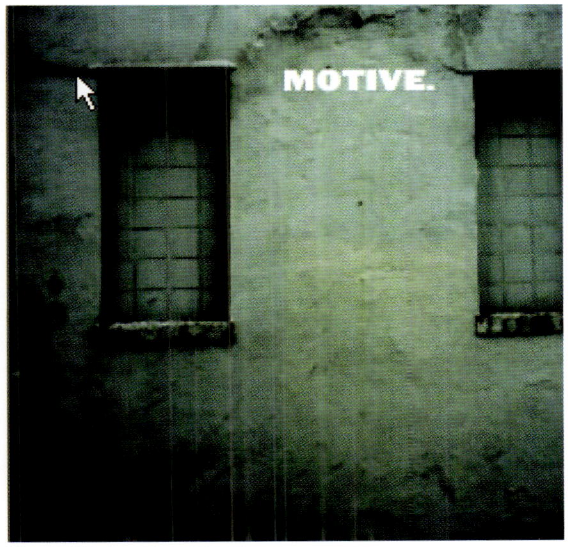

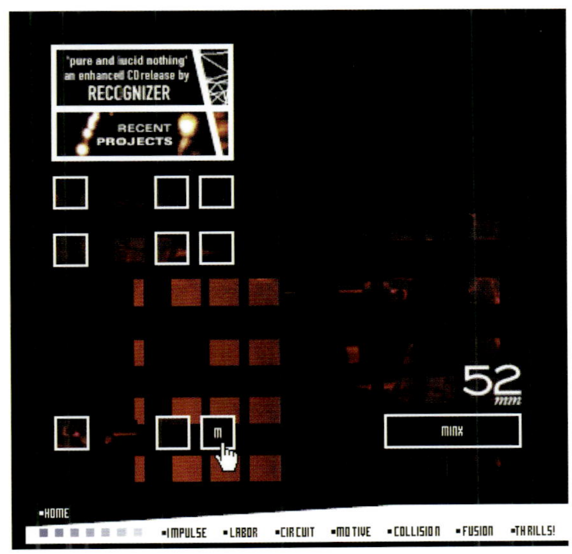

Title
52 mm
URL
www.52mm.com/
Design Firm
52 mm

A small bar on the bottom of the pop-up window navigates this whole site. The somewhat traditional navigation bar provides contrast on this unconventional site.

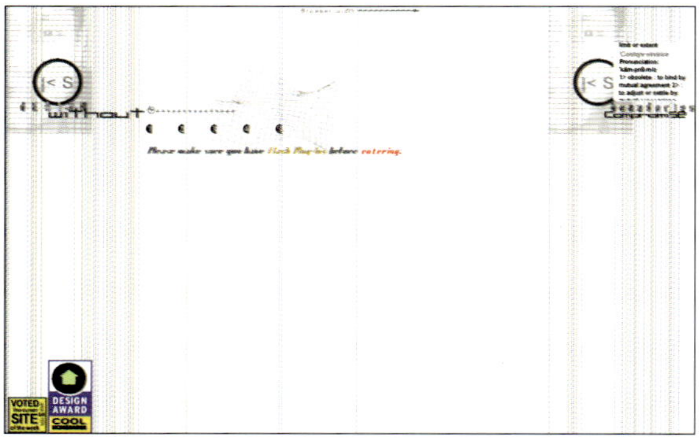

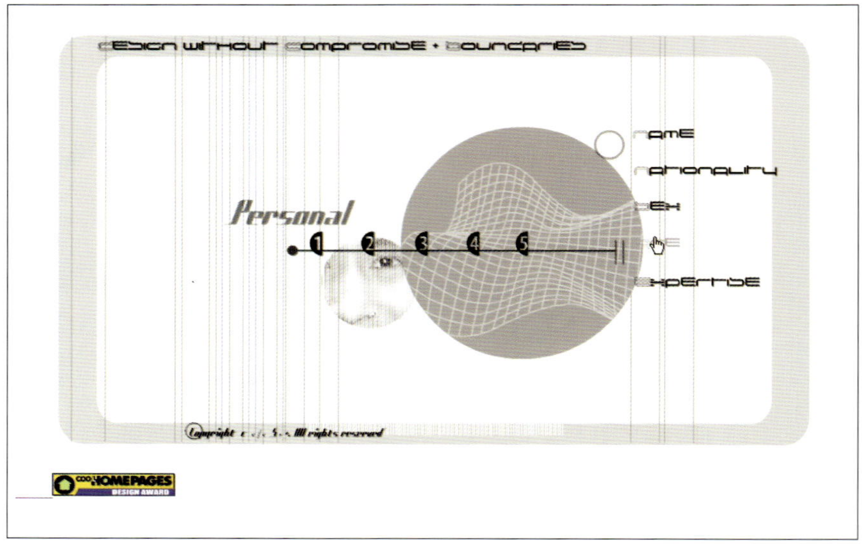

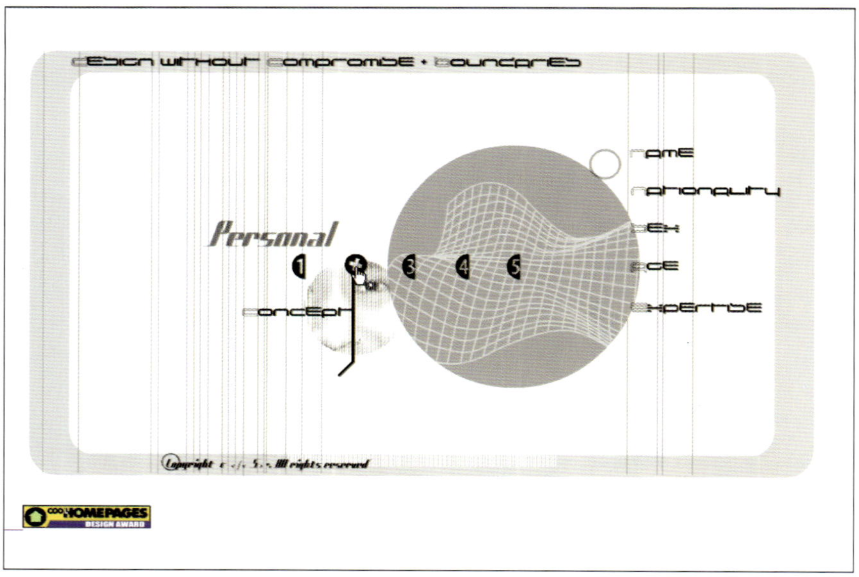

Title
Kim Seng
URL
www.freshdsign.com/kimseng
Design Firm
Consortio Inc.

Using Flash, Kim Seng creates buttons that move. On mouse-over, the buttons reveal their purpose. The buttons do take a second to find on this busy site, but when you do scroll over them, you can't miss them.

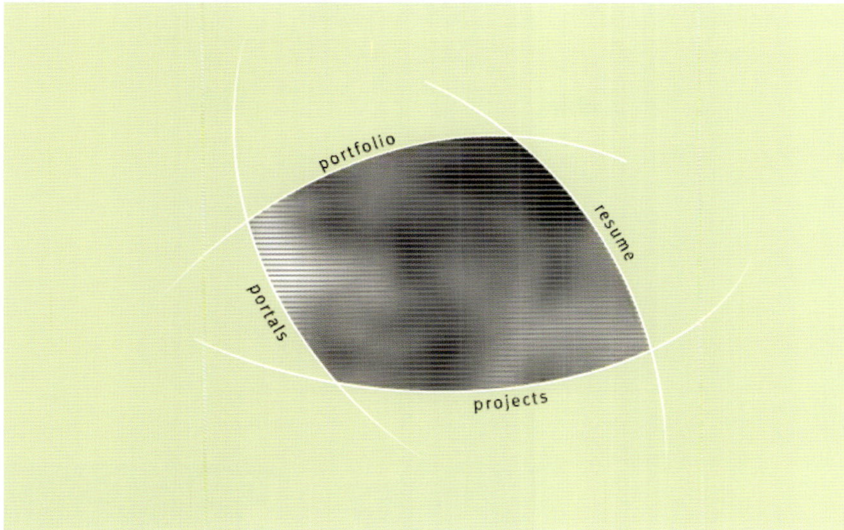

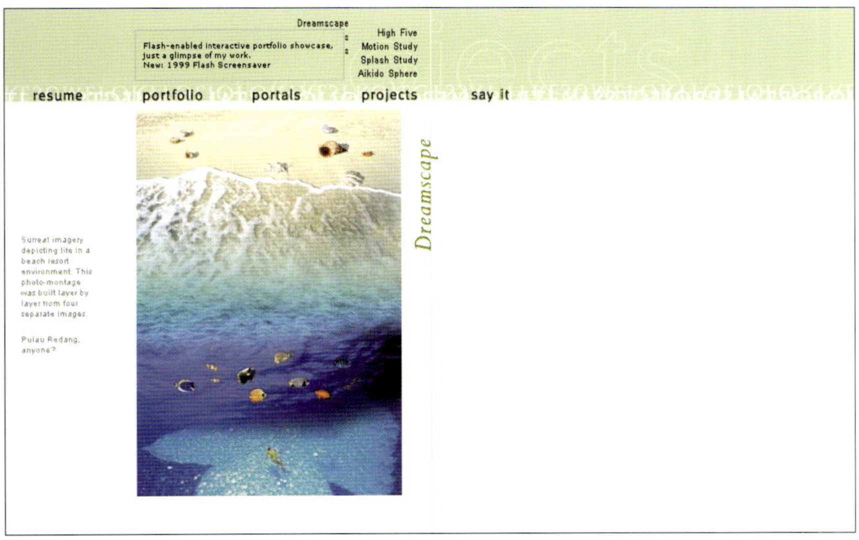

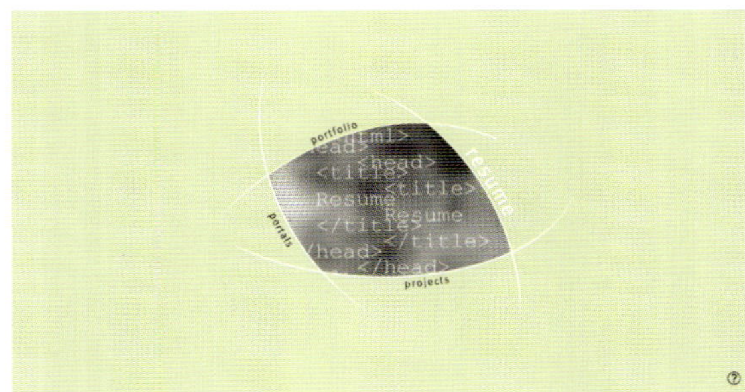

Title
Andy Lim
URL
andy.artdirectors.com/
Design Firm
Embedded Wireless Labs

Andy Lim created another Flash interface that creates interesting movements on mouse-over. The interface features four buttons that trigger animations in the center window.

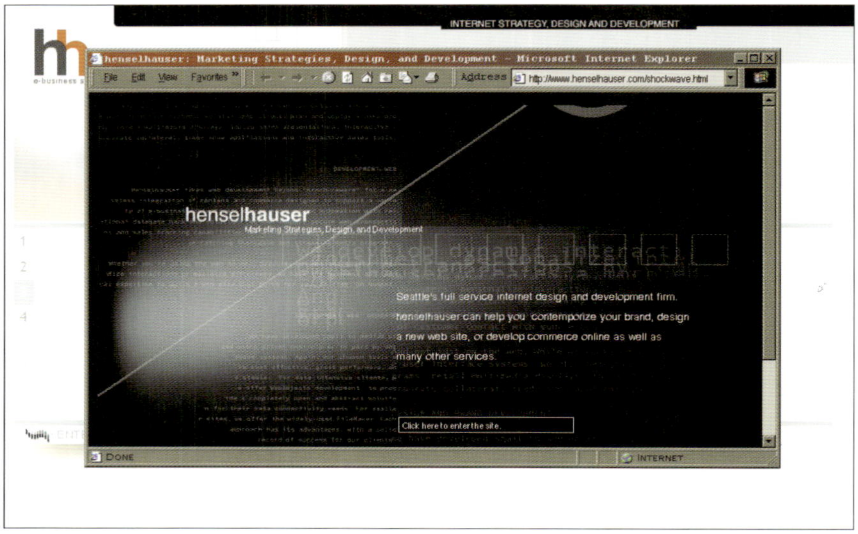

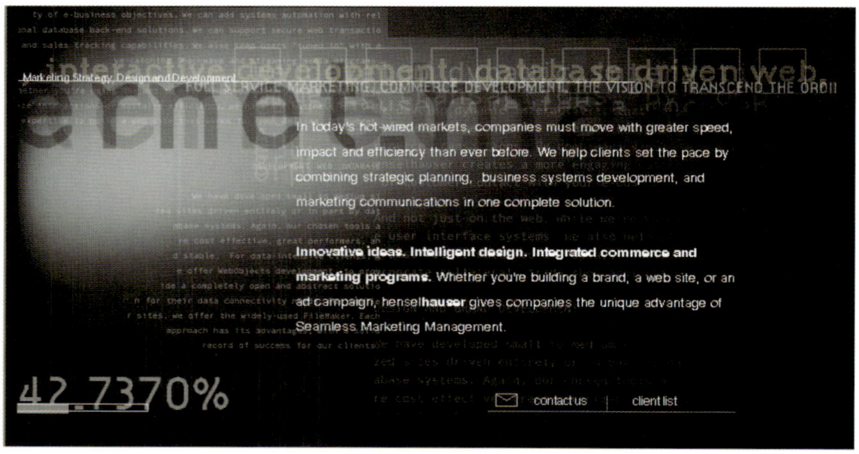

Title
Hensel Hauser
URL
www.henselhauser.com/
Design Firm
Hensel Hauser
Designer
Todd Hauser

Hensel Hauser is an impressively easy site to navigate, particularly in light of the extensive use of Flash. The new types of interfaces work extremely naturally, while the traditional ones are traditional. The nontraditional interfaces include design examples that feature thumbnails in a row. The thumbnails actually move in response to your cursor and highlight on mouse-over. Click on the image to enlarge.

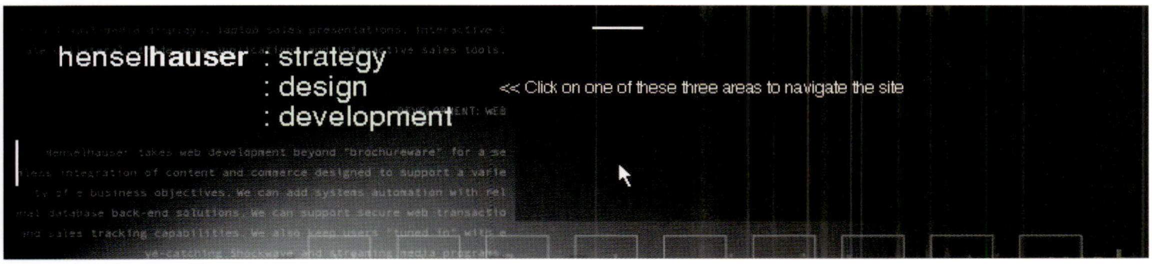
henselhauser : strategy
: design
: development
<< Click on one of these three areas to navigate the site

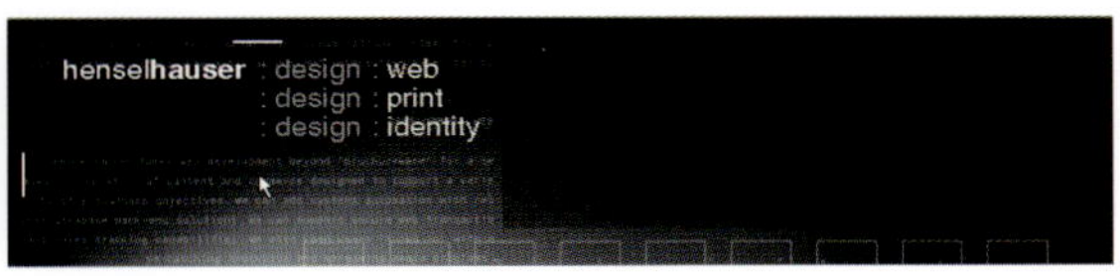
henselhauser : design : web
: design : print
: design : identity

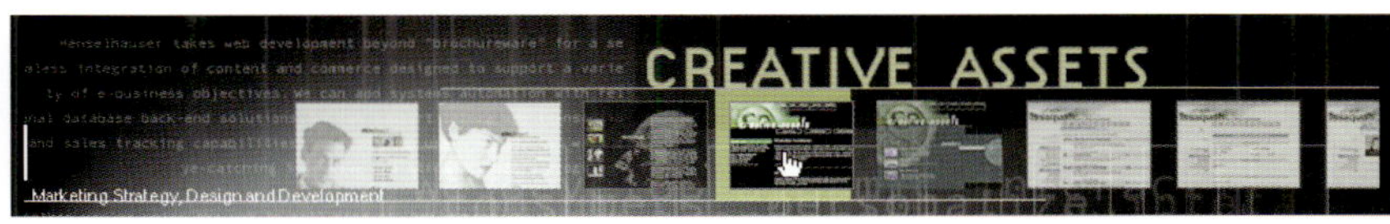
CREATIVE ASSETS
Marketing Strategy, Design and Development

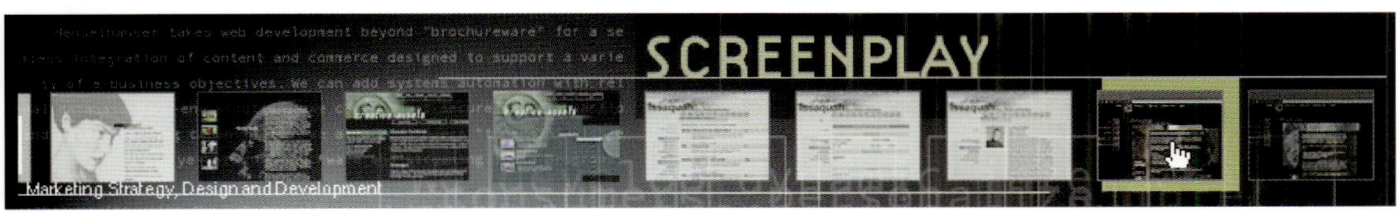
SCREENPLAY
Marketing Strategy, Design and Development

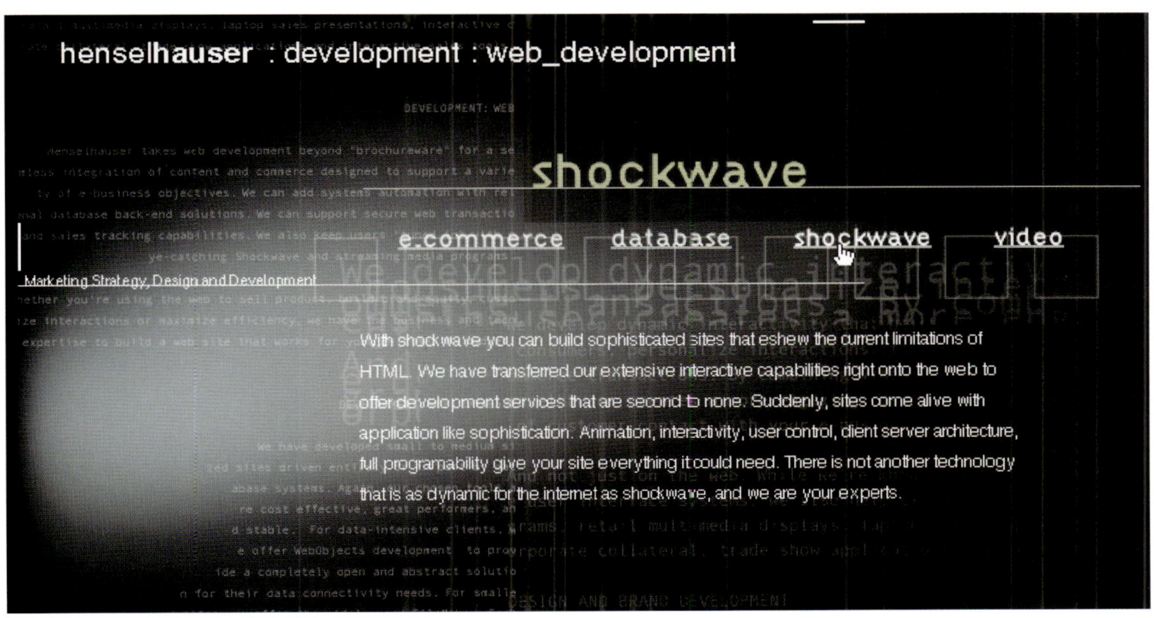
henselhauser : development : web_development
shockwave
e.commerce
database
shockwave
video
Marketing Strategy, Design and Development
With shockwave you can build sophisticated sites that eshew the current limitations of HTML. We have transferred our extensive interactive capabilities right onto the web to offer development services that are second to none. Suddenly, sites come alive with application like sophistication. Animation, interactivity, user control, client server architecture, full programability give your site everything it could need. There is not another technology that is as dynamic for the internet as shockwave, and we are your experts.

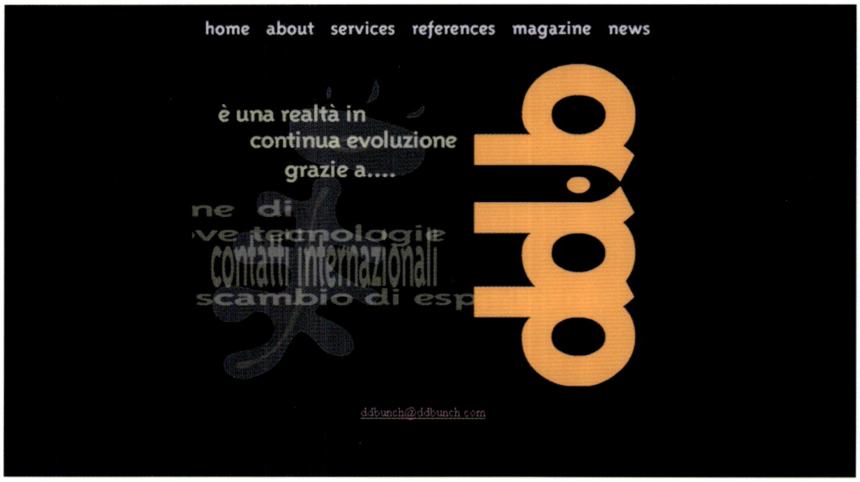

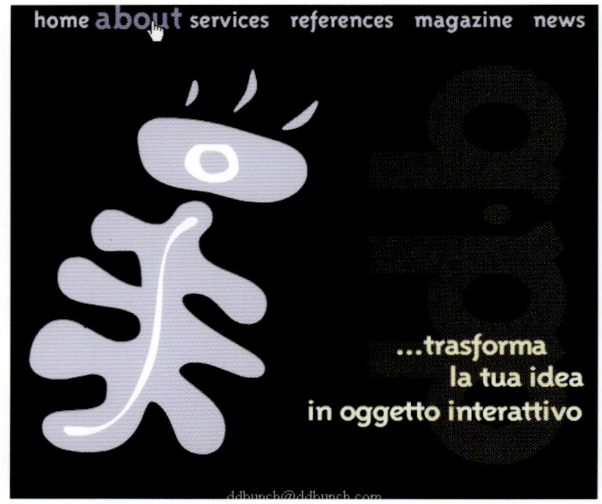

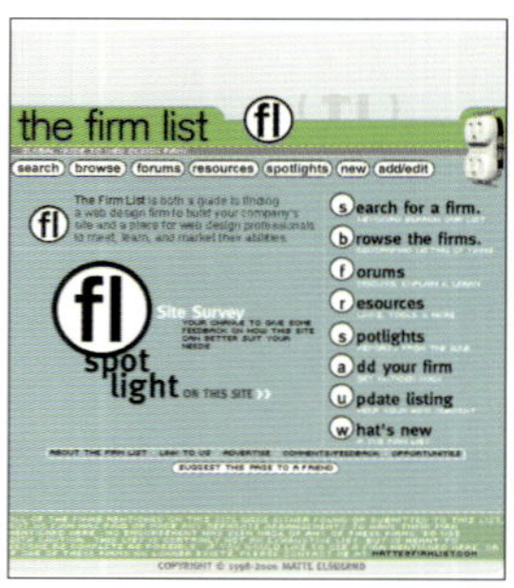

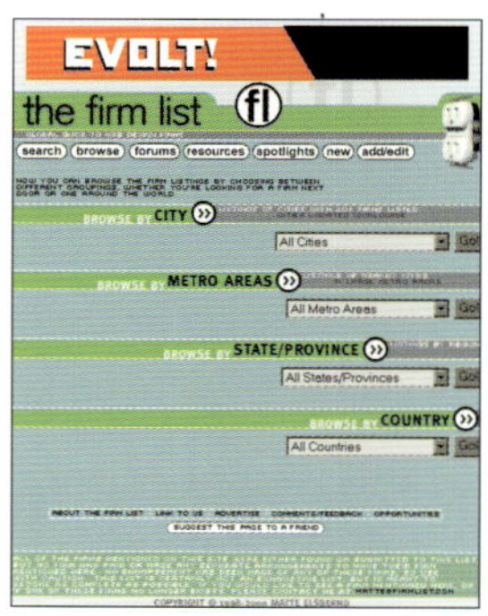

Title
DDBunch
URL
www.ddbunch.com/
Design Firm
Diciamo Digital Bunch SBL

The navigation bar across the top of this site is standard to every page. The navigation is somewhat traditional, unambiguous, and easy to use as a result.

Title
The Firm List
URL
www.thefirmlist.com/main.htm
Design Firm
The Firm List

If you are going to create a directory to Web-design firms, then you had better design the site well. The Firm List includes a lot of buttons that could become confusing if not for the intelligent design.

Title
gary venter
URL
www.gva.net.au/
Design firm
gary venter Architect

This site has four main buttons that reveal a lot of information on mouse-over. The text explaining your destination is more than typical, but the design works and is certainly easy to navigate.

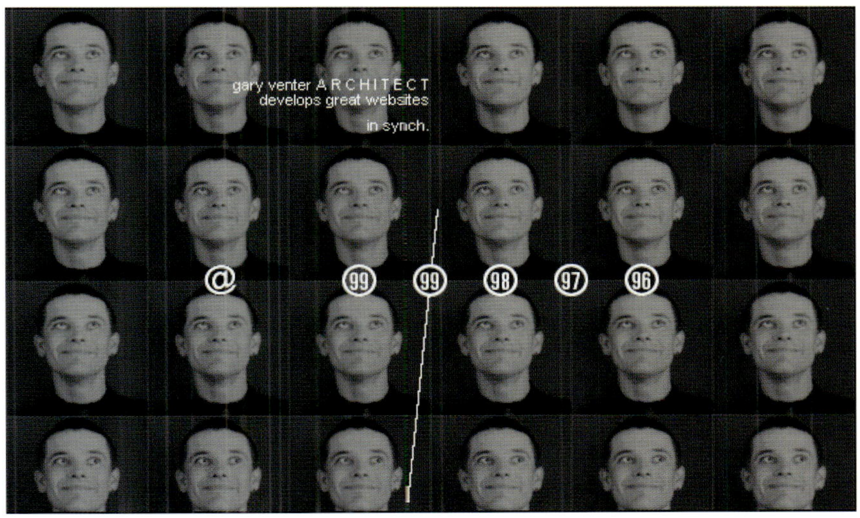

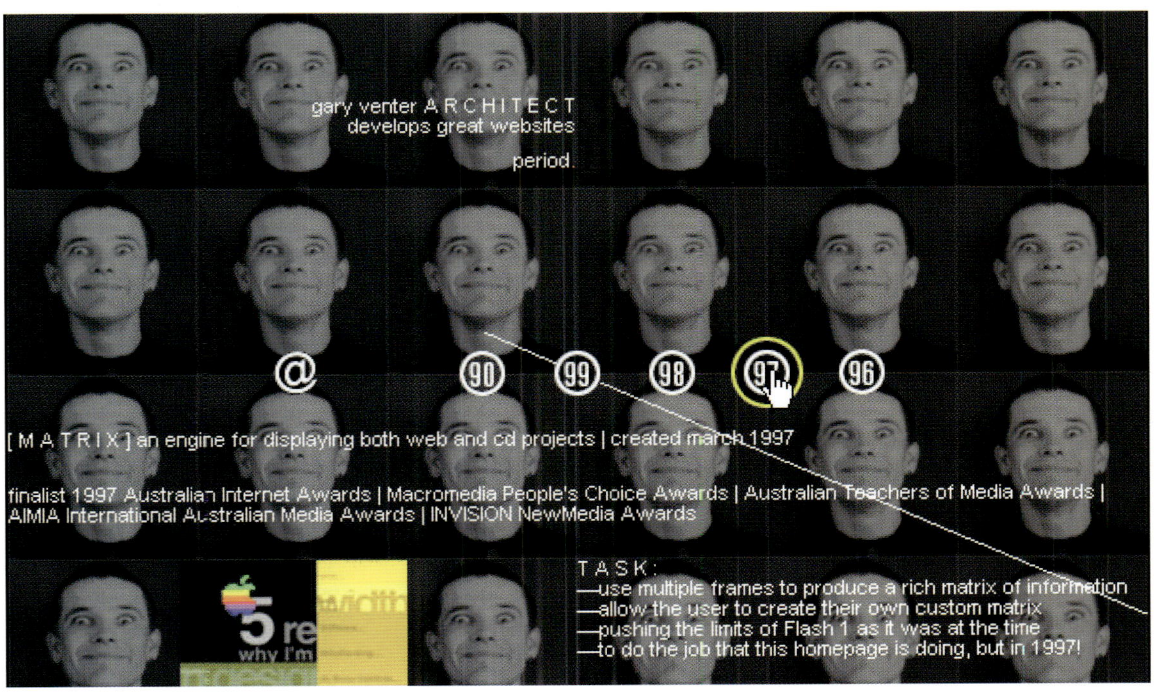

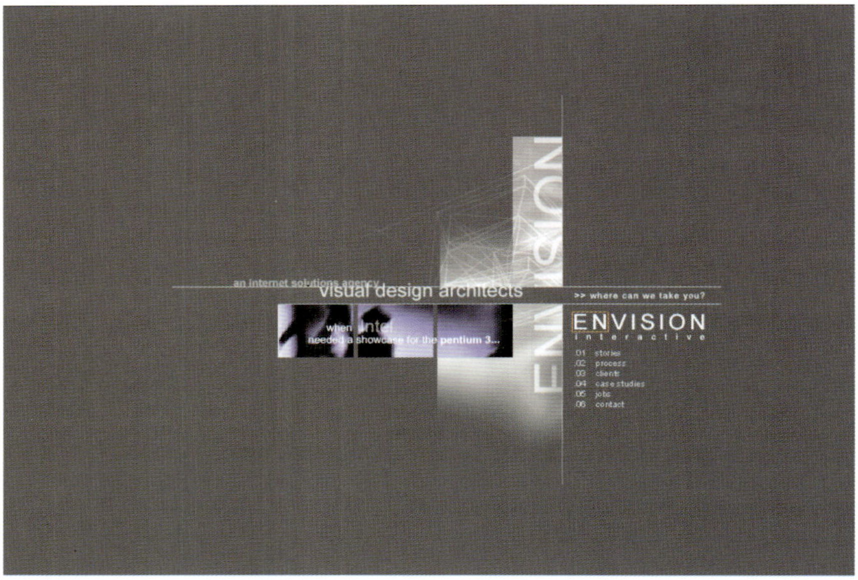

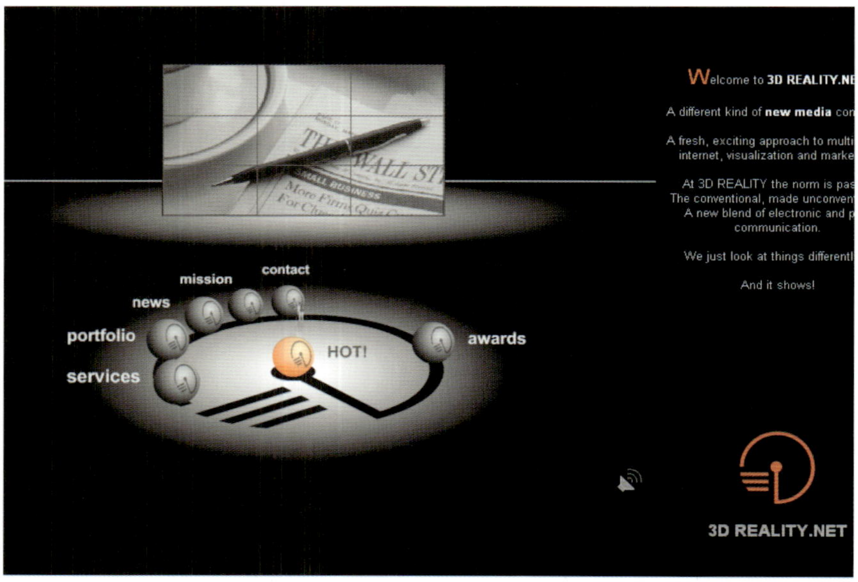

Title
3D Reality
URL
www.3dreality.net/main.htm
Design Firm
3D Reality.net
Designers
Les Fram, R. Tyler Smith

The main page has buttons that are highlighted by spotlights and a hot button that becomes hotter on mouse-over. The feeling of a large, important boardroom gives the site a professional flavor.

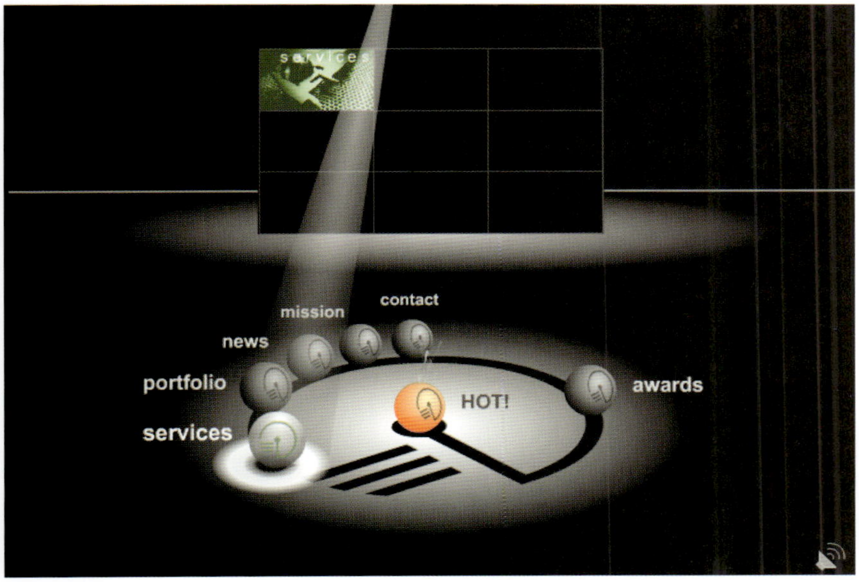
services
contact
mission
news
portfolio
awards
HOT!
services

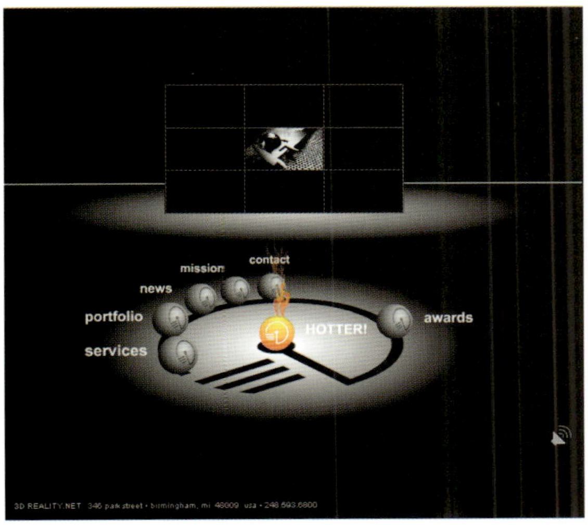
contact
mission
news
portfolio
HOTTER!
awards
services

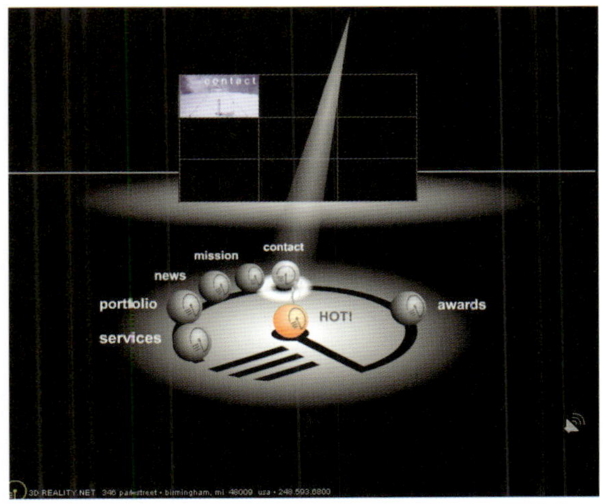
contact
mission
contact
news
portfolio
HOT!
awards
services

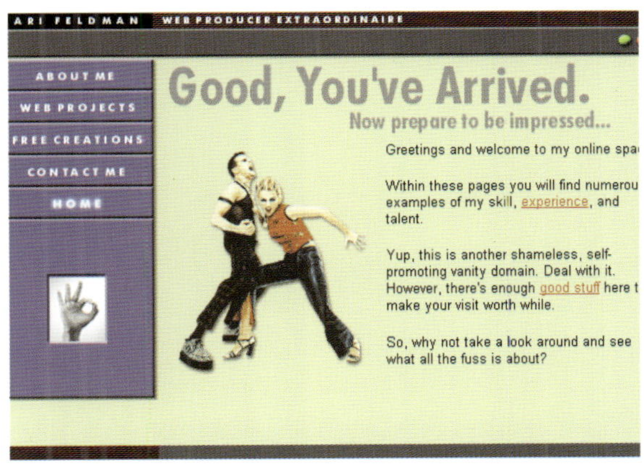
ARI FELDMAN
WEB PRODUCER EXTRAORDINAIRE
ABOUT ME
WEB PROJECTS
FREE CREATIONS
CONTACT ME
HOME
Good, You've Arrived.
Now prepare to be impressed...
Greetings and welcome to my online spa
Within these pages you will find numerou examples of my skill, experience, and talent.
Yup, this is another shameless, self-promoting vanity domain. Deal with it. However, there's enough good stuff here t make your visit worth while.
So, why not take a look around and see what all the fuss is about?

Title
Asmussen Interactive
URL
www.turtleshell.com/asm
Design Firm
Asmussen Interactive

The Asmussen Interactive interface has three buttons that serve as gateways to the rest of the site. The mouse-over reveals—in no uncertain terms—where each leads.

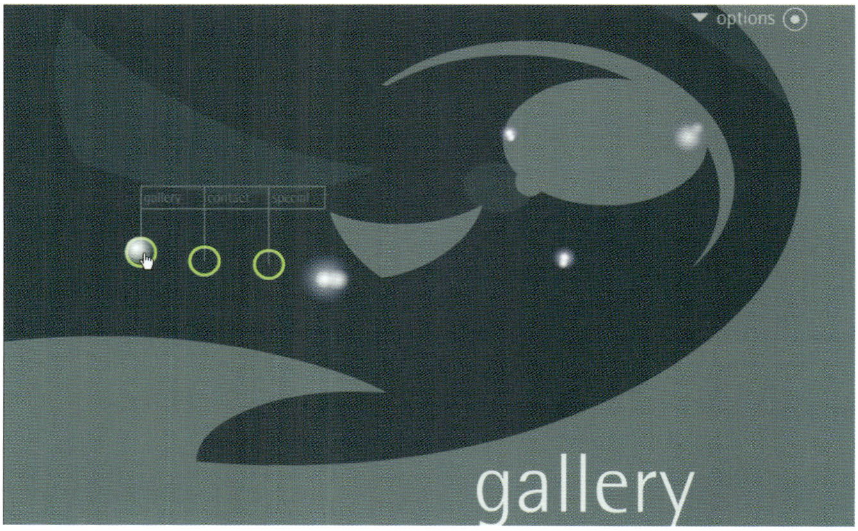

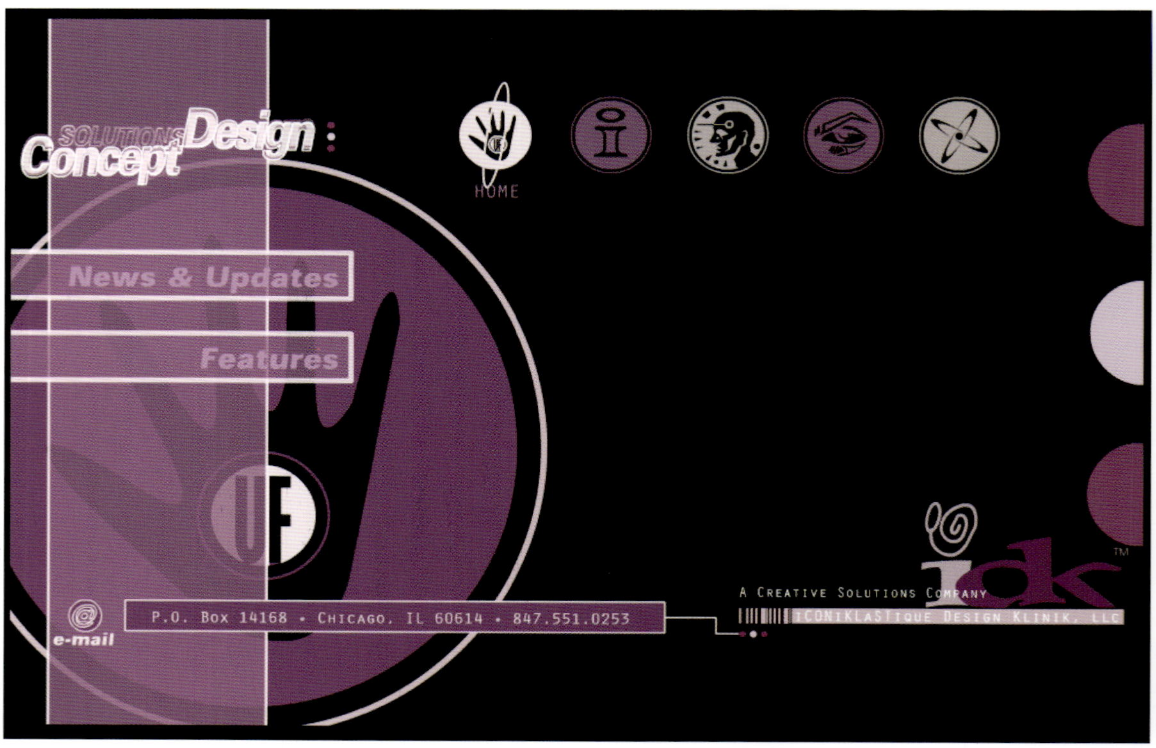

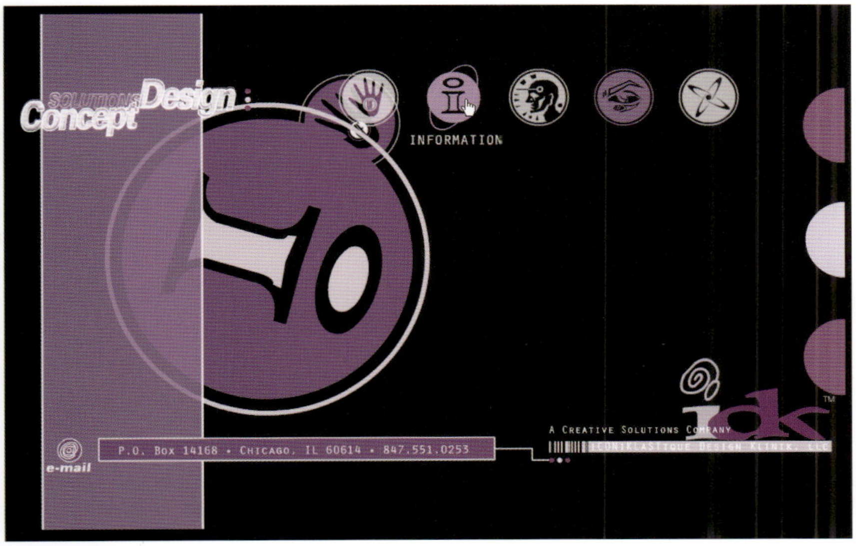

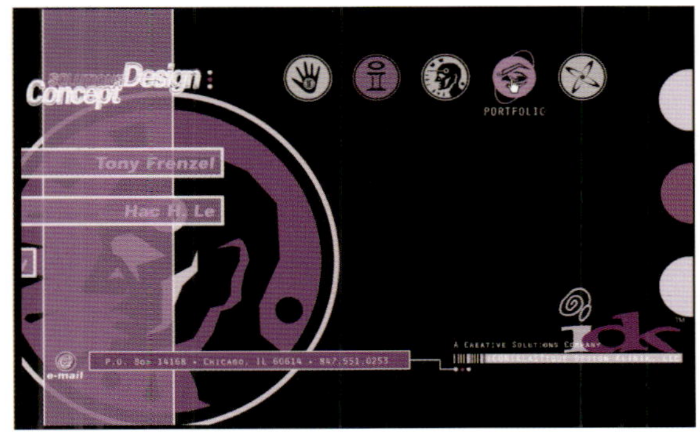

Title
Iconiklastique
URL
www.ida-a-ok.com/
Design firm
Iconiklastique Design Klinik, LLC

Click on the buttons; they rise up and become the main image. This is a good use of Flash, which loads an image and can then be resized without any additional download time.

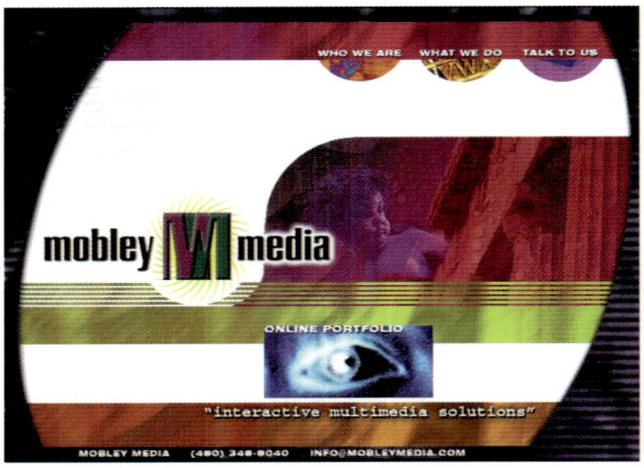

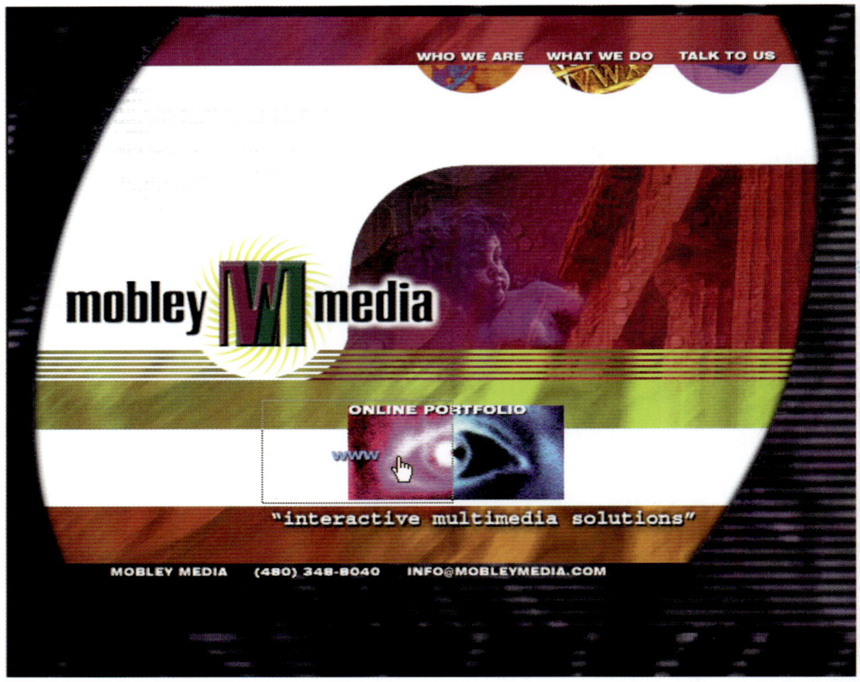

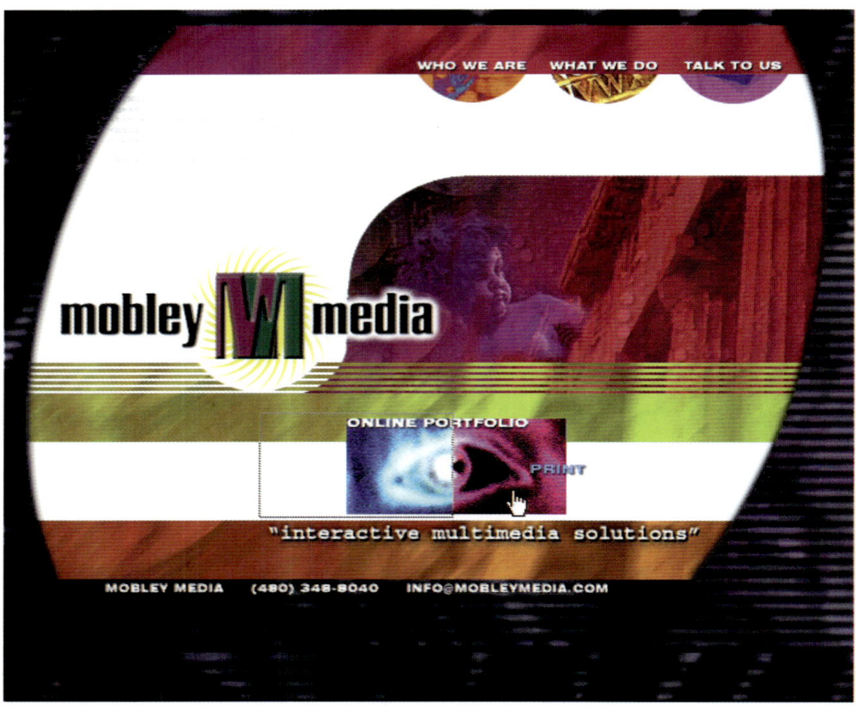

Title
Mobley Media
URL
www.mobleymedia.com/
Design Firm
Mobley Media
Designer
Margie Mobley

Great colors that change on mouse-over show you where you're going on this lushly illustrated site.

directiv
signer
sion Media Group, Inc./producer
lmer Erana

The great navigation bar along the right side of this site features four animated buttons. Four more buttons sit in the middle of the page.

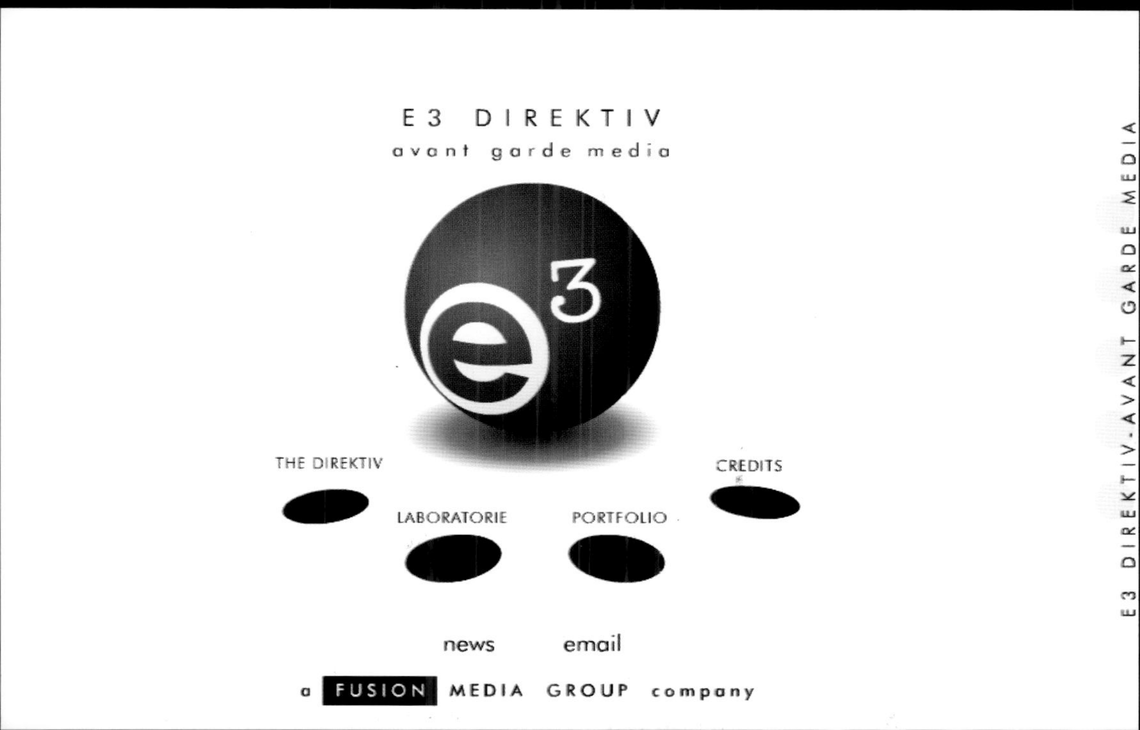

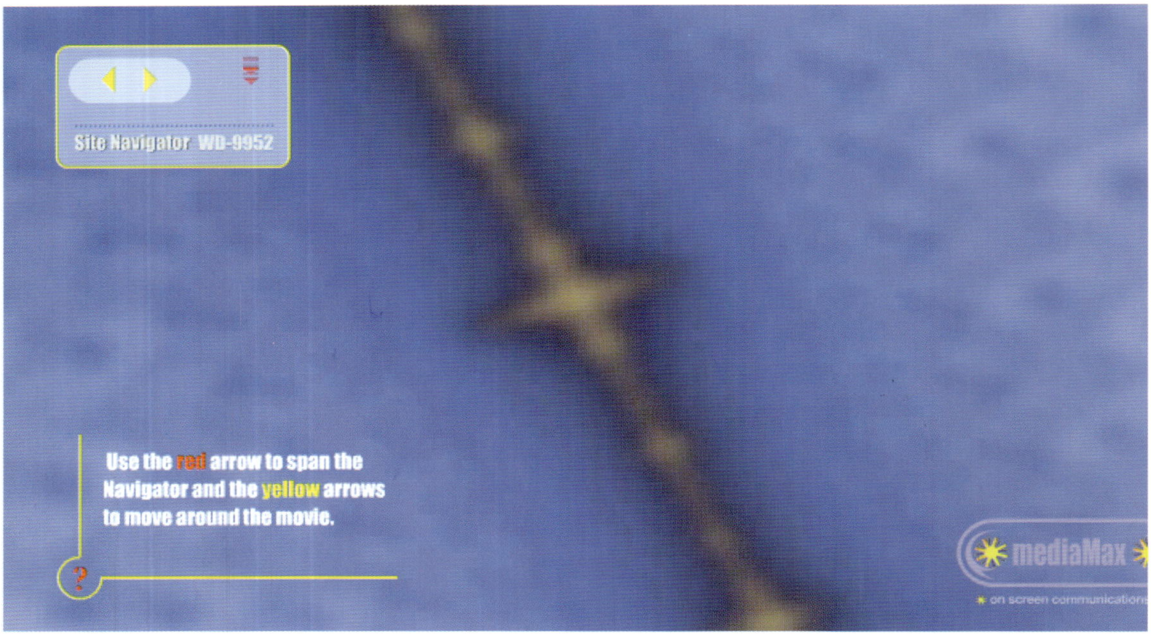

Title
Mediamax
URL
www.mediamax.gr
Design Firm
Mediamax

Mediamax features a unique interface that takes a moment to get used to, but once you do, it allows for seamless navigation. The interface shows a thumbnail of the page, and when you click on it, it takes you there.

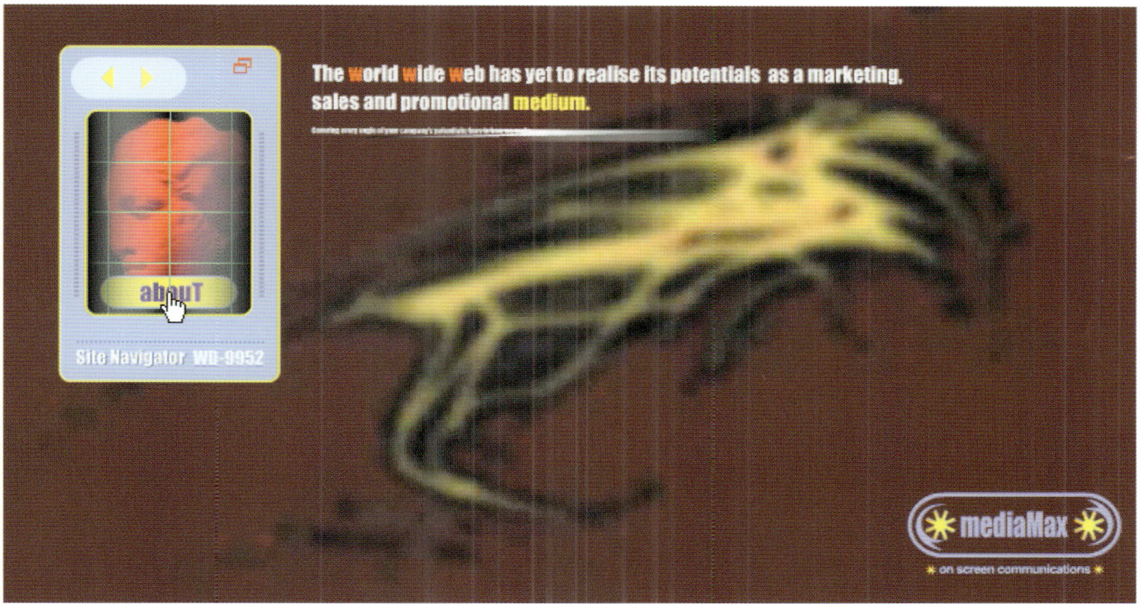

abouT
Site Navigator WD-9952
The world wide web has yet to realise its potentials as a marketing, sales and promotional medium.
mediaMax
on screen communications

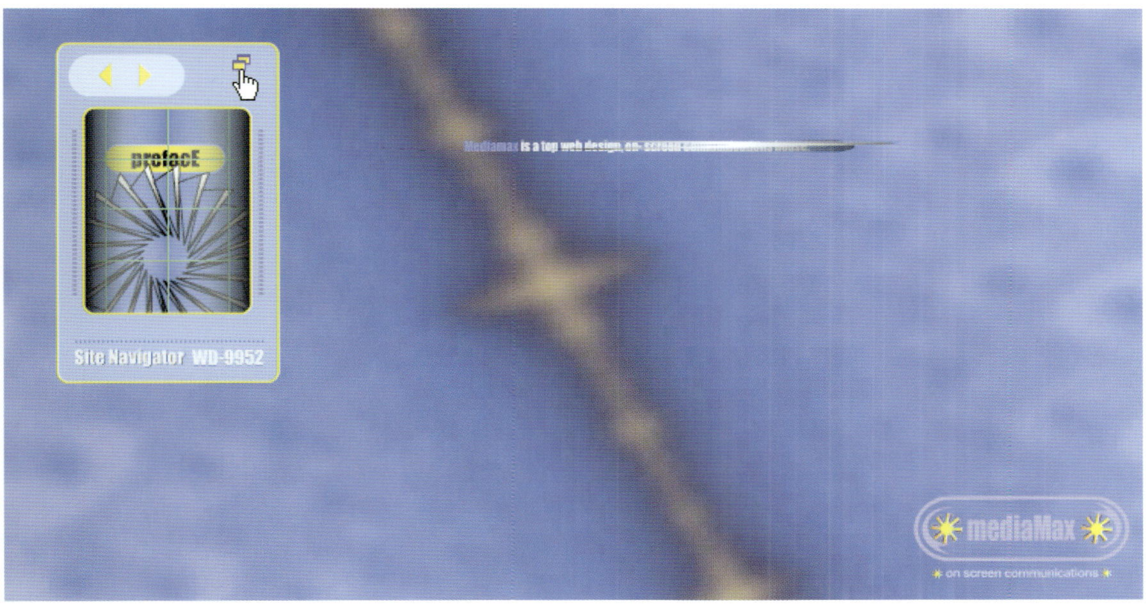

prefacE
Site Navigator WD-9952
mediaMax
on screen communications

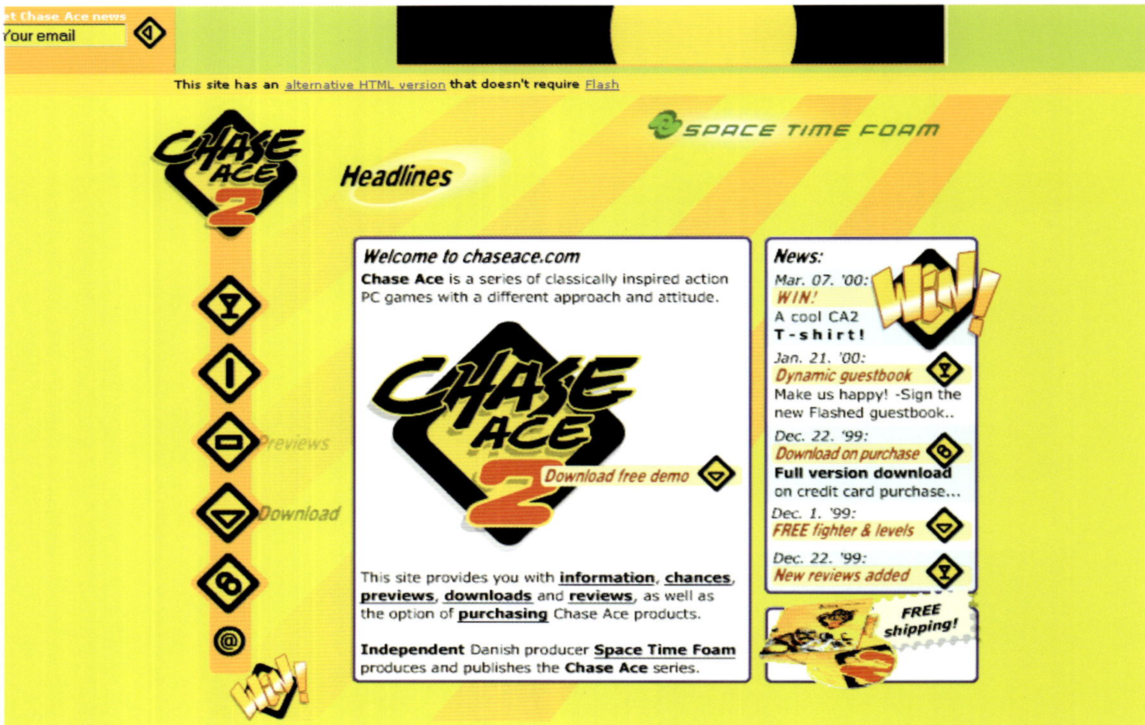

Title
chase Ace
URL
www.chaseace.com/
Design Firm
petergrafik/space Time Foam
Designer
peter Holm

The destinations of these buttons scroll by constantly and come into focus on mouse-over. All the information that you need to navigate this site is on the main page.

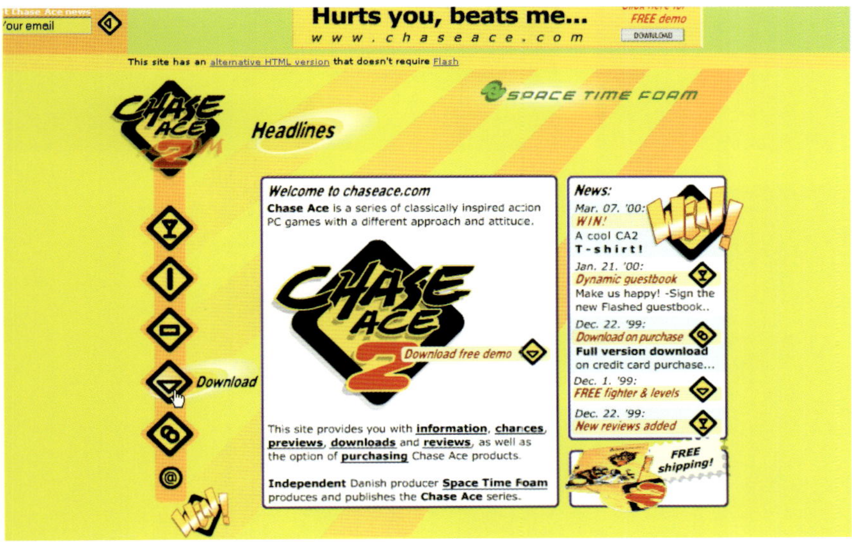
Your email
Hurts you, beats me...
w w w . c h a s e a c e . c o m
FREE demo
DOWNLOAD
This site has an alternative HTML version that doesn't require Flash
SPACE TIME FOAM
Headlines
Welcome to chaseace.com
Chase Ace is a series of classically inspired action PC games with a different approach and attitude.
Download free demo
Download
This site provides you with information, chances, previews, downloads and reviews, as well as the option of purchasing Chase Ace products.
Independent Danish producer Space Time Foam produces and publishes the Chase Ace series.
News:
Mar. 07. '00:
WIN!
A cool CA2
T-shirt!
Jan. 21. '00:
Dynamic guestbook
Make us happy! -Sign the new Flashed guestbook..
Dec. 22. '99:
Download on purchase
Full version download on credit card purchase...
Dec. 1. '99:
FREE fighter & levels
Dec. 22. '99:
New reviews added
FREE shipping!

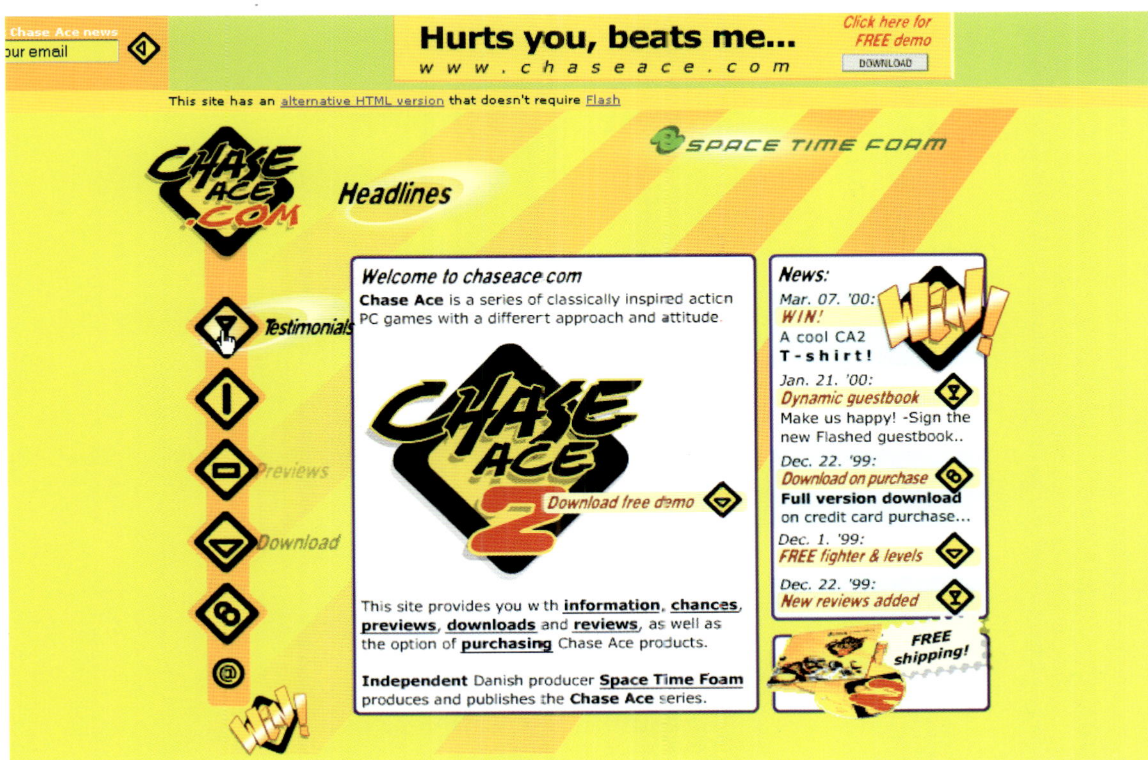
Chase Ace news
our email
Hurts you, beats me...
w w w . c h a s e a c e . c o m
Click here for
FREE demo
DOWNLOAD
This site has an alternative HTML version that doesn't require Flash
SPACE TIME FOAM
Headlines
Testimonials
Previews
Download
Welcome to chaseace.com
Chase Ace is a series of classically inspired action PC games with a different approach and attitude.
Download free demo
This site provides you with information, chances, previews, downloads and reviews, as well as the option of purchasing Chase Ace products.
Independent Danish producer Space Time Foam produces and publishes the Chase Ace series.
News:
Mar. 07. '00:
WIN!
A cool CA2
T-shirt!
Jan. 21. '00:
Dynamic guestbook
Make us happy! -Sign the new Flashed guestbook..
Dec. 22. '99:
Download on purchase
Full version download on credit card purchase...
Dec. 1. '99:
FREE fighter & levels
Dec. 22. '99:
New reviews added
FREE shipping!

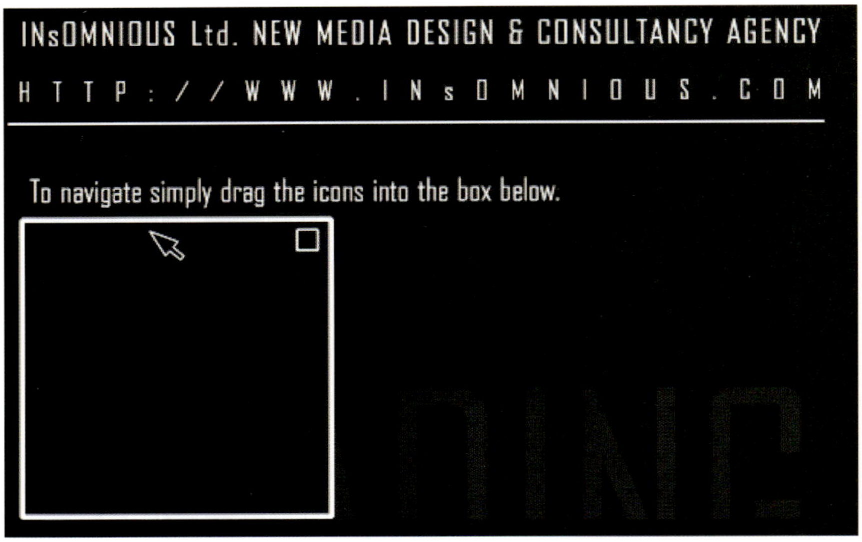

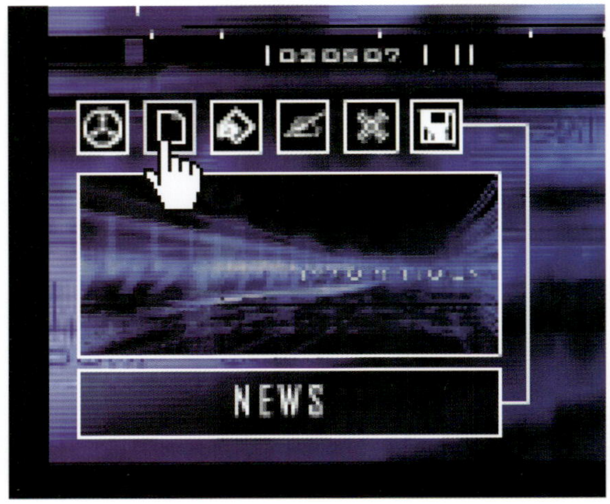

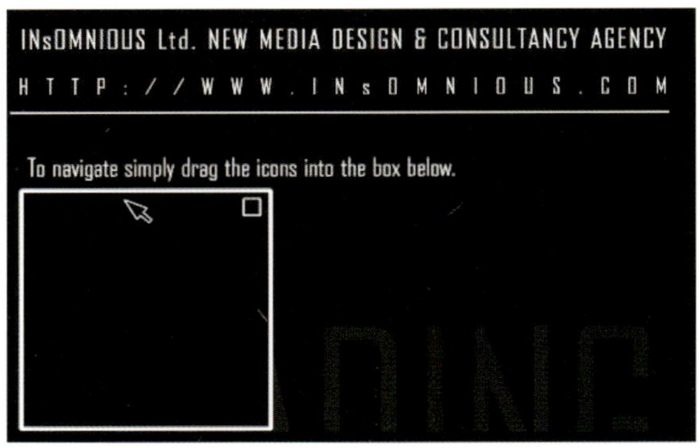

Title
insomnius
URL
www.insomnious.com/
Design firm
Insomnious, Ltd.

Insomnious designed one of the most creative interfaces on the Internet. Click on the button and drag it into the adjacent box. Then the window with the information that you want will mimic the button.

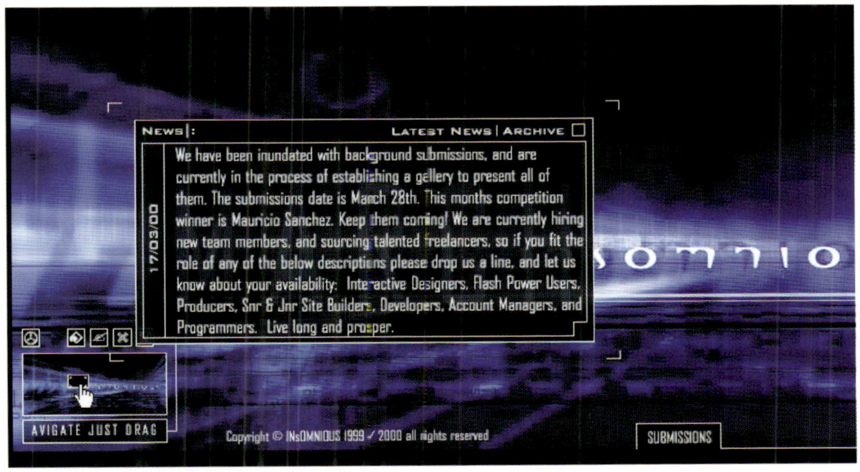
News |:
Latest News | Archive
17/03/00
We have been inundated with background submissions, and are currently in the process of establishing a gallery to present all of them. The submissions date is March 28th. This months competition winner is Mauricio Sanchez. Keep them coming! We are currently hiring new team members, and sourcing talented freelancers, so if you fit the role of any of the below descriptions please drop us a line, and let us know about your availability: Interactive Designers, Flash Power Users, Producers, Snr & Jnr Site Builders, Developers, Account Managers, and Programmers. Live long and prosper.
AVIGATE JUST DRAG
Copyright © INsOMNIOUS 1999 / 2000 all rights reserved
SUBMISSIONS

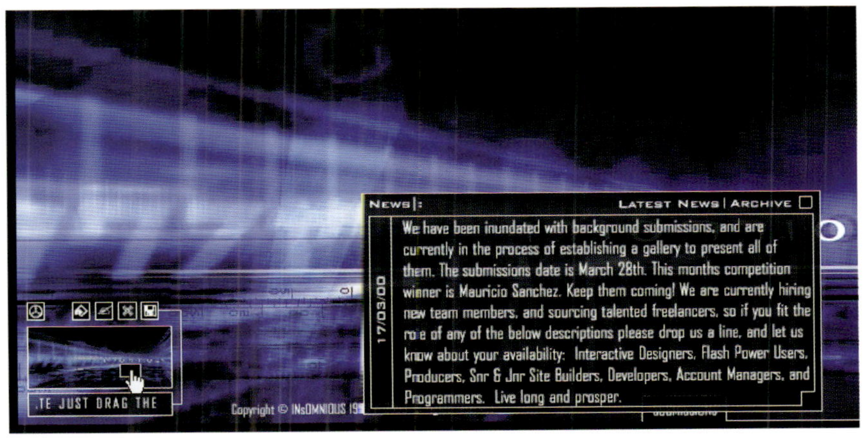
News |:
Latest News | Archive
17/03/00
We have been inundated with background submissions, and are currently in the process of establishing a gallery to present all of them. The submissions date is March 28th. This months competition winner is Mauricio Sanchez. Keep them coming! We are currently hiring new team members, and sourcing talented freelancers, so if you fit the role of any of the below descriptions please drop us a line, and let us know about your availability: Interactive Designers, Flash Power Users, Producers, Snr & Jnr Site Builders, Developers, Account Managers, and Programmers. Live long and prosper.
TE JUST DRAG THE

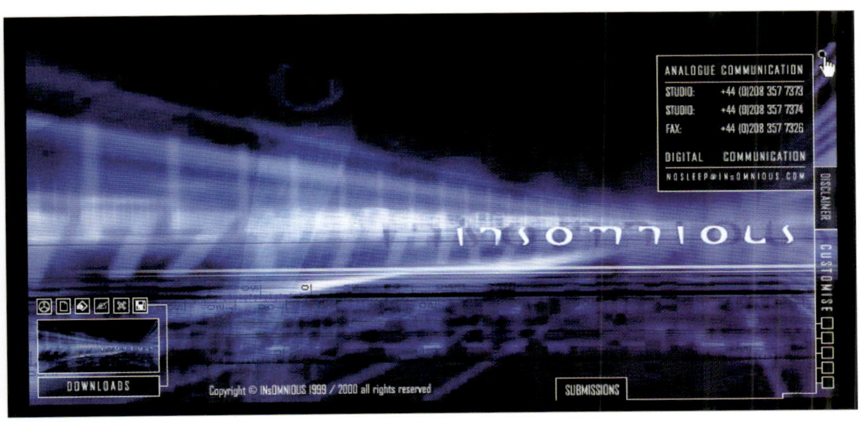
ANALOGUE COMMUNICATION
STUDIO: +44 (0)208 357 7373
STUDIO: +44 (0)208 357 7374
FAX: +44 (0)208 357 7326
DIGITAL COMMUNICATION
NOSLEEP@INsOMNIOUS.COM
DISCLAIMER
CUSTOMISE
DOWNLOADS
Copyright © INsOMNIOUS 1999 / 2000 all rights reserved
SUBMISSIONS

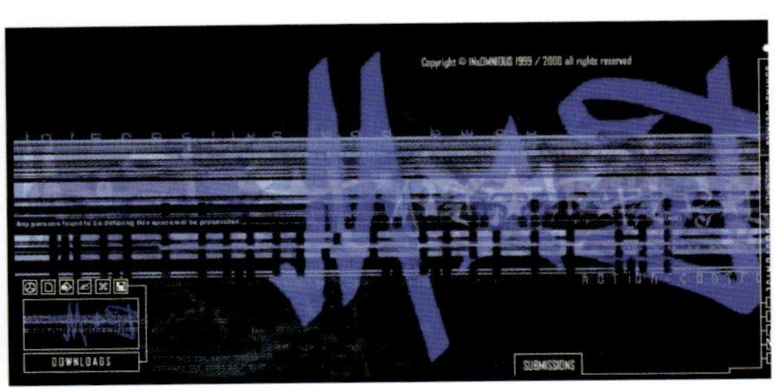
DOWNLOADS
SUBMISSIONS

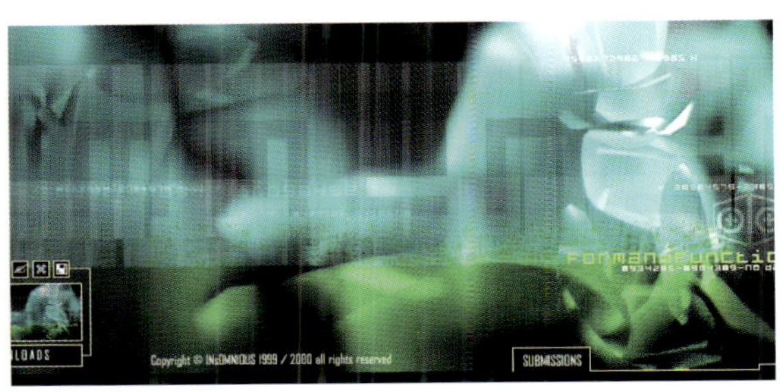
Copyright © INsOMNIOUS 1999 / 2000 all rights reserved
SUBMISSIONS

Title
King Led
URL
www3.sympatico.ca/kingled/
Design Firm
King Led Comics
Designer
Louis Douzepis

The main page interface works as a frame that borders the rest of the images. The buttons are clear and simple. The use of extremely lush .jpeg images and a black background make this a very pretty site.

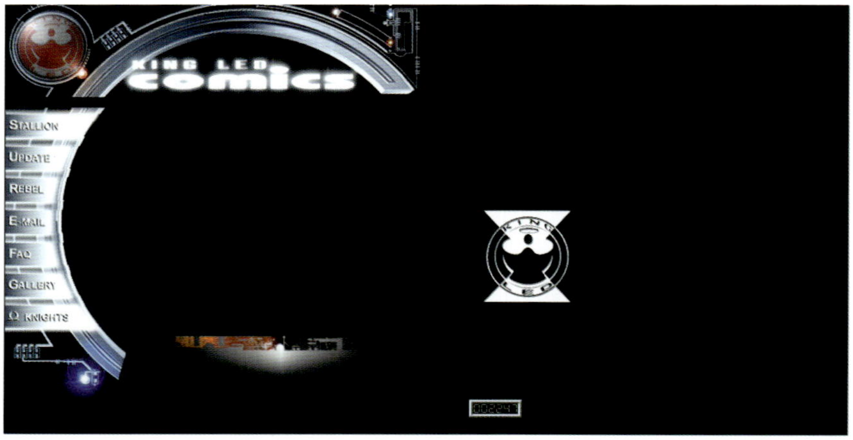

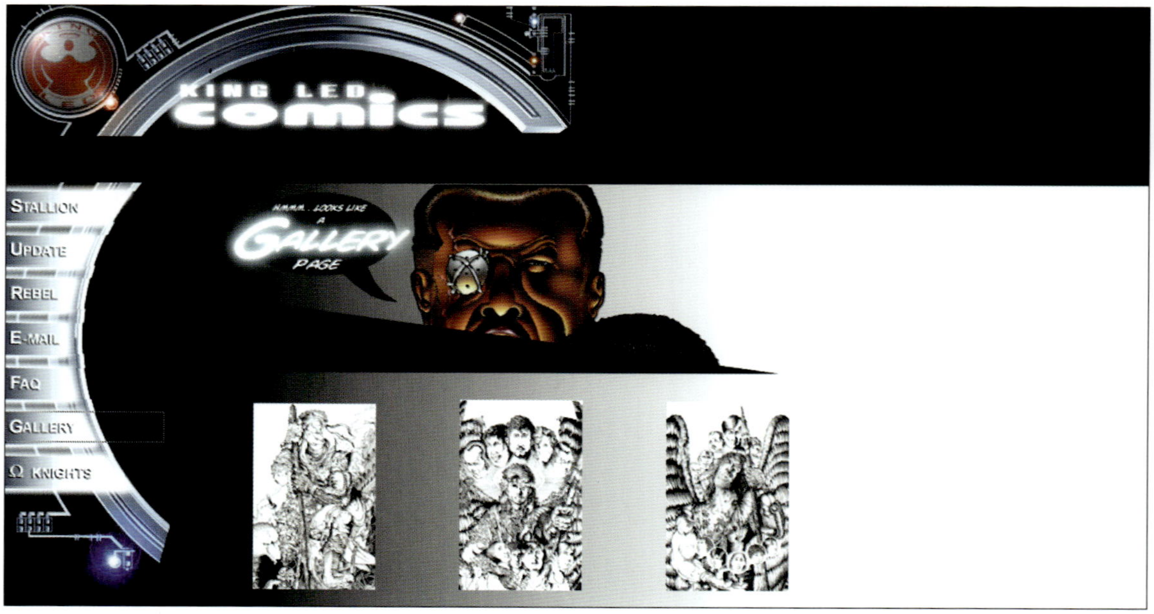

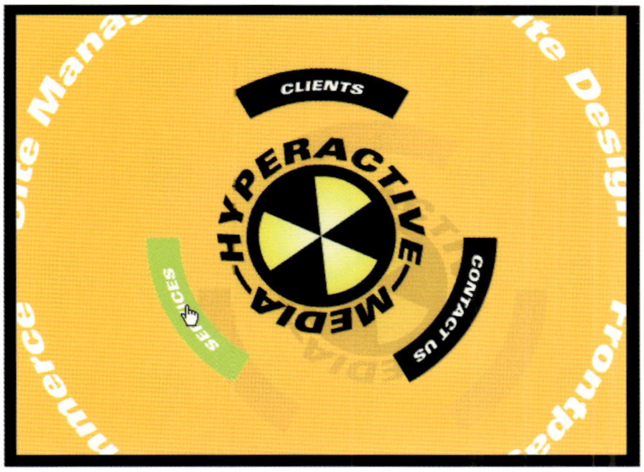

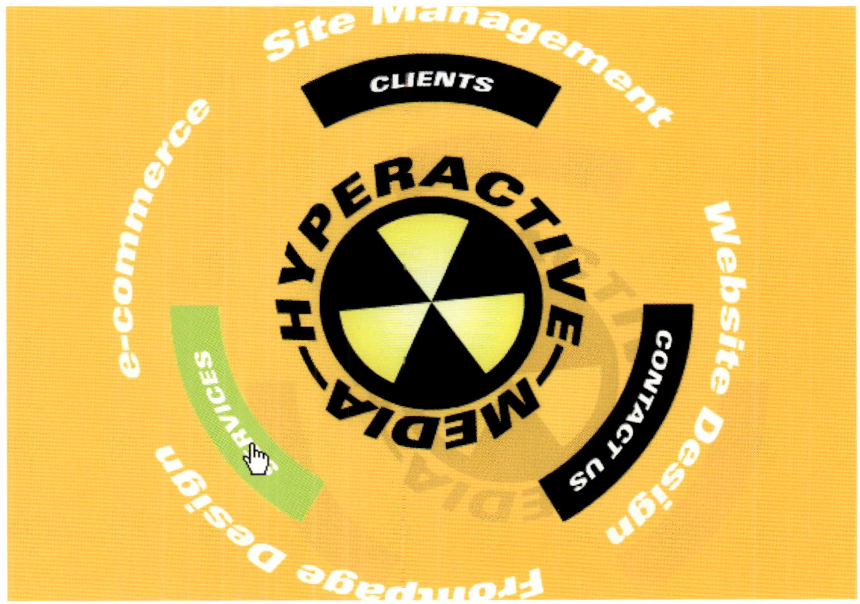

Title
Hyper-Active (BSI)
URL
www.bsimedia.com/
Design Firm
BSI Media

The three buttons on this site are totally Flash driven. Click on one and the information comes flying down from outside the animation window.

index

About the Authors

Richard Karl Danielson is a freelance writer and artist living in Cambridge, Massachusetts. He has produced live theater, cut a record of his own songs, and written for a variety of media—electronic and print. He studied history and writing at Marlboro College. He is a Web designer by avocation and is fascinated with the Internet revolution. He is currently producing a short movie for the Web and writing a book on cinematography.

Glenn Fleishman has written about technology and its use in several publications, including *InfoWorld* and *NetGuide.* He was a founding contributing editor and columnist at the print edition of *Web Developer* and is a contributing editor and columnist for *Adobe Magazine,* where he writes the Web Watcher column. Glenn was course manager at the legendary Kodak Center for Creative Imaging in Camden, Maine, and later worked doing scanning and color correction at High Resolution Inc. He founded one of the first Web development companies, Point of Presence Company (POPCO), offering firms Web site programming and hosting. While at POPCO, he helped broadcast the first feature film over the Internet. Glenn has also worked at Amazon.com Books and Open House. He now works as a consult ant, conference chair, writer, and itinerant perl programmer. Glenn co-authored the second edition of *Real World Scanning and Halftones.* <http://www.glenns.org>

In 1995 **Toby Malina** joined Thunder Lizard Productions, a Seattle-based conference production company, as editorial/technical director. At Thunder Lizard, she worked in collaboration with the editorial staff and outside experts in the desktop publishing and Web design fields to develop editorial content for *The Photoshop Conference*, *The Adobe Internet Conferences*, and *Web Design: HTML and Beyond*, among others. In addition, Toby was responsible for the coordination and execution of all conference audio/visual, including computer systems, lighting, sound, and projection. If it broke, she fixed it. In 1997 she served as product manager for *Technique: Digital Artists at Work* and *The PageMaker Summit*.

For the past ten years, Toby has also worked independently as a graphic designer and Macintosh consultant. Her multifaceted roles have included art director, production artist, MIS manager, software/systems trainer, and mental health professional. Her greatest triumph: wrenching a motherboard from the jaws of a client's basset hound and successfully reseating it.

Jeff Carlson spent several years doing desktop publishing before jumping into the Web publishing arena by founding and editing eSCENE, the Internet's only yearly anthology of the best short fiction appearing on the Web. A stint as managing editor at a small Seattle-based book publisher convinced Adam and Tonya Engst that they should tap him for the same position at the widely read newsletter *TidBITS*. Jeff has published articles in *HOW* magazine, *Macworld*, and *Adobe Magazine*, and was a contributing editor and columnist for Adobe's online venture, *adobe.mag*. He is also the author of *The Palm III/PalmPilot Visual QuickStart Guide*. In addition to writing and editing, he's an accomplished Web designer and consultant through his company Never Enough Coffee Creations. People around him seem to possess urges to constantly ask him questions. <http://www.necoffee.com>